Environmental Health and Safety Audits

8th Edition

Lawrence B. Cahill
Raymond W. Kane
Thomas R. Vetrano
James C. Mauch
Marc E. Gold
Michael M. Meloy
Brian P. Riedel
Lori Benson Michelin

Government Institutes
Rockville, Maryland

 **Government Institutes**

Published by Government Institutes
An imprint of The Scarecrow Press, Inc.
A wholly owned subsidary of The Rowman & Littlefield Publishing Group, Inc.
4501 Forbes Boulevard, Suite 200, Lanham, Maryland 20706
http://www.govinstpress.com

Estover Road, Plymouth PL6 7PY, United Kingdom

British Library Cataloguing in Publication Information Available

Library of Congress Cataloging-in-Publication Data

Environmental, health and safety audits / Lawrence B. Cahill ... [et al.]
  p. cm.
Includes bibliographical references.
ISBN: 978-0-86587-825-9
  1. Environmental auditing—United States. I. Cahill, Lawrence B. II. Environmental audits.
TD194.7.E597 2001
658.4'08—dc21   00-054830

Printed in the United States of America

To Claire, Brendon, and Bryan, always there when I return....

SUMMARY OF CONTENTS

PART I. MANAGING A PROGRAM

PART II: CONDUCTING THE AUDIT

PART III: SPECIAL AUDITING TOPICS

APPENDICES

TABLE OF CONTENTS

Chapter 3: Legal Considerations 47

Chapter 4: Elements of a Successful Program 65

PART II: CONDUCTING THE AUDIT

Chapter 21: Achieving Quality Environmental Audits: Twenty Tips For Success 319

PART III: SPECIAL AUDITING TOPICS

Chapter 22: Property Transfer Assessments 331

APPENDICES

LIST OF FIGURES

PREFACE

It has been five years since Government Institutes published the seventh edition of *Environmental Audits*. Since that time, we have continued to see the Environmental, Health, and Safety auditing field mature and blossom. During the preparation of the previous edition, the ISO 14000 Standards and Guidelines were still a year away from issuance, the U.S. EPA had only just released its 1995 Self-Policing Policy to say nothing of the Agency's 2000 Policy, and there was no such thing as a Board of Environmental, Health, and Safety Auditor Certifications. There were also only 13,100 pages of U.S. Federal environmental regulations then; there are now over 17,000 pages, which is a growth of 30 percent.

As a consequence, the seventh edition, like all previous editions, was becoming very outdated. This was problematic for me as the book is the principal tool used in the ABS Group, Government Institutes Division's Environmental, Health, and Safety Audits training course, which I have been leading since 1983.

I have always said to the course attendees that once the supplementary materials become thicker than the course text, then I know it's time for a new edition. Well, for the past couple of years that has been the case as we've attempted to keep the course current. However, it has taken me these same two years to store up enough energy to put out another edition. I started planning for this edition in 1998. Those of you who have attempted to write and edit a technical book while maintaining a full-time job and family responsibilities will know why it took a while to mobilize. The work on this book was done late at night and on weekends, and not always in the United States.

The eighth edition maintains the same basic three-part structure of the seventh: Managing a Program, Conducting the Audit, and Special Auditing Topics. As in the past, the new edition stands alone as a complete document; where information from the previous edition was determined to be no longer relevant, this material was removed. Moreover, no chapter in the eighth edition went untouched as we attempted to improve the quality and provide the most current information.

There are now twenty-seven chapters in the book as opposed to twenty-five. We have removed one chapter and added three new chapters: Chapter 6 on ISO 14000 and its Potential Effect on Auditing Programs, Chapter 18 on Auditors' Dilemmas, and Chapter 21 on Twenty Tips for Conducting Successful Audits. Yet, probably the real added value in the eighth edition is the audit tools we have added, principally in the Appendices. These include:

· A model EH&S Audit Program Manual

· A new model Pre-Audit Questionnaire

· A model Pre-Audit Checklist

- A model EH&S Audit Opening Conference Presentation
- A model Environmental Audit Report (reflective of ISO 14000 expectations)
- A model EH&S Audit Appraisal Questionnaire
- A model Management Report.

These tools can be tailored to fit any EH&S audit program and represent a "fast-start" kit for anyone developing a program from scratch.

Finally, throughout the text we discuss new developments in information generation and availability, especially Internet sites, which can add real value to a program.

Through the efforts of my co-authors, we believe we have addressed the issues currently impacting EH&S audits and audit programs. It is a very dynamic setting in late 2000 and further changes likely are ahead of us.

Lawrence B. Cahill
November 2000

ABOUT THE EDITOR
AND PRINCIPAL AUTHOR

Mr. Lawrence B. Cahill, CPEA is a Principal in ERM's Business Integration Group located in Exton, PA. Mr. Cahill has over twenty-five years of professional EH&S experience with industry and consulting. Principally for Fortune 500 Companies such as DuPont, Exxon, BFGoodrich, Colgate-Palmolive, Hercules, Bristol-Myers Squibb, TRW, and Hughes Aircraft, he has developed, evaluated, and certified audit programs; conducted hundreds of audits; and trained literally thousands of people in auditing skills all over the world, including Asia-Pacific, South America, Africa, Europe, and North America. He has provided an "auditor's opinion letter" formally certifying the efficacy of EH&S audit programs for DuPont, Eastman Kodak, Occidental Petroleum, TRW, Honeywell, and Bristol-Myers Squibb, among others. These letters have routinely appeared in the companies' annual environmental reports.

Mr. Cahill has been awarded Distinguished Instructor status by Government Institutes. He has taught Government Institutes' Environmental, Health and Safety Audits course since 1983. He is a member of the Environmental, Health and Safety Auditing Roundtable (EAR) and was on the original Board of Directors of the Board of Environmental, Health and Safety Auditor Certifications (BEAC). He is a Certified Professional Environmental Auditor, with Master Certification.

Mr. Cahill holds a B.S. in mechanical engineering from Northeastern University, an M.S. in environmental health engineering from Northwestern University, and an M.B.A. in Public Management from the Wharton School of Business at the University of Pennsylvania. He previously was a Project Engineer with Exxon Research and Engineering where he audited plants in the U.S., Canada, and Europe.

CONTRIBUTING AUTHORS

RAYMOND W. KANE
Independent Consultant
Environmental Management Consulting
Mr. Kane wrote all or parts of Chapters 5, 15, 16, and 23.

Mr. Kane is currently senior vice president at Marsh Risk Consulting. He deals with EH&S compliance audits, audit program development, third-party review of EH&S audit and management programs, EH&S training, ISO 14000 environmental management consulting, and environmental due diligence. Previously, Mr. Kane was a consultant with Environmental Management Consulting in Philadelphia, PA, and vice president at McLaren/Hart Environmental Engineering Corporation. There he developed and conducted major environmental audit and compliance programs for private industry and federal organizations such as the National Institutes of Health and the U.S. Air Force. Mr. Kane received his B.S. and M.S. in Civil/Environmental Engineering from Villanova University and served for four years in the U.S. Navy as a submarine officer.

MARC E. GOLD
Partner
Manko, Gold & Katcher
Mr. Gold co-authored Chapter 3.

Marc E. Gold is a founding partner of Manko, Gold & Katcher, L.L.P., a twenty-lawyer firm that concentrates its practice exclusively in environmental law. Formerly, Mr. Gold served as a Section Chief in the Legal Branch of the U.S. EPA, Region 3, and was a partner in the Environmental Department of a major Philadelphia law firm. In addition, Mr. Gold was an Adjunct Assistant Professor at Temple University's School of Engineering where he taught environmental regulation. Mr. Gold has more than twenty years of experience in environmental law. His practice focuses on all aspects of environmental regulation and counseling covering hazardous waste, air and water pollution, and site remediation issues. Mr. Gold has been involved in several multi-facility environmental audits and has participated in the development of corporate environmental policies and procedures. Mr. Gold received his law degree from Villanova University School of Law and his B.A. from The American University.

MICHAEL M. MELOY
Partner
Manko, Gold & Katcher
Mr. Meloy co-authored Chapter 3.

Michael M. Meloy is a partner at Manko, Gold & Katcher, LLP, a law firm concentrating in environmental and land use law. Mr. Meloy brings both a legal and engineering background to bear in regularly advising clients with respect to a broad spectrum of environmental regulatory and litigation issues. He has been actively involved in the development and implementation of the residual waste and hazardous waste programs in Pennsylvania. He has also been actively involved in the development of self-evaluative privilege legislation for Pennsylvania. In addition, as part of his practice, Mr. Meloy has advised clients regarding health and safety issues arising under the Occupational Safety and Health Act. Mr. Meloy is a member of the Natural Resources, Energy, and Environmental Law Section, American Bar Association; the Environmental, Mineral, and Natural Resources Section, Pennsylvania Bar Association; and the Environmental Law Committee of the Philadelphia Bar Association. Mr. Meloy earned his bachelor's degree in civil engineering, summa cum laude, from the University of Delaware in 1980. He was admitted to the Pennsylvania Bar in 1983 after graduating cum laude from Harvard Law School.

BRIAN P. RIEDEL
U.S. Environmental Protection Agency
Mr. Riedel wrote Chapter 2.

Brian P. Riedel is counsel for the U.S. EPA's Office of Planning and Policy Analysis (OPPA) which serves the Assistant Administrator for Enforcement and Compliance Assurance (OECA). Mr. Riedel is co-author of EPA's interim and final environmental self-policing policies. He is co-chair of the Quick Response Team responsible for making recommendations regarding interpretation and application of the policies. In addition, Mr. Riedel is the OECA lead on enforcement and compliance matters relating to ISO 14001 standards for environmental management systems. He is a member of the U.S. Technical Advisory Group (TAG) to ISO Technical Committee 207 on environmental management. Before moving to EPA, Mr. Riedel practiced environmental law with the Washington, D.C. law firm of Newman & Holtzinger. He received his law degree from the University of Wisconsin and A.B. from the University of Michigan.

JAMES C. MAUCH
Vice President
Vista Environmental Information, Inc.
Mr. Mauch co-authored Chapter 22 with Mr. Cahill.

Mr. Mauch was vice president for Vista Information Solutions, Inc., in Louisville, KY. He was also an attorney and was in private practice for five years with a Midwest general practice and litigation law firm. His practice involved trial work and commercial litigation, and focused in part on environmental and mineral rights issues affecting land use transactions. While at Vista, Mr. Mauch was involved in federal legislative initiations and published articles on the appropriate standards for Phase I environmental real estate assessments. Mr. Mauch was an active member of ASTM's E-50.02 subcommittee, which developed the Site Assessment Standards, and he was chairman of the Public Records Task Group of that subcommittee.

LORI BENSON MICHELIN
Manager of Knowledge Management
Colgate-Palmolive Company
Ms. Michelin co-authored Chapter 21 with Mr. Cahill.

Lori Benson Michelin has more than twelve years of professional environmental experience. Ms. Michelin works for Colgate-Palmolive Company and was instrumental in developing and implementing Colgate-Palmolive's EH&S Audit Program, which is now under way in every region of the world. She served in a dual role as the Corporate Audit Program manager and Environmental Engineering Manager. Her environmental engineering group provided direct technical support to new and existing manufacturing facilities in key areas such as wastewater treatment, air permits, and waste management. Prior to joining Colgate-Palmolive, Ms. Michelin worked as an EH&S Manager for Ocean Spray Cranberries, Inc. She also worked as an environmental consultant on projects related to waste collection and treatment, water distribution, and land use while she was employed at BCM Engineers and Carrol Engineering. Ms. Michelin received her M.S. in Civil and Environmental Engineering from Villanova University and her B.S. in Civil Engineering from Pennsylvania State University. She has a Professional Engineering license.

THOMAS R. VETRANO
Principal
ENVIRON Corporation
Mr. Vetrano contributed to both Chapters 24 and 27.

Mr. Vetrano is a principal at ENVIRON Corporation in Princeton, NJ, which provides international environmental and health risk management consulting services. He has over twelve years experience in strategic international environmental, health, safety, and risk management consulting. He has managed and conducted numerous environmental due diligence, site assessment, and compliance audit programs for Fortune 500 companies in over twenty-five countries on six continents. Mr. Vetrano has extensive experience in designing environmental compliance, auditing, and risk management programs for a wide range of companies, including aerospace, electronics/computer, chemical, pharmaceutical, and consumer products companies. Mr. Vetrano has directed environmental due diligence programs for hundreds of merger/acquisitions, diventures, and corporate transactions totaling over $30 billion on behalf of corporations, law firms, and financial institutions. He has also designed and implemented commercial waste management vendor assessment programs for multinational clients. Prior to joining ENVIRON, Mr. Vetrano served as vice president and managing director of Kroll International, an international environment consulting and risk management firm. He also served as western regional manager for HART Environmental Management Corporation, directing HART's nationwide environmental assessment and auditing practice. Mr. Vetrano received a B.S. in Environmental Studies from Rutgers University and an M.S. in Environmental Engineering and Toxicology from the New Jersey Institute of Technology.

ACKNOWLEDGMENTS

I wish to thank the contributing authors for their efforts in delivering a quality product on time. Well, at least in delivering a quality product. Working with the staff at ABS Group / Government Institutes Division in preparing the manuscript was a pleasure. All the authors had to do was email rough electronic versions of the material to Government Institutes and, believe me, that was challenge enough. Thank you Charlene at Government Institutes for the encouragement (or was it harassment?) it took to produce the eighth edition. Nothing gets done well without help.

PART I

MANAGING A PROGRAM

Chapter 1

PERSPECTIVES IN EH&S AUDITING

Eyes are more accurate witnesses than ears.

– Heraclitus, c. 540-480 B.C.

WHY AUDIT?

Managing compliance in today's regulatory setting has become an overwhelming exercise, involving more and more regulations, and affecting more and more organizations. In the United States, we have gone well beyond the straightforward regulation of air emissions and wastewater effluents, which were the prevalent command and control initiatives in the legislation and regulations of the 1970s. Hazardous wastes and hazardous materials are now tightly controlled, and their discharges are freely and openly reported through community and worker right-to-know regulations. The U.S. can no longer assume that it is at the leading edge of environmental regulation. Many countries have adopted U.S. regulations as a baseline and have built an even more stringent platform from there.

The traditional approach of regulating only major industry groups has also long passed us by. In this day and age, environmental rules affect neighborhood dry cleaners, liquor stores, auto parts stores and body shops, amusement parks, and, in some states, your local supermarket.

Even more disturbing, we find no safe harbor from these complicated and pervasive issues while sitting at home. Consider the following:

- **Could your home contain friable asbestos?** Although asbestos insulation was outlawed around 1974, the U.S. EPA estimates that thousands of public buildings and innumerable homes still contain asbestos.

- **Was your home built over an abandoned landfill?** Love Canal is the classic case, and there are now 30,000 documented abandoned waste disposal sites across the country.

3

■ **Could there be radon in the basement?** U.S. EPA has reported that millions of U.S. homes are potentially tainted with unsafe radon levels. Scientists estimate that thousands of lung cancer deaths a year may be caused by radon.

■ **Could your drinking water supply be contaminated?** A study by the Center for Responsive Law found that nearly one in five public drinking water systems is contaminated with chemicals, some of them toxic. Many in-home supplies are contaminated with excessive levels of lead, abraded from the lead solder used to connect copper piping.

■ **Could fluorescent lights be a source of PCBs and mercury?** Light ballasts manufactured before 1976 will likely contain PCBs. The tubes themselves can contain trace amounts of mercury.

Growth of Regulations

This continuous emergence of new environmental risks has resulted in the regular enactment of laws designed to protect both public health and the environment. As Figure 1.1 demonstrates, we have seen a dramatic growth in federal environmental regulations, even during periods of "regulatory reform." National environmental regulations under Title 40 of the Code of Federal Regulations (CFR) now total over 17,000 pages and have grown by over 50 percent in the 1990s alone! Health and safety regulations promulgated under Title 29 add another 2,700 pages. Can 20,000 total pages be far off? Well interestingly enough, there could be a barometer that might answer this question. If we review the statistics reported by both the U.S. EPA and OSHA, we note that there is roughly one employee or full-time equivalent per page of regulation at each agency (see Figure 1.2). Does this tell us anything? Perhaps.

The stifling federal regulatory oversight is not likely to abate for some time, even with the new, more cooperative approach to regulation that evolved in the mid-1990s. In November 2000 the U.S. EPA reported in its short-term agenda that it had some 449 regulations under development, revision, or review (see Figure 1.3). Almost half of these are regulations to be promulgated under the Clean Air Act, arguably one of the most complex pieces of legislation ever passed by Congress. Over this same time period, OSHA has reported that it is expected to add another 54 regulations.

Of course, all of this is to say nothing of state and local EH&S regulations. Often lost in the glare of the national regulatory setting is the increasing impact that states have on compliance management. Although states generally are required to adopt federal standards as the bare minimum of regulation, many states go beyond what is required by federal regulations. For example, Proposition 65 in California and the Industrial Site Restoration Act (ISRA) in New Jersey not only carve out new regulatory frontiers but are often viewed as model legislation that could be, and

Figure 1.1 Growth of Environmental Regulations

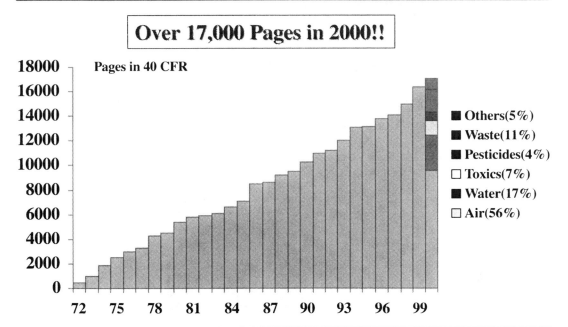

Over 17,000 Pages in 2000!!

Pages in 40 CFR

- ■ Others(5%)
- ■ Waste(11%)
- ■ Pesticides(4%)
- □ Toxics(7%)
- ■ Water(17%)
- □ Air(56%)

Figure 1.2 Comparing U.S. EPA and OSHA Staff Size

Comparing U.S. EPA and OSHA Staff Size

FTE (2001 FY Budget)

2,384

18,050

- ■ EPA
- □ OSHA

Figure 1.3 U.S. EPA's Short-Term Agenda

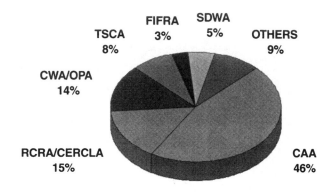

U.S. EPA's Short Term Agenda
(November 30, 2000)

449 Regulations Under Development (OSHA-54)

have been, adopted by other states. For organizations with facilities in more than one state, compliance assurance can be difficult if not impossible. As can be seen in Figure 1.4, states will vary in their regulatory stringency; thus, it is typically quite a challenge to stay current on regulations promulgated in multiple states. With the proliferation of community right-to-know legislation in the last few years, local fire departments and county agencies have become players in the game.

Moreover, the regulatory environment varies significantly from country to country. Figure 1.5 begs the question: Are there fewer lawyers per capita in other countries because the countries are less litigious by nature, or are other countries less litigious because they have fewer lawyers? The United States is known to be a very litigious society with an overwhelming regulatory framework. Other countries have a more cooperative relationship between the regulators and the regulated, and are much less litigious. For multi-national companies, the need for different rulebooks can be very challenging.

Figure 1.4 State Regulatory Stringency

Most
Stringent

AK: 46
HI: 24

Source: Institute for Southern Studies

Figure 1.5 Concentration of Lawyers in Developed Countries

Concentration of Lawyers in Developed Countries

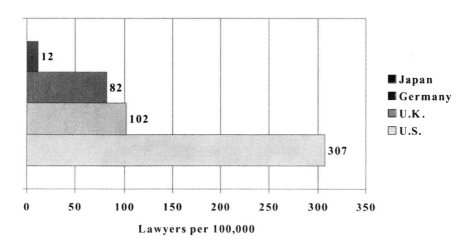

Lawyers per 100,000

Legend: Japan, Germany, U.K., U.S.

Values: 12, 82, 102, 307

Growth in Visibility

It was not so long ago that a company's EH&S information was known only to them and to the regulatory agencies. This is no longer true. With the advent of community and worker right-to-know legislation, and the Internet, EH&S data are available to all citizens with the click of a mouse. For example, the three following Internet sites provide detailed information on a facility's historical compliance:

- **www.epa.gov/enviro** – Provides U.S. EPA historical data on all environmental media for each regulated facility.

- **www.scorecard.org** – Developed by the Environmental Defense Fund, provides historical data on Community Right-to-Know Toxic Release Inventory Facility Reports.

- **www.osha.gov/oshstats** – Provides OSHA inspection data for each inspected facility.

Information can be gathered and analyzed quite easily using available data. For example, Figures 1.6 and 1.7 provide interesting state-by-state and year-by-year comparisons of Toxic Release Inventory data. This is only the "tip of the iceberg." There is little that is not known or that could not be obtained about EH&S compliance at a given facility.

Figure 1.6 1998 TRI Reporting — Total Releases by State

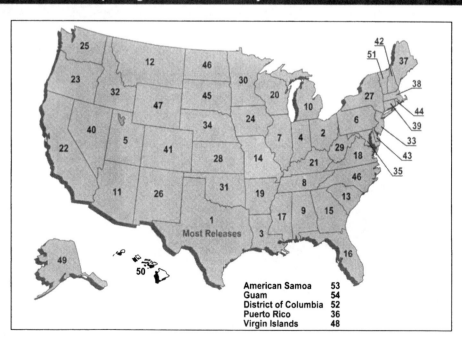

American Samoa	53
Guam	54
District of Columbia	52
Puerto Rico	36
Virgin Islands	48

Figure 1.7 1998 TRI Reporting — Strong Early Reductions in Total Releases

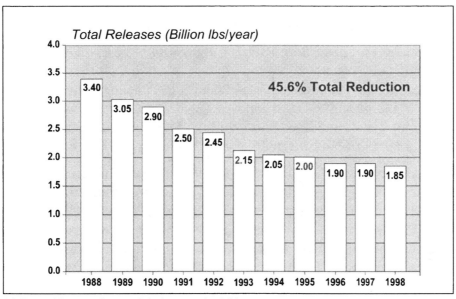

*Adjusted for regulatory deletions and additions

Growth in Enforcement

In this regulatory setting, one can only wonder if "fail-safe" management of compliance is, indeed, an achievable objective. Yet, the penalties for not complying are far too intimidating to risk applying anything but extreme diligence towards meeting standards and applying good management practices. Civil penalties of up to $25,000 per day are common in most statutes.

In addition, the U.S. EPA has reemphasized its enforcement role and has moved toward a policy of taking enforcement action against corporate officials as well as their companies. The following cases are some of the more unique and interesting examples of that policy reported by the U.S. EPA in 1998.[1] Note that several of the cases actually involve companies that were in the business of environmental management and protection.

- ■ *GTE Corporation.* In January 1998 the largest settlement under the U.S. EPA's Audit Policy (see Chapter 2) was reached when GTE agreed to resolve 600 violations at 314 facilities in 21 states. The company paid a fine of

[1] Taken from U.S. EPA's Enforcement and Compliance Assurance Accomplishments Report—FY 1998, June 1999.

about $50,000; the U.S. EPA waived another $2.38 million in potential penalties. However, the U.S. EPA did undertake an enforcement initiative against ten other telecommunications companies, essentially GTE's competitors, to determine if similar violations existed at their sites.

■ *United States v. Louisiana Pacific Corporation.* The Louisiana Pacific Corporation (LPC) operated a wood products plant in Colorado. An indictment alleged that the plant manager and plant superintendent violated the Clean Air Act and committed mail and wire fraud. The Company was convicted of 18 felony counts and fined $36.5 million. The plant manager was sentenced to ten months of jail time and the superintendent, six months.

■ *United States v. Safewastes, Inc.* In 1993 the Sacramento, California Fire Department inspected a warehouse which led to the discovery of illegally stored hazardous wastes and rocket motors, warheads, 17,000 artillery shells, and 7,500 pounds of explosives. The two principals involved were charged with illegal storage and transportation of hazardous wastes, among other firearms infractions, and were given 21 and 51 months of jail time.

■ *United States v. Hess Environmental Laboratories, Inc.* Investigations by federal and state regulatory agencies revealed that this lab in Pennsylvania was providing fraudulent analyses of environmental samples to its customers. The lab was fined $5 million and the director was sentenced to 12 months of jail time. In May of 1997 the lab closed and terminated its business.

■ *United States v. Barry Shields, et al.* The IEMC Environmental Group was contracted to remove asbestos-containing materials from the Hess Department Store in Louisville. As a result of improper removal, the storeowner was ordered to conduct an emergency cleanup, which cost about $1 million. The IEMC project manager was sentenced to 51 months in prison and the onsite supervisor, ten months.

■ *United States v. Warner Lambert Company, Inc.* This company was convicted of falsifying discharge monitoring reports in 1998. The receiving waters were used by poor area residents for drinking water and recreational purposes. The company was fined $3 million and the plant manager was sentenced to 21 months in prison.

■ *United States. v. Royal Caribbean Cruise Lines, Ltd.* In October 1994, the U.S. Coast Guard observed the cruise ship *Sovereign of the Seas* emitting an oil sheen off the coast of Puerto Rico. When boarded by the Coast Guard, a false logbook was presented. Additionally, under orders of a senior officer, the oil-water separator bypass pipe was removed. The disposal of this pipe was documented by a Coast Guard videotape. The cruise line paid over $9 million in fines and was convicted of witness tampering, destruction of evidence, and conspiracy.

■ *United States v. City Sales, Ltd., et al.* In 1993 and 1994, City Sales, a Canadian auto parts dealership, illegally imported 246 tons of CFC-12 into the U.S. They never possessed the CAA consumptive allowances and made false declarations on import invoices. The City Sales owner was sentenced to 15 months in prison. His wife was also convicted.

Placement of notices in local newspapers is another approach that regulatory agencies are using with increasing frequency. As an example, Figure 1.8 is a copy of a full-page notice placed in the Sunday *Los Angeles Times*, as mandated by the Los Angeles Toxic Waste Strike Force.

The sum total of the EPA's enforcement efforts is shown in Figure 1.9. Note that the amount of fines and the number of defendants charged have grown substantially over the past 20 years. No company, no matter how apparently innocuous its operations, is immune. Figure 1.10 notes the Walt Disney Corporation's record in the late 1980s and early 1990s.

As if all this weren't enough to heighten the anxiety of corporate managers, they may also face the ire of stockholders if the company's stock price is adversely affected by compliance problems. This is a real risk, as indicated by Figure 1.11, which shows the short-term price drops of four public companies suffering through environmental incidents. The classic case in this regard is Union Carbide's Bhopal tragedy in late 1984. The impacts of more recent asbestos claims are just as substantial.

IMPACT ON THE REGULATED COMMUNITY

What are the implications of these policies and trends for management? With the high probability of continued controversy and complexity in the EH&S arena, it is very important to avoid complacency and to pay attention to compliance matters. Management's ability to anticipate and respond to government and private actions aimed at addressing real or perceived EH&S problems must remain undiminished. Yet, corporate outlays for environmental management, including those for staffing, generally have been reduced, as have expenditures for many other business activities in the competitive economic climate of the last decade. Thus, many companies may be less than ideally prepared to face a future regulatory environment that will continue to be complex and onerous.

The task of business, then, in this climate of uncertainty, is to assure minimal vulnerability in compliance-related matters and to do so in the most efficient and cost-effective way. One solution to this problem is the development or vigorous maintenance of a formal EH&S audit program that evaluates compliance with regu-

Figure 1.8 Warning of Illegal Disposal

WARNING

THE ILLEGAL DISPOSAL OF TOXIC WASTES WILL RESULT IN JAIL.

WE SHOULD KNOW WE GOT CAUGHT!

February 12, 1983

XYZ Corporation

Dear Businesses and Residents of the City & County of Los Angeles:

Pollution of our environment has become a crisis.

Intentional clandestine acts of illegal disposal of hazardous waste, or "midnight dumping" are violent crimes against the community.

Over the past 2 years almost a dozen Chief Executive Officers of both large and small corporations have been sent to jail by the L.A. Toxic Waste Strike Force.

They have also been required to pay huge fines; pay for cleanups; speak in public about their misdeeds, and in some cases place ads publicizing their crime and punishment.

THE RISKS OF BEING CAUGHT ARE TOO HIGH — AND THE CONSEQUENCES IF CAUGHT ARE NOT WORTH IT!

We are paying the price, TODAY, while you read this ad our President and Vice President are serving time in JAIL and we were forced to place this ad.

PLEASE TAKE THE LEGAL ALTERNATIVE AND PROTECT OUR ENVIRONMENT.

Very Truly Yours,

XYZ Corporation
Los Angeles, CA 90031

Figure 1.9 Trends in U.S. EPA Environment Enforcement

Trends in USEPA Enforcement

77 78 79 80 81 82 83 84 85 86 87 88 89 90 91 92 93 94 95 96 97 98 99 0

■ **Defendants Charged** ■ **Civil/Criminal Penalties ($MM)**

Figure 1.10 Incidents at Walt Disney Corporation

Incidents at
Walt Disney Corporation

Date	Incident	Fines
7/90	Waste Disposal	$550,000
4/90	Sewage Discharge	$300,000
1/90	Vulture Kill	$10,000
1989	PCB Transport	$2,500
1988	Waste Storage	$150,000
Totals		$1,012,500

Figure 1.11 Financial Impacts of Industry Incidents

Financial Impacts ...

The 1984 Union Carbide Bhopal Incident

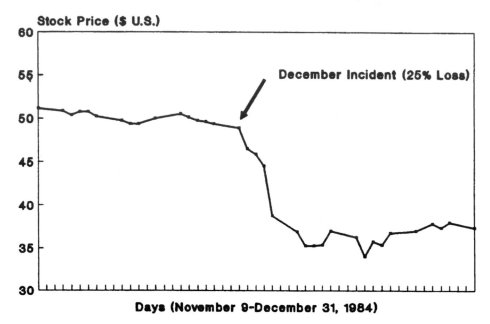

Days (November 9-December 31, 1984)

Financial Impacts ...

The 1989 Phillips Houston Incident

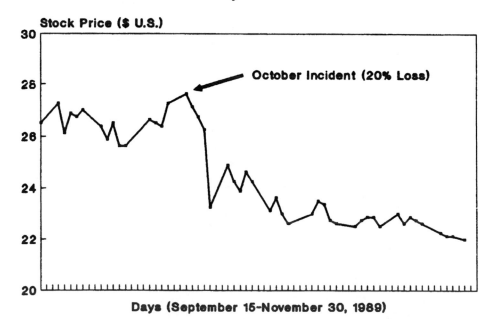

Days (September 15-November 30, 1989)

Figure 1.11 *(cont'd.)*

Financial Impacts ...
The 1986 Sandoz Rhine River Incident

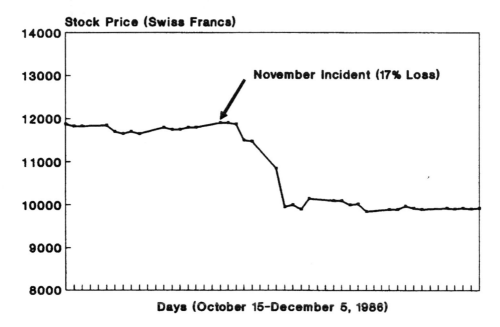

Stock Price (Swiss Francs)

November Incident (17% Loss)

Days (October 15–December 5, 1986)

Financial Impacts ...
The 1990 Arco Channelview Incident

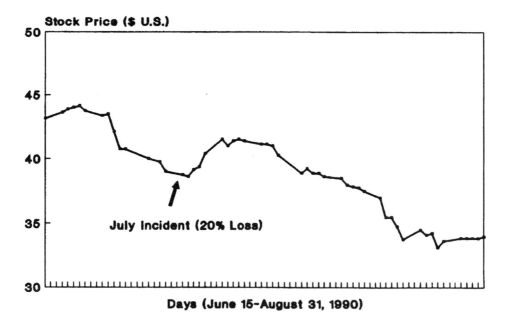

Stock Price ($ U.S.)

July Incident (20% Loss)

Days (June 15–August 31, 1990)

Figure 1.11 *(cont'd.)*

The 1999 Asbestos Class-Action Lawsuits and Settlement Agreements

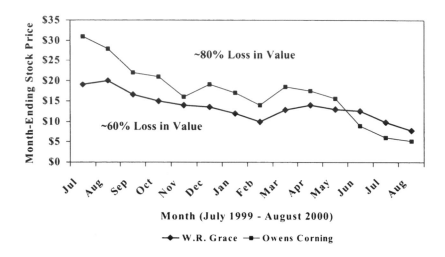

Month (July 1999 - August 2000)

W.R. Grace — Owens Corning

latory requirements, good management practices, and corporate policies and procedures at all facilities.

EVOLUTION OF ENVIRONMENTAL AUDITING

As a separate and distinct compliance management tool, environmental auditing had its beginnings in the late 1970s and early 1980s. These beginnings were stimulated principally by the Securities and Exchange Commission (SEC) actions against three companies: U.S. Steel (1977), Allied Chemical (1979), and Occidental Petroleum (1980).[2] The SEC required each of these public companies to undertake corporate-wide audits to determine accurately the extent of the environmental liabilities they faced. In essence, the SEC believed that each company was vastly understating its liabilities in its annual report to stockholders. Since that original SEC audit, each company has had an effective environmental audit program in place.

In the 1990s, the SEC once again raised this issue of inaccurate reporting of environmental liabilities by public companies in annual reports. Most recently, the

---

[2] *SEC v. Allied Chemical Corp.*, No. 77-0373 (D.D.C., March 4, 1977); *SEC v. U.S. Steel Corp.*, (1979-1980 Transfer Binder) Fed. Sec. L. Rep. (CCH) 82,319 (1979); *SEC v. Occidental Petroleum Corp.*, (1980 Transfer Binder) Fed. Sec. L. Rep. (CCH) 82,622 (1980).

SEC has stated that it believes companies are not portraying their potential Superfund liabilities properly. It is possible that another round of SEC actions could occur in the near future, unless the perceived systemic discrepancies are remedied.

On the heels of the SEC audits came the implementation of major hazardous waste rules that were promulgated in the late 1970s and put into effect beginning in 1980. These rules were comprehensive, administratively complex, and potentially costly if not adhered to. Because of the nature of the industry, the large chemically intensive corporations were the first to develop audit programs to better respond to these rules. In recent years, many Fortune 500 diversified manufacturing companies have begun to adopt the concept. Even government agencies have seen the light and are developing programs that focus both on compliance for operating facilities and defining liabilities where property is bought or sold.

Today, in the new millenium, environmental auditing has reached a certain level of maturity. Applicability has spread beyond the basic chemical industry to all types of industries and even government agencies.[3] Even simple properties are undergoing audits or assessments prior to sale. Additionally, most generators of hazardous waste are auditing the sites to which their wastes are being transported for handling and disposal by third parties.

EH&S AUDITING ORGANIZATIONS

Although now a widespread practice, auditing is still an evolving discipline. As a result, several associations have been organized to further the profession of EH&S auditing. Two of the better known are discussed below. The discussions are based on descriptions provided by the associations.

EH&S Auditing Roundtable

The EH&S Auditing Roundtable (EHSAR) is a professional organization dedicated to furthering the development and professional practice of environmental auditing. The EAR dates back to January 1982, when managers of several environmental audit programs met informally to discuss their auditing programs and practices, as well as policy and regulatory actions related to auditing.

The original group soon increased to ten managers who held quarterly meetings during 1982 and 1983. Meetings were opened to all interested persons in September 1984, with the original ten members serving as the organization's first steering committee. At that time, the organization adopted the name Environmental Auditing Roundtable and developed a statement of purpose and organizational principles.

---

[3] Government agencies certainly have reason to pause over environmental contamination. It has been reported that it may cost up to $110 billion and take nearly 60 years to clean up the Department of Energy's nuclear weapons manufacturing facilities.

In June 1987, EAR participants adopted a code of ethics and bylaws that, among other things, established general membership criteria and a five-member board of directors elected by the membership at large. Following peer review and vote by the membership, EAR adopted Standards for the Performance of Environmental Audits in 1993.

Most EAR members are practicing EH&S auditors with extensive field experience. While EAR focuses primarily on meeting the needs of industry, membership is open to anyone with a professional interest in the practice of EH&S auditing. Since June 1984, EAR has continued to hold regular national and regional meetings. The EAR has more than 800 members. For more information about EAR, contact:

Environmental, Health & Safety Auditing Roundtable
15111 N. Hayden Road
Suite No. 160355
Scottsdale, AZ 85260-2555
Phone: (480) 659-3738
Fax: (480) 659-3739
http://www.auditear.org

The Board of EH&S Auditor Certifications

In 1997 the Board of EH&S Auditor Certifications (BEAC) was established as a joint venture of the Institute of Internal Auditors (IIA) and the EH&S Auditing Roundtable to provide certification programs for the professional practice of EH&S auditing. The BEAC is an international, independent, non-profit association dedicated to advancing the professional development of the individual EH&S auditor and the EH&S auditing profession. BEAC offers three Certified Professional Auditor (CPEA) designations: EMS 14000 Plus, environmental compliance, and health and safety. For more information about the BEAC, contact:

Board of EH&S Auditor Certifications
249 Maitland Avenue
Altamonte Springs, FL 32701-4201
Phone: (407) 831-7727
Fax: (407) 830-7495
http://www.beac.org

DEFINING ENVIRONMENTAL AUDITS

Precisely defining environmental audits is a difficult exercise. In part, this is due to the evolving nature of the concept, its rather recent appearance as a formal management tool, and the need to tailor programs to the sponsoring organization. It also has to do with the fact that audit programs are typically designed to meet one or more of the following objectives:

- Assuring compliance with regulations
- Determining liabilities
- Protecting against liabilities for company officials
- Fact-finding for acquisitions and divestitures
- Tracking and reporting of compliance costs
- Transferring information among operating units
- Increasing environmental awareness
- Tracking accountability of managers.

Yet, within these broad boundaries, definitions can be framed. The U.S. EPA defines environmental auditing as "a systematic, documented, periodic and objective review by regulated entities[4] of facility operations and practices related to meeting environmental requirements."[5]

An alternative definition is that audits can be said to verify the existence and use of:

Adequate...Systems...Competently...Applied.

Simply put, an audit program is first and foremost a *verification* program. It is not meant to replace existing environmental management systems at the corporate (e.g., regulatory updating), division (e.g., capital planning for pollution control expenditures), or plant (e.g., NPDES discharge monitoring) levels. Indeed, the program should be designed to verify that these environmental management *systems* do, in fact, *exist* and are *in use*. These systems, whether they are to assure compliance or define liabilities, need to be *adequate*, in that they should acknowledge and respond directly to the regulatory and internal requirements that define compliance or liability.

The systems should also be *applied*, meaning that procedures are not simply "bookshelf exercises," out-of-date and out-of-use before the ink dries. Finally, the systems must be applied *competently*. All plant managers, environmental coordinators, and unit operators must have an awareness of environmental compliance, and conduct their responsibilities accordingly.

---

[4] "Regulated entitites" include private firms and public agencies with facilities subject to environmental regulation. Public agencies can include federal, state, and local agencies as well as special-purpose organizations such as regional sewage commissions.

[5] Taken from U.S. EPA's final Environmental Auditing Policy Statement.

ADVANTAGES AND DISADVANTAGES

Like most anything in life, audit programs can be characterized by both advantages and disadvantages. On the positive side, audits can result in a number of significant benefits, including:

- Better compliance

- Fewer surprises

- Fewer fines and suits

- Better public image with the community and regulators

- Potential cost savings

- Improved information transfer

- Increased environmental awareness.

However, these benefits can be offset by some real and potential costs (which will be discussed in more detail in other chapters in this book):

- The commitment of resources to run the program

- Temporary disruption of plant operations

- Increased ammunition for regulators

- Increased liability where one is unable to respond to audit recommendations involving significant capital expenditures.

The last two disadvantages raise a special issue associated with EH&S audits. Even where programs are operated under legal protections (e.g., attorney-client privilege) as discussed in another chapter, there is a chance that audit reports could be "discovered" in a legal proceeding. Thus, it is vital management understands that if a program is initiated, the company must be serious about fixing the problems that are identified in the reports. Otherwise, the report could be most incriminating in a court case or administrative proceeding.

Notwithstanding these drawbacks, most firms, faced with the question of whether or not to undertake an audit program, have opted to do so. The general theory is that in this day of increased litigation and possible criminal suits, it is better to know your liabilities than to remain oblivious to them. As stated some time ago by a former U.S. EPA General Counsel: "Management ignorance is no defense!"[6]

---

[6] R.V. Zener, In *Environmental Reporter,* Bureau of National Affairs, Current Developments (June 26, 1981).

TRENDS IN EH&S AUDITING

In the past few years, a number of interesting trends have surfaced within the environmental auditing discipline. These include:

- **A Push for Standards.** With the development of several professional organizations, as described earlier in this chapter, we have seen a push by some segments of the auditing profession towards the development of standards and possibly national and international registration or certification. As discussed in a later chapter, standards such as ISO 14000 and the European Eco-Management and Audit Scheme and the like are proliferating. The thought is that standards will help to improve the quality of both audits and auditors and to more clearly define the acceptable EH&S audit—presently a nebulous concept. Given the varying types of audits and the multiple objectives a program can be designed to achieve, the development of standards will be a challenging exercise. Nonetheless, as shown in Figure 1.12, the U.S. EPA, the U.S. Department of Justice, the European Union, and the International Organization for Standardization (ISO) have developed standards and guidelines defining an acceptable environmental audit program.

- **The Use of Computers.** Computers are now being used in a variety of ways to support audit programs. They help to maintain online regulatory databases and audit protocols; they store audit reports, action plans, and facility schedules; and portables are increasingly used in the field to develop debriefing documents and draft reports. In some cases, permit and other regulatory information, such as training records, are being filed centrally on computers and accessed as part of the audit's pre-visit activities.

- **An Emphasis on Management Audits.** Through the EH&S audit, many companies have found that inadequate attention to management systems has been central to the most significant compliance problems identified at operating facilities. Two examples are in the areas of maintenance and emergency response. Lack of an adequate maintenance program can turn a "gold-plated" pollution control facility into a continuing compliance headache. The lack of a "working" emergency response system can turn a small spill or release into a major remediation project. Thus, many companies are now focusing their audit efforts on assuring that environmental management systems are in place and functioning. The development of the ISO 14000 standards has fostered this approach.

- **An Integration of Compliance Management Programs.** Because of overlapping requirements (e.g., Material Safety Data Sheets, emergency response) and the desire to avoid overwhelming facilities with "the audit of the month," many companies with separate programs are reviewing the possibility of

Figure 1.12 Common External Expectations for Environmental Audit Programs

(Check Mark Indicates Explicit Mention of that Expectation in the Guideline or Policy)

EXPECTATION	USEPA Policy[1]	USSC Guidelines[2]	EMAS Regulation[3]	ISO 14000 Guidelines[4]
Top Management Support	✔		✔	
Auditor Independence	✔	✔	✔	✔
Specified Audit Frequency	"periodic"	"frequent"	3 Yrs (Max)	risk-based
Auditor Training	✔	✔	✔	✔
Explicit Objectives	✔	✔	✔	✔
Written Reports	✔	✔	✔	✔
QA Program	✔		✔	✔
Follow-up System	✔	✔	✔	✔
Surprise Audits		✔		
Reporting w/o Retribution		✔		

[1] U.S. EPA, "Environmental Auditing Policy Statement," Final Policy Statement (July 9, 1986); and "Incentives for Self-Policing: Discovery, Disclosure, Correction and Prevention of Violations," Final Policy Statement (January 22, 1996).

[2] U.S. Sentencing Commission, "Draft Corporate Sentencing Guidelines for Environmental Violations" (November 16, 1993).

[3] European Union Regulation 1836/93, *Allowing Voluntary Participation in an Eco-Management and Audit Scheme (EMAS)*, O.J.L. 168/1 (July 10, 1993).

[4] International Organization for Standardization (ISO), "Guidelines for Environmental Auditing, ISO 14010 (General Principles), 14011 (Audit Procedures) and 14012 (Qualification Criteria for Environmental Auditors)" (Fall 1996).

combining environmental, health, and safety compliance and audit programs. In some companies, this will require a re-engineering of the organization, because the health and safety program "grew up" in the Human Resources Department while the environmental program, which arrived much later, often had a life of its own.

While "doing more with less" today may be an understandable attitude and even a worthwhile goal, any fundamental relaxation of compliance efforts by companies presents an unjustifiable risk. EH&S auditing is a sound way to prevent damaging situations from occurring. Its value should not be neglected by management.

Chapter 2

GOVERNMENT PERSPECTIVE[1]

The environmentalists beat up on it. Congress beats up on it.
The Administration usually ignores it. In a curious way, the
strongest supporters of a forceful EPA are the industries it
regulates. They want government to set reasonable standards,
and they want the public to know they are being enforced.

– William D. Ruckelshaus, 1988[2]

INTRODUCTION

"Know thyself," the admonition of the oracle of Apollo at Delphi, is particularly sage advice regarding environmental affairs. Apparently, this wisdom is being followed in the regulated community. Rates of environmental auditing among American corporations are approximately 75 percent to 90 percent overall and 96 percent to 98 percent within the manufacturing sector, according to surveys of corporate environmental practices.[3]

Many sound business reasons support having an auditing program. The vast majority of respondents to the 1995 Price Waterhouse survey cited the following reasons for performing environmental audits:

- To improve the company's overall environmental program, and make it more proactive (94 percent) (selected most frequently as the primary reason)

- To identify problems internally and correct them before they are discovered by an agency (96 percent)

---

[1] This chapter was written by Brian P. Riedel and reflects the views of the author and not necessarily those of the U.S. Environmental Protection Agency or any other government entity.

[2] "Here Comes the Big New Cleanup," *Fortune Magazine* (November 21, 1988): 110.

[3] The Voluntary Environmental Audit Survey of U.S. Business, Price Waterhouse LLP, March 1995; 1996 Corporate Environmental Profiles Directory, Investor Responsibility Research Center; Environmental Audit Policies and Practices—A Manufacturers Alliance Survey, February 1995; Progress on the Environmental Challenge, A Survey of Corporate America's Environmental Accounting and Management, Price Waterhouse LLP, 1994.

- To provide assurance to management that control systems are functioning (91 percent)

- To decrease the company's operating and financial risks (88 percent).

Other business reasons for environmental auditing include the following:

- Provide evidence of meeting customers' environmental expectations

- Help maintain good public relations

- Satisfy investor criteria and improve access to capital

- Help secure insurance at reasonable cost

- Enhance an entity's image and market share

- Provide the basis for meeting vendor certification criteria

- Demonstrate reasonable care

- Facilitate conservation of input materials and energy

- Improve relations with government.

An auditing program is also one of many tools needed to develop and maintain an effective environmental management program. But identification of the deficiencies in compliance and management is only the first step. An organization must be willing to correct violations and other deficiencies and root causes in order to achieve improved results. If an organization is unwilling to act upon the discovered deficiencies, the audits may become a source of damaging evidence of liability.

An *effective* environmental auditing program is a very important piece of the overall environmental management puzzle.[3] Auditing can serve as a quality assurance check to help improve the performance of basic environmental management systems and programs by assessing whether necessary control systems and management practices are in place, functioning, and adequate. Environmental audits evaluate—but do not substitute for—direct compliance activities such as obtaining permits, installing controls, monitoring compliance, reporting violations, and keeping records. Although they cannot replace regulatory inspections, audits can supplement conventional federal, state, and local government oversight and point toward more efficient allocation of enforcement resources.

The U.S. Environmental Protection Agency (EPA) has defined environmental auditing as a systematic, documented, periodic, and objective review of facility op-

---

[3] For additional reading on broader environmental management practices see Jack E. Daugherty's *Industrial Environmental Management: A Practical Handbook* (Rockville, MD: Government Institutes, 1996).

erations and practices related to meeting environmental requirements.[4] In Europe, the International Chamber of Commerce has adopted essentially the same definition in its position paper on environmental auditing.[5] Whether domestic or international, an environmental audit can be designed to accomplish any of a number of objectives, including verifying compliance with environmental requirements; evaluating the effectiveness of environmental management systems already in place; and assessing risks from regulated and unregulated materials, wastes, and practices.

Environmental auditing has been developed for sound business reasons, particularly as a means to help manage pollution control affirmatively over time instead of reacting to crises. Auditing can improve facility performance *before* the regulatory inspector arrives. More importantly, it can help indicate effective solutions to common environmental problems, focus facility managers' attention on current and upcoming regulatory requirements, and generate protocols and checklists that help facilities manage themselves better. Auditing also can result in improved management of risks, since auditors frequently identify environmental liabilities that go beyond regulatory compliance.

In 1983, the U.S. EPA began promoting environmental auditing through a less structured approach labeled "endorsement, analysis, and assistance." The agency endorsed auditing at workshops and conferences, analyzed the attributes and benefits of effective audit programs, and assisted those interested in pursuing specific auditing approaches, especially federal agencies.

U.S. EPA, DOJ, AND OSHA[6] POLICIES ENCOURAGE ENVIRONMENTAL AUDITING

In general, the U.S. EPA encourages sound environmental management practices to help improve environmental results. In particular, implementation of an environmental auditing program can result in better identification, resolution, and avoidance of environmental problems. U.S. EPA policy encourages auditing whether done by an independent internal group, but a third party, or by some combination of both. (Larger organizations generally have greater resources to devote to an internal audit team, while smaller ones might be more likely to use outside auditors.)

Although environmental laws do not require auditing, ultimate responsibility for facility environmental performance lies with top corporate managers, who are responsible for taking all necessary steps to ensure compliance with environmental

---

[4] U.S. EPA, "Environmental Auditing Policy Statement," July 9, 1986 (51 *FR* 25004).

[5] International Chamber of Commerce, Commission on Environment, 38 Cours Albert ler, 75008 Paris, France, Document No. 210/285 Rev. 2 (December 7, 1988).

[6] A discussion of OSHA's 2000 Self-Audit Policy is at the end of this chapter.

requirements. This creates a strong incentive to use reasonable means, such as environmental auditing, to secure reliable information about facility compliance status. In other words, it's better to manage problems before they surface than to constantly react after the fact and face legal liabilities that could have been avoided.

The U.S. EPA does not seek to dictate or interfere with the environmental management practices of private or public organizations in its policy or elsewhere. Neither does the U.S. EPA intend to mandate auditing, though in certain instances the U.S. EPA will seek to include provisions for environmental auditing in settlement agreements. Environmental auditing systems have been widely adopted on a voluntary basis in the past. Because audit quality depends to a large degree upon genuine management commitment to the program and its objectives, auditing should remain a voluntary activity.

The U.S. EPA and the U.S. Department of Justice (DOJ) recognize that environmental auditing—and sound environmental management generally—can be powerful tools in protecting public health and the environment. EPA and DOJ have developed criminal environmental enforcement guidance documents designed to encourage use of these tools.

On July 1, 1991, the DOJ issued guidance entitled, "Factors In Decisions On Criminal Prosecutions For Environmental Violations In The Context of Significant Voluntary Compliance Or Disclosure Efforts By the Violator." The guidance sets the general DOJ policy on auditing: "It is the policy of the Department of Justice to encourage self-auditing, self-policing, and voluntary disclosure of environmental violations by the regulated community by indicating that these activities are viewed as mitigating factors in the Department's exercise of criminal enforcement discretion." In addition to "voluntary disclosure" and "cooperation," the DOJ guidance identifies "preventive measures and compliance programs," such as the existence and scope of a compliance audit program or compliance management system, as factors DOJ will consider in determining whether and how to prosecute an entity for suspected environmental violations.

On January 12, 1994, EPA issued guidance entitled, "The Exercise of Investigative Discretion," which sets forth specific factors that distinguish cases meriting criminal investigation from those more appropriately pursued under administrative or civil judicial authorities. In discussing the many factors to be considered, the guidance states,

> When self-auditing has been conducted (followed up by prompt
> remediation of the noncompliance and any resulting harm) and full,
> complete disclosure has occurred, the company's constructive activities
> should be considered as mitigating factors in EPA's exercise of investiga-
> tive discretion. Therefore, a violation that is voluntarily revealed and fully
> and promptly remedied as part of a corporations's systematic and compre-
> hensive self-evaluation program generally will not be a candidate for the
> expenditure of scarce criminal investigative resources.

As discussed in greater detail below, EPA has issued the 1986 "Environmental Auditing Policy Statement" ("1986 Auditing Statement") and the 1995 and 2000 "Incentives for Self-Policing: Discovery, Disclosure, Correction, and Prevention of Violations" ("Audit Policy"). In addition to making statements generally encouraging the use of environmental auditing, the 1986 policy sets forth the widely accepted core criteria for conducting environmental audits. These criteria or elements have provided an important guide for entities wishing to develop and implement auditing programs.

In contrast, the EPA Audit Policy is an enforcement policy. Under this policy, entities that meet the policy conditions for voluntary discovery, prompt disclosure and expeditious correction will receive zero or greatly reduced civil penalties and will not be recommended for criminal prosecution.

U.S. EPA's 1986 AUDITING STATEMENT AND ELEMENTS OF EFFECTIVE AUDIT PROGRAMS

On July 9, 1986, the U.S. EPA published its environmental auditing policy statement. Perhaps the most important contribution of this policy is the listing of the essential elements of effective auditing programs. In addition to addressing audit related policy issues, the U.S. EPA's policy statement also sets forth the essential elements of effective auditing programs. In doing so, the agency hopes to accomplish several objectives. A general description of elements in effective, mature audit programs may help those starting audit programs. Regulatory agencies may also use them when negotiating environmental auditing provisions for administrative consent orders or judicial consent decrees. Finally, they may help guide states and localities considering their own auditing initiatives.

Private sector environmental audits of facilities have been conducted for several years and have taken a variety of forms, in part to accommodate unique organizational structures and circumstances. Nevertheless, effective environmental audits appear to have certain discernible characteristics in common with other kinds of audits, for which standards have been documented extensively. The U.S. EPA, when setting standards for environmental audits, drew heavily on two of these documents: *Compendium of Audit Standards*[6] and *Standards for the Professional Practice of Internal Auditing.*[7] The U.S. EPA's standards also reflect findings from agency analyses conducted over several years and comments from corporate environmental audit managers, especially those active in the Environmental Auditing Roundtable.

An effective environmental auditing system will likely include the following general elements:

---

[6] Walter Willborn (Milwaukee: American Society for Quality Control, 1983).

[7] The Institute of Internal Auditors, Inc. (Altamonte Springs, FL: The Institute of Internal Auditors, 1974).

■ *Explicit top management support for environmental auditing and commitment to follow-up on audit findings.* Such support could be demonstrated by sanctioning the role of the audit program in a written management policy statement on environmental protection, buttressed with specific, tangible implementing actions.

■ *An environmental auditing function independent of audited activities.* The status or organizational focus of environmental auditors should be sufficient to ensure objective and unobstructed inquiry, observation, and testing. Auditor objectivity should not be impaired by personal relationships, financial or other conflicts of interest, interference with free inquiry or judgment, or fear of potential retribution.

■ *Adequate team staffing and auditor training.* Environmental auditors should possess or have ready access to the knowledge, skills, and disciplines needed to accomplish audit objectives. Each individual auditor should comply with professional standards of conduct. Auditors, whether full-time or part-time, should maintain their technical and analytical competence through continuing education and training.

■ *Explicit audit program objectives, scope, resources, and frequency.* At a minimum, audit objectives should include assessing compliance with applicable environmental laws and evaluating the adequacy of internal compliance systems to carry out assigned responsibilities. Explicit written audit procedures should generally be used. Auditors should be provided with all internal policies and federal, state, and local permits and regulations pertinent to the facility, as well as checklists or protocols addressing specific features that must be evaluated.

■ *A process that collects, analyzes, interprets and documents information sufficient to achieve audit objectives.* Information should be collected before and during an on-site visit regarding matters related to audit objectives and scope. This information should be sufficient, reliable, relevant, and useful enough to provide a sound basis for audit findings and recommendations.

In furtherance of the development and implementation of effective environmental compliance audit programs, the U.S. EPA has developed 13 sets of protocols for conducting environmental compliance audits under different environmental statutes. These protocols may be found at www.epa.gov/oeca/ccsmd/profile.html, and are available from Government Institutes.

U.S. EPA'S AUDIT POLICY

 On April 11, 2000, the U.S. EPA announced the "Incentives for Self-Policing: Discovery, Disclosure, Correction and Prevention of Violations"[8] policy which refines and supersedes the policy dated December 22, 1995 by the same name.[9] With the exception of a longer prompt disclosure period (21 days instead of 10 days), the 2000 policy is identical to the 1995 policy in all major respects.

Under the Audit Policy, the agency will greatly reduce civil penalties and limit liability for criminal prosecution for regulated entities that meet the policy's conditions for discovery, disclosure, and correction.[10]

Audit Policy Incentives

Under the policy, the U.S. EPA will not seek gravity-based[11] civil penalties for violations that meet all of the policy's nine conditions for systematic and voluntary discovery, prompt disclosure, and expeditious correction. *Systematic discovery* means detection of the violation through an environmental audit or a compliance management system (CMS). Where violations are discovered by means other than an environmental audit or CMS, the U.S. EPA will reduce gravity-based penalties by 75 percent provided the other eight policy conditions are met. The agency will generally not recommend to the DOJ that criminal charges be brought against entities that meet the policy conditions, although failure to meet the *systematic discovery* condition will not necessarily disqualify entities for such treatment. Finally, the policy restates the U.S. EPA's policy and practice of not routinely requesting environmental audit reports.

Safeguards

While the Audit Policy contains significant incentives for encouraging discovery, disclosure, and correction of violations, it also contains very important safeguards to deter irresponsible behavior and protect the public and the environment. For example, the policy requires entities to take steps to prevent recurrence of the violation and to remediate any harm caused by the violation. In addition, the policy does not apply to violations that resulted in serious actual harm or may have presented an

---

[8] April 11, 2000 (65 *FR* 19617).

[9] December 22, 1995 (60 *FR* 66706). This policy, in turn, revised the "Voluntary Environmental Self-Policing and Self-Disclosure Interim Policy Statement" announced on April 3, 1995 at 60 *FR* 16875

[10] The 2000 Audit Policy appears in Appendix B.

[11] The "gravity" component of a penalty represents the "seriousness" or "punitive" portion of penalties. The other major part of a penalty, the economic benefit component, represents the economic advantage a violator gains through its noncompliance.

imminent and substantial endangerment to human health or the environment. More-over, entities are not eligible for relief under the policy for repeated violations. The policy does not apply to individual criminal acts, or to violations that involve a prevalent philosophy or practice to condone or conceal the violations, or a conscious, high-level, corporate or managerial involvement in or willful blindness to the violations. Finally, the U.S. EPA retains its discretion to collect any economic benefit gained from noncompliance in order to provide an incentive for timely compliance and to preserve a "level playing field" for complying entities.[12]

Additional Incentives and Behavior

The Audit Policy provides additional incentives for entities to utilize the critical compliance tools of environmental auditing and compliance management systems. These incentives add to the many existing business reasons for entities to develop and maintain environmental auditing and compliance management systems, as discussed earlier in this chapter.

In 1986, the U.S. EPA announced that it was the agency's policy to encourage environmental auditing as a means to help achieve and maintain regulatory compliance.[13] Toward that end, the 1986 policy sets forth the basic elements of effective environmental auditing programs.

As memorialized in the Audit Policy, the U.S. EPA's policy toward encouraging the use of compliance tools such as auditing and management systems had evolved into incentives for penalty mitigation and protections related to criminal prosecution. It is important to recognize that this evolution is likely to continue as organizations develop more effective tools to manage the environmental aspects and impacts

---

[12] Under the Audit Policy, the U.S. EPA may waive the entire penalty for violations that, in the U.S. EPA's opinion, do not merit any penalty due to the insignificant amount of any economic benefit.

Some environmental statutes require the U.S. EPA, in assessing penalties, to consider the economic benefit a violator gains from noncompliance. *See* CAA §313(e), CWA §309(g), and SDWA §1423(c). The U.S. EPA's longstanding policy has been to collect significant economic benefit gained from noncompliance. *See* "Calculation of the Economic Benefit of Noncompliance in EPA's Civil Penalty Enforcement Cases," June 18, 1999 (64 *FR* 32948); and "A Framework for Statute-Specific Approaches to [Civil] Penalty Assessments: Implementing EPA's Policy on Civil Penalties," EPA General Enforcement Policy #GM-22, February 16, 1984. *See also* the approximately 24 U.S. EPA media and program-specific penalty and enforcement response policies. Two reasons justify collecting economic benefit. First, the prospect that the U.S. EPA will recoup the economic benefit of noncompliance provides an incentive for regulated entities to comply on time. Recovery of economic benefit can be likened to the IRS requirement of paying interest or fees on taxes paid late. Second, collection of economic benefit protects law-abiding entities from being undercut by non-complying competitors; that is, recovery of economic benefit will help preserve a "level playing field."

[13] Environmental Auditing Policy Statement, July 9, 1986 (51 *FR* 25004). *See* earlier discussion.

of their activities, services and products. Environmental management system (EMS) standards such as ISO 14001 and supporting standards hold promise as a means of improving environmental performance.[14] The U.S. EPA is exploring possible incentives for encouraging the use of such standards insofar as the incentives do not jeopardize protection of human health and the environment.[15]

Open and Inclusive Process Utilized to Develop the Audit Policy

In May of 1994, the Administrator asked the Office of Enforcement and Compliance Assurance (OECA) to determine whether additional incentives are needed to encourage entities to disclose and correct violations uncovered during environmental audits.[16] Over the next 18 months, stakeholders representing a spectrum of interests actively participated in the process to develop the 1995 policy. This process included a Washington, D.C. public meeting in July 1994, a San Francisco stakeholder dialogue in January 1995, Chicago stakeholder dialogues in June 1995, and a Washington, D.C. stakeholder dialogue in September 1995. The American Bar Association Section on Natural Resources and Environmental and Energy Law (ABA-SONREEL) hosted the Chicago and Washington, D.C. stakeholder dialogues.

Stakeholders represented state attorneys general and environmental commissioners, district attorneys, industry and trade groups, public interest and citizen groups, and professional auditing groups. In addition, the U.S. EPA established and maintained the Audit Policy Docket, which makes publicly available hundreds of comments, letters, and documents relating to environmental auditing. The open and inclusive process by which the policy was developed was a very important part of gaining support for the policy.

Widespread Use of the Audit Policy to Date with High Satisfaction Rate

To date, approximately 1150 regulated entities have disclosed actual or potential environmental violations at over 5400 facilities under the Audit Policy since 1995. The number of disclosures increased each of the six years the policy has been in effect. Results of the 1998 Audit Policy User's Survey revealed very high satisfaction rates among users, with 88 percent of respondents stating that they would use

---

[14] *See* "EPA Position Statement on Environmental Management Systems and ISO 14001 and a Request for Comments on the Nature of the Data to Be Collected from Environmental Management System/ISO 14001 Pilots," March 12, 1998 (63 *FR* 12094).

[15] *See* this author's chapter, "A Regulatory Enforcement Perspective of ISO 14001," in *Implementing ISO 14000: A Practical, Comprehensive Guide to the ISO 14000 Environmental Management Standards*, Eds. Tom Tibor and Ira Feldman (Burr Ridge, IL: Irwin Professional Publishing, 1997). *See also* the U.S. EPA's National Environmental Performance Track program.

[16] *See* June 20, 1994 *Federal Register* notice (59 *FR* 31914).

the policy again and 84 percent stating that they would recommend the policy to clients and/or their counterparts. No respondents stated an unwillingness to use the policy again or to recommend its use to others.

Audit Policy Conditions

1. **Systematic Discovery—Entity must discover the violation through an environmental audit or compliance management system to obtain full gravity penalty mitigation.**

The Audit Policy provides full mitigation of gravity-based civil penalties if the disclosed violations are detected through an environmental audit or a CMS, provided the other policy conditions are met. Entities that do not discover the violations through an audit or CMS—that is, "randomly discovered" violations—would still obtain 75 percent gravity mitigation as long as the other conditions are met.

The Audit Policy defines an *environmental audit* the same way as it is defined in the 1986 auditing policy: "a systematic, documented, periodic and objective review by regulated entities of facility operations and practices related to meeting environmental requirements." Note that this definition covers several types of environmental audits including risk, pollution prevention, and EMS audits as well as compliance audits.

A CMS under the policy is defined as an "entity's documented systematic efforts, appropriate to the size and nature of its business, to prevent, detect and correct violations" through the following CMS criteria:

■ compliance policies, standards, and procedures that identify how employees and agents are to meet regulatory requirements;

■ assignment of responsibility to oversee conformance with these policies, standards, and procedures;

■ mechanisms including monitoring and auditing of compliance and the CMS to assure the policies, standards, and procedures are being carried out;

■ training to communicate the standards and procedures;

■ employee incentives to perform in accordance with the compliance policies, standards, and procedures; and

■ procedures for the prompt and appropriate correction of violations including program modifications needed to prevent future violations.

These CMS (or due diligence) criteria were adapted from codes of practice, especially Chapter Eight of the U.S. Sentencing Guidelines for organizational defendants that has been effective since 1991.[17] The Sentencing Guidelines have had an enormous impact in encouraging the development and implementation of CMSs in the United States.

Stakeholder written and oral comments indicated that ongoing, comprehensive, and systematic efforts to prevent, detect, and correct violations should be rewarded at least as much as environmental auditing. The difference between a compliance audit and a CMS can be likened to the difference between a snapshot and a video.

It is also significant that the U.S. EPA may require, as a condition for penalty mitigation, that a description of an entity's CMS be made publicly available. This type of public disclosure has the potential to push the state-of-art in CMS development and encourage benchmarking among suppliers and competitors. The public availability of CMS descriptions can also provide valuable information for insurers, financial markets, investors, and lenders, providing the basis for "quasi" market-based incentives.

2. **Voluntary Discovery—The violation was voluntarily discovered and not through legally mandated monitoring or sampling (e.g., CEM, DMRs).**

The violation must have been discovered voluntarily and not through monitoring or sampling required by statute, regulation, permit, judicial or administrative order, or consent agreement. Examples of discovery that is not voluntary include emissions violations detected through continuous emission monitors required by permit, or violations of National Pollutant Discharge Elimination System discharge limits detected through sampling required by a consent decree. However, the voluntary discovery requirement does not extend to an audit that is a component of agreement terms to implement a comprehensive EMS. The basis for this exception is to encourage, or not discourage, entities from agreeing to implement a comprehensive EMS.

In some instances, violations of the New Source Review and Prevention of Significant Deterioration requirements of the Clean Air Act may be eligible for Audit Policy relief if the violations were discovered, disclosed, and corrected by an entity prior to issuance of a Title V permit. This clarification or guidance is relevant to companies that are conducting annual compliance certifications necessary to obtain Title V operating permits. The guidance memorandum, dated September 30, 1999, is available at www.epa.gov/oeca/ore/apolguid.html.

---

[17] U.S. Sentencing Commission Guidelines Manual, Chapter 8C Sentencing of Organizations, Part AC General Application Principles (effective November 1, 1991).

3. Prompt Disclosure—Entity discloses the violation in writing to the U.S. EPA generally within 21 days after discovery.

Under the policy, the entity must fully disclose in writing to the U.S. EPA that a violation has occurred or may have occurred, within 21 calendar days after discovery. The 21-day disclosure period begins when any officer, director, employee, or agent of the facility has an objectively reasonable basis for believing that a violation has, or may have, occurred. If a statute or regulation requires the entity to report the violation in fewer than 21 days, disclosure must be made within the time limit established by law.[18] In the acquisitions context, the 21-day disclosure period begins on the date of discovery by the acquiring entity, but in no case will the period begin earlier than the date of acquisition. Disclosures under the Audit Policy should be made be made to the appropriate U.S. EPA regional office or, where multiple regions are involved, to U.S. EPA Headquarters. Audit policy contacts for disclosure are listed in the *Audit Policy Update* newsletter available at http://es.epa.gov/oeca/ore/apolguid.html.

If an entity might not be able to disclose the violation within the 21-day period, the entity should contact the appropriate U.S. EPA office to develop disclosure terms acceptable to the U.S. EPA. The U.S. EPA would ordinarily extend the disclosure period to allow reasonable time to audit multiple facilities, provided that the facilities to be audited are identified in advance, and the U.S. EPA and the entity agree in advance on the timing and scope of the audits. The U.S. EPA may also extend the disclosure period in exceptional circumstances, such as in a complex situation where the U.S. EPA believes that the violation cannot be identified and disclosed within 21 days, or in an acquisitions situation.

The 21-day disclosure period is a new change to the policy, which had previously required disclosure within 10 days. In response to comments and based on the 1998 Audit Policy Users Survey, the U.S. EPA lengthened the disclosure period from 10 to 21 days to provide organizations with additional time to analyze discoveries of potential violations and determine whether to make a disclosure under the Audit Policy. Twenty-one of the 29 sets of comments received during the 60-day comment period supported lengthening the disclosure period to at least 21 days. According to the User's Survey, the most frequently suggested change to the policy (18 percent) was to lengthen the disclosure period. Out of the first 274 disclosures received, 53 (or 19 percent) were late and approximately half of those met all of the conditions except for the 10-day prompt disclosure condition. Failure to meet the prompt disclosure condition was the most frequent reason for ineligibility under the policy.

---

[18] For example, unpermitted releases of hazardous substances must be reported immediately under 42 USC § 9603.

Regarding the length of the disclosure period, the U.S. EPA considered the fact that, under the User's Survey, 58 percent of the late disclosures were made between 10 and 20 days after discovery. The U.S. EPA selected 21 days to capture these late disclosures and because 21 is a multiple of seven so that if discovery was made on a business day, the 21-day disclosure deadline would also fall on a business day.

4. **Discovery and Disclosure Independent of Government or Third-Party Plaintiff—The entity must disclose the violation prior to discovery or imminent discovery by the government.**

The entity must identify and disclose the violation before the government has discovered or will discover the violation. Thus, the entity must disclose the violation prior to commencement of a government inspection or investigation, issuance of an information request, notice of citizen suit, filing of a third-party complaint, or reporting by a whistle-blower. However, for entities that own or operate multiple facilities, the fact that one facility is already under investigation does not automatically preclude Audit Policy credit for other facilities owned or operated by the same entity.

5. **Correction and Remediation—The entity must correct the violation within 60 days or as expeditiously as possible, and remedy harm.**

The entity must correct the violation expeditiously and within 60 days certify correction and take appropriate measures to remedy any harm caused by the violation. If more than 60 days is needed to correct the violation, the entity must notify the U.S. EPA before the 60-day period has passed. Where appropriate, the U.S. EPA may require a written agreement, order, or decree to satisfy requirements for correction, remediation, or prevention measures especially where such measures are complex or lengthy.

6. **Prevent Recurrence—The entity must agree to take steps to prevent recurrence of the violation.**

The entity's efforts to prevent recurrence of the violation may involve modifying its environmental auditing program or compliance management system.

7. **No Repeat Violations—The specific or closely related violation has not occurred at the same facility within the past three years or is not part of a pattern of violations at the parent company within the past five years.**

The policy does not apply to repeat violators. The U.S. EPA has established "bright lines" to determine when a prior violation constitutes a "repeat violation." Under the policy, the specific or closely related violation must not have occurred at the same facility within the past three years or is not part of a pattern of violations at the facility's parent organization within the past five years. The applicable three- or five-year period begins to run when the government or third party has given the violator clear notice of the specific or closely related violation, regardless of when the prior violation occurred. The existence of a violation prior to a new acquisition does not trigger the repeat violation exclusion. This policy exclusion provides entities with a continuing incentive to prevent violations and avoids the unfairness of granting policy relief repeatedly for the same or similar violation.

8. **Other Violations Excluded—The violation is not one that has resulted in serious actual harm or may have presented an imminent and substantial endangerment, or violates the specific terms of an order or agreement.**

The policy does not apply to violations that resulted in serious actual harm or may have presented an imminent and substantial endangerment to human health or the environment. Extending coverage of the policy to such violations would undermine deterrence and reward entities for delinquent management of their environmental activities. The policy also does not apply to violations of the specific terms of any administrative or judicial order or consent or plea agreement. This is necessary to preserve incentives to comply with the orders or agreements.

9. **Cooperation—The entity must cooperate with the U.S. EPA.**

The entity must cooperate and provide whatever information EPA requests to determine applicability of the Audit Policy.

Relationship to State Laws, Regulations, and Policies

Approximately 26 states[19] have enacted laws or policies with provisions that establish an evidentiary environmental audit privilege and/or limited immunity from prosecution or penalties for disclosed violations discovered through environmental audits. Under federal law, states must have adequate enforcement authority to enforce the requirements of any federal programs they are authorized to administer. Some state audit privilege and/or immunity laws have placed restrictions on the ability of states to obtain penalties and injunctive relief for violations of federal program requirements, or to obtain information that may be needed to determine compliance status. Using the "Statement of Principles, Effect of State Audit Immunity/Privilege Laws on Enforcement Authority for Federal Programs," dated February 14, 1997,[20] EPA worked with states where audit privilege/immunity legislation was pending or had been enacted. In approximately 20 of these states, the state and EPA had worked together to remove the legal impediments posed by the audit privilege/immunity legislation, which allowed EPA to approve, authorize or delegate the programs in

---

[19] *See* Appendix A at the end of this chapter.

[20] This Memorandum may be found at www.epa.gov/oeca/oppa.

the respective states. As of date of publication, EPA is working with approximately six states to remove the legal impediments posed by their respective audit laws.

The U.S. EPA has worked and continues to work with states to encourage their adoption of policies that reflect the incentives and conditions outlined in the Audit Policy. Approximately 16 states[21] have issued self-disclosure policies, some of which, in final or draft form, provided models for the U.S. EPA Audit Policy.

The U.S. EPA remains opposed to environmental audit privileges that would provide a cloak of secrecy over evidence of environmental violations and that contradict the public's right to know. The U.S. EPA also remains opposed to blanket immunities or amnesty for violations that reflect criminal conduct, present serious threats or actual harm to health or the environment, allow non-complying entities to gain an economic advantage over their competitors, or reflect a repeated failure to comply with federal law. Law enforcement, citizen, environmental, and other groups have successfully thwarted efforts to enact audit privilege/immunity legislation at the federal level.

Applicability and Effective Date

The Audit Policy applies to the settlement of any alleged violations of federal environmental laws that the U.S. EPA administers, and supersedes any inconsistent provisions of the U.S. EPA's media and program-specific penalty and enforcement response policies. The Audit Policy operates in conjunction with other U.S. EPA enforcement policies to the extent they are not inconsistent with the policy. However, an entity may not receive additional penalty mitigation for having met the same or similar conditions under other enforcement policies, nor will the Audit Policy apply to violations that have received penalty mitigation under other enforcement policies. The policy is intended to be utilized for settlement of administrative and judicial enforcement actions, not for pleading purposes. The 2000 Audit Policy became effective on May 11, 2000.

Policy Redresses Industry Concerns

The policy redresses three general problem areas perceived by some in the regulated community. First, industry representatives asserted that the U.S. EPA's enforcement response to self-disclosed violations under the U.S. EPA's approximately 24 media-specific enforcement policies was not consistent and predictable. Second, there were perceptions in the regulated community that audit reports generated through proactive efforts to detect violations would provide a "roadmap" to areas of potential civil and criminal liability that will be used by the U.S. EPA and U.S. DOJ

---

[21] See Appendix B at the end of this chapter.

investigators and prosecutors. Therefore, it was argued, documented auditing activity (and other documented environmental management activity) actually increases a company's exposure to civil and criminal liability. These concerns are sometimes collectively referred to as the "seek and ye shall be fined" perceived phenomenon. Third, some in industry were concerned that criminal acts of "rogue employees" could trigger corporate criminal liability under the general law of agency, and could inculpate corporate officers under the "responsible corporate officer doctrine," where the corporation and individual corporate officers are not otherwise culpable.

As outlined above, the Audit Policy establishes a multi-media, consistent, and certain enforcement response for entities that discover, disclose, and correct environmental violations and meet the other safeguards under the policy. Since 1995, hundreds of entities have taken advantage of the policy, and, based on the 1998 User's Survey, there is a very high satisfaction rate among the users.

Regarding the concerns that audit reports would be used as liability "roadmaps," the U.S. EPA believes that these perceptions were not supported by the facts. For example, the U.S. EPA and U.S. DOJ were not able to identify a single federal or state criminal prosecution of a regulated entity for violations uncovered through an audit and self-disclosed before an independent government investigation was underway. Moreover, the following findings from the 1995 Price Waterhouse survey support the conclusion that U.S. EPA policies and practices have not discouraged environmental auditing: 1) environmental auditing is prevalent among large corporations; 2) the respondents that do not audit generally do not perceive any need to audit; and 3) concern about confidentiality of audit information is one of the least important factors in their decisions not to audit. In fact, corporate respondents indicated that U.S. EPA activity contributed to their decision to audit; 96 percent of the corporate respondents that audit stated that they do so in order to find and correct violations before the violations are found by government inspectors.

In addition, the Audit Policy restates U.S. EPA's policy and practice since 1986 of not requesting or using an environmental audit report to initiate a civil or criminal investigation of the entity. Thus, consistent with past practice, the U.S. EPA will not request audit reports during routine inspections. If the U.S. EPA has reason independent of the audit report to believe that a violation has occurred, however, the U.S. EPA may seek the relevant information needed to determine liability or the extent of any harm. This policy restatement should further reassure the regulated community that investigators and prosecutors will not abuse their discretion regarding the request for and use of audit reports.

With respect to industry's "rogue employee" concern relating to increased criminal liability, the Audit Policy makes it clear that as long as conditions two through nine are satisfied (regardless of whether the violation was systematically discovered), the U.S. EPA will not recommend to the U.S. DOJ that criminal charges be brought against the entity. This protection is available as long as the violation does not involve a prevalent philosophy or practice to condone or conceal the violations, or a conscious, high-level, corporate or managerial involvement in, or willful blindness to, the violations. The U.S. EPA reserves the right to recommend prosecution for the criminal acts of individuals. The U.S. EPA has not referred a criminal case for prosecution of corporate officers, nor has the U.S. DOJ criminally prosecuted corporate officers, solely on the basis of the corporate officer's position in the company.

Use of Audit Policy in Corporate-Wide Audit Agreements and Compliance Incentive Programs

Corporate-Wide Audit Agreements

The U.S. EPA encourages companies with multiple facilities to take advantage of the Audit Policy to conduct corporate-wide audits and develop corporate-wide compliance systems. Corporate-Wide Audit Agreements have proven to be a mutually advantageous means of addressing potential environmental noncompliance. A Corporate-Wide Audit Agreement is an up-front agreement between a company and the U.S. EPA regarding the scope and timing of the audit, as well as disclosure and compliance schedules. Under the agreement, penalties for disclosed violations may be stipulated on a per violation and/or aggregate basis. Stipulation as to economic benefit is also possible. The agreement may address policy eligibility and treatment of certain types of violations.

From a company's perspective, Corporate-Wide Audit Agreements can offer many benefits. They can provide certainty regarding the size of anticipated penalties and whether the Audit Policy would apply at all by negotiating disclosure periods longer than 21 days. Companies participating in Corporate-Wide Audit Agreements have one point of contact within the Agency, which is a significant benefit in some cases. Corporate-Wide Audit Agreements offer companies an opportunity to evaluate corporate policies and compliance status without the stigma of enforcement action. These agreements also remove the uncertainty and cost of litigation and attorneys' fees. Typically, Corporate-Wide Audit Agreements are particularly effective where violations are suspected within multiple facilities involving homogeneous operations, or even at a very large facility.

From the U.S. EPA's perspective, Corporate-Wide Audit Agreements are an efficient and economical means of improving and ensuring compliance.

Since 1999, the U.S. EPA has entered into Corporate-Wide Audit Agreements with a number of different types of companies. Examples include agreements with 10 telecommunications companies involving the audit, disclosure, and correction of approximately 1300 CWA Spill Prevention and Control and Countermeasure and EPCRA violations at 400 facilities. These telecommunications companies collectively paid approximately $129,000 in penalties, which represent their economic benefit gained from noncompliance. The U.S. EPA waived approximately $4.2 million in gravity-based penalties that otherwise would have been assessed.

Another Corporate-Wide Audit Agreement with a major airline involved the audit, disclosure, and correction of CAA §211 fuel standard violations. The airline paid $95,000 representing economic benefit, and the U.S. EPA waived approximately $1.4 million in gravity-based penalties that otherwise would have been assessed. Other Corporate-Wide Audit Agreements involve the audit of a natural gas facility for PCB violations, the audit of two major chemical companies for TSCA violations, and the audit of 40 manufacturing facilities for CAA New Source Review violations.

Compliance Incentive Programs

The U.S. EPA has utilized the Audit Policy as a key tool in Compliance Incentive Programs. In contrast to Corporate-Wide Audit Agreements, Compliance Incentive Programs apply to entire sectors; individual companies have limited or no ability to influence the specific terms of the program. The initiation of the programs usually begins when the U.S. EPA has detected high levels of noncompliance within a certain sector. Generally, the U.S. EPA sends letters to invite members of the sector to participate in the program and also reaches out to relevant trade associations.

The terms of Compliance Incentive Programs vary, but usually provide that gravity-based penalties will be waived if the audit, disclosure, correction, and other program terms are met. Typically the disclosure period is longer than 21 days. In some programs, stipulated penalties are available. Participation in the programs is typically opt-in with a deadline. If a member of the sector chooses not to participate in the Compliance Incentive Program, the company may face an increased inspection frequency within that sector. Of course, non-participants face full exposure to gravity-based liability and the stigma attached to enforcement action. Occasionally, a Compliance Incentive Program will result in the execution of a Corporate-Wide Audit Agreement with members of the target sector.

Some of the Compliance Incentive Programs have focused on above-ground storage tanks, wetlands (U.S. EPA Region 4), universities (Regions 1, 2, 3, and 9), nitrate compounds, non-road engines, grain producers, telecommunications industry, airlines, iron and steel minimills, and pork producers.

Audit Policy Information Resources

A wealth of information regarding the Audit Policy and its implementation is available on U.S. EPA's website at http://es.epa.gov/oeca/ore/apolguid.html. This website contains the Audit Policy Interpretive Guidance, *Audit Policy Update* newsletters, an optional form for submitting disclosures, policy memoranda regarding application of the policy in the context of criminal and certain Clean Air Act disclosures, findings of the Audit Policy Evaluation, and other information. In addition, copies of executed settlement documents involving Audit Policy disclosures, as well as descriptions of CMSs submitted under the first condition of the Audit Policy, are available in the Audit Policy Docket by calling (202) 564-2614.

U.S. EPA'S SMALL BUSINESS COMPLIANCE POLICY

On April 11, 2000, EPA published the "Small Business Compliance Policy" (65 *FR* 19630), which is substantively identical to the 2000 EPA Audit Policy, with the following exceptions: the Small Business Compliance Policy 1) only applies to facilities owned by businesses that employee 100 or fewer individuals; 2) provides 100 percent mitigation of gravity-based penalties for violations discovered by any voluntary means, including non-systematic discovery and discovery through government sponsored on-site compliance assistance; 3) allows a longer correction period of 180 days (instead of 60 days), or 360 days if the correction involves pollution prevention modifications; 4) contains several differences regarding ineligibility for repeat violators; and 5) does not apply to criminal conduct.

CONCLUSIONS

Judging by the thousands of disclosures by hundreds of users and the high user-satisfaction rate, the U.S. EPA Audit Policy has been successful in encouraging voluntary and systematic discovery, prompt disclosure, and expeditious correction of environmental violations. The policy incentives include the elimination of gravity-based penalties for entities that meet the policy's safeguards. As an enforcement tool, the U.S. EPA has also utilized the Audit Policy in the context of Corporate-Wide Audit Agreements and Compliance Incentives Programs. These agreements and programs have provided greater enforcement certainty for their participants, and the U.S. EPA has used these agreements and programs to effectively leverage enforcement resources. In the future, the U.S. EPA will continue to develop effective and innovative ways to protect human health and the environment.

OSHA'S 2000 SELF-AUDIT POLICY

In July 1999, the Occupational Safety and Health Administration (OSHA) conducted a telephone survey of about 500 employers and found that over 85 percent of them were conducting safety and health self-inspections or audits. The respondents stated that companies conducted the audits to reduce injury and illness rates, do the right thing, and be in compliance with OSHA regulations.

Much like the U.S. EPA, OSHA is very supportive of these employer self-audits. In order to clarify its position on self-audits, on July 28, 2000, OSHA published in the *Federal Register* its Final Self-Audit Policy.[21] The Policy contains four basic provisions:

---

[21] "Final Policy Concerning the Occupational Safety and Health Administration's Treatment of Voluntary Employer Safety and Health Self-Audits," July 28, 2000 (65 *FR* 46498-46503).

1. It explains that OSHA will refrain from routinely requesting reports of voluntary self-audits at the initiation of an enforcement inspection.

2. It explains that OSHA will refrain from issuing a citation for a violative condition that an employer has discovered through a voluntary self-audit and has corrected prior to the initiation of an OSHA inspection (or a related accident, illness, or injury that triggers the inspection), even if the violative condition existed within the six month limitation's period during which OSHA is authorized to issue citations. The employer must also have taken appropriate steps to prevent the recurrence of the condition.

3. It contains a safe-harbor provision under which, if an employer is responding in good faith to a violative condition identified in a voluntary self-audit report and OSHA discovers the violation during an enforcement inspection, OSHA will not treat that portion of the report as evidence of willfulness.

4. It describes how an employer's response to a voluntary self-audit may be considered evidence of good faith, qualifying the employer for a substantial civil penalty reduction, up to 25 percent, when OSHA determines a proposed penalty.

The policy also states that all OSHA personnel applying the policy will receive instruction in order to ensure the consistent and appropriate application of the policy.

Appendix A: States with Audit Privilege and Immunity Laws: July 5, 2000

The following states have enacted environmental audit privilege and/or penalty immunity laws. The first date contained in the parenthetical indicates when the law was enacted; the subsequent dates reference actions to satisfy minimum requirements for federally authorized, delegated or approved environmental programs (i.e., sunset, amendment, memorandum of agreement and/or attorney general statement).

Privilege Only	Privilege and Immunity	
1. Oregon (11/93)	1. Kansas (7/95)	11. Michigan (3/96, 11/97)*
2. Mississippi (7/95)	2. Kentucky (7/94)	12. Ohio (12/96, 7/98)*
3. Illinois (1/95)***	3. Alaska (5/97)	13. Montana (5/97, 12/99)*
4. Arkansas (2/95, 3/99)*	4. Nevada (7/97)	14. Minnesota (1/95, 5/99)*
5. Indiana (7/94, 5/99)*	5. Nebraska (4/98)	15. Wyoming (2/95, 3/98)*
	6. Iowa (4/98)	16. Utah (3/95, 5/97)*
Immunity Only	7. Colorado (6/94, 5/00)*	17. Texas (5/95, 5/97)*
1. Rhode Island (7/97)	8. South Carolina (6/96, 5/00)*	18. South Dakota (3/96, 2/99, 3/99)*
	9. New Hampshire (7/96, 5/99)*	19. Arizona (4/00)**
	10. Virginia (7/95, 1/98)*	20. Idaho (7/95, sunset 12/97)

Note: Oklahoma has adopted a regulation (6/97) allowing penalty immunity under certain conditions.

*State has enacted statutory revisions and/or issued a clarifying Attorney General's statement and/or entered into a Memorandum of Agreement with the U.S. EPA to satisfy minimum requirements for federally authorized, delegated, or approved environmental programs.

**State has enacted a law that contains elements of audit privilege and/or immunity in the context of encouraging environmental management systems. Law satisfies minimum requirements for federally authorized, delegated, or approved environmental programs.

***Illinois and the U.S. EPA have reached an understanding as to necessary statutory revisions and the state has issued a clarifying Attorney General's statement. Once the amendments are enacted, the state will satisfy minimum requirements for federally authorized, delegated, or approved environmental programs.

Appendix B: States with Self-Disclosure Policies: July 5, 2000

The following states have adopted self-disclosure policies. The first date contained in the parenthetical indicates when the policy was adopted; subsequent dates reflect policy revisions.

California (7/8/96, 12/98)	Tennessee (11/27/96)
Connecticut (10/30/96, 3/27/00)	Vermont (12/14/96)
Delaware (4/11/97)	Washington (12/20/94)
Florida (4/1/96)	Minnesota (1/24/95)
Maryland (6/24/97)	New Mexico (2/5/99)
Massachusetts (4/26/97)	New York (8/12/99)*
North Carolina (9/1/95)	Oregon (2/18/99)
Pennsylvania (9/25/96)	Indiana (4/5/99)

* (only applicable to small businesses)

Chapter 3

LEGAL CONSIDERATIONS[1]

Laws too gentle are seldom obeyed; too severe, seldom executed.

    – Benjamin Franklin, Poor Richard's Almanac, 1732-57

INTRODUCTION

Over the past 25 years, the United States has witnessed a veritable explosion of environmental laws and regulations at the federal, state, and local levels. As a result, businesses in all sectors of the economy are subject to environmental requirements that affect a broad spectrum of activities. Many of the environmental programs that are now in place rely on "command and control" strategies applicable to specified classes of substances and activities. For example, the generation, transportation, storage, treatment, disposal, and recycling of hazardous wastes are subject to complex federal and state requirements; discharges from point sources to surface waters are subject to permit requirements and limitations that are regularly revised; and sources of air pollutants are subject to pervasive regulatory controls and a myriad of permitting requirements based upon fluctuating thresholds. Frequent revisions to these and other environmental regulatory and statutory schemes compound the challenge of maintaining compliance with environmental laws and regulations.

Virtually all of the major environmental statutes vest the government (usually both federal and state governments) with broad enforcement powers. Those found to have violated environmental requirements may be subject to civil penalties, criminal sanctions, and enforcement orders. The potential exposure for relatively minor violations of environmental requirements can often be quite significant. Civil penalties under many of the major environmental statutes can range up to $25,000 per day of violation. Each day of a continuing violation is typically treated as a separate violation. Criminal sanctions can also be quite severe.

---

[1] Note: This chapter was written by Marc E. Gold, Esquire and Michael M. Meloy, Esquire, Manko, Gold & Katcher, LLP, Suite 500, 401 City Avenue, Bala Cynwyd, PA 19004, mgold@mgklaw.com.

In response to the broad spectrum of environmental requirements that are now in place, many businesses have developed new and innovative ways to ensure that their operations are being conducted in conformance with applicable environmental requirements. Environmental assessments, including formal environmental compliance audits and compliance management systems, represent a critically important tool to achieve these goals.

A similar evaluation has occurred in the area of workplace health and safety requirements. The Occupational Safety and Health Administration (OSHA) administers programs aimed at reducing workplace accidents, illness, and injuries; and encourages compliance through a myriad of initiatives. The legal considerations described below with respect to environmental issues apply equally to potential workplace liabilities defined by OSHA.

FUNCTION OF ENVIRONMENTAL ASSESSMENTS[2]

Environmental assessments or audits typically are designed to evaluate whether specific activities or operations are being conducted in conformance with applicable regulatory requirements and whether associated equipment and facilities meet environmental standards. They may be used to evaluate whether changes must be made in operations or equipment to achieve environmental compliance or whether such changes will otherwise lead to reductions in environmental risks. In this regard, environmental assessments may help businesses make informed decisions regarding the appropriate deployment of capital and personnel. They are also useful to identify opportunities for reducing emissions and minimizing the generation of wastes. Additional examples of the function of environmental assessments include:

- minimizing the potential for governmental enforcement actions or third party lawsuits such as toxic tort actions;

- evaluating whether nonregulatory standards such as internal corporate environmental goals and industry standards are being achieved;

- preparing for due diligence or divestitures; and

- satisfying internal stakeholders.

Environmental assessments may be performed as part of an overall compliance program designed to meet the ISO 14001 environmental management system standard developed by the International Organization of Standardization. Satisfying this

---

[2] While the chapter uses the term "Environmental Assessments," the same considerations apply to Health and Safety Assessments. In many cases, compliance assessments at a facility will cover both environmental requirements and health and safety requirements. Moreover, most corporate programs manage environmental, health, and safety liabilities in a single unit.

standard may be necessary to participate in certain sectors of the global market-place. Environmental assessments may be performed due to marketing or public relations considerations or to improve relationships with neighbors and customers. Finally, environmental assessments may be performed to facilitate compliance with non-environmental legal requirements such as disclosure and reporting obligations administered by the Securities and Exchange Commission.

Whatever the motivators may be, environmental assessments provide businesses with a powerful tool to facilitate compliance; however, they can (and often do) identify areas of noncompliance or other facts that could lead to substantial legal liability. This dynamic potentially creates significant disincentives to performing environmental assessments. For example, the results of an environmental assessment may:

1. provide a ready basis for a governmental enforcement action or a citizen's suit;

2. be used against the party conducting the assessment in other types of litigation such as toxic tort actions, property damage suits, and personal injury actions; or

3. trigger reporting and disclosure requirements under applicable laws and regulations leading to the unanticipated expenditure of significant funds.

For some businesses, concerns over the potential exposure to enforcement actions and other litigation predicated on self-identified violations outweigh the benefits to be gained from environmental assessments, thereby eliminating an otherwise useful mechanism to foster compliance. Other businesses have sought to strike a balance between these competing considerations by structuring environmental assessments to maximize the potential for maintaining the confidentiality of the results of the assessment.

ROLE OF ENVIRONMENTAL ASSESSMENTS

One of the principles undergirding federal and state environmental programs is that compliance with environmental requirements represents an important benchmark for evaluating overall environmental performance. The same theory applies to legally mandated health and safety requirements. Assuming that these requirements represent societal standards for how members of the regulated community ought to conduct their activities, a critical question then becomes how best to foster a high level of compliance with such requirements. As the environmental regulatory programs have matured, regulatory agencies have generally recognized that multiple approaches to facilitate compliance are necessary. This is in marked contrast to the view that an aggressive enforcement program, by itself, is the lynch pin to promoting compliance. While enforcement actions remain an important component of the overall framework of the environmental programs, they can be confrontational, expensive, resource intensive, and time consuming.

During the past several years, the U.S. EPA and many states have embraced the view that voluntary efforts by the regulated community are critical to achieving a high level of environmental compliance. Moreover, agencies have recognized that environmental assessments are a fundamental tool to accomplish this goal. There is broad consensus regarding the importance of encouraging members of the regulated community to conduct compliance self-assessments, even though there has been considerable debate over the most appropriate methods to use to achieve this goal.

The U.S. EPA and some states have embraced the view that incentives to perform environmental assessments should be based on the concept that those who voluntarily identify, disclose, and correct environmental violations should be entitled to some reduced level of punishment. The reward for performing the environmental assessment, and disclosing and correcting the violations, is the knowledge that civil penalties will be reduced. By contrast, many members of the regulated community as well as a number of states have endorsed the concept that those who engage in environmental assessments should be entitled to protect the confidentiality of the results of such assessments, provided that the identified environmental violations are promptly corrected. This concept rests on the notion of one or more of the following legal privileges: the attorney-client privilege, the attorney work-product privilege, and the "self-evaluative privilege." The U.S. EPA has actively attacked this concept as antithetical to the open exchange of information, which in the U.S. EPA's view is an important aspect of most environmental regulatory programs.

This is the general backdrop for evaluating the legal issues associated with environmental assessments. If we assume that performing environmental assessments is a positive step in assuring compliance and improving environmental performance, then should the results of the environmental assessments be promptly disclosed based on the promise of more lenient enforcement, or should they be privileged and subject only to a duty to address areas of identified noncompliance? The tension between these two approaches is the subject of the remainder of this chapter and is the root of the legal conundrum.

FEDERAL POLICIES ENCOURAGING ENVIRONMENTAL ASSESSMENTS[3]

Overview and Evolution of U.S. EPA Policies

Both the U.S. EPA and the U.S. Department of Justice (DOJ) have issued formal policy statements encouraging the use of environmental audits and assessments.

---

[3] In addition to the U.S. EPA and U.S. DOJ policies discussed in detail in this chapter, OSHA published an audit policy entitled "Final Policy Concerning the Occupational Safety and Health Administration's Treatment of Voluntary Employer Safety and Health Self-Audits," 65 *FR* 46498 (July 28, 2000).

Neither the U.S. EPA nor the U.S. DOJ, however, has taken the step of insulating the results of environmental audits and assessments from disclosure.

On July 9, 1986, the U.S. EPA issued a document entitled *Environmental Auditing Policy Statement*. This document identifies factors that in the U.S. EPA's opinion are necessary for implementing a successful environmental auditing program. The U.S. EPA also took the position in this document that as a matter of policy, it would not routinely request environmental audit reports, although it reserved its ability to seek such reports on a case-by-case basis where necessary to accomplish its "statutory mission," or where deemed to be material to a criminal investigation.

On January 12, 1994, the U.S. EPA issued a guidance document relating to the exercise of its investigative discretion. This document sets forth internal guidelines for distinguishing cases meriting criminal investigation from those more appropriately pursued under administrative and civil judicial authorities. Pursuant to this guidance document, environmental audits followed by prompt remediation of any noncompliance and appropriate disclosure is to be considered as a mitigating factor by the U.S. EPA in its exercise of investigative discretion. Accordingly, an appropriate self-evaluation program may help protect a business from criminal sanctions for environmental noncompliance.

On April 3, 1995, the U.S. EPA published for public comment a document entitled "Voluntary Environmental Self-Policing and Self-Disclosure Interim Policy Statement" ("Interim Policy Statement") (60 *FR* 16875). The Interim Policy Statement reflected the U.S. EPA's reassessment of its position regarding voluntary compliance evaluations conducted by the regulated community. The Interim Policy Statement recognized the importance of voluntary self-evaluations in promoting compliance with environmental requirements and attempted to strike a balance between encouraging such evaluations and retaining appropriate enforcement authority. Key components of the Interim Policy Statement are:

1. The U.S. EPA indicated that it would eliminate or substantially reduce the gravity component of civil penalties assessed for violations discovered and disclosed to the U.S. EPA, provided that the disclosing entity could meet seven conditions set forth in the Interim Policy Statement. By contrast, the Interim Policy Statement did not disturb the U.S. EPA's authority to seek the economic benefit component of a civil penalty assessed in such circumstances.

2. The U.S. EPA indicated that it would not recommend that criminal charges be brought against the disclosing entity so long as the entity was acting in good faith to identify, disclose, and correct violations, and no serious actual harm occurred as a result of the disclosed violations. However, the Interim Policy Statement did not provide a safe harbor against prosecution of individual managers or employees for their criminal acts.

3. The U.S. EPA indicated that it would no longer request the results of voluntary environmental evaluations to trigger enforcement investigations as part of routine inspections. However, the U.S. EPA reserved the right to seek any information, including environmental audit reports, if it believed that a violation existed or occurred and the information might be relevant to such violations.

While the Interim Policy Statement represented a significant step by the U.S. EPA to encourage voluntary environmental assessments and audits, its extensive qualifying conditions limited its effectiveness. The U.S. EPA received more than 250 sets of comments on the Interim Policy Statement expressing concerns and reactions to the positions articulated.

On June 23, 1995, the U.S. EPA published for public comment a document entitled "Interim Policy on Compliance Incentives for Small Businesses" (60 *FR* 32675). This policy is designed to facilitate compliance with environmental requirements by small businesses (those with no more than 100 employees). It authorized the U.S. EPA to mitigate or eliminate civil penalties in circumstances where a small business has made a good faith effort to comply with environmental requirements, as demonstrated by detecting violations, while receiving compliance assistance from a non-confidential government program or government-supported program that offers services to small businesses. The policy also included a number of additional conditions that must be satisfied in order to gain the benefits conferred thereby.

On December 22, 1995, the U.S. EPA published a policy regarding incentives that it will provide to the regulated community to voluntarily discover, disclose, and correct violations of environmental requirements. This policy, entitled "Incentives for Self-Policing: Discovery, Disclosure, Correction and Prevention of Violations" ("1995 Audit Policy") (60 *FR* 66706), replaced and superceded the Interim Policy Statement and contained a number of important changes responding to concerns raised by the regulated community in comments regarding the Interim Policy Statement. The 1995 Audit Policy went into effect on January 22, 1996.

On April 11, 2000, the U.S. EPA issued revisions to the 1995 Audit Policy addressing some of the concerns raised as a result of the collective experiences with that policy. The most recent version of the policy, entitled "Incentives for Self-Policing: Discovery, Disclosure, Correction and Prevention of Violations" ("Audit Policy") (65 *FR* 19617), is discussed in detail below.

The Audit Policy provides three major incentives for the regulated community to engage in self-evaluative activities designed to voluntarily discover, disclose, correct, and prevent violations of federal environmental requirements.

1. The U.S. EPA will not seek the gravity component of civil penalties associated with violations discovered during an environmental audit or as a result of due diligence efforts provided that the violations are promptly disclosed to the U.S. EPA and corrected. (The U.S. EPA will reduce by 75 percent the gravity compo-

nent of civil penalties associated with violations voluntarily discovered through other means and are promptly disclosed and corrected.)

2. The U.S. EPA will not recommend criminal prosecution of the disclosing entity as long as the disclosed violation is not indicative of (1) a prevalent management philosophy to conceal or condone environmental violations, or (2) management's conscious involvement in or willful ignorance of environmental violations. The U.S. EPA also has reserved the right to recommend prosecution of individual employees and managers for their criminal acts.

3. The U.S. EPA will not request or use an environmental audit report to initiate a civil or criminal investigation of the disclosing entity unless the U.S. EPA has an independent basis to believe that a violation has occurred.

The U.S. EPA's Audit Policy sets forth a list of nine conditions which must be satisfied to qualify for a waiver of the gravity-based component of a civil penalty and to prevent the possibility of a criminal referral by the U.S. EPA to the U.S. DOJ. These nine conditions are summarized below.

1. The violation must be discovered through an environmental audit or a compliance management system.

2. The discovery of the violation must be voluntary, e.g., not the result of a legally mandated monitoring or sampling requirement prescribed by statute, regulation, permit, judicial or administrative order, or consent agreement. Significantly, the policy applies to all voluntarily discovered violations regardless of whether the violations thereby uncovered are subject to independent reporting requirements under applicable environmental laws.

3. The violation must be disclosed in writing to the U.S. EPA within 21 days after its discovery unless a shorter period is provided for by an applicable reporting requirement.

4. The discovery and disclosure of the violation must occur prior to a government inspection, investigation, information request, notice of citizen suit, or other third-party action.

5. The violation must be corrected within 60 days and appropriate measures must be taken to remedy any harm caused by the violation. If required, additional time may be requested. The U.S. EPA is authorized under the policy to enter into written agreements, administrative consent orders, and consent decrees to provide for extended compliance schedules.

6. The disclosing entity must agree in writing to take steps to prevent a recurrence of the violation.

7. The disclosed violation must not be a repeat violation. To demonstrate that a violation is not a repeat violation, the disclosing entity must show that the specific violation or a closely related violation has not occurred within the past three years at the same facility or that the violation is not part of a pattern of federal, state, or local violations by the facility's parent organization.

8. The disclosed violation must not have resulted in serious actual harm or present an imminent and substantial endangerment to human health or the environment, and the disclosed violation must not have been a violation of the specific terms of a judicial or administrative order or consent agreement.

9. The disclosing entity must cooperate with the U.S. EPA and provide the U.S. EPA with any information necessary to determine the applicability of the policy. The duty to cooperate includes providing all requested documents, access to employees, and assistance in investigating the violation, any noncompliance problems related to the disclosure, and any environmental consequences related to the violation.

For purposes of its Audit Policy, the U.S. EPA has defined an environmental audit as a "systematic, documented, periodic and objective review by regulated entities of facility operations and practices related to meeting environmental requirements." This definition mirrors the definition contained in the 1986 *Environmental Auditing Policy Statement*. The U.S. EPA has defined "compliance management system" for purposes of the Audit Policy as "documented systematic efforts, appropriate to the size and nature of [the regulated entity's] business, designed to prevent, detect and correct violations." ("Due diligence" was the term used in the 1995 Audit Policy.) Qualifying for the full benefits of the Audit Policy depends on meeting these conditions.

If a regulated entity cannot demonstrate that the violation disclosed to the U.S. EPA was discovered through either an environmental audit or compliance management system as defined in the Audit Policy, the disclosing entity can still qualify for a 75 percent reduction in the gravity component of the civil penalty provided that the disclosing entity meets the other eight conditions described in the Audit Policy. The policy also makes clear U.S. EPA's position that it fully reserves its rights to recover the economic benefit component of any civil penalty in order to preserve a "level playing field" for the regulated community. The policy includes U.S. EPA's views opposing statutes that either encourage voluntary environmental compliance by creating privileges to protect the confidentiality of the results of environmental audits and assessments, or provide immunity for environmental violations that are inconsistent with the positions taken by the U.S. EPA in its Audit Policy.

While the U.S. EPA is quite proud of its Audit Policy and there have been some positive results, it does not go far enough and may amount to a policy-based regulatory program vesting broad discretion in the U.S. EPA. There are two principle procedural problems with the approach taken by the U.S. EPA: (1) a company must first perceive some threat of U.S. EPA enforcement before it will view the policy as an opportunity to obtain relief; and (2) because of the subjective criteria within the policy, a company reporting violations to the U.S. EPA will not know if it qualifies for penalty relief until *after* the disclosure is made. That would appear to be a little too late, especially if there is a risk that the U.S. EPA will deny the requested relief.

Recent experience has suggested a third problem that is a bit more draconian. Once disclosure to the U.S. EPA is made, the U.S. EPA has shown a tendency to use that information as a blueprint for enforcement against (or "invitations" to voluntarily disclose by) other companies within the disclosing company's industry, and to saddle all subsequent disclosers with legal and regulatory interpretations established as part of the resolution achieved with the company that made the initial disclosure. Results such as these are likely to provide a substantial disincentive for industry to self-disclose and could significantly undercut the objectives that the Audit Policy is intended to accomplish.

U.S. DOJ Policy

On July 1, 1991, the U.S. DOJ issued a document entitled "Factors in Decisions on Criminal Prosecutions for Environmental Violations in the Context of Significant Voluntary Compliance or Disclosure Efforts by the Violator." This document describes the factors that the U.S. DOJ considers in deciding whether to prosecute a business or individual for an environmental violation. The document contains a broad policy statement by the U.S. DOJ that it encourages self-auditing, self-policing, and voluntary disclosure of environmental violations by the regulated community. According to the document, these activities are viewed by the U.S. DOJ as mitigating factors in the U.S. DOJ's exercise of criminal enforcement discretion. However, the document only provides general guidelines for the U.S. DOJ and does not afford the regulated community any specific comfort that in a particular case, the U.S. DOJ will not proceed with a criminal prosecution notwithstanding the presence of a vigorous environmental self-evaluation program.

PROTECTION OF THE CONFIDENTIALITY OF ENVIRONMENTAL ASSESSMENTS UNDER EXISTING LAW

Businesses that seek to protect the results of environmental assessments from disclosure have typically invoked the attorney-client privilege and/or the work-product doctrine. In certain circumstances, these alternatives have insulated the results of an environmental assessment from disclosure. However, neither the attorney-client privilege nor the work-product doctrine provides a reliable mechanism for protecting environmental assessments in all circumstances.

Attorney-Client Privilege

The attorney-client privilege has long been recognized as a means to foster the full and free disclosure of information between clients and attorneys. As a policy matter, it is generally recognized that clients should have the ability to speak freely with their attorneys without the fear that such communications will later be disclosed and potentially used against them. Generally, the attorney-client privilege is established where legal advice of any kind is sought from an attorney in the attorney's capacity as such and where the client makes the communication in confidence. Such a disclosure is entitled to confidential treatment under the attorney-client privilege provided the protection is not waived.[4]

For a communication to be protected by the attorney-client privilege, it must meet a variety of requirements. For example, the communication between the client and the attorney must be for the purpose of obtaining legal advice. Communications directed to an attorney for other purposes such as monitoring ongoing activities or soliciting business advice may not be subject to protection. Moreover, the communication must have been made in confidence (generally outside the presence of third parties) and made by the client. The privilege may also be lost if appropriate steps are not taken to prevent the waiver of the privilege by disclosure of the communication to a third party. Communications made to non-attorneys may be protected if the person to whom the communication is made is under the direction and control of an attorney and the communication is offered to facilitate obtaining legal advice from that attorney. For example, a communication made to an environmental consultant under the direction and control of an environmental attorney for purposes of assisting the attorney in rendering legal advice would likely be protected under the attorney-client privilege as long as the other requirements for the privilege were satisfied.[5]

Courts interpreting the attorney-client privilege have often differentiated between communications, which are protected, and underlying facts, which are not. This distinction can become extremely problematic in the environmental context. For example, sampling data cannot be protected, but the evaluation of the data or a discussion of the potential sources of the contamination may be protected. Generally, however, a client cannot insulate from disclosure an underlying fact within his or her knowledge merely because it was communicated to an attorney even though the contents of the discussions with the attorney are subject to protection.

---

[4] See generally *Swidler & Berlin v. United States*, 118 S.Ct. 2081 (1998); *Upjohn Co. v. United States*, 449 U.S. 313 (1981); *Montgomery County v. Microvate Corp.*, 175 F.3d 296 (3d Cir. 1999).

[5] *Olson v. Accessory Controls and Equipment Corporation*, 254 Conn. 145, 757 A.2d 14 (2000); *Consolidated Rail Corporation v. Pennsylvania Department of Environmental Protection*, 1999 EHB 204 (1999), and *Andritz Sprout-Bauer, Inc. v. Beazer East, Inc.*, 174 F.R.D. 609 (M.D. Pa. 1997).

In order to maximize the probability that a court would find the results of an environmental assessment to be protected by the attorney-client privilege, the business conducting the assessment must ensure that the assessment is structured to meet the legal prerequisites and standards. This can significantly encumber the investigative process to the point where, in some instances, the benefits to be obtained from the assessment may be limited by the constraints placed on the investigative process. For example, the assessment typically should be controlled by outside counsel with authority to direct the inquiries made and to assimilate the responses obtained. Confidentiality must be maintained at each step of the way and the assessment must be structured to ensure that its focus is the provision of legal advice to the business being evaluated. Technical personnel assisting in the assessment must perform their duties under the direction and control of the attorneys running the assessment. While each of these safeguards may serve to encumber the process, it is obvious that they cannot be superimposed on the audit results after the fact.

Work-Product Doctrine

The work-product doctrine offers a second potential avenue for protecting the results of an environmental assessment. Under the work-product doctrine, the mental impressions, conclusions, opinions, and legal theories concerning actual or anticipated litigation of an attorney or other representative of a party are generally subject to a qualified immunity from discovery. Unlike the attorney-client privilege, this immunity may be overcome by a showing of sufficient need.

The principles supporting the work-product doctrine were articulated in *Hickman v. Taylor*, 329 U.S. 495 (1947) and have been incorporated into Fed. R. Civ. P. 26(b)(3), which provides in pertinent part as follows:

> [A] party may obtain discovery of documents and tangible things otherwise discoverable . . . and prepared in anticipation of litigation or for trial by or for another party or by or for that other party's representative (including the other party's attorney, consultant, surety, indemnitor, insurer or agent) only upon a showing that the party seeking discovery has substantial need of the materials in the preparation of the party's case and that the party is unable without undue hardship to obtain the substantial equivalent of the materials by other means. In ordering discovery of such materials when the required showing has been made, the court shall protect against disclosure of the mental impressions, conclusions, opinions, or legal theories of an attorney or other representative of a party concerning the litigation.

The work-product doctrine is limited in that it applies only to work performed "in anticipation of litigation." Accordingly, in the absence of litigation or anticipated litigation, the work-product doctrine does not offer protection to environmental assessments.

Even when an environmental assessment is conducted "in anticipation of litigation," it generally cannot be used to protect underlying facts, but only the conclusions and impressions to be drawn from those facts. To be protected under the work-product doctrine, the primary motivating purpose for collecting information or generating a report must be to assist in actual or anticipated litigation. Routine investigations conducted in the ordinary course of business generally do not meet this standard. Accordingly, if a business routinely conducts environmental assessments to determine whether it is in compliance, those assessments are likely not protected under the work-product doctrine. By contrast, if a business waits until an enforcement action or citizens' suit is threatened or pending before conducting an assessment and the assessment is used to help formulate a litigation strategy, the likelihood of protecting the assessment under the work-product doctrine improves.

The viability of using the attorney-client privilege or the work-product doctrine to protect the results of environmental assessments, including formal audits, suffers from the fact that neither the attorney-client privilege nor the work-product doctrine is designed specifically to achieve these ends. Instead, these mechanisms have been used, albeit somewhat imperfectly, to achieve a modicum of protection for environmental assessments conducted in certain circumstances and for certain purposes. Because of the uncertainty as to whether these mechanisms will actually work in a particular situation, businesses have tended to err on the side of caution and operate under the assumption that environmental assessment reports may ultimately be required to be disclosed.

Self-Evaluative Privilege

Over the past two decades, the courts have begun to recognize that in certain instances, it is sound public policy to encourage candid and frank self-evaluation leading to the identification and correction of internal problems. Accordingly, in certain instances, the courts have insulated reports and documents from disclosure relying on a concept called the "self-evaluative privilege" or the "critical self-analysis doctrine."

The self-evaluative privilege was first recognized in a medical malpractice case where a district court ruled that confidential hospital staff meeting minutes, recorded for the purpose of self-improvement, were entitled to a qualified privilege on the basis of the compelling public interest in facilitating peer review of physician performance. *Bredice v. Doctor's Hospital, Inc.*, 50 F.R.D. 249 (D.D.C. 1970), *aff'd*, 479 F.2d 920 (D.C. Cir. 1973). Since that time, the self-evaluative privilege has been examined in other contexts, including auditing functions to enhance environmental compliance.

In *Reichhold Chemicals, Inc. v. Textron, Inc.*, 157 F.R.D. 522, 39 E.R.C. 1328 (N.D. Fla. 1994), the court held that the self-evaluative privilege protected reports concerning retrospective analyses of past conduct, practices, and occurrences, and the resulting environmental consequences, as long as the reports were prepared for the purpose of candid self-evaluation with the expectation that the reports would remain confidential and such confidentiality was in fact maintained. The court also found that the privilege was a qualified rather than an absolute privilege; it could be overcome by a showing of extraordinary circumstances or special need.

The court noted that the self-evaluative privilege was rooted in public policy considerations designed to allow individuals or businesses to candidly assess their compliance with regulatory and legal requirements without creating evidence that might be used against them by their opponents in future litigation. The court indicated that the privilege protects an organization or individual from the "Hobson's choice" of aggressively investigating accidents or possible regulatory violations, ascertaining the causes and results, and correcting violations or dangerous conditions, but thereby creating a self-incriminating record that could be evidence of liability; or deliberately avoiding making a record on the subject (and possibly leaving the public exposed to danger) in order to lessen the risk of civil liability. The *Reichhold Chemicals* court applied a four-part test for determining whether to protect self-evaluative materials from disclosure: (1) the information must result from a critical self-analysis undertaken by the party seeking protection; (2) the public must have a strong interest in preserving the free flow of the information sought; (3) the information must be of a type whose flow would be curtailed if discovery was allowed; and (4) the information must be generated with the expectation that it will be kept confidential and the information must be so maintained.

In contrast to the *Reichhold Chemicals* decision, certain other courts have taken a narrow view of the self-evaluative privilege in the context of environmental reports and documentation. In *Koppers Company, Inc. v. Aetna Casualty and Surety Company*, 847 F. Supp. 361, 364 (W.D. Pa. 1994), the court held that the self-evaluative privilege "does not apply *a fortiori* to environmental reports, records, and memoranda. Indeed, we disagree that a corporation would face a Hobson's choice between due diligence and self-incrimination in the tightly regulated environmental context, for that context requires strict attention to environmental affairs. We doubt that today potential polluters will violate regulations requiring environmental diligence for fear of these documents being used against them tomorrow."

In *Grand Jury Proceedings*, 861 F.Supp. 386 (D. Md. 1994), the court refused to protect audits conducted by a company to determine whether it was in compliance with requirements under the Food, Drug and Cosmetics Act. The court held that the results of such audits had to be produced in response to a grand jury subpoena. In reaching this decision, the court indicated that it was aware of no case in which the self-evaluative privilege had been applied to thwart a governmental request for documents. If this aspect of the decision is followed, it may severely undercut the utility of the self-evaluative privilege as fashioned by the courts in the context of environmental audits.

STATE ENVIRONMENTAL AUDIT LEGISLATION AND POLICY

A number of states have intervened and adopted statutes recognizing the self-evaluative privilege for environmental assessments in light of the increasing utilization of environmental assessments to facilitate compliance with environmental requirements, the continuing concerns relating to the potential disclosure of the results of such assessments, and the mixed results that businesses and individuals have experienced in seeking to protect the results of environmental assessments under traditional common law concepts. Typically, these statutes have been designed to cover formal voluntary environmental compliance audits and generally do not extend to health and safety audits.

In 1993, Oregon became the first state legislature to create a qualified privilege for voluntary environmental audits. The law was adopted as part of an omnibus environmental crimes package and the audit provisions were considered to be part of an overall systemic solution to the need to reform Oregon's environmental requirements. Since Oregon took action other states have followed suit.

Self-evaluative privilege legislation at the state level has taken a variety of forms. However, there are certain common threads evident in such legislation. Typically, such legislation addresses the following issues:

1. the types of activities and documents subject to the privilege;

2. the scope of the privilege;

3. the manner in which the privilege can be lost or waived;

4. the mechanisms for asserting the privilege; and

5. the protections, if any, to be afforded for reporting and correcting items of non-compliance.

Self-evaluative privilege legislation generally includes a series of provisions defining key terms such as "environmental audit" and "environmental audit report." These definitions can be extremely important in determining what types of information and documents are subject to the self-evaluative privilege. For example, a number of statutes provide that an environmental audit must be a voluntary undertaking designed to evaluate the compliance status of facilities, activities, and/or management systems relating to those facilities or activities. In considering the definition of an "audit," some have proposed that health and safety audits as well as environmental audits be subject to the privilege. Generally, the narrower approach has been followed. Likewise, investigations of environmental conditions at particular parcels of property have typically not been covered by the definition of an environmental audit.

Self-evaluative privilege legislation almost invariably contains provisions delineating the scope of the protection afforded. For example, most but not all privilege laws expressly provide that reports generated by an environmental evaluation are neither discoverable nor admissible. The protections afforded such reports and related documents have also been extended in certain instances to provide a testimonial privilege to protect persons involved in the evaluative process from testifying as to the results of the review. Most self-evaluative privilege legislation excludes certain types of information from protection. For example, information that is otherwise required to be developed, maintained, reported, or made available to a regulatory agency is typically not subject to protection. Similarly, information obtained by a regulatory agency through observation, sampling, or monitoring, or information obtained from an independent source, is generally not subject to protection.

Self-evaluative privilege legislation typically contains provisions specifying certain conditions in which the privilege can be either lost or overridden. For example, as a general rule, the self-evaluative privilege will be lost if the privilege is asserted for a fraudulent purpose or if an audit or assessment reveals areas of noncompliance and corrective steps are not promptly initiated and pursued with reasonable diligence. In addition, in some instances, the self-evaluative privilege can be overridden upon a showing of compelling need for the results of the audit or assessment. In statutes that contain such a provision, it highlights the qualified nature of the privilege. In other instances, the privilege may be lost if an audit or assessment shows that a clear, present, and impending danger to public health or the environment exists. Most self-evaluative privilege legislation also provides for the waiver of the privilege, either by express action or by implication.

In some instances, self-evaluative privilege legislation contains "safe harbor" provisions, which protect businesses and individuals from enforcement actions where the results of an audit or assessment show noncompliance with environmental requirements, steps are promptly taken to correct the noncompliance, and the noncompliance is reported. In essence, "safe harbor" provisions afford those that voluntarily conduct environmental assessments, including formal audits, a measure of comfort that if they find areas of noncompliance, they can take steps to correct the problems and report the noncompliance to the government without running the risk that the self-discovered and self-reported violations will result in civil penalties or criminal sanctions.

PRACTICAL CONSIDERATIONS AND RECOMMENDATIONS FOR PERFORMING SELF-ASSESSMENTS

The overall benefits of performing regular environmental assessments are clear and the incentives created by the U.S. EPA, the U.S. DOJ, OSHA, and state governments either in the form of legislation or policy, support the process. Below are a number of recommendations for optimizing these opportunities.

1. Any self-assessment should be carefully planned. It is essential that a company develops the assessment process with a full understanding of the available legal protections, whether they be audit policies, statutes, or common law privileges. It will be impossible to retrofit the assessment to incorporate the procedures necessary to qualify for these legal protections. In planning the assessment, care should be taken to ensure that the assessment fits within the types of activities covered by the relevant policies. For example, if a regulated entity is setting up a compliance management system, it should overlay the Audit Policy definition and any key terms from state law or policy to ensure that all of the various components of the applicable definitions are being met.

2. The team of professionals who will be involved in the self-assessment should be identified beforehand and should include, at a minimum, a representative of the regulated entity with knowledge concerning the operations to be evaluated, a technical consultant (or in-house environmental staff person), and an environmental attorney. Input from each of these disciplines is quite important.

3. The time frames for disclosure set forth in the Audit Policy are short. Therefore, it is critical that the team of professionals conducting the assessment be kept directly apprised of the results of the assessment. Depending on the information generated by the assessment, there may be only a narrow window of time to evaluate the factual and legal predicates to determine whether a violation exists before disclosure may be necessary to preserve the benefits of the U.S. EPA's or OSHA's policy.

4. Depending on the circumstances, a regulated entity may wish to conduct assessments either in discrete phases or of discrete aspects of its operations. By dividing an assessment into "bite size pieces," it may be easier to ensure that issues are identified and resolved in a timely and prudent fashion. There also may be less potential for creating paralysis of decision-making resulting from the identification of a host of compliance problems in a single report. Finally, by separating the process into phases, it may be easier to separate "legal advice" from "business advice" and thereby come within the attorney-client privilege.

5. The assessment team should understand the legal framework applicable to the operations being evaluated. For example, it is important to identify beforehand whether federal or state law (or both) provide the governing requirements. This may influence whether disclosure of any violations discovered should be made to the U.S. EPA, OSHA, and/or the state.

6. Before conducting an assessment, the regulated entity must be committed to addressing the issues that are likely to be identified. Performing an assessment and ignoring the results is likely to leave the regulated entity in a markedly worse set of circumstances than not performing the assessment at all.

7. Take care in preparing any written documentation of assessment findings to avoid speculation and unnecessary legal conclusions. Auditors are fact-finders, which is quite a different function (requiring specific expertise) than drawing compliance and legal conclusions from the identified facts.

Environmental, health, and safety laws and regulations are extremely complex and ever changing. Environmental, health, and safety assessments can serve a pivotal function both in assuring compliance and in establishing protocols to determine areas of noncompliance. These are two different goals, both equally important, that can be achieved through a thoughtful, well developed environmental, health, and safety auditing program.

Chapter 4

ELEMENTS OF A
SUCCESSFUL PROGRAM

"For example" is not proof.

– Yiddish Proverb

PRINCIPLES OF AN AUDIT PROGRAM

The principles of an EH&S audit program are well known, but may be usefully summarized in the following five points. The audit team, comprising knowledgeable professionals (either in-house staff, third parties, or both), carries out such duties as:

- Understanding and ascertaining maintenance of schedules and records with respect to all operations having EH&S compliance requirements

- Inspecting facilities, equipment, and personnel performance to evaluate adherence to institutional standards

- Submitting written status reports to appropriate senior management

- Explaining deviations from the norm and recommending corrective action

- Operating independently of all audited functions, at a peer level with their management.

As these points make clear, the essence of an EH&S audit program is to provide assurance to top-level company management and company stockholders that all relevant regulatory requirements are being met in accordance with the company's operating philosophy.

In order to accomplish this goal, an audit program must contain certain key elements around which an individualized structure can be developed. These elements and the relationship between them are shown in Figure 4.1. An audit program must be planned carefully and have the appropriate supportive tools and staff. Audits must be conducted on a continuous basis with additional sampling used only when and where necessary. Finally, the results must be evaluated and turned into solutions and corrective actions. Each of these elements is important to the successful implementation of the program. Accordingly, this chapter presents a detailed discussion of each of the elements within the context of the overall program.

Figure 4.1 Elements of an Audit Program

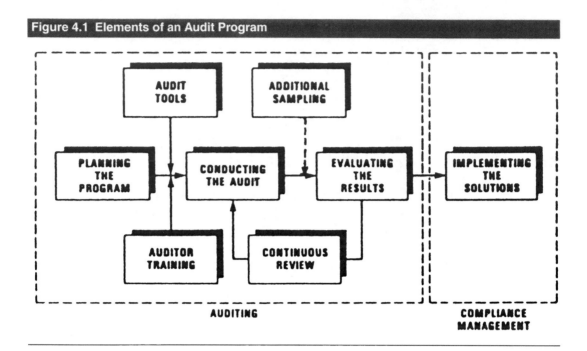

PLANNING THE PROGRAM

An important first step is planning a program. Among the decisions to be made are: what is the objective to be achieved, who will be involved, how often will audits be conducted, what laws and regulations will be covered, and should information be kept confidential. As indicated by the list below, the issues to be resolved are numerous and often complex:

■ Program Objectives
  - Assurance of compliance
  - Management of liabilities
  - Accountability of management
  - Tracking of compliance costs

■ Organization of the Program
- Corporate control with full-time corporate auditors
- Corporate control with part-time auditors selected from divisions
- A small corporate oversight group with delegation of the audit function to the operating divisions
- A small corporate oversight group with the use of external, independent auditors

■ Legal Issues
- Written vs. oral reports
- Retained documentation
- Corporate counsel involvement
- Protection from discovery
- Report format and watchwords

■ Program Scope and Coverage
- Frequency of audits
- All regulations
- All plants, random sample, or directed sample
- Past practices
- Vendor audits
- Waste contractor audits

■ Process Issues
- Pre-visit questionnaire
- Number of auditors
- Duration of audits
- Pre-visit, on-site, and post-visit procedures
- Sampling procedures
- Interview technique
- Inspection procedures
- Use of portable computers

■ Auditor Selection and Training
- Skills required
- Attorney's role
- Training procedures
- Full-time vs. part-time auditor

■ Management Issues
- Expectations of senior management
- Measures of successful performance
- Unannounced visits
- Reporting protocols
- Supportive vs. combative style

- Supporting Tools
  - Pre-visit questionnaire
  - Compliance checklists
  - Regulatory updates
  - Audit reports
  - Guidance/procedures manual
  - Follow-up reports
  - Computer support

Although this book and other sources can provide guidance on what might be considered the "standard" approach to the issues listed above, each company considering a program must decide for itself the optimal program structure. There is no one best answer.

Most companies will develop audit guidance manuals to set the framework for the program and to ensure the consistency, efficiency, and completeness of all audits. A complete model audit manual is presented in Appendix F. Audit manuals typically address essential programmatic issues and include a variety of audit tools, including model opening conference presentations, pre-audit questionnaires, model audit reports, and audit checklists or protocols. Examples of each of these are also provided in the appendices. Essentially, audit manuals are designed to communicate the structure of the program to both the auditors and those audited, in order to remove any mystery from the program.

The next few sections discuss the keys to implementing a successful program. They touch upon many of the issues listed above and provide some guidance on preferred approaches. These are the central points that should be addressed in the program's guidance manual.

Program Objectives

An audit program can achieve a variety of objectives. Historically, in most companies, compliance assurance has been the principal objective, with other, secondary objectives evolving along the way. This is confirmed by a 1994 Manufacturers' Alliance Survey of industry, which showed that 99 percent of programs surveyed stated that compliance assurance was one of the main program goals. As shown in Figure 4.2, non-regulatory risk assessment followed closely behind at ninety-one percent. This implies that companies are also addressing corporate standards and good management practices.

Figure 4.2 Why Audit? Industry's Response to Audit Program Objectives

Audit Program Objective	Industry's Response
Compliance Assurance	99%
Non-Regulatory Risk Management	91%
Financial Liability	22%
Others (e.g., Awareness, Pollution Prevention)	23%

Yet, it is important to note that companies will frame a program to meet individual needs, and these can vary significantly. One company's programs include the following five objectives:

- Provide assurance of adequate EH&S performance and continuous improvement to the board of directors

- Ensure division and facility compliance with federal, state, and local EH&S regulations and corporate policies and procedures

- Ensure division management accountability for correcting compliance deficiencies identified on audits

- Increase EH&S awareness and continuous learning by audited personnel and auditors

- Transfer EH&S technological and administrative innovations across the corporation.

Note that the compliance assurance objective is one of the five listed. But the additional objectives are quite intriguing. For example, the program is also designed to provide assurance and confirmation of continuous improvement of environmental performance to the board of directors. This objective is very consistent with the international standards discussed elsewhere in this book.

Further, the program is designed to hold division management, not the audit program manager, accountable for correcting deficiencies. This applies the compliance pressure to the appropriate organization. And note that it does not hold line management accountable for an excellent rating on any given audit. What it does ask of line management is that, where problems are identified, they be corrected promptly.

Further, the program is designed to be a training tool for both rotating auditors and those who are audited. This is a very common objective for auditing programs and is easily achieved. In probably every instance, an auditor and those being audited can walk away from the audit and say "I learned something from that exercise."

Finally, the program is expected to communicate "best practices" throughout the corporation. Auditors are in a great position to do this as they review practices in different businesses and geographical regions. Before the advent of communications tools such as Lotus Notes, this kind of communication was quite difficult.

As mentioned above, these are only a few of the objectives an EH&S audit program can achieve. Individual organizations must decide for themselves which objectives are appropriate. Whatever is decided, the objectives should be stated in such a way that clear performance measures can be established. One must be able to periodically evaluate the program's performance to determine where improvements need to be made.

Roles and Responsibilities

One of the early keys to developing a successful program, regardless of the strategy selected, is commitment. Top management's role at this stage is critical. Before any audits are conducted, management must develop and communicate a policy that supports the *concept* of an audit program. To be successful, the policy must portray the program as a positive move towards helping facility managers enhance compliance and reduce liabilities. Senior management should dismiss explicitly the notion that the program is designed to "check up" on facility managers and operators. In fact, under a properly designed audit program, employees have as much, if not more, to gain than corporate managers do.

In addition, early in the development of the program, corporate management should designate a senior executive or staff member as the audit program director. This director should be senior enough to establish and maintain the program's credibility.

The specific structure of the audit program will vary, depending upon the individual organization. Probably the most prevalent, though not the only, approach is to appoint a corporate audit program director and to assign a small group to this individual. This group might include a regulatory specialist and one or more, or no, audit team leaders. The auditors and/or team leaders could come from other corporate groups and division and plant EH&S staffs and would conduct a few audits per year while retaining full-time EH&S responsibilities in their respective organizations. Quite often such audit teams are supplemented by third parties (e.g., consultants) that can provide specialized expertise (e.g., process safety) or an added independence to the program. This "rotating auditor" approach requires significant "buy-in" from line management, which is achieved when there is indeed top management support for the program.

An example of an organizational structure for an audit program is shown in the Model Audit Program Manual in Appendix F. Note that, in that case, the audit program manager is tied closely to the board of directors through the chief executive officer. Also, the law department provides significant input but is not directly in control of the program. The audit program director has organized a small group of audit program managers who serve as team leaders. Qualified auditors can come from anywhere in the organization, but must successfully complete an internal auditor-training program.

However the audit program is structured, roles and responsibilities should be defined for each of the participant categories. These categories include:

- Senior or executive management

- The audit program manager and staff

- The legal department

- Division management
  - Facility management and staff
  - Audit team leaders
  - Auditors.

A set of roles and responsibilities for the audit program director or manager, for example, might include:

- Determining, on an annual basis, the sites to be audited, consistent with the corporate audit frequency policy

- Maintaining and updating program materials, including the program guidance manual, the pre-audit questionnaire, and the audit protocols

- Maintaining the auditor training program, including updating the qualified auditor database

- Reviewing all draft and final audit reports to ensure that reports meet quality standards and are submitted on time

- Tracking the status of corrective action plans and formally "closing out" audits when all findings are corrected

- Providing the audit teams, on an as needed basis, with country or state regulatory information

- Conducting an annual evaluation of the program

- Periodically reporting on program status to the board of directors

- With the advice of counsel, managing the program files consistent with the corporation's established record retention policy.

Roles and responsibilities for other participants can be established in a similar fashion (See Appendix F). As with the program objectives, the individual participants' responsibilities should be framed so that performance can be measured.

Legal Protections[1]

The legal protection issue is one of great concern to most companies and, therefore, each organization must decide on the approach that best fits its philosophy. And the best approach is not always invoking maximum legal protections for the program. As shown in Figure 4.3, not all companies invoke formal attorney-client privilege protections for audit reports and documents. The results of the Manufacturers' Alliance Survey of Industry suggest that only 50 percent of the surveyed organizations use attorney-client privilege for all documents.

Figure 4.3 Industry's Response to Audit Confidentiality

Confidentiality Approach	Industry's Response
Treat Audit Documents as Confidential	70%
Use Attorney-Client Privilege Veil for ALL Documents	50%
Use Attorney-Client Privilege Veil for SOME Documents	20%

Why is there such disparity in approaches? Well, most companies do want to protect their audit reports but some are not sure that it is worth the trouble of invoking formal protection privileges. Use of the privilege puts the legal department, or outside counsel, at the center of the program, not in a review and advisory role. Such extensive legal involvement has often meant a more expensive and elaborate program, and perhaps more importantly, can slow down the report distribution process substantially. Companies that do not invoke the privilege believe that the risk of disclosure is not improved substantially by attorney-client privilege, since the underlying facts are not protected in any event. Moreover, any protections gained are viewed as more than offset by the increased bureaucracy of the program and the inability to produce and distribute reports expeditiously. U.S. EPA's Audit Policy and State Audit Privilege and Immunity Legislation will continue to affect how companies view this issue. (See Chapters 2 and 3 for more detailed discussions.)

Scope and Coverage

Any audit program must have some bounds under which it operates. Someone must decide which facilities are audited, what they are audited against, and what type of audits will be conducted.

---

[1] An entire chapter in this book is devoted to legal issues associated with audit programs. This section discusses the management consequences of various legal protection approaches.

Quite often one of the most difficult tasks for an audit program manager is determining the inventory of facilities subject to the program. With all the mergers, acquisitions, and divestitures taking place in the U.S. and overseas, the structure of any organization can change very quickly. In general, audit programs will be responsible for auditing the following facility types:

☐ Manufacturing facilities owned and operated

☐ Manufacturing facilities operated but on leased property

☐ Captive and shared contract manufacturing facilities

☐ Joint ventures with majority ownership and operational responsibility

☐ Joint ventures with minority ownership and operational responsibility

☐ Warehouses and distribution centers owned and operated

☐ Administrative and office buildings owned and operated

☐ Real estate owned.

For other facility types (such as joint ventures with majority or minority ownership and no operational responsibility, or leased warehouses), the company will attempt to influence the partner(s) to participate in the audit program or ensure that the partner(s) has an equivalent program.

Most audit programs are designed to cover major operating facilities. Other types of facilities that have to be addressed, however, are acquisitions and divestitures, suppliers, commercial waste disposal contractors, and captive toll manufacturers. These are all risk situations in need of some kind of independent review. In some companies, these reviews are considered a formal part of the audit program, and in other companies they are addressed separately but coordinated with the corporate audit program manager.

The second audit scope issue relates to regulatory coverage. Program managers must decide what regulations are to be addressed. Will EH&S issues be combined into one integrated audit program? There are as many examples of companies with separate environmental audit programs as there are with integrated EH&S audit programs. Other regulatory issues must be addressed as well. Certain laws such as the Toxic Substances Control Act (TSCA) are not easily audited at the facility level. Certain programs created to respond to TSCA requirements such as Pre-Manufacture Notification exist more at the business unit level. Companies sometimes develop focused or target audits to address these issues thoroughly but independently of the facility audit program. Similarly, the Chemical Diversion and Trafficking Act (CDTA) is not really an environmental act but can be audited quite easily at the facility level. As a consequence, CDTA requirements are sometimes "piggy-backed" onto the EH&S audit program.

Once the company has decided on the regulatory scope of the program, it can then decide on the types of audits that can best meet the program's objectives. This may result in the creation of specialized audits, designed to address multi-organizational issues, as well as the more traditional facility audits. Such specialized audits will be discussed in later chapters.

Facility Audit Schedules

When first faced with the "audit or not" question, many corporate EH&S departments wonder where the significant, additional resources will come from. In an economic environment that is shouting "do more with less," some initial planning and priority setting can help the compliance manager meet the often conflicting objectives of: (1) increased EH&S compliance and (2) reduction of the resources committed to that goal. Fortunately, there are some steps managers can take to better understand the operations within the company that pose the greater risks and to design an audit program that addresses those risks within the context of resource constraints.

Setting facility audit schedules based on a sense of risk can do much to assure a cost-effective program. According to the results of the Manufacturers' Alliance Survey, audit frequency varies considerably among companies (see Figure 4.4).

Figure 4.4 Industry's Response to Frequency of Audits

Audit Frequency	Industry's Response
Annual	22%
Two Years or Less	28%
Three Years or Less	23%
Greater Than Three Years	27%

Unfortunately, there is no general guidance on what is an acceptable frequency. The U.S. EPA's landmark 1986 Policy Statement, British Standard 7750 and the ISO 14000 Guidelines are notably silent on the issue. However, the Eco-Management and Audit Scheme (EMAS) in Europe has established audit frequencies as follows:

■ One year for activities with a high environmental impact

■ Two years for activities with a moderate environmental impact

■ Three years for activities with a low environmental impact.

Notwithstanding the EMAS-prescribed frequencies, many companies that have mature audit programs have settled in on a three-year frequency for major facilities. This is after each facility has been audited at least once or twice.

There are several ways to establish a frequency for auditing. One way is shown in Table 4 of Appendix F. This method establishes factors that can be used to set a site-audit frequency for each of three major categories. Some judgment is required in using this method because an overall categorization results from an evaluation of how often a site can be placed in one of the categories. That is, a given site may have three factors in Category I, two in Category II, and the remainder in Category III. The auditor then has to determine the relative weight of each placement in terms of an overall classification.

There are, of course, other approaches to ranking facilities by risk. Generally, site risk factors can be viewed as two-fold: inherent and external. First, there are indeed inherent risks of operation, which can involve the materials handled, the age of the facility, and the complexity of the process. These risks are important but perhaps more controllable[2] than the second class of external risks that may include the company's compliance history, the community and environmental setting, and the state agency's regulatory stringency.

If one views these two classes of risk in concert, as in Figure 4.5, a facility-by-facility risk evaluation can be conducted. We can find fairly large facilities, such as Facility G, that pose high risks, and efforts can be undertaken to reduce both inherent and external risks to move this facility into either a relatively safe or controllable situation. Such efforts might include increasing measures to reduce noncompliance or investigating the possibility of materials substitution. For another facility, such as Facility E, which poses only modest inherent risk, but is in so unstable an external environment that it is vulnerable to unwanted surprises, a public relations or compliance improvement program can be developed that will move the facility to the "relatively safe" category.

In much the same way, all facilities or units can be evaluated for their relative risk potential. Corrective action programs can then be fine tuned to address the nature and extent of the risk with the most cost-effective solution. One of these solutions could be the development of an environmental audit program which uses the material and facility risk assessment techniques discussed previously as priority setting tools. As shown in Figure 4.6, the scope, frequency, and resource commitment can be assigned based on an estimate of risks posed by the facility and the materials handled at the facility. In this way, resources are committed cost effectively. That is, the number of auditors and the facilities being audited at any one time are minimized.

---

[2] In this context, controllable means those items that are under the purview of management to change, including the substitution of materials, modifying processes, and upgrading process units.

Figure 4.5 Assessing Risk in a Multi-Plant or Multi-Unit Setting

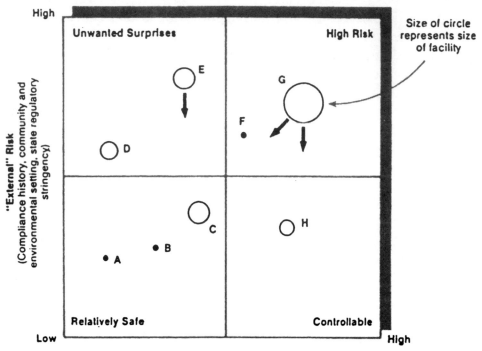

Figure 4.6 Sample Site Visit Schedule

ELEMENTS OF A PROGRAM

| Site | Description | Site Classification* | | | | Overall Rating & Class | Principal Scope | Frequency of Audit | Duration of Audit | No. of Auditors |
		Incident History	Materials Handled	Process Complexity	Environ Sensitivity					
I	Large AG-CHEM Processing Facility	4	3	3	3	13 A	RCRA/ FIFRA	Semi-Annual	One Week	4
II	Machine Tool Plant	3	3	2	4	12 B	CWA	Annual	2-3 days	3
III	Drum Storage Facility	1	2	1	3	7 C	RCRA	Every 3 Years	Half Day	1
IV	Truck Terminal	0	1	1	1	3 D	All	Every 5 Years	Half Day	1

*Sites are ranked from 0-4 (4 being highest potential risk) in each of four categories.

Overall rating is determined by total score as follows:
Score 1-4 (D), Score 5-8 (C), Score 9-12 (B), Score 13-16 (A)

Figure 4.6 can also be used as a resource planning tool. Once the company's inventory of facilities to be audited is established and a frequency, audit duration, and team size is assigned to each facility, the manpower loading for field audits can be determined for any given year. Further, if the number of field hours is increased by 50 percent or so to account for audit preparation and report writing, the result should indicate full cost accounting for the program, except for management and administration time.

Compiling this information on a spreadsheet will allow the program manager to manipulate critical factors, such as audit frequency, to determine the financial or budgetary impacts of increasing or decreasing the frequency.

Auditor Selection and Training

Thus far, in the brief history of EH&S auditing, companies have tended to design their audit function using one of four fundamental organizational approaches. The first of these, appropriate for larger companies, is to set up a corporate audit function. Under this option, full-time auditors are hired or transferred permanently into a corporate staff unit. This staff function alone is responsible for conducting company-wide audits. This particular strategy can be found in companies where management responsibilities are quite centralized.

The second approach, also most appropriate for large companies, involves establishing audit functions at the division or subsidiary levels. Here, the auditors from one division assess the facilities of other divisions and vice versa. Each audit team reports the results of its assessments to corporate headquarters. This strategy is typically used within the operating divisions.

A third tactic is to have each plant audit itself using common guidelines. This approach amounts to self-reporting and is used by some larger companies as well as by one-plant corporations.

Finally, some companies use outside contractors or consultants to (1) develop and manage their audit programs, (2) conduct individual facility audits, or (3) complete periodic third-party reviews of their in-house facility audits. Quite naturally, each of the above approaches has its advantages and disadvantages. Choosing from among them is a difficult exercise with no clear choice emerging.

Independent of the chosen organizational style of an EH&S audit program are the questions of who and how many staff should make up a given audit team. Since the assessment team is the heart of each company's program, the success of the program depends in large part on the skill, judgment, and perception of the team members.

Typically, the size of a given assessment team will depend upon the size of the facility, the complexity of the environmental issues, and the time that has elapsed since the last assessment. Experience has shown that four to six people are needed for a week to review complex facilities, with an equal amount of additional time off-site to prepare, write the final report, and respond to inquiries. On the other hand, certain facilities, such as storage facilities or warehouses, can be reviewed by one person in half a day.

Team composition will be dictated, to a large extent, by the type of facility, the EH&S issues, and the size of the team. In formulating the team, care should be given to balancing the skills of the team members to include knowledge of:

■ The audit process

■ The applicable environmental regulations

■ Corporate policies

■ The individual facility operations.

Because of the range of knowledge required, it is not surprising that companies will select from among a number of disciplines, including operations managers, engineers, scientists, attorneys, and accountants (because of their experience with financial audits). However, it is safe to say that the majority of audit teams consist of an operations or EH&S manager as team leader who is supported by engineers and scientists familiar with EH&S issues. Where a sensitive legal situation dictates, an attorney may provide on- or off-site counsel directly to the audit team.

Audit Procedures

Establishing procedures for the program is obviously an essential element in the planning process. In fact, an entire chapter of this book is dedicated to this issue. Here, it suffices to say that procedures should be carefully documented so that there is a common understanding among all participants in the program. (See also Appendix F)

One of the key planning issues is defining the time line for individual audits. An example site environmental audit process timeline is shown in Figure 4.7. The timeline shows the entire audit process from initial notification to the site by the audit team leader to submission of the corrective action plan by the site management. All of the interim steps are shown as well. This depiction can be useful in explaining how the process works to the uninitiated.

Audit Reports and Documentation

Audit programs generate a significant number of documents, many of which can pose significant liabilities to the organization. Thus, document management and retention are critical issues for the program manager. Each company must decide for itself the appropriate document retention procedures. Listed in Tables 6 and 7 of Appendix F are the classes of documents that are typically generated. Listed also are the functions that are commonly responsible for generation of the documents, the document due dates, the likely recipients of the documents, and their ultimate disposition or destruction. The tables present document management approaches

Figure 4.7 Example Site Environmental Audit Process Timeline

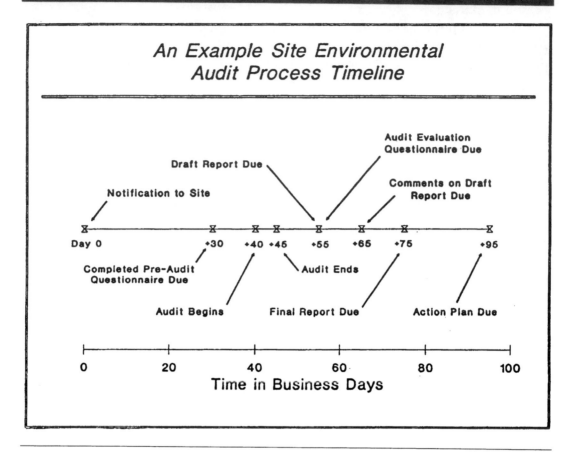

An Example Site Environmental Audit Process Timeline

typically used in industry; other approaches than those proposed are, of course, acceptable. Efficient ways of handling this process are discussed elsewhere in this book; but it is important to note here that proper document management is one of the most critical aspects of any audit program.

Audit Program Management & Evaluation

Any management program should be evaluated on a periodic basis. Each year, the audit program manager should report to senior management on the successes and failures of the program. The submittals, concise reports on the status of the program, should contain the following information at a minimum:

- Number of audits completed during the time period and number planned for the next time period

- Highlights of liabilities most affecting the corporation

- Trends in the types of noncompliance items to identify potential corporate-wide issues

- Trends in the number or percentage of repeat findings

- Statistics on business success rates in meeting corrective action plan schedules or percent of on-time closure of audit findings

- Results of formal feedback from those who are audited

- Development and implementation of an auditor training program

- Timeliness and quality of audit reports

- Periodic information exchange reports focusing on key findings and root-cause analysis

- Annual update of the program guidance manual and audit protocols.

The program evaluation can be done internally or by a third party, and should be completed annually. A model Audit Program Management Report is provided in Appendix K.

Audit Program Support Tools

The principal audit program tools include the guidance manual, corporate EH&S standards, regulatory databases, model presentations and reports, and the auditors' checklists or protocols. The protocols are clearly a critical tool. These are the actual working documents for the auditors. The checklists pose questions relating to:

(1) compliance with federal and state regulatory requirements
  (the "paper" audit)

(2) effective organizational controls (the "management" audit), and

(3) proper on-site and off-site unit operations (the "technical" audit).

These three areas are reviewed to determine whether: (1) specific regulatory requirements are known and complied with; (2) an organization is in place which can monitor compliance, respond to upsets or emergencies, and anticipate regulatory changes; and (3) compliance procedures are carried out by unit operators.

Protocols should be developed for key compliance areas and should integrate any federal, state, or local requirements influencing the facility. Specific protocols should be developed for at least the following compliance areas, if they are applicable to the facility:

- Water and Wastewater

- Air emissions

- Solid and hazardous wastes

- Above and underground storage tanks

- Special pollutants (e.g., PCBs, asbestos, universal wastes, pesticides)

- Hazardous materials management

- Emergency response and spill control

- Community right-to-know

- Worker right-to-know

- Industrial hygiene (e.g., respiratory protection)

- Worker safety (e.g., confined space, hazardous energy)

- Process safety

- Product stewardship.

These are considered the major EH&S areas affecting most industrial facilities and should be viewed as a baseline group of requirements for which protocols are required. Other protocols can be added to the program as conditions change and new regulations emerge.

The following elements should be part of a good audit protocol:

- It should provide the auditor with an abstract or overview of the key federal, state, and local regulations and requirements relevant to each compliance area at the facility being audited.

- It should highlight those key definitions that help the auditor conduct the audit without having to refer to the full text copies of the applicable regulations. The importance of definitions in verifying regulatory compliance areas cannot be over-emphasized.

■ It should include all the items strictly required by federal, state, and local statutory laws and their associated regulations.

■ It should include inspection items that permit evaluation of the plant's vulnerability to "common law" environmental problems (i.e., noise, odor, nuisances, community impacts).

■ It should provide an opportunity to verify that internal company environmental management procedures are understood and adhered to by plant staff.

■ It should give the auditor specific action steps so that compliance can be properly evaluated. Use of action verbs such as "examine," "inspect," "calculate," and the like should be used in the protocol so that the auditor understands clearly what must be done.

■ The protocol should provide a space in which comments can be written by the auditor. These notes are then readily available when writing the audit report. This also discourages the use of loose papers and notes that could be misplaced.

Within these guidelines, individual approaches can vary. One example of a particularly good approach is provided in Appendix C, which is an audit protocol developed by the U.S. EPA to conduct assessments of Community Right-to-Know requirements. It and many others are available for free on the EPA's web site (www.epa.gov). While using a protocol developed by the regulators is by no means a "fail-safe" approach toward assuring compliance, it does provide an internal system of checks consistent with external Federal expectations.[3]

Remember that in using any protocol, they are designed as an aid and should not be considered exhaustive. The auditor's judgment should continue to play a role in determining the focus and extent of further investigation.

The development of an appropriate set of audit protocols is, at a minimum, a challenging task. Prior to the selection of a particular style, the manual developer should think long and hard about the specific objectives of the overall corporate audit program, the demands a particular style may place on plant staff and their willingness to accommodate these demands, and the capabilities of the staff who will be designated, either temporarily or permanently, as auditors.

Before developing protocols for an organization, the following steps should be taken:

■ **Decide on the scope of the audits.** Which laws and regulations will be reviewed? Will the checklists include state and local requirements?

---

[3] However, it is important to realize that state and local regulations are often the governing requirements, and are frequently more stringent than federal regulations.

■ **Review your facilities against these standards.** Do you have any NPDES permits or are all plants discharged to municipal systems? Do you have any RCRA disposal facilities? Not all regulations will need checklists if you have no facilities regulated by the standards.

■ **Decide on checklist format.** Use the following sources to choose or develop your style of checklist:

- U.S. EPA/NEIC reports
- U.S. EPA protocols
- Government Institutes/U.S. EPA inspection manuals
- Published literature
- Forums such as the Environmental Auditing Roundtable.

■ **Develop one checklist.** Pick a compliance area (wastewater discharges) and develop the checklist.

■ **Test the checklist.** Before proceeding with the remaining checklists, test the first one. It's surprising sometimes how the logic developed in the office is found wanting in the field.

■ **Develop and test the remaining checklists.** Complete and test the remaining checklists, looking for a balance between completeness and manageability.

The end result of this exercise should be checklists that meet the specific organizational objectives.

A KEY PROGRAM ISSUE: CORPORATE STANDARDS AND GUIDELINES

One of the most useful aids for any audit program is a sound set of corporate environmental standards and guidelines. Generally, there are numerous environmental management standards that can be developed to enable a company to more effectively manage its environmentally related activities. Such standards might involve requiring secondary containment for all drum and tank storage, and transferring hazardous materials and wastes, regardless of local regulatory requirements.

Development of a common set of corporate expectations gives the audit team a firm foundation for making risk-based recommendations. For example, in a case where there are no regulatory or corporate requirements for secondary containment of hazardous materials, auditors might receive significant "push-back" from the site if they were to recommend such corrective action, even in cases where the risk clearly justifies construction of containment. Several environmental management standards or procedures that could be developed in any organization are discussed below. Certainly many more procedures could be developed as well. Some will relate to administrative requirements and others might relate to minimally acceptable physical facilities.

Development of Waste Discharge Inventories

Many companies require that their sites develop air emissions inventories, water balances, and waste inventories. Defining a baseline of discharges assists greatly in measuring environmental improvement and pollution prevention successes. In the U.S., documentation of these inventories is almost mandatory due to the Emergency Planning and Community Right-to-Know Act (EPCRA), the Clean Air Act (CAA), and other recent legislation.

The inventories also are valuable tools for audit teams as they provide a map or guide for the review. This is particularly true for air emissions audits, which can be quite a challenge for the auditor if the site has never completed an inventory. For instance, at large chemical plants, the number of stacks, vents, and other release points can number in the tens of thousands if fugitive sources are included. In fact, on many an audit where there is no documented site air emissions inventory, this lack of an inventory becomes the first finding of the audit team, since it is difficult for the site to determine regulatory applicability if there is no general understanding of site-wide quality and quantity of air releases.

Secondary Containment for Hazardous Materials and Wastes

It is sometimes surprising how little regulation there is worldwide regarding secondary containment of both liquid hazardous wastes and materials. Even in the U.S., there is no federal requirement that hazardous waste accumulation points incorporate secondary containment. However, storage of these materials can pose substantial risk to the organization if there is a release to soils, surface waters or groundwater.

Accordingly, many multinational companies have developed global secondary containment standards for hazardous waste, and material containers and tanks. These standards are fairly straightforward and address both containment integrity (e.g., no cracks or open sumps) and capacity (e.g., the area must hold the contents of the largest container or 10 percent of the entire contained volume, whichever is greater, plus an allowance for rainfall if there is no overhead protection). If there is valved drainage associated with the containment area, the standards also require that the valves be closed and locked under normal conditions and that there be a formal, documented procedure for release of accumulated rainwater.

Such corporate standards and audits go hand in glove. They minimize overall corporate risks and provide the legitimacy an audit team requires when making recommendations to install secondary containment measures. Using the "it's a good management practice" argument is often not viewed as compelling by the site management.

Internal Reporting of Environmentally Related Incidents

During the course of the year, facilities will experience violations, excursions, spills or other environmental incidents. These occurrences must be brought to the attention of corporate headquarters on a timely basis. The objective of the internal reporting procedure is to provide a mechanism for the prompt reporting of these incidents as well as to define responsibilities throughout the company for the reports.

The information, when received by headquarters, is typically compiled into a database so that the total liability of the corporation can be readily determined. This policy is not geared toward the periodic reporting requirements of regulatory agencies as stipulated in permits and other regulations. Rather, this procedure should emphasize the proper reporting of a violation from the point at which it happens, up through the chain of command to the corporate headquarters officer responsible for environmental affairs.

All facilities need to develop standard forms and distribute them along with instructions for completing and submitting them to headquarters when a violation occurs. Large companies commonly develop a management information system (preferably computer-based) to store records of the reported violations at corporate headquarters. This system gives corporate headquarters the "real time" information it needs to effectively manage the environmental affairs of the company and helps auditors better understand the environmental management issues at the site.

Environmental Recordkeeping/Records Retention Procedures

The objective of this management procedure is to specify environmentally related data, records, reports, and files that should be maintained by the company. Environmentally related data, records, reports, and files should be interpreted broadly to include all materials strictly required by statute, rule, or regulation, as well as those written materials useful and necessary for the company to manage its environmental compliance program but not required by law. The procedure should also identify responsibilities for maintenance and custody of environmental records, including minimum retention periods.

In some cases, joint custody of particular records should be established between departments that share responsibility for compliance activities. Some records and reports must be maintained for specified periods of time as stipulated in various statues, rules, and regulations. Many records, however, have no statutory requirements for retention, and, therefore, good management practice considerations should be used to establish the retention periods.

Records are normally maintained in a central location. Maintaining them in this manner will aid in retrieval of environmental compliance-related information, and will enhance the site's ability to respond to internal audits and external regulatory inspections.

External Regulatory Inspection Procedures

The objective of this management procedure is to specify procedures to be followed when compliance inspections are conducted by external regulatory agencies. Most federal and state agencies have broad statutory authority to conduct inspections at industrial facilities.

Companies should develop a procedure that includes steps for dealing with these visits. The procedure will deal with items that should be covered prior to, during, and after the inspection. Plant management should have clear guidance on: (1) limits of authority of inspectors, (2) objective and scope of the inspection, (3) plant personnel who will accompany the inspector, and (4) legal counsel participation.

During the inspection, plant personnel should have guidance on how they should respond to deficiencies found, what notes they should take during the inspection, and what their general attitude should be in dealing with inspectors.

After the inspection, plant personnel should have instructions from corporate headquarters on preparing memoranda for the record and developing an action plan for resolving identified deficiencies.

The common elements of a compliance inspection procedure can be grouped into five procedural categories: (1) pre-inspection preparation, (2) entry of inspector, (3) opening conference, (4) physical inspection, and (5) closing conference. These categories will be discussed at length in various chapters of this book.

ADDITIONAL SAMPLING

There is no real consensus on whether or not to conduct sampling as part of an audit and most companies do not do so. These companies typically focus on verifying compliance in this area through a review of the site's sampling and analysis quality assurance/quality control (QA/QC) program. If that program is found to be strong, then duplicate (split) sampling is considered unnecessary.

However, some companies do collect split samples and send one set of samples to an outside, independent laboratory to further verify their QA/QC program.

In a third approach, the audit team conducts analyses during the audit with pH probes and the like to determine whether the stream is in compliance that day. This approach is used in only limited cases, and is not generally believed to be an effective means of verification.

CONTINUOUS REVIEW

Auditing is not something that is done once and forgotten for ten years. Noncompliance can surface quickly. Therefore, audits should be conducted on a regular basis. As the audit program evolves into an integral part of operations, senior management should periodically review the program to assure that it is continuing to meet its originally stated objectives. In fact, some companies use outside firms periodically to conduct audits as a mid-course review on their program.

EVALUATING THE RESULTS AND IMPLEMENTING THE SOLUTIONS

These two elements must both be included for a successful program. Corporations are most liable where compliance problems have been identified, yet no solutions are planned. These solutions must be documented, even where management initially can only commit to a phased response for a needed major capital expenditure. It is vital that senior management have a system in place to assure that where violations have been noted, the facility operator is, in fact, on the way towards achieving compliance. History indicates that the corporation and its executives are at great risk where violations have been identified and no plan is in place to remedy the situation.

In recent years there has been a particular trend to (1) assure that corrective-action plans are, in fact, just that and (2) to provide formal briefings for senior management, including the board of directors, on the status of the audit program. Automated tracking systems have been put in place in most companies. These systems produce monthly status reports for each facility's action plan and, subsequently, produce statistics (similar to safety program reporting) for senior management on those items completed ahead of, on, or behind schedule. This kind of reporting to senior management has done much to increase the internal credibility of the audit program; after all, senior management can no longer escape the civil and criminal liability associated with noncompliance.

Chapter 5

IMPACT OF INTERNATIONAL STANDARDS ON EH&S AUDIT PROGRAMS[1]

Opinions have vested interests just as men have.

– Samuel Butler, 1835-1902

What do General Motors, The Episcopal Diocese of Massachusetts, and Ben and Jerry's Homemade Ice Cream have in common? All three organizations have endorsed the CERES Principles, a model corporate code of environmental conduct developed by the Coalition for Environmentally Responsible Economies (CERES). This "model code" generally goes well beyond what is now typically required of industry to maintain compliance with already stringent requirements established by regulatory agencies.

The CERES Principles are not the only game in town. Many other environmental initiatives have surfaced both in the U.S. and abroad over the past years (See Figure 5.1). Expectations for corporations are rising even as these initiatives compete for recognition and acceptance. Notable disasters such as Bhopal and the Exxon *Valdez* accidents, as well as more chronic environmental issues such as deforestation and depletion of the ozone layer, have done much to heighten the world's concerns over the environment by generating support for establishing a "global-level playing field" that protects the environment while allowing for sustainable development. It is this concept that is really considered to be the underlying driver for all of the increased pressure on transnational companies to rethink their performance. Sustainable development in its basic form is the process of meeting the needs of the present without interfering with the ability of future generations to meet their needs.

Presently, there are numerous sets of initiatives that will likely shape the future of corporate EH&S performance expectations and, specifically, EH&S auditing programs. These are:

---

[1] Adapted and updated from an article originally published in *Total Quality Environmental Management* (New York: Executive Enterprises, Inc., 1994).

Figure 5.1 Corporate Performance Judged beyond Compliance

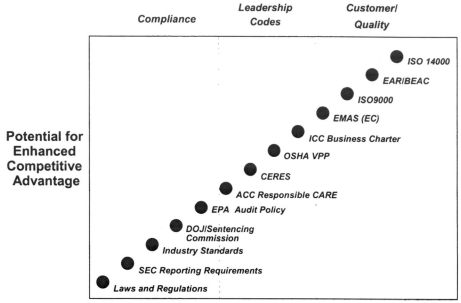

Corporate Performance Judged Beyond Compliance: Global Initiatives Forcing Response

■ The CERES Principles

■ International Organization for Standardization (ISO) Environmental Management System Standards

■ The European Community Eco-Audit Management and Audit Scheme (EMAS)

■ The Chemical Industry Responsible Care Program

■ U.S. EPA and OSHA Audit Policies and Performance Programs

■ The U.S. Sentencing Commission's Mitigating Factors Guidelines

■ The Environmental, Health, and Safety Auditing Roundtable Audit Standards

■ The Board of EH&S Auditor Certifications Audit Standards

This chapter discusses these initiatives and provides some thoughts on what companies are doing presently to prepare for the future.

THE KEY INITIATIVES

The dissimilarity and fragmentation of the initiatives will be the major challenge facing those who wish to comply with the progressive requirements, although there has been some historical coordination among the originating organizations. This dilemma is similar to that of facility emergency response planning in the U.S., where separate plans with separate requirements can be required under the Clean Air Act, the Clean Water Act, the Resource Conservation and Recovery Act, the Emergency Response and Community Right-to-Know Act, and the Occupational Safety and Health Act. How then does one assure that a site's emergency response planning efforts will respond to individual requirements while resulting in a program that will indeed work if there is an emergency? One could ask the same question about the environmental management initiatives under discussion.

The CERES Principles[2]

CERES is a nonprofit membership organization comprised of leading social investors, major environmental groups, public pension funds, labor organizations, and public interest groups. Together this coalition represents over $150 billion in invested assets. Thus the power it wields in making investment choices can be significant.

CERES began as a result of the Exxon *Valdez* incident that occurred in March 1989. In fact, the principles were originally called the Valdez Principles. As shown in Figure 5.2, the consequences of the *Valdez* incident on Exxon's stock price were measurable, resulting in roughly a ten-dollar-per-share shortfall a little over a year after the incident when compared to five major Exxon competitors. Investor strategies likely had a significant bearing on this shortfall.

The ten CERES Principles, listed below, demand that companies that endorse the principles pledge to go voluntarily beyond the requirements of the law. The ten CERES Principles are:

- Protection of the Biosphere
- Sustainable Use of Natural Resources
- Reduction and Disposal of Wastes
- Energy Conservation
- Risk Reduction
- Safe Products and Services
- Environmental Restoration

---

[2] Information on CERES has been obtained from their web site, www.ceres.org.

Figure 5.2 Consequences of the Exxon Valdez Incident

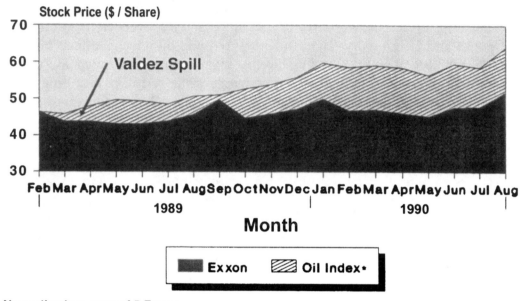

Exxon Stock Growth
Did Valdez Hurt???

Stock Price ($ / Share)

Valdez Spill

FebMar AprMay Jun Jul AugSepOctNovDec Jan FebMar AprMay Jun Jul Aug

1989   1990

Month

Exxon   Oil Index•

**• Normalized average of 5 Exxon
Competitors**

- Informing the Public
- Management Commitment
- Audits and Reports.

One noteworthy Principle is the Management Commitment, which requires that a company's board of directors and chief executive officer be fully informed about pertinent environmental issues. Directly or indirectly, this has resulted in many cases where companies now have appointed environmental experts on their boards of directors. This trend is discussed in more detail later in the chapter.

Further, the CERES Principles require the adoption of an audit program. Companies must commit to an annual self-evaluation on the progress against meeting the Principles. Companies must also support the timely creation of generally accepted environmental audit procedures and annually complete a "CERES Report." Not surprisingly, reporting to the public on environmental issues is troubling to many companies. However, it is a trend that can be found in several of the initiatives (e.g., the European Eco-Audit Program), all of which have been preceded in the U.S. by the public reporting requirements of federal Community Right-to-Know legislation passed in 1986.

As of the end of 2000, over 50 companies had endorsed the CERES Principles. They include:

- American Airlines
- Baxter International
- Bethlehem Steel
- The Body Shop
- Ben & Jerry's
- Coca-Cola USA
- Ford
- GM

- H.B. Fuller
- Louisville Sewer District
- Northeast Utilities
- Polaroid
- Sunoco
- Timberland Company
- Westchester County, NY
- U.S. Trust Company of Boston

The endorsement language of each company must be read quite carefully—GM and Sun, in their statements, stop short of adopting the principles, an original requirement of the CERES coalition. For example, Sun's statement is as follows: "In February 1993, Sun Company, Inc. became the first Fortune 500 firm to endorse the health, environmental, and safety principles of CERES. In addition, CERES has recognized Sun's Principles of health, environment, and safety as being consistent with their own."[3] Sun's CEO has been heard on radio and television talking about his company's commitment to the environment and the CERES Principles—perhaps the most pro-active effort to date by a Fortune 500 company in getting its message to the public.

Similarly, GM's endorsement statement as reported by *The New York Times* was as follows: "GM said on February 3, 1994 that it would uphold the CERES Principles. In return for support of the Principles, CERES endorsed GM's own principles as consistent with the goals of the CERES Principles."[4] The skeptic might wonder what is really being said here. Nonetheless, the endorsement by several Fortune 500 companies has likely provided an impetus for the endorsement or adoption of the CERES Principles by others.

International Organization for Standardization (ISO) Environmental Standards

The standards that probably have the most potential long-term impact are those that have been crafted by the International Organization for Standardization (ISO). ISO

---

[3] Taken from an undated Sun Company brochure.

[4] *The New York Times*, February 4, 1994.

has a long history of developing quality standards (i.e., the ISO 9000 series) that are firmly entrenched in the developed world, including the U.S. In some industries (e.g., automotive, electronics) becoming a registered ISO 9000 company is almost a mandatory requirement. In time, a facility seeking ISO 9000 quality registration may be required to have or be seeking ISO 14000 environmental registration as well.

Early in 1993, ISO constituted a new technical committee (TC 207) charged with developing international standards in the field of environmental tools and systems. ISO/TC 207 was the result of a two-year study by ISO's Strategic Advisory Group on the Environment (SAGE), which concluded that international environmental management standards would:

- Promote a common approach to environmental management, similar to quality management and the ISO 9000 series

- Enhance organizations' ability to attain and measure improvements in environmental performance

- Facilitate trade and remove trade barriers.

In mid-1993, several ISO/TC 207 subcommittees were established to address particular aspects of environmental management systems. These subcommittees and the countries designated to lead the effort are:

- Environmental Management Systems (United Kingdom)

- Environmental Auditing (The Netherlands)

- Environmental Labeling (Australia)

- Environmental Performance Evaluation (U.S.)

- Life-Cycle Assessment (France)

- Terms and Definitions (Norway)

- Environmental Aspects in Product Standards (Germany)

Official ISO 14000 Standards related to management systems and auditing were finalized in the fall of 1996. The environmental auditing standards are really comprised of three separate guidelines, which are:

- ISO 14010 - General Principles of Environmental Management Systems (EMS) Auditing

- ISO 14011 - EMS Auditing Procedures

- ISO 14012 - Qualification Criteria for Environmental Auditors

It should be noted that the ISO 14000 auditing guidelines are just that, guidelines. This is to distinguish them from the ISO 14001 Environmental Management Systems (EMS) specification, which carries with it the "shall" descriptor. Also, the ISO 14000 Standards are only environmental standards, as opposed to health and safety standards, and will only be required if the global marketplace calls for them. In other words, ISO 9000 Standards have been adopted principally because customers of multinational companies have demanded it or because the manufacturers have viewed their adoption as providing a competitive advantage. The same is true of the ISO 14000 Standards.

The European Community Eco-Management and Audit Scheme

The European Community Eco-Management and Audit Scheme (EMAS) was adopted in mid-1993 and became effective in April 1995. It is designed to "promote continuous improvement in the environmental performance of industry."[5] This "voluntary" regulation affects only European Union (EU) members, and if a company operating in one of these countries wishes to participate, only individual sites can be registered. In order to participate, the following requirements must be met:

- An environmental policy must be adopted consistent with requirements listed in the EMAS regulations.

- The company must conduct an initial site review.

- An environmental management system must be developed consistent with requirements listed in the EMAS regulations.

- Independent, ISO 10011-consistent audits must be conducted at least every three years, using internal, but site-independent, staff or third parties.

- An environmental statement must be prepared annually.

- The environmental statement must be verified by an independent third party that was not involved in the audit.

- The environmental statement is to be released to the public.

Arguably, the most controversial provision of the EMAS regulations is the last requirement: release of the environmental statement to the public. The reason is that the statement is likely to contain sensitive information. The statement is to have the following organization:

- Overview of site activities

---

[5] "Council Regulation (EEC) No. 1836/93 of 29 June 1993 allowing voluntary participation by companies in the industrial sector in a Community eco-management and audit scheme," *Official Journal of the European Communities*, No. L 168/1 (July 10, 1993): 2.

- Assessment of significant environmental issues

- Summary data on emissions and releases

- Other environmental performance data

- Company environmental policy and overview of environmental management systems

- Deadline for issuance of next environmental statement

- Name of verifier.

There are additional controversies associated with the EMAS regulations, such as setting accreditation standards for the third-party verifiers. However, the apparent momentum is such that major companies operating facilities in the EU will be compelled to comply. Facilities that do participate will be allowed to use the EMAS logo on their stationery but not on their products or in their advertisements.

The Chemical Industry's Responsible Care Program

The chemical industry worldwide has historically been under tremendous scrutiny related to its EH&S practices. In an effort to better manage its environmental liabilities, the industry developed the Responsible Care Program a few years ago. In the U.S., this has been spearheaded by the American Chemistry Council (ACC), which includes in its membership all major U.S. chemical companies. Presently, the adoption of the Responsible Care Codes of Practice is a requirement for membership in the ACC. The six codes are:

- Community Awareness and Emergency Response

- Process Safety

- Product Safety

- Employee Health and Safety

- Distribution

- Pollution Prevention.

Each of the codes prescribes the management systems that should be expected in a company in order to meet the objectives of a sound program. Each year, member companies are required to evaluate or audit how far along they are towards full implementation of an effective program.

In order to enhance the credibility of the Responsible Care Program, the ACC has developed a Management Systems Verification (MSV) process. The process provides participating companies with an *external* review of the effectiveness of their management systems for carrying out Responsible Care and helps to demonstrate the integrity of the initiative to key audiences.

The Responsible Care Program is a good indicator of how and why expectations can become fragmented and confusing. The Responsible Care concept was initially developed by the Canadian Chemical Producers' Association (CCPA) and modified by CMA for use in the U.S.

The CCPA codes include:

- Community Awareness and Emergency Response

- Research and Development

- Manufacturing

- Transportation

- Distribution

- Hazardous Waste Management

While the U.S. and Canadian codes are similar, they are not identical. Variations have typically occurred in standard-setting programs, either due to the variation in geo-politics of the individual country or because, frankly, most organizations wish to place their own particular signature on developing trends.

U.S. EPA and OSHA Audit Policies and Performance Programs

The 1986, 1996, and 2000 U.S. EPA and 2000 OSHA Audit Policies are discussed elsewhere in this text. Here it is important to highlight only that the U.S. EPA was the first organization to define the elements of an effective environmental audit program in its 1986 Policy. In summary form, the seven basic "Elements of an Effective Environmental Auditing Program," set forth in the Appendix to the Policy Statement, are:

1. Explicit top management support for environmental auditing, and a commitment to follow up on audit findings

2. Environmental auditing function must be independent of the audited activities

3. Adequate team staffing and auditor training

4. Explicit audit program objectives, scope, resources, and frequency

5. A process that collects, analyzes, interprets, and documents information sufficient to achieve audit objectives, with particular emphasis on the efficiency and reliability of the information gathered

6. Preparation of candid, clear and appropriate written reports including audit findings, corrective actions, and schedules for implementation

7. Quality assurance procedures to assure accuracy and thoroughness of environmental audits.

These elements have been used as the building blocks of audit expectation statements made by many other organizations.

In addition to the audit policies, both the U.S. EPA and OSHA have launched programs that are designed to recognize and promote exceptional environmental, health, and safety performance in the regulated community. The OSHA Voluntary Protection Program (or Star Program) pre-dates the U.S. EPA National Environmental Performance Track Program, which was launched in December 2000. In both cases, however, participants are expected to have designed and implemented outstanding environmental or health and safety programs, respectively. The adequacy of these programs is verified by agency reviews. The benefits to participants include public recognition, fewer compliance inspections, and potential penalty mitigation where compliance deficiencies do occur. These programs are an attempt to foster exceptional performance through the use of incentives as opposed to enforcement. As such, they represent a changing attitude among the regulatory agencies and a movement away from strict command and control approaches. Detailed information on each program can be found on the agencies' websites, www.epa.gov or www.osha.gov.

The U.S. Sentencing Commission's (USSC) Guidelines for Mitigating Factors

In 1993, the USSC published a draft of proposed sanctions for organizations convicted of environmental offenses. Although these guidelines have yet to be published in final form, they do provide some insight into what audit-related factors the U.S. Department of Justice might consider in mitigating a sentence. To be considered for mitigation the organization must, among other efforts, have designed and implemented, with sufficient authority, personnel, and other resources, the systems and programs that are necessary for:

■ frequent auditing (with appropriate independence from line management) and inspection (including random, and when necessary, surprise audits and inspections) of its principal operations and all pollution control facilities to assess, in detail, their compliance with all applicable environmental requirements and the organization's internal policies, standards and procedures, as well as internal investigations and implementation of appropriate, follow-up countermeasures with respect to all significant incidents of noncompliance;

■ continuous on-site monitoring, by specifically trained compliance personnel and by other means, of key operations and pollution control facilities that are either subject to significant environmental regulation, or where the nature or history of such operations or facilities suggests a significant potential for noncompliance;

■ internal reporting (e.g., hotlines) without fear of retribution, of potential non-compliance to those responsible for investigating and correcting such incidents;

■ tracking the status of responses to identified compliance issues to enable expeditious, effective, and documented resolution of environmental compliance issues by line management; and

■ redundant, independent checks on the status of compliance, particularly in those operations, facilities, or processes where the organization knows, or has reason to believe, that employees or agents may have, in the past, concealed noncompliance through falsification or other means, and in the those operations, facilities or processes where the organization reasonably believes such potential exists.

Environmental, Health, and Safety Auditing Roundtable (EAR) Auditing Standards[6]

In 1993 and 1997 the EAR published two auditing standards–one for conducting effective audits, the other related to program design. These are highlighted below.

Standards for Performance of EH&S Audits (February 1993)

This standard was adopted by EAR in February 1993. The Standards Committee undertook a "five-year review" of this standard during 1998, which included a survey of the entire membership for comments. Based on the results of that survey and the independent evaluation by the Standards Committee, it was concluded that the standards remained appropriate without revision.

The purpose of these standards, as stated in the introduction, is "to provide minimum criteria for the conduct of EH&S audits. These are the generally accepted auditing standards that EAR members believe are necessary for the professional conduct of EHS audits." They are deliberately concise and are intended to "define *what* is required to conduct a competent audit, not *how* to implement each aspect of the standard." The standards can be used in connection with transactional or due diligence audits as well as the conduct of an audit as part of an ongoing management process or system.

The standards "define good commercial and customary practices for performing audits" while recognizing that there may be "specific circumstances that might mandate a departure from the standards established here." The one-page EAR "Code of Ethics" is a companion document to the standards and defines the honesty, objectivity, and diligence that are essential qualities of the environmental auditor. These

---

[6] The EAR information was obtained directly from that organization's website, www.auditear.org.

include avoiding bias or prejudice and respect for confidential information. In particular, these standards address the following topics:

- Auditor proficiency, including technical knowledge, training and qualifications to conduct an audit

- Knowledge of the legal and regulatory requirements and environmental policies applicable to the facility that is being audited

- The use of due professional care, diligence, and skill in performing the audit

- Objectivity and independence of the audit site or activity to be audited, free of conflict of interest or internal or external pressure that might influence any auditor's findings

- Clear and explicit objectives for the audit

- Systematic plans and procedures for conducting the audit, including the use of written protocols, checklists, and similar tools

- Planning and supervision of the field work, including the organization and deployment of the audit team and the procedures for gathering the necessary information sufficient to support all findings, conclusions, and recommendations

- Audit quality control and assurance

- Documentation, including the preparation and retention of working papers

- Clear and appropriate reporting, including findings, conclusions, supporting evidence as appropriate, and, where part of the task, recommendations with respect to the correction of any deficiencies.

Standard for the Design and Implementation of an EH&S Audit Program (January 1997)

This standard was initially adopted by the EAR Board on a provisional basis in January 1995, and was given full approval on January 12, 1997. It is designed to "establish criteria for the design and implementation of EH&S audit programs, including both compliance and management systems audit programs." As such, it complements the *Standards for the Performance of EH&S Audits* described above. The standard is intended to describe the basic elements to be included in EH&S audit programs. "Key requirements and best practices are defined, but detailed implementation steps are intentionally not prescribed. Specific circumstances justifying a departure from the key requirements of this standard, must be documented."

Both EAR standards make clear that the words "must" and "shall" denote mandatory practices or key requirements, while "should" denotes a desired "best practice" recommendation. The standard provides definitions of basic terms and proceeds to discuss the following principal elements of a sound and effective EH&S audit program:

Senior management commitment to the program

Written policies or procedures to describe the scope and operation of the program and the audit activities to ensure compliance

Clearly stated scope and objectives of the audit program

■ Program organization, including a program manager, auditor qualifications and training requirements, and independence of the audit function.

Procedures for selection of sites to be audited, subjects to be covered, and frequency, including a sensible basis for prioritizing sites that may need more frequent audits than others

The use of protocols, checklists, and guidance documents, including mechanisms to ensure that these documents reflect all current and applicable laws, regulations, organization policies, and other elements that define the scope and purpose of the audit, and a procedure to keep these materials current

Pre-audit activities

Procedures for reporting the results of the audit and document management

■ Corrective action planning and tracking to ensure that reasonable and necessary corrective measures are identified and that their timely implementation is assured

Quality assurance, both as to the program and the quality of the program managers and auditors.

The Board of EH&S Auditor Certifications (BEAC) Auditing Standards

In 2000, BEAC published *Standards for the Professional Practice of EH&S Auditing*. The BEAC Standards provide the basis for development and operation of EH&S audit programs. The purpose of the Standards is to impart an understanding of the roles and responsibilities of EH&S auditing to all levels of management, boards of directors, public bodies, external auditors, and related professional organizations. The Standards are intended to establish a basis for guidance and measurement of EH&S auditing performance, improve the practice, and advance the profession of EH&S auditing.

The General Standards and Performance Standards are the first two parts of a three-tiered set of standards and practices. The General Standards are brief and mandatory, although not specific. Performance Standards are a means of conformance with the General Standards and are recommended but not mandatory. Performance Practices are "useful and suitable means of meeting a General or Performance Standard," according to the BEAC Auditing Standards. The scope of the Standards includes independence, professional proficiency, performance of audit work, scope of the audit program, and management of the EH&S auditing function.

CORPORATE RESPONSES

In many ways, the future expectations for environmental excellence can be overwhelming to corporate executives. Nonetheless, the likelihood that all of this will simply go away is quite remote. Thus, corporations have already begun to change the way they operate, anticipating an increasingly challenging future. Four rather interesting developments are:

- Appointment of environmental experts to corporate boards
- Voluntary public reporting
- Third-party program evaluations and certifications
- Benchmarking studies.

Each of these is discussed briefly below.

Appointment of Environmental Experts to Corporate Boards

As previously mentioned, investor groups have requested that U.S. companies adopt certain principles to help ensure sound environmental management. One of the principles asks that companies appoint members of environmental organizations or, at a minimum, environmental experts to company boards. In fact, this is happening.

A listing of several companies and the environmental experts on their boards is shown in Figure 5.3.[7] It is a diverse group of companies and a diverse group of board members, including several previous administrators of the U.S. EPA. Moreover, more than 50 company executives are also on the boards of national environmental organizations; Union Carbide, for example, has had its directors on the boards of the World Wildlife Fund, World Resources Institute, and the Natural Resources Defense Council.

Voluntary Public Reporting

Public reporting of environmental issues is something that creates great angst among chief executives in major corporations. In the U.S., however, with the passage of the

---

[7] The figure first appeared in L.B. Cahill and S.P. Engelman, "Bolstering the Board's Environmental Focus," *Directors and Boards Magazine*, vol. 18, no. 1 (Fall 1993): 23-5. Some Board members may have changed; however, the trend remains.

Figure 5.3 Environmentalists on Boards of Directors

Environmentalists on Boards

Company	Environmental Director	Affiliation
Ashland Oil Inc.	Patrick Noonan	President, Conservation Fund
Atlantic Richfield Co.	Frank Boren	Conservation Fellow, World Wildlife Fund/ Conservation Fund
Baxter International Inc.	James Ebert	Director, Chesapeake Bay Institute
Chevron Corp.	Bruce Smart	Senior Counselor, World Resources Institute
Dexter Corp.	Jean-François Saglio	Former Director, French Administration of Environment Protection
Du Pont Co.	William Reilly	Former Administrator, U.S. Environmental Protection Agency
Exxon Corp.	John Steele	Senior Scientist, Woods Hole Oceanographic Institution
Metaclad Corp.	Allan John Borner	Founding Director, National Association for Environmental Management
Monsanto Co.	William Ruckelshaus	Former Administrator, EPA
Niagara Mohawk Power Corp.	Bonnie Guiton	President and CEO, Earth Conservation Corps
Union Carbide Corp.	Russell Train	Chairman, World Wildlife Fund; Former Administrator, EPA
Waste Management Inc.	Kathryn Fuller	President, World Wildlife Fund and Conservation Foundation (presently on leave from the board)
Weyerhaueser Co.	William Ruckelshaus	Former Administrator, EPA

Sources: Directors & Boards; Directorship; The Wall Street Journal

Emergency Planning and Community Right-to-Know Act (EPCRA) in 1986, public reporting is here and here to stay. It is now quite simple to identify and rank the top ten companies that release EPCRA-listed toxic chemicals. This is one top-ten list that companies will attempt to avoid.

While these toxic release reports are mandated by regulation, many companies have now concluded that it might be better to produce voluntary comparable information, along with any positive developments, in an annual environmental report, since this information will be reported to the public by independent environmental organizations and newspapers. As a result, annual environmental reports are becoming commonplace among progressive companies. Over 70 companies in North America, Europe, and Japan have produced freestanding environmental reports.[8] These reports typically are being produced in response to new regulations; emerging business requirements, including the need to report environmental liabilities accurately; and changing public expectations.

In recognition of the growing demand for these environmental reports, in 1992 a number of companies worked on developing suitable guidelines for reporting. The result was the *Public Environmental Reporting Initiative (PERI) Guidelines*. These Guidelines were developed to improve environmental reporting by companies, and are consistent with the expectations of related initiatives such as CERES reporting. The Guidelines propose that the following elements be considered for inclusion in environmental reports:

- Organizational profile
- Environmental policy
- Environmental management
- Environmental releases
- Resource conservation
- Environmental risk management
- Environmental compliance
- Product stewardship
- Employee recognition
- Stakeholder involvement.

The goal is to standardize the process as much as possible while still allowing each reporting organization the flexibility to determine how best to address each element.

---

[8] Deloitte Touche Tohmatsu International, The International Institute for Sustainable Development, and Sustainability, *Coming Clean: Corporate Environmental Reporting* (1993).

Third-Party Program Evaluations and Certifications[9]

Consistent with good Total Quality Management practices, many companies are now having outside consultants (i.e., third parties) or their internal audit departments (i.e., second parties) evaluate their EH&S audit programs on a periodic basis. The annual or biennial studies help the companies both meet their "continuous improvement" objectives and answer to the increasing pressure by stakeholders to provide assurances that the company is identifying and remedying its EH&S issues.

Within these companies' environmental reports, the evaluation of the EH&S audit programs is increasingly being addressed. For example, from 1992 through 1999, DuPont has provided the results of the third-party evaluation of its SHE Audit Program on its website. Each year, the summaries of the last three year's evaluations are available. Eastman Kodak, Bristol-Myers Squibb, and numerous other companies provide similar information as part of their annual environmental reporting.

Benchmarking Studies

Finally, one might ask how environmental expectations should be managed appropriately in the future. Companies have important strategic choices: they can be leading edge, middle-of-the-pack, or follower companies. Depending on a variety of factors, each of these strategies could be appropriate. One of the key challenges, however, is defining at any given time what each means. The rules and expectations are changing constantly; leading edge this year could be follower next year.

Conducting regular benchmarks of comparable companies can help to better define the situation. As an example, Figure 5.4 displays the results of an analysis of four audit program elements taken from a survey of 15 companies. Note that the entire programs were not benchmarked, only certain elements were, such as the classification of findings, the presence of an auditor's summary opinion in the audit report, the use of attorney-client privilege, and organizational program reporting. Conducting simple benchmarking studies such as this can help audit program managers make better decisions about the direction they should take and can also help them understand the possible consequences of those decisions.

---

[9] Also discussed in Chapter 8, "Benchmarking Environmental Audit Programs: Best Practices and Biggest Challenges."

Figure 5.4   Environmental Audit Benchmarking Study

Environmental Audit Benchmarking Study
Classifying Findings by Significance

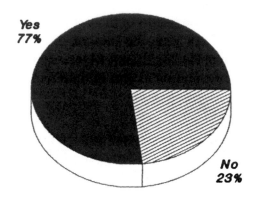

Yes
77%

No
23%

Do You Classify Findings?

Environmental Audit Benchmarking Study
Use of Attorney-Client Privilege

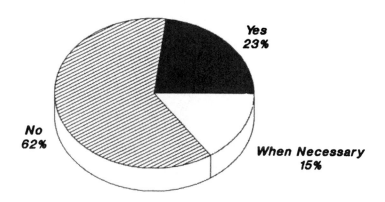

Yes
23%

No
62%

When Necessary
15%

Do You Utilize Attorney-Client Privilege Protections?

Figure 5.4 *(cont'd)*

Environmental Audit Benchmarking Study
Auditor's Summary Opinion

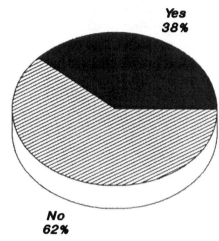

**Do Your Reports Include an
Auditor's Summary Opinion?**

Environmental Audit Benchmarking Study
Organizational Program Reporting

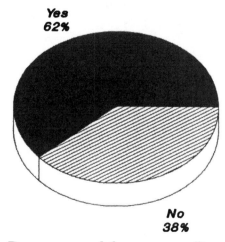

**Does Program Manager Report to
a Corporate VP or Higher?**

CONCLUSION

In summary, stakeholder expectations of corporations are increasing at a rapid rate. Environmental management initiatives are exploding worldwide, resulting in a confusing and challenging geopolitical setting that is not likely to change any time in the near future. Progressive companies are taking action now to respond to present and future demands. They have gotten the message that was delivered at the February 1990 World Economic Forum, where 650 industry and government leaders ranked the environment as the number one challenge for business. Sustainable development is no longer a fashionable cliché. The corporate performance expectations and emerging initiatives discussed in this chapter have made it a reality.

Notes: Any discussion of a company's individual environmental audit program approaches in this chapter is based on information provided to the public at large through technical papers, presentations, and the like. Any discussion of a commercially available audit product does not imply an endorsement of that product.

Chapter 6

THE CHALLENGES OF MEETING ISO 14000 AUDITING GUIDELINES: AUDIT PROGRAM GAPS

Only dead fish swim with the stream.

– Anonymous

The ISO 14000 Environmental Management System Standards and Guidelines were first issued in the fall of 1996 in final form and have been accepted in the U.S. and elsewhere as official national standards. The Auditing Guidelines portion of the Standards and Guidelines consisted of:

- Guidelines for environmental auditing - General principles (ISO 14010: 1996(E))

- Guidelines for environmental auditing - Audit procedures - Auditing of environmental management systems (ISO 14011: 1996(E))

- Guidelines for environmental auditing - Qualification criteria for environmental auditors (ISO 14012: 1996(E)).

Unlike the Environmental Management System (EMS) Standard (ISO 14001), the Auditing Guidelines are just that, guidelines. Their strict adoption is not necessarily required for an organization to be registered to ISO 14000. However, there is a strong implication that any audit program that is an integral part of an effective management system should be consistent with the ISO auditing guidance.

The ISO 14000 Auditing Guidelines are not long documents; ISO 14010 is three pages, ISO 14011 is five pages, and ISO 14012 is three pages. However, if one reviews the Auditing Guidelines in detail, and at face value, there are a number of program and procedural requirements that are not specifically addressed in a typical audit program. This chapter highlights ten of these program-related requirements and makes suggestions on how to remedy the deficiencies efficiently. Addressing these deficiencies will help to assure full conformance with the Guidelines. It should be noted that this chapter focuses principally, but not exclusively, on the *program* requirements discussed in 14010 and 14011. Many of the auditor qualifications and training issues have been discussed elsewhere.[1]

I. A Process to Evaluate the Adequacy of Resources

Section 3 of the General Principles Guideline (14010) requires that "the audit should only be undertaken if, after consultation with the client, it is the lead auditor's opinion that there are adequate resources to support the audit process." This requirement could be interpreted to mean a number of things. Are there a sufficient number of trained auditors assigned given the audit scope and size of the operation? Are there a sufficient number of days allocated? Are audit protocols and other program tools current and adequate?

If we were evaluating compliance status on the audit, one would also ask a question related to the adequacy of regulatory resources available to the auditors. But since we are only concerned here with management systems audits, the regulatory resources question likely does not apply. Or does it? In the U.S., there has been considerable discussion among interested parties as to what extent regulatory compliance is evaluated on EMS audits. Most believe that some verification of compliance is necessary to determine the adequacy of the EMS. This hypothesis is supported, by inference, by the logic of the ISO 14000 standards themselves.

That is, according to the EMS Standards and Auditing Guidelines, an EMS audit is designed to determine the adequacy of the EMS. This EMS is defined as "part of an overall management system that includes organizational structure, planning activities, responsibilities, practices, procedures, processes and resources for developing, implementing, achieving, reviewing, and maintaining *environmental policy*." Further, ISO 14001 requires that an environmental policy include "a commitment to comply with relevant environmental legislation and regulations." There is indeed a strong inference here that the EMS include a commitment to regulatory compliance and that the EMS audits determine the status of that commitment. This sounds remarkably like a compliance audit and the extent to which compliance is evaluated on an EMS audit will dictate additional resource needs (e.g., compliance checklists, auditor regulatory training).

Most companies can respond to the audit length and team size requirement quite well with general program material already provided in program guidance documents. That is, in mature audit programs there is typically enough experience, since each site has been audited at least once for compliance, to know how many auditors are required and for how long. This experience helps to decide the level of auditor

---

[1] L.B. Cahill and D.P. Schomer, "The Potential Effect of ISO 14000 Standards on Environmental Audit Training in the United States," *Total Quality Environmental Management,* vol. 4, no. 3 (New York: John Wiley and Sons, Inc., 1995).

commitment required for separate EMS audits or those conducted in conjunction with a compliance audit. Many companies also require that all auditors be trained, if not certified, prior to conducting an audit. If one holds true to this training requirement, and training is documented, there should be no problem in complying with the intent of ISO 14000 in this regard.

The second resource question, related to the adequacy of program tools, should be covered by the development of an EMS audit protocol (and possibly compliance audit protocols). The EMS audit protocols can be developed in-house or purchased from vendors. For example, Specialty Technical Publishers, the Global Environmental Management Initiative (GEMI), the U.S. Department of Energy (DOE), the American Society for Testing and Materials (ASTM), and NSF International are among many organizations that have published and offer EMS audit protocols or guides. Whether a company uses these external resources or develops its own audit protocol, some protocol or guide needs to be utilized to assure the EMS audits are comprehensive and consistent. Remember that an audit protocol is typically more than a checklist for evaluating conformance with applicable standards; it includes audit methodologies and procedures as well.

2. A Process to Evaluate Auditee Cooperation

Section 3 of the Auditing Principles Guideline (14011) requires the lead auditor to form an opinion that "there is adequate cooperation from the auditee." Now, how does one make this determination in a practical and constructive way? This is less problematical than it appears. Here, the response is pretty straightforward and hinges on a few key factors. Did the site agree to the audit at the appropriate frequency? Did the site complete the pre-audit questionnaire and return it to the team leader well in advance of the audit? Was the environmental coordinator(s) available to the audit team during the week? Did the Plant Manager attend the opening and closing conferences? Did the site complete a corrective action plan in a timely manner? If the answer to all these questions is yes, then you can say with confidence that adequate cooperation was achieved.

Note that the issue of "did the auditee agree with all of the findings" is not what is meant by "cooperation" in this context. So, you can have all the disagreements you want as long as the auditee participates actively in the process and the audit team leader achieves appropriate closure on any outstanding issues.

It may not be necessary to develop a formal procedure to respond to the ISO 14010 requirement discussed above, but if you think you do, a simple checklist, which is presented as Figure 6.1, can be utilized. It is difficult to anticipate how much additional documentation ISO 14000 will require, but checklists such as the one presented will make an ISO 14000 registrar's evaluation much easier to conduct and, as any auditor knows, that is a good thing.

Figure 6.1 Questionnaire to Determine the Adequacy of Audit Resources and the Level of Cooperation of the Audit

Question	Yes	No
1. Were there a sufficient number of auditors on the audit so that all pre-defined scope areas were covered?		
2. Was the audit of sufficient length so that all pre-defined scope areas were covered?		
3. Had all auditors been trained?		
4. Was the full scope of the audit completed?		
5. Was the EMS protocol less than a year old?		
6. Did the site agree to the audit at the appropriate frequency?		
7. Did the site complete the pre-audit questionnaire and return it to the team leader well in advance of the audit?		
8. Was the EH&S coordinator(s) available to the audit team during the week?		
9. Did the Plant Manager attend the opening conference?		
10. Did the Plant Manager attend the closing conference?		

3. A List of Auditees in the Audit Report

Section 4.7 of the General Principles Guideline (14010) and Section 5.4.2 of the Auditing Procedures Guideline (14011) require that the audit report include "the identification of the audit-team members and the identification of the auditee's representatives participating in the audit." Typically, audit reports include a list of auditors but not auditees. Although some have questioned the need for providing a list of both auditors and auditees in the audit report, the listing can be quite helpful to the readers of the audit report and to future auditors. For example, knowing that the auditors interviewed all the key managers at a facility is essential in determining the adequacy of the EMS review. Also, for subsequent EMS audits a listing of both the auditors and auditees can be very useful to the team leader and his team. For instance, if many of the key site managers are no longer in their previous roles, this would affect the strategy and approach of the audit.

Responding to this requirement for listing auditors and auditees in the report is, of course, straightforward. One can simply add a table in the audit report, either in the introduction or in an attachment, of the site individuals involved in the audit. Generally, the table should list the key individuals from the site, not necessarily every individual who was interviewed or attended the opening or closing conferences. On large sites, this could include as many as 30-40 people and including them is probably not the intention of the requirement. The key word for deciding whom to include among the auditees is "participation" in the audit. There is some participation threshold below which involvement is not significant. Figure 6.2 provides a generic audit report introduction that allows for a list of both auditors and auditees.

4. Identification of "Obstacles Encountered" in the Audit Report

Section 4.7 of the General Principles Guideline (14010) and Section 5.4.2 of the Audit Procedures Guideline (14011) require that the audit report include "a summary of the audit process including any obstacles encountered." At first glance, this requirement appears quite negative in connotation, creates unnecessary liabilities and might not be appropriate for an audit report. "Obstacles encountered" implies that the site "put up road blocks" to prevent the audit team from completing the audit. This is not necessarily the interpretation that should be made. The real issue here is whether the scope of the audit, as designed, was completed. If so, then no significant obstacles were encountered. For an EMS audit, there are some obstacles that could prevent the team from completing the scope and these typically arise through coincidence not malice. For example, the plant manager might be called out of town on an emergency before his interview process is complete. Also, the computer system containing many of the site's policies and procedures could "crash" during the audit, resulting in an incomplete document review.

On one audit that the author conducted of a major chemical plant, the hazardous waste accumulation area inspection logs were maintained on the inspector's computer. During the audit, the inspector became hospitalized due to a severe car accident. Although the site staff did attempt to communicate with this individual to obtain his "password" so that the files could be accessed, he was incoherent due to medication, which made obtaining the necessary information impossible. Perhaps the auditor's judgment was harsh but the audit finding was that there was no system in place to demonstrate that the inspections were occurring.

In summary, whatever does or does not happen on the audit, the "obstacles encountered" statement should be linked with the designed scope and any needed qualifier should be placed in the introduction. See Figure 6.2 for an example.

Figure 6.2 Sample EMS Audit Report Introduction

INTRODUCTION

An Environmental Management Systems audit was conducted at *[Plant or Organization Name and Location]* on *[Provide Dates]*. The objectives of the audit were: (1) to determine whether the organization's EMS conforms to the ISO 14001 EMS audit criteria, (2) to determine whether the system is properly implemented and maintained, and (3) to determine if the internal management review process is able to ensure the continuing suitability and effectiveness of the EMS. The audit team generally reviewed records and performance since the last audit, which occurred the week of *[Provide Dates]*.

The audit team leader was *[Provide Name]*. Audit team members are shown below with their areas of responsibility on the audit:

Team Member	Organization	Responsible Areas

The audit required substantial participation by the site staff. Principal participants included:

Site Staff	Title	Responsible Areas

Figure 6.2 *(cont'd)*

The audit was conducted consistent with the requirements of the corporate EMS Audit Guidance Manual. The audit team in assessing conformance with ISO 14001 utilized the company's standard EMS protocol. The process included a review of records, interviews with site staff and physical observation of facilities. All findings were verified. Consistent with generally accepted audit practices, in some cases the audit team may have reviewed only a representative sample of records or equipment. Therefore, no absolute assurances can be made with respect to areas that were not found deficient. No obstacles were encountered that prevented the audit team from completing the audit as designed.

This report presents the results of the audit. The report is considered company confidential. It is not to be released to a third party without prior written approval from the Legal Department. The remainder of the report contains two sections. An Executive Summary is provided and a detailed discussion of findings with appropriate recommendations is presented. Findings are classified by priority. *[Explain prioritization scheme].* It should be noted that this is an exception report in that only deficiencies are recorded as findings. Where especially innovative or commendable practices are identified, these are highlighted in the Executive Summary.

5. Documentation of "Findings of Conformity"

Section 5.4.2 of the Audit Procedures Guideline (14011) states that the audit report should include conclusions such as "EMS conformance to the EMS audit criteria." A note to Section 5.3.3 also states that "if within the agreed scope, details of audit findings of conformity may also be documented, but with due care to avoid any implication of absolute assurance." These two statements appear mildly contradictory and should be interpreted in the way that best suits the company and audit customers. The Guidelines appear to provide the option of discussing only findings of non-conformity, which is consistent with current practice in the U.S. Generally, most auditors and companies prefer to develop exception-based audit reports, discussing only the non-conformities. This makes for a shorter and more user-friendly report that avoids a lot of cloudy language stating where the system is in conformance. However, in responding to the Section 5.4.2 requirement, one might want to place a statement in the introduction that says, where non-conformance is not mentioned, conformance can be implied although no "absolute assurances" can be assumed. Once again, see Figure 6.2 for a model statement.

6. An Appropriate Code of Ethics

Section 10 of the Auditor Qualifications Criteria Guideline (ISO 14012) states that auditors should "adhere to an appropriate code of ethics." Most auditors will have not formally committed to a code of ethics although in some corporations employees are required to sign a general ethics statement. In order to meet this requirement, a code of ethics will have to be developed or, alternatively, staff who are members of certain technical societies may have already committed to an appropriate code of ethics through their membership in these societies. For example, the Environmental, Health, and Safety Auditing Roundtable issued a Code of Ethics for environmental auditors in 1993. The Roundtable's code, applicable to all members, includes six articles covering Professional Conduct for auditors as well as five articles covering the Conduct of Members. This Code would meet the intent of ISO 14000 and could be adapted to corporate audit programs, where deemed necessary.

7. A Non-Disclosure or Records Retention Policy

The ISO 14000 Auditing Guidelines have several requirements related to non-disclosure and records retention. Section 4.3 of the General Principles (14010) states that "unless required by law, the audit-team members should not disclose information or documents obtained during the audit, or the final report, to any third-party, without the express approval of the client and, where appropriate, the approval of the auditee." Section 5.2.3 of the Audit Procedures Guideline (14011) states that documents "involving confidential or proprietary information should be suitably safeguarded by the audit-team members." Section 5.4.4 of the Audit Procedures Guideline (14011) states, "all working documents and draft and final reports pertaining to the audit should be retained by agreement between the client, the lead auditor and the auditee, and in accordance with any applicable requirements."

These requirements provide tremendous flexibility in managing audit documentation. However, that flexibility should not be interpreted as the absence of concern, particularly in the litigious U.S. With the 1996 and 2000 issuances of the U.S. EPA Audit Policy[2] and numerous state audit privilege laws, records retention is critical. Unfortunately, many audit programs are still not rigorous in their management of critical audit documents. On a recent oversight audit conducted by the author, there were key managers at the site who had never seen the previous audit report. At the same time, contained in the environmental coordinator's files were copies of various draft and final audit reports covering a ten-year period. Neither of these situations was compliant with corporate policy. Organizations should have a records retention policy for all documents generated on an audit (e.g., pre-audit questionnaires, checklists, working papers, draft and final reports, corrective-action plans, periodic status reports) and should regularly determine if this policy is being implemented.

---

[2] U.S. EPA, "Incentives for Self-Policing: Discovery, Disclosure, Corrective and Prevention of Violations" (2000).

8. A Formal Audit Plan

Section 5.2.1 of the Audit Procedures Guideline (14011) states that an "audit plan should, if applicable, include:

a) the audit objectives and scope

b) the audit criteria

c) identification of the auditee's organizational and functional units to be audited

d) identification of the functions and/or individuals within the auditee's organization having significant direct responsibilities regarding the auditee's EMS

e) identification of those elements of the auditee's EMS that are of high audit priority

f) the procedures for auditing the auditee's EMS elements as appropriate for the auditee's organization

g) the working and reporting languages of the audit

h) identification of reference documents

i) the expected time and duration for major audit activities

j) the dates and places where the audit is to be conducted

k) identification of audit-team members

l) the schedule of meetings to be held with the auditee's management

m) confidentiality requirements

n) report content and format, expected date of issue and distribution of the audit report

o) document retention requirements

The audit plan should be communicated to the client, the audit-team members, and the auditee. The client should review and approve the plan."

Most organizations will begin each audit with a memo from the audit team leader to the auditee. The memo will typically include some but not all of the fifteen elements listed above. Each has value and should be considered for inclusion in the announcement memo. Audits should not be a secretive process and presenting in advance a discussion of methodology and approach can only make the process more effective and efficient.

9. Auditor Independence

Section 4.2 of the General Principles Guideline (14010) states that "the members of the audit team should be independent of the activities they audit. They should be objective and free from bias and conflict of interest throughout the process." Normally, meeting the test of auditor independence is not a problem for most organizations. There is one common difficulty faced by corporate staff, however. That is where these individuals are not truly independent of the activities they audit. Quite often, for example, the corporate Toxic Substances Control Act (TSCA) expert will not only assist a business unit in developing a TSCA management system but, because there are so few people in a given organization who are comfortable with the TSCA topic, this person is also asked to audit the business unit's program that they helped develop. This is clearly a conflict of interest (COI) and should be avoided. Companies should have specific COI procedures to prevent this from happening. These procedures might suggest the use of external resources to conduct audits of areas where the internal resources are insufficient.

10. Sufficient Program Guidance Documentation

Section 4.4 of the General Principles Guideline (14010) states that "the environmental audit should be conducted according to documented and well-defined methodologies and systematic procedures." The key word here is "documented." It is surprising how many organizations still operate their audit program without a formal guidance manual. ISO 14000 rightly implies that this is not acceptable. Formal, documented guidance is required. The guidance should be designed to assist clients, auditors, and auditees understand the workings of the program. There should be no secrets about what the auditors will do when they visit the site or an organization. Guidance documents do not have to be tomes; they can be as short as 20-25 pages. However, they should include as many sample tools as possible, including:

- Sample announcement memo or letter
- Audit protocols and sample pre-audit questionnaire
- Model opening and closing conference presentations
- Sample audit report and corrective action plan.

Including these tools in the documentation will help auditors design an approach that is comprehensive, consistent and meets the expectations of ISO 14000.

Chapter 7

A REVIEW OF SOME TYPICAL PROGRAMS

Our plant managers like the reviews; they give them some security.

– Edward W. Callahan, Vice President, Allied Corporation, 1980

Although most EH&S audit programs exhibit the same basic structure, individual program approaches are usually tailor-made to meet the objectives and constraints of the sponsoring organization. Thus, one can find distinctly different programs in the same basic industry. Over time, one can even find a dramatically changed program in the same company; the changes can occur due to reorganization, mid-course program evaluations, or, in these days of mergers and acquisitions, a major restructuring of business lines.

A survey of over twenty programs indicated that the extent of fine-tuning varies, but is significant in some cases. The survey, which was a combination of literature review and phone interviews, evaluated the programs against the following twelve factors:

- Program overview and scope
  - Program name
  - Start date
  - Purpose
  - Program organization
  - Program scope

- Program methodology
  - Audit methodology
  - Reporting findings
  - Follow-up mechanisms

- Program operations
  - Audit staffing
  - Audit duration
  - Number of plants per year audited
  - Frequency of audits.

Summaries of the individual programs can be found in Appendix E, but company names are not listed in order to protect the confidential nature of some of the information. Descriptions of the companies' sizes and types of business are also provided. Presented in this chapter is an assessment of the survey for each of the evaluation factors; the highlights are presented in Figure 7.1.

PROGRAM OVERVIEW AND SCOPE

Program Name

While the majority of companies use the word *audit* to describe the nature of the program, several companies use surrogate words, such as *assessment, surveillance*, and *systems review*. Some of the reasons given for using surrogates are that (1) audits can connote a more rigorous approach (vis-a-vis financial audits) than is typically the case; (2) the word *audit* (meaning "to examine, verify, or correct accounts, records, or claims") has an accusatory flavor to it; and (3) environmental reviews are more than the paperwork exercises that financial audits imply.

Figure 7.1 Summary of the Review of 20 Environmental Audit Programs

Program Overview and Scope		
Evaluation Factor	**Most Common Response**	**Range of Other Responses**
Program Name	Audit	Surveillance, Review
Start Date	1985	1976–1988
Purpose	Compliance with regulations and company standards	Compliance with good management practices; awareness; technology transfer; risk control
Organization	Corporate environmental audit department with 2–4 full-time auditors	Most programs placed in corporate with 1–30 staff; some programs delegated to divisions with corporate oversight
Program Scope	U.S.; environmental separate from health and safety a little more than half the time; multi-media reviews; recent emphasis on management systems and global roll-out	Special issues such as medical and product stewardship sometimes included; some focused, single-media reviews

Figure 7.1 *(cont'd)*

Program Methodology		
Evaluation Factor	**Most Common Response**	**Range of Other Responses**
Audit Methodology	Standard pre-audit, onsite, and post-audit activities; use of computers for in-field report writing	Surprise audits when needed; infrequent physical sampling; use of spill response drills; community participation on some audits
Reporting	Reports due within 30 days; brief exception reports; recommendations included; findings classified by significance; legal review initially and as needed thereafter; periodic summary reports to management	Highly variable; verbal reporting only in unique cases
Follow-up	Formal plant response required within 60 days of audit; formal calendar-based quarterly tracking; a real challenge	Informal response in some cases; red tag plant shut down procedure in one case; follow-up verification audits conducted

Program Operations		
Evaluation Factor	**Most Common Response**	**Range of Other Responses**
Audit Staffing	3 technical staff	1–8 staff (some legal)
Audit Duration	3 days	1–15 days
Plants/Year Audited	20	5–80
Frequency of Audits	Every 2 years; slowly moving to once every 3 years	1–5 year cycle

Start Date

Estimating the program start date is difficult because most companies have had informal programs for some time, and the formal programs have had several stages of development. Notwithstanding these constraints, most companies estimate that their program, as it exists today, roughly started anywhere between 1978 and 1988—the beginning of which coincidentally spans the time when SEC required Allied (1977), U.S. Steel (1979), and Occidental (1980) to complete costs-of-compliance audits, and the first set of RCRA hazardous waste regulations was promulgated (1980). Later in the 1980s and 1990s, programs were re-engineered to take advantage of the lessons learned.

Purpose

More often than not, the stated purpose of the program is to attain and maintain compliance with federal, state, and local regulations. Most (but not all) companies also state explicitly the objective of meeting good management practices (GMPs) and corporate policies and procedures. In the past few years, there has been widespread development of corporate environmental standards and guidelines, which developed in part to take the guesswork and judgment out of GMPs. This has helped to improve the rigor of environmental audits, especially in third-world countries where there are few environmental regulations. While most companies recognize there are other benefits (e.g., technology transfer, increased awareness), these benefits are typically seen as the "icing on the cake."

Recently, several companies have re-designed their programs to emphasize reviews of management systems. This focus is an attempt to remedy the underlying causes of noncompliance and is consistent with ISO 14000 environmental management systems standards.

Program Organization

A certain amount of independence is seen as an essential element of a program, so almost every company has established a corporate audit function that is responsible for the program. This function is usually housed in the corporate environmental (or health and safety) department. Other options include a function in the financial department (where the financial auditing function is located) or in the legal department (ostensibly to provide as much protection from report discovery as possible).

The size of a corporate audit staff varies considerably. In some companies, one or two people on staff provide an oversight function, drawing on a pool of division and plant staff and consultants to conduct the audits. In other cases, a small group (two to three) of corporate staff conduct the audits but with help from division and staff people. Finally, some companies have a corporate staff of as many as thirty whose responsibility it is to run the program and conduct the audits (without assistance). In all cases, however, audit teams are comprised of staff who are organizationally independent of the plant audited.

Program Scope

Most companies have focused on their U.S. facilities historically, although there is an increasing trend to broaden the program to all facilities worldwide. The Bhopal tragedy has done much to accelerate this trend. One company has developed checklists and protocols in Spanish in its effort to audit South American plants. Several companies have left the implementation of the overseas audit program to regional environmental coordinators; audit teams are selected from trained staff within the particular region. This approach can minimize cultural and language problems. Still other companies conduct all their overseas audits using U.S. staff.

Companies are divided fairly evenly as to whether their program should be strictly environmental or should be broader to include other areas, such as hazard communication and product stewardship. However, those companies that have strictly environmental audit programs usually have companion or separate health and safety audit programs as well.

The great majority of companies do perform multimedia audits (i.e., water, solid and hazardous wastes, PCBs, and pesticides), but as the programs have evolved and facilities have been audited several times, there has been a tendency to reduce the scope of the audit to those media that present the greatest liability at that plant site.

PROGRAM METHODOLOGY

Audit Methodology

There has evolved over time a "standard" audit methodology that most companies in this survey used. It involves the three phases shown in Figure 7.2. With only a few exceptions, companies with existing audit programs use this approach. Some of the more significant exceptions include:

- Surprise audits—used by some companies where situations warrant them

- Effluent/emissions sampling—some audit teams conduct these independently

- Ranking of facilities based on a scoring system—some companies use this

- Vendor/Supplier audits—normally the plant's responsibility, but occasionally the audit team will do this as well

- Emergency response drills during an audit—their use is becoming more prevalent

- Community participation on selected audits—used by some companies, such as DuPont

Figure 7.2 Standard Environmental Audit Methodology

Phase	Steps
I. Pre-Audit	- Organize the audit team - Assign responsibilities - Notify the site - Review relevant regulations - Review the last audit, protocols, and pre-audit questionnaire
II. Audit	- In-brief site management - Meet with environmental staff - Participate in orientation tour - Review records and management systems - Interview site personnel - Inspect facilities - Brief site daily - Debrief site management
III. Post-Audit	- Draft audit report - Respond to reviews - Submit final audit report - Enter report findings into follow-up tracking system - Close-out audit

Although the use of detailed checklists and procedures is pretty much universal, the format for the checklists is typically unique to the company. The main components of the checklists include the basic protocol, a topical outline, a detailed audit guide, a yes or no questionnaire, an open-ended questionnaire, and a scored questionnaire or rating sheet.

How the checklists are used varies as well. Some auditors use them religiously as they review, inspect, and interview. Other auditors, perhaps those with more experience, use them as references at the beginning and end of each day to assure themselves that they are not overlooking anything. Still others use the checklists as the source for a one-page list (per medium) of important items to review during the audit. Each of these approaches has merit; their use must depend on the skill and preferences of the auditors and the audit team leader.

A final point concerns the use of computers. Most companies are now outfitting their audit teams with laptop computers. The objective is to develop both a debriefing document and a draft report before the audit team leaves the site. The more preformatted the audit report, the easier it is to accomplish. One company goes so far as to have the audit team telecommunicate (via modem) the debriefing document and draft report to the corporate audit staff and the legal department prior to releasing it to the site management.

Reporting Findings

Most audit reports are brief (five to twenty pages), but some can be as long as fifty pages. Increasingly, audit teams attempt to draft a preliminary report before leaving the site. When developed, these are used to debrief site management. At a minimum, most companies strive to develop a formal list of findings and prepare them so they can be inserted into the audit report.

There is no clear consensus on whether audit reports should discuss good performance as well as out-of-compliance issues. Some companies believe that good performance should be incorporated because the report, as a stand-alone document, will provide a more accurate picture of total compliance. These companies are also concerned that the audit reports are legally "discoverable" and could wind up in the hands of the public. The alternative philosophy is that audit reports should not be political, lengthy, or self-congratulatory documents, but should instead be straightforward, factual summaries of compliance items in need of attention. For the most part, audit programs use the exception-report format.

There is also no consensus on whether audit reports should contain recommendations on how to fix the stated problem. Some companies include recommendations because they believe the process and report are "cleaner" that way; for every identified problem, there is a solution. This approach avoids the situation where the audit report is "discovered" without a companion piece stating the company's planned efforts to remedy the problems.

The alternative approach is for no recommendations to be included in the audit report because this responsibility is thought to be that of the plant manager. The underlying philosophy is that the auditors are responsible for simply identifying noncompliance and should not dictate to the plant manager their particular suggestions on how to resolve the problem. One company resolved the "recommendations" dilemma by having the auditors state only their findings in the report but leaving room (after each finding, for inclusion at a later date) for the plant manager's proposed solution. Hence, auditors do not dictate to the plant staff, but each audit report is a complete document with recommendations.

Finally, the companies are split once again on whether pro forma legal review of draft audit reports is required. Some companies have their legal department review all audit reports, while others have legal review only when the audit team leader deems it necessary.

Follow-Up Mechanisms

Detailed follow-up systems have evolved rapidly and are discussed elsewhere in this book. Most companies, at a minimum, require a formal response from the plant within thirty to sixty days. This response would consist of a detailed action plan for remedying all identified problems. The trend presently is to load all action plans onto a computer system that generates monthly "tickler" reports, which in turn report on the status of the action plan items. One company goes so far as to "score" each plant on its action item completion rate and submits those scores to senior management. One company has a "red tag" procedure, whereby a unit can be shut down if follow-up is deemed non-responsive. Although used sparingly, this procedure has been used successfully in the past. Presently, the mere threat of its use seems sufficient leverage to obtain adequate responses.

PROGRAM OPERATIONS

Audit Staffing

Audits are viewed by most companies as principally a technical exercise with regulatory overtones. Thus audit teams consist almost exclusively of experienced technical staff (e.g., engineers, scientists, environmental professionals). In some instances, lawyers are part of the audit team, but this is more the exception than the rule. On average, two to three staff make up the audit team, but the range includes anywhere from one to eight, depending upon the audit objectives and the size and complexity of the facility.

Audit Duration

On average, audits will take three to four days, but the range can be anywhere from one day to three weeks; again, this depends upon the audit objectives and the size and complexity of the facility.

Number of Plants Per Year Audited

The number of plants per year that are audited varies considerably. One company may audit as few as six facilities, but these audits include checks on hazard communication and product stewardship. On the other hand, another company may audit as many as seventy-five facilities per year, but this company does strictly environmental audits and has ten full-time corporate audit staff members. Of course, the number of facilities audited annually also has a lot to do with the size of the organization, so it is difficult to create a measure of appropriateness.

Frequency of Audits

Generally, the goal for companies is to audit major production facilities once every two years and to audit minor facilities (e.g., warehouses, distribution centers) once every three to five years. However, there is a trend in companies with mature audit programs to extend the frequency of audits from once every two years to once every three years.

CONCLUSION

It is clear that within the overall concept of environmental auditing, each company must design a program to meet its own identified needs and objectives. This program must be structured so that it is consistent with available resources. This "simple" exercise of matching objectives with available resources is, in large part, the reason for the variety of programs encountered today.

Chapter 8

BENCHMARKING EH&S AUDIT PROGRAMS: BEST PRACTICES AND BIGGEST CHALLENGES[1]

In the country of the blind, the one-eyed man is king.

– Michael Apostolius, Proverbs, 15th Century

A few years ago, I was leading an audit of a coalmine in Wyoming. In preparing for the upcoming closing conference with the president of the company, I mentioned to their EH&S director that several programs were operating quite well and, therefore, we would have no findings in those areas. I said casually, "If it ain't broke, don't fix it." I thought the EH&S director would have a coronary on the spot. It seemed that the president was a big supporter of the then new concept of Total Quality Management (TQM) and had lectured his staff incessantly on the need for continuous improvement. My director friend suggested that I would be thrown out on my ear if I made the same casual comment in the closing conference. So went my first exposure to TQM.

Since that time, TQM has become an important concept in learning how to manage EH&S audit programs more effectively. An especially useful TQM tool has been competitive benchmarking. Companies are using benchmarking studies to identify "best practices" that could be incorporated into their programs. In conducting benchmarking studies, evaluators often also identify the biggest common challenges facing audit program managers.

This chapter discusses these best practices and biggest challenges associated with environmental audit programs. The conclusions are based on a number of benchmarking studies and third-party evaluations of corporate audit programs. As the sources are necessarily limited to the author's own experiences, there are no

---

[1] Originally published in *Total Quality Environmental Management*, (New York: Executive Enterprises, Inc., 1994). Updated for this edition.

doubt many other best practices, in particular, that are not discussed in this chapter. These will surface over time.

OVERVIEW OF BENCHMARKING

The concept of competitive benchmarking has received considerable attention in the literature of the past few years.[2] As defined by the Xerox Corporation in its Leadership through Quality Program, *competitive benchmarking* is "the continuous process of measuring company products, services and practices against the toughest competitors or those companies recognized as leaders." The steps used in a benchmarking study are relatively straightforward and are shown in Figure 8.1. It is not the intent of this chapter to provide a discourse on each of the steps involved in the benchmarking process; that is better handled through other sources. However, based on previous environmental audit program benchmarking experiences, five steps were found to be key when conducting a successful study. Those five steps are discussed below.

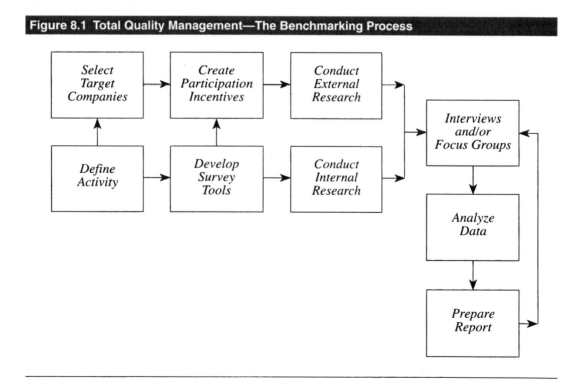

Figure 8.1 Total Quality Management—The Benchmarking Process

[2] For example, see K.H.J. Leibfried and C.J. McNair, *Benchmarking: A Tool for Continuous Improvement*, The Coopers and Lybrand Performance Solutions Series (New York: Harper Collins, 1992).

Precisely Define the Scope

One can benchmark any and all components of an audit program. For example, a chemical company that was in the midst of a reorganization wished to determine the best reporting relationship for its audit program. Thus their goal in a benchmarking study was to determine just that: among a dozen targeted companies, to whom did the corporate audit program manager typically report?

More broad-based studies can help as well. However, there are many components to an audit program, and it is probably best to define and analyze only those that are most crucial (e.g., use of attorney-client privilege, frequency of audits, follow-up systems).

Select Target Companies Using a Variety of Techniques

One can select among companies in similar businesses, industry in general, or companies with known "best-in-class" audit programs. Any of these approaches would suffice, depending on the objectives of the study. An example of one type of technique that can be used is shown in Figure 8.2. In this figure, fourteen companies are evaluated against one another using three criteria: company size, return on equity,

Figure 8.2 Competitor Financial Evaluation

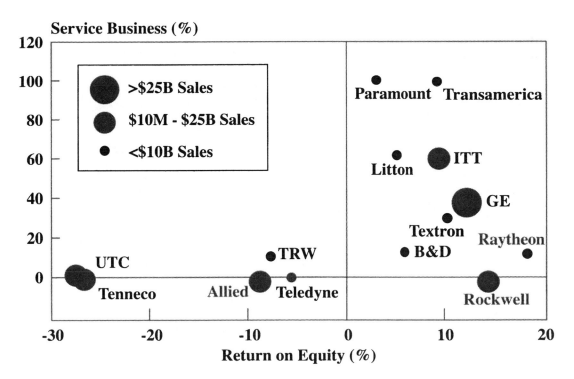

Competitor Financial Evaluation

and the percent of the company's sales that are in service businesses. Other criteria can be used as well (e.g., percent of business that is outside the U.S.), but the idea is to find groupings of companies that are similar, based on key financial criteria against which to benchmark.

Create Participation Incentives

Benchmarking has become a common business analysis technique, so quite often it is not difficult to identify willing participants. However, some incentive will usually be required. This can be a report summarizing the results of the study, although in order for a participant to receive the full analysis, some financial participation in the study is usually expected.

Develop Measurable Criteria

This can be a difficult challenge, especially if one is evaluating the "softer" components of a program. However, developing measurable criteria in advance is crucial to comparing results from disparate companies. These criteria might include the following:

- Frequency of audits for major facilities

- Type of report, if any, left with site staff at the close of the field audit

- Draft and final audit report types (e.g., exception reporting only) and schedules

- Frequency and type of follow-up system

- Use of legal protections

- Frequency and type of reporting to management

- Organizational levels between the audit program manager and the chief executive officer

- Budget for audit program per unit of company sales.

Each of the above criteria is generally quite measurable and requires short cryptic responses. The evaluator can then make broad conclusions based on the results (e.g., 50 percent of the benchmarked companies use attorney-client privilege protections to protect their audit reports).

Utilize Focus-Group Sessions

Bringing together the participants of a benchmarking study for a day can be an extremely useful exercise. It can help to assure that individuals are not discussing apples and oranges when addressing complex program issues. The technique can also help to identify subtle nuances in programs that otherwise might not surface during a one-on-one interview. If participants have difficulty assembling in one location, teleconferencing can be a suitable substitute.

BEST PRACTICES

In benchmarking audit programs over the past few years, a number of "best practices" have surfaced. Not all of these might be applied effectively to a given audit program, but using them selectively should result in an improved program that meets the ever-increasing expectations of stakeholders. This section describes a number of those practices.

Reports to Management

Reporting health and safety statistics to executive management has been a common practice in U.S. industry for many years. More recently, overall EH&S performance is being reported not only to executives, but to the public as well. Annual environmental reports are commonplace among progressive companies.[3] Within these reports, environmental audit programs are occasionally, but increasingly, addressed. For example, DuPont provides the executive summaries from the past three annual third-party evaluations of the company's corporate SHE audit program on its website.

For environmental audit programs to be successful, some form of reporting to the company's executives is paramount. In a few companies, like Occidental Petroleum, the chief executive has shown enough interest that he reviews every report, and calls are made to line managers where it is perceived that individual issues are not being resolved quickly enough. This demonstrates the top management commitment that the U.S. EPA calls for in its Environmental Auditing Policy Statement.[4] More commonly, senior management might receive a quarterly or semi-annual briefing on issues identified by the audits. These issues might be noncompliance problems that cut across the corporation and are in need of a systemic remedy; statistics among business units on timely resolution of findings; or instances where the audit program saved the company money through, for example, the avoidance of fines or substitution of less toxic materials.

Relationship to Compensation

In order to assure support for an EH&S audit program, many companies will factor audit results into the bonus equation used for plant and/or environmental managers.

---

[3] For example, see Deloitte Touche Tohmatsu International, The International Institute for Sustainable Development, and Sustainability, *Coming Clean: Corporate Environmental Reporting* (1993).

[4] U.S. EPA, *Environmental Auditing Policy Statement,* FR25003, vol. 51, no. 131 (July 9, 1986).

This usually gets the attention of the individuals principally responsible for remedying problems; however, some caveats are in order.

First, managers should be held more accountable for fixing identified problems than for the results of the first audit at a given facility. This first audit usually sets the baseline and should not be a "witch hunt." How well the site staff respond after the audit is really what should be evaluated.

Second, one has to be careful of falling into the trap of numerically scoring the results of an audit in order to apportion compensation. For one thing, it is difficult to compare facilities and their audit performance. There are many factors beyond the plant manager's control, such as the regulatory stringency of the state in which the plant is located; the type, age, and size of the facility; the toxicity of the materials used; and the nature of the property (e.g., the presence of wetlands). Also, using a scoring system tied to compensation can heighten the tension of an audit because the plant staff will typically be more argumentative about the number and significance of findings. Where scoring is used, too much time is typically spent on whether the resultant score is an 81 or a 79 or whether the score is higher than the last audit. This takes away from the real purpose of the audit.

Use of Spill Drills

One of the most important EH&S compliance areas to audit is emergency response. A good response program can save both money and lives. Moreover, emergency response is now an integral component of regulations, promulgated under a variety of statutes:

- Spill Prevention Control and Countermeasure Plans under the Clean Water Act (CWA)

- Contingency Plans under the Resource Conservation and Recovery Act (RCRA)

- Hazardous Waste Operations Emergency Response Planning (HAZWOPER) under the Occupational Safety and Health Act (OSHA)

- Hazard Identification and Release Reporting under the Emergency Planning and Community Right-to-Know Act (EPCRA)

- Risk Management Planning under the Clean Air Act (CAA) Amendments.

This has made developing an effective emergency response program a complex exercise. The more progressive audit programs will not only verify that the emergency response program meets regulatory requirements but, more importantly, that the program will also work when needed. To provide these assurances, firms like Safety Kleen actually have conducted "spill drills" during their audits, and many of these take place in the early hours of the morning. As a suitable but less direct alternative, many audit programs will review the results of spill drills conducted during the year, assessing whether deficiencies were identified and remedied. Either way, emergency response programs should include drills, or simulations at a minimum, and audit programs should assess how the site responded to the results of those exercises.

Red Tag Shutdowns

This was quite an interesting approach used by a West Coast aerospace company. Essentially, their auditors carried with them red equipment tags that could be attached to an individual unit to shut the operation down if observed noncompliance issues seemed to warrant it. The technique proved to be very powerful—it was used only once. Subsequently, the mere threat of its use provided sufficient leverage to obtain adequate responses.

Community Participation

In 1992, DuPont initiated a demonstration program in which a community member participates in a select number of audits each year. This program appears to be unique among U.S. corporations. The rationale is as follows: "As one element of our efforts to understand and respond to community concerns, drive improved environmental performance, build trust, and continue to achieve this consent, we will consider community participation in each corporate environmental review."[5] Selected audit team members must come from the local Community Advisory Panel (CAP), and their participation does not typically extend to employee interviews because such participation "might inhibit the free flow of information essential for an environmental review and compromise employee rights."[6] The demonstration program continues to this day.

Next Site Participation

One way to reduce the anxiety of being audited is to have a site environmental manager participate in an audit, as a team member, directly prior to the audit of his or her site. Some companies use this technique to help the individual better understand the process and prepare effectively for the audit of his or her site.

Use of Portable Computers, Intranets, and the Internet

Use of portable computers is becoming almost mandatory for audits. Computers are used in a variety of ways. Some companies use commercially available automated

---

[5] DuPont, *DuPont Environmental Auditing: Corporate Guidelines*, Appendix B, Community Participation in Corporate Environmental Reviews (June 4, 1992).

[6] Ibid.

audit protocols to directly insert findings generated from a review of the checklists into a report skeleton. The checklists also contain regulatory digests so that the multi-volume *Code of Federal Regulations* does not have to be carried to every audit. In general, computers are used for three purposes on audits: (1) access to an online, CD-ROM, or floppy-disk-based regulatory database, (2) generation of reports prior to leaving the site, and (3) use of automated checklists in the field. The ability to leave a draft report with the site, in particular, is especially valuable in that it helps to maintain the momentum of the audit. Computers are also helpful for keeping in touch with the home office through email.

The use of the Internet and company intranets to support EH&S audit programs has virtually exploded in the past few years. The Internet can be and is used to access publicly available regulatory information on a given site. Both the U.S. EPA (www.epa.gov/enviro) and OSHA (www.osha.gov/oshstats) have accessible databases containing large volumes of reporting and inspection information. Many firms will access these database sites prior to the audit to help the team prepare. This information is also given to the site so that they might review it and, just as important, determine whether it is indeed correct and current. The Internet is often used to obtain the following additional logistical information:

- Inexpensive airline tickets (www.priceline.com)

- Weather at the plant site (www.weather.com)

- Directions to the hotel and plant site (www.mapquest.com)

- Information on facilities available at and near the hotel (hotel chain websites)

Company intranets also provide a tremendous resource to audit teams. On these sites one can find site addresses and phone numbers, audit protocols, procedures and schedules, model plans and reports, lists of best practices identified on audits throughout the corporation, and corporate standards and guidelines. Bristol-Myers Squibb is one company that has taken full advantage of its intranet. Sites are now linked worldwide.

This ready availability of critical information on the Internet and company intranets has truly revolutionized how EH&S audits are done. Organizations not taking advantage will clearly be left behind.

Assessment of Ancillary Operations

Most audits rightfully focus on the site's line operations. However, the better programs address certain ancillary operations as well. These include:

- ■ **Off-site hazardous waste treatment, storage, and disposal (TSD) facilities.** This is an especially important area to review. Audit teams typically are not expected to visit off-site TSD facilities. At a minimum, however, the audit team should check to assure that the site is using only corporate-approved facilities, and/or the facilities have been visited at a frequency consistent with corporate guidance.

- **Purchasing.** Purchasing staff should be interviewed to determine if they use any environmental guidelines in procuring materials. For example, one company's policy requires the purchasing of materials in 55-gallon drums on an exception basis only. Other companies have a similar policy for chlorinated solvents. The two relevant audit questions are: Is purchasing required to meet any environmental guidelines, and if so, are these guidelines being followed consistently?

- **Maintenance.** This function is almost always audited; however, the depth of the audit can at times be quite shallow. Key environmental issues to address include the use and disposal of maintenance chemicals. The safety of the maintenance equipment (e.g., grinders, lathes, and drill presses) should also be reviewed. An area often overlooked is the storage and application of pesticides.

- **On-site contractors.** The audit team should review temporary and permanent on-site contractors, such as asbestos removal companies. Their contracts should also be reviewed to verify that appropriate EH&S provisions are included and that they are being followed.

- **Nearby warehouses used by the site.** Off-site owned or leased warehouses can create liabilities for companies and, therefore, should be audited on occasion. If the warehouse is nearby, many audit programs will include it in the site audit.

- **Local publicly owned treatment works (POTWs).** Quite often a site will discharge some or all of its wastewater into a local sewer system. Visiting the local POTW can provide the audit team with insight into the municipality's view of the company's compliance status and the likelihood of forthcoming changes in the effluent standards or surcharges.

Addressing these ancillary areas does add time to the audit. However, many companies believe that this is time well spent.

Use of Verification Audits

One of the biggest challenges associated with audit programs is assuring that problems are corrected in a timely fashion. Companies typically set up sophisticated databases to track the status of corrective actions. How data are entered into these databases, however, is the real challenge. Typically, sites send quarterly status reports to a central location and the data are entered there. This approach works reasonably well except in the instance where site management's perception of a "fix" diverges from that of the audit team.

One interesting approach, used by Colgate-Palmolive, is to conduct verification audits of a select number (e.g., 5 to 10 percent) of sites with outstanding corrective actions. The audits would involve only one or two auditors on site for one or two days. Their sole objective is to review the status of completed and outstanding corrective actions from the previous audit report. These audits help to "verify" the accuracy of the quarterly data being submitted and assist in resolving any problems the site might be having with interpretation of a finding. They also help to "keep the responses honest" because sites recognize that there is some possibility each year that they will be the recipient of a verification audit.

Site-Satisfaction Questionnaire

One way for the audit program manager to assure that the program is achieving its objectives is to have the site staff being audited complete a questionnaire evaluating the audit team's performance. This questionnaire is typically given to the site management at the close of the audit, and it is mailed back to the audit program manager, not the team leader. Survey topics include the competency and reasonableness of the team, the adequacy of the interpersonal skills of the team, the depth of the audit, the perceived value of the audit, and any improvements that could be made. See Appendix J for a model questionnaire.

Companies like Bristol-Myers Squibb keep extensive statistics on the returned questionnaires, which are used to make adjustments to the program. It should be noted, however, that the completed questionnaires must be reviewed very carefully. One has to be cautious if the site responses are overly positive or negative. While a high-scoring questionnaire might be a good result, it could also mean that the audit team was quite lenient in its dealings with the site management. Conversely, should a questionnaire come back with excessively low scores, it could mean that the team was ineffectual but it could also mean that there were numerous, serious (and justified) findings and the plant staff "took it out on the auditors" when completing the questionnaire. It's only human nature to react emotionally in these situations.

Periodic Third-Party Evaluations

Consistent with good TQM practices, many companies are now having outside consultants (i.e., third parties) or their internal audit departments (i.e., second parties) evaluate their EH&S audit programs on a periodic basis. The annual or biennial studies help the companies meet their "continuous improvement" objectives and help relieve the increasing pressure by stakeholders to provide assurances that the company is identifying and remedying its EH&S issues.

Third-party evaluations conducted in the U.S. usually include a review of program documentation, including audit reports and corrective action plans, interviews with key program participants, and observation of a representative number of audits. Programs typically are compared with the Elements of Effective Environmental Auditing Programs provided as an Appendix in U.S. EPA's 1986 Auditing Policy Statement,[7] as well as with other companies' programs and internally developed standards and policies.

In Europe, third-party reviews should be much more prevalent and formalized because the European Community's Eco-Management and Audit Scheme (EMAS) became effective in April 1995. This program requires site environmental statements and audits to be validated through an external environmental verifier. Although the EMAS is voluntary, companies like DuPont have committed to implementing the scheme for facilities in the European Community.

Development of a Program Newsletter

There should be no secrets about the objectives, implementation, and operation of an environmental audit program. Most programs have guidance manuals that describe the workings of the audit process. The manuals provide a needed program constancy, should the audit program manager be reassigned. Some companies, like Bristol-Myers Squibb take this one step further and have developed program newsletters. The newsletter can do much to advertise the program in a very positive light and to communicate important information, such as new corporate standards, chronic deficiencies, and exceptional EH&S programs that might otherwise go unrecognized.

There are surely other best practices among audit programs that have not been identified in this chapter. If one is interested in identifying other techniques that are being used, these could be identified, surprisingly enough, through a benchmarking study.

BIGGEST CHALLENGES

Benchmarking studies and third-party evaluations identify not only best practices, but usually the biggest challenges as well. Listed below are a few items that seem to recur time and again as deficiencies in EH&S audit programs.

The Program Manual

Putting together an EH&S audit program manual can be an onerous task and quite often, as a result, it is not done formally. Some programs will have no written guidance document whatsoever, while others might have a presentation package describing the program that is used in the opening conferences on audits. The lack of a program manual does not necessarily mean that a given program is not operating well; however, a manual does help document and communicate the program's ob-

---

[7] U.S. EPA, *Op.Cit.*, U.S. EPA Auditing Policy Statement (1986): 25008–25010.

jectives and procedures. Further, it is difficult to assess the relative successes or failures of a program without some written guidelines against which this evaluation can be made. Consistent with TQM principles, all programs should be evaluated on a periodic basis. Finally, a manual helps to guide the program during the transition that would occur if the program manager were to vacate the position.

Protocol Updating

The problem with audit checklists or protocols is that they are typically out-of-date once they are reproduced. This poses a problem because auditors who rely heavily on the checklists, and not a fundamental knowledge of the regulations, may not be evaluating a site based on the most recently applicable requirements. Many audit program managers do find it difficult to allocate the resources or the time to update protocols more than once every couple of years. An update, at least annually, is consistent with good audit practices.

Use of commercially available automated checklists[8] can help to avoid the problem of outdated program documents. These checklists are updated automatically by the company providing the product. The initial investment in the checklists may seem high, but this update service can be very cost-effective.

State Regulatory Review

It is imperative that audit teams independently evaluate a site's compliance against both federal and state requirements. The federal government establishes only a regulatory floor from which state agencies can and do develop more stringent requirements, although these state requirements are not always addressed appropriately on audits. Because many audit checklists and protocols emphasize only the federal requirements, too often the auditors rely on the site EH&S manager's knowledge of the applicable state requirements, and this is clearly not an independent assessment. There are now several regulatory databases available that allow for an independent review of state regulations prior to an audit.[9] State requirements must be addressed and addressed independently.

---

[8] There are several commercial offerings of automated EH&S audit protocols. The most noteworthy are EH&S Compliance guides by Specialty Technical Publishers, Vancouver, British Columbia; Dakota Auditor by Dakota Software, Rochester, NY, and AuditPro by Arthur D. Little, Cambridge, MA. Each provides regular updates as part of the maintenance contract.

[9] There are numerous automated regulatory databases offered in the marketplace. Some of the more well known are Enflex, BNA, and RegScan.

Unclear or Unknown Corporate Standards

Most companies audit compliance with both regulations and corporate standards or guidelines. Audit teams quite often have a difficult time with the latter. Corporate standards may be vague, unclear, or not well communicated throughout the organization. Moreover, a distinction is often not made between mandatory standards and optional guidelines.

DuPont has addressed this challenge by placing all corporate standards and guidelines on the company's intranet. This is the "official" version so there are no excuses related to having outdated paper copies at the plant sites. In addition, all mandatory requirements are either in italics or use the words "shall" or "must". Guidelines are not in italics and use the word "should." Auditors can only assess against standards.

Misleading Closing Conferences

The closing conference is one of the most difficult elements of the audit process. There is a strong tendency to "sugar coat" the findings in order to keep from antagonizing site management and to make the meeting go smoothly. All too many closing conferences begin with an extended discourse on how wonderful the site staff are and how well the site is operated. On one audit, in particular, the team leader opened with the statement that the large chemical plant "was found to be in compliance." Whereupon the plant manager left the meeting, leaving the EH&S manager to deal with the forty or so findings that the audit team subsequently raised. Audit team leaders must have the fortitude to make sure that plant management gets the right message. If there are significant findings, they should be raised early in the meeting and given their rightful emphasis.

Timeliness and Quality of the Report

Considering the emphasis that most companies place on the audit report, one would think that there would be few problems in this area. However, this is not the case. With established programs, there are generally more problems with late reports than anything else. Late reports can destroy the momentum gained by the audit and can create liabilities for the organization. Quality is always an issue with any program; yet, after a few reports have been developed, there are typically adequate models to follow. A good technique that is used by many companies is to develop an audit program writing manual, which provides general guidance and samples of acceptable findings and complete reports (See Appendix I). Eastman Kodak has developed one of these manuals and gone one step further. The company has a database containing hundreds of findings, taken from previous reports, that auditors have access to in the field. Finally, any audit training that is conducted as part of the program should stress the written report as much as anything else.

Insufficient Follow-Up

This is a chronic problem in most any program. Audit reports are developed; corrective action plans follow; and then many systems break down. There are no systematic assurances that findings are being corrected in a timely fashion. This, of course, can create major liabilities for the organization. Development of a sound database, which allows periodic (e.g., quarterly) tracking of corrective action status, can help to alleviate this problem. Verification audits, as practiced by Colgate-Palmolive and discussed earlier in this chapter, are another useful technique. One should not wait until the next scheduled audit, which might be three or more years later, to verify completion of corrective actions; although the closure of findings from a previous audit should be a formal part of any audit.

Lack of Program Metrics

It has been rather ironic to observe how few EH&S audit programs have developed performance metrics for the program's activities, given that the operations that are audited by the program have innumerable metrics against which they are routinely evaluated. In this day and age, metrics should be the rule not the exception. Good examples of factors to consider include:

- Scheduling audits so that established frequencies are met
- Completing scheduled audits on time (on average)
- Issuing reports on time
- Assuring that all auditors have received auditor training
- Soliciting and receiving formal site feedback
- Developing and reporting statistics on findings closure
- Maintaining up-to-date protocols and procedures

There are, of course other metrics that can be developed. Suffice it to say that EH&S audit programs should be viewed as any other program. There should be a way to measure success or failure.

Notes: Any discussion of a company's individual EH&S audit program approaches in this chapter is based on information provided to the public at large through technical papers, presentations, and the like. Any discussion of a commercially available audit product does not imply an endorsement of that product.

Chapter 9

ENVIRONMENTAL AUDITOR QUALIFICATIONS: GREAT EXPECTATIONS[1]

Blessed is he who expects nothing, for he shall never be disappointed.

– Alexander Pope, Letter to John Gay, October 6, 1727

There continues to be much discussion lately in the profession about certifying EH&S auditors based on certain performance criteria. But how does one evaluate for such important measures as "physical stamina"?

This chapter discusses the qualifications that EH&S auditors should have if they are to lead or conduct a quality audit. It becomes evident after reviewing these expectations that certifying auditors only through a traditional written examination might ignore some of the most important skills an auditor should possess. Before certifying organizations progress too far down the "tight restrictions," written-exam road, they should determine how these other skills are to be assessed. For instance, no amount of "book learning" can overcome the drawbacks of a poor or combative interviewer, or even of an exhausted auditor. On the other hand, some years ago an exceptional auditor with a masters degree in regional planning could not become a registered environmental assessor in California because she did not have a degree in engineering, science, or law. Thankfully, that restriction has since been relaxed, but these kinds of arbitrary restrictions are not appropriate. Environmental, health, and safety auditing is a demanding profession that requires a whole range of skills. Thankfully, this is now being widely recognized. For example, the ISO 14012 Qualification Criteria for Environmental Auditors state that "auditors should possess personal attributes and skills that include, but are not limited to, the following:

---

[1] Excerpted and updated from an article originally published in *Total Quality Environmental Management* (New York: Executive Enterprises, Inc., 1994).

(a) competence in clearly expressing concepts and ideas, orally and in writing;

(b) interpersonal skills conducive to the effective and efficient performance of the audit, such as diplomacy, tact, and the ability to listen;

(c) the ability to maintain independence and objectivity sufficient to permit the accomplishment of auditor responsibilities;

(d) skills of personal organization necessary to the effective and efficient performance of the audit;

(e) the ability to reach sound judgements based on objective evidence; and

(f) the ability to react with sensitivity to the conventions and culture or region in which the audit is performed."[2]

This chapter will further explore these skills and attributes that are necessary for good auditing.

CORE SKILLS

There are certain "core" skills that every auditor should have. Some of these can be easily learned; others are inherent in an individual's character.

Learned Skills

First, the learned skills—a working knowledge of the regulations, a familiarity with the facilities being audited, and, in today's world, computer literacy.

Auditors should have a working knowledge of the applicable regulations. This knowledge can certainly be acquired through courses, textbooks, and the review and application of audit checklists or protocols. This last way of learning about regulations brings up an important point. Regulations do not have to be, and more importantly, cannot be committed to memory. As of 2000, there were over 17,000 pages of federal environmental regulations in Title 40 of the *Code of Federal Regulations* and another 3,000 pages of health and safety regulations in Title 29. Therefore, the term "working knowledge" is just that. Auditors should be familiar enough with the regulations to be able to use a protocol effectively and the protocols need to be detailed enough to support the auditor's efforts.

---

[2] International Organization for Standardization (ISO), "Personal Attributes and Skills, Section 7," *Guidelines for Environmental Auditing, Qualification Criteria for Environmental Auditors*, ISO 14012:1996(E) (1996).

There is a secondary issue related to regulatory knowledge. Auditors too often limit themselves to their very defined area of expertise. It is important that auditors also become comfortable reviewing areas *related* to those in which they are expert. This makes them more valuable and flexible as team members and allows them to "pinch hit" should one of the team members become indisposed during an audit.

The auditor should also be familiar with the facilities being audited and should be comfortable in a plant setting. This does not mean, however, that to be effective every auditor of a chemical plant must be a chemical engineer with twenty years of plant experience. In fact, a good, solid, smart professional with an unabashed, natural curiosity and some familiarity with the facility being audited is probably the best candidate to do a quality audit. Further, there is no one particular educational background that is best suited for auditing. Engineers, scientists, lawyers, managers, and, yes, even financial auditors can bring valuable skills to the table.

More recently, auditors are finding that computer literacy is also a necessary core skill, for several reasons. First, it has become routinely expected that a working draft report be prepared on a laptop computer before the team leaves the site. Also, some companies are now using automated checklists or protocols loaded onto laptop computers. Further, computerized regulatory databases are providing additional field support to audit teams. Finally, plant data files (e.g., training records, discharge monitoring reports) are now more frequently automated. Thus, it is presently difficult to get by on an audit without some familiarity with computers.

Inherent Skills

All of the above skills can be acquired with a little effort and dedication. However, there are other core skills that are more difficult to attain unless there are existing, fundamental "building blocks" within the auditor's personality. The two that come to mind are interpersonal traits and physical stamina.

Good interpersonal skills go a long way in conducting quality audits. In fact, of all the core skills required, these are clearly the most important. Such skills include being able to interview people effectively, having a high degree of curiosity, adjusting smoothly to changes in schedule, responding professionally to challenges made to your verbal and written statements, working well under pressure, and generally keeping a cool head when everybody around you is panicking. The "bottom line" is that an auditor must be both a good communicator and an excellent listener. This takes sincerity, patience and, at times, a great sense of humor.

While certainly these skills can be learned through experience, many individuals will never attain them to a sufficient level to work effectively as an EH&S auditor. Remember that audits, unlike regulatory agency inspections, are meant to be a supportive function and, therefore, individuals who are inherently brusque, volatile, argumentative, and overly egocentric will not be successful.

It may sound ludicrous to place a strong emphasis on physical stamina as an important trait for auditors. However, any of us who have participated in audits know how important this can be. Consider the pace of an audit. Auditors are often traveling on the weekends or late at night. They climb towers and buildings all day, which can be exhausting. They are under constant pressure to perform and to assure that they are diligent and thorough in the investigation.

The most taxing tasks of all are the daily late-night team meetings to discuss observations and findings. When a draft report is to be prepared prior to leaving the site—a general trend these days—the night before the day of the closing conference can flow into the early hours of the morning if the data-gathering phase has not been completed sufficiently early. Attempting to craft an articulate, accurate, and precise finding at 1:00 am is no simple feat.

OBSERVATIONS IN THE FIELD

Now, how do these skills and attributes actually contribute to or hinder the quality of an audit? As an audit team leader or program manager, what should you be looking for, or watching out for, in an auditor. Examples of the worst and best behaviors are discussed below.

The Worst Attributes

No auditor is perfect. However, there are certain behaviors that clearly should be avoided.

Insufficient Records Review. Too many auditors want to do a field inspection immediately upon beginning an audit. Records must be reviewed first to determine the applicable requirements. This problem is often a result of a lack of familiarity or comfort with the regulations or corporate standards. An auditor should take the time early to determine the requirements.

Too Much Records Review. This often occurs when auditors are intimidated by the size or complexity of the site and just don't know where to begin. They will bury themselves in the records and not come up for air. A better approach would be to first get a "windshield" tour of the facility, and then cut off small chunks of the operation and visit appropriate locations in a modular fashion.

Identification of Symptoms. A very common problem arises when the auditor becomes too dependent on the checklist: he or she focuses on symptoms instead of causes. Auditors add value when they address underlying or root causes. They should take some time to think through what really might be happening at the site to cause the identified problems. Answer the "why" as well as the "what" question.

Jumping to Conclusions. This is the opposite of the problem discussed above. Some auditors have a tendency to draw broad conclusions before all the evidence is in. Auditors can sometimes let their egos get in the way of doing a thorough analysis and verifying their findings. They've seen it all before and they simply "know" what is causing the problem. This results in statements such as "the hazardous waste management system at the site is deficient," which is not a very articulate or helpful finding. Auditors need to take a step back and make sure that there is evidence to support the conclusion.

Poor Time Management. There are auditors who never seem to finish on time. This often occurs when they are given more than one compliance area to cover and spend 90 percent of their time on the area where they feel the most comfortable. Make sure that auditors attack compliance areas in parallel, not in series. It is risky to leave one area for the last day of the audit.

"In My State" Syndrome. Nothing annoys site staff more than having auditors preach to them about how things are done in their state or at their location. Auditors should research the appropriate state regulations for the site, audit the site against those regulations. They should, of course, tactfully report on what is being done at their site if it might be a helpful suggestion on improving performance.

Too Easy/Too Tough. Auditors must strike a fine balance between being supportive and providing an honest assessment of the site's performance. Over the years, auditing programs do have a tendency to swing back and forth between "good cop/bad cop" scenarios. When the plants scream that the program is becoming punitive, then the "white hats" go on and the reports become so vague that management can't tell if there's a problem or not. There is no easy solution here, nor should there be. Auditors should not, however, pull any punches in the closing conference or report. Site managers need to understand all of the ramifications of their actions.

The Best Attributes

What is it that makes an individual a good auditor? Communication skills certainly count, but other characteristics contribute as well.

An Even Disposition. Volatile personalities do not make good auditors. This is a very stressful occupation and requires a level head and an ability to adjust to new people and surroundings and constant change.

Flexibility. Audits never go quite as planned. An auditor needs to be flexible to adjust to changing dates, schedules, situations, and the like.

Natural Curiosity. Mentioned previously, this is an important trait. Some would say that the better descriptor would be a "healthy skepticism." In either case a natural inquisitiveness is important.

High Energy Level. There is no time to relax on an audit. Days typically start at 7:00 a.m. with a breakfast meeting and end at 9:00 p.m. or later with a discussion of findings. This can be very taxing, and an auditor has to enter into the process understanding that.

Grace under Fire. Site staff constantly challenge auditors during an audit. It is simply the nature of the process. Auditors must be able to handle this with professionalism. This is especially true during the closing conference when those doing the challenging are more likely to be senior staff.

Under-Control Ego. A healthy ego is probably an asset for an auditor, who must present his findings confidently, but a "know-it-all" attitude is not helpful.

MAKING GOOD THINGS HAPPEN

How does one assure that auditors do indeed have the appropriate skills? Most firms accomplish this through a variety of techniques.

First, there are certain individuals who can be eliminated because of their personalities. This does not necessarily mean that they are not good performers, just that they might not be suited to be auditors.

Second, most firms require that auditors attend a formal training program. These programs can be tailored to address those issues most in need of attention. In fact, some companies have both basic and refresher seminars. The best basic programs usually include a "mock audit" of an actual plant so that auditor candidates can get a true feel for the experience. Such programs feature simulated opening and closing conferences, and actual interviews, records reviews, and facility inspections. Improving communication skills through role-playing and group exercises is usually an essential element of the program.

The refresher programs can focus on historical problems experienced in the field by the audit teams. These problems can be identified using several techniques. For example, audit team leaders can and do critique both the process and the auditors. And they should be confident enough to do this during the audit, as well as after it is complete. On-the-spot, *constructive* feedback is one of the best ways to improve performance. Further, as part of a quality assurance program, some companies will have an oversight auditor participate on a select number of audits during the year to evaluate the process. Lastly, site feedback questionnaires are used to identify problems from a "customer" perspective.

CONCLUSION

Attaining and maintaining good auditor skills is a challenging and never-ending task. To be effective, auditors need more than just knowledge of the regulations. The challenge is to assure that auditors are trained properly and receive continuous feedback. Third-party certifying organizations must assure that auditors they certify have the full arsenal of skills necessary to conduct a quality audit.

Chapter 10

TRAINING EH&S AUDITORS

The vanity of teaching doth oft tempt a man to forget
that he is a blockhead.

– George Saville, Marquess de Halifax, 1633-1695

THE NEED

Auditor training is an essential element of any audit program. Sending poorly trained staff to conduct audits at operating facilities can create technical, legal, and organizational problems, particularly in cases where companies or institutions are attempting to establish the credibility of a corporate or headquarters audit program. Moreover, some states, such as California, have developed formal training criteria for the voluntary registration of environmental auditors. That is, the criteria assume only trained individuals will be registered.

There is also a continuing groundswell within the EH&S auditing profession that some independent certification program should be developed and this has occurred (e.g., BEAC certifications). Thus, there are externally driven, as well as inherently logical, reasons for assuring that an organization's auditors are formally trained.

Fortunately, with a modest investment of effort up front, management can feel comfortable knowing that the auditing staff are at least trained in the fundamentals of manufacturing operations, regulatory requirements, interviewing and inspection techniques, and perhaps most importantly, dealing effectively with plant management.

Choosing the best training approach is a decision that must be made by management for their particular organization. There is no one solution that fits each and every case. However, the EH&S manager can go through the following analytical process to define the training needs of the organization. The steps include:[1]

---

[1] P.G. Friedman and E.A. Yarbrough, *Training Strategies from Start to Finish* (Englewood Cliffs, NJ: Prentice-Hall, Inc., 1985).

- ■ Diagnosing the situation
  - What is the status quo?
  - What discrepancy exists between the current behavior of then trainees and what is desired?
  - What are the realistic goals for training?
  - What methods are needed to achieve the instructional objectives?

- ■ Developing the instructional plan
  - Title?
  - Trainer(s)?
  - Sponsoring organization?
  - Participants?
  - Dates and times?
  - Places?
  - Overall training objectives?
  - Training plan?
    - Time period
    - Goal
    - Method
    - Materials needed
  - Evaluation procedure?

- ■ Implementing and monitoring
  - Frequency?
  - Updating?
  - Annual evaluations?

The remainder of this chapter attempts to provide some insight into how management might go about answering these programmatic questions. The chapter addresses issues such as who should do the training, who should be trained, where the training should take place, and what techniques should be used. Several suggestions for ensuring that the training is effective are included, along with a training "starter kit."

SELECTING THE TRAINERS

There are three basic choices involved in selecting the trainers for an audit program. These are:

- ■ Using experienced in-house auditors to train junior staff

- ■ Sending inexperienced staff to publicly available courses on environmental auditing

- ■ Hiring consultants to come in and train staff in groups.

The first option can be done formally or it can be provided on the job. That is, junior staff can be teamed with more senior staff on actual audits. As they gain experience, they can be given additional responsibilities. Using the in-house option has the advantage of giving the auditors company-specific training. However, it can be taxing on the lead auditors. It also does not expose trainees to how other companies handle the variety of issues that auditing presents, and thus may stifle program advances.

There are several publicly available courses that can be used as training vehicles for auditors. In fact, this book is used as the text for one of those courses. The course approach has merit because it exposes auditors to other organizations' programs and to the wide variety of strategic and operational approaches used by these organizations. However, in order to cram a considerable amount of material into one, two, or three days, these courses cannot tailor the program to an individual company's needs, and typically cannot include field exercises as part of the agenda, unless a particular hotel is more accommodating than most.

A third approach is to contract with consultants experienced in EH&S auditing. The consultant can conduct a training seminar for one, two, or three days that not only highlights the broad issues but is also tailored to meet specific program requirements. The consultant can also take photographs in advance of typical plant situations to add realism to the training. This seminar can be held at a plant site or, in larger companies, during an annual EH&S management meeting, and might include several field exercises as well as classroom instruction. As worthwhile as this approach is, it is also probably the most expensive approach and would be beneficial only if there were a sufficient number of auditors to train on an initial and ongoing basis.

SELECTING THE TRAINEES

Obviously, those staff members who will be conducting the audits should be trained prior to their first audit. In addition, however, refresher training of all auditors should be considered. This ongoing training can be accomplished through conventional courses or through participation in organizations such as the Environmental, Health & Safety Auditing Roundtable (EAR). Management should also consider including those people who will be on the receiving end of the audit (e.g., plant managers, EH&S coordinators) in the training programs so that they are aware of the objectives of the environmental auditing program.

SELECTING THE SETTING

With instructional courses and on-the-job training, management has little control over the setting in which the training is conducted. That setting is either in the cities where the courses are offered or in the plants where the audits are conducted. However, when a formal in-house classroom approach is selected, there are some choices:

- At headquarters
- At a plant site
- At a training center.

Each of these options has its advantages and disadvantages. The headquarters location is usually more accessible to most staff than a particular plant site. Moreover, there are often periodic meetings of one kind or another at headquarters that could provide a forum for a training program. However, a plant site offers a real-world setting for incorporating field exercises into the training program (e.g., conducting a mock audit of the hazardous waste storage area). Some companies have regional training centers that provide effective locations for a program, particularly if they are close to a plant site. One of the real advantages of a training center, regional or otherwise, is the resource it offers in the way of rooms, audio-visual equipment, and other amenities.

SELECTING THE TECHNIQUES

A variety of teaching techniques are available for structuring an EH&S auditor training program. Those that are most appropriate are outlined below.

Lecture

Probably the most commonly used technique, the lecture, can be useful in explaining the fundamentals of EH&S auditing. Lectures can be supported by visuals to make them more interesting. In particular, the use of photographs and slides to portray typical situations an auditor might find in a plant can be especially informative. The biggest risk with lectures is overusing them. The communication that occurs during a lecture is only one-way. Lectures need to be supported by more interactive techniques in order to make the entire training experience valuable.

Problem Solving

We have each learned (some of us the hard way) that there is nothing like problem solving to help us better understand the subject at hand. Several examples of problem-solving exercises are included in Appendix D under the category of "auditing techniques." These exercises simulate actual situations an auditor might experience in the field, including situations that might occur while he or she is conducting audits of environmental or health and safety issues. These exercises are not only meant to instruct staff on how to conduct audits of compliance areas, but to present the trainee with a variety of unusual circumstances that can arise during an audit. Chapter 18 provides insight into the challenges that auditors might face.

Role-Playing

Role-playing can be a valuable and enjoyable supporting technique in any training program. It allows program participants to more directly experience situations that occur during audits.

Role-playing exercises that can be used to strengthen auditing skills are presented in the Appendices. One exercise is a scripted one in which two auditors, each with an entirely different and purposely exaggerated approach, interview a plant engineer on the issue of hazardous waste management.

The training approach for this exercise is to have training volunteers role-play through the situations first. Then the performance of the "auditors" is evaluated. The evaluation should be done in a constructive way, and should come from the class participants, with the process facilitated by an experienced trainer.

Keys to Making It Work

Developing and implementing a successful training program is not easy. Some of the keys to making a success of the program are:

- **Be Prepared.** Adequate preparation is essential. The program planner needs to outline the objectives, develop the agenda, select the trainers and audience, select the methods, and develop the training tools in advance. Don't be afraid to perform a "dry-run" of the materials. If there are field exercises, survey the facilities before the training session. Attend to details; make sure audio-visual equipment is available, is in working condition, and has all the necessary spare parts (e.g., light bulbs).

- **Make It Fun.** Don't rely too heavily on lectures. Use interactive techniques such as in-class problem solving, role-playing, and field exercises.

- **Evaluate the Program.** Always prepare an evaluation sheet to assess the program. Training programs should not be static. Improvements should be made constantly. Feedback is essential.

- **Leave the Trainees with a "To Do" List.** In many training programs, the trainee receives a barrage of materials and can easily become overwhelmed by the volume and complexity of the issues. It's important to sum up the training by focusing on the most important points a trainee should take from the training. Examples could include:

  - Develop a checklist for yourself on what you need to accomplish during the pre-audit phase.

  - Develop a list of the materials you need to take with you on any audit.

  - Spend at least four hours a week reviewing the EH&S literature in order to keep up on regulatory trends.

These exercises can help trainees identify the most important techniques to be learned from the training.

Chapter 11

EH&S AUDIT TRAINING IN THE ASIA PACIFIC[1]

Many shall run to and fro, and knowledge shall be increased.

– Daniel 12:4

With many auditors in the environmental profession doing more international work these days, it might be helpful to describe the highlights of a two-and-a-half week training experience in Singapore and Japan.

There is a certain heightened anxiety in doing any assignment overseas. And frankly, if you aren't just a bit anxious about teaching auditing in different cultures, particularly issues such as how to conduct an effective closing conference or prepare an adequate audit report, you just haven't thought the challenge through. It is quite a different experience than taking a short plane ride in the U.S. to conduct a seminar, knowing that the class shares a common background and that you are only a short trip from home or office. If you have forgotten something on a U.S. assignment, you know you can have it shipped or faxed rather easily. This is not the case for overseas assignments. Overseas communications are much easier now than they used to be, but it is still not quite the same as in the U.S.

You want to have certain bulky items, such as course manuals (which may need to be translated as well), shipped ahead of time—this should be done far enough in advance so that you can confirm that the materials have reached their destination. Care should be taken in such places as Singapore; there can be heavy censorship. Although the content of the training materials, as such, should not be offensive, the customs review of items such as videotapes can hold up their arrival for a considerable time. I was able to send certain non-critical course materials in advance to both Singapore and Japan by an express delivery service and, much to my amazement, they did arrive—three days after I expected them. This experience was quite similar

---

[1] This chapter is an account of Mr. Cahill's experiences as recorded in his travel journal during his trip to the Asia Pacific.

to one I had in the early 1970s when my noise analysis equipment, which was crucial to completing my work, was tied up in French customs for three days.

How do you pack for two weeks so that you only need one carry-on bag? It was difficult to do for this trip since Singapore, only 80 miles north of the equator, is a casual-dress business environment with average daily maximum and minimum temperatures in April of 88° F. and 75° F., and Japan is a formal-dress business environment with average daily maximum and minimum temperatures of 62° F. and 46° F., for the part of the country that I was going to visit. Two very different types of clothing were required.

This trip took over thirty hours from Philadelphia to Singapore, via San Francisco and then Tokyo, on three separate jets. Local Singapore time was twelve hours different from U.S. Eastern Time, so jet lag was brutal. It was five nights before I slept through a complete night.

FIRST STOP: SINGAPORE

Singapore turned out to be quite a surprise. It is a very rich but small (2.7 million people and 225 square miles) independent city-state just off the southern coast of Malaysia. It is about half the size of Los Angeles with about 80 percent of the population. The population is seventy-six percent Chinese, fifteen percent Malaysian and seven percent Indian. The official business language is English. The currency is the Singaporean dollar, worth about three-quarters of the U.S. dollar.

Traveling in Singapore presented its challenges. In the British tradition, they, of course, drive on the left side of the road. It takes a while to get used to sitting in the left front passenger seat with no steering wheel in front of you. Singapore also has a number of interesting laws, such as no spitting and no jay walking.

Communicating with home by phone was incredibly easy with the new direct dial systems, and the quality of the connections made you feel like the person on the other end was sitting in the next room. Water and food were not a problem; the Chinese food is excellent, but there are fifty-seven McDonalds in Singapore if you need a taste of home.

On this trip, I was traveling with a colleague and co-trainer, Darwin Wika of DuPont, who had lived in Singapore for three and a half years, while on assignment. I must admit, as a result of this and the Anglicized environment, I had a relatively easy time adjusting on this leg of the trip.

My assignment while in each of the countries was to conduct a week-long environmental audit training program. The first two days would be classroom training and the last three would be an actual audit of the plant site, aided by the recently trained class. This was a difficult two-fold objective, complicated further by the need to produce a draft, typed audit report by the end of each week.

There were about fifteen people in the Singapore class, who came from Korea, Taiwan, New Zealand, and Singapore. All spoke at least some English, and although we did have difficulties with language, the interaction was excellent.

Good interaction overseas is not always the case, even when the class members are supposed to understand English. Even the most fluent are sometimes timid in using a second language in public forums, such as training classes. I am reminded of a training seminar I gave in Europe a few years ago. An attendee raised his hand early in the training and I became excited because I thought we might actually have an interactive session. He said quite seriously: "Mr. Cahill, could you please hurry up and slow down?" When I asked that he clarify his request, I found out that what he meant was that I was speaking too quickly for him, so I should slow down my speech, but, at the same time, he wanted me to get through all the material, so could I hurry it up. Upon reflection, I found it quite an interesting and fair request.

The training session in Singapore went quite well, although we did face the usual problems. It seems that the site was undergoing an ISO 9000 audit at the same time as our visit. Although this did constrain us somewhat, it demonstrated to the class that they must learn to be flexible. On the positive side, when given classroom assignments the students attacked the problems with tremendous energy. They had a wonderful sense of humor and were also quite prompt, sometimes arriving as much as a half-hour ahead of time. This trait is greatly appreciated by trainers trying to live up to a pre-set agenda.

The mock field audit worked especially well, although things can become complicated when just-trained people are unleashed on a site. As a rule, I prefer to have enough trained coaches from the client's staff so that each field team has someone who can guide them through the investigative process. There were three coaches, including myself, in this program. In Singapore this turned out to be enough "seasoned" coaches. In Japan, during the second week, this became more problematic, because these same coaches were Americans and many of the team members were not very fluent in English. Forcing the students to conduct the audit in English constrained the process too much, so the mock audit was conducted mostly in Japanese. This allowed for only an occasional review of progress by the coaches.

For the most part, the course materials worked well. I brought over 300 35mm slides, including many facility photographs portraying typical noncompliance situations. These included pictures of visible emissions, spills, lack of secondary containment, rusting drums, etc. Without exception, the students preferred these images to the word slides describing what one should focus on during an EH&S audit.

The course manual was also helpful as it contained, among other things, numerous class exercises. These exercises, or case studies, allow for a break from lecturing for both the instructor and the students, and can really add value to the training experience by reinforcing the lecture points. The Harvard Business School knew what it was doing when it decided years ago to use the case-study approach as its principal teaching tool. Course evaluations received from students often say that the best part of the training was the interaction with the other students during the exercises. These are intelligent people, who, with a little advance work on my part, basically teach themselves through use of the exercises.

We conducted mock opening and closing conferences with the plant manager. These mock conferences worked extremely well in exposing the students to the difficult questions that they might encounter on an audit. The plant manager was fed a number of "loaded" questions, including:

- I won't be around for the closing conference. Is that okay?

- We just got word there's to be an agency inspection this week. Can you postpone the audit?

- How would you rank my facility against the others you've audited?

- If I fix some of the deficiencies today, can they be removed from the report?

- If I fix all of the items you've identified, and later have an agency inspection, can you guarantee we'll get a "clean bill of health"?

This plant manager played his role so well that the students could not tell the planted questions from the real ones. However, this did complicate the situation. Recall that the training program had two objectives—to train internal staff and to actually conduct an audit of the site. With some effort, we did work through this issue.

The training ended with the presentation of a draft report to plant management in a closing conference. The three teams were given forms to use in writing and classifying their findings and recommendations. Because the class generally followed directions in completing the form (one form per finding), it was easy to incorporate the findings into a report skeleton that was prepared in advance. It did make for a long Thursday night for the person responsible for completing and critiquing the report, but the advantages of being done with the draft report before leaving a site half way around the world greatly outweighed the extra effort one had to make.

The plant manager raised one interesting and legitimate accountability issue during the closing conference. It seems that the wastewater treatment plant had exceeded its daily flow limits about fifty percent of the time over the previous month. The team presented this as a serious finding. The plant manager's question, then, was should he shut the entire facility down if he had every reason to believe that tomorrow the treatment plant would once again exceed its permit limits? We suggested to the class that the most appropriate response for the audit team is to simply state that, if the plant were allowed to operate under these circumstances, yet another noncompliance incident would occur. It is the plant management's responsibility to decide on the relative risks of the various alternative actions and to make a business decision based on his assessment of these risks. Beyond tomorrow, however, something should be done by plant management to mitigate, if not eliminate the problem (e.g., reporting the exceedances, revising the permit, installing a retention pond or tank, or examining possible infiltration or cross-connections in the process sewer system).

We finished up the closing conference by discussing the next steps in the process, including finalizing the report and corrective action plans. The plant manager was not elated that we had found some real issues, but that is the nature of the audit process.

THE TRANSITION: SINGAPORE TO JAPAN

The flight from Singapore to Tokyo was six hours, a relatively short hop compared to the trip from the U.S., but still a length with which most auditors are unfamiliar.

Much of what we hear about Japan is indeed true. Sushi is quite popular, so get used to raw fish. One does sit on the floor for formal, traditional dinners. Shoes are removed upon entering a residence or restaurant. Also, it is very impolite for you to refill your own beer or wineglass. Your dinner companion does this. And, of course, it is your responsibility to keep their glass full as well. Unless you are careful, this can make for a challenging and foggy evening.

The Japanese take business card exchanges very seriously. You should have your business cards ready. The Japanese are able to present theirs to you with the same speed that Wyatt Earp drew his six-shooter. And, it *is* a presentation. The cards are presented with two hands with the words facing the recipient. You then read the card, acknowledge the individual, and place the card in a pocket of importance, which is not your pants' hip pocket. You return the favor by presenting your card in a similar fashion. In Japan, sliding cards across a meeting table, as though you were playing poker, is quite the insult.

I did notice that the Japanese seemed to be a very forgiving people when an American makes a cultural mistake, and you *will* make some. As long as you make an effort to comply with the customs, and to enjoy them, the Japanese will forgive your mistakes and will, at times, find them quite humorous.

SECOND STOP: JAPAN

We conducted the training in Japan similar to the way we did in Singapore: two days of lecture (in a local hotel this time) and two and a half days of a mock audit at a site. There was an extra challenge in Japan, however. Because of language problems with some, but not all, of the class, all program materials had to be translated into Japanese. This posed an interesting quandary when using word-slide overhead transparencies. As an instructor, should you put up the English version, which has the same page number as the Japanese version in the class manuals, and so can be followed by the class? This method allows the instructor to better recall the issues he needs to address or highlight. Or, should you put up the Japanese version, which is better for the class, but can be confusing to the instructor? We opted to use a mixed approach depending on the subject matter.

All of our lectures had to be translated into Japanese as we went along. This was done for each slide, so that there was first the lecturer's discussion and then a translation of that discussion. This made the presentations almost twice as long as normal. It did curtail discussion of some of the audit "war stories" that instructors use to enliven presentations. But, in some ways there were unforeseen advantages in having the translations. The most significant of these advantages is the one to two minute respite occurring during the translation that allows the American instructor to think about anything important that was missed or prepare for the next slide. This made for a very organized and thoughtful presentation.

Observing and participating in the translation process was very interesting for many reasons; two of which are worth particular mention. First, our instructors became very sympathetic towards the translator, who was a senior staffer for the Asia-Pacific environmental group of the client organization. We, the instructors, could relax half the time. The translator, however, had to not only do the translating, but also had to pay attention during the English presentation so that he could, in fact, translate. Thus, the translator was the only person in the room who had to be focused 100 percent of the time. Our translator was still enthusiastic but very tired after two days.

Second, it turned out that many in the class understood English quite well. We found this out when many of the students would laugh at our funny remarks before the translation even occurred. Once I began to understand this, I would periodically ask one of the students in English if the translations were accurate. He would always tell me the same story. They were mostly accurate but sometimes the translator would add some of his own comments and sometimes he would delete some of my comments—a consequence of having a professional environmental staffer as the translator. Actually, however, this was a bonus. Our translator was confident enough to ad lib on occasion because he had attended all of the lectures in Singapore the week before. This was an invaluable preparation step that considerably improved the quality of the Japanese program.

I must say that the punctuality of the Japanese trainees was marvelous and, at times, almost disconcerting. As the scheduled start time of 9:00 am approached on the first day of the training, all twenty-five students were at their places, with course materials in front of them and hands folded, waiting for us to begin. This was different from the U.S. or Europe, where instructors must call people into the room for most classes. Also, in the U.S. you often have to use "tricks" with the class to get them to return from breaks on time. One of these, for example, is giving the class a thirteen-minute break rather than a fifteen-minute break to reinforce the idea of punctuality. These tricks are unnecessary in Japan.

I did have a difficult time remembering students' names in Japan. I require name tents, filled out with bold magic-markers, to be placed by each student for all courses that I teach. Name badges do not work because they cannot be read from the front of a class. Even with the name tents, however, name recollection was quite a challenge in Japan. The Japanese go by their last names followed by the salutation *san*—so I was known as Cahill-san and Darwin was known as Wika-san. A sample roll call of the course attendees is: Yoshimura-san, Watanabe-san, Inuizawa-san, Takekawa-san. While not overly difficult, it was still a challenge for me.

The value of class exercises or case studies was something we were concerned about in Japan. Many of the class exercises that we typically use require considerable interplay between the instructors and the class. In Japan, the two-way translation process would impede a free-flowing conversation. Instead, we redesigned the exercises to incorporate more visual report backs. For example, in the U.S. (and in Singapore) after a lecture on air emissions auditing, I would typically break the class into groups of five or six students and ask them in an open-ended way how they would perform an air emissions audit at a particular site. A case study would be given to them with specific questions related to this hypothetical site. In Japan, we reworked the questions so they were more closed-ended and the answers could be easily posted on a flip chart, easel, or white board. For example, the case studies posed specific questions like:

- How many air sources would you review?

- Would you go up on (1) all roofs, (2) some roofs, or (3) no roofs?

- Would you talk directly to an asbestos contractor working at the site?

Each of the four teams would then post the answers on the board, which was initially turned away from the class. Then, once the exercise was over for the teams, the instructor would discuss his evaluation of the results with the entire class. This minimized the amount of needed translation without significantly compromising the value of the case studies. We designed one case study on the first day in this way and took a vote in class on the value of the approach. There was an overwhelmingly positive response, so we spent that evening redesigning the remainder of the case studies. We completed four more in this fashion on the second day.

The mock audit at the site went well, although most of it was conducted in Japanese. Each of the three American coaches joined one of the three audit teams (air, water, or waste). One of the coaches was the Asia-Pacific Safety, Health, and Environmental Director for the client organization (a U.S. citizen) so his involvement helped him get to know the Japanese staff better and it was more cost-effective than sending a third person from the U.S. There was at least one student on each team who was bilingual, so the three coaches were able to check progress every now and again.

Although the Japanese were disciplined and organized, it appeared that they were not as probing as a comparable team of U.S. auditors. Americans are suspicious about everything, but in the Japanese culture it is not proper to be suspicious in a public setting. As a result, the verification process was probably not as rigorous as we might expect in the U.S.

We had an interesting time prioritizing the findings of the mock audit—both the commendable activities and the deficiencies. We had each of the teams list on a white board, in Japanese, their top three or four "good and bad" findings. We had a quick verbal translation and then a vote by the entire group. Each person was allowed to vote three times for his or her choice of priority findings. It was remarkable how quickly this stratified the results, and before we knew it, we had our executive summary.

After the fact gathering and analysis, our goal was to prepare a draft report and distribute it during the closing conference. Again, as in Singapore, we used a prescribed form for each of the findings and the teams were quite responsive in completing it accurately and fully. We had prepared the introduction and background material in advance, so it was simply a matter of inserting the twenty or so findings into the report on Thursday evening. Our translator took the forms filled out in Japanese, translated them "on-the-fly," and inserted a rough English version into the report. I then edited this version for technical correctness and language usage. With all the right adapters and consistent software, this part of the process flowed smoothly. In my experience around the world, this process does not always work as well, although you can always seem to finagle some kind of computer support.

We did however commit one of the cardinal sins of auditing on the mock audit. We allowed the site to schedule the group dinner on Thursday evening, the night on which the audit team normally puts together the draft report or draft set of findings. Adding a three-hour formal dinner onto the schedule for this night makes for one very long evening.

Our last responsibility was to conduct the closing conference. I introduced the process and summarized the results, being sure to emphasize that we had a dual mission—to train people and to conduct an audit that would be as thorough as possible, given the time constraints. Each of the teams presented their findings in Japanese to the twenty or so site people attending the meeting. We concluded our meeting, ate our last sushi meal and gracefully departed.

Chapter 12

INFORMATION MANAGEMENT

Environmental managers are discovering that manual methods of data management are no longer adequate.

– R. Raybourn and W. Rappaport, 1985[1]

Ensuring EH&S compliance has become a paperwork nightmare. Companies typically need to generate and track a variety of documents such as permit applications, manifests, monthly and annual operating reports, exception reports, audit action item reports, and the like. In addition, they need to manage the incoming information stream generated by federal, state, and local regulatory agencies in their continuing efforts to promulgate standards, regulations, and guidance.

In response to this ever-increasing flood of paper, corporate EH&S auditing staffs are developing in house, or purchasing from vendors, computerized data management systems. For audit programs these systems generally fall into four classes:

■ Federal, state, and international regulatory databases

■ Automated audit checklists

■ Environmental property information databases

■ Program management software.

This chapter addresses the first two classes of systems: regulatory databases and automated checklists. Environmental property information databases and program management software are discussed in other chapters of this book. For the two classes presented in this chapter, the discussion focuses on the factors that should be considered when evaluating any given package or approach.

Because the environmental software field is so dynamic, this chapter does not evaluate individual products or online services. For detailed reviews and compari-

---

[1] "Computerizing Environmental Information: What to Look for in Systems," *Pollution Engineering* (January 1985).

sons of current products, the reader should refer to environmental software buyer guides that can be found in environmental periodicals.

REGULATORY DATABASES

Current information on most federal and state regulations is easily accessed on a variety of "user friendly" computerized databases. The data is either provided online (e.g., EarthLaw, Lexis/Nexis) or on CD-ROM (e.g., Government Institutes, Enflex, RegScan). More and more auditors are using these systems, both in preparation for an audit and during the on-site activities. This on-site use means, of course, that the audit team must have access to a computer during the audit and that the computer must have either a modem to connect with an online service or a CD-ROM reader. The regulatory databases are especially important in identifying applicable state regulations as many audit protocols will address only the federal regulations.

Automated regulatory databases should incorporate the following characteristics:

- **Coverage.** All major federal EH&S regulations should be a part of the system. This includes regulations on the environment (Title 40), health and safety (Title 29), and hazardous materials transportation (Title 49). In addition, most advanced products now include the EH&S regulations for all fifty states. As discussed above, this state coverage is essential. Some of the products also offer international coverage (e.g., the European Union, individual countries). As audit programs go global, this added feature is becoming more important.

- **Currency.** The systems should be relatively current; updating should occur at least every six months, if not more frequently. More frequent updating at the federal or national level should be expected. In the United States, the *Federal Register* provides an expedited means of doing so. Updating of individual state regulations is more problematic since many states are not as systematized in codifying their regulations.

- **Ease of Use.** These systems should be, and for the most part are, user friendly. Moreover, they should be friendly to both the casual and power user. The Microsoft Windows environment has done much to improve the usability of several of the systems, such as Enflex.

- **Flexibility.** Systems should be designed for single-user applications, local-area networks, wide-area networks, and the evolving groupware software. A user should be able to access the database from other software such as Lotus Notes and Microsoft Windows. The provider should be willing to arrange for a corporate license that responds to these varying needs without breaking the corporate bank.

■ **Powerful Search Capabilities.** The programs should incorporate some kind of search engine (e.g., Fulcrum Technologies' SearchServer) that allows for easy and powerful searching in a variety of ways, including searches by key word, acronym, citation number, and subject. The user should be allowed to search across multiple jurisdictions simultaneously.

■ **Notation of Changes.** Some of the databases have incorporated a feature that marks text to show the user exactly what has been added, deleted, or amended since the last update. This is especially useful for auditors who need to keep abreast of changing requirements in an efficient manner.

■ **Online Help.** The database should have online help that is easy to access and simple to understand.

■ **Speed and More Speed.** With tens of thousands of pages of regulations now on the books, the database should work very quickly in its searches.

■ **Ease of Exporting or Printing.** Although this certainly is the computer age, it is still sometimes helpful to be able to print hard copy or otherwise output the regulations that are being researched. The database should have a printer and/or export function that will allow regulations to be printed in a high-quality format (including tables) and/or be directly inserted into reports.

Although computerized regulatory databases are powerful tools for auditors, sometimes it is still helpful to actually talk to a fellow human being for interpretations of requirements. The U.S. EPA offers several hotlines that can be called for these regulatory interpretations. These numbers can be called anonymously. The lines are usually staffed by contractors, not U.S. EPA employees and it is important to note that the advice is not the "official voice" of the agency. For particularly complex issues, it is probably a good idea to call the applicable hotline twice and determine whether the interpretations are consistent.

Finally, it should be noted that EH&S regulatory data can be accessed for free on the Internet. There are several sites, including www.epa.gov and www.osha.gov, that provide regulatory information. However, these sites often do not provide the ancillary tools, such as high-powered search engines, that are the foundation of the better commercial products.

AUTOMATED CHECKLISTS

Auditors' checklists or protocols are a key component of any audit program. The checklists typically contain hundreds, if not thousands, of questions related to applicable government regulations, company standards and guidelines, and good management practices. Historically, checklists have been fairly large hard-copy documents, making it difficult and costly for companies both to develop and then routinely update these checklists. Because of this and other difficulties associated with maintaining audit checklists, several software development companies have developed automated checklists (e.g., Dakota Software's Dakota Auditor, Specialty Technical Publishers' EH&S Compliance Guides). These checklists can be loaded onto a portable computer and used as the principal audit protocol tool in the field. The automated checklists have their uses but do not come without some disadvantages, both of which are discussed below.

Advantages

The automated checklists offer a number of key advantages, including:

- **Regulatory Coverage.** The checklists typically cover the major EH&S federal regulations that would be of concern to most any organization. In some cases, state requirements are addressed as well.

- **Regulatory Searches.** The automated checklists are generally contained in a linked database that provides the actual regulations that drive the audit requirement. The user can quickly access these regulations by using a "hot key." The user has access to a detailed interpretation of the requirement without having to refer to a separate document, system, or regulatory database.

- **Currency.** One of the real advantages of the automated checklists is that they are kept current by the supplier. Most checklists are updated every three to six months, incorporating new regulatory requirements. Updated computer disks or CD-ROMs are routinely distributed to customers.

- **Consistency.** In providing each auditor with a comprehensive set of audit protocols, the company is likely to achieve more consistent auditing over time.

- **Training.** The checklists can be an invaluable training device. They contain a wealth of information on regulatory requirements, and particular areas of interest can be accessed quickly. The checklists are quite often used as part of site self-assessment programs in which site environmental coordinators select one or more compliance areas to audit every other month or so.

- **Report Generators.** Most of the automated checklists contain report generators, which can automatically incorporate findings through "red-flag" triggers. That is, the audit questions are structured so that certain answers will trigger a finding, and these are imported into the report generator automatically. Some advanced users have been able to use this powerful red-flag tool in a Windows environment and have transferred the findings to a more traditional word processing software.

Disadvantages

The automated checklists bring with them a number of challenges that must be overcome.

- **State Coverage.** Not all the automated checklists contain the EH&S regulatory requirements at the state level. This can be a significant drawback because ensuring adequate state coverage is a key component of any EH&S audit. The programs do allow for incorporating additional questions in each module, which can be questions addressing corporate standards and guidelines, as well as state requirements. Adding these components to the checklists will increase their value, but updating them will burden the purchaser of the product.

- **Small-Site Applicability.** In order to be comprehensive, the automated checklists can contain several thousand questions. This comprehensiveness can be a problem when auditing a small manufacturing site or laboratory. An auditor does not usually have the time to review several thousand questions on a one- or two-day audit of these smaller facilities. As a consequence, the programs often provide for an initial screening of the areas in need of review and also have the ability to follow up with a more focused audit. Nonetheless, auditors sometimes feel more comfortable with a paper checklist so that screening and culling can be accomplished more quickly and effectively.

- **Multiple-User Costs.** Like any software product, the commercial automated checklists have become much more cost-competitive over the past few years. However, if a large corporation adopts one of these packages as a universal audit tool, the costs can become significant because each user requires a separate license. The software companies will work with purchasers of multiple systems to develop a corporate license that can reduce significantly the cost per user.

- **The Occasional User.** Automated checklists work best when auditors use them often enough to become very familiar with their capabilities. The packages are more of a challenge when auditors use them only occasionally. Such occasional usage is very common with audit programs that use part-time auditors from divisions and plants. It is difficult to become facile with a software package when one uses it only once or twice a year as many of these part-time auditors do.

- **Interference with the Audit.** One of the most often-communicated problems associated with the automated checklists is that they interfere with the normal audit process. Sometimes auditors become so engrossed with interacting with and completing the checklists that they do not spend sufficient time interviewing staff, reviewing records, or inspecting the facility.

It should be noted here as well that the Internet provides competitive products, and for free. For example, the U.S. EPA has developed and is developing compliance audit checklists for its major regulatory programs. Although not the classical "automated" protocols, they are excellent auditor tools. They can be found on www.epa.gov

In sum, automated checklists are definitely worth exploring, especially for programs where self-audits will be expected. There are some risks in adopting this approach, however. Careful planning can do much to mitigate these risks.

EVALUATING AUDITING SOFTWARE SYSTEMS

Choosing an audit system from the numerous commercially available environmental auditing software systems is not easy. Some systems can be purchased outright for less than $1,000. Others, if they were to be purchased and used company-wide, might cost as much as $100,000 or more for a corporate license. Yet, these more expensive systems are more flexible and usable throughout the corporation.

To select from among the options offered, in general, potential purchasers should first develop program specifications and requirements and then evaluate the offerings against these specifications. For example, a buyer might want an audit program management system to meet some or all of the following requirements. That is, in a perfect world, the system should be able to:

- Be operated on the company's hardware configuration and be accessible from portable computers with a modem

- Allow for widespread access to environmental regulatory databases

- Load and sort company-designed or commercial federal and state compliance checklists

- Allow easy updating of the checklists

- Load (at times by modem from the field) and search audit reports

- Produce tabular audit-findings reports

- Produce periodic "incomplete action items" reports, across all facilities

- Code and retrieve findings by class (e.g., air emissions), location, year, organization, and severity (e.g., low, medium, and high risk)

- Calculate simple statistics (e.g., number of significant air compliance issues in California) across all audits

- Produce graphics-oriented management reports, using data across all audits

- Provide for selective data security.

Once the above design specifications are further refined, staff need to evaluate any offering against the following criteria:

Is the program truly pre-existing, or will the buyer be paying for its design or major modifications?

Can the system readily meet the design specifications?

Is the system flexible?

Is it user friendly?

What type of reports can be generated?

Are search capabilities broad enough?

Is documentation complete and clear?

■ Can the system handle text (e.g., checklists) as well as numeric data?

Will it have on-screen help?

Can data be transferred among modules?

Are presentation graphics available?

Is updating or upgrading the program design easy or a major undertaking?

It is possible that an otherwise attractive system may not fulfill all these requirements in its current form. However, the question really is: can the system be modified readily to take into account the needs of the company? If so, many of these software packages can add significantly to the auditor's tool set.

Chapter 13

USING GROUPWARE TO MANAGE THE EH&S AUDIT PROGRAM DOCUMENTATION PROCESS[1]

We're drowning in information and starving for knowledge.

– Rutherford D. Rogers, 1915-

THE IMPORTANCE OF SOUND INFORMATION MANAGEMENT

Environmental, health, and safety audits are used by the regulated community to help assure continued compliance with laws and regulations, company policies and procedures, and good management practices. One of the biggest challenges for any program is to ensure effective management, control, and distribution of the information and data generated by the audit.

Several critically sensitive documents are generated as a result of each audit. These include: (1) draft and final audit reports prepared by the audit team, which document the deficiencies or findings at the site or within the audited organization or system, (2) a plan generated by the audited entity, which defines the measures needed to correct the deficiencies, and (3) a report that continuously tracks the status of all proposed corrective actions for all audits. It is generally the responsibility of the corporate (or headquarters) EH&S audit program manager to monitor and analyze the data and information generated by these audit reports and plans.

One of the more important challenges for an EH&S audit program manager is to provide documented assurances to the corporation that the sites' corrective actions are being completed on time and are consistent with the findings of the audit teams. It has been stated many times by attorneys and regulators that one is better off not

---

[1] Originally published in *Total Quality Environmental Management* (New York: John Wiley and Sons, 1995). Updated for this edition.

implementing an audit program if the corporation cannot assure that identified deficiencies are corrected in a timely fashion. In sum, organizations need to reach *verifiable* closure on all audit findings.

A second critical documentation issue for the audit program manager is determining whether audit reports and documents can be protected from discovery in a legal proceeding and, if not, deciding what should be done to minimize liabilities to the corporation posed by a potential release of these sensitive documents. In 1986, the U.S. EPA stated only that they "will not routinely request audit reports."[2] This has been reinforced in the EPA's subsequent 1996 and 2000 policies. Moreover, many states have enacted audit immunity and privilege laws, regulations, and policies.

These initiatives demand that audit program managers treat the management, retention, and destruction of records very seriously. Historically, this has been an arduous task since most programs principally used paper-filing systems. In the past few years, automation has made some breakthroughs, particularly in the area of tracking audit reports and the status of corrective action plans. New software technology—that is, groupware—if used properly can revolutionize the management of audit program documentation.

TRADITIONAL RESPONSES TO AUDIT DOCUMENT MANAGEMENT

The audit report documentation process can be quite complex and involved in many organizations. As shown in Figure 13.1, the process typically involves staff at the corporate and site level as well as the audit team.

Typically, as a first step, the audit team develops a draft list of findings and draft and final audit reports. These receive extensive reviews by site staff, line management, corporate environmental affairs staff, and corporate legal staff. In some companies, these reviews are conducted simultaneously, which accelerates the process, but at the risk of the audit team receiving conflicting comments.

In other companies, corporate environmental affairs and legal staff must receive copies of the draft reports first (even draft findings sometimes), and comments must be incorporated before the site or line management receive their copies. This helps to protect the auditors and the corporation, but the process often bogs down substantially, with the site at times not receiving draft reports for several months.

There are similar challenges associated with the corrective action planning process. Typically, the site develops a draft corrective action plan (CAP) and submits it to the corporate audit program manager for review. The legal department usually receives a copy as well. Comments are incorporated and a final CAP distributed. The corporate audit program manager is responsible for tracking the progress of

---

[2] U.S. Environmental Protection Agency, "Environmental Auditing Policy Statement: Notice," *Federal Register* 51, no. 131 (July 9, 1986).

Figure 13.1 Audit Reporting Process Organizational Responsibilities

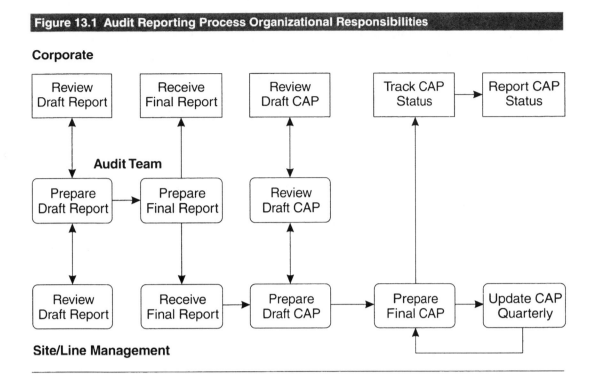

each CAP, and this is usually accomplished through the development and distribution of quarterly or semi-annual status reports by the sites.

In an organization with scores of sites, one can imagine how quickly the document management process can get out of control. At any given time, there are a variety of document types for each site, in various stages of completion, winding their way through the organization. As an example, take a company with twenty sites, each on a two-year audit cycle. After six years, the organization will have developed sixty draft audit reports, sixty final audit reports, sixty draft CAPs, sixty final CAPs, as many as 480 quarterly status reports, and numerous other program documents. Is it any wonder that most programs can't seem to meet their established scheduling standards for report and CAP completion?[3]

As a result of these challenges, many companies have increased their reliance on portable computers in the field. Field use of computers allows audit teams to develop the skeleton of a report prior to visiting the site. This can accelerate the report-generation process.

---

[3] Report timeliness and quality, and insufficient follow-up have been identified previously as two of the top six deficiencies typically observed in environmental audit programs. See L.B. Cahill, "Benchmarking Environmental Audit Programs: Best Practices and Biggest Challenges," In *Total Quality Environmental Management* vol. 3, no. 4. (New York: Executive Enterprises, Inc., 1994).

Companies also have instituted automated audit tracking systems. These systems rely on commercially available databases, such as Microsoft Access, to monitor the generation of audit reports and codify individual findings and their associated corrective actions. For example, Colgate-Palmolive has co-developed with Marsh Risk Management the software program "Trend Tracker." This is a system that allows tracking of the closure of audit findings from facilities located all over the world. This is especially important for Colgate-Palmolive as only 30 percent of their facilities are located in the U.S. With this system, Colgate is able to report to management the percent of audit findings closed on time by division or region.

Using these systems, audit program managers can monitor the progress of draft and final audit reports and periodically (usually quarterly) review the status of all outstanding corrective actions. Audit reports, where all corrective actions are completed, will be formally closed out and the program manager will "red flag" those planned actions that are behind schedule.

Examples of the types of data that are tracked are shown in Figure 13.2. Many factors associated with each finding and corrective action must be tracked.

For the corporate periodic tracking to be effective, the audited entities must submit a status report of some kind, which is usually entered manually into the database and then updated. Examples of the types of output typically generated from the submitted reports are discussed later in this chapter.

In addition, the data are also reviewed to determine the progress the site has made toward completing the corrective actions by the original target date. In fact, timely completion of corrective actions is probably the most critical performance factor for the site that was audited, even more so than other factors, such as the number of deficiencies observed by the audit team.

Unfortunately, many of the current audit automation systems in use are cumbersome and not easily maintained and updated. For example, audit reports will be completed using a word processing program, tracking data are maintained on a relational database, and performance charts are developed using a charting program. Although many of these programs can be used relatively seamlessly, the links are often manual. That is, a clerk re-enters the data from the audit report into a database and, subsequently, enters key elements of the database into the charting program. Not surprisingly, without a true champion, the databases, quarterly reporting, and tracking often fall by the wayside.

THE GROUPWARE SOLUTION

Groupware such as Lotus Notes can make the audit tracking process much more manageable and effective. "Groupware allows groups of users to work together by sharing information across a network. The information can include files created in the groupware, files from other software packages, comments attached to those files, and a variety of other file formats and types of information. You can also combine

Figure 13.2 Audit Reporting Process Critical Data Elements for Tracking

Audit Report	*CAP*	*Tracking Report*
For Each Finding:	For Each Corrective Action:	For Each Site:
Description	Description	Findings Statistics
Audit Date	Planned End Date	CA Statistics
Compliance Area	Actual End Date	Root Cause Analysis
Priority	Current Status	CA Close-Out
Classification	Responsible Party	Statistics
Citation		Exceptional Practices
Root Cause		
Site		
For Each Report:	For Each Report:	For Each Report:
Report Dates	Report Dates	Report Dates
Distribution	Distribution	Distribution
Closure Dates	Closure Dates	Closure Dates

different types of information and different file formats into a single document or database."[4] In a *Fortune* magazine article, Ray Ozzie, the inventor of Lotus Notes, said that the intention of groupware is to "enable people in business to collaborate with one another and to share knowledge or expertise unbounded by factors such as distance or time zone differences.[5]

"One of the special powers of Lotus Notes, in particular, is in its replication capability. Performing replication passes your changes to a document to the shared database, and/or receives other user's changes from the shared database."[6] Replication routines assure that common files are periodically updated globally.

---

[4] Allen W. Sim, *Lotus Notes® for Novices—A Guide for the Perplexed*. (New York: Ballantine Books, 1994), 2.

[5] David Kirkpatrick, "Why Microsoft Can't Stop Lotus Notes," *Fortune* (December 12, 1994), 142.

[6] Sim, 161.

Conceptually, groupware could be a very powerful tool for managing an audit program. If taken to its full potential, groupware could allow for a *paperless* audit documentation system. Let's explore some of the possibilities.

Under the groupware scenario, findings from audits can be loaded directly onto the system network during the audit, allowing for real-time review of the audit reports by the site and other interested parties (e.g., corporate legal). This would allow the legal department to review a draft audit report the evening before the closing conference and to have any proposed changes incorporated into the report prior to the meeting. The same could be done by the corporate audit program manager, and all comments could be incorporated and the file replicated so that all recipients have the same version. In fact, where all relevant parties have access to the report findings, there may be no need for a written report, although a printed set of findings might be useful for the closing conference at the site.

Further, the corrective action plan can be quite easily loaded onto the groupware system and keyed to the audit findings and report. Screens can be designed so that for each audit, individual findings with their proposed corrective actions can be shown together. Real time adjustments can be made here as well.

One of the more powerful ways to use groupware is in the continuous updating of corrective action plans. There really would no longer be a need for formal, quarterly status reports. Updating can be done at the site level since actions are completed through direct input into the network as opposed to transmitting status reports by paper or electronic mail and then manually entered into a database.

It might be prudent to exercise certain controls or security measures over the corrective-action updating process, because the corporation may not want to allow uncontrolled modification of the corrective action plans. That is, only certain individuals should be given authority to update the plans. Establishing read-only files for most users of the audit reports and corrective action plans would be an appropriate security measure. This is quite easy to accomplish with groupware.

Finally, groupware allows the audit program manager to easily develop and update the periodic tracking reports and distribute the reports directly and electronically to the interested parties.

With groupware, audit program output reports can take a variety of forms. Graphical presentations can be developed from the fundamental tracking tool, the audit finding.

As shown in Appendix K, a Model Management Report, certain important program characteristics such as root causes, report timeliness, and the type and significance of findings can be developed and analyzed. The audit program manager should decide in advance which characteristics are appropriate to analyze and display for his or her organization. Some companies will statistically analyze each plant's performance, others will assess only a division's performance, while still others will "roll-up" the data to show only overall corporate performance. These strategic views can help the audit program manager better understand the relative strengths and weaknesses of the organization's EH&S program.

CONCLUSION

At first blush, the EH&S audit document management process appears to be an ideal application for groupware. It is vitally important that audit tracking systems are put in place and operate effectively. Groupware can help achieve this objective.

Chapter 14

MANAGING AND CRITIQUING AN AUDIT PROGRAM

A company must evaluate a number of general considerations in devising a rational and cost-effective environmental audit program tailored to its unique needs.

– W.N. Hall, 1985[1]

Assuring regulatory compliance is a complex challenge for today's industrial manager. Shaping EH&S audit programs to help meet this challenge is no less a challenge. Programs must be well thought out and receive the support of senior managers.

This chapter is directed at those managers who will be given the complex chore of developing or managing an EH&S audit program within a corporate structure. The chapter first presents an approach for developing a program, consisting of eight steps, beginning with a policy setting and planning exercise and ending with full implementation of the program. Using this as a starting point, the remainder of the chapter discusses a variety of management techniques that can be used to control, assess, and evaluate an ongoing audit program.

BEGINNING A PROGRAM

As one is immersed in the complex and pliable concept of EH&S auditing, one can become overwhelmed with the choices that need to be made in setting up a comprehensive yet workable program. It is often useful to attack the problem one step at a time. Presented below is an outline of one step-by-step approach that could be used in creating a successful audit program.

---

[1] "Environmental Audits—A Corporate Response to Bhopal," *Environmental Forum* (August 1985).

Develop an EH&S Audit Policy and Procedure

Successful EH&S audit programs uniformly receive strong support from senior management. The explicit backing of the program by senior managers creates a supportive attitude throughout all levels of a company. Thus, quite often the first step in any program is the development and distribution of a policy statement, signed by a senior corporate executive, describing and supporting the initiation of a formal EH&S auditing program. This policy statement sets the tone of the program.

The policy statement should include a set of program procedures, which is a natural follow-up to the policy. These procedures deal with key planning and structural issues, such as those suggested in Figure 14.1. The statement should be responsive to the criteria selected by the organization, as appropriate. These criteria might include the U.S. EPA Environmental Auditing Policy, the U.S. Sentencing Commission Guidelines, ISO 14000 Auditing Guidelines, and/or the European Union Eco-Management and Audit Scheme.

The successful EH&S audit program should also respond to any Total Quality Management (TQM) principles established by the organization. Some that come to mind include:

Focus on Customers. Define the customers of the program. They include corporate management, line management, EH&S management, and site staff. In some cases, shareholders are included as well. Make sure that key documents, such as the facility audit reports and third-party certifications, respond appropriately to those customers.

Figure 14.1 Key Audit Program Planning Issues

Type	Issues
Policy	Objective of the program Expectations of senior management Measures of successful performance
Management	Corporate vs. divisional control Internal vs. external auditors Unannounced visits Reporting protocols
Legal	Written oral reports Retained documentation Corporate counsel involvement
Coverage	Frequency of audits All regulations All plants, random sample, directed sample Past practices

Improve Constantly. The program should be evaluated annually to determine if it has met pre-established objectives. Moreover, a new set of objectives should be established each year, which should correspond to program improvements. It is especially important that line management perceives that the program is adding value each year and not simply becoming "more picky" on each subsequent audit.

Drive Out Fear. Although it is difficult to remove the "performance evaluation" flavor of an environmental audit completely, the program should focus on management systems and site procedures and performance. Depersonalizing the program can drive out the fear at the site level.

Remove Staff Barriers. The audit program can help the sites understand that environmental compliance is not simply the responsibility of EH&S managers. Line management has a clear role in achieving compliance. With line and staff organizations working together, more can be accomplished.

Eliminate Slogans and Quotas. Audit programs should be careful about incorporating broad, unachievable objectives, such as, "compliance will be improved." The audit program is only part of that equation. One should also be careful to put quotas on the number of audits that need to be conducted each year, without some risk categorization of the sites being audited.

De-emphasize Mass Inspections. There is a common tendency for organizations to "count up" the number of findings on each audit and compare one site against another. This should be avoided since each site is different and not generally comparable. One comparison that can be made is how a site performs on audits over time. Are deficiencies being corrected? Is the site performing better over time?

Institute Training. Most companies have a requirement that auditors must be formally trained prior to their first audit and that experienced auditors receive refresher training and periodic updates on relevant regulatory issues. This is a good practice and consistent with ISO 14012 expectations.

Don't Buy on Price Alone. In reviewing ancillary operations during an audit, make sure that the site is purchasing services and equipment that aren't always the low-cost providers. Many companies' sites have been compromised environmentally by low-bid, onsite contractors.

Set Up the Organization

The second step on the agenda is deciding how to organize the audit program. For larger, multi-division companies, there are a variety of options, including:

- A corporate audit function with full-time corporate auditors

■ A corporate audit function with part-time auditors selected from divisions

■ A small corporate oversight group with delegation of the audit function to the operating division

■ A small corporate oversight group with self-auditing conducted by plant staff

■ A small corporate oversight group with the use of external, independent auditors.

Even in smaller companies, similar organizational issues arise. Beyond the choices listed above, the types of individuals who should serve as auditors must be selected (e.g., engineers vs. attorneys). It must also be decided how corporate counsel is to be involved in the audit. Further, should auditors be full-time, full-time rotation, or part-time; and who is to have ultimate responsibility *and* authority for running the program?

Unfortunately, there is no standard organizational solution for the management of an audit program. Each company must investigate the strengths and weaknesses of the variety of options open to it and select accordingly.

Develop Tools

The third part of program planning process is the early development of the audit tools. Many of the tools and techniques commonly used in industry have been discussed elsewhere in this book. These include:

■ Statement of policy

■ Pre-visit and audit evaluation questionnaires

■ Site visit and opening/closing conference protocols

■ Audit checklists and protocols

■ Audit report, corrective action plan, and status report formats.

Each of these tools should be developed in a standard and compatible way to ensure consistency within and among individual audits. Eventually, they can be included in an all-encompassing audit manual that will serve as a training device, as well as the audit working document.

Train Staff

The fourth step in the process is auditor training. A certain amount of auditor training will be required early in the program. The extent and nature of the training will vary depending upon the backgrounds of the individual auditors (e.g., corporate environmental staff vs. plant environmental engineers vs. corporate attorneys). Additionally, the frequency of recurring training will vary depending upon the organizational choice selected earlier. That is, the training of full-time auditors is pretty much a one-time effort, while the use of full-time rotational or part-time auditors will require training on a regular basis.

Understandably, auditors must be trained technically to be able to deal with very complex compliance management requirements. But perhaps more importantly, they must also develop skills in conducting probing interviews with personnel having a wide variety of educational and employment backgrounds. Auditors must walk a fine line between being supportive to plant supervisors in their management of environmental affairs and being assertive in their probing for areas of known or suspected noncompliance. It is a task requiring both diplomacy and firmness.

A final point on training—and this is an area where outside help may be useful. Audit consultants can bring a large number of experiences to a training exercise and can provide the expertise or program start-up. These may be otherwise unavailable to the organization.

Test the Program

With the organization, tools, and trained auditors in place, the fifth step is to test the program. Testing involves conducting one or more practice audits at plant sites. In this light, the audit program manager may want to test the auditors' abilities to conduct an investigation commensurate with the potential liabilities associated with the range of company sites. Therefore, he may want to select one large, complex facility and one small, fairly risk-free facility (e.g., warehouse and distribution center) to audit. The intensity and duration of the investigations for these facilities should vary considerably and, therefore, testing the audit method at each site would be a useful exercise.

Set Review Schedule

With the program fully tested, the sixth step is to set a schedule for reviewing all of the company's sites. To provide some rationale for determining how often sites are to be audited, for how long, and by how many auditors, many companies rank sites based on risk-potential criteria. An example of how this is typically done is shown in Chapter 4. In the example, each of four sites was first classified based on risk potential. The resulting classifications were then used to determine frequency of audit, duration of audit, and audit team size. This type of exercise can be completed for all facilities to help assure that audit resources are applied effectively and efficiently.

Conduct Audits

With all preparatory tools in place and a schedule set for facility audits, the seventh step is to actually conduct the audit using the tools and timetable developed. The approach used to conduct individual site audits is discussed in detail in Chapter 15.

Implement Full Program

The central purpose of an EH&S audit program is to assure continued compliance with regulatory requirements. Audits are not one-time efforts but must be followed up on a regular basis. As has been stated, where instances of noncompliance have been identified, these must be corrected within a reasonable length of time so that corporate vulnerability is not exacerbated. Thus, in implementing the full program, most companies have designed a follow-up mechanism to monitor subsequent corrections made to eliminate noncompliance. One approach has been to develop brief "exception reports" or "action item reports" as a result of each and every audit. These reports would then be entered into a computer, together with a program that would produce monthly status reports on completion of action items. As corrective actions are taken at sites, these are noted. In addition, semi-annual or annual reports are generated that summarize key compliance management statistics such as: items of noncompliance per facility type; type and cost of corrective measures; lag time between identification of noncompliance and implementation of corrective action; and so forth.

MANAGING A PROGRAM

Too often the value of a management technique, such as an EH&S audit program, is lost to an organization because of execution. This can happen even in cases where the program planning exercise has been extremely successful. The management techniques discussed below can be useful in keeping a program on track.

Assessment Tools

Audit programs often are implemented without any *a priori* consideration given to how program success might be measured. This is not a good management practice. Truly successful programs will typically incorporate several monitoring and evaluation techniques. Most of these use the reduction over time of noncompliance items as a yardstick.

The formal incorporation of compliance measures into the performance standards of plant and division managers is a technique sometimes used. Since community complaints, excursions, notices of violation (NOVs), and fines are, in fact, measurable events, management can be held accountable. In some observed cases, plant managers have maintained graphs on their office walls depicting historical compliance at the facility. As demonstrated by Figure 14.2, these graphs can depict the trend in both overall and individual media environmental compliance.

Incorporating these techniques into the management system, and evaluating managers based on successful execution, will help to ensure that risks and liabilities are understood and handled appropriately. It establishes a clear message that environmental management is taken seriously at high levels within the organization.

Management Reports

Top management's role in assuring EH&S compliance is crucial. Constructive EH&S policies and procedures must be developed *and* communicated. Recent history is filled with examples of employees illegally dumping wastes and falsifying compliance records, all done "in the best interests of the company." Senior management must demonstrate a serious commitment to assuring compliance.

In addition to being involved in the setting of policies and procedures, senior management also must be apprised of the successes and failures that occur during program operation. In organizations where the reporting of audit results does not go beyond the corporate environmental manager, this manager has, in some cases, found himself in a troubling situation. He may lack the institutional leverage needed to convince line managers—often his peers—that expenditures for achieving environmental compliance should be budgeted on par with normal operating expenditures.

One way to ensure management awareness and commitment is to design an audit program that formally requires reports to be delivered to senior management. Precedence for this can be found in corporate safety programs in which summary safety statistics are routinely reported to levels as high as the Board of Directors. Environmental reports could (and should) be a part of this process.

A key to making the "reports to management" idea work is to design a report that provides useful information efficiently. Most senior executives are not in a position to read all audit reports, and even if they did, they would typically be unable to reach any strategic conclusions without some supporting trend or snap-shot analyses.

Typically, then, reports to management should be brief tabular and graphical presentations, transmitting the maximum amount of information in the minimum number of pages. Assuming that these reports would probably be quarterly, they might contain the following information:

- Number of audits completed in the quarter (by organizational unit)

- Highlights of liabilities most affecting the firm (*e.g.*, new or pending underground storage regulations)

- Trends in noncompliance items identified

- Statistics on success rates in meeting "action item" schedules

- Specific instances where audit program findings and recommendations have resulted in significant cost savings (e.g., major potential fines avoided or substitution of non-hazardous materials for hazardous materials). See Appendix K.

Figure 14.2 Compliance Monitoring

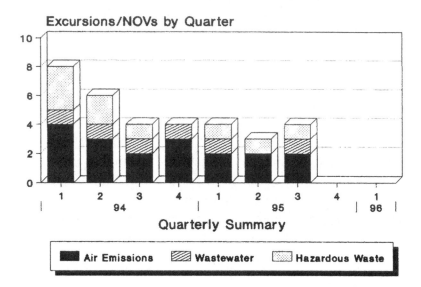

Plant Manager Tracking System

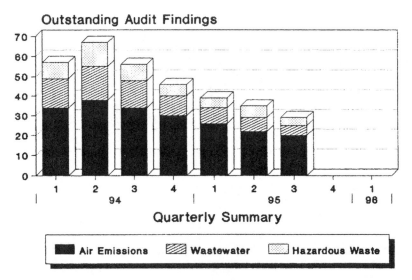

Quarterly Report to Management

Presenting this information in a concise, digestible format will aid the EH&S audit program manager in his efforts to establish and maintain corporate credibility for his program.

Staff Management

The role of an EH&S auditor is a difficult one. Even under the auspices of a supportive program, much of what an auditor does involves evaluating the performance of the company's environmental and operational staff. Constantly "dinging" facilities (and their management) in written audit reports can become a fatiguing exercise (although some people, for better or worse, seem born to it). Also, in most situations, extensive travel is required. While this seems glamorous at first, regularly spending weeks in Nowhere, U.S.A. can add to the fatigue.

In order to maintain a motivating environment for auditors, the program manager should initiate some efforts to counter the downsides of auditing. These could include:

- **Rotating Staff.** Most companies rotate audit staff on a regular basis. This helps to keep auditors fresh and enthusiastic and will also help to spread EH&S awareness among a large group of individuals.

- **Establishing Career-Progression Tracks.** Supplementing the need for rotation is the need to convince staff that the EH&S auditing slot is a logical step in one's career and not a "dead end" or "holding pattern." One company, in fact, has a standing pool of corporate "fast trackers" who, as part of their individual development plans, will serve as EH&S auditors for a period of time. The goal is to create a sense of EH&S awareness in the managers of the future.

- **Maintaining the Technical Edge.** Keeping up with EH&S trends is an overwhelming task. It seems that every month one significant federal EH&S regulation is either proposed or promulgated. Audit staff need to do more than read the *Federal Register* (a task to be reserved for strong hearts and sharp eyes) to keep abreast of developments. Participation in regular seminars (e.g., the Environmental, Health, and Safety Auditing Roundtable) will maintain a cutting edge in staff, put auditors in a setting with auditors from other companies, and provide a perquisite that can enhance morale.

There are, of course, many other traditional techniques that managers can use to motivate staff (e.g., good salary increases for good performance), and they should indeed be used. Over time an audit program is only as strong as its people.

Quality Assurance

One of the key challenges with any program is to ensure it meets or exceeds its stated objectives. Assuring a quality program requires regular performance reviews.

One way to accomplish this is to have an annual self-evaluation. The evaluation can be completed as part of the year-end planning and scheduling for next year's site visits, which is done by most companies. Thus, the planning exercise should not only be a look forward but a look backward as well.

- What have we accomplished?

- Did we meet our objectives?

- Where did we exceed our plan?

- Where did we come up short? Why?

- What changes can we make to improve our program?

In addition to the self-evaluation, programs also benefit from occasional third-party evaluations. For a modest expenditure to an outside firm, a company could conduct an audit of their audit program. This audit could include requesting that the third party observe an actual audit or review audit reports for substance, format, and language.

Lastly, the program manager is faced with a very difficult quality assurance challenge in order to keep current with changing EH&S regulations. Most programs use some form of audit checklist drawn from current standards and regulations. If no effort is made to keep these checklists updated, they will quickly be viewed as irrelevant, and the program's viability will be jeopardized. As discussed in an earlier chapter, some mechanism for regulatory updating must be chosen *and* used.

Maintaining Awareness

It is frequently surprising how much selling is a part of a job—any job. We all must sell ideas, approaches, plans, strategies, and the like to our bosses, our peers, and even our staff. Strong-arming goes only so far. Running a successful audit program is no different. Senior management and line managers must be convinced of its value. And perhaps most importantly, plant operators, through the audit program, must understand the EH&S consequences of their actions. They are where "the rubber meets the road." Techniques companies have used to make this happen include the posting of important notices and procedures in the workspace of unit operators. Too often emergency response procedures, spill procedures, and target effluent limitations are found as blueprints on the shelves in office buildings but not in the operating environment where they would be the most useful. Also, regular training and orientation of both new and seasoned employees is an important awareness technique for management. This should include not simply classroom exercises but practice drills for spills and upsets. Finally, advertising good environmental practices in the way safety performance has been traditionally rewarded will help improve the visibility and credibility of the EH&S audit program.

CONCLUSION

This chapter has been designed to assist company managers and staff in developing and running audit programs to monitor compliance at their plant sites—be it one site or fifty. It is our hope that the concepts and approaches presented herein will guide the development of efficient and effective programs that will minimize both the liability exposure of corporate managers and the pollution exposure of the public at large.

PART II

CONDUCTING THE AUDIT

Chapter 15

CONDUCTING THE
EH&S AUDIT

Management ignorance is no defense.

– Robert V. Zener, Former U.S. EPA General Counsel, 1981[1]

INTRODUCTION

The core of any audit program lies in the actual completion of individual facility audits. Audits must be conducted efficiently, consistently, and comprehensively by competent auditors who must elicit the cooperation of plant managers and staff. This can be a tall order for uniquely complex facilities whose basic day-to-day operations fully tax on-site staff resources.

Accordingly, this and the following chapter discuss the detailed steps and procedures that are typically undertaken in the course of an EH&S audit. It should be noted, however, that every facility is different, and this chapter can only address those elements of an audit that are common to most facilities and programs. That is, some of what is presented here may not be applicable to certain programs and, conversely, there may be some EH&S compliance issues that are not included here that are of concern to your operations.

Nevertheless, these next two chapters will provide insights and perspectives into the conduct of an EH&S audit from the "typical" plant viewpoint. The following key questions will be addressed:

- How should I prepare for the audit?

- What records and documentation should I review?

- What part of the plant should I inspect and what compliance issues are key?

---

[1] In *Environmental Reporter*, Current Developments (June 26, 1981).

- Who should I interview and how should I do it?

- How do I communicate my findings to the site?

- What should be done after the audit is completed?

There are three major phases to an EH&S audit. They are: (1) pre-audit activities, (2) on-site activities, and (3) post-audit activities. Because of the distinct procedural differences in each of these phases, the remainder of this chapter addresses each separately. The next chapter discusses specific examples of inspection items and compliance problems that one might observe at a facility.

PRE-AUDIT ACTIVITIES

There are several key activities that should be completed before an audit team arrives on site. They include:

- Team selection and formation

- Completion and review of the pre-audit questionnaire

- Review of relevant regulations

- Audit scope definition and establishment of team responsibilities

- Review of audit protocols

- Development of a detailed agenda.

This stage of the process should not be underestimated. There has been many an audit that has failed due to inadequate preparation. This is especially true where a company relies on part time auditors from divisions or plants. These are typically very busy people and quite often begin preparation for the audit when they climb aboard the plane. This is too late and often results in peculiar behaviors such as "herding," where the team members follow the team leader around all day because they have not been assigned individual tasks or protocols (very inefficient). In order to assist auditors in better preparing for the audit a pre-audit checklist is provided in Figure 15.1. Take the time to prepare; it will provide substantial rewards.

Figure 15.1 Model Pre-Audit Checklist

AUDIT BACKGOUND	
Site Name:	
Site Location:	
Audit Type:	
Audit Dates:	
Team Leader:	
Team Members:	

NO.	PRE-AUDIT PLANNING ACTIVITY	DONE (?)
	Team Leader Only	
1.	Define the Audit Objectives, Scope, and Schedule	o
2.	Form the Audit Team	o
3.	Contact Site Six (6) Weeks in Advance to Discuss the Audit. Address the Following:	o
3a.	• Audit Objectives, Scope, and Schedule	o
3b.	• Availability of Site Manager for Opening/Closing Conferences	o
3c.	• Identification of Any Current SHE Litigation	o
3d.	• Completion of Pre-Audit Questionnaire (PAQ)	o
3e.	• Team Room Availability	o
3f.	• Phone Availability	o
3g.	• Site Intranet Access	o
3h.	• Printer Availability	o
3i	• AV Equipment Availability (e.g., Overhead and/or Computer Projectors)	o
3j.	• On-Site Lunch Availability (Optional)	o

Figure 15.1 *(cont'd)*

NO.	PRE-AUDIT PLANNING ACTIVITY	DONE (?)
	Team Leader Only *(cont'd)*	
3k.	• Site Contact Name(s) and Phone/Fax Numbers	o
3l.	• Directions to the Site	o
3m.	• Ground Transportation Needs	o
3n.	• Hotel Recommendations	o
3o.	• Dress Code and PPE Requirements	o
4.	Send PAQ to Site	o
5.	Assign Areas of Review to Team Members	o
6.	Distribute Completed PAQ and Previous Audit Report to Team	o
7.	Develop Detailed Audit Agenda, Including Timing for Opening/Closing Conferences	o
8.	Distribute Agenda to Site Staff and Team Members	o
9.	Develop/Tailor Opening Conference Presentation	o
10.	Hold Pre-Audit Team Meeting. Address the Following:	o
10a.	• Areas of Responsibility	o
10b.	• Report Writing Responsibility and Expectations	o
10c.	• Need for Portable Computer(s)	o
10d.	• Review of Completed PAQ and Previous Audit Report	o
10e.	• Dress Code and PPE Requirements	o
10f.	• Arrival Time and Means of Transportation	o
10g.	• Departure Time and Means of Transportation	o
10h.	• Site Contact Name(s) and Phone/Fax Numbers	o
10i.	• Hotel Name, Location, and Phone/Fax Numbers	o
10j.	• Site and Hotel Directions	o

Figure 15.1 *(cont'd)*

NO.	PRE-AUDIT PLANNING ACTIVITY	DONE (?)
	All Team Members (Including the Team Leader)	
1.	Determine Scope, Objectives, and Schedule	o
2.	Identify Personal Areas of Review	o
3	Participate in the Pre-Audit Team Meeting	o
4.	Assure the above Items 10a-10j Are Covered by the Team Leader in the Meeting	o
5.	Obtain and Review Applicable Pre-Audit Information, Including:	o
5a.	• Completed PAQ or Equivalent	o
5b.	• Company Auditing Standard or Guidelines	o
5c.	• Applicable National or Federal Regulations	o
5d.	• Applicable State or Regional Regulations	o
5e.	• Previous Audit Report	o
5f.	• Applicable Audit Protocols	o
5g.	• Applicable Corporate EH&S Policies, Standards, and Guidelines	o
6.	Obtain Local Weather Forecast (e.g., using www.cnn.com)	o
7.	Research Country Customs and Norms (If Applicable)	o
8.	Bring Language Dictionary (If Applicable)	o
9.	Determine/Comply with Passport, Visa, and Vaccination Requirements (If Applicable)	o
10.	Determine Electrical Adapter Requirements (If Applicable)	o

A detailed discussion of each of the pre-audit activities is presented below.

Team Selection and Formation

The audit program manager selects the audit team leader and together they typically select the remainder of the team members. Team members should have complementary and overlapping skills, if at all possible. As discussed elsewhere in this book, auditors should be prepared for any circumstance in the field. Auditors can become ill, especially overseas, or otherwise indisposed. One is sometimes asked to pitch in and cover the areas that one of the team is not addressing.

Thought should also be given to paring relatively inexperienced auditors with suitable mentors; not every audit should get the "A" team, otherwise the experienced auditor pool will never expand.

In the U.S., it is helpful to have one or more auditors on the team from the same state but independent of the site. This aids in conducting an independent review of state regulatory applicability.

Some companies assign to the audit team the EH&S coordinator from the next site to be audited. This gives that person a good idea of the process and will help him or her be better prepared for the upcoming visit.

One should also consider language when creating an audit team. Even in North America this issue can come into play. Having an auditor who can speak French on an audit in Quebec or an auditor who can speak Spanish on an audit in Mexico or Puerto Rico can be very advantageous. For better or worse, cultural issues should be considered, at least to some extent. On one recent third-party review of a corporate audit program, one of the criticisms of the audits was that "corporate keeps sending these Yankees with attitudes down here to audit us. We don't appreciate it." Cultural diversity on audit teams can be a wonderful asset when auditing a wide geographic and culturally diverse area.

Finally, once the audit team is selected, there should be a team meeting prior to the audit. This can be handled in a variety of ways. A face-to-face meeting is preferred but not always possible. A teleconference or video conference is an acceptable substitute. The team may also schedule a meeting for the evening before the audit. This approach should be used sparingly because it might be too late at this time to make any last minute adjustments. And there is always the risk that one or more auditors' flights will be late and the meeting will never take place.

Completion and Review of the Pre-Audit Questionnaire

The purpose of the pre-audit questionnaire is twofold. First, it enables the audit team to become familiar with the general EH&S-related activities and operations before they arrive on site. Second, it serves as a timely alert to the facility manager so that he may better prepare himself and his staff for the audit.

An important element of a good pre-audit questionnaire should be its brevity. Normally fifteen to twenty-five pages is sufficient. The pre-audit questionnaire should ask only for general information on the facility. Its primary purpose is to enable the audit team to be sufficiently aware of plant EH&S activities so that relevant regulations and requirements can be obtained and reviewed. An example of an environmental pre-audit questionnaire is included as Appendix G.

Several important lessons on pre-audit questionnaires are worth mentioning. If the audit team wants the questionnaire completed, make sure it is simple and straightforward. For example, the questionnaire should not require the site to provide reams of performance data that can be reviewed better when the audit team arrives on site. Make sure it is distributed to the site well in advance. Most importantly, each member of the team must review the questionnaire prior to the on-site activities. There is nothing more inconsiderate than to require the site to complete a questionnaire and then realize that it has not been reviewed by the team in advance of the audit.

Review of Relevant Regulations

There are numerous regulatory requirements that are administered by federal, state, and local authorities. Once the pre-audit questionnaire has been returned to the audit team, a thorough review of the relevant regulations affecting the facility should be undertaken. There are several methods that can be used to obtain the regulations. Direct contact with regulatory agencies and asking for copies of the regulations is an appropriate technique. This is particularly useful on the local level for such items as sewer ordinances, county/city effluent limitations, air emission regulations promulgated by air quality management districts, and flammable/combustible storage and handling regulations issued by local health or fire departments.

In the U.S., there are numerous computerized regulatory database systems available that provide for fast retrieval of federal and state regulations through the use of key words (e.g, Government Institutes, Enflex, BNA, RegScan). These products have become quite cost-effective in the past few years. Most provide regulatory information on CDs or the same information can be loaded onto a company's Intranet. Auditors often bring the CDs into the field. More details on these systems are presented in the chapter on information management. Internationally, teams can access country regulations through books, the Internet, local consultants, embassies, and to a limited extent the computerized regulatory database systems (e.g., Enflex maintains regulations for six countries). Simply because it is an international audit does not mean that regulatory data gathering should be ignored. In almost all cases, at least limited regulatory information is available.

Suffice it so say, audit teams must have some access to national, state, and local regulations during the course of the audit. Protocols and checklists only go so far.

Definition of Audit Scope and Establishment of Team Responsibilities

An important pre-audit activity is to define clearly the audit scope and audit team responsibilities. It is not necessary that all areas be audited during the site visit if it is felt that time would be better spent concentrating on a few compliance areas that represent a higher exposure. An EH&S audit scope could consist of any or all categories shown in Figure 15.2.

Once the team decides on the areas that will be the subject of the audit, each team member should be given a specific assignment and responsibility to serve as the auditor for that compliance area. The auditor can then prepare to be fully ready to start his or her portions of the audit efficiently once the team arrives on site.

Figure 15.2 Typical Compliance Areas on an EH&S Audit

Air Emissions
Incinerators
VOC sources
Hazardous air pollutants
Fuel burners
Fugitive emissions
Vehicle emissions

Wastewater Discharges

Direct discharges (NPDES)
Indirect discharges (POTW)
Stormwater discharges
Treatment plant operations
Certification/licenses

Hazardous Waste

Generator requirements
Universal wastes
TSD requirements
Manifests/records
Off-site disposal

Oil Spill Control

SPCC/FRP Plans
Spill reporting
Training

Solid Waste
Permitted facilities
Monitoring for segregation
Proper disposal

PCBs

In-use equipment inspection
Temporary storage
Permanent storage facility
Disposal

Pesticides

Application certification
Storage and handling
Disposal

USTs/ASTs

Registration of tanks
Leak detection
Monitoring and reporting
Overfill protection

Drinking Water

Water use permits
Backflow prevention/cross connects
Sampling/analysis

In some cases, it may be appropriate to have two members of the team audit the more complex compliance areas. This should be decided by the team before the audit commences.

Other issues that should be discussed by the audit team before the on-site activities start are whether staff organization and company management systems, procedures, and policies are going to be reviewed during the audit. For instance, is this audit going to look past the "strict regulatory requirements" and evaluate the attitude and effectiveness of the plant EH&S staff? And should the team review potential liabilities under common law that could create exposure for the plant? Will the team assess the need for improved EH&S management procedures at the facility? These items, which go beyond the traditional regulatory requirements, are typical of the questions the audit team should discuss during their pre-audit activities.

Figure 15.2 *(cont'd)* **Typical Compliance Areas on an EH&S Audit**

Hazardous Materials

Flammable/combustible storage/handling
Acid and caustic storage/handling
Gas cylinder storage/handling

Hazard Communication

Training
MSDSs
Labeling

Community Right-to-Know

Inventory monitoring & reporting
Reporting of releases
Emergency response planning

Occupational Health

Ventilation systems
Exposure monitoring
Training
Illness/Injury Recordkeeping
PPE/Respirators
Hearing conservation
Medical surveillance
Bloodborne pathogens
Heat and cold stress

Confined Spaces

Written program
Identification of spaces/signs
Annual program audit
Completed permits
Training and recordkeeping

Hazardous Energy

Written program
Training and recordkeeping
Annual program audit
Contractor Training and Checking

Fire Prevention

Prevention and evacuation plan
Fire extinguishers
Drills and training
Flammables storage and grounding

Ergonomics

Management commitment
Employee involvement
Training and communication
Engineering controls
Administrative controls
Medical management

Development of a Detailed Audit Agenda or Plan

The success of the on-site audit will depend largely on how well the audit team has prepared itself and the facility staff. A good technique is to develop a daily agenda that describes the activities planned for each day of the audit. A typical daily agenda for an environmental audit is shown in Figure 15.3. The agenda allows the facility manager to alert key facility staff when they will be required to talk with the auditors and, generally, the audit topics that will be covered.

Figure 15.3 Sample Itinerary for an Audit

Day 1—Monday a.m.

The audit team meets with the host facility manager and environmental manager to make introductions and review purpose of the audit. Refine schedules for interviews, tours, and special requirements.

The environmental coordinator makes a brief presentation to the audit team, highlighting major facilities and features of the facility.

There is a general tour of the facility to provide audit team with orientation of overall facility. This is a brief "ride through" of key areas on the facility.

Day 1—Monday p.m.

The team conducts a detailed audit of *wastewater discharge* compliance. Physically inspect discharge points, treatment facilities, NPDES permits, monitoring records, and other related data. Conduct interviews with key facility staff.

The team conducts a detailed audit of *air emissions* compliance. Physically inspect fuel burning facilities, incinerators, sources of VOC emissions, and other air emission sources. Review air monitoring records, inspection records, permits, and licenses. Conduct interviews with key facility staff.

The team meets at the end of the day, without site environmental staff, to discuss interim findings and general observations.

Day 2—Tuesday a.m.

The audit team briefs the site environmental staff on interim findings and they plan the daily agenda.

Conduct audit of *hazardous waste management* compliance. Physically inspect hazardous waste generation points (e.g., shops, process areas, storage yards, warehouses). Inspect manifests, waste analysis records, RCRA permits, groundwater monitoring, and inspection plans/schedules. Conduct interviews with key facility staff. (Depending on facility size and hazardous waste activities, this audit could take a full day or more.)

Day 2—Tuesday p.m.

Conduct audit of *hazardous materials management* compliance. Physically inspect hazardous waste chemical storage areas and warehouses. Review spill contingency plans, spill reporting procedures, and incident reports. Conduct interviews with key staff.

Conduct audit of *fuel/oil storage and spill response* compliance. Physically inspect oil storage areas, tank farms, and drum storage areas. Review oil spill contingency plans, spill reports, and SPCC Plans. Conduct interviews with key staff.

The team meets at the end of the day, without site environmental staff, to discuss interim findings and general observations.

Day 3—Wednesday a.m.

The audit team briefs the site environmental staff on interim findings and they plan the daily agenda.

Figure 15.3 *(cont'd)* **Sample Itinerary for an Audit**

The team conducts an audit of *PCB handling/storage* compliance. Physically inspect areas where transformers/capacitors are maintained. Review records of testing for PCB content, inspection logs, annual reports, and disposal records. Conduct interviews with key staff.

The team conducts an audit of *pesticides handling/storage* compliance. Physically inspect pesticide storage areas. Review records of pesticide applications, certifications for applicators, and disposal records. Conduct interviews with key staff.

Day 3—Wednesday p.m.
The team conducts an audit of *water supply/distribution* compliance. Physically inspect well facilities and pump house treatment facilities. Review records of water quality monitoring, water withdrawal, distribution system inspection records, and conduct interviews with key staff.

The team conducts an audit of *solid waste handling/disposal* compliance. Physically inspect areas of facility with asbestos insulation. Inspect handling/disposal procedures. Review records of disposal of asbestos. Conduct interviews with key staff.

The team meets at the end of the day, without site environmental staff, to discuss interim findings and general observations.

Day 4—Thursday a.m.
The audit team briefs the site environmental staff on interim findings and they plan the daily agenda.

The team conducts a general inspection of areas just outside facility boundaries, especially residential areas. Look for potential "common law" environmental nuisance problems (i.e., emissions, noise, odor, etc.).

The team continues audits as before.

Day 4—Thursday p.m.
This period is reserved to conduct audits of any special areas that are uncovered once the team is on site. It is a period to review the previous days' activities. Additional data or information needs are identified and any unfinished items are completed. Perhaps a second visit to an area on site is needed or some discussion on the applicability of certain regulations is required. This period is also used by the audit team to develop a preliminary list of audit findings for an information briefing to key staff.

Day 5—Friday a.m.
The audit team makes an informal briefing to key environmental staff on preliminary findings of audit. The purpose of this briefing is to alert the staff of any significant compliance problems found so that corrective actions may be initiated. The meeting is also used to verify the validity of the findings with site environmental management prior to meeting with the facility manager.

The audit team conducts a formal closing briefing to facility manager.

The audit team departs the facility.

Review of Audit Protocols

Audit protocols are typically used with some discretion. More experienced auditors will often use the checklists as reference documents, reviewing them in detail each morning and evening, to assure themselves that they are not overlooking any aspect of compliance. These auditors sometimes develop one-page reminder sheets that cover the major compliance categories for each area. Other, perhaps less-experienced, auditors will use the checklists verbatim during the course of the inspections and interviews.

The advantages of the first approach are the increased flexibility for the auditor and his ability to interview staff without the intimidating presence of a checklist. Although these advantages are typically lost in the second approach, use of the more rigorous second approach is less likely to result in the auditor overlooking noncompliance items.

There are some companies and organizations that have decided to utilize the commercial, computerized audit protocols available in the marketplace. These are excellent tools, both comprehensive and current. However, one should be wary of their use in the field. Teams that are required to answer every protocol question in order to generate a report, find that protocol completion can interfere with the conduct of the audit. The team will often spend too much time behind the computer screen and not enough reviewing records, observing the facility and its activities, and otherwise verifying compliance.

Regardless of the protocol techniques selected, the auditor should familiarize himself or herself thoroughly with the protocol prior to the audit. If the auditor chooses the first approach (i.e., using the protocols as reference tools), he or she probably should develop the one-page summary sheets prior to the site visit. It is also important to include compliance items on the protocols that reflect local regulatory requirements (e.g., city, county, and region).

Arrange Logistics

Logistics is not a trivial concern on EH&S audits. The pre-audit checklist provided in Figure 15.1 lists any number of items that must be addressed, including hotels, rental cars, and safety gear. The team leader must discuss these items with the site staff well in advance of the audit. It is not fun to stay at a hotel that is 90 minutes from the plant site because there is a NASCAR race in town and nearby hotels were sold out. Also, the team should take advantage of the Internet whenever possible. There are websites for inexpensive airline reservations (e.g., www.priceline.com), hotels (e.g., www.marriott.com), weather forecasts (e.g., www.weather.com), and driving directions (e.g., www.mapquest.com). Utilizing the resources at hand will help to assure that the team arrives on time, prepared, and rested.

ON-SITE ACTIVITIES

On-site activities during an EH&S audit will include the following primary functions:

- Opening conference
- Orientation tour
- Records/documentation review
- Staff interviews
- Physical inspection of facilities
- Daily reviews
- Closing conference
- Development of the audit report.

Not all of the above activities are, strictly speaking, auditing. Be aware that the three principal auditing verification tasks, records reviews, interviews, and facility inspections, represent only about 50 percent of the time spent in the field on an audit. So a five-day audit involves about two and a half days of actual auditing. This takes many first-time auditors by surprise.

Opening Conference

Each audit should begin with an opening conference involving the audit team and site operational and EH&S management. This meeting, while it might begin with a welcome by the plant manager, is the responsibility of the audit team leader, who sets the agenda and keeps it running on time. Advice on how to run the opening conference is presented in Chapter 17 of this book and a model opening conference presentation is provided in Appendix H. One of the most important things to remember about the opening conference is to *arrive on time*. The audit will not proceed smoothly if the audit team is late and the site's management team is wasting time waiting for them to arrive. Late arrivals occur more than one might imagine.

Orientation Tour

After the opening conference, the audit team is usually taken on an orientation tour. This allows the team to gain an appreciation for the relative complexity of the site and the operations. Some tips for completing this tour are:

1. Give the site escort a time limit for the tour (usually about one hour) and, for subsequent scheduling purposes, assume you will run over by 15 minutes. Tell the escort what you would like to see. Use the pre-audit questionnaire to help focus the exercise.

2. For environmental (as opposed to health and safety) audits, work from the outside of the facility inwards. Focus on the following general areas:

   ■ The fence line

   ■ Stormwater and wastewater outfalls

   ■ Critical environmental areas (e.g., wetlands)

   ■ On-site disposal and equipment "boneyards"

   ■ Critical storm drainage areas

   ■ The wastewater treatment plant

   ■ Major tank farms and materials loading/unloading areas

   ■ Underground storage tank locations

   ■ Major liquid materials tank and container areas

   ■ Solid/hazardous waste tank and container areas

   ■ Hazardous waste treatment systems (e.g., neutralization, incineration)

   ■ Used oil and solvent storage areas

   ■ The powerhouse and electrical substations

   ■ Maintenance (e.g., shops, pesticide storage)

   ■ Laboratories and medical clinics

   ■ Process and manufacturing areas.

3. If you need to request a vehicle to observe remote areas, do so. Generally, you will be able to return to most plant areas later, but for remote areas this may not be the case. Make careful initial observations in these situations.

4. Be careful not to spend too much time in the process or manufacturing areas. Auditors generally find these areas personally fascinating, but detailed observation of manufacturing does not always provide substantial EH&S compliance or performance information, except for certain topics such as personal protective equipment, machine guarding, and the like.

5. If the audit, because of the size of the site, requires a large team (more than four), split the team in two and request two escorts. Organize the orientations based on relative areas of interest among the two audit sub-teams.

6. Take notes when on the tour, but other than for remote areas, do not get into too much detail. It will slow down the process. Try to note particular areas you would like the team to re-visit.

7. Bring a one-page plot plan or site map with you to help with the site orientation.

8. If feasible, do not retrace your steps so that you see as much of the facility in as short a time as possible. For example, try not to return to the office by the same route you left.

9. Try to have the team stay together as much as possible. There will be a tendency for team members to wander off. This not only slows down the process but the escort often makes significant comments during the tour, which some team members might not hear.

10. Arrive at the plant early on the first day of the audit and attempt to drive along the site boundary to obtain a different perspective. This may help during the orientation tour.

Records/Documentation Review

As noted earlier, a good audit protocol will provide the auditor instructions on the records, files, and reports he or she should request during the audit. More importantly, it should help the auditor understand what he or she should be looking for when the documentation is reviewed. Normally, records should be reviewed just before conducting interviews and inspecting facilities. However, often it is useful to review documentation at the same time an interview is being conducted or an operation is being inspected. This will depend on the area being audited and the individual style of the auditors. As a general rule, however, auditors should spend their initial efforts reviewing the records and files associated with the specific compliance area, to gain a better understanding of the key compliance issues at the facility.

Figure 15.4 lists some of the most significant records, files, and reports that should be reviewed by the auditors. They are broken down by the typical compliance areas and operations normally found at industrial facilities.

One of the important things to remember when reviewing documentation is that many compliance requirements are contained within the records. For example, an NPDES permit may have numerous conditions in the boiler-plate on Best Management Practices (BMPs). The auditor will need to scan these documents, looking specifically for applicable terms, conditions, or requirements, and then verify that these requirements are being met.

When appropriate, auditors should obtain copies of relevant documentation uncovered during the audit when it is felt that this can aid them in evaluating the compliance status of the facility. Also, it is useful as reference material to write the audit report at the conclusion of the audit.

During the course of the audit, a file of working papers will develop. It is not uncommon for an audit team to leave the facility with a thick file of records, reports, or other documentation. However, the rule-of-thumb is to make copies only of those

Figure 15.4 EH&S Compliance Audit Program Example Documents to Review

General

Corporate policies and procedures
Site organization chart
Site standard operating procedures
Management of change procedure
Illness and injury reports
Incident response reports
Notices of violation
Agency inspection reports
General EH&S correspondence
Self-audits
Training records and job descriptions
Emergency response plan

Air

Title V Permit
O&M records
Source emission inventory
Boiler opacity records
Stack emission test records
Fuel use reports
Stack/vent operating certificates

Occupational Health

Respiratory protection program
Hearing conservation program
Hazard communication program
MSDSs
Bloodborne pathogen program
PPE assessment
Ergonomics program
Sanitation inspections
Exposure monitoring records

Water

NPDES Permit
Discharge monitoring reports
Exception reports
Laboratory certifications
Sludge disposal permit
Off-site disposal records
Operator training certifications
O&M records
Stormwater management plan
SPCC/FRP Plan
Potable water inspection records

Waste

Hazardous waste manifests
Biennial/annual reports
Manifest exception reports
Waste analysis test results
Contingency plan
Inspection records
Medical waste records
Training records
Waste minimization plan
Treatment/disposal permit

General Safety

Confined space entry program
Completed permits
Hazardous energy program
Fire prevention program
Emergency response equipment inspections
OSHA 200 log
Machine guarding inspections
Fork lift truck inspections
Rope and chain inspections
Harness inspections
Crain and hoist inspections

materials that the audit team needs to perform a complete and thorough evaluation of the facility's compliance status. Finally, be careful about leaving the site with documents in your possession, which you have yet to review. This may mean that you have not completed your review and it will be difficult to conduct a follow-up verification of apparent deficiencies once back in your office.

Some helpful guidance on developing an effective document review strategy is:

- **Obtain what you can ahead of time, within reason.** Asking for a copy of the site's RCRA Part B Permit to be sent ahead of time is not typically feasible. However, requesting a copy of the site's written confined space entry procedure is more reasonable.

- **Review records first.** Many auditable requirements (e.g., inspections, maintenance procedures) are found in the documents.

- **Don't get overwhelmed with the task at hand.** There will typically be thousands of pages of records. Start with strategic documents in each of the compliance areas (e.g., written programs and procedures) and see where that leads you.

- **Ask for quiet time if you need it.** Nobody wants to be watched while they read. When a site person is hovering next to you, concentrating becomes difficult.

- **Develop a list of verifiable requirements.** These are items such as training, inspections, and the like that you will want to assure the site is completing consistent with the requirements.

Remember, reviewing records is a critical, if tedious, audit task. Do it completely, but do it efficiently.

Interviews with Facility Staff

Proper interviewing during an EH&S audit is perhaps the single most important aspect of the audit process. Yet, too often, lack of attention to the subtleties of interviewing results in less than optimal results. There are a number of interviewing skills and techniques that, if followed, can enhance the outcome of the audit.

Schedule Interviews Ahead of Time

Popping in on busy superintendents or shop supervisors is a sure way to cause ill feelings and poor audit results. An interview should be scheduled well ahead of time so that the person being interviewed is prepared and ready for the auditor. If possible, the interviewee should be told ahead of time the purpose of the audit, the general types of questions that will be asked, and the types of documentation the auditor will want to review. Often the interviewee will suggest that someone else in the shop be available for the interview because the auditor's questions can be better answered by that person. This is to be encouraged because the whole purpose of the interview is to obtain the best evidence available, relative to the compliance status of the facility. If at all possible, at least a one-day advance notice should be given to all interviewees.

However, there are exceptions to this rule of notification. In some instances, the auditor might want to simply walk the shop floor and ask operators or technicians a few questions. Examples include:

■ What would you do in case of an emergency or a spill?

■ Do you attend any safety meetings?

■ What PPE is required in the various areas?

■ Is there any difference in what you do when you rotate onto the night shift?

You should receive permission first to conduct these "casual" interviews, especially in union shops, but they should be part of your audit process. Don't be too concerned about the unannounced nature of the interviews; everyone at the site will be on high alert as you can be assured that they have been notified of your presence well in advance.

Conduct Interviews in the Workspaces

Conducting interviews in the workspace of the interviewee serves several purposes. First of all, the person being interviewed is more relaxed and less defensive than he might be if summoned to the plant manager's office or other similar location for the interview. Second, key records and files are often maintained in the workspace and will be more readily available to the auditor. Third, the auditor has an opportunity to observe first-hand actual workplace conditions, attitudes of plant staff, and other subtleties that would not be observable in the plant manager's office or conference room.

The one disadvantage to conducting interviews in the workplace is that distractions and interruptions likely will occur. The interviewee will face phone calls, employees with a problem, and other similar distractions. Also, it is often noisy in many workplaces and difficult to communicate.

The auditor should make it clear to the interviewee that he would like his attention and would appreciate some uninterrupted time. An opening statement may be appropriate such as, "Hello Mr. Smith, I know you have a tight schedule, as I do. If you could put your telephone calls on hold and minimize interruptions from your staff, I know I can be finished with these questions in short order and let you get back to work."

Be Sensitive to the Interviewee's Nervousness and Defensiveness

This may seem obvious, but often is not perceived by auditors. There is a normal negative reaction associated with an audit of any kind regardless of the auditor's plea that "I'm only here to help you." The auditor must continue to reassure the interviewee that the purpose of the audit is to uncover the areas that need more attention, resources, staff training, and the like in order to comply with the law and/ or corporate expectations. It is not an audit of the interviewee, but rather an evaluation of the systems that are needed to help him or her do his or her job better and more efficiently.

Some people will view the auditor as a threat to their job security. The auditor should be sensitive to this and ask questions in a constructive, respectful, and unemotional manner. If an interviewee becomes overly negative, sarcastic, or uncooperative, it is better to terminate the interview at that point and discuss the problem with the team's site host. Most people who are interviewed are nervous to begin with and become more so if they sense their responses to the auditor's questions are not the correct ones. Sometimes, they will dig a hole for themselves as they try and grope for the right answer. When the interviewee is struggling, the auditor should change the subject rather than probe more deeply. Move on to either other audit questions or perhaps curtail the audit temporarily and talk about some other topic to relax the interviewee.

Avoid Yes/No Responses to Questions

Questions asked during an audit should be focused on getting the interviewee to open up and discuss compliance issues. That is, ask open-ended questions. Avoid closed-ended questions that give the person an easy "yes/no" response. "Do you inspect the PCB storage facility every 30 days as the regulations require?" may result in a simple "yes" because he assumes that's what he is supposed to do. He may not even be aware of any requirement to inspect PCB storage facilities. "Tell me about your procedures to ensure your PCB equipment isn't leaking" is a more open-ended question, which will reveal much more about the interviewee's knowledge of PCB inspection requirements.

In summary, if these suggestions are followed, auditors will obtain more precise information about the conditions at the facility. Interviewing is a personal, interactive process. Each auditor will have his or her own unique style and attitude. As an aid, a list of recommendations that all auditors should review before conducting interviews is provided here:

- ■ Call the interviewee and schedule the exact time and place of the interview at least a few hours ahead of time.

- ■ Upon meeting the interviewee, introduce yourself and explain who you are, where you are from, and why you are auditing the facility.

- ■ First, relax the interviewee and get him to explain who he is and his roles and responsibilities.

■ Don't become captive to your checklist so that effective communication is hampered.

■ Ask open-ended questions; avoid questions that require only a yes or no answer.

■ Don't ask questions about compliance items that can be better evaluated by physical inspection or documentation review at a later stage of the audit.

■ Don't preach to or intimidate the interviewee by your knowledge of the regulations. Don't quote or give citations unless this information is requested and you think it will help the interviewing process.

■ Ask the interviewee about previous audits/inspections relative to the compliance area you are auditing. This is a good place to start.

■ Solicit input from the interviewee about how the audit should be conducted for maximum effectiveness. Make him a part of the audit process not the subject of it.

■ Be careful not to tell or order the interviewee to do anything during the interview. Remember you are there to obtain information and identify problems, not to solve them during the audit. That will come later.

■ When appropriate, and if it helps the interview to proceed more effectively, make general comments that are instructional in nature as long as they are not construed to be directives from the auditor.

■ At the time that noncompliance items are being identified, don't make the interviewee uncomfortable by your reaction. Continue to assure him that the audit is not intended to be a personal inquisition but a process to identify problems that are typically found at facilities.

■ Be empathetic as you talk to the interviewee but don't cross the line and become too sympathetic to his or her problems. The interview could last longer than it needs to.

■ Be quick to distinguish the "hostile interviewee" who doesn't want to cooperate, from the "nervous interviewee" who is simply uptight about being questioned.

Physical Inspection of Facilities

There are many facilities, operations, pieces of equipment, and other physical systems that need to be observed or inspected during an audit. In this section some fundamental concepts relating to audit techniques that should be employed during the on-site inspection will be discussed. The next chapter will present more specific examples of inspection items and typical compliance problems that auditors should look for in several compliance areas.

Inspect Remote Areas

Many facilities will have remote areas that in the past or perhaps currently have been used for storage or handling of hazardous materials. It is important that the auditor thoroughly review the facility for these locations, because the plant staff may not realize they represent potential problems. A good example is shown in Figure 15.5, a picture all too common at industrial facilities. Trailers like the one shown in the picture are favorite hiding places for forgotten drums of hazardous materials. The drums shown stacked are empty according to the plant staff, but are they? Why does the road seem oily? Do the transformers contain PCBs?

Areas like the one shown in the picture may have become part of the landscape to people working at the facility. The auditor's job is to diligently inspect the area to determine if potential problems exist.

The same can be said for remote buildings or buildings that are said to contain no hazardous materials or operations, as shown in Figure 15. 6. Is this building truly free of hazardous materials? Are any liquid chemicals, including oils, stored near

Figure 15.5 Inspecting Remote Areas

floor drains? What about asbestos? Has the building been surveyed? What about the floor drains? Where do they go? Do employees work in this building? What are the PPE requirements? Is there a working ventilation system? Are there eyewashes, emergency showers, or fire extinguishers that need to be inspected?

Observations Must Be Timed to Verify Compliance

There are inspections of certain compliance areas that can only be verified adequately if the inspection is timed to occur at the optimal moment. This is normally related to equipment operation inspection items. For example, air quality regulations in most states usually allow no visible emissions except during periods of start-up, maintenance, or trouble-shooting. During these events, short periods (four to six minutes/hour) of opacity are permitted. If the auditor does not observe the stack shown in Figure 15.7 during one of these events, a true verification of compliance may not be obtained. Observing the air emission source only during the period it is running in a steady-state condition may lead the auditor to the conclusion that the facility is always in compliance. A good technique, therefore, is to schedule the inspection of the source shown in Figure 15.7 at a period when it is started up for the day or during a maintenance period.

Some examples of critical activities that should be observed by an audit team if at all possible include:

- Safety meetings
- New construction or demolition
- Emergency response drills
- Inspections and sampling
- Loading and unloading
- Materials handling and transfer
- Process equipment startups and shutdowns
- Waste packing and pickup
- Confined space entries
- Lock, tag, and try.

For most of these activities (e.g., loading and unloading, confined space entries), the auditor must answer two key questions: First, does the formal procedure meet the company or regulatory requirements? Second, is it being followed? Physical observation of these activities helps to answer the second question. Too often, audit teams focus only on answering the first question.

Figure 15.6 Inspecting Buildings

Figure 15.7 Timing Inspections

Figure 15.8 Inspecting the Fence Line

Inspection of Facilities

Observe the Facility from the Outside

The facility shown in Figure 15.8 may look different to the auditor from the outside looking in than it does from a perspective inside the plant. Nuisance conditions that are sometimes more obvious from a distance include odors, fumes, mists, excessive noise, fugitive dust, and even unknown discharges or runoff under the fence line. With the growing interest and awareness by the public of the community right-to-know legislation and their rights under these regulations, it is more important than ever that industrial facilities use the audits as an opportunity to evaluate and monitor the environmental profile they create in the neighboring community.

Observe Emergency Response Plans in Action

Many EH&S regulations require industrial facilities to prepare and maintain emergency response plans that should include specific response actions in the event of inadvertent spills, discharges, fires, or other unplanned events. Clearly, as part of the records review phase of the audit discussed earlier in this chapter, the auditor conducts an evaluation of the emergency response plans for completeness. What is also perhaps more revealing to observe first hand is how staff at the facility actually respond when an incident occurs.

If at all possible, a drill or exercise should be scheduled during the audit, so that the auditor can observe how the facility personnel react and if the plan is understood by those who are responsible for responding (see Figure 15.9). A drill or exercise may not be necessary if the auditor happens to be on site when an actual emergency release or unpermitted discharge or leak occurs. If this happens during the inspection, the auditor should immediately seize this opportunity, stand back and observe how the facility employees carry out the procedures in the contingency plan.

Yet, it is more likely that a drill cannot be staged during the audit. In these cases, the team should assure itself that drills are routinely conducted by the site, and there should be documents prepared and available for review discussing any opportunities for improvement and actions needed to implement those improvements.

Observe Sampling/Monitoring Procedures

In some cases, chemical or physical sampling and analysis is included as part of an audit, as in the case of taking split samples of a wastewater discharge to verify NPDES permit compliance. However, the majority of audits being conducted today do not include this activity as part of the audit protocol. The prevailing attitude is that a one-shot grab sample is not a valid technique in evaluating compliance on a

Figure 15.9 Emergency Response Drills

Demonstration of Contingency Plan

daily basis. Most firms seem to focus on auditing proper sampling and analysis methodology during the audit rather than expending resources on actual analysis of samples.

As shown in Figure 15.10, the technician is observed by the auditor to verify if proper sampling protocols are followed. Items observed would include: (1) use of

Figure 15.10 Auditing Sampling Procedures Evidence Gathering

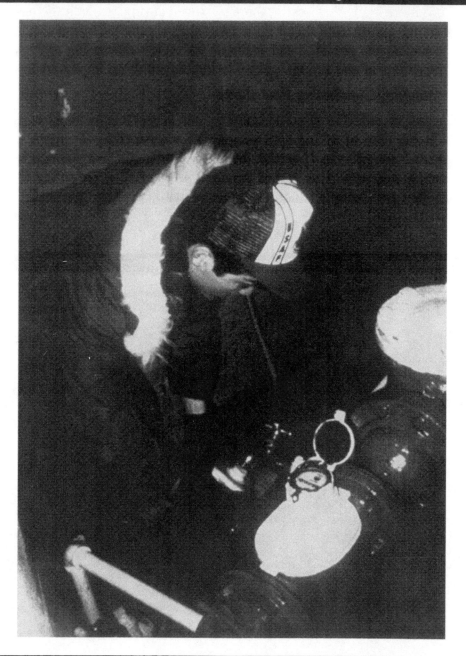

clean sterile sampling containers, (2) not exceeding holding times and temperatures, (3) proper chain of custody procedures, and (4) samples sent to certified laboratories.

These fundamental audit techniques are considered to be effective mechanisms to verify compliance when auditors are conducting on-site physical inspections. Obviously, they must be used with judgment depending on the audit objectives, scope, resources available, size of facility, and other related factors.

There are two key questions auditors often have with respect to the evidence gathering phase of the audit. The first is, how do I really spend my time in the field to assure proper verification? The second is, do I have to review everything? Some thoughts on these two questions are provided below.

During the course of an audit, there are three principal evidence-gathering techniques: records review, interviews, and physical inspections. A good rule of thumb for the auditor is the law of thirds. That is, the auditor's verification efforts should be split equally among the three evidence-gathering techniques. Many auditors have a difficult time doing this. Quite often, interviews suffer because an auditor is much more comfortable reviewing documents and "kicking the tires." Sitting across from an individual with the intent of asking probing questions about potential deficiencies is not an easy task, but it must be done.

Auditors must be thorough in their field investigations. This is true whether the investigation is a review of paperwork or a physical inspection of the plant equipment. However, this does not necessarily mean that the auditor must review each of several thousand hazardous waste manifests or several hundred air emission sources, for example, to meet the thoroughness objective.

Sampling is a common technique used during EH&S audits when a large universe of items needs to be reviewed. Statistical sampling can provide a means to identifying the number of items to be reviewed to be fairly confident the results are representative of the universe. Auditors should be at least knowledgeable of statistical sampling techniques and can use the information in Figure 15.11 to determine a representative sample. Where sampling techniques are utilized on an audit, teams should be careful to document the approach taken.

It is important to note, however, that the use of statistical sampling on EH&S audits is more the exception than the rule. This is mostly due to the small population size of EH&S activities. Note that in order to achieve a 95 percent confidence level that the selected sample represents the total items, the minimum expectation of most statisticians, an auditor would have to review 80 of 100 items. Most would justifiably ask, why not review the entire population?

Regardless of whether statistical sampling techniques are utilized, it is important to note that auditors will not review all records or pieces of equipment during the course of an audit. Thus, it is quite important to communicate the approach taken. Auditors should keep three numbers in mind when communicating results: the population (e.g., the total number of fire extinguishers on site), the sample size

Figure 15.11 Selecting a Sample Size on EH&S Audits

Population Size	Suggested Minimum Sample Size		
	A	B	C
10	98%	88%	72%
25	94%	74%	49%
50	89%	58%	32%
100	80%	41%	19%
250	61%	21%	8%
500	43%	12%	4%
1000	28%	6%	2%
2000	16%	3%	1%

Source: Inman, R.L. and Conover, W.J., *A Modern Approach to Statistics* (1983), and Cochran, W.G., *Sampling Techniques, Second Edition,* New York: John Wiley & Sons, Inc., (1977).

A - Suggested minimum sample size for a population(s) being reviewed that is considered to be extremely important in terms of verifying compliance with applicable requirements, and/or is of critical concern to the corporation in terms of potential or actual impacts associated with noncompliance. A confidence level of 95 percent is assumed.

B - Suggested minimum sample size for a population(s) being reviewed that will provide additional information to substantiate compliance or noncompliance and/or is of considerable importance to the corporation in terms of potential or actual impacts associated with non-compliance. A confidence level of 90 percent is assumed.

C - Suggested minimum sample size for a population(s) being reviewed that will provide ancillary information in terms of verifying compliance with a requirement. A confidence level of 85 percent is assumed.

(e.g., the number of extinguishers inspected), and the number deficient (e.g., the number of extinguishers that had not received the monthly inspection). This puts the finding in perspective and also avoids misleading site management into believing that the audit team inspected every fire extinguisher and only those identified had not been inspected.

Daily Reviews and Pre-Closing Conference

It is important that the audit team meet with the site EH&S staff daily to discuss progress and interim findings. Based on experience, these meetings are better held in the morning rather than the afternoon. This gives the audit team the night before to organize and cross-check the validity of each auditor's findings. These daily reviews are an important part of the four-step process of communicating findings to plant management and staff. Each and every finding should be communicated:

- When first observed
- At the daily meetings
- At a pre-closing conference
- At the closing conference.

The objective is to have free and open communication during the process and to make the closing conference as boring as possible. If findings are communicated throughout the week, then there should be common agreement during the closing conference with the plant manager. The closing conference is not the time for fireworks.

On the last day of the audit, a pre-closing conference is typically held in place of the daily review meeting. This is essentially a dress rehearsal for the closing conference with site management. Most often, only the key site EH&S managers attend this meeting with the audit team. If there is to be a "bloody" meeting this is it. Any misinterpretations or misunderstandings should be sorted out in this meeting, prior to the official closing conference.

The Closing Conference

A closing conference should take place at the facility being audited before the audit team leaves the site. This is typically a formal meeting and involves the site manager, who may not have been involved in the process since the opening conference. Some thoughts on preparing for and conducting the closing conference are provided below. Further thoughts can be found in Chapter 17.

Preparing for the Closing Conference

1. Determine the time, place, and invitees as soon as possible so that all parties are given proper notice.

2. Organize findings by compliance areas (e.g., air, wastewater, hazardous waste) and prepare a brief handout for people attending the meeting.

3. Plan the meeting to be relatively brief (less than one hour) and focus only on key compliance problems. Leave details to the audit report.

4. Organize findings by type: (1) regulatory, (2) company policy or standard, and (3) company guideline or good management practice.

5. Organize findings by priority, minor, major, or significant, depending on degree of risk, health impact, or other similar criteria.

6. Focus findings on the root causes of the compliance problems, not the symptoms.

7. Rehearse the closing conference with other audit team members and challenge each other to be sure that the findings are valid.

Conducting the Closing Conference

8. Introduce the audit team and state the objectives of the audit and the format for the meeting.

9. Express appreciation to plant management for their cooperation and assistance.

10. Try to avoid using specific names of plant staff when presenting negative findings but specify individuals' names when presenting commendable findings.

11. Avoid confrontation during the meeting with any member of the plant staff who may disagree with your findings.

12. Avoid comparisons to another plant's performance unless it is helpful to make a point.

13. Resist requests to "re-audit" an area before the audit team departs the site so that findings can be left out of the audit report.

14. Discuss the follow-up requirements for the draft and final reports, the corrective action plan, and periodic status reports.

If care is taken to prepare adequately for the closing conference, there should be little to be concerned about. It is principally the communication of factual findings that have been fully verified and previously communicated to site EH&S staff.

The Audit Report

Just about every audit results in a written audit report. This topic is so important that it is the principal topic of another chapter in this book (See Chapter 19 and Appendix I). In general, most audit programs are now attempting to develop draft audit reports or draft audit findings, at a minimum, before the team leaves the site. This helps to maintain the momentum that has been generated by the audit. The team will usually have a report skeleton loaded onto a portable computer, which is brought to the audit. The introduction and facility background sections can even be written before the on-site activities take place. Preparing reports on site can make for some long evenings during the week, but this cost is more than offset by the fact that no (or very little) written work is required of the team once they leave the site.

Chapter 16

TYPICAL COMPLIANCE PROBLEMS FOUND DURING AUDITS

The emerging lesson in a company that ignores environmental requirements is that the middle of the corporate ladder can be a perilous place to perch. At the lower end...the "Nuremberg Defense" can be an effective escape.... And top management may be too far removed from actual or constructive knowledge of polluting activities.

– Michael P. Last, 1989[1]

In this chapter, typical compliance problems and inspection items are presented for each of several areas that may be a part of the scope of an environmental, health, and safety audit. This listing is not intended to be all-inclusive.

In the first section, for each of a variety of compliance areas, the compliance problems most often uncovered during audits are listed. The second section highlights many of the key inspection items associated with these same compliance areas. Photographs of typical plant facilities illustrate the inspection items that an auditor should address when on site.

Finally, at the end of the chapter is an auditor's checklist, which can be used by the team leader as he or she prepares for and conducts an audit.

EH&S AUDITS: WHAT CAN GO WRONG?

The answer to the "what can go wrong?" question is simple, plenty. Audits are not always a successful enterprise. Some of the more typical failings are a result of auditors losing perspective of their role. We can leave the "police officer" approach to the regulatory agency inspectors. Auditors are there to add value and contribute to site improvement and the ultimate goal of zero incidents. What should be your frame of mind when you visit a site as an auditor?

---

[1] "Toxic Torts Put CEOs at Risk," *Environmental Liability* (July/August 1989).

THE "POLICE OFFICER" APPROACH	THE "VALUE-ADDED" APPROACH
We're there to find problems.	We're there to help the site improve.
They will hide things from us; we must be suspicious.	They will be open and candid; still, we should be thorough.
We'll hit the ground running on Monday; real-time planning is the way to go.	We must be sensitive to the site's scheduling needs; we should set an agenda prior to the audit.
The findings are mine; the site doesn't have to agree.	We can negotiate the findings, but the final call is mine.
Findings can be based on my opinion; after all, that's why they're paying me.	My findings should be defensible and based on specific regulatory and company requirements.
We are secretive with the findings until the closing conference.	We communicate openly and freely throughout the on-site process.
We leave nothing behind; a draft report in two weeks is good enough.	We leave at least draft findings so the site can get started.
It's okay if there are new findings in the report that were not discussed while the team was on site.	New findings will be very unlikely; where it happens, we will alert the site prior to issuance of the draft report.
The closing conference will be scheduled based on my travel wishes.	The closing conference will be scheduled to assure that we're done and the plant manager can attend.
Overall. . . We were relentless in identifying, justifying, and reporting the site's deficiencies.	Overall. . . We made a substantial difference in improving the safety and environmental performance at the site.

COMMON COMPLIANCE PROBLEMS

PCB Management

- ■ PCBs in hydraulic systems or heat transfer systems not known
- ■ PCB transformers not inspected quarterly and inspection records incomplete
- ■ PCB transformers not registered with local fire department
- ■ No knowledge of PCB content of utility-owned transformer located on property
- ■ No labeling of PCB-free or PCB-contaminated transformers (making it difficult to identify all PCB transformers)
- ■ Combustible materials stored next to PCB transformers

Out-of-service PCB storage facility not designed properly, including lack of secondary containment, presence of drains and cracked floors, and lack of spill cleanup materials

PCB-contaminated equipment and large, out-of-service PCB high-voltage capacitors stored outside PCB storage facilities, not stored on pallets, and not inspected weekly

Liquid PCBs not stored in U.S. DOT-approved containers

PCB annual reports missing or not prepared in accordance with U.S. EPA regulations

Disposal records/manifests not available or incomplete.

Wastewater Discharges

NPDES permit out of date, or re-application not submitted six months prior to expiration date

Proper sampling procedures not followed

Monitoring equipment not calibrated

Discharge monitoring reports not submitted on time

Occasional exceedances of discharge limits

Excursions not reported immediately to regulatory agencies

Changes in plant operations or discharges not reflected in permit revisions or renewals

Inoperative or poorly maintained monitoring equipment

Unpermitted process wastewaters in shop areas discharging to sewer lines, septic tanks, or streams

Runoff from hazardous materials storage areas discharging to sewer lines or streams

Discharges to a publicly owned treatment works (POTW) contain materials that are fire or explosion hazards, corrosive hazards, or flow obstructions

Unpermitted septic tanks, leach fields, or other on-site wastewater disposal areas

Unpermitted stormwater contaminated discharges to storm sewer or streams

QA/QC procedures not followed by analytical lab; lab not certified.

Air Emissions

■ Air emission points not completely identified, including stacks, vents, wall fans, exhaust ports, incinerators, and fume hoods

■ Air emissions inventory not available or incomplete

■ Air emissions sources not permitted or exemption letters not available

■ Performance testing records not available

■ Monitoring equipment not calibrated or maintained properly

■ Vapor control systems not installed on required sources

■ Submerged fill pipes not installed on gasoline fuel tanks

■ Modifications to air sources not reported to regulators

■ Air pollution alert and emergency plan not available or incomplete

■ Sulfur content of fuel oil not in conformance with regulatory limitations for fuel burners; no certificate of analysis for sulfur content

■ Fugitive dust impacting neighborhood areas

■ Asbestos abatement or demolition activities not reported to regulatory agencies prior to the event

■ Incinerator operations not maintained at correct temperature requirements and charging rates.

Oil Spill Control

■ Spill prevention control and countermeasure (SPCC) plan not signed by a registered professional engineer

■ SPCC plan not updated in the past three years and not consistent with oil storage facilities at the plant

■ No evidence of spill response training

■ Lack of adequate spill control equipment and materials

■ Lack of specific procedures for handling used oil

■ Appropriate containment measures (e.g., dikes, berms) not installed around oil facilities

■ Secondary containment structures cracked, drains present, or signage inadequate for volume of oil present

■ Valves for secondary containment structures left in the open position

■ No procedure for the assessment and disposition of accumulated rainwater in containment structures

■ Oil/water separators not installed before stormwater is discharged to stream or sewer

■ Oil/water separators not maintained and cleaned periodically for efficient operation

■ Aboveground tanks over certain capacities not leak-tested and inspected periodically.

Hazardous Waste Generation

■ Inadequate waste analysis plan, resulting in hazardous waste being handled as nonhazardous waste

■ Satellite accumulation drums improperly labeled and kept in open condition, venting to the atmosphere

■ Hazardous waste manifests file incomplete; return copies or land disposal restrictions notifications/certifications missing

■ Hazardous waste containers stored longer than 90 days

■ Accumulation start dates and other required information missing or incomplete on hazardous waste containers

■ Open top funnels and missing bungs on hazardous waste drums

■ Grounding clips and wires missing on stored drums of flammable hazardous waste

■ Accumulation point not maintained, with improper segregation of incompatible wastes, insufficient aisle space, and unsafe stacking height

■ Accumulation point manager not specifically designated in writing and not properly trained

■ Weekly inspection records of accumulation points not available, incomplete, or missing

■ Emergency response equipment and material not available or inadequate at the accumulation point

■ Contingency plan not available or not maintained at the accumulation point.

Community Right-to-Know

■ Notification not made to state and local authorities

- List of chemicals stored on site not reported to local emergency planning committee

- Hazardous chemical inventories (TIER I and TIER II) not submitted on an annual basis

- Toxic chemical release inventory (TRI) form (FORM R) not submitted by July 1 for previous year to local regulatory authority

- Selected chemicals missing from Tier I, Tier II, and TRI inventories.

Worker Health and Hazard Communication

- Baseline exposure monitoring for hazardous chemicals in the workplace not properly documented for all affected employees

- No documentation available for employee noise exposures

- Periodic noise level measurements not routinely taken

- Written respiratory protection program not documented

- Emergency self-contained breathing apparatus (SCBA) equipment not maintained, tested, or stored properly

- Hazard warning labels not placed on chemical containers in shop areas

- Material identification labels missing on chemical containers in shop areas

- Personal exposure monitoring system not established for exposure to X-rays

- Written hazard communication plan incomplete or out of date, not updated for changes in operations and use and handling of hazardous chemicals in shop areas

- Employee notification of health monitoring results not given in a timely manner

- MSDS sheets not complete for chemicals in the workplace and MSDS files not maintained in an area accessible to employees

- Hazard communication training for employees not conducted or documented

- Food-only refrigerators contain chemicals.

Employee Safety

- Records and certificates for personnel trained in first aid and CPR not available for inspection

- Ventilation systems not routinely maintained, air flow rate not regularly tested, and filters not regularly changed

Machine guards removed by employees or not properly installed

Overhead cranes and lifting equipment not labeled with tonnage rating

Completed confined space entry permits lack selected information

No safety manual or guidelines promulgated or posted for employees access

Fire-fighting piping and hoses not hydrostatically tested or physically inspected on an annual basis

Annual fire extinguisher training for employees not conducted or documented

■ All exits not marked with illuminated signs, and exit paths not clearly marked

Work-related injuries and illnesses records (OSHA 200 LOGS) not maintained properly

Hard-hat, safety-shoes and safety-glasses procedures not uniformly monitored and enforced by plant management

Eye washes, emergency showers, fire extinguishers, fork lift trucks, cranes and hoists, and slings and harnesses not routinely inspected.

Pesticide Management

Pesticide applicators not state-certified or properly trained

Health monitoring for pesticide-handling personnel not conducted or documented

Pesticide-application records not maintained at the plant

■ Pesticide storage facilities not segregated from other non-related spaces

Concentrated pesticides improperly released to sanitary wastewater or stormwater drains

Use of banned pesticides

Pesticide storage not in a dry, well-ventilated area designed for two air changes per hour

Personal protective clothing, such as respirators, masks, gloves, coveralls, and equipment, not available

Restrictions on application of "restricted use" pesticides not followed.

Underground and Aboveground Storage Tanks

Tanks not registered with state regulatory agency

Monthly monitoring not conducted for new tanks

■ Monthly inventory control and tank tightness testing not conducted every five years or as required

■ New tanks not installed with proper corrosion protection

■ New tanks not constructed with proper spill/overfill protection

■ New and existing suction piping not tested every three years

■ New and existing pressurized piping not outfitted with automatic flow restriction, automatic shut-off device, or continuous alarm system; no annual line testing or monthly monitoring.

Hazardous Materials Storage

■ Inside bulk storage of flammable materials not in compliance with design standards (e.g., containment, ventilation, self-closing doors, explosion-proof lighting)

■ Flammable/combustible bulk storage inside buildings not meeting stack heights, aisle space, and quantity restrictions

■ Outside storage areas for flammable/combustible materials not graded or contained to keep spills away from buildings

■ NFPA-approved metal cabinets not used for incidental storage of flammable materials around shops and work areas

■ Flammable materials not put in NFPA-approved safety cans when used around shop areas

■ Dispensing areas for flammable materials missing drip pans under containers

■ Grounding clips missing on containers of highly flammable materials

■ Compressed gas cylinders not tied down and stored in segregated area in one-story building

■ Spills of reportable quantities of hazardous materials not reported to the National Response Center and Coast Guard.

Drinking Water

■ Water withdrawal permits not obtained from regulatory agencies

■ Water treatment plant operators not properly trained or certified, or documentation not available

■ Drinking water not monitored for all required parameters (i.e., nitrates, fluoride, bacteriological, turbidity, radiological, trihalomethanes)

■ Drinking water systems not checked for corrosivity

■ Backflow prevention devices not installed or inspected annually

☐ Exceedances of primary drinking water standards not reported to state within seven days

☐ Public notification procedures not followed when maximum contaminant limits (MCLs) are exceeded

☐ Monthly monitoring reports not sent to state regulatory authorities for bacteriological and turbidity analysis

■ Annual monitoring reports not sent to state regulatory authorities for radiological and chemical analysis.

Solid Waste Disposal

☐ Solid waste disposed of or buried on site without permit or approval from local regulatory agency

☐ Use of off-site disposal facilities that are not properly permitted for solid waste stream

☐ No knowledge of identity of off-site solid waste facilities being used by haulers

☐ Solid waste containing asbestos not sealed in leakproof containers and not disposed of at approved disposal facilities

☐ Solid waste receptacles not meeting design and operational specifications

☐ No procedures to insure that only nonhazardous waste materials are placed in solid waste receptacles

☐ Ash residues or sludges not tested for hazardous constituents before being disposed of as a solid waste

☐ Used oils contaminated with hazardous constituents being disposed of as a nonhazardous waste

■ Ineffective management program for universal wastes.

TYPICAL INSPECTION AREAS

The following pages contain photographs of facilities normally inspected during an EH&S audit. On the page facing each photograph is a list of the key inspection items the auditor should cover during the audit. These photographs are only a representative sample of some of the more common inspection areas; many more facilities, activities, and operations will be inspected during an actual audit.

Figure 16.1 In-Service PCB Transformer

Key Compliance Issue: Labeling and Inspection of PCB Transformers

Figure 16.1 Typical Inspection Items

1. Compare PCB inventory with PCB equipment on the facility for consistency.

2. Inspect PCB transformer locations, look for PCB labels affixed to equipment. They should contain phone numbers or other contact information for emergency response.

3. Look for presence of drains adjacent to PCB transformers and evidence of leaks from equipment.

4. Inspect any PCB transformer locations that pose an exposure risk to food and feed. Ensure weekly inspections are conducted for these units.

5. Inspect logs to ensure all other PCB transformers are inspected quarterly for leaks.

6. For PCB transformers found to be leaking, ensure cleanup is initiated within 48 hours.

Figure 16.2 PCB Transformers Out of Service and Awaiting Disposal

Key Compliance Issue: PCB Storage Facility Standards and Requirements

Figure 16.2 Typical Inspection Items

1. Inspect PCB storage facility for the following:
   - Roof/walls to exclude rainfall
   - 6-inch curb or containment
   - No drains, valves, joints, or openings
   - Floors/curbing continuous and impervious
   - Doors locked or access controlled.

2. Verify that inspection of PCB storage facility is conducted at least every 30 days.

3. Observe presence of cleanup/absorbent materials in storage facility.

4. Observe that all PCB equipment in storage facility is marked with the date it was placed in storage. Disposal must occur within one year.

5. Observe that containers used for storage of PCB liquids do not have removable heads. Typical U.S. DOT specs are 5, 5B, and 17C.

6. Observe that PCB equipment found leaking is contained and cleanup is initiated immediately.

7. Observe that hazardous waste labels are affixed to PCB equipment awaiting disposal.

8. Observe PPE and warning signs at the entrance to the building.

Figure 16.3 Wastewater Treatment Facilities

Key Compliance Issue: Proper Operation and Maintenance to Meet Effluent Limitations

Figure 16.3 Typical Inspection Items

1. Observe general housekeeping, plant conditions, and presence of odors.

2. Observe provision for standby power and look for adequate alarm systems in case of equipment failure.

3. Observe proper operation of all treatment units.

4. Observe spare parts inventory for critical equipment.

5. Inspect O&M manual for consistency with actual plant configuration.

6. Inspect operator and superintendent state certifications.

7. Inspect daily plant operating logs for neatness and clarity.

8. Observe daily sampling procedures at sampling points.

9. Observe effluent bypass points and discuss instances of any hydraulic or organic over-loads at the plant.

10. Observe any on-site sludge disposal areas. Look for evidence of disease vectors, sur-face runoff control, seeding, or other cover measures.

11. Observe posting of safety or occupational hazards and contingency measures.

Figure 16.4 Stormwater Discharges

Key Compliance Issue: Contaminated Stormwater Discharge

Figure 16.4 Typical Inspection Items

1. Observe outfall for obvious signs of contamination (e.g., odors, discoloration, oil sheen).

2. Observe location for possible sources of contamination upstream of discharge point.

3. If permit is required, verify location is as described in permit.

4. If monitoring is required in permit, observe location of sampling points and proper operation of measuring for sampling device.

5. Observe sampling procedure of field technician, looking for properly cleaned sample containers, proper preservation techniques, hold times, and chain-of-custody procedures.

6. Inspect any upstream oil/water separators for proper operation and maintenance.

Figure 16.5 Hazardous Waste Accumulation in Drums

Key Compliance Issue: Labeling and Container Standards

Figure 16.5 Typical Inspection Items

1. Inspect containers awaiting transport off site for leaks, corrosion, and bulges.

2. Inspect labels on drums for accurate description of waste. Ensure "Hazardous Waste" label is clearly visible.

3. Observe that accumulation start dates are on each container. Ninety days is the maximum period for storage; a permit is required.

4. Observe that containers are tightly sealed. Open funnels are not permitted. Bungs should be closed.

5. Containers of highly flammable waste should be electrically grounded.

6. Inspect accumulation points for presence of:
   - Telephone
   - Fire extinguishers
   - Spill cleanup equipment
   - Warning signs.

7. Observe that drums are on pallets and adequate aisle space is maintained.

8. Observe that any containers holding ignitable or reactive waste are located at least 50 feet from property line.

Figure 16.6 Hazardous Waste Storage Facility

Key Compliance Issue: Storage Facility, Security, Emergency, and Contingency Requirements

Figure 16.6 Typical Inspection Items

1. Observe facility is secured with locked doors and fenced areas, and is monitored by security guards.

2. Observe that signs with wording "DANGER—UNAUTHORIZED PERSONNEL KEEP OUT" and "HAZARDOUS WASTE STORAGE AREA" are posted at each entrance.

3. Observe that communications equipment (e.g., telephone, radio) is present and operating.

4. Inspect safety and emergency equipment for proper operation.

5. Inspect the inspection log. Verify that entries are properly recorded:
   - Date/time of inspection
   - Name of inspector
   - Notation of observances
   - Date/nature of repairs.

6. Inspect containers for tight seals, leaking, bulging, or rusting.

7. Inspect storage area for adequate aisle space.

8. Observe storage area for containment system:
   - Base is free from cracks and gaps, and impervious to spills or leaks.
   - Base is sloped to drain spills or leaks.
   - Containers are elevated to prevent contact with spilled liquids.
   - Capacity of containment system is adequate to contain 10 percent of the volume of the container.

Figure 16.7 Aboveground Oil Storage Tank

Key Compliance Issue: Spill Containment and Inclusion in SPCC Plan

Figure 16.7 Typical Inspection Items

1. Inspect oil storage facilities and ensure that all facilities are included in SPCC Plan.

2. Observe if any changes to oil storage/handling facilities have been included in amended SPCC Plan.

3. Observe that appropriate containment (i.e., berms, dikes) is present to prevent discharge of petroleum products.

4. Observe that the containment drainage valves are in the locked, closed position.

5. Inspect condition of dikes for cracks or overflow.

6. For tanks over 660 gallons, observe that secondary containment for entire contents is provided.

7. Observe that dikes areas are impervious to spilled contents.

8. Observe that appropriate cleanup equipment is available at the facility:
   - Absorbent materials
   - Oil retention brooms
   - Sand bags
   - Fuel recovery pumps
   - Protective gear (boots, gloves, respirators)

Figure 16.8 Aboveground Storage Tank Seal Inspection

Key Compliance Issue: Compliance with Confined Space Entry Permit Procedure

Figure 16.8 Typical Inspection Items

1. Determine if a permit has been completely filled out, authorized, and posted. Observe compliance with permit conditions.

2. Observe if tank is labeled as a confined space.

3. Determine if employees or contractors have been trained in confined space entry procedures.

4. Observe if an atmospheric monitoring device is available and has been checked and calibrated.

5. Observe if the atmosphere is tested prior to and during the entry.

6. Observe whether respiratory protection equipment has been inspected and tested.

7. Observe whether rescue equipment has been inspected and tested.

8. Determine if the attendant has been trained in rescue procedure, including practice rescues.

Figure 16.9 Solid Waste Incinerator

Key Compliance Issue: Particulate and Visible Emissions

Figure 16.9 Typical Inspection Items

1. Determine that incinerator is on facility emissions inventory.

2. Determine that emissions estimate has been calculated correctly.

3. Observe that permit to operate incinerator is posted and effective.

4. Observe that incinerator has multiple chambers fired by supplemental fuel.

5. Observe that timing/control mechanism for supplemental fuel feed operates properly to ensure complete combustion.

6. Observe visible emissions during combustion for exceedance of emissions limitations.

7. Observe that security measures (e.g., fence, locks) are in place.

8. Observe area around stack for excess ash.

9. Observe allowable permit limitations for temperature or charging rates are followed during operation.

Figure 16.10 Solvent Metal Cleaner

Key Compliance Issue: VOC Emissions

Figure 16.10 Typical Inspection Items

1. Observe that cover is always in closed position when not handling parts in the cleaner.

2. Provisions for draining parts must be internal to degreaser.

3. Cleaned parts are allowed to drain for 15 seconds or until dripping stops.

4. Operating instructions are posted near the cleaner.

5. Solvent stream does not splash above freeboard level.

6. If solvent vapor pressure is more than 0.6 pounds/psi, or if temperature is above 120°F, check for either a water cover over the solvent, or a freeboard ratio of 0.7 or less. (Freeboard ratio is measured by dividing the height of the freeboard by the width of the tank.)

7. Observe operation of any thermostats or safety switches.

Figure 16.11 Pesticide Storage Facility

Key Compliance Issue: Proper Facility Design Standards and Storage Requirements

Figure 16.11 Typical Inspection Items

1. Observe that the pesticide storage facility is not also used by non-related functions.

2. Observe that storage, mixing, and preparation areas are separate from laundry, office, showers, and locker rooms.

3. Observe that facility is dry and well-ventilated with no drains or cracks in floor.

4. Observe that curbing or other containment is provided for mixing areas or decontamination areas.

5. Observe that all rinse or washwaters are contained and do not connect to sanitary or stormwater lines.

6. Inspect mixing area ventilation for six changes of air per hour.

7. Inspect storage area ventilation for two air changes per hour.

8. Observe that personnel protective clothing and equipment is provided:
    ■ Respirators
    ■ Masks
    ■ Gloves
    ■ Safety shoes.

9. Observe that no smoking, food consumption, or drinking is allowed in pesticide storage areas.

10. Observe that pesticide containers are kept closed when not in use and stored upright above the facility floor with all labels plainly visible.

11. Observe that signs which read "DANGER—POISON, PESTICIDE STORAGE" are posted near entries to storage facilities.

Figure 16.12 Hazardous Materials Dispensing Area for Shop Use

Key Compliance Issue: Proper Storage Spill Containment Procedures

Figure 16.12 Typical Inspection Items

1. Observe that drums/containers are not leaking and are tightly sealed when not in use.

2. Drip pans or absorbent materials should be placed under containers.

3. Observe that all containers are clearly marked with contents, and incompatible materials are separated.

4. Observe that dispensing areas are not located near catch basins or storm drains.

5. Observe that highly flammable (Class I) materials are electrically grounded.

6. Observe that approved safety cans are used for transporting and dispensing flammable liquids in quantities of 5 gallons or less.

7. Observe that chemical dispensing areas are located away from adjacent property lines.

8. Observe that "NO SMOKING" signs are posted near areas where flammable materials are dispensed.

Figure 16.13 Flammable/Combustible Materials Storage Facility

Key Compliance Issue: Facility Design Standards and Specifications

Figure 16.13 Typical Inspection Items

1. Observe that walls meet NFPA Fire Resistant Standards (2 HR) NFPA 251-1969.

2. Observe that wall/floor joints are liquid tight.

3. Observe that electrical wiring and equipment meet NFPA standards (i.e., explosion-proof).

4. Observe that make-up air is vented directly to exterior of building.

5. Observe that exhaust air is vented directly to exterior of building.

6. Observe that exterior markings and warning signs are posted on building.

7. Observe that stacked containers are separated by dunnage or pallets, and stacks are no closer than 3 feet to nearest beam, girder, or sprinkler.

8. Observe that all containers are marked with contents and hazard markings.

9. Observe that at least one 10-BC-rated fire extinguisher is located outside and within 10 feet of opening.

10. Observe that all positive sources of ignition (e.g., open flames, cutting, welding, radiant heat) are prevented near the storage facility.

Figure 16.14 Solid Waste Disposal Facility

Key Compliance Issue: Proper Segregation and Disposal of Solid Waste

Figure 16.14 Typical Inspection Items

1. Inspect sample of solid waste receptacles.

2. Observe that solid wastes receptacles are vermin-proof and waterproof, and have functioning lids.

3. Observe that any ash residues or sludges disposed of as a solid waste have been tested for hazardous characteristics.

4. Observe that asbestos wastes are disposed of in leakproof containers, and are properly labeled. Verify that disposal facility is approved to accept asbestos waste.

5. Inspect plans of solid waste disposal facility. Verify that its operations are in compliance with permit conditions.

6. Observe that proper solid waste disposal procedures are current and posted for all employees.

7. Interview shop personnel for awareness of solid waste and hazardous waste segregation procedures.

Figure 16.15 Drinking Water Sampling Point

Key Compliance Issue: Proper Sampling Procedures and Protocols

Figure 16.15 Typical Inspection Items

1. Observe sampling procedures for the following:
   - Containers are clean, sterile.
   - Water is allowed to flow freely before sample is taken.
   - Record of sample is properly documented, including source of sample, time of collection, purpose of sample, and person collecting sample.

2. Inspect sampling points to verify they are representative of entire water supply system.

3. Observe wellhouse facilities. Look for sources of possible contamination to well casing.

4. Inspect chemical, bacteriological, and other analytical data for exceedances of primary drinking water standards. Discuss causes or sources of exceedances and remedial action taken.

5. Observe state certification of lab.

6. Observe certifications of treatment facility operators.

AUDITOR'S REMINDER CHECKLIST

Conducting an EH&S audit is a complex exercise. It involves mobilization of a team, conduction of detailed regulatory reviews, coordination with site management, a relatively short on-site visit, and team preparation of a report.

In preparing for an audit, the team leader, in particular, will have numerous details to consider. The following is a checklist of items that will guide the team leader through the process. See also Chapter 15 for a detailed checklist that focuses strictly on pre-audit activities

Preparing for the Audit

1. What is the scope of the audit?

   ■ Location of site (e.g., state, county)

   ■ Acreage of site

   ■ Square feet of manufacturing space

   ■ Overview of operations

   ■ Number of employees

   ■ Age of facility.

2. What should be decided beforehand?

   ■ Audit coverage (i.e., EPA, OSHA, DOT, etc.)

   ■ Team members (number and checklist responsibilities)

   ■ Duration of audit

   ■ Days of audit

   ■ Agenda

   ■ Hotel, cars

   ■ Handling of working papers (e.g., bound journals)

   ■ Assigning a team member to every section of the audit report, including introduction and facility overview.

3. What should be done prior to the audit?

   ■ Establish plant contact

   ■ Send pre-audit questionnaire

   ■ Establish need and desire for:
   - Hard hats

- Work clothes
- Safety glasses
- Work boots
- Cameras
- Security requirements

- Set exact time of arrival

- Get directions to facility

- Get hotel recommendations

- Request office space and telephone

- Obtain names and phone numbers of state and county/city agencies

- Make airline reservations, early, and for arrival the night before

- Make sure plant will be operating during the audit

- Ask that paperwork be assembled

- Identify all key site staff

- Ask if emergency response drill could be scheduled during the audit.

4. What should be reviewed before the audit?

- Previous audit

- Pre-audit questionnaire

- Checklists

- State/local regulations

- New federal regulations

- Plant background reports.

5. What problems should be anticipated?

- Didn't guarantee hotel room for late arrival

- Pre-audit questionnaire not returned

- One team member inexperienced or unprepared

- Last minute request to delay the audit

- One or more team members confused about responsibilities and/or arrangements

- Team leader forgets to make confirming phone call the Friday before the audit week.

Conducting the Audit

1. Brief the site management.

   ■ Introductions

   ■ Team member responsibilities

   ■ Identify escort and key interview candidates

   ■ Purpose of the audit; supportive but thorough

   ■ Who initiated the audit

   ■ Audit approach (e.g., review of records, interviews, field inspections)

   ■ Program approach (i.e., how long it will take to complete the report, who gets it, what do facility staff need to do?)

   ■ Protocol if imminent hazard (e.g., uncontrolled spill) is observed

   ■ Approximate schedule for debriefing

   ■ Who to call with concerns about the audit.

2. Become oriented to facility.

   ■ Obtain plot plan

   ■ Ask for overview of manufacturing/processing operations

   ■ Ask for orientation tour.

3. Review paperwork.

   ■ Review important paperwork first (e.g., permits)

   ■ Ask about making copies and keeping copies for review

   ■ Read local newspaper.

4. Interview staff.

   ■ Interview all key players

   ■ Be courteous; schedule ahead

   ■ Ask open-ended questions

   ■ Interview staff in their workplace

   ■ Be supportive.

5. Inspect facility.

   ■ "Leave no stone unturned"

   ■ Walk the fenceline

    ☐ Walk key roofs

    ☐ Respect (but visit) secured areas

    ☐ Identify all adjacent property uses

    ☐ Visit during evening or night shifts

    ☐ Schedule emergency response drill.

6. Conduct debriefing.

    ☐ Conduct complete dry-run with team first

    ☐ Acknowledge assistance of plant staff

    ☐ Provide overall statement of performance

    ☐ Have each team member present his or her findings

    ☐ Be supportive, precise, thorough, and practical.

7. Complete report.

    ☐ Decide on format and outline

    ☐ Assign every section

    ■ Decide on report manager

    ☐ Set schedule for first draft

    ☐ Set schedule for final draft and distribution.

8. Anticipate problems.

    ☐ Team members spend too much time reviewing records and not enough time interviewing or inspecting operations

    ☐ Lukewarm reception by plant staff

    ☐ No office available

    ☐ Site is more complicated than anticipated

    ☐ Paperwork was not properly assembled

    ☐ Audit team member addressing compliance areas in sequence and not in parallel; leaving one important area for the last day

    ■ Escort was unaware of agenda or need for his or her significant involvement

    ☐ A significant compliance issue is raised by a plant staff member but there is no corroborative evidence

- One team member can't seem to complete his or her report sections on time

- A team member is imprecise in the debriefing, raising questions about the general competence of the audit team.

Chapter 17

CONDUCTING EFFECTIVE OPENING AND CLOSING CONFERENCES[1]

Though it be honest, it is never good to bring bad news.

– William Shakespeare, 1564-1616

The room was filling slowly for the Friday afternoon meeting. There was a feeling of nervous anticipation among the staff of the large chemical plant located in Texas. Just then, the audit team leader announced that the closing conference would begin. The plant manager and his fifteen staff members took their seats alongside the five-person audit team. The team leader, noticeably on edge himself, began with "We found this site to be in compliance..." and paused for effect. As he paused, his team members looked at each other in masked disbelief. The plant manager did much the same, whispered a comment to his deputy, and left the room, seemingly satisfied that all was well. He returned two hours later, as the meeting was breaking up, and after the audit team had presented some thirty significant findings resulting from the audit. Due to a misleading opening, the plant manager had missed the true message of the audit—all was *not* well at his facility.

This is a true story and took place in the 1990s during an audit at a Fortune 100 Company with a well developed EH&S audit program. It demonstrates that, if not handled correctly, a closing conference can jeopardize an otherwise excellent effort. Both opening and closing conferences are crucial elements of an effective EH&S audit program. In fact, closing conferences, in particular, have been cited as one of the six biggest challenges in maintaining an effective audit program.[2] As many firms

---

[1] Originally published in *Total Quality Environmental Management,* (New York: John Wiley and Sons, Inc., 1994). Updated for this edition.

[2] L.B. Cahill, "Benchmarking Environmental Audit Programs: Best Practices and Biggest Challenges," *Total Quality Environmental Management*, vol. 4, no. 3 (New York: Executive Enterprises, Inc., 1994), 457-467.

go about re-engineering[3] their audit process, focusing on the beginning and end points of the on-site process makes eminent sense.

This chapter discusses a variety of issues that often arise during the preparation and conduct of opening and closing conferences. If these issues are dealt with appropriately, the audit will have a greater potential for success.

OPENING CONFERENCES

The opening conference, not surprisingly, occurs at the very beginning of the audit. It typically involves the full audit team, the site manager, the site EH&S manager, and selected site staff. The basic intent is to provide face-to-face introductions, establish the audit objectives, set the agenda for the audit, and to discuss, in a preliminary fashion, issues raised by a review of pre-audit information. The meeting quite often has two phases: the first, shorter phase involves the plant or site manager and is followed by a longer phase during which issues are discussed and the site manager may or may not be present.

The opening conference sets the tone for the entire audit. It is a meeting that can be stressful and is filled with potential "land mines" for the audit team. If the following six recommendations are kept in mind by the audit team, many of the mines can be avoided.

Take Charge of the Meeting

This may seem to be a simple point, but it is often lost on the audit team leader. The opening conference or meeting should be orchestrated by the audit team, not by site management. This can be especially difficult with a domineering site manager who is several positions higher than the team leader in the organizational hierarchy.

Certainly, the site manager will most often want to welcome the team, make general introductions, and provide an overview of the site's history and operations. But after this is accomplished, the team leader should take over, based on an agenda that has been discussed previously with site management. This is not to say that site staff don't have a major contribution to make during the meeting—they do indeed. However, the audit team is on-site only for a short while and will have quite an ambitious agenda; therefore, any substantial deflections can jeopardize meeting the objectives of the audit. One must keep the audit on track at all times.

Be Organized

Once the team leader assumes responsibility for the flow of the meeting, he or she should conduct the meeting in an organized fashion. A pre-developed series of slides

---

[3] For more information see M. Hammer and J. Champy, *Reengineering the Corporation—A Manifesto for Business Revolution* (New York: Harper Collins, 1993).

and/or handouts works well to keep things moving ahead and to assure that all audits, regardless of the makeup of the team, are conducted consistently. See Appendix H for a model presentation. This somewhat formal method is especially useful when discussing the audit objectives, approach, results, and follow-up. Quite often, companies develop the handouts as part of the audit program guidance document so that they are generally available to all auditors.

A list of topics that should be covered in the opening conference includes:

Audit objectives and scope

Audit "flow" including follow-up and closure

Identification of key interview candidates and availability (including obtaining relevant organization charts)

A summary review of the operations at the facility (including obtaining plot plans)

■ Identification of important site activities occurring during the week

A review of the pre-audit information

■ Scheduling the daily and closing conferences

Identification of the audit team workroom and phone protocol

Identification of site work hours and visitor safety and security protocols

Identification of computer/printer support

Discussion of the site escort protocol for visitors.

A couple of points here need to be kept in mind. The meeting should be crisp and to the point. The team's questions and inquiries should clearly reflect that they have done their homework; that the pre-audit information has been read and digested well in advance of the audit. There is no greater insult to the site staff than to have them realize that one or more audit team members has not reviewed (in detail) the pre-audit information that they so painstakingly prepared.

Finally, remember that not all questions will be answered in full during the opening meeting. Don't involve ten or so people in a protracted discussion of an issue that can be resolved much more easily and quickly in a follow-up, one-on-one discussion.

Discuss Logistics

One of the biggest challenges during the audit week is to manage the logistics of the effort. During the opening conference, the pre-set agenda should be modified as appropriate, and actual names of interview candidates and escorts should be placed in the "time blocks" of the agenda.

Notwithstanding this noble objective, one can be assured that within two hours of the formal initiation of the audit, a change to the agenda will need to be made. A new interview candidate will be identified, another will be called away for a day, or a surprise regulatory agency inspection will occur, justifiably deflecting the attention of the site staff.

The audit team needs to be responsive to the various incidents that might require schedule changes; flexibility and common courtesy are paramount. Several techniques are useful in this regard. First, the audit team should leave some open time near the end of the audit agenda. This can be used to accommodate needed changes. This time never seems to go to waste.

Second, the auditor should address compliance areas in parallel, not in series. In other words, if an individual audit team member is responsible for several areas, such as wastewater, PCBs and spills, confined space, lock-out, tag-out, and machine guarding, some work on each of these areas should begin early in the process, even if it is simply to review paperwork and schedule interviews. This accomplishes two things. It allows for better time management, minimizing the chance that an area will not be addressed at all if completely left to the morning of the last day. It also avoids the issue of having the key site staff member take a holiday on the last day of the audit, without the knowledge of the auditor.

Third, don't think of the audit as only taking place from 8:00 a.m. to 5:00 p.m. each day. Conflicts in scheduling can sometimes be remedied through breakfast and dinner meetings. After all, what else is there to do far from home in a hotel two miles from the plant?

Find Out What's Happening at the Site

Far too often, audit teams miss opportunities to observe important activities that might occur during the week of the audit. Examples include:

- A spill drill
- A hazardous waste pickup
- Startup of a boiler
- Monthly wastewater or stormwater sampling
- Weekly or quarterly inspections
- A line breaking
- A confined space entry
- A fuel or chemical delivery.

There is no better verification technique than to actually watch to see if something is done consistent with written procedures. These activities should be observed if at all possible.

Interesting things can happen during the verification process. On one audit, there was an interview with the director of a medical research laboratory who was discussing the lab's wonderful waste segregation procedures—each station had both a "black-bag" and a "red-bag" container, which allowed for complete segregation of infectious wastes. As the procedures were being discussed with the director, the auditor noticed a technician at a nearby lab hood seemingly discarding waste with no distinction being made between infectious and non-infectious wastes. Later, when interviewed separately, the technician stated that he thought the different bag colors were simply a result of the medical center's desire to "liven up the place!"

The team may never have uncovered this issue without actually being there to observe the activity as it took place. Take some time in the opening conference to schedule real-time observation of as many activities as possible; written procedures and what managers believe happen are not always consistent with reality.

Schedule Additional Conferences

Most mature audit programs include not only opening and closing conferences, but daily audit team and site EH&S staff meetings as well. During the opening conference, a tentative time should be set for the closing conference and the daily meetings with the site.

The daily meetings do take time away from the actual audit, but they are crucial in maintaining adequate communications. These meetings allow participants to review findings to date, resolve any misunderstandings early, and revise the audit agenda as needed. Based on numerous observations, the daily meetings with site staff appear to work better early in the morning as opposed to late in the afternoon, which is the more traditional approach. That way, the morning meetings occur when people are fresh and not fatigued by the day. People on both sides of the table are often more articulate and patient. The morning meeting also allows the audit team to have some time alone the evening before to prepare and compare notes.

Address Important Topics

There are certain special topics that should be addressed during the opening conference. If they are ignored, misunderstandings can arise. These topics are as follows:

- **There will be findings (or no site is perfect).** Site staff need to be told that an audit will result in findings, no matter how well managed the site is. Stated another way, audit findings in and of themselves are not necessarily reflective of poor management; it is more the number of significant or repeat findings.

- **Audits require verification.** Acceptable audit methods require verification; hearsay evidence is generally not sufficient. This implies that when a site employee claims, for example, that all staff members have received appropriate training, the auditor typically will not or cannot take that statement at face value; audit records will have to be reviewed. However, unless site staff are made aware of the need for verification, any given individual could be insulted if the auditor seemingly does not believe his or her statements.

■ ***All areas must be covered.*** Simply because the completed pre-audit questionnaire stated, for example, that there were no underground storage tanks, permitted confined spaces, or PCB-containing equipment at the site, does not mean that the audit team can ignore those areas. The person completing the questionnaire might not have considered a septic tank serving the maintenance shop as an "underground storage tank," might not have thought a 5-foot construction trench was a confined space, or might not have known that fluorescent light fixtures sometimes have PCB-containing ballasts. These issues can be important and cannot be ignored.

■ ***How will "fixed" findings be handled?*** It is quite likely that some identified deficiencies will be remedied during the course of the audit. The audit team needs to inform the site staff on how these are to be handled in the report. Site staff typically will request that the fixed findings not be included in the report; however, most audit programs do include them but indicate that they were remedied during the audit. This approach is generally preferred because the findings, as trivial as they might be to the site staff, could sometimes be symptoms of a much larger site issue or even a corporate-wide issue. The larger issues could be lost if the symptoms are not included in the report.

■ ***How will "significant" issues be handled?*** There may be, on occasion, a truly significant issue (e.g., an uncontrolled PCB spill, operating without a permit) identified by the audit team. The team should not wait until the end of the audit before raising these issues with site management. Site management should be told that if a significant issue is uncovered, it will be brought to their attention immediately and the audit may be temporarily suspended until a plan of action is implemented.

As can be gathered from the above comments, the "bottom line" for opening conferences is free and open communication.

CLOSING CONFERENCES

The closing conference is the final on-site activity of the audit process. It typically involves the full audit team, the site manager, the site EH&S manager, and selected site staff; the participant makeup is thus pretty much identical to the opening conference. The basic intent of the meeting is for the audit team to report back to the site on the findings of the audit. The meeting should be crisp and to the point; a one-hour goal (not including the inevitable questions and comments) is usually appropriate.

More often than not, a final working meeting with site EH&S staff directly precedes the closing conference. This meeting is where most, if not all, of the "differing points of view" are resolved; it is not unlike the daily meetings discussed previously.

The closing conference can be a stressful meeting, especially if the audit team is working right up to the last minute to produce a typed, formal list of findings or a draft report, as many audit teams are directed to do. Keeping the following points in mind can help to reduce, but not eliminate, the stress.

Take Charge of the Meeting

Having the audit team take control of the closing conference is an even more important issue than for the opening conference, so it's a point worth repeating. The same issues discussed with respect to the opening conference apply here as well. An agenda should be established by the team leader; there should be an allowance for significant input by site staff; and the team should respect the position of the plant manager without being overly deferential.

Further, the correct message must be communicated to plant management, and this can only be done if (1) the team leader is in charge and (2) the plant manager is present. If, in fact, the plant manager is unavoidably absent, the team leader should find some way to communicate the findings to him or her separately, whether by phone or face-to-face at a different time or location. This direct communication is essential because no matter how well-intentioned the site EH&S staff is in relaying the information, there will always be a filtering or screening of the findings when transmitted secondhand.

Be Organized

The audit team must certainly be organized for the closing conference; most often, time with the plant manager, in particular, is limited. It would not hurt to once again review the audit objectives, scope, approach, report format, and follow-up requirements. Using the formal overheads or transparencies developed for the program, as discussed previously, is a useful technique. Although much of this information was transmitted in the opening conference, a second review is recommended because there may be additional site staff in attendance at the closing conference and the staff who were in attendance at the opening conference may not have retained all of the information in the days that have transpired since then.

A proposed agenda for the meeting might be:

■ General re-introductions

■ Statement of objectives, scope, and approach

■ Overall summary of the audit, highlighting particularly commendable items and significant deficiencies

- Review of findings by individual compliance area

- Discussion of the audit report format and schedule

- Discussion of the corrective action report format and schedule.

The organizational question that arises is: who should present the findings for the individual compliance areas? The audit team leader could make all the presentations himself or herself, or each auditor could discuss his or her individual compliance area. In most cases, it is advisable to have the individual team members present their own findings, even if their presentation skills are not quite as good as those of the team leader. Using typed transparencies of the findings is a good support tool, even for experienced presenters, and it should be considered.

Having individual auditors present their own material is advantageous for several reasons. If the auditors know that at the end of the audit they will be standing before a demanding audience and defending their findings, they are more likely to be careful about both the accuracy and precision of each finding. They are also the persons who directly observed the deficiency and should be better able to respond to questions. Lastly, each of these closing conferences is an opportunity to improve presentation skills and, ultimately, to groom future lead auditors.

Be Appreciative but Don't Bury the Message

It is very difficult to stand up in front of ten to twenty people who might also be fellow employees and colleagues and go into detail about all the things they are doing wrong. Thus, more often than not, closing conferences begin with a speech by the audit team leader, thanking virtually everyone on the site for their help on the audit and praising them for their extensive knowledge and expertise. This is certainly courteous behavior and is appreciated by the site staff, but if the praise becomes too effusive, site management can misinterpret what is being said. Managers will focus on the recognized expertise of their staff and assume the deficiencies or findings are trivial, administrative shortcomings, whether or not this is true. Auditors should not overdo the thanks and acknowledgments; be courteous but be straight and to the point.

Set Priorities

On audits where there are numerous findings, some prioritization is in order. Many programs distinguish between regulatory, company policy, and "good management practice" findings. Each of these finding types are often classified by level of significance as well.[4] In the closing conference, some similar organizational structure

---

[4] See L.B. Cahill, "Preparing Quality Audit Reports: Ten Steps (and Some Leaps) to Improve Auditing," *Total Quality Environmental Management*, vol. 4, no. 2 (New York: Executive Enterprises, Inc., 1994), 319–324.

is needed. The site manager should know before leaving the meeting whether there are any so-called "show-stopper" findings. These significant findings should be addressed either at the very beginning or the very end of the meeting.

Minimize Praise for "Acceptable" Performance

In school, scoring a 95 out of a possible 100 will get you an A+. In regulatory compliance, it could get you a major fine or jail time. People often forget this important distinction. Audit team leaders need to stress that 100 percent compliance with EH&S rules and regulations is the expectation of enforcement agencies. Sites should not receive effusive praise for being "mostly" in compliance. This philosophy is quite consistent with total quality management principles of continuous improvement, no-defects production, and "six sigma" quality control.

Respond Professionally to Challenges

It is the goal of each audit team to resolve all conflicts with site staff prior to the closing conference. This is done mostly in the daily meetings and the final preparatory meeting with site EH&S staff. However, it is possible that controversies will arise in the closing conference.

The most important thing to remember in the closing conference is that the audit team should respond professionally to any challenge of the findings. A few years ago, a member of an audit team was convinced through interviews that the required quarterly inspections of PCB equipment were not being performed at the site being audited. This was brought up as a finding in the closing conference and found to be incorrect; the auditor never interviewed the correct individual—the site electrician. This "error" had to be handled quite delicately.

In dealing with these potential controversies, it is helpful to use the guidance given in the classic 1981 book on negotiation, *Getting to Yes.*[5] In this text, the authors propose that it is best to argue your "underlying interest," not your "position." In the context of an audit, the team leader's position is quite often that "there will be no successful challenges to the team's findings during the closing conference." The position of the site staff might be that "there will be no significant findings resulting from the audit." If both parties enter the meeting with these positions in mind, it could be a difficult session. If, on the other hand, the team leader can convince participants, as well as himself or herself, that the underlying interest of all is to have a fair, thorough, and accurate audit of the site, things might work out a bit better.

---

[5] R. Fisher and W. Ury, *Getting to Yes: Negotiating Agreement Without Giving In* (Boston: Houghton Mifflin, 1981).

Focus on Root Causes but Avoid Evaluations of Staff Performance

There is now a general trend in auditing to get behind the symptoms and to identify the root causes of the problems. This quite often results in a focus on management and organizational systems. The advantage of this approach is that focusing on root causes will more likely result in long-term fixes.

For example, a label could be missing from a drum containing hazardous waste. If this is reported as a finding, the site's response will most probably be to stick a label on the drum and be done with it. Yet, the audit team focusing on root causes would attempt to identify not only the "what" but also the "why" of the problem (e.g., why was the label missing), and there could be half a dozen reasons. Focusing on these why's, such as lack of training, no ownership of the drum, poor labels, and so forth, should result in more appropriate corrective actions.

Yet, as valuable a tool as root cause analysis can be, it can also more directly identify an individual's or group's lack of performance as being at the core of the problem. This is a much more difficult point to raise in the closing conference and should be handled with great care. The old adage "praise in public, admonish in private" should apply. If there is indeed a sense on the part of the audit team that there is a chronic performance problem, the team might want to (1) make absolutely sure it's true (e.g., maybe the individual did not receive the appropriate training) and (2) deal with it outside the public arena of the closing conference.

Understand How to Handle Repeat Findings

Every audit program should have a policy on how to handle findings that arise repeatedly from audit to audit. Many organizations will escalate the significance of the finding simply because it has not been corrected since the last audit. There is also the issue of how these findings are handled in audit reports. Some programs will specifically identify them as repeat findings, while others prohibit this practice because they are concerned about the potential liabilities of apparent "willful and knowing" noncompliance. Should there be any repeat findings on the audit, the audit team leader should be ready to address these issues consistent with corporate policy during the closing conference.

Avoid Comparisons

Whether they ask the question or not, site managers are always curious about how their operations measure up with others in the organization. Responding to this question in the closing conference is generally a no-win proposition for the audit team leader. If the team leader states that the site is exceptional by comparison, then any message of significance is lost on the site management. Also, the "about average" or "lower quartile" responses are almost never taken at face value without challenges.

Some programs do require the audit team to score the facility, and this is done in a variety of ways for a variety of reasons. This is occasionally done against an absolute four-point scale, such as:

- In compliance (4.0)

- Generally in compliance (3.0)

- Needs improvement (2.0)

- Substantially out of compliance (1.0).

Even this more simplified scoring can create disputes and arguments, however, given the competitive nature of most organizations.

Notwithstanding the above policies of scoring of some companies, it is best for the audit team not to provide comparative judgements when, in fact, sites cannot be evaluated fairly against one another. Sites handle different materials, use different technologies, are of varying ages, and are located in different physical and regulatory settings (e.g., wetlands, non-attainment areas for air pollutants.)

Avoid Guarantees

Another wish of the site manager is that the audit will identify any and all problems so that if a regulatory agency inspection were to occur within a short time after the audit, no surprises would result. The team leader should never make this guarantee. An audit, especially a systems audit, is a spot check of the facility's operations using statistical and/or representative sampling techniques. That is, it occurs over a limited period of time, with a limited scope, and not *all* records are necessarily reviewed. It is quite possible that an agency inspector could subsequently review a certain compliance area in considerably more depth. The inspector could, therefore, come across a compliance problem not identified by the audit team.

Leave Written Findings

It is remarkable to observe the look on the site EH&S manager's face when told by the audit team leader during the closing conference that the team will leave no written record of the findings with the site. There is usually a look of bewilderment and disappointment, and one can sense that the momentum built up during the week of the audit is in jeopardy of being lost.

Some believe that providing a verbal debriefing alone should indeed be sufficient feedback to the site during the audit. After all, the site staff is hearing the essence of the message. These same people would prefer that any written report, be it a draft list of findings or a draft report, receive an independent (legal) review before even a limited distribution to the site and others.

There are at least two problems with this approach. First, momentum can be lost as the site waits anywhere from two weeks to three months for the draft report. The lack of on-site written documentation lessens the likelihood of quick or immediate responses. One could argue that the liability stemming from not addressing an issue in a timely fashion as one awaits the draft report is greater than the liability associated with leaving a draft list of findings with the site, which may need legal "massaging" later. And in point of fact, the audit team leader should stress that if there are to be changes of significance between the draft list of findings and the draft or final report, site staff will be alerted prior to distribution of the report. This is common courtesy.

Second, there is quite often a major difference between the spoken and written word. Time and again people will agree with what the auditor is saying in a closing conference, yet once they see it in written form, they will disagree with both form and substance. This is because there are communications filters between the observation, the verbalization of the observation, and the documentation of the observation. Misinterpretations caused by these filters should be resolved face-to-face in the closing conference, not by "email missiles."

Discuss the Next Steps

It is important for the audit team leader to close the meeting with a precise discussion of the next steps in the process. These steps relate principally to any follow-up work required of the audit team, schedule and distribution of the draft and final reports, and schedule and distribution of the corrective action plan. The team leader should explain that much is expected of the site in the final phase of the audit process. The site really determines the success of the audit in their dedication to correcting identified deficiencies in a timely manner. If all participants leave the meeting agreeing to the importance of this commitment, the audit has been a success.

Solicit Site Feedback

Many companies require that audit teams solicit formal feedback from the site on the value of the audit. This is often done through the use of a questionnaire. A model questionnaire is provided in Appendix J. It is appropriate and valuable to solicit feedback formally. The completed questionnaire should be returned, not to the team leader, but to the audit program manager. Be careful about misinterpreting the results. A high-scoring result could mean an excellent audit or it could mean that the team was too lenient. Conversely, a low-scoring result could mean a poorly performing team or a site that was not pleased with the justifiable rigor applied to evaluating its EH&S performance.

Acknowledgment: The author wishes to thank Ray Kane, with whom he has led scores of environmental audit training seminars over the years. Many of the ideas and issues raised in this chapter have been brought up not only on audits but also during these seminars.

Chapter 18

AUDITING DILEMMAS

What does not destroy me, makes me stronger.

– Friedrich Wilhelm Nietzsche, 1844-1900

Audit team leaders and members are often faced with challenging dilemmas during their visits to sites. This is true in spite of the clear direction routinely provided by government regulations and corporate standards. Resolving these dilemmas often requires astute judgement and practical resolution of difficult issues. How an audit team handles these issues can often make or break an audit.

In this chapter ten dilemmas are discussed. There is no right or wrong answer for any of them. They are presented here to simply demonstrate that all is not always as it seems. As an audit team leader or member, think about how you would handle the dilemmas. Each is based on an actual experience.

1. The Management Systems Defense

You have just completed an audit of the boiler operations at a major industrial facility. There is a large above ground heating oil tank that supplies fuel to the boilers (see Figure 18.1). The company standards require that this tank have secondary containment. It does have containment but the estimated capacity would hold only half of the tank's contents when full. Containment volume cannot be increased due to physical constraints. You notice that a broad black line has been drawn across the tank about half way up its height. The site EH&S coordinator tells you that they have put in place an administrative management system (e.g., level indicator, training), which assures that the tank is never filled above the black line, implying that the secondary containment capacity is acceptable. He also tells you that, because they have become more reliant on natural gas, there really is no need to fill the tank beyond halfway. As an auditor, you have the following options. Which do you choose?

Figure 18.1 Aboveground Storage Tank with Horizontal Fill Line Drawn

Option	Description	Select (✔)
1.	Accept the site's management systems solution.	
2.	Have the site install an overfill vent pipe just above the black line so that if the oil reaches this pipe it will spill out into the containment area.	
3.	Require that physical systems (e.g., high level alarms and automatic cutoff devices) be put in place to assure that the tank is never filled more than half way. (Note: there is a risk that the site could deactivate these controls.)	
4.	Require decommissioning of the existing tank and the purchase and installation of a new tank half as large.	

2. The De Minimis Issue

As a team member, you have been given the responsibility to review the site's hazard communication program. You have just completed your review of the MSDS file. Material safety data sheets were available for all chemicals used at the site and they were generally up-to-date. There was one exception, though. The MSDS for a biocide used only occasionally in treating boiler water was not available. There was one 30-gallon container of this chemical stored in the boiler house. The site obtained the MSDS during the audit and placed it in the file. Is this an audit finding that should be documented in the report?

3. Virtual Compliance

You are conducting an audit of a manufacturing facility overseas. The average daily BOD discharge concentration from the wastewater treatment plant is about 40 mg/l. The effluent standard is 30 mg/l. They are out of compliance. The site manager tells you that the plant is considered a model for the region and they have never been cited. Other companies up and down that stretch of the river, which is basically an open sewer, are discharging without treatment and BOD effluent concentrations can be as much as several hundred mg/l. The local environmental agency has issued an environmental citizenship award to the site (a plaque is mounted in the lobby) and the agency director routinely brings other companies' management to the site to show them "how it should be done." It will cost about $250,000 to upgrade the plant to meet the 30 mg/l limit. As an auditor, do you report this as a finding and recommend that the capital be spent to upgrade the facility? The plant manager is definitely opposed to spending the money on what he believes to already be a "best in class" operation for his city.

4. Unobtainable Verification

You are conducting a health and safety audit of a chemical plant. Fire extinguishers must be inspected every month. The site recently switched over to a computerized inspection system so there are no tags on the extinguishers to determine if they have been inspected. All the extinguishers look great and you're convinced they are being inspected. You later find out that the inspector was recently "hit by a truck" and is in the hospital recovering. To verify whether the inspections are being conducted, you request to review the computer records. Unfortunately, site staff cannot get to the records because they don't have the inspector's password. A call to the hospital is not successful; the inspector is too incoherent to remember his name, never mind his password. How do you handle this as an auditor?

5. Non-Specific Corporate Standards

You have been asked by the team leader to visit the site's aboveground storage tank farm. There is a 1,000-gallon diesel oil tank in the area that does not have secondary containment (see Figure 8.2). There is no regulatory requirement that any secondary containment be provided. The Corporate Environmental Standard states that sites must be designed and operated so as to "protect groundwater." Is this enough

Figure 18.2 Diesel Oil Tank without Secondary Containment

for you to conclude that secondary containment is required? What else, if anything, might you want to consider in your deliberations? What if the tank contained a chlorinated solvent or caustic soda? Would that change your conclusions?

6.   Conflicts Between Country Regulations and Corporate Standards

You are conducting an environmental audit overseas. In the laboratory, you note that there are two 5-gallon sealed metal containers inside one of the hoods. They are labeled waste xylene and waste toluene, respectively. The containers are in secondary containment pans. Everything seems to be consistent with the recently promulgated federal hazardous waste management regulations, which have been modeled after the U.S. version of the Resource Conservation and Recovery Act (RCRA). When you ask about disposal, the site tells you that the containers are placed in the trash dumpsters when full. There reportedly is no treatment or disposal technology in the country that can handle these wastes and so, for now anyway, the government accepts this method of disposal. Corporate standards require that all hazardous waste be disposed of *properly*. Is this a finding? If yes, what is the appropriate corrective action? If no, why not?

7.   Repeat Findings

You are in the middle of an environmental audit. One of your responsibilities is to determine if any of your findings have been repeated from the last audit, conducted three years ago. You have observed that three of the twenty drums in the site's sole hazardous waste accumulation area did not have the required labels (see Figure 8.3). The report from three years ago includes the following finding: "Two of ten drums in the 90-day hazardous waste accumulation area did not have the required labels." You have determined that none of the 20 current drums were at the site three years ago; the old drums were transported off site for disposal. Is this a repeat finding? If yes, do you think the site management will feel the same way? Why or why not? Could the original finding been written in an alternative way to make the "repeat finding" question more clear?

8.   Just-in-Time Compliance

As part of your evaluation activities on an assessment, you are requested to review the site's confined space program. You first request a copy of the site's procedure or written program, which is given to you without hesitation. The procedure tracks the OSHA regulations exactly. However, the effective date of the procedure is three

Figure 18.3 Inspecting a Hazardous Waste Accumulation Area

days prior to the audit you are now conducting. The EH&S coordinator admits that the procedure is brand new and was completed in anticipation of the assessment. When you ask about the required training, the coordinator tells you it is scheduled for next week. They had to wait until issuance of the final procedure and could not do it during the assessment week. Next week was the first available time. There is a fully documented training plan for next week. You also ask if you can review any completed entry permits and are told that, since the procedure is so new, no completed permits are available. There are some old completed forms in the file that were used under a previous more informal system. Upon review of a sample of the forms, you note that they seem rather complete but do not address all of the elements of a safe entry.

Next you travel out to the manufacturing and storage areas and note that many, but not all, confined spaces have the appropriate warning signs. Here again, the coordinator says that they are in the process of placing the signs on the appropriate tanks and vessels. In fact, you notice that by the end of the assessment week this task has been completed. Finally, you ask if you can observe an entry while you are onsite. The coordinator says that there are no entries scheduled for this week but several will be done next week as part of the training.

The bottom line is that they seem to be knowledgeable of the requirements and are putting an excellent program in place. It's just not fully implemented. Is there a finding here? What would it be? Other than reviewing the program again on the next audit scheduled in three years, is there a way you can be sure that the program is real and not just an audit smoke screen?

9. Regulatory Intent

You're responsible for auditing the hazard communication program at a site in the U.S. In reviewing your regulatory database you note that the training provisions of the regulations (29 CFR 1910.1200 (h)(2)), "require that employees shall be informed of the location and availability of the written hazard communication program, including the required list(s) of hazardous chemicals and MSDSs required by this section." In interviewing four employees, you note that each is able to tell you where the nearest MSDSs are located. Moreover, when requested, each is able to locate a specific MSDS for a fairly obscure water treatment chemical and they know how to "read" the MSDS. However, when you ask all four employees where they might find the written hazard communication program, each and every one looks at you with a blank stare. Do you have a finding here?

10. Vague Regulatory Definitions

It's November 2000 and you are auditing a site in the U.S., which has 250 employees and about 20 different job classes. In assessing the EH&S training programs, you note that an excellent needs assessment matrix has been developed for all applicable training modules and for all job classes; computerized and pretty impressive at first glance. You check on ten employees' records and note that three of them have missed their required annual hazardous waste training for 2000. You are told by the EH&S coordinator, who didn't seem to be aware of these deficiencies, not to worry that this was due to summer vacations. The employees will make up the training in December, which means that some employees will have an interval of 18 months between sessions. Their last training was in June 1999. Is this a finding?

Chapter 19

PREPARING QUALITY EH&S AUDIT REPORTS[1]

Vigorous writing is concise. A sentence should contain no unnecessary words, a paragraph no unnecessary sentences, for the same reason that a drawing should have no unnecessary lines and a machine no unnecessary parts. This requires not that the writer make all his sentences short, or that he avoid all detail and treat his subject only in outline, but that every word tell.

– William Strunk, Jr., *The Elements of Style, Third Edition*

There has been much written on developing effective EH&S audit reports. Unfortunately, authoring a chapter on how to write effective audit reports is a bit like giving a speech on how to be an effective speaker. Anything but perfection will not be tolerated.

Notwithstanding this heart-felt reservation, this chapter examines a variety of issues that need to be considered when developing an audit report. These are issues that never quite seem to go away, no matter how many reports are written or how often the frustrated audit team leader refers an auditor to the classic Strunk and White book, *The Elements of Style*, which is an excellent source and should be used by every auditor. The audit report is the document in which the findings of the audit team are presented with respect to the compliance status of the facility. As such, it is the key document of the audit program. The audit report should be a working, supportive document that will assist the facility staff in attaining and maintaining compliance.

Assuring that an audit report is accurate, precise, thorough, and helpful to facility staff is a considerable challenge. It requires proper preparation during the audit,

---

[1] Parts of this chapter are adapted from L.B. Cahill, "Preparing Quality Audit Reports: Ten Steps (and Some Leaps) to Improve Auditing," *Total Quality Environmental Management*, vol. 4, no. 2 (New York: Executive Enterprises, Inc., 1994): 319-324.

deliberate efforts in the week following the audit, and a consistent follow-up program. This chapter discusses each of these equally important phases.

FIELD PREPARATION

Preparing well in the field is vital to developing a useful audit report. In most cases, a return trip to the site to gather overlooked information is infeasible. Follow-up phone calls are about the only avenue open to the auditor and the information gathered from these remote efforts is not sufficiently verified. Yet, there are several things that an auditor can do to help assure that sufficient data has been obtained to write the report without following up with the site later.

Keep the Customer in Mind

One of the key tenets of Total Quality Management, "keeping the customer in mind," is often forgotten in the heat of the battle. Audit reports should be written principally for the site management—in particular, those responsible for correcting the deficiencies.

Yes, there are other customers. Senior management should have a sense of whether they have a problem site on their hands after reading the executive summary. There should indeed be an executive summary, for quite often that is all some reviewers will read.

However, the body of the report, the findings, must be written so that the reader both understands the nature of the problem and can readily envision a corrective action. Thus, when the team leader reviews the report, he or she should put his or her "plant hat" on and ask, for every finding, do I understand the problem well enough to know how to fix it? If the answer is yes, then the auditor has done the job of serving the customer.

Look for Underlying Causes

It is generally the responsibility of the auditor to determine the root cause of identified deficiencies. This will help the site in defining corrective actions that will address the underlying cause, not the symptom. This enhances the likelihood of implementing a true and lasting fix. Where auditors do not have the available time to address root causes for each and every finding, the site should be held accountable for completing this exercise.

Root cause analysis is a value-added effort and should not be ignored for efficiency sake. For example, the lack of secondary containment at a hazardous waste storage facility might be due to:

1. an untrained site manager who is unaware of the requirement,

2. the permitted use of a temporary location while a permanent one is being built,

3. a disapproved capital improvement request by division management, or;

4. a general uncaring attitude on the part of site management.

The recommended corrective action will vary depending upon which of the above is the underlying cause. In a case where site staff are not trained in the applicable requirements, simply constructing a dike or berm will not likely avoid the possibility of additional problems (e.g., wall penetrations) arising in the future.

Organize Daily

An individual auditor can produce hundreds of pages of field notes during the course of the on-site work. How these field notes are recorded should be left to the personal preferences of each auditor. Some will use bound journals, some loose papers, and others loose-leaf or spiral-bound notebooks. Regardless of the technique that is used, it is imperative that the auditor take some time daily to organize his or her thoughts and findings. Otherwise, the auditor will probably be unable to decipher his own work when it comes time to write the report. Daily organizing of the working papers also allows the auditor to determine whether any particular compliance area has been overlooked. This organization task may require allocating some time each evening in a hotel room, but this will be time well spent.

Bottom-Line Interviews

An auditor might interview scores of people during the on-site effort. Interviewing is probably the most important of the field activities. During an interview, an auditor is typically very busy; especially where, as is often the case, the auditor is conducting the interview alone. The auditor will be referring to the protocols, asking questions, hopefully listening to the answers, and taking notes. Too often, auditors are thinking about what the next question should be, as opposed to truly listening to the answer. The auditor should not be intimidated by "dead air time" during the course of the interview; take some time to allow your notes to catch up with the conversation.

Quite often auditors question whether a small, pocket tape recorder might not help in documenting interviews. In general, this is not an effective approach. Interviewees quickly "clam-up" when a recorder is present. If the auditor later wishes to record notes to himself on the tape recorder as a way to document findings, though, this would be acceptable.

Probably the most important thing an auditor can do is pinpoint the "bottom-line" of the interview, immediately following the interview itself. In other words, interviews should be scheduled so that time is available after the session to quickly summarize the results of the interview. The benefits of this effort will be realized later when the auditor attempts to write the report using field notes.

Another effective technique is to summarize the results of the interview at the end with the interviewee; that is, repeat back to the individual your perception of the key findings resulting from the conversation. The auditor will often find out that the recap has lost something in the translation, and this gives the interviewee a final opportunity to clarify any misunderstandings.

Develop an Annotated Outline

The auditor should begin to develop an annotated outline of his or her sections of the report, beginning the very first day. This will help to prepare for the debriefing and will be a check to assure that all areas the auditor is responsible for are covered adequately. This effort will also aid in organizing field notes properly, as discussed above.

Challenge Each Other

In most cases, the audit team will be required to debrief site management as a way of concluding the fieldwork. It can be almost guaranteed that the audit team's findings will be challenged in this meeting. Therefore, it is important that the team members challenge each other's findings throughout the fieldwork in preparation for the debriefing. This often proves to be a valuable exercise and will result in more precise findings and in double-checking sources of information. Each team member should be aware of the benefits of this internal challenging and should not immediately become defensive if another team member questions a finding.

Develop a Consistent Debriefing Approach

The debriefing is a vital part of the entire process. It informs facility staff of significant findings and clears up any misunderstandings held by the audit team. If the debriefing is structured properly, it can also provide the basis for the audit report.

One good way to assure that proper findings are eventually developed is to use a four-step process in communicating findings to site staff and management. Each finding should be communicated:

(a) when first observed

(b) during a daily meeting with site EH&S staff

(c) during a pre-closing conference with site EH&S staff

(d) during the closing conference with site management.

If the auditing team strictly adheres to this process, the closing conference should not be a contentious exercise.

REPORT PREPARATION

Having properly done everything in the field, the auditor is now prepared to undertake what for many is the most difficult part of the process: writing the report. The audit report typically includes a discussion of the audit process, an overview of the facility, an executive summary, and a presentation of findings and recommendations. The report addresses both regulatory and procedural findings. A regulatory deficiency is one involving federal, state, or local regulations. A procedural deficiency is one involving internal requirements or good management practices. Findings are often classified as significant, major, or minor. Where a finding is corrected prior to the departure of the audit team, the report will contain the finding but will indicate it as corrected.

Audit team members will write those sections of the report that relate to the compliance areas reviewed. The audit team leader is responsible for assigning other sections of the report to himself or other team members (e.g., Introduction, Facility Overview, and Executive Summary). Based on past experiences, team members would do well to adhere to the following guidance.

Organize for Monitoring

Many reports are rambling narratives in which it is difficult to sort background information from the findings. This does little to help the site or to allow for later tracking of corrective actions.

The audit report should be organized so that the findings are broken down, listed, and codified. It is normally best to list only findings that are deficiencies. It makes little sense to codify a finding that requires no corrective action. If positive findings are listed, there will be a numbering gap in the sequencing of corrective actions that can confuse those responsible for managing the closeout process. Save the positive findings and commendable items for the executive summary.

One company assigns each finding of each report a two-field numerical code, which includes the year of the audit and the number of the finding. When coupled with a code for the plant that was audited, this allows for computerized tracking of the closure of all findings. This closure step is critical to the success of a program. In independent reviews of audit programs, problems with the management of the findings follow-up and closure system is one of the most commonly observed deficiencies.

Start Early

When the auditor returns to his office, he always does so with good intentions; the first order of business is to complete the audit report. However, most people who have been away from the office for an extended period of time will spend the first couple of days back returning phone calls, reading mail, and catching up with the latest office politics. It is crucial not to let these distractions prevent the auditor from completing the report in a timely fashion. To paraphrase what Yogi Berra might say in this regard, "The more you put it off, the more you'll put it off." Procrastination builds on itself.

As an auditor, you do not want to be in the position of committing to write a report in the field as you undertake yet another audit. Nor do you want to be back at your office with several reports due to team leaders. You can become quite confused in trying to recall exactly what you observed at any given site.

There are several approaches that may help the auditor quickly complete the report. Developing an annotated outline before one leaves the site is a technique that works well. One of the more interesting approaches is the increasing use of laptop computers in the field. In some cases, draft reports are basically completed before the team leaves the site. The laptops are also helpful in developing very impressive debriefing packages.

In summary, however, each auditor must do what works best for him or her. For many of us, simply taking an hour to organize our notes for one compliance area and writing the first paragraph is enough to get us going. If we continue to struggle, reviewing a previous audit report should be a source of ideas on how to approach the material.

Establish a Report Format

Regardless of the report format chosen, it should be adhered to consistently so that subsequent audit reports are prepared in the same manner. This allows comparison of reports among different facilities to be made against common elements. It also allows for easier assessment of how a specific facility is improving its compliance status over time by comparing findings in one report to the findings in the subsequent audit report.

A model audit report is provided in Appendix I. Although there is no one correct approach, many companies follow the outline presented. The philosophy of the report should be to make it as short as possible without compromising on necessary details. Long reports slow down the process markedly and jeopardize the relevance and currency of the findings. One should aim to produce reports with fewer than twenty-five pages, if at all possible.

The audit report should contain the same information as that found in the report presented in Appendix I. Section 1.0 is a brief executive summary written for upper management that highlights the key findings and recommendations of the audit report and any especially commendable items. Section 2.0 stipulates the who, what, where, and when information to familiarize the reader with the administrative aspects of the audit. Section 3.0 provides general background on the facility.

Section 4.0, Audit Findings and Recommendations, should be written with respect to noncompliance items as a first priority. Many companies take the viewpoint that the audit report should be an exception report; that is, the report should only document those items that were found to be deficient. Conditions found in compliance are not documented, and an individual section begins with a phrase along the lines of, "The facility was found to be generally in compliance with hazardous waste regulations with the following exceptions. . ." Other companies take the view that all findings, good and bad, should be documented.

The exception report approach appears to be the most prevalent form of documentation of audit findings by companies with audit programs. When reporting findings, every effort should be made to specify the regulatory citation that applies to the finding. This can be a federal citation (e.g., 40 CFR 761.50), a state citation (e.g., Pennsylvania Department of Environmental Resources Regulation 150.50), or a local regulation (e.g., City of Philadelphia Sewer Ordinance 115).

Recommendations typically stipulate the auditor's suggestions on actions needed to come into compliance. These may range from simple administrative suggestions to recommendations for a capital improvement project (e.g., a treatment plant upgrade). The recommendations may also focus on the need for additional investigation or further analysis before a final solution is chosen to correct the noncompliance condition observed.

One of the significant issues of concern to companies with audit programs is the liability created when recommendations documented in an audit report are not implemented. The only guidance that can be given is to document only recommendations that are known to be implementable by the facility. If there is some doubt that the audit's recommendations will be carried out (due to lack of resources, staffing, or funds), then it would be better to recommend that the facility management come up with their own action plan to address the problems. In these cases, the auditors should focus on the "what" and not the "how."

Specifying a responsible party and a time limit or date for a recommendation is more often left to the site's corrective action plan. The concern of having a recommendation in an audit report, which can't be implemented, is a valid one. Audit report writers should be sensitive to the positions that they potentially are putting facility managers into when they pose their recommendations.

Supporting data are sometimes included as attachments in the report to provide certain relevant backup information, such as tables of analytical data, copies of Notices of Violations (NOVs), plot plans, schematics, or photographs. There is great variability among audit programs regarding inclusion of this material in a report. Photographs, in particular, are excluded from many audit reports because they are considered to be potentially damaging and provide only a snapshot of the facility.

The benefits of including supplementary materials in a report should be weighed against the impact the material might have on the reader of the report. A picture may be worth a thousand words, but it might also be worth a thousand words to a plaintiff's attorney in the event the report is used as evidence in a lawsuit. A simple rule of thumb is to include only supplementary information that is absolutely needed to convey the point to the reader. If the point can be made clearly and completely in the body of the report, the use of supplementary material to support the finding should be discouraged.

Pay Attention to Repeat Findings

The handling of findings that remain uncorrected from the previous audit is quite a challenge for most programs. Many lawyers will argue, rightfully, that labeling them as "repeat" findings in the audit report creates added liabilities for the organization.

Yet, for senior managers, it is important to know if documented problems are being corrected. Some would say that not knowing whether problems are being fixed is an even greater liability than documenting repeat findings.

One company, DuPont, has a specific and proactive policy regarding repeat findings. The policy calls for auditors to pay particular attention to problems identified in the previous audit that have not been corrected. In classifying these findings, auditors are asked to consider assigning them a higher risk priority than otherwise would be the case.

Be Careful of "Good Practices"

Most audit programs classify findings into one of three types: regulatory, company policy, or good management practice (GMP), sometimes also called good engineering practice or observations. Difficulty often arises in crafting effective GMP findings.

Hour-long discussions (or, more precisely, arguments) have occurred between the audit team and site management over the validity of a single GMP finding. The discussion usually centers on the justification for the finding. When the auditor says "that's the way we do it at our site" or "we will accept nothing less than best practice procedures," this usually raises the hair on the back of the site manager's neck.

There is a place for GMPs in an audit report. Regulations or company policies do not always address all practices that might pose a risk to the organization. However, there needs to be solid justification for each GMP finding.

One way to develop that justification is to frame GMP findings in the same way as suggested above for repeat findings. What is the situation? What is the requirement (e.g., protection of groundwater)? Too often, GMP findings begin with phrases such as, "The site should...", "The site needs to...", and the like. These are *not* findings; they are really "soft" recommendations. This is the trap that many auditors fall into, crafting GMP findings as recommendations with no supporting justification.

Set Priorities

Not all findings are created equal. Some are more important than others, although all need to be addressed. Thus, it is usually helpful to categorize findings by significance. Some companies do this by bringing forward the most important findings into the executive summary. In other cases, individual findings are classified by level of significance. This can, of course, create heartburn among the legal profession, but it can be a valuable tool for management.

Some organizations (e.g., the U.S. Air Force) use a scheme that is based on a classification system suggested by the U.S. EPA in its Federal Facilities Compliance Strategy. This results in a three-tiered classification, as follows:

Significant. A problem categorized as significant requires immediate action. It poses, or has a high likelihood of posing, a direct and immediate threat to human health or safety, the environment, or the installation mission. Some administrative issues can be categorized as significant. For example, failure to ensure that hazardous waste is destined for a permitted facility, failure to report when required, and failure to meet a compliance schedule are all significant deficiencies.

Major. A problem categorized as major requires action, but not necessarily immediate action. This category of deficiencies usually results in a notice of violation from regulatory agencies. Major deficiencies may pose a future threat to human health or safety, or the environment. Immediate threats, however, must be categorized as significant.

Minor. Minor deficiencies are mostly administrative in nature. They may involve temporary or occasional instances of noncompliance.

The above classification scheme can be helpful because the definitions are based on the U.S. EPA's sense of significance, and it allows the auditor to highlight truly significant findings.

DuPont has taken this scheme and modified it to serve the purposes of its own environmental audit program. This classification has been helpful in setting facility action priorities within DuPont. DuPont classifies its audit findings as follows:

Level I: Highest Priority Action Required. Situations that could result in substantial risk to the environment, the public, employees, stockholders, customers, the company or its reputation, or in criminal or civil liability for knowing violations.

Level II: Priority Action Required. Does not meet the criteria for Level I, but is more than an isolated or occasional situation. Should not continue beyond the short term.

Level III: Action Required. Findings may be administrative in nature or involve an isolated or occasional situation.

No matter what approach is used, however, there should be some way to establish priorities among findings and to highlight those items that are truly in need of immediate attention.

Be Clear and Concise

A good audit report should not be an attempt to write the great American novel. Reports should not include gripping, suspenseful, or emotional stories. Findings should be written in a simple and straightforward manner based solely on observation, tests, or interviews. Use of general or vague statements will do little to help the reader understand the magnitude and nature of the compliance problems found during the audit. Best put, the writer should put himself in the facility manager's place and ask the question: If I were to read this report, would I know the exact nature of the problem and would I know how to resolve it? Again, the auditor needs to be precise and accurate about underlying causes.

The importance of writing clear and precise audit reports and findings has been discussed at length in the classical audit texts. Here, the intent is to reinforce the importance of the topic and to suggest an approach to writing findings that can help achieve a quality product. Most audit findings can be broken up into three components: the situation, the requirement, and the reference. A sample finding written in this format is presented below.

The Situation: At the Building 27 90-day hazardous waste accumulation point, there was one drum containing waste solvents that had an open-top funnel.

The Requirement: RCRA requires that containers holding hazardous waste be closed except when adding or removing waste.

The Reference: 40 CFR 265.173(a)

Now, each finding does not have to be organized with the three headings listed as shown. But the intent of the organization is to first, in one to two sentences, precisely describe the *situation* so that the reader could readily go to the location in question (e.g., Building 27) and locate the deficiency (e.g., the drum with the funnel). By paraphrasing or even quoting the *requirement*, the auditor is also helping the site staff understand what is needed. Finally, listing the *reference* allows them to conduct additional research if necessary. With a little more effort, even management systems findings can be handled in this way. Note that Figure 19.1 demonstrates a way to efficiently utilize this format on audits. This paper or electronic form drives a consistency among audit team members, a worthwhile goal.

When using numbers to quantify a finding, put the information into its proper perspective. There are generally three distinct numbers that are important in a quantitative finding: the universe of items at the site (e.g., 300 total fire extinguishers), the number evaluated by the audit team (e.g., the team reviewed 30), and the number that were deficient (e.g., the access to three was partially or fully blocked).

Finding three improperly completed manifests on an audit may or may not mean that the facility has a major problem. One could simply report that there were discrepancies in manifest management at the site, leaving the reader to wonder if this is a major problem. However, if 500 manifests were reviewed and the problem was an incorrect abbreviation for drum versus missing return copies, the problem may, in fact, be trivial. This clarifying information should be included in the written finding.

The use of indefinite adjectives should be discouraged or minimized in audit reports. "Very," "some," "significant," "small," "high," and the like are often found throughout audit reports and their meaning and intent are wrongly left to the interpretation of the reader. One tip is to spend the time to count items when it is appropriate. For example, it is often a good idea to count drums at hazardous waste accu-

Figure 19.1 EH&S Audit Findings Form

Description of Finding:

Statement of Observation:
The site had no documentation available of inspections of the hazardous waste accumulation point located on the south side of Building A23

Statement of Requirement:
RCRA requires the site to inspect "areas where containers are stored, at least weekly, looking for leaks and for deterioration caused by corrosion and other factors."

Citation/Source:	**Compliance Area:**
40 CFR 265.174	Hazardous Waste

Type: [✔] Regulatory   [ ] Company Policy   [ ] Guidance
Level: [ ] Level I   [✔] Level II   [ ] Level III

Recommendation (Immediate/Long-term):

Provide the appropriate assurances that the inspections are occurring or develop and implement a verifiable inspection procedure. Begin the inspections immediately.

Code:	**Auditor:**	**Date:**
S12-99-04	C. M. Sweat	October 2, 2000

mulation areas. Then, when it is reported that five drums were stored past the ninety-day deadline, the auditor can state whether it is 5 of 10 or 5 of 200. There is a difference.

The auditor should not attempt to prove a point using sensational language or hyperbole in an audit report. Words such as "dangerous," "negligent," "willful," "criminal," and the like are often over-statements and imprecise, and can lead to misinterpretation by the reader.

The auditor should also use proper English and avoid slang and excessive use of acronyms. The average length of sentences, according to writing experts, should be in the range of fifteen to eighteen words; that is, short, crisp sentences make the technical information easily digestible by the reader. Where acronyms are necessary, they should be spelled-out the first time they are used, or the auditor should include a table of acronyms in the report.

De-emphasize Numbers

Total Quality Management principles suggest that numerical quotas should be eliminated. In the context of an audit report, this suggests that one has to be very careful how the number of findings is handled within the organization. It seems that no matter what is said or done, line managers and others have a tendency to add up the findings and compare. This is neither a meaningful nor constructive exercise and should be discouraged by senior management.

It is nearly impossible to make effective performance evaluations solely by keeping track of the number of findings. First, individual site situations, even within the same class of facility, differ greatly due to such factors as the surrounding area (e.g., wetlands, and non-attainment areas) and the state in which the facility is located (e.g., regulatory stringency).

Second, audit teams differ in composition and makeup. One can send two different audit teams to the same location and have them audit something as straightforward as an accumulation point and return with a wide variance in the number, priority, and type of findings.

Finally, as audit programs have evolved over the past few years, there has been a movement towards evaluating management systems. This has resulted in the "rolling up" of individual compliance findings into an overall system finding. This makes quantitative comparisons over time even more difficult.

In summary, using the number of audit findings as a measure of performance is fraught with problems. As an alternative, some companies have asked audit teams to classify the site overall. An example ranking system, based in part on a scheme sometimes used by financial auditors, might be to classify the site as follows:

- Good

- Qualified

- Needs Improvement

- Unacceptable.

This approach is more compelling, although each of the classifications would have to be defined.

Use Evidence in the Discussion of Findings

During the course of the audit, evidence will be obtained using one of three methods: inquiry, observation, and test. Inquiry is evidence gained through interviews; observation through, not surprisingly, visual inspection; and test through means such as running an emergency response drill or physical sampling. When writing findings in the audit report, the method of discovery should be inherent to the language used. For example, where appropriate, phrases such as "It was observed that..." or "It was reported that..." should be used. This phrasing gives more meaning to the auditor's findings.

The auditor should be very careful to avoid outright conjecture, or conclusions deduced by guesswork. This is a common pitfall in auditing. There should be at least one solid piece of evidence for each finding and probably two pieces of evidence for each significant finding. Speculation on the part of a maintenance supervisor that there was a fifty-gallon spill of perchloroethylene fifteen years ago is not sufficient evidence. The supervisor may have been reprimanded recently and possibly is looking to damage the reputation of the plant manager. When the auditor does run into this kind of situation, an effort should be made to find corroborative evidence. This could include independent confirmation by another facility staff member, a spill report, or regulatory agency correspondence. Where no confirmation can be made, the auditor should raise this issue at the debriefing. Usually the issue will be resolved one way or the other in this forum.

Avoid Common Pitfalls

Each of us falls into writing traps that we cannot seem to avoid. Presented below are some of the more typical problems evident in audit reports. Twenty sentences or paragraphs are listed and the problems with each are listed directly afterwards. There may be other problems as well, but the problems pointed out are probably the most important ones to remember.

Pitfall Examples

1. The chemical hygiene program was deficient and could be improved. This is a serious concern. *(This is a soft recommendation ("could be"); How was the program deficient? "Serious concern" is a conclusion, not a fact.)*

2. The audit team inspected 20 eyewashes and ten emergency showers. Three of these were not operating adequately. *(There is use of an indefinite modifier; which three were they? "Adequately" is an improper audit word, explain further.)*

3. Several of the waste drums at the hazardous materials storage area had no labels, as required by the Federal Hazardous Waste regulations. *("Several" is an improper audit word; the statement literally says, "no labels are required." The literal corrective action would be to remove the labels from the rest of the drums.)*

4. Three fire extinguishers at the site did not have the required inspection tags. *(Which three?)*

5. The hazardous waste storage area directly outside the north side of Building A101 had no secondary containment. Any releases would spill onto the soil and enter the groundwater. *(Is containment required? The second sentence is speculation. Stick to the facts; explain the potential consequences in the closing conference.)*

6. Not all aboveground storage tanks have high-level alarms. Company standards require that all aboveground storage tanks have high-level alarms and automatic shut-off devices. *("Not all" is not definitive enough. The requirement statement*

adds "shut-off devices" when there is no mention in the finding of the status of the devices.)

7. A unit operator reported that attendants occasionally leave their station during confined space entries. This violates the site's confined space entry permit program. *(This is hearsay evidence. "Violates" is not an appropriate audit word; it is a legal conclusion.)*

8. Because of the possibility of solvent releases into the sewers, the wastewater treatment ponds might have to be permitted as a hazardous waste surface impoundment. *(This is conjecture. "Might have to be" is a soft recommendation.)*

9. The infectious disease program should be improved to reflect the most recent Company standards. *("Should be improved" is a soft recommendation. How is the program now deficient?)*

10. The permitted hazardous waste storage facility at Building 51 was recently inspected by the U.S. EPA and found to be in compliance with applicable standards. *(This is not a finding. The auditor is relying on the government inspection.)*

11. The hazardous waste program does not meet all applicable federal requirements. The site should use the model program developed by the Morristown, NJ facility as a guide to develop a more complete program. *(How does the program not meet the requirements; "In my state" or "at my facility" is not an appropriate audit approach.)*

12. The team was told that there have been several spills of hazardous materials by forklift operators. The audit team recommends that these individuals be disciplined and retrained. *(This is hearsay evidence and an inappropriate recommendation.)*

13. During the facility tour, the team observed employees not wearing hearing protection in high noise areas. During 1995, the facility did not comply with the OSHA annual hearing conservation training requirements. Several employees did not receive the annual training. *(These are unconnected findings. How many employees did not have protection; "several" is not an appropriate audit word.)*

14. It appears that there is insufficient aisle space in the soap plant. *("Appears" and "insufficient" are not appropriate audit words.)*

15. Only 20 percent of the workers in the 500-person workforce could locate a specific MSDS on the Haznet Computer System. *(This implies that the auditor interviewed all 500 employees. It is likely that the auditor interviewed only five or ten employees and found only one or two, respectively, who could locate an MSDS. Is the Haznet Computer System the only accepted approach for locating MSDSs; there may be manuals as well.)*

16. A filthy 8710 disposable respirator was noted on a desk in the plating department, obviously in direct violation of regulatory requirements. (29 CFR 1910.134.) *("Filthy" is not an appropriate audit word. "In direct violation" is a conclusion and legal opinion.)*

17. Based on the lack of documented training records in their personnel files, it appears that Robert Atwell, David Lee Perry, and Rodrigo Munoz have not received the required annual hazardous waste training. *(Do not indict individuals. "Appears" is not an appropriate audit word.)*

18. Almost all of the employees working in Assembly Room B were not wearing the required hearing protection. *("Almost all" is not an appropriate audit phrase.)*

19. Due to PTS, TTS, high dBA in the CPS range, in addition to presbycusis, it appears to this CIH that established NRRs may not be adequate. *(Too many acronyms and abbreviations are used.)*

20. As part of the hazardous waste audit, we went to the point where the flammable hazardous wastes are stored at the site and we reviewed whether the drums had labels and whether each was inspected weekly and whether the electrical equipment was explosion proof and whether adequate ventilation existed and weather grounding and bonding requirements were complied with. Their were a plethora of violations. *(A wonderful example with a few small problems, including a run-on sentence, use of slang (e.g., regs), a misspelled word (their), use of pretentious words (e.g., plethora), use of volatile words (e.g., violations), and ending a sentence with a preposition (with). Also, the auditor is writing the report as he did the audit; he should separate the process from the product. Finally, the report is written in the first person; most audit reports are written in the third person.)*

REPORT FOLLOW-UP

With the report now completed, one could assume that the process is complete. It is not. Audit follow-up is a crucial part of the entire process. Without adequate follow-up, the system is likely to fail. One should pay special attention to the following few items in particular.

Assure Legal Review of Reports

Some companies manage their audit programs through their legal departments, due to concerns about protecting the confidentiality of the findings. Potential protections such as attorney-client privilege, work product doctrine, and the principle of self-evaluation privilege are discussed in Chapter 3. Whether or not the audits are done under these mechanisms for protection, it is most prudent to have a lawyer review the draft audit report. The lawyer can help to ensure that legal references in the report are correctly stated and applied. More importantly, the lawyer can make suggestions relative to the wording and tone of the report from a legal view. It is a good rule of thumb to assume that the audit report may be discoverable in a subsequent legal proceeding against the company. Review of the draft report by the lawyer may be very helpful in the event that he or she is required to defend the company in environmental litigation.

Limit Distribution of the Report

The draft report should be sent to the facility manager and his immediate supervisor for review. This report should be distributed within two weeks of the audit. A time limit should be stipulated for responses so that any disagreements can be resolved quickly. The plant staff should have no longer than a week to respond. Upon review, a final report should be issued, together with an action plan. The final report should be distributed to upper management as well as to the facility manager and his immediate supervisor.

Producing more copies of the audit report than those needed, as stated above, should be discouraged. These extra copies tend to find their way to people who don't necessarily have a need to know. Many companies number the copies so that distribution can be controlled and persons held accountable for their copies of the report. Once a final report has been issued, many companies have adopted a policy of destroying the draft copies. Final reports are kept either indefinitely or until the next audit report is issued for that site. The auditors' notes and working papers are normally destroyed after the audit report has been issued. Obviously, it is a good idea to develop a formal records-retention policy covering audit reports and associated documents and papers.

Accept No Mistakes

Not much needs to be said here. Audit reports should be mistake-free. Even the smallest typographical error should not be allowed, not even in a draft report. In fact, in the audit business, much like the consulting business, there is really no such thing as a draft report. If it is to be sent to the client or customer, it should be considered final, no matter if words like draft or preliminary are used.

Every report should have a third-party review by someone not on the audit team. Also, do not rely solely on computer software spell checks to eliminate all typos; they will not. A human must conduct the final check.

Based on experience, it is better to take the heat for a report being a day or two late than for it being sloppy. People will remember a report with all the typos for ten years and will forget the perfect report within a month.

Remove Barriers to Efficiency

Auditors must be given the tools to be able to develop a quality report. This includes a sample audit report to be used as a guide. Many companies, such as Eastman

Kodak, have also developed a separate audit report-writing guide, which typically includes a discussion of the writing process, pitfalls to avoid, and a sample report with sample findings. Kodak has gone one step further and developed a database of over one thousand written findings from past reports, codified by category, which assist auditors in the field. Also, in-field use of laptop computers has done much to improve the efficiency of the process. Draft reports can be developed "on-the-fly."

Develop Action Plans

Approaches to follow-up actions on audit findings vary among companies. Still, this is viewed as one of the key factors in having a successful program. As discussed elsewhere, each audit report typically results in an action-item table generated by the site, which lists each finding, the associated recommended remedial action, the responsible party, and the expected date of completion. Tracking can be accomplished by follow-up phone calls to facility management or by expedited follow-up audits.

Recently, the action-item tables quite often have been entered onto a computer database, and quarterly tracking reports are generated to monitor progress. Responsibility for this monitoring usually rests with the audit program leader, who may delegate it to audit team leaders for particular sites. Whether plant staff have the ability to revise information on the database is an option that is handled in a variety of ways. In some cases, the system is secured from entry by anyone but an auditor.

Regardless of which method is used, the audit process is not complete unless some formal measures are instituted to ensure that each of the audit findings and recommendations are being addressed by the facility staff. Clearly, some recommendations made in an audit report may involve large capital expenditures that cannot be made immediately. In this case, placing the item on a subsequent year's capital expenditure plan is an appropriate step to take, as long as this action does not implicitly condone continuing noncompliance. All corrective actions do not necessarily have to take place immediately. As long as the facility management has a reasonable schedule for completion and is tracking the status of corrective measures, it can demonstrate a good faith effort to operate in a responsible manner.

Train the Auditors

Train, train, and retrain! All auditors should receive formal training before they embark on their first audit. A good part of this training should be on report writing, or at minimum, on the writing of individual findings. Providing on-the-job training on how to write findings at an inopportune time (e.g., on a Thursday night at 11:00 p.m.) for someone's first audit is no fun. Unfortunately, though, it happens too much.

Preparing a quality audit report is a difficult task. It takes time, effort, and lucidity. But the effort is well worth it. The report is *the* decision-making document for the EH&S audit program.

Note: Any discussion of a company's individual EH&S audit program approaches in this chapter is based on information provided to the public at large through technical papers, presentations, and the like.

Chapter 20

ENVIRONMENTAL AUDITING: A MODERN FABLE[1]

What you don't know will hurt you.

– F. Friedman, Vice President,
Occidental Petroleum Corporation, 1983

THE COMPANY

The year was 2050 and times were good at PEP, Inc. The firm was indeed living up to its name (Purchase Everything Possible) and had just passed the two largest law firms in the United States to assume the number one position on the Fortune 500 list. It was the first time in ten years a law firm wasn't number one.

A not insignificant reason for the rapid growth of PEP was the performance of its newest subsidiary—Moon Rock, Inc. The founders of MRI had discovered that if certain rocks on the moon were ground to dust, refined using a special solvent, and combined with several "active" ingredients, the resultant product (sold as Klairol's Hairall) would arrest male-pattern-baldness. Not surprisingly, since the discovery five years ago, MRI's revenues had grown by 1,000 percent each year.

Yet, Hairall could not be manufactured without some risk. Processing had to take place in an oxygen-free environment, so both mining and manufacturing had to occur on the moon. This wouldn't have been so bad if the special solvent, methyl ethyl death, and one of the active ingredients, pandemonium trichloride, weren't so difficult to transport and handle. As a consequence, MRI was having difficulty booking cargo space on the weekly moon shuttle, and several environmental groups, particularly Citizens for a Clean Universe, were questioning the benefit of hair to men when compared with the potential cost of a spill in transit or processing. Risk

---

[1] This story is a fictional case study. Any terms that may relate to existing organizations or products is purely coincidental.

assessments and cost-benefit analyses conducted to date were inconclusive in this regard.

These and other concerns resulted in the establishment of a corporate environmental audit program by PEP management. The U.S. EPA under its voluntary registration procedure, which was first proposed just before the turn of the century but only recently implemented, had recently certified this program. There was after all a 25-year public comment period for all new environmental regulations.

THE AUDIT

As luck would have it, MRI had thus far escaped being audited, mostly due to the somewhat remote location. PEP had first focused on domestic facilities, then international, and now, finally, the corporation was hitting its NEB (non-earthbound) facilities. It was soon to be MRI's turn.

Two of PEP's more experienced auditors had been assigned to the MRI audit. Although experienced, each typically had a different approach to the work. I.M. Fair (Irene, as she was known) viewed audits as a way for facility managers to help themselves do the right thing. On the other hand C.M. Sweat (affectionately known as Charlie, or by some as "that Cretin") saw auditing as a temporary stop-over on his way to top management; he was determined to demonstrate his ability to implement the "lean and mean" philosophy of the current management.

Irene understood the importance of the assignment and was already in the midst of her preparations. Although she was on temporary duty in Europe, she called Charlie at corporate headquarters in Washington, D.C. (PEP had relocated to the long-since abandoned Waterside Mall complex.)

"Charlie," she said, "We really should get ready for this MRI audit. I'm pretty excited by the trip to the moon, and I want to do a great job. I'll be getting my checklists, a completed pre-visit questionnaire, and a plant profile sent here to London. And..."

"Whoa," said Charlie, "Aren't we getting ahead of ourselves. After all, the audit isn't for two months."

"I don't think so," responded Irene, "You remember how much more preparation we needed to conduct the international audits, don't you?"

"Oh yeah," said Charlie.

"If it's okay with you," said Irene, "I'll take responsibility for hazardous materials, water, and sanitary wastes. That will leave you with solid and hazardous wastes. Oh, by the way, I need you to coordinate with the MRI plant manager. He needs to know our schedule, agenda, and scope. He also needs to help us with logistics. You know, like providing an escort, security clearances, access to a phone, availability of an office, and so on. Charlie, are you still there?..."

Charlie was still there but he was beginning to think that this trip might not be the cakewalk he originally had thought. These guys at MRI are supposed to be the hotshots of PEP; why should he spend his precious time coordinating the trip with *them*. It should be the other way around. And if Irene thinks she's going to unload all this preparatory work on him, well...

"...Charlie?"

"Yeah Irene, I hear you," responded Charlie. "Don't you worry your pretty little head. I'll take care of those details for us. I'll meet you on the shuttle leaving on the 14th. See you then."

As she heard the click, Irene was now starting to think along the same lines as Charlie—this was not going to be an easy assignment. It would be the last time that Irene and Charlie would have anything close to similar thoughts.

THE BEGINNING

It was now the 14th, and although Charlie had not gone over his checklist or the pre-visit questionnaire, or anything else for that matter, he had had his secretary pack those materials and call the MRI plant manager, Dr. Demanding, to coordinate the audit with him. He felt good about his preparation steps and his ability to delegate. He could always go over the paperwork on the trip.

Irene, on the other hand, was edgy. Much like an athlete before the big game, she never quite settled down until the audit had begun. She had read all her materials but felt uncomfortable having left the plant coordination to Charlie. As it turned out, she had very good instincts.

The trip to MRI proved uneventful except for one problem. Although Charlie and Irene spent considerable useful time discussing the forthcoming audit, it occurred to Charlie that he had left his background materials in his luggage, which was not retrievable during the flight. He was able to review Irene's copy of the questionnaire and the plant profile but Irene had only brought the checklists and regulatory citations for the areas she was to cover. Charlie had always prided himself in his ability to "wing it," and this assignment would once again test that skill.

THE FIRST MEETING

It was the 15th, the morning of the first day of the audit, although "morning" on the moon was strictly a man-made convention. Charlie and Irene had had a good breakfast at the visitors' quarters; they now were waiting in the MRI reception area for the arrival of Dr. Demanding. Irene was reading that day's edition of the *Moon News* to see if there was anything of note that might help her on the audit. Charlie was reviewing his stocks in the *Wall Street Journal*.

Suddenly Dr. Demanding turned the corner, walked up to them, and said brusquely, "Your secretary told me you were to be here yesterday. Where the hell were you?"

Irene looked at Charlie who was a bit flustered, but upon regrouping, said, "Doctor, I think she probably confused the arrival date with the date we were to start the audit. You see, we arrived yesterday and..."

"Well, if you and I had talked," Dr. Demanding interrupted, "This might not have happened. I'll be able to make adjustments today, but we won't be able to get started for another two hours. You can sit in my office until then."

Attempting to calm things down, Charlie said, "Well, we don't want to inconvenience you, so why don't we sit in the office you've allocated to us for our stay."

"Say what!?," responded Dr. Demanding.

"You know, the office we'll work out of while...didn't my secretary mention we'll need an office?"

"No, she didn't! What else didn't she tell me?"

Irene thought it was about time to interject. "Sorry for the misunderstanding, Dr. Demanding. But it would be easier on all of us if we had a workspace to spread-out in and access to a phone, and if you're too busy I'm sure one of your staff could be an effective escort for us. We really do want to minimize any disruptions to your operations."

This seemed to quell Dr. Demanding's mounting anger. Although maybe all it did was transfer it to Charlie who was thinking he would "get" Demanding for being so unreasonable and would certainly make Irene's life miserable for making him look bad.

Two hours later the briefing with plant management seemed to be going well. Everyone came to understand the scope of the audit and Irene was able to ask several very relevant questions because of the research she had done on the facility prior to the audit.

While things were going better, Charlie was still having his problems. In an attempt at conciliation, he began his opening remarks with his favorite cliché, "We're from corporate and we're here to help you." This went over like the proverbial lead balloon.

THE FIELD WORK

Upon completion of the briefing, Charlie and Irene stated that they would next like to review the environmental records and then begin their physical inspection of the facilities. More problems surfaced due to the lack of preparation, of course. They were told that some of the permits were kept back on earth for security reasons and there were no available spacesuits for either Charlie or Irene so their inspections of the mining operations would have to be canceled. However, Irene was once again ahead of the game. In her research she became aware of both problems and obtained copies of the permits and had been fitted on earth for a spacesuit, which was due the next day. Her phone call one-month ago to Charlie on these issues went unanswered.

They both reviewed the paperwork and most everything seemed to be in order. Charlie did note that a new waste disposal cell had been constructed and was about to receive its first load of waste material that week. He suggested that Irene schedule her fieldwork in a way that would allow her to see this operation. Irene agreed wholeheartedly. Charlie also reviewed the hazardous waste disposal permit and a dozen manifests, one of which had two errors, an incorrect abbreviation for drum and the lack of a signature. He noted these in his logbook. Irene noted that the Spill Plan was close to three years old and would be in need of updating and re-certification within three months. Although this was not strictly a noncompliance finding, she thought she might mention it in the debriefing and note it in the report. She felt that plant management should begin the update process right away in order not to miss the forthcoming expiration date.

It took pretty much all day for the team to review the paperwork. Both Charlie and Irene were following the prescribed checklists during their reviews. Notes were put into their bound journals as required by corporate procedure.

THAT NIGHT

Towards the end of the day Irene went searching for Dr. Demanding to see if he would be available for an early dinner that evening. The good Doctor was very receptive to the idea since his family had remained on earth during his six months of moon duty, and he still had three months to go. Irene always attempted to have at least one dinner with the site or environmental manager as she saw this as an opportunity to learn more about the person and the facility she was auditing. She also made sure this dinner was not on the evening before the closing conference, as this was usually a late night involving significant preparation.

Of course, Irene assumed Charlie would join them. She was learning, however, that assuming anything with Charlie was a mistake.

"No, I don't think I can join you tonight," he said. "I really need to go over my checklists and regulatory abstracts before we begin the field work tomorrow."

"Charlie!" shouted Irene, "If you had done that when you should have, you wouldn't have to miss this dinner! It's important."

"Oh, I'm sure you can handle it for the both of us," Charlie responded. "It's just not that critical."

That night Irene learned more about the facility's operations than she had in all her previous work. Dr. Demanding turned out to be quite a character and very sociable outside the work environment. He even took Irene to see the plant on the night shift, which raised some questions in both their minds about the adequacy of the Emergency Response Plan. Meanwhile, Charlie ordered room service, ate, watched television (100-year-old reruns of *The Honeymooners*), and promptly fell asleep without reviewing his checklists.

THE NEXT DAY

Charlie and Irene were now ready to undertake their fieldwork. They were to review the tank farms, the processing areas, the materials storage areas, and the waste disposal areas. In addition, Irene was to take a moon-rover out to the mining operations. Each had an escort as they went their separate ways. Charlie relied principally on observation and spent little time asking questions of his escort or the unit operators. When he did ask questions, they went something like:

"Do you inspect weekly?"

"Are staff here competent?"

"Have you ever had a spill that you didn't report?"

After a while Charlie even stopped asking these types of questions because, for some reason, the responses were not helpful.

Based on his evaluation against the checklists, Charlie noted several problems:

Poorly labeled drums

Lack of containment in the tank farms

Insufficient liners in the waste disposal cells.

He was finally starting to enjoy the audit.

Meanwhile, Irene was having more success with her approach. While each auditor's observation skills were roughly equivalent, Irene was having better luck discussing operations with staff. She was using open-ended questions like:

"Can you explain to me what you do here?"

"What are some of your concerns in achieving successful operational performance?"

"Do the environmental requirements you face always make sense operationally?"

Irene believed that if she was able to get staff to open up, she might understand better what transpires on a typical day as opposed to the day or days when there is an audit or inspection. She felt that the one-day snapshot approach was too restrictive. She also believed that audits were not just inspections of records and physical facilities, but of management systems as well; she had noticed on other audits that if management and staff were not environmentally sensitive and aware, there would eventually be a problem no matter how sound the physical systems.

In her evaluation of sanitary discharges and hazardous materials she did observe:

The potential for water/wastewater sewer cross-connections

Potentially uncontrolled releases through drains

Poor inventory control practices (last-in, first-out) resulting in the accumulation of expired raw materials in deteriorating drums.

She noted these in her journal and on plant drawings so she would remember exactly where in the facility she observed the problems. It was a big place.

FINISHING

Upon completion of three days of inspection, Charlie and Irene, sat down to discuss their findings. They agreed that during the debriefing Irene would take the lead as she seemed to have fostered a stronger relationship with Dr. Demanding, and just about everybody else for that matter.

They each developed a detailed set of notes from which they would speak on the next morning. Irene found the going easier since each evening she spent some time in her room compiling the previous day's findings. As a result, Irene felt that her findings were sound but that Charlie was being less than precise in several areas. She pressed him on these issues but his defensiveness caused her to back down. She would wait until tomorrow and do her best to support Charlie in the meeting. Her patience was wearing thin and she was glad tomorrow was the final day of the audit.

Charlie, on the other hand, couldn't understand what was bothering Irene. He had seen all he needed to. Yes, he had observed several significant issues, and, yes, he was going to fix somebody's wagon tomorrow.

THE BRIEFING

The next morning came and the 10:00 a.m. ESET (Eastern Standard Earth Time) meeting began promptly. Irene began by thanking the plant people for their hospitality and stated, by way of summary, that the plant is generally in compliance.

Irene then highlighted her findings, taking pains to be thorough and accurate but not overemphasizing unnecessary details. She realized that most of the people in the room wanted to hear the "bottom line" and would be willing to review the details later in the report. Her main points were the following:

> "The Spill Plan must be updated and re-certified in three months. Much has changed at the facility in the past three years, so the update will not be a trivial exercise. You should begin this task immediately."

> "Your 97-6A hazardous materials storage area contains several deteriorating drums with potentially expired materials. These drums should be removed and the materials recovered or disposed before the situation worsens. This is not strictly a compliance problem now, but it could be if left unattended."

> "Based on a review of drawings and my observation of the facility, you have a potential for a cross-connection of drinking water lines with sani-

tary lines in area 92-7B. There are also five floor drains in this area not on the drawings. No one on the unit knew where these drains discharged. They could be the cause of the contamination detected by the continuous monitoring soil detection (CMSD) system installed below the foundation of the AY Complex."

And so Irene went on....

Dr. Demanding responded favorably to Irene's findings. She was precise, thorough, anticipatory, and offered new insights into problems that had been a "thorn in his saddle," as he liked to say.

Now it was Charlie's turn. He was bolstered by management's response to Irene and was really feeling good about himself. He began.

"Your hazardous waste manifests are not filled out correctly, and this could result in fines and citations. Further..."

"Hold on," Dr. Demanding interrupted, "We must fill out a thousand manifests a year. Are you telling me that they're all filled out incorrectly? And what is it about them that's wrong?"

"Well," Charlie began, "Of those I reviewed, several had problems including no signature and the wrong abbreviation for drum."

"Certainly the signature being missing is a problem," Dr. Demanding responded, "But I need to know if this is a chronic problem or not. How many manifests did you review and how many had problems?"

"Uh, I only had time to review a dozen, but it was enough for me to come to a conclusion."

"You mean to tell me," shouted Dr. Demanding, "that of the 5,000 manifests we've generated in the last five years you inspected 12? You must be joking!...Oh, never mind, go on."

"Well, I'm sure you understand we only have a short time up here. Besides, my other findings are better substantiated. Irene will back me up in that regard."

Irene was beginning to feel like the heroine in the movie she had recently seen in the Hollywood Archives Museum. What was it called, she asked herself? Oh, *Aliens*, that was it.

Charlie continued, feeling a nervousness he had not anticipated. "I also noted that several of your hazardous waste drums were not labeled. This is, as you know, a serious violation that has cost PEP some money at other plants."

"I agree with you Charlie about the seriousness of the violation," said Dr. Demanding. "If you can tell me the details of where and how many, I will send one of my staff out now to remedy the problem."

Charlie immediately began shuffling through his notes but could not find any reference to where his "problem drums" were. His nervousness was increasing, coupled now with a sense of agitation caused by Dr. Demanding's continuous challenges.

"I can't find my notes on the labeling problem right now. I'll have to get back to you on that one. Let me go on if I can," said Charlie.

"Okay," said Dr. Demanding, "But I want these issues resolved before you return home."

"Fine," responded Charlie, "I only have one more finding and then we can wrap up."

About this time, Dr. Demanding was thinking of wrapping *Charlie* up and jettisoning him into deep space.

"With respect to your hazardous waste storage and disposal, I noticed that your three tanks do not have the appropriate diking, and that the disposal cells do not have double electrosynthetic liners. This added protection is required by the 2044 amendments to the Resource Conservation and Recovery Act Scrolls. Actions to remedy the situations should take place immediately."

As Charlie was rather smugly stating his final finding, Dr. Demanding was reaching for his tranquilizers. Demanding could not believe the idiocy portrayed by this corporate hotshot. He vowed that if he ever had the chance, Charlie Sweat would do just that in the last remaining coal mine on earth.

Dr. Demanding began, having lost all patience by now, "Mr. Sweat, how can you be so...so...stupid!? The tanks you mentioned do not need diking because they are double-walled tanks on a special foundation. We have an exemption from the diking requirement, which if you had asked anybody out at the storage area they would have gladly shown to you. Didn't you talk to anybody out there?

"As for the disposal cell," he continued, "The preemptive local regulations allow for single liners on the moon since a leak presents few risks to us or the environment. We have no groundwater to protect, remember!? Didn't you review the local regulations before you began this audit?"

Charlie was shell-shocked. His only thought was of something his brother the poet had once said to him. He had quoted an ancient philosopher named Thoreau who had said, "The mass of men lead lives of quiet desperation." He hadn't understood it then, but he understood it now.

Dr. Demanding wasn't about to wait for Charlie's response. He said as he was leaving the meeting taking his staff with him, "You two had best do some regrouping before you leave this facility. If you have anything else to report, do it to me privately. I don't want to waste my staff's time. Otherwise, I'll wait to see the draft report, which by the way, had best be more accurate than your briefing. Good day!"

Irene was furious! Not only was she caught up with this loser, but she was now going to have to stay an extra day to fix the problems Charlie had caused. This would mean that she would miss her husband's birthday.

Charlie was now regaining this composure. He turned to Irene and said matter of factly, "I don't understand what his problem is. So I missed a few things. Nobody's perfect."

"Charlie, haven't you learned anything from this mess you've created?" asked Irene.

"Well, yeah," Charlie responded, "Plant people sure can be arrogant."

"No, Charlie," shouted Irene, "This is what you should have learned:

> **Attend to Details.** Don't leave important communications and logistics to your secretary. If you have no choice, at least follow up with a phone call.

> **Be Prepared.** Spend some time up-front understanding the facility and the regulations. Bring what you need to get the job done, even if it means an extra suitcase.

> **Communicate.** Spend the time it takes to understand the problems these people face. For God's sake, talk to them.

> **Commit the Effort.** This is not a 9 to 5 assignment. Meet these people for dinner, visit the plant during the off-shifts, and read the local newspaper.

> **Be Thorough.** Reviewing a dozen of 5,000 manifests is not sufficient. Pick a much larger sample, particularly if you begin seeing problems.

> **Be Precise.** If you see a problem make sure you're able to describe it so management can act on it. "Some drums somewhere" just won't do.

> **Be Supportive.** We're all on the same team. Dr. Demanding is clearly trying to do the right thing. We are here to help him follow through on that commitment.

Finally,

> **Be a Little Scared.** Don't be so cavalier about these audits. These assignments are not as simple as you make them out to be. There's a lot riding on our ability to do a good job, particularly here on the moon, which many people on earth believe should have never been commercially mined in the first place. PEP faces some serious liabilities if MRI is operating outside of standards, whether it's intentional or not."

Charlie did his best to pay attention, but he couldn't help but think Irene was over-reacting. What was the "Be a little scared" nonsense all about, anyway? What could possibly happen to PEP if they had missed a couple of items? However, to placate Irene, he mentioned that he had indeed learned his lesson.

And so it appeared for the remainder of the audit. Charlie and Irene re-audited the hazardous waste area on the next day, successfully debriefed Dr. Demanding, and made plans to return to earth.

THE REPORT

On the shuttle on the way back, Irene and Charlie talked about the audit report. They agreed that the outline proposed in the corporate guidelines would work well for the MRI audit. They decided on the following responsibilities:

Introduction and Summary

- Audit Background (Charlie)

- Facility Overview (Charlie)

- Regulatory Setting (Irene)

- Summary of Findings (Irene)

Findings of the Audit

- Paperwork (Charlie)

- Environmental Management (Irene)

- Water and Wastewater (Irene)

- Hazardous Materials (Irene)

- Hazardous Wastes (Charlie)

- Solid Wastes (Charlie)

- Housekeeping and Nuisances (Charlie)

The audit background would discuss the who, what, when, where, and why of the audit. This was to be followed by two brief sections—one presenting an overview of the facility and the second presenting any special regulatory requirements associated with MRI's operation on the moon. These two sections were generally well received because many of the report reviewers typically had either never been to the audited facility or had not been there for quite some time.

The findings section would address both noncompliance and poor management practices, clearly delineating between the two. Also, recommendations on corrective actions would not be included, as it was corporate policy to leave this responsibility to facility management. Most people in the audit program felt the company could have gone either way on this particular issue but, in the end, management decided that because of its decentralized organizational approach this responsibility was best placed at the plant level. A plant follow-up action item report was formally instituted as a result of this decision.

Based on her experience to date, Irene agreed to take responsibility for producing the report. A draft was due to corporate and MRI in 30 days and somehow she felt Charlie just might miss that deadline if he had to pull it all together.

Upon landing, they went their separate ways; Charlie believing the assignment was pretty much over, and Irene thinking, to some extent, that the most difficult part was ahead of her. It turned out she was right, but not for the reason she expected.

Two weeks after the audit, Irene hadn't heard from Charlie and so she called him to find out how he was progressing.

"Hello?"

"Charlie, this is Irene. How's the MRI report coming? I'm done with all my sections except for the executive summary."

That figures, thought Charlie. "Well, Irene, I'm about half done with my sections, and I should be finished in two weeks. My boss has really been pushing me on some other projects since we got back."

"Charlie!" shouted Irene, who realized she shouted more at Charlie over a two-week period than she did at her husband over a year. "Charlie," she repeated, "The report is due in two weeks. How am I supposed to turn it in on time if I get your material on the date it's due?"

"Hey, no sweat," responded Charlie, "My sections won't be that long. Just leave room for them on the word processor and have a secretary insert them, and then use electronic mail to distribute the report. You shouldn't be more than a day late."

What is this "*You* shouldn't be more than a day late" nonsense, Irene thought? It was clear Charlie was already disassociating himself from the audit.

They finished their phone conversation, but it left Irene unsettled. She had reason to be. Charlie had told a pretty common white lie. He was not really half done. He had only finished one of his six sections, but he always felt that getting started was half the battle, so, therefore, he told her he was half done.

This sounded pretty logical to Charlie especially given his present difficulty. Charlie was having a real problem completing his sections because he realized, too late, that his notes were not detailed enough to write a precise and accurate report. He had less than a photographic memory, and he was having difficulty recalling several important observations he had made. He was in a bind because he was not about to admit to Irene or Dr. Demanding that he needed more information. If only he had done what Irene had done: develop an annotated outline before he had left.

Charlie eventually worked his way through his sections. They turned out to be very superficial, and he was two weeks late in submitting them to Irene. Dr. Demanding, based on his previous experience, accurately suspected the root cause of the delay but corporate management was laying the blame on Irene since she was responsible for producing the report. Maintaining silence like a good corporate soldier, she could only hope that all good things come to those who wait. It turned out it was well worth the wait.

EPILOGUE

It was three months later and the Chief Executive Officer of PEP, INC had summoned Charlie. It was 7:00 p.m., and Charlie had no idea what Mr. Vance Hall Wharton wanted. He presumed it was to congratulate him on the fine work he was doing. Charlie continued to view himself as a "fast-tracker."

Charlie was surprised to find both Dr. Demanding and Irene in the meeting. Their facial expressions did not bode well.

Mr. Wharton began, "Charlie, I understand that you conducted an environmental audit of the MRI operation a few months ago. Is that right?"

"Yes, sir, with Irene."

"Was it you who was to assess compliance with hazardous waste regulations?"

"Yes, why?"

"Well, it seems we have a problem on our hands. You see, we recently had a U.S. EPA inspection and we were told that, although our waste disposal cells were in compliance with all standards, we were disposing a waste in the cells that is prohibited. It seems that six months ago the U.S. EPA issued a land disposal restriction on the newest formulation of methyl ethyl death (MED-1,1,4), our special solvent used in manufacturing Hairall. Fortunately, we've only been using 1,1,4 for about four months; we began about a month before you did your audit. However, the restriction applies especially to the moon because trace amounts of MED-1,1,4 can set up a chain reaction in the moon's geologic formations, causing a breakdown in the structural integrity of the strata. Are you still with me, Charlie?"

"Uh, yes, I think?"

"What this means Charlie is that if our liners fail we could have the entire processing facility swallowed up in a sink hole, people and all. We have now been operating at risk for over four months. Didn't you know about this restriction when you did the audit? Didn't you do any research on recently issued regulations that might not have made it into our checklists yet?"

"Well, I did some research, but..."

"Obviously, you overlooked something fairly obvious and critically important, don't you agree?"

"Yessir."

"Fortunately Dr. Demanding and Irene found a way to identify, excavate and treat the MED-1,1,4 before any problems occurred. However, the U.S. EPA has decided to assess the maximum penalty possible for the violation, which because of the risks posed is $500,000 per day, or $60 million." (It turned out that the dollar amount of statutory environmental penalties had basically tracked with inflation over the past 50 years.)

"Charlie, because of your incompetence, you have cost us $60 million and put scores of people at risk. Firing is too good for you. You still have three years on your contract with us, is that right?"

"Yessir."

"Well, let me have Dr. Demanding, our new Executive Vice President for Environmental Management, tell you what we have in mind for your next assignment."

"Charlie," began Dr. Demanding, "I must admit I can't take full credit for this idea. Mrs. Fair, here, my new Director of Compliance Management, is really responsible. Mr. Wharton and I must get to another meeting so I'll leave it to Irene to brief you on the assignment. Oh, and Charlie, don't even think about reneging on your contract because we'll see to it that you don't find another job on the face of the earth!"

As they left, Irene began. "I won't belabor this Charlie. You have been designated the permanent environmental coordinator for the new sulfur mine on Venus...."

"You can't do this to me!," protested Charlie, "that mine is a hell hole. Temperatures on Venus reach 480 degrees centigrade, and I hear that the operation uses mostly convicts to mine the sulfur. Women aren't allowed because some unknown source of radiation affects their reproductive capabilities. And..."

"Oh Charlie," responded Irene gleefully, "I'm sure it can't be all that bad. You're a tough guy, you can put up with anything for three years, can't you? Good night, Charlie."

"Good night, Irene, good night."

Chapter 21

ACHIEVING QUALITY ENVIRONMENTAL AUDITS: TWENTY TIPS FOR SUCCESS[1]

It is one thing to show a man that he is in error, and another to put him in the possession of the truth.

– John Locke, 1632-1704.

In rolling out Colgate-Palmolive's re-engineered environmental audit program, a two-day training program was coupled with a three-day audit. Whether in Asia-Pacific, South America, Europe, or the U.S., auditor trainees always seemed to fall into the same traps time and again. In order to facilitate the learning process, a list of 20 tips was compiled that was used at the beginning and end of all the training programs and audits. Reinforcing these messages seemed to improve the quality of the audits. Here are the 20 golden rules:

1. Do Not Ignore or Underestimate the Need to Prepare for and Plan the Audit and Its Logistics.

This is especially true overseas. Make sure that communications with the site continue right up to the time you and your team leave for the airport. Try to be as explicit as possible about the arrangements. We developed a comprehensive list of requirements (e.g., audio/visual equipment, computers, printers, room lighting control, flip charts and marking pens, copier capabilities, blank transparencies, name tents, safety equipment) for each of our sessions, which we faxed ahead of time to the site hosting the audit or training session.

Even using these detailed instructions, our preparation did not always result in perfection. On one of our training sessions that was combined with an audit, the room arrangements were less than ideal as there was no effective way to eliminate the sunlight from entering the room. This made slide presentations quite challeng-

---

[1] Originally published by Mr. Cahill and Ms. Michelin in *Total Quality Environmental Management* (New York: John Wiley and Sons, Inc., 1996).

ing. Conducting the training from midnight to dawn was not an option, although given our jet lag it might have been preferable. We also found that some of the older carousel projectors cannot accept 140-slide (versus 80-slide) trays. This meant that many of the training modules had to be transferred to another tray prior to use. As they say, "The devil is in the details."

Also, if you are sending materials ahead of time, do it well in advance. Customs agents have a way of slowing things down. Auditor trainees do like to have certain documents, like audit protocols, in front of them as you explain the audit process.

Compiling the appropriate regulations ahead of time is especially helpful on an audit, although not always doable on international audits, especially in the developing world. These regulations will do little good if they're in a language that no one on the audit team can understand. There will be surprises. We had more success in finding paperwork in English in Singapore and Malaysia than we did in Brazil and Denmark. Moreover, we found that most people from Spanish-speaking South America do not understand Portuguese, so Brazil was a challenge. And, while most Europeans speak several languages, Danish was not usually one of them.

2. Develop and Maintain a "Living" Agenda throughout the Audit.

Audits consist of records reviews, interviews, and physical observations sandwiched in between an opening and closing conference. Generally, records are reviewed right after the opening meeting and facility orientation tour. If the team is tasked with developing a draft report or draft set of findings while on site, there is usually a period of time needed to prepare these findings. This occurs just before the closing conference and sometimes late at night. Auditors should develop an agenda that allows for this logical approach. This agenda should be sent to the site ahead of time so that appropriate interviews and location visits can be scheduled. The agenda should be adjusted constantly during the audit, depending upon what the audit team is finding and any changes in the daily work schedules of the site staff.

Leave an open slot in the agenda just before you are scheduled to prepare the findings. This time will never go to waste. There will be additional people to interview, records to review and locations to visit to further verify your findings.

3. You Will Never Finish So Manage Your Time Wisely.

We have never been on an audit where the team was able to review every single EH&S document or interview all site staff involved in environmental compliance. If nothing else, there is simply not enough time on an audit to cover over a dozen compliance areas with a census-type approach. Moreover, audit sampling (statistical or otherwise) is a time-honored approach that allows one to capture the salient issues on the relevant topics. This sampling of records or interview candidates does not mean that the audit was incomplete but it does mean that audit teams need to use their time wisely, spending more time on higher priority issues. So, use your "living agenda" to continuously set your priorities.

Remember, it is better to address all areas to some extent than to ignore one or two areas entirely. Thus, the audit agenda should be structured so that each team member is conducting his or her assessments in parallel, not in series. For example, if one team member is tasked with reviewing pesticides, PCBs, drinking water, and underground storage tanks, he or she should do some initial review on each area on the first day of the audit and not leave one area to the last day. By reviewing each of the areas up front, time priorities can be established based on the relative risks identified. The auditor will not be caught in the uncomfortable position of not leaving enough time for one or more full compliance areas. This parallel approach will also help to identify whether any key site individuals might not be available later in the week. Their interviews can then be moved up.

4.   Keep a Balance between Records Review, Interviews, and Observation.

The audit team leader is always challenged by the different tendencies of individual team members. Some auditors are bored or intimidated by paperwork and are ready to undertake the physical audit almost immediately. This can be very risky even where the auditor has encyclopedic knowledge of regulations and company policies. Many requirements are found in site permits and licenses; ignoring these before you interview and observe activities can be perilous. Review records first.

On one recent audit of a Fortune 500 Company,[2] it was noted that the NPDES wastewater permit required secondary containment where four or more containers of liquid hazardous materials are stored outside. This was a very peculiar requirement to be included in the best management practices section of a wastewater permit but was there nonetheless. If an auditor goes into the field prior to learning about this requirement, he or she will not be looking for situations that might fall under this requirement. One is left in the unenviable position of having to repeat the facility inspection.

On the other hand, some auditors can be intimidated by the interviewing process or the physical facility itself. These auditors will pore over records until they have them virtually memorized. The team leader needs to push these individuals into the field to assure an adequate verification process.

As with most things in life, balance is the key. Try to avoid your own tendencies towards one or two of the three core audit activities.

---

[2]   Some of the examples used in this article come from experiences on audits for companies other than Colgate-Palmolive. This is one of those examples.

5. "Things" Will Happen on the Audit. Be Flexible.

Have you ever had an auditor become unavailable in the middle of an audit because of an allergic reaction to a bee sting, or get food poisoning, or be called back to his or her office? Has there ever been a surprise agency inspection on an audit in which you participated? Has your otherwise reliable computer gone on the fritz as you were preparing the draft report? If you audit long enough, any or all of these things will happen to you.

Be flexible and have a contingency plan for unexpected occurrences. If you are on an audit because of your hazardous waste expertise, do not be surprised if you're asked to help out on confined space entry, especially if you finish early. That's why organizations develop audit protocols, to help guide the auditor through a compliance and/or systems review.

There might also be an agency inspection or other outside activities (e.g., ISO 9000 audit) taking place during the week. With some adept scheduling or scoping changes, the impact of these distractions can be minimized. It is generally not appropriate to postpone or cancel the audit once the team is on site.

If you rely on automation, always have some kind of back-up approach for your computer or printer, especially overseas. Check ahead of time to see if the site has compatible computer capabilities. Typed draft reports are impressive; having the site staff stand around a computer screen because you don't have the correct printer driver is not. One option is to have findings neatly written on a pre-printed form as they are developed. These forms can be inserted into the report if time allows, but can also be used as presentation handouts if technology fails.

If you intend to develop a typed draft report for the closing conference, as many organizations do, schedule the audit so that the report can be printed and copied the night before. Giving yourself two hours on a Friday morning to accomplish the final editing, printing, and copying of the report or handout materials is flirting with catastrophe. A late night on Thursday can decrease the team's anxiety considerably. It is also usually better to work through the final stages at the facility and have a late dinner as opposed to having dinner and then working on the report. A lot of momentum and energy can be lost after dinner.

And be careful about designing a program approach that assures the team will work until 2:00 a.m. the night before the closing conference. Aside from those individuals who relish the pain of a late night, this is typically not a morale booster for audit team members and does not have to be an integral part of each audit

6. Always Be On Time Even When the Site Staff Are Not.

One of us was recently on an audit for a $1 billion natural resources company, where the audit team was large enough that two vehicles were required. Upon arriving at the airport, the team split up for the 3-hour drive to the plant site. The team knew that it would be cutting it close for the opening conference but, barring unusual traffic problems, there should have been no problems. As an added precaution, one group grabbed a quick lunch at a fast-food "drive-thru." Unfortunately, the other group decided a sit-down meal was in order. Well, as you might have guessed, the second group was a half-hour late for the opening meeting. This is bad enough under normal circumstances but the part of the team that did arrive on time had to sit in the room with the plant manager and his staff and continuously apologize for their teammates. Always, always be on time during audits.

On the other hand, the audit team may find that site staff might not always be available for the pre-scheduled interviews. This can happen because of normal day-to-day interruptions. Remember, site staff still have to perform their job duties during the audit. Unless the lateness or no-show problem becomes chronic, the audit team should "grin and bear it."

7. Remember Site Staff Will Always Consider Audits a Performance Evaluation.

As much as we kid about the saying, "We're from corporate and we're here to help you," second- or third-party audits are generally intended to be a supportive exercise. Yet, there is no way to avoid completely the site staff feeling that their personal performance is being evaluated. That is probably because it's true, especially on management systems audits. Auditors should never forget this and should, therefore strive to be empathetic (the action of understanding, being aware of, being sensitive to the feelings, thoughts and experiences of another) without becoming sympathetic (a feeling of loyalty; a tendency to favor or support).

8. In Spite of the Existence of Governmental Regulations and Company Standards, Considerable Judgment Is Still Required.

Isn't it comfortable to know that the corporation has prepared audit protocols for us that define precisely the government regulations and company standards against which we will audit? It takes all the guesswork out of the review, right? Well, of course it doesn't. Probably a good 25 percent of all findings on an audit have very little to do with requirements definitively prescribed in protocols. Even where requirements are provided, sometimes the specific site applicability is complex. One also has to be cognizant of the fact that even detailed regulatory protocols only serve as a guide because they can never be completely up to date. As a consequence, auditors should always receive some sort of training prior to that first audit. This will help immeasurably in their learning to apply practical interpretations to complicated situations.

9. Every Country, State, or Region Is Different.

Audit teams need to reflect the differences in local requirements on every audit. Yet, the lack of an independent review of state, regional, or local regulations is one of the most common deficiencies observed in audit programs.[3] Audit protocols typically address federal requirements and company standards; a few, but not many, companies actually develop state-level protocols. Auditors, then, are often expected to conduct an independent review of regional, state, or local requirements prior to the audit. Fortunately, a rigorous state regulatory review is becoming much easier to conduct in the U.S. through the commercial databases now available (e.g., BNA, Enflex). Audit teams are upgrading their laptop computers to include a CD-ROM reader in order to have access to these databases in the field, as well as prior to the audit.

The challenge of undertaking an adequate regulatory review is magnified when conducting an overseas audit. Even national-level regulations are difficult to obtain and will often require extensive translation. Some of the commercial databases in the U.S. (e.g., BNA, Enflex) have recognized this problem and compiled EH&S regulations for a number of developed countries. There are also now consortia of companies who have developed summaries of country regulations through third parties (e.g., World Environment Center). Yet, the fact is, presently there is no known complete source for international environmental regulations.

10. Learn and Apply the Audit Protocols, but Don't Forget to Use Your Common Sense and Natural Curiosity.

It is comforting for most auditors to have access to an extensive set of audit protocols. It is literally impossible to have total recall of all regulatory requirements and company policies on any given audit, even where the auditor might be responsible for only one compliance area (e.g., hazardous waste). The protocols will guide the review but they do not replace common sense and natural curiosity. Asking naive, open-ended questions, not in the protocol, can result in some remarkable answers. Examples include: Where does this drain lead to and how do you know? What if this vessel were to rupture? Why doesn't your boiler need a permit? What if the environmental coordinator isn't on site when a release occurs? Auditors should let their natural instincts guide them in their interviews.

11. Try to Observe Things as They Happen.

Verification is what auditing is all about but this is not always accomplished effectively by audit teams. This can be a special challenge overseas. Different cultures have different value systems and individuals may react in surprising ways to requests for verification. It may seem perfectly logical in the U.S. to request training

---

[3] Cahill, L.B., "Preparing Quality Reports: Ten Steps (and Some Leaps) to Improve Auditing," *Total Quality Environmental Management*, L.B. Cahill, "Benchmarking Environmental Audit Programs: Best Practices and Biggest Challenges," *Total Quality Environmental Management*, vol. 3, no. 4 (New York: Executive Enterprises, Inc., New York, NY, Volume 3, No. 3, Spring 1994.1994).

records to verify the statement by the site environmental coordinator that staff have been trained properly. This same request could be considered an insult in other cultures.

To maximize the verification process, auditors should attempt to observe key activities as they occur. These activities could include spill drills, wastewater and air emissions sampling, routine inspections, chemicals loading and unloading, and waste pickups by contractors. It is one thing to read in the standard operating procedures how these activities are to be conducted (e.g., "There will always be a company person attending all loading and unloading of hazardous chemicals or wastes"); it is quite another actually to observe them in practice.

Auditors should review both the design *and* implementation or operation of physical and management systems. Many an emergency response plan has met the regulatory requirements but, because of a lack of training or drills, the plan is ineffectual when tested during a real emergency. It is common to observe on an audit situations where perfectly acceptable secondary containment systems' designs have been compromised by poor operating practices (e.g., valves kept in the open position, containers stored on or outside the dike wall, breaches in the containment wall created to allow fork trucks to enter the area). The engineer had the right design in mind originally but the operators, because of other demands, will have negated the effectiveness of the system. The bottom line for the auditor is to make sure that all the plans and procedures that have been created in response to regulatory and company requirements actually are practiced in the field. Test the systems.

12. Observe Ancillary Operations.

On too many audits, the auditors fall into the trap of spending most of their time with the EH&S coordinator and, to a lesser extent, line managers and operators. Not only should more time be spent with line operations but the team also should increase its efforts in reviewing ancillary operations such as maintenance, site purchasing, laboratories, and on-site contractors.

For example, maintenance, which is usually assessed for its safety compliance (e.g., machine guarding, confined space entry), also handles numerous hazardous chemicals including oils, degreasers and chlorinated fluorocarbons used in the air conditioning system. Not only should auditors assure that these chemicals are handled properly by department staff but they need to also assure that the chemicals have been included in any regulatory threshold determinations (e.g., Spill Prevention Control and Countermeasure (SPCC) Planning; Community Right-to-Know §311, §312, and §313 Reporting). Maintenance is often overlooked when making these determinations.

Site purchasing can also pose quite the challenge to site compliance. A classic component of any audit of management systems is to assure that there is a procedure in place for purchasing to notify the site environmental staff when new chemicals arrive on site. If there is proper notification, Material Safety Data Sheet (MSDS) books and systems can be updated and, as discussed above, regulatory threshold determinations can be made and the chemicals can be added to any regulatory reports, if and when required. The auditors should also determine if there are ways quantities of chemicals can arrive on site without going through on-site purchasing. At times, a tenant business unit can acquire materials through central or divisional purchasing, thereby bypassing on-site purchasing. Research and development laboratory staff occasionally obtain small quantities of new chemicals from distributors and bring them on site in their personal vehicles. These potential channels of acquisition must be explored on audits.

13. Observe, Articulate, and Write, in That Order.

Auditing is a process that, hopefully, results in clearly articulated findings. Some auditors forget that an effective process begins and ends with an observation in the field that must be then presented orally in the closing conference and then written into the report. When auditors don't take detailed notes about what they have observed, they often find themselves in serious trouble. Reporting in the closing conference that there "were some hazardous waste drums without labels" or that "several MSDS's were missing from the maintenance shop book" is both improper investigation and not helpful to the site in determining the appropriate response. Auditors must clearly define what they observe in the field and translate it precisely and accurately in the closing conference and audit report. Clear definitions come from meticulous note taking.

At Colgate, a findings form has been developed to force the auditors into a prescribed format that minimizes the occasional vagueness in written findings. The form requires the auditor to formally complete, for each finding, a statement of the observation (e.g., "At the 90-day hazardous waste accumulation point, there was one drum containing waste solvents with an open-top funnel) and a statement of the requirement (e.g., RCRA requires that containers holding hazardous waste be closed except when adding or removing waste). This rigor is applied to both compliance and management system findings.

14. True and Complete Root-Cause Analysis Can Be Complex, Difficult, and Time Consuming.

Just about everyone these days is espousing the need to undertake root-cause analysis on EH&S audits. The belief is that audit teams should do more than just identify the symptoms of the deficiency (e.g., missing labels). They should also explain why the symptom exists (e.g., inadequate training). This is especially true where one is conducting a management systems audit where the corrective actions are expected to focus on permanent fixes.

We propose, however, that the audit team should do in-depth root-cause analysis only where the risks dictate it. Comprehensive root-cause analysis can be complex and beyond the resources of a small audit team on site for three to five days. Even in the simple case of the missing label, there could be easily a half-dozen reasons why it was missing and tracking down the correct one could take the better part of the audit for one of the team members. There is simply not enough time on an audit to do this for every issue.

In most cases, it will be the audit team's responsibility to identify the deficiency and it will be the site's responsibility to identify underlying or root causes and to effect long-term and permanent solutions. The audit team and audit program manager should follow up and assure that the site has identified and implemented the right solution. The acid test will occur on the next audit.

15. Writing Is the Hardest Part; Developing "Bullet-Proof" Findings Is an Elusive Goal.

Findings are verified statements of fact. Auditors should leave the conjecture, speculation, hearsay, and editorializing for other endeavors. Sounds simple enough, doesn't it? This is, of course, easier said than done.[4] Developing unassailable findings is the most difficult part of the entire process, especially as audit programs move more towards management systems reviews. How does one communicate that an organization is not very effective in achieving its goals? Not easily. Nonetheless, each auditor should have as a goal the development of findings that, when challenged, will withstand the intense scrutiny from the site. Appropriate evidence gathering and verification, as discussed above, will provide the foundation upon which an auditor can build an effective case.

16. Write the Findings as You Go.

Experienced auditors have found that it is one thing to verbally communicate a finding in a closing conference; it is quite another to communicate it in a draft report. Many times when the site reads the written findings for the first time a few weeks after the audit, the response is "but that's not what you said in the meeting." Accordingly, many audit programs have as a goal the preparation and distribution of a draft report for the closing conference. This is a considerable amount of extra work but is generally worth the effort as the site can respond to the actual report that will be distributed to management. This approach will mean that the audit team must prepare written findings as they go to prevent an "all nighter" the evening before the closing conference. This also adds discipline to the audit process and means that the audit team leader will not have to rely on team members preparing audit findings once they have returned to their respective offices, a risky proposition at best. Many companies use a standard form to compile individual findings and a portable computer and report "skeleton" to expedite the process.

---

[4] Cahill, L.B., "Preparing Quality Reports: Ten Steps (and Some Leaps) to Improve Auditing," *Total Quality Environmental Management*, vol. 3, no. 3 (New York: Executive Enterprises, Inc., 1994).

17. Prepare Well for the Opening and Closing Conferences.

Opening and closing conferences are key elements for establishing audit team credibility. They are the main interface between site management and the audit team. The team is often judged by its performance in these forums. Good presentation skills and communicating technically correct information are the keys to success. The conferences work better when auditors use standard presentation tools developed by the corporate audit group. Auditors should also listen attentively to questions and respond directly. If you don't know the answer, admit it, and commit to gathering the information needed to respond.

18. Make Sure the Site Hears the Real Story in the Closing Conference.

There will be a tendency to want to soften the findings in a closing conference. The environment can be very intimidating, in part, due to the fact that the audit team leader is reporting findings to the site manager who might be several positions higher in the organizational hierarchy. As a consequence, most closing conferences begin with high praise for the site staff and operations. While this approach is fine, if warranted, the site manager must also hear any significant issues clearly. This will mean that the audit team leader should separate these issues from the rest and communicate them with emphasis. It is best to highlight these priority issues together as a group early in the closing conference. If one waits to the end to "wrap-up" with the high-priority issues, there is some risk that the plant manager might have been called out of the meeting and may miss the importance of the message.

19. Plan to Be Done When You Depart.

The audit team should minimize the number of issues requiring future analysis. The site staff will want to be assured that what they are hearing in the closing conference is what will appear in the final report. Although the audit team should make no guarantees in this regard, the team should be close to 100 percent complete before leaving the site. If findings surface later, it is common courtesy for the audit team leader to communicate those to the site environmental manager prior to their appearing in the draft or final reports.

20. Enjoy Yourself!!!

Environmental, health, and safety auditing is hard work but personally and professionally rewarding. There is always something new to learn on an audit, no matter how many you've done. And take advantage of the trip; experience the countryside, whether it's the United States Midwest or Asia Pacific. You might never return to that location again.

PART III

SPECIAL AUDITING TOPICS

Chapter 22

PROPERTY TRANSFER ASSESSMENTS

Advice is seldom welcome; and those who want it the most always like it the least.

- Lor d Chesterfield, 1694-1773

INTRODUCTION

There continues to be a remarkable increase in property transfers, mergers, acquisitions, and divestitures in the U.S. and elsewhere, resulting in new ventures for the players. Some of the more interesting completed and attempted recent mergers include:

- Exxon/Mobil (Bring back Standard Oil)

- United Airlines/U.S. Airways (Watch out fliers)

- MCI/Worldcom (Wasn't the AT&T monopoly better?)

- Warner Communications/Time, Inc./AOL (Is Newsweek next?)

- Compac/Digital Equipment (Super computers fall to mass marketing)

- GE/Honeywell/AlliedSignal (Wasn't Allied a chemical company not so long ago?)

- Walt Disney/ABC (Mickey is sold)

- Glaxo Wellcome/SmithKline Beecham (Drugs become an even bigger business)

- USX/Marathon Oil (Steel and oil?)

- R.J. Reynolds/Nabisco (Tobacco and Oreos?)

At the same time we see major divestitures as well, as companies return to their "core competencies." Notable examples here are DuPont's divestiture of Conoco and Eastman Kodak's sale of Eastman Chemical and Sterling Drug. Many outright acquisitions are intriguing; Unilever, owners of the Breyers brand of ice cream, purchased Ben & Jerry's.

In many years, there are several transactions of at least one billion dollars, and in today's U.S. economic setting of uncertainty, the changing patterns of ownership likely will continue for some time.

Yet, even in this "pro-merger climate, it is significant that it has been estimated that one-third of all corporate acquisitions fail, and 70 percent are disappointing to the acquiring corporation."[1] As evidenced by the three noteworthy examples below, undisclosed environmental problems have had some impact on this lack of success:

■ In 1968, Occidental Petroleum Corporation purchased Hooker Chemical Company and the subsequent liabilities associated with Love Canal. Less than ten years later, the Love Canal became the genesis of the federal Superfund program.

■ Also in 1968, Northwest Industries, Inc. purchased Velsicol Chemical Company, and throughout the 1970s experienced incidents "like the inadvertent use of polybrominated biphenyl for cattle-feed supplement in Michigan, the claims of neurological injury to plant works in Bayport, Texas, and charges of contamination from dump sites in several locations." Velsicol was subsequently divested by Northwest.[2]

■ In 1966, Nalco Chemical Company acquired Industrial Biotest Laboratories (IBT), which has been swamped with lawsuits claiming laboratory analyses throughout the early 1970s had been purposefully and improperly performed and documented. Nalco took a $13 million write-off.

These past problems with property transfers have not gone unnoticed by regulators, particularly given the ever-expanding problem of abandoned waste sites. A handful of states enacted laws designed to prevent certain property transfers without government approval. For example, the State of New Jersey, in 1984, passed the Environmental Cleanup and Responsibility Act (ECRA), which required "that any place of business where hazardous materials were stored or handled in any way be given a clean bill of health by the state before a transfer of ownership or change of operation take place." ECRA was supplanted with the passage of the Industrial Site Recovery Act (ISRA), Public Law 1993, Chapter 139, in 1993. In essence, ISRA and its predecessor require companies to notify the New Jersey Department of Environmental Protection, within thirty days of an announcement of a pending sale, that it has completed an evaluation of its property—groundwater as well as surface conditions—including a history of spills, together with a detailed description of its

---

[1] B. Kennedy, "The Need for Environmental Audits," Pollution Engineering (July, 1982).

[2] "Velsicol Still Striving to Live Down Old Image," Chemical Week (May 14, 1980): 29.

testing protocols, and so on. The state then reviews the submission, and can hold up any sale until it issues an approval that the site is not contaminated.[3] As a result of the New Jersey initiative, other states have enacted similar statutes (e.g., buyer protection laws and superlien provisions) for their jurisdictions.

At both the federal and state level, property owners face tremendous liabilities under environmental cleanup statutes such as the federal Comprehensive Environmental Response, Compensation and Liability Act (CERCLA), otherwise known as Superfund. Superfund, and its state counterparts, allow for recovery of cleanup costs by the enforcing agencies at sites contaminated by past hazardous waste disposal. There are now over 75,000 sites nationwide that are under investigation by the U.S. EPA and state environmental agencies for potential cleanup, and almost 7,000 sites that currently require cleanup under one or more of the environmental cleanup programs. Surveys sponsored by the U.S. Congress suggest that the number of cleanup sites could approach a half million before all is said and done. Even worse, the U.S. EPA estimates that the average cost of cleaning up a Superfund site under CERCLA currently exceeds $42 million; but even "small" cleanups can result in seven-figure costs.

A more perplexing problem for the business community is that cost recovery under these laws is based on joint and several, and strict liability. In other words, liability for cleanup is independent of the volume of waste disposed by a particular company or whether the disposing company was acting in compliance with all rules and regulations in effect at the time. In fact, a property owner, or someone with operational control over the property like a tenant, is liable under Superfund. This is based solely on ownership or control of the property and regardless of whether the owner or operator contributed to the contamination or whether the owner or operator knew the property was contaminated at the time of acquisition or possession. Yet, the Superfund Amendments and Reauthorization Act of 1986 (SARA) does provide some protection for property owners and operators. The "innocent landowner" provision of SARA can shield an owner or operator from environmental liabilities if "all appropriate inquiry into the previous ownership and uses of the property" is made prior to the purchase. Many of the state cleanup statutes have similar "innocent landowner" provisions.

All this activity in mergers and acquisitions has given senior corporate managers pause for thought. Most companies now have an internal policy requiring that various environmental investigations be conducted prior to completion of an acquisition or facility lease. In addition, because of several court cases in the last decade,[4]

---

[3] "Environmental Audit Letter" (May and June 1984): 1.

[4] See *Environmental Law Handbook, Sixteenth Edition* (Rockville, MD: Government Institutes, 2001). Precedent cases include *Midatlantic National Bank v. New Jersey Department of Environmental Protection* (1986), *United States v. Mirabile* (1985), *United States and Trust* (1986), and *United States v. Fleet Factors* (1988).

banks and lending institutions are requiring similar due diligence investigations where they are providing refinancing or initial financing of a project or leveraged buy out. Developers, as well, are assessing "virgin" properties for signs of indiscriminate past waste disposal, excessive use of pesticides, or the presence of wetlands.

APPROACH OVERVIEW

Superfund and similar laws have encouraged most parties involved in commercial real estate transactions to conduct an environmental assessment of the property, usually called a Phase I environmental site assessment, prior to transfer. These assessments are driven by due diligence considerations similar to the more traditional facility compliance audits, but they differ significantly in both the objective and the scope. These differences are outlined below.

SCOPE AND THE ASTM STANDARD

The scope of a property transfer assessment varied from one region of the country and one transaction to the next until 1993. In May of 1993, ASTM (formerly the American Society of Testing and Materials) published standard E-1527 for Phase I Environmental Site Assessments in Commercial Real Estate Transactions. The standard has been amended since its original publication. As this text is being written the most recent version is dated July 2000. The ASTM standard, in essence, codified the current practice for conducting Phase I assessments, with certain limitations. By design, the standard sets out a minimum scope of services for the assessment and, depending on the nature of the property or the transaction, a more thorough scope of work may be necessary. As a minimum scope of work, the standard implicitly assumes that no environmental risks are known or suspected at the start of the project, so that the ASTM procedure can appear extremely elementary on industrial sites with known practices involving the use and disposal of hazardous substances. Also, the ASTM standard only addresses risks associated with CERCLA defined hazardous substances and RCRA defined petroleum products. Other common environmental issues associated with property transfers and ownership, such as asbestos, radon, wetlands, cultural and historical resources, regulatory compliance, industrial hygiene, health and safety, ecological resources, endangered species, indoor air quality, high voltage power lines, lead in drinking water, and lead in paint, are not covered by the standard.

ASSESSMENT TEAM

For property transfer, or Phase I, assessments, use of senior staff is essential. Acquisitions, in particular, often require the utmost discretion from staff involved in the process. Disclosure of sensitive information can significantly affect the purchase price or even the likelihood of a successful agreement. Thus, environmental auditors involved in the acquisition must appreciate the distinction between a Phase I assessment for a real estate transfer, and a facility compliance audit. Auditors will often be required to review the facility(ies) on very short notice, in the absence of any pre-assessment information and in the presence of a hostile or unaware host facility. Auditors may also be reviewing facilities or operations with which they have little familiarity because the acquisition may be an attempt at significant diversification (e.g., U.S. Steel and Marathon Oil). Finally, on occasion, external third-party auditors may be necessary where: (1) special expertise (e.g., groundwater monitoring and modeling) is required; (2) internal staff is otherwise occupied; or (3) external financing or insurance coverage might demand it. (The ASTM standard requires that a Phase I be performed by an "environmental professional," which is defined as someone with the training and experience to form conclusions about environmental risk on the property and an opinion as to the impact of the environmental risks to the property.)

EXTERNAL CONTACTS

During the course of a compliance audit, environmental audit teams might not call regulatory agencies. This is done for one of two reasons: either to "let sleeping dogs lie" or because it is thought that regulatory agency contact is best left in the hands of facility staff. However, under the ASTM Phase I procedure, a review of certain federal and state agency databases and calls to certain local regulatory agencies are required. In the case of the federal and state databases, the information can be obtained from private commercial companies that specialize in environmental information to thereby avoid "tipping off" the agency through the inquiry. The ASTM standard identifies specific databases that must be reviewed and designates search distances for each database. The private services can generate a report that satisfies these requirements and provides a map of the area that shows the locations of the risk sites in the neighborhood. A sample copy of a federal and state database report that meets the requirements of the ASTM standard is provided in Appendix L.

There are also ways regulatory agency contacts can be made without revealing the purpose of the call. For example, the assessor can make a blind call stating that a survey of the region's industry is being conducted and that a part of that survey is assessing the reputation of the major firms relative to one another. This way, no one firm is singled out as the target of the call, and the regulator is put in a more comfortable position. Keep in mind that the ASTM standard directs the interviewer to request information about the environmental condition of the property in question, so ultimately the questions will identify the property. In some states, compliance and compliance history records on any firm are commonly made available to the public if a request is made. These are usually readily available, except that some agencies are now requiring that formal Freedom of Information Act (FOIA) requests be made. This can delay the process from four to eight weeks. Once again, private information companies often collect compliance information in addition to the Phase I databases, and they can typically produce reports in 24 to 72 hours.

Finally, for this facet of the assessment, it may be best to use a third-party (e.g., consultant or law firm) so that internal staff are not compromised when asked the name of their employer during a phone call or office visit. Also, each caller should understand the agreed to protocol (e.g., whether the company's name is specifically mentioned and in what context) before the calls are made.

THE THREE PHASES

Within these guidelines, the approach to property transfer assessments is to divide the program for a site into three sequential phases of effort:

Phase I. The ASTM assessment consists of historical property use research, government records research, interviews with key site managers and local agency officials, and a detailed site inspection.

Phase II. Selective sampling of areas suspected of being potential environmental liabilities.

Phase III. Strategy for site utilization and/or potential environmental remediation or cleanup.

It is important to understand, as shown in Figure 22.1, that all three phases will not be required for each property. For example, at a minimum, every property will undergo a Phase I assessment. If the records, available data, interviews, and inspection show no indications of environmental concerns associated with hazardous substances or toxic wastes and materials use and disposal on the property, then there is

Figure 22.1 Approach to Conducting Site Environmental Assessments

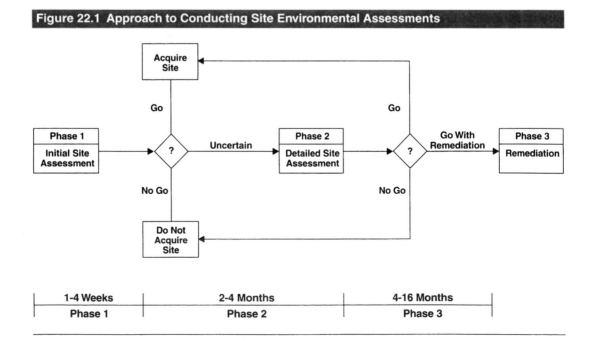

no need to proceed with Phases II and III. However, if the Phase I investigation shows that selected areas of the property may now, or in the future, pose environmental questions and/or liabilities, then samples (soil, groundwater, surface water, vegetation, etc.) should be taken and analyzed as part of Phase II efforts.

Based upon the Phase II analytical results, conclusions can be drawn as to the environmental condition of the property. It is possible that in isolated cases, a purchaser may wish to proceed with a project even though the site does, or most likely will, represent environmental responsibilities (i.e., clean-up). In these instances, as part of a Phase III level of service, the assessor would undertake a more comprehensive sampling and site assessment program, and would estimate the remedial actions and capital and operating costs for the property as a basis of negotiations for lease or purchase. In many instances, this type of property transaction must be consummated not only with the full cognizance of owner and buyer, but also with approvals from appropriate state, regional, and federal agencies.

PHASE I

As previously discussed, a Phase I assessment includes a compilation and review of available historical records pertaining to the specific property uses and surrounding property uses. The ASTM standard lists eight sources for historical property use information: historical aerial photographs, fire insurance maps, property tax files, land title records, historical topography maps, local street directories, building department records, and zoning/land-use records. Other sources may also be consulted, such as site plans/maps and interviews with neighboring property owners.

FEDERAL DATABASES	SEARCH DISTANCES
National Priorities List (NPL)	1 mile
CERCLIS List	0.5 miles
RCRA TSDs	
If CORRACTS facilities	1 mile
If non-CORRACTS	0.5 miles
RCRA Generators	Prop. & Adj. Prop.
Emergency Response Notification System	Prop. only
STATE DATABASES	
State Priorities List (SPL)	1 mile
State 'CERCLIS' equivalent	0.5 miles
Registered Underground Storage Tanks	Prop. & Adj. Prop.
Leaking Underground Storage Tanks	0.5 miles
Solid Waste/Landfill Facilities	0.5 miles

In addition, the ASTM standard identifies the federal and state agency databases shown in the table on the previous page as essential research sources.[5]

Evaluation of these files can provide a chronology of site operations and conditions for at least as long as the relevant agency has regulated the facility. The search distance refers to a search distance around the subject property, and it is measured from the border of the subject property. "Prop. & Adj. Prop." refers to a search distance that encompasses both the subject property and adjacent properties, which are those that are contiguous to, or separated only by a street or other right-of-way from, the subject property. The report must state the environmental professional's judgment about the significance of any listing found to the analysis of the environmental condition of the property.

The next step in an ASTM Phase I is interviews with key site managers (typically the same person who is interviewed for a compliance audit at the facility) and local agency officials. The contacts with the key site manager should also include a request for documents such as prior assessment and audit reports; environmental permits, registrations, and notices; MSDSs; community right-to-know plans and safety and preparedness plans; reports of hydrogeological conditions; and notices of violation or other environmental compliance issues.

Local agency officials should be asked for general information regarding the existence or use of hazardous substances or petroleum products on the property or in the neighborhood around the property. (Use the federal and state government database search distances as a guide.) Following the historical and government records research and the interviews, a visual site inspection is conducted to observe the most recent conditions of the site. For small parcels, the visual inspection should be conducted on foot. For large properties, a vehicle search or even a brief helicopter fly-over can be a first step and, if necessary, can be followed by a more selective and closer examination of specific areas of concern viewed from the air. If very recent aerial photos are available, it may not be necessary to perform another visual inspection from the air.

As discussed above, the ASTM standard does not address certain issues that may be appropriate for a comprehensive assessment. Nevertheless, the Phase I assessment should be designed to identify the potential presence of these "non-scope" hazards.

These issues are not solely the problem of industry. Environmental contamination has become every property owner's concern in view of real cases where: (1) groups of homes are sinking because they were built over landfills (Philadelphia), (2) major office buildings are being abandoned because of PCB contamination caused by electrical explosions and fires (San Francisco), and (3) public water supplies have been contaminated (Woburn, Massachusetts).

---

[5] CERCLIS files are available, with some struggle, from U.S. EPA. However, several database firms maintain a current CERCLIS database that can be accessed for a fee.

· As a guide to those conducting Phase I assessments, a hierarchical assessment of five property types is presented in Figure 22.2. The five property types are:

■ Undeveloped land

■ Single-family residences

■ Multi-family residences

■ Commercial buildings

■ Industrial manufacturing facilities.

The figure assesses the potential investment consequences of the most commonly observed risk-posing situations, such as the presence of discarded drums on the property. The potential risks to the investors are described and a recommendation is made for each situation as to whether a follow-up and more detailed site assessment by an environmental specialist is essential, advisable, or not generally required.

In general, each of the five property types poses the same liabilities as that type preceding it, along with some additional liabilities. For example, in the hierarchy, industrial manufacturing facilities present the most comprehensive set of potential liabilities one might discover with any of the other property types (e.g., asbestos or radon accumulation). Thus, the assessment tables build on one another, beginning with an assessment of undeveloped land.

Lenders and buyers can use the tables to screen investment properties to identify real and potential environmental liabilities. The tables can also be used to assure that all potential liabilities are investigated and reported where an environmental specialist is used to assess a site.

At the conclusion of Phase I, a draft report is issued documenting the data and information gathered and the conclusions regarding the environmental status of the site. In the parlance of the ASTM standard, the report must identify the existence of "recognized environmental conditions," which are defined as a past, present, or threat of a future release of hazardous substances or petroleum products on the property. The assessor also must state his or her opinion as to the potential impact of those conditions on the property. In other words, a "recognized environmental condition" could be found, but its potential impact will vary depending on many other conditions at the property. It also must be appreciated that Phase I results may be inconclusive due to the limited extent of available data and/or may include the recommendation to proceed to Phase II activities in order to conduct additional research for certain issues to reach more definitive conclusions on the site's environmental condition.

Figure 22.2 Potential Risks Posed by Real Estate Transactions

POTENTIAL ENVIRONMENTAL RISKS POSED TO THE PURCHASER/LENDER
BY REAL ESTATE TRANSACTIONS:
A HIERARCHICAL ASSESSMENT OF FIVE PROPERTY TYPES

Hazard Class	Situation	Potential Consequences	Risks Posed	Need For a Detailed Assessment*
UNDEVELOPED LAND				
Waste Disposal	(1) Property is abandoned waste disposal site or former military/ industrial site	Contamination of soils and/or ground water from past usage	Potential deal killer; especially if neighborhood water supply is on individual wells	Essential
	(2) Located within 1 mile of active waste disposal site	Past or future contamination of ground water	No direct culpability but potential for serious legal entanglements	Advisable
	(3) Located within 1 mile of abandoned waste disposal site	Past or future contamination of ground water	No direct culpability but potential for serious legal entanglements	Advisable
	(4) Located adjacent to high-risk neighbor (e.g., gas station	Past or future contamination of ground water	No direct culpability but potential for serious legal entanglements	Advisable
	(5) Presence of discarded drums, cans, and/or evidence of stressed vegetation and stained soils	Contamination of soils and/or ground water from past usage	Potential deal killer; especially if neighborhood water supply is on individual wells	Essential

* Evaluates the need for a detailed assessment (to include a review by an environmental specialist and physical sampling) if the described situation exists or has a good probability of existing.

Figure 22.2 *(cont'd)*

Hazard Class	Situation	Potential Consequences	Risks Posed	Need For a Detailed Assessment*
Underground Storage Tanks	(1) Existence of abandoned UST's on property	Contamination of soils and/or ground water from past leaks	Potential deal killer if tanks have leaked in the past	Essential
Pesticides	(1) Past significant use of agricultural or landscaping pesticides	Contamination of soils and/or ground water from past practices	Potential deal killer; especially if neighborhood is on individual wells	Essential
SINGLE FAMILY RESIDENCES				
	All of the above plus …			
Asbestos	(1) Use of asbestos spray-on or bulk insulation or other construction materials (only likely in pre-1975) construction	If asbestos is damaged (i.e., friable), it can become airborne and inhaled by occupants	Asbestos can be removed or encapsulated, but remediation could be costly	Essential
Drinking Water	(1) Chemical contamination from on-site plumbing (especially lead)	Drinking water contamination	Lead plumbing can be replaced, but at high cost	Advisable
Radon	(1) Possible radon pocket	Buildings could accumulate radon, especially in the basements	Ventilation improvements in basements might be required	Advisable
Others	(1) Use of lead-based paint	Children have tendency to eat paint	Risks only in cases where children have access	Not Generally Required
	(2) Use of area formaldehyde insulation	Possibility of airborne formaldehyde particles	Uncertain; conclusions on the relative risks of formaldehyde unclear	Not Generally Required

Figure 22.2 *(cont'd)*

Hazard Class	Situation	Potential Consequences	Risks Posed	Need For a Detailed Assessment*
MULTI-FAMILY RESIDENCES				
	All of the above plus ...			
PCB's	(1) Presence of PCBs in electrical transformers and/or fluorescent light fixture ballasts (only likely in pre-1976 equipment)	Past or future contamination of soils, ground water, or buildings from leaks (transformers may be owned by local electric utility)	Soils must be cleaned to 1 ppm in most cases; could be expensive, even if principal responsible party is utility	Advisable
Septic Tanks	(1) Poor operation and/or disposal of chemicals down the drain, especially where commercial establishments (e.g., dry cleaners) occupy building	Contamination of soils and/or ground water from past practices	Potential deal killer if substantial quantities are involved, especially if neighborhood is on individual wells	Essential
COMMERCIAL BUILDINGS				
	All of the above plus ...			
Hazardous Chemicals	(1) Use, spillage, or in-discriminate disposal of chemicals and/or oils by: - schools and laboratories - dry cleaners - auto repair shops - paint shops - gas stations	Contamination of building, soils, and/or ground water from past practices	Potential deal killer, especially if neighborhood is on individual wells	Essential
Trash	(1) Disposal of substantial quantities of hazardous chemicals in trash stream	Hazardous wastes being improperly/illegally sent to local landfill	Potential lawsuit or involvement in landfill cleanup	Advisable

Figure 22.2 *(cont'd)*

Hazard Class	Situation	Potential Consequences	Risks Posed	Need For a Detailed Assessment*
INDUSTRIAL MANUFACTURING FACILITIES	All of the above plus …			
Air Emissions	(1) Presence of regulated emission sources (e.g., stacks, vents)	Exceedance of U.S. EPA emissions standards (community)	Possible need for installation of expensive control equipment	Essential
	(2) Presence of workplace odors and/or emissions	Exceedance of OSHA workplace standards	Same as above plus workmen's compensation suits where health is impacted	Essential
Stormwater	(1) Presence of combined sewers or possibility of spills entering storm/floor drains	Discharge of contaminated storm runoff to soils, surface, or ground water	Potential deal killer if substantial quantities are involved, especially if neighborhood is on individual wells	Essential
Wastewater	(1) Process wastewater discharge to sewers	Exceedance of U.S. EPA or municipal effluent standards	Possible need for installation of expensive control equipment	Essential
	(2) On-site generation of wastewater sludge	Land disposal of contaminated sludge	Possible need to remedy land disposal site; very costly	Essential
Waste Disposal	(1) Presence of active or closed on-site land disposal facilities	Contamination of soils and/or ground water from past practices	Potential deal killer, especially if neighborhood is on individual wells	Essential
	(2) Past use of troubled contractor's waste disposal site	Contamination of soils and/or ground water from past practices	Could be brought into Superfund case as responsible party	Essential
Chemicals/Waste Management	(1) Significant use, storage, or manufacture of toxic and hazardous chemicals	Noncompliance with CAA, CWA, RCRA, SARA, TSCA, FIFRA, SDWA, or other environmental statutes	Possible historic noncompliance and future need for costly new programs and facilities	Essential

PHASE II

If, at the conclusion of the Phase I assessment, it appears that more information is required to explain such things as soil discoloration, large earth disturbances, or nearby/surrounding property concerns (e.g., well water odors or contamination, colored seepage, abandoned dump sites), then Phase II soil and/or groundwater sampling should be conducted.

A sampling plan (locations, type, chemical analyses, etc.), schedule, and cost estimate need to be proposed. Analyses should be conducted by a laboratory that is accredited in the state where the site is located.

Normally, any underground storage tank (UST) that had not been tested in the year prior to the assessment will either be tested or the subsurface soils analyzed under a Phase II program. Also, any suspected asbestos-containing material (ACM) will be sampled and analyzed under a Phase II effort. If the site is known to contain USTs and/or suspected ACMs prior to the Phase I assessment, then the tank testing and ACM sampling can be accomplished during the Phase I site visit.

An ASTM committee worked for three years on a Phase II standard, which was published in 1998. The standard, ASTM E-1903, provides broad guidelines for Phase II activities but, unlike the Phase I standard, does not include detailed Phase II procedures.

Presently, there is no universal agreement about whether shallow soil or soil gas sampling should be conducted on all assessments. Many professionals feel that sampling during the Phase I assessment, without additional information about contaminants, is a wasted effort, since assessors cannot determine what to test for and where to test. Nonetheless, some companies require limited soil sampling regardless of the results of a Phase I effort. In extreme cases, some companies also require groundwater monitoring (one up-gradient and two down-gradient wells) for any acquisition as a matter of policy. In general, however, the standard property transfer assessment approach is to test all USTs, sample all suspected ACMs, and to sample/monitor soils and groundwater only where the results of a Phase I assessment warrant it.

PHASE III

In certain cases, the purchaser may decide to proceed with a purchase even though the site represents present or future environmental liabilities as determined by Phase I or II assessments. If so, an engineer would develop a work plan, schedules, and fee estimates to conduct a comprehensive site assessment, including capital and operating cost estimates for future site remedial or cleanup actions. It should be clearly understood that such a detailed site assessment is relatively costly and time-consuming, and the resultant cost estimates are approximations.

ASSESSMENT ISSUES

The use of environmental assessments in real estate transactions has given rise to a number of thought-provoking issues, which are not strictly technical issues, as is evidenced by those questions posed below. If you are about to undertake an assessment using a third party, you should consider the following:

How Do I Know What Rules and Regulations Apply?

This is, unfortunately, a moving target. Superlien, buyer protection, and state transfer statutes are being passed and revised regularly in states throughout the U.S. In addition, the more traditional environmental laws (e.g., the Resource Conservation and Recovery Act) and their related rules are being modified as well. By the end of 2000, the U.S. EPA alone had over 450 separate regulations under development, revision, or review. The best bet is to consult with an attorney who is familiar with federal environmental laws as well as laws in the state in which a deal is being consummated. A good alternate source is the environmental assessment consultant.

How Can I Be Sure That the Consultant I Retain Is Qualified?

There are several ways. For example, in some states special certifications are required to do asbestos assessment work. Check these certifications. If underground storage tanks are to be tested, the tester should be familiar with the techniques. Also, consultants will be more than willing to provide statements of qualifications. But beware—you may be inundated with paper. Probably the best way to attain a certain level of comfort is to check references. Any consultant should be able to provide you with three references for whom he or she performed similar work.

Do I Need a Big Firm or Will an Individual Consultant Suffice?

Within the constraints listed above, individual consultants could be perfectly acceptable. However, they need broad-based capabilities; the skills needed to assess asbestos issues are often very distinct from those of soil contamination. Also, larger firms might have turn-key capabilities that you might need (e.g., the ability to sample *and* analyze soils, the ability to remove friable asbestos or test underground storage tanks). Larger firms will also have multiple offices, so if the investments cover a wide geographic range, you might want to consider this fact. One might also contract only with firms that have errors and omissions insurance coverage, in the event that a particular liability is not uncovered during the assessment. Firms that do not provide this protection can only protect the client with its assets.

Can I Get a "Clean Bill of Health" Certification?

No. Nor should you look for a certification that the site is clean. Any consultant willing to broadly certify sites, by definition, has suspect qualifications. This is particularly true with respect to soil or groundwater contamination. A site cannot be assumed to be universally clean without turning the landscape into "Swiss cheese" in an effort to test every particle of soil for every conceivable contaminant. There could always be that small pocket of undetected contamination where a ten-gallon pail of solvent was spilled three years ago. What you *can* get from your consultant, however, is a qualified certification, one that typically states that "using generally accepted sampling and testing techniques, the site was found to be essentially free of contamination." This can qualify as protection under the innocent landowner defense.

If There Is Some Contamination, How Do I Know If There Is a Problem? In Other Words, "How Clean Is Clean?"

This is a tough question. The U.S. EPA has yet to resolve it conclusively in determining cleanup standards for Superfund sites. The answer to the question is often a matter of judgment and may have to be negotiated with regulatory agencies. For groundwater, there are federal drinking water standards, but these presently cover only a very few contaminants. Many states today have developed "action levels" or guidelines for acceptable levels of contaminants in soil or groundwater.

Some Deals Develop Quickly. How Much Advance Warning Do I Have to Give the Consultant?

The more the better, of course. You should be able to obtain a consultant for a Phase I assessment with only a few days' notice, and a Phase I on a small site can be completed in a week, with certain limitations on access to public records. Consultants are prepared to mobilize quickly. There have been cases where several hundred sites have been assessed in four to six weeks. It is best for both parties, however, if the client has a standing contract with the consultant so that contractual terms and conditions don't impede progress.

What If the Assessment Identifies That Corrective Actions Are Necessary?

The need for corrective action should not necessarily be a deal killer. Removal of a damaged UST or ACMs can often be accomplished in a way as to eliminate any residual liability. Groundwater or soil remediation can be another story, however, due to the complexity of the problem and the time needed for remediation. Yet, even these issues can be resolved with the creative use of contractual warranties, covenants, and indemnifications; that is, the seller may have to assume some ongoing cleanup responsibilities or be contractually responsible for part or all of any contamination discovered in subsequent years. Or, in the alternative, the selling price could be discounted based on estimated liabilities. (The classic case is the Exxon corporate headquarters building in New York, which was sold in the 1980s for substantially less than its market value because of the widespread presence of asbestos.) The key is to understand the costs of continuing liabilities and to factor these into the agreement of sale.

What Situations Might Constitute Deal Killers?

This can be a very judgmental decision. Some lenders, for instance, will not provide financing on any property that contains asbestos, regardless of its condition. Others take a more reasoned approach. In general, the presence of one or more of the following conditions could be considered unacceptable to the buyer or lender:[6]

- The structure is built over a closed sanitary landfill or other solid, hazardous, or municipal waste disposal site.

- There is a presence of friable asbestos-containing materials; or substantial amounts of non-friable asbestos that can't be safely encapsulated and/or removed or won't be routinely inspected and maintained by the owner/operator.

- There is a presence of high-risk neighbors with evidence of spills or soil/groundwater contamination on or around their properties.

- There is documented soils/groundwater contamination on the subject property and/or a documented tank leak greater than 0.05 gal/hr (the National Fire Protection Association standard), and any of the following four situations exist:
  - Physical constraints posed by the site-specific geology, geohydrology, or subsurface structure render corrective actions technically unfeasible

  - Constraints render treatment processes or disposal options prohibitively expensive; that is, beyond the financial capabilities of the owner

  - Potentially responsible parties are unwilling or financially incapable of instituting corrective actions on neighboring properties

  - Soil or groundwater sampling values are above the state or federal guidelines.

- There is PCB contamination where:
  - Physical constraints posed by the site-specific geology, geohydrology, or subsurface structure render corrective actions technically impossible

  - Constraints render treatment processes or disposal options prohibitively expensive.

---

[6] This material is abstracted from guidelines developed by the Federal National Mortgage Association for its Multifamily Delegated Underwriting and Servicing Program.

■ High radon levels (i.e., greater than> 4 pCi/l) can only be corrected through large capital improvements and/or extensive on-going maintenance programs that are beyond the financial, organizational, or technical capability of the owner.

■ Conditions represent material violations of applicable local, state, or federal environmental or public health statutes or laws (although this is not a function of a typical Phase I assessment).

■ Properties are currently the subject of environmental or public health litigation or administrative action from private parties or public agencies.

What Do I Do With the Report If the Deal Is Killed?

If there were no significant environmental issues identified, then this becomes a moot issue. If, however, some significant issues were raised, then you should consult your lawyers. Many environmental laws have specific reporting requirements where real or potential environmental contamination could occur or has occurred. Although you may have no regulatory reporting obligations yourself, the property owner might have had to do so, and now you have knowledge of this fact. This has even more significance in the unlikely event that an imminent health hazard has been identified.

Who Should Hire the Assessor?

In cases where only a buyer and seller are involved, each party might want to hire its own assessor. More typically, however, the buyer will contract with an assessor (or use in-house staff) and the seller will make sure that its representatives (i.e., trained in-house or consulting staff) are on site during the site inspection—in essence, assessing the assessors.

More complicated assessments could include a buyer, a seller, attorneys representing each, and a bank providing financial support to the buyer. In these cases, the contractual relationship among the parties can become quite confused. This is particularly true where the assessor is working for both the buyer and its bank. These two parties have similar, but not always identical, objectives in the transaction. More often than not, the buyer will be willing to tolerate more risk and/or unknowns than the bank. In these cases, it should be made clear for whom the assessor is working.

Experience seems to indicate that the most troublesome relationship occurs when the assessor is hired by an owner, at the request of a bank, where the owner is in need of financing. In that event, it is obviously in the owner's best interest to have the assessor report the site to be essentially free of environmental liabilities. On the other hand, the bank that required the assessment and probably recommended the firm being used by the owner prefers to have every single liability identified and priced, regardless of significance. Given the judgmental nature of these assessments, this often puts the assessor in a direct conflict-of-interest situation. There have even been cases where owners have offered bribes to assessors to downplay the significance of the findings. The best solution to this problem is to have the bank choose and hire the consultant and be willing to absorb the costs if the deal falls through.

What If an Imminent Hazard Is Identified during the Assessment?

During the course of an assessment, an assessor might uncover an imminent hazard. A leaking PCB transformer or the presence of significant quantities of friable asbestos in a work area would be two examples. Assessors are not likely to uncover these hazards very often, but they should be prepared to respond appropriately when and if it happens.

Typically, responses will have to be handled on a case-by-case basis, and attorneys should be consulted. In the absence of any better guidance, the policy should be to inform the owner/operator immediately. This notification does not have to be made by the assessor directly, but can be made through an intermediary such as the owner's legal counsel or the lender.

Under most reporting requirements, the assessor has no personal responsibility to report an incident to a regulatory agency. However, today some jurisdictions impose reporting requirements for releases of hazardous substances on *anyone* with knowledge. Also, in cases where assessors are not satisfied that an intermediary will carry the word forward or that the response will be adequate, the situation becomes much more cloudy. In these situations, in particular, legal counsel should be sought.

What Are the General Approaches for Assessing Asbestos?

Asbestos is a mineral fiber that, prior to the mid-1970s, was considered a "miracle" product used in building construction due to its insulation, acoustic, tensile, and decorative properties. In buildings, asbestos has been used as sprayed-on acoustic material; pipe, boiler, tank, and duct insulation; adhesives, fillers, and sealers; and roofing felt and shingles. If material-containing asbestos remains intact, the asbestos presents no immediate hazards to those who live or work in its vicinity. However, when the material is damaged or disturbed, asbestos fibers are released, presenting a potential health risk to building occupants. While the use of asbestos-containing materials in construction has been mostly eliminated since 1975, some products are still made with asbestos as a component (e.g., asbestos-cement pipe, vinyl asbestos floor tile, pipe joint compound, automobile brake pads). Material is considered asbestos-containing if asbestos constitutes more than 1 percent of the total composite.

The presence or absence of asbestos can be determined in several ways, including:

- Review of "as built" engineering drawings and specifications
- Review of a previous asbestos assessment

■ Certification that a newly constructed building (e.g., newer than 1975-1979) was completed without use of asbestos-containing products

■ A bulk sampling program.

The challenge, then, for assessors on many sites is to be able to rely on the first three approaches listed above during a Phase I assessment. Simple physical observation will not be sufficient to make a negative finding, because much asbestos material can be hidden above dropped-ceiling panels or behind interior walls. The Phase I assessment is generally a "non-intrusive" procedure where, because of the risks of exposure, ceiling panels and the like are not routinely disturbed. Dried, friable, fallen sprayed-on asbestos can sometimes be laying on top of the panels, and any disturbance could release substantial amounts of fibers into the living or work space.

The assessor should recommend a bulk sampling program as part of or after a Phase I assessment when there is no documentation that the site is asbestos-free; observation of visible insulation is inconclusive (recall that materials with more than 1 percent asbestos are considered asbestos-containing materials); or the assessor is unable to access all areas of the building safely. Should a bulk sampling program be recommended, it should be completed by a certified asbestos inspector. In some locations, such as New York City, this is required. Also, ASTM publishes asbestos sampling standards (D-3879 and D-2590) and, as of this writing, an ASTM Subcommittee (Task Group E.50.02.07) is working on a standard for asbestos site assessments for commercial properties.

How Is Radon Assessed?

Radon is a naturally occurring gas produced by the radioactive decay of the element radium. Recently, the occurrence of radon in buildings, especially in residential structures, has received increasing attention. Radon can be found in the air space in buildings and in the water supply. With the construction of "tighter" homes and the decreased ventilation as a result, indoor air pollutants such as radon can accumulate to unsafe levels. The U.S. EPA estimates that radon exposure causes as many as 20,000 lung cancer deaths a year in the U.S.

Radon is not a localized issue. It can be found at high levels throughout the country. Radon concentrations are typically highest in basements, although there are some exceptions to this rule. Radon can also be very selective; neighboring homes can have decidedly different concentrations. Average annual radon concentrations below 4 pCi/l are thought to be safe.

In a Phase I assessment, the assessor can conduct a risk screening for radon that could include:

■ Contacting the local or county agencies to determine whether the area is believed to be a radon "hot spot"

■ Assessing the relative risks of the structure (e.g., determining whether there are basement apartments or offices where radon could accumulate).

In addition to the approaches listed above, there are also specific measurement techniques recommended by the U.S. EPA. In general, the method of choice is the charcoal canister, readily available in the marketplace for $15–$25. This canister should be left in place for two to three days, with winter conditions being simulated (i.e., windows and doors remaining closed). The canisters are then closed and sent to a laboratory for analysis.

In using the canisters, the assessor faces two problems. Because the assessor may not be on site for two to three days, he or she must rely on occupants to reseal the canister and mail it to the laboratory. Second, the assessor will have no verification that the canister was not moved to a lower-risk location during the two-to-three-day period. This lack of control can jeopardize the integrity of the results. Thus, canisters should be used with some discretion until such time as cost-effective, real-time monitoring equipment is available.

Are Wetlands Important?

Yes. The wetlands issue is receiving considerably more attention from regulatory agencies such as the U.S. EPA. In the 1980s, the U.S. EPA adopted a national goal of no-net-loss for wetland areas. There are now many cases where development projects have been stopped dead in their tracks because wetlands had been destroyed during construction and no permit had been obtained. In several instances, the developers have been required to purchase and dedicate, in perpetuity, other wetlands on a two-for-one trade; that is, two dedicated acres for each acre destroyed.

Thus, assessors may need to determine whether greenfield properties and properties where facility expansions are being planned contain wetlands. Determining whether a given property contains a wetland may require the eyes of an expert or consultation with the U.S. Army Corps of Engineers or county agencies. Wetlands are not always easily defined by the casual observer, or even a trained environmental assessor.

Can Farmland Pose Liabilities?

Assessors may be requested to conduct assessments of farmland, particularly in cases where the land will be converted to residences, commercial buildings, or industrial plants. Farmland can present substantial environmental liabilities. The issues of importance at these sites are underground storage tanks; spills of oils, lubricants, and hazardous chemicals; and past application of pesticides. Many common pesticides are classified as acute hazardous wastes under RCRA, and therefore they present significant health risks to humans, even at low exposures.

With regard to the pesticide issue, the assessor can conduct a Phase I screening that would address past pesticide use (e.g., type—particularly restricted-use or banned pesticides—and application rate and method), crop type, soil type, depth to groundwater, and prevalence of use of groundwater as potable water. This screening should provide some sense of whether past practices involved significant use of fairly toxic pesticides (e.g., chlordane, DDT) and whether this use has a low or high probability of contaminating an important groundwater source. Yet, without actual groundwater testing, one can never be sure. Because of the extreme toxicity of many pesticides, sampling groundwater is usually recommended where significant long-term application of pesticides is found, or where the level of use is unknown.

What about Urea Formaldehyde?[7]

Urea formaldehyde foam insulation (UFFI) and certain other building products such as some paneling and particle-board flooring have been used historically in building construction. UFFI, in particular, has been used extensively as a retrofit wall insulation. Volatile releases of formaldehyde from these products can cause respiratory problems in humans sensitive to the material. Trailer homes have been of particular concern due to the high use of formaldehyde products and the "tightness" of the homes.

In 1982, the Consumer Product Safety Commission banned the use of UFFI in residential and school buildings. However, due to the lack of definitive public health data, the ban was challenged and overturned by the courts almost immediately. Nonetheless, the consequences of the regulatory attention paid to formaldehyde makes it an issue in property transfer assessments. As a consequence, the assessor should identify whether any formaldehyde products, especially UFFI, are present on the property. The assessor should not overstate the impact of the presence of UFFI; it is presently not an issue on a par with asbestos. But the buyer or lender should be aware that the material is present so that susceptible individuals can be alerted.

What about Lead-Based Paint?

The presence of paints with high lead concentrations can create liabilities in buildings, particularly residences. Some children have an abnormal craving to eat substances not fit for food, such as clay, soils, and paints. This abnormality is known as pica. Thus, if lead-based paints exist in a building where children can be exposed to them, there is a legal risk to the building owner. Children are especially susceptible to lead poisoning. This issue has received special attention from the U.S. Department of Housing and Urban Development (HUD), and new regulations, effective October 31, 1995, require that lead in paint be tested in multifamily property. HUD housing project managers also must provide notification to tenants where lead-based paint exists.

---

[7] It is interesting to note that, in addition to asbestos and urea formaldehyde foam insulation, U.S. EPA is considering listing fiberglass as a possible human carcinogen and mineral wool as a probable human carcinogen.

Fortunately, use of paints with high lead content in residential applications was prohibited over ten years ago. However, older buildings where multiple coats of paint still exist do present a hazard if the paint layers are peeling. This issue should not arise that often; yet, the assessor should be aware of it when assessing an older single-family or multifamily residence. Use of lead-based paints in apartments and hallways should be identified, particularly on wall areas less than five feet off the floor.

What about Drinking Water?

The drinking water for a facility can be supplied through bottled water, an on-site well, or by a private or municipal water distribution system. The riskiest option is the on-site well, and where this is the case, some lenders will not, as a matter of policy, provide financing. However, even the presence of a municipal system cannot guarantee a safe water supply since some contaminants may not be removed effectively by a treatment system, or contaminants may enter the distribution system on route to the property through line-break infiltration or pipe corrosion and scaling.

Lead is a contaminant of particular concern. Several recent surveys have detected lead levels in public drinking water supplies significantly above the 50ppb standard. In many cases, the contamination is coming from lead solder used to connect copper tubing. Thus, the municipality may be providing a perfectly safe supply, but piping within the building may be the cause of contamination.

The lead issue does not mean that every site must have its drinking water sampled as part of a property transfer assessment. However, testing might have to be done where children are present (the lead poisoning issue), the piping system is old, or there have been complaints about the municipal drinking water or the drinking water in the building.

CONCLUSION

Conducting property transfer or Phase I assessments is essential in these days of increasing corporate and personal liability. This assessment will do much to identify any liabilities that might come hand-in-hand with the assets of the target; yet, assessments are not guarantees. If something is overlooked, there is typically recourse through the agreement of sale, which may contain a statement made by the seller that no material information has been withheld. Of course, this is a legal remedy with the potential for protracted litigation. It is best to understand the potential liabilities in the beginning through both financial and environmental assessments.

Chapter 23

THE TOP TEN REASONS WHY PHASE I ENVIRONMENTAL ASSESSMENT REPORTS MISS THE MARK[1]

Writing is easy. All you do is stare at a blank sheet of paper until drops of blood form on your forehead.

– Gene Fowler, 1890-1960

Historically, there has been considerable professional concern over many of the issues associated with environmental due diligence assessments, including report writing. This chapter discusses how reports can be vastly improved to help interested parties evaluate risks and make better business decisions on property transactions. The guidance can be applied to a broad range of auditing and assessment activity to improve the understanding of environmental issues.

Environmental assessments of property transactions are now routine. Typically, buyers and investors wish to identify any environmental (or health and safety) liabilities that could affect the value of the acquisition or investment. Even sellers have a vested interest in having assessments conducted. The assessments establish an environmental baseline that can protect the seller should future regulatory agency investigations identify significant problems at the site.

Almost all environmental assessments result in a written report. In virtually no cases will these reports state that there are absolutely no environmental problems posed by the site. Thus, the document is the principal tool that parties use to determine if the identified environmental issues at the site are significant enough to affect the financial structure or viability of the deal. As such, the report is critical in helping buyers and investors make an intelligent business decision.

Although there are nationally recognized standards and guidelines on what constitutes the content of an acceptable report, experience dictates that report quality varies considerably. Even with the ASTM guidance, buyers and investors are quite

---

[1] Originally published in *Total Quality Environmental Management* (New York: Executive Enterprises, Inc., 1993). Updated for this edition.

often left with the unenviable task of hiring a second environmental consultant to interpret the report of the consultant who conducted the initial assessment. The reports are sometimes so deficient that the second consultant must revisit the site, a costly and unnecessary expense.

The ASTM Standard does suggest a report outline, which is as follows:

1. Summary

2. Introduction

3. Site Description

4. User-Provided Information

5. Records Review

6. Site Reconnaissance

7. Interviews

8. Findings

9. Opinion

10. Conclusions

11. Deviations

12. Additional Services

13. References

14. Signature(s) of Environmental Professional(s)

15. Qualification(s) of Environmental Professional(s)

16. Appendices[2]

As a consequence, the ASTM Standard has added considerable discipline to report writing in the auditing profession. Yet, the ASTM Standard does not meet the full needs of the "due diligence" customer. For example, ASTM specifically omits the following environmental issues from consideration:

- Asbestos-containing materials
- Radon
- Lead-based paint
- Lead in drinking water

---

[2] Ibid., Appendix X2, Recommended Table of Contents and Report Format.

- Wetlands
- Regulatory compliance
- Cultural and historic resources
- Industrial hygiene
- Health and safety
- Ecological resources
- Endangered resources
- Indoor air quality
- High voltage power lines[3]

Obviously, these ASTM "non-scope" issues can pose significant liabilities to the purchaser and/or lender.

The ASTM efforts notwithstanding, there remains considerable variability in assessment and report quality. Simply providing an outline for the assessment report, as the ASTM standard does quite well, can only go so far in assuring a product that meets current and future expectations. In an effort to provide guidance on what constitutes a good assessment report, this chapter discusses some of the most common report writing problems and how to deal with them.

1. Failure To Maintain Independence and Objectivity

The assessor must be diligent in attaining a high degree of objectivity when writing the report. This is easier said than done once the draft report is submitted to the client. The seller typically would prefer to see a clean bill of health and, in many cases, will put considerable pressure on the assessor to soften or eliminate findings. There are instances where the seller has refused to pay the assessor unless changes are made. This presents an ethical dilemma for the assessor that can only be prevented if full payment is made in advance. After the fact, the choices are to make the changes, write off the client and the costs, or sue for damages. This is why doing assessments for sellers can be risky.

Conversely, the buyer will wish to see every single environmental problem identified and costed, in order to use the information to reduce the price of the property. The risk here for the assessor is that the site will be so fraught with problems that the buyer will walk away with no intention of throwing good money after bad.

Assessors should also remember that their roles are different from environmental attorneys representing buyers, sellers, or lenders. Attorneys are advocates for

---

[3] Ibid., Section 12, Non-Scope Considerations.

their clients and, as the client's agent, may put considerable pressure on the assessor to make changes or use softer language in the report. Assessors should be independent, third-party analysts providing an accurate accounting of the environmental liabilities posed by the site. There is a distinct difference.

Notwithstanding the risks of maintaining objectivity, the assessor is generally better off, in the long run, holding firm on technically sound findings. There is less chance for a damaged reputation and less likelihood of a lawsuit in which the assessor must defend an unsound report.

Aside from this concern about pressure being applied to modify report findings, there is a more fundamental reason to use independent and objective assessors. Every effort should be made to use environmental professionals who are not familiar with the property. Without even meaning to, people who are too familiar with the property may overlook problems that have become background conditions to them. Using independent assessors helps to assure a fresh set of eyes and ears are not going to miss things from over-familiarity.

2.   Failure To Define The Exact Scope of Work

In spite of the ASTM standards of practice and the other Phase I assessment guidelines, there still can be miscommunication regarding the scope and format of the Phase I report. There should be a thorough discussion of the contents of the report before the actual work begins. One way of clearing up any differences is for the consultant to include a table of contents of the Phase I report in the proposal so that the client understands early in the process what to expect when the report is submitted. Yet, as discussed above, a table of contents only helps the client understand the format, not the content. Developing and submitting a "sanitized" report from a previous assessment is also an approach worth considering, although consultants are usually reticent to provide a past report due to standing confidentiality agreements and/or the risk of inadvertently leaving something in the edited version that would permit identification of the site or client. On assignments where multiple sites are to be assessed, it is good practice to conduct a pilot assessment of one site and submit the report for that site before beginning any other site reports. This minimizes the need to substantially revise multiple reports.

Some report issues that need to be resolved early in the process include the level of detail of the findings. It must be determined, whether to present only exceptions or problems that were found, or to report all investigated areas, even if no problems were encountered. Recommendations are often requested and presented in Phase I reports, but sometimes they are not required or desired. These and related issues need to be discussed before the report is submitted to avoid costly and time-consuming rewrites.

It should also be noted that simply adopting a scope proposed by a recognized authority, such as ASTM, might not be sufficient in all cases. Remember that because the ASTM standard focuses exclusively on CERCLA-defined liabilities, adopting the ASTM approach can lead to omission of key environmental areas of concern. That is, the ASTM standard does not address investigation of asbestos, radon, lead-based paint, lead in drinking water, and wetlands because these are not considered CERCLA issues. This would be considered a serious oversight by most investors and buyers who still may be held liable for these sources of potential environmental liability.

3. Use of Conjecture in Report Findings

Hearsay evidence and unsubstantiated information are often incorrectly used in judgments and opinions in Phase I reports. This can lead to findings that may either understate or overstate the environmental problem described. For example, a maintenance person at a site might suggest to the assessor that several drums of hazardous waste were dumped in a nearby culvert some months ago. While this might have been the case, it also might not be true. The interviewee could be mistaken (the drums may have been filled with rainwater), or he could be deliberately misrepresenting the facts because his job is in jeopardy if the company is sold. It is the assessor's responsibility to obtain confirming evidence before presenting this spill as an undisputed fact.

It is often difficult to obtain completely reliable and thorough information when conducting property assessments. Partial and incomplete information is often the norm. It is important, however, that the parties conducting the Phase I assessment try to obtain as much corroborating evidence as possible about a potential environmental problem before including it in the Phase I assessment report. All sources of evidence, including personnel interviewed at the site as well as at neighboring properties, records and files reviewed, and physical inspections performed, must be used to insure that the findings are defensible. If real uncertainty exists about the extent of the environmental problem, some level of Phase II investigation may be needed. However, all efforts to identify and describe the environmental problem using Phase I evidence should be exerted first. Do not jump into Phase II recommendations when more diligence in the Phase I tasks will answer the question.

4. Use of Imprecise Language

In the rush to complete environmental assessments on schedule, the assessor may not be diligent enough in gathering field data, and this will result in an imprecise report. Assessors must strive to provide quantitative site information where possible. Too often statements like those given below are included in audit reports:

■ There were a few drums behind the maintenance shed. (How many drums? Were they protected from rain on a contained pad? Were they full or empty? What shape were they in? What was in them?)

■ There was evidence of past spills on the ground. (What exactly was the evidence? How big an area was affected? What materials might have been involved? Is runoff a problem or infiltration into the soils and groundwater or both? Is the groundwater resource used for potable water?)

■ The building was constructed in the seventies. (When in the seventies? Asbestos and PCB manufacture was prohibited in the mid-seventies. There could be a significant difference if the building was constructed in 1971 rather than 1979.)

■ There were a number of stacks and vents protruding from the roof. (How many stacks and vents? What shape were they in? Did any show signs of deterioration? What sources were associated with each stack? Did any need permits?)

When conducting field investigations, assessors must spend the time to quantify what they observe. This quantification should be translated directly into the report.

On the other hand, in an effort to be complete and thorough, the assessor must be careful not to use categorical phrases that are not supported by the evidence. For example, the statement "there are no underground storage tanks on the site" should never be made in an assessment report. One could almost never be completely assured of the truth of this statement. If, at a later date, a 50-year-old abandoned tank is discovered 20 feet below the surface in a remote area of the property, one can be assured that litigation will follow shortly thereafter.

There are better ways to state this particular finding, such as: "Based on interviews with the site supervisor, a review of the site's records, and a walk-over, there is no indication of any underground fuel oil tanks at the site."

5. Failure to Distinguish "Compliance" Findings From "Liability" Findings

In the mid-1980s, when Phase I environmental assessments were first becoming a part of real estate transactions, the focus was typically on identifying major sources of contamination at the site (i.e., spills, leaks, dumps). These sources were often seen as the "big ticket" items that could make or break a deal. Gradually, evaluating the property and the operations and activities at the property for compliance with EH&S regulations has become of equal interest to buyers, sellers, and lenders. Buyers and lenders, in particular, have become keenly aware of the potential for $25,000-per-day fines for compliance violations, which can quickly add up to substantial amounts.

Moreover, compliance issues can result from what might be considered progressive environmental actions, and therefore can be masked at a site that seems to be doing all the right things. For example, many sites over the past few years have been removing their fuel oil underground storage tanks and replacing them with aboveground tanks. Although this practice theoretically helps to prevent groundwater contamination, many sites now have to comply with Spill Prevention Control and Countermeasure (SPCC) requirements promulgated under the Clean Water Act. This has occurred because the SPCC underground regulatory threshold (greater than 42,000 gallons) is so much greater than the aboveground threshold (greater than 1,320 gallons). Given that SPCC regulations could require secondary containment systems for all tank and drum storage of oils and fuels, it would be a substantial oversight to omit this issue from an assessment report.

Thus, it is important that for Phase I assessments, the report clearly presents the findings in categories that distinguish them according to their type and significance. A useful scheme is to break findings and recommendations into three categories:

- **Required by regulation.** Environmental concerns identified as regulatory deficiencies are primarily compliance items mandated by federal, state, county, or municipal laws and/or regulations. Regulatory deficiencies may be related to paper violations (e.g., failure to submit an annual hazardous waste generation report), which carry only monetary penalties, while others may pose a significant environmental concern (e.g., unpermitted discharges of pollutants to groundwater).

- **Environmental liabilities.** Environmental concerns identified as potential liabilities are items or operational practices that are not currently regulated by federal, state, county, or local agencies but may have current or historic adverse impacts on the environment (e.g., an abandoned industrial septic system on site or the use of a CERCLA-listed site for disposal of hazardous waste). Usually these issues are candidates for Phase II investigations.

- **Best management practices.** These are items identified during the course of the Phase I assessment that, although not required by law or regulation, would limit the potential liability associated with the operation of the facility (e.g., secondary containment around aboveground storage tanks).

6. Documented Sources

Evidence is gathered on environmental assessments in one of three ways: interviews, records review, and physical observation. The assessment report must be clear about the source of evidence for each conclusion. Where evidence is not fully provided in the report itself, the project's files must contain complete documentation. There are now cases where poor document management has jeopardized the position of a client and consultant in subsequent litigation.

Assessors must obtain the names, titles, and affiliations of people interviewed and document the dates of the interviews," locations of the interviews, and whether the interviews were was conducted face-to-face or over the phone. Interview logs and forms are excellent for assuring that all appropriate background information is obtained.

Written sources must be documented accurately and thoroughly. Written records are typically obtained from a variety of sources: the site, local municipal authorities (e.g., the county health department, the city water department), state and federal regulatory agencies, federal information agencies, and third-party providers of general site and area compliance data. Written records must be referenced thoroughly in the report and copies included where it would be helpful to the reader. For example, where the records show that the site had never received a fine for a hazardous waste violation, the effective date of that finding is important to include. If there is a recent fine that the dated records do not reflect, the assessor would be rightfully challenged if this information is unearthed by someone else through other means.

Finally, any physical observation must be described accurately and should include appropriate parameters (e.g., time of day, weather, status of the site's manufacturing operations) when necessary to understand the issue.

7. Failure to State Assumptions Regarding Cost Estimates in Assessment Reports

There is usually high interest by the buyer, seller, or lender for the Phase I report to include estimates of costs to conduct additional Phase II investigations or costs to clean up or remediate the environmental problems found. This is not unjustified. After all, the real reason for conducting the assessment is to determine how environmental liabilities might affect the value of the property.

This issue often leads to conflict. The buyer or seller would prefer to have the assessment conducted as cheaply as possible but often expects any cost estimates for remedies to be quite precise. These two objectives are, for the most part, conflicting. The assessment firm's cost estimates are typically order-of-magnitude or approximate estimates. They often are based on generic unit cost estimating factors or rules of thumb to give the property owner some idea of the potential future costs. The buyer, seller, or lender who has requested the assessment is outraged at the assessment firm when the actual cleanup or remediation costs solicited from construction or remedial firms are significantly higher than the cost estimates in the report.

To prevent this conflict, it is imperative that all cost estimates for future Phase II or cleanup activities be presented with the complete list of assumptions that were used to generate the estimate. Three types of assumption that should be clearly stated for each cost estimate are:

■ **Quantity assumptions.** This refers to cost estimates that are based on volume of soil to be excavated, area of asbestos to be removed, quantity of liquids in tanks, and similar types of quantity-derived cost estimates. All assumptions (including whether quantities are based on actual measurement, calculated mathematically, or taken from another source of information) that provide a basis for the reader to understand the reliability of the estimate should be stated in the report. This will also provide a defense for the assessment firm if a subsequent cost estimate by another party is different from the cost estimate in the Phase I report.

■ **Replacement cost assumptions.** This mistake is often made by assessment report writers because they typically are viewing the cost estimates only as environmental cleanup costs, not construction costs. Replacing tanks, fuel lines, or new ceiling tiles and flooring that were removed to get to a source of contamination are examples of real costs that the owner will see in a construction company's estimate. Care should be taken to list the replacement or field-construction-related costs that will be incurred. Make clear in the Phase I report that these costs are not a part of the estimate.

■ **Unit cost assumptions.** There are several cost estimating guides that provide unit cost estimates for items such as:

– Cubic foot of soil removed

– Hundred gallons of water pumped

– Drum removed

– Square foot of asbestos removed.

It is important that the source of any unit costs provided be clearly stated in the Phase I report. If the costs came from a published cost estimating guide, the specific name of the document and the edition used should be listed. If the unit costs came from quotes from construction or remedial firms, they should be noted in the report.

Stating assumptions used in deriving costs based on unit cost factors, whatever their source, will help to prevent conflicts between the owner of the property and the assessment firm about the validity and reliability of cost estimates presented in the Phase I report.

8. Lack of Editing and a Quality Assurance Review

Every Phase I report should be reviewed by a qualified third party. This must be someone qualified to give an independent and objective reaction to the report in three key areas:

■ Technical accuracy

■ Readability

■ Defensibility

A senior member of the assessment firm should normally conduct the quality assurance review. The writer of the report needs to leave his ego at the door and accept the comments of the editor for the purpose intended—to improve the value of the report to the client.

Certainly the report should be technically accurate. As stated earlier, words such as "some," "widespread," and "a few" should be eliminated. The writer should also demonstrate a clear understanding of how state and local regulations, in particular, might affect the site and any proposed remedies.

Readability means just that. Is the report simple and clear? Are acronyms defined? Are too many polysyllabic words used? Writing in the active voice is not critical, but it tends to be more direct and descriptive for the reader. Remember the readers of the Phase I report have probably not been to the site. The report needs to help the reader visualize the issues and conditions. Unlike compliance audits, Phase I assessment reports routinely contain photographs to aid the reader.

For the report to be defensible, the findings must be supported by hard evidence. The editor of the report should challenge the writer if findings appear to be unsubstantiated. Defensibility also can be viewed in the legal sense. More and more transactions that have gone bad are being argued in court based on what the Phase I environmental assessment report did or did not say.

9.   Disputes Over Disclaimers

This issue typically becomes a tug of war between the buyer, seller, and lender—which prefer that no disclaimers be included in the report—and the firm conducting the assessment—which prefers as complete a disclaimer as possible. As with most things in life, an equitable compromise usually can be reached.

There are typically three disclaimer issues that arise in an assessment report. The first is certification. From the assessment firm's perspective, there should be no expectation that they "certify" or "guarantee" the site is "clean." This is simply too absolute, and no responsible firm will agree to make the certification. There are softer certification statements that can be made that both parties would find acceptable. These usually center on the certification that the Phase I assessment was conducted "in accordance with industry standards."

Second, the assessment firm should not be expected to warrant that documents, records, and reports prepared by others not under the direction of the assessment firm, and which are used by the assessment firm in determining findings, are accurate or up-to-date. These records are necessary for the assessment process, but they may contain errors or may not be complete. This can happen with records obtained from federal, state, and local regulatory agencies as well as materials prepared by private companies or their consultants.

Third, the assessment firm should be able to disclaim knowledge of any environmental problems that were not apparent during the assessment but came to light some time after the assessment was completed. Judgment is, of course, needed here. Not identifying that a leaking underground tank was on the property during the audit, which eventually creates cleanup liability for the owner months later when it is discovered, should not be covered under a disclaimer. However, the presence of twenty rusty, leaking drums behind a warehouse, which may have been placed there weeks or months after the assessment, should be viewed as a possible disclaimer issue for the assessment firm.

Other than the three areas of potential disclaimer use mentioned above, the assessment firm should be held accountable for all findings or lack of findings in the assessment report.

10. Failure to Write the Report as a Business-Decision Tool

Engineers and scientists generally write Phase I assessment reports. They are primarily concerned about environmental impacts and risks. Consequently, their reports are full of details and information about everything they did and observed during the Phase I assessment. Too often this information, although well intended and documented, is extraneous and not useful to the reader, who is generally a businessperson simply trying to make a business decision.

As an example, a report that forces the reader to struggle through three pages of a description of the geologic subsurface conditions and each underlying rock strata and hydrogeologic characteristic of the site is really not serving the client's needs. For example, the important point that might need to be made here is that "local groundwater, which is not a drinking water source, is about 200 feet below the surface with a 10-foot layer of dense clay in between, making potential contamination of groundwater virtually impossible."

Another good example comes from a report that states that the soils underlying an underground storage tank were tested and found to contain 1 percent total petroleum hydrocarbons (TPH), but does not state the significance of this finding. In this case, the buyer, unalarmed, was left to interpret the meaning of this finding. When he discovered later that the 10,000 ppm concentrations were 100 times that state's guidelines for TPH in soil, he was rightfully angry that he was unaware of the situation.

Another trap that writers of Phase I reports sometimes fall into is the quantification of the environmental risk. Unlike health-based risk assessments, for example, where quantification of risk in incremental cancer-caused deaths is a normal practice, quantification of environmental risks in Phase I assessments is much less practiced. Many lenders and buyers would like to see statements like "there is a 95 percent chance that the underground tank will not leak in the next five years" or "there is a 10 percent risk that groundwater will be contaminated from the chemical spill." These statements, however, are difficult to defend unless a clearly defined methodology based on statistics or computer modeling has been used to generate the numbers. Using qualitative definitions of risk potential and severity of risk, based on the assessment firm's professional judgment, is generally a better approach. This still provides the owner a sense of the risk potential in a way that helps him or her make the business decision.

Business people are accustomed to making decisions based on risks. Writing the report in the simplest way possible allows them to make informed judgments about the risks associated with the transaction.

Chapter 24

WASTE CONTRACTOR AUDITS

Those who cannot remember the past are condemned to repeat it.

— George Santayana, 1863-1952

It has become the norm, rather than the exception, for generators of solid and hazardous wastes to be concerned about the companies that treat, store, or dispose of their solid and hazardous wastes. Many corporations spend hundreds of thousands of dollars annually to ensure that their waste is being handled properly. Until the late 1970s, before the proliferation of environmental legislation controlling these activities, the transportation and off-site disposal of what was then referred to as "garbage and chemical wastes" represented little more than a minor line item, if that, on a corporation's annual operating budget. In many cases, small contractors and vendors who operated local waste disposal businesses handled almost any type of waste offered to them, including trash, drums of waste oils and solvents, treatment sludges, and other by-products of manufacturing and industrial operations.

Many of these chemical wastes generated from manufacturing operations, such as solvents and oils, were mixed with domestic trash and placed in municipal landfills. Worse yet, they were taken to inactive quarries, warehouses, farmland, or other remote areas and simply abandoned or buried. There was little concern on behalf of the waste generator about the ultimate disposition and fate of these wastes, since their disposal costs were low, and regulations did not exist at the time to prevent or control these activities. In fact, many companies sought to find the most inexpensive waste disposal option, regardless of the technology employed.

In the late 1970s and early 1980s, three key factors combined to abruptly change corporate America's waste disposal practices forever:

1. the discovery of toxic waste disposal sites such as Love Canal and Kin-Buc landfill, where the illicit disposal of industrial wastes posed a real threat to human health and welfare;

2. the passage of landmark environmental legislation controlling the generation, handling, and treatment/disposal of toxic and hazardous wastes (RCRA); and

3. the establishment of legislation aimed at cleaning up those properties already contaminated with hazardous substances (CERCLA, Superfund).

The Superfund legislation allows the U.S. EPA, under certain conditions, to impose severe, retroactive, strict, and joint and several liability upon any party responsible for the release of hazardous substances into the environment. Strict liability means that parties can be found liable regardless of fault or extent of negligence. Joint and several liability means that any one responsible party can be held liable for the entire cost of site investigation, cleanup, and other damages. The average cost to investigate and remediate a contaminated site on the CERCLA National Priorities List (NPL) is approximately $25 million, exclusive of legal costs. There are many former waste disposal sites, such as the Stringfellow site in southern California and the Lowery Landfill in Colorado, where the costs are much greater. Responsible parties can include current or previous owners or operators of a waste treatment, storage, or disposal (TSD) facility; transporters or contractors that selected the disposal facilities; and, most importantly, the generators who provided the hazardous wastes. Waste generators are the most susceptible to joint and several liability for several reasons, which are:

■ The previous or current site owners may not have the financial resources to meet the cost of the damages.

■ Due to the complex nature of many Superfund sites, in some cases it becomes very difficult to accurately allocate responsibilities among owners, operators, and generators, so all of the responsible parties are forced to contribute. Legal costs for prolonged negotiation and discovery can prove insurmountable, forcing companies to settle.

■ Industrial corporations that generated the wastes often represent the "deep pocket" at the site, making them the most likely target for both CERCLA cost-recovery actions and private party "toxic tort" suits.

It should be noted that potential liabilities for generators associated with the disposal of waste are not solely limited to the use of the off-site TSD facilities. CERCLA liability can also be assigned to parties that transported or arranged for the disposal of the wastes. As a result, transporters and waste "brokers" can be held accountable as "potentially responsible parties" (PRPs) under CERCLA. In today's environment, with a decreasing number of waste disposal options available to a generator, many generators are relying more heavily on the use of multiple transporters and waste brokers to remove and dispose of wastes. In many cases, waste brokers are actually selecting the disposal site for the generator's waste, potentially exposing the generator to additional future liability if the site is poorly managed, operated, or financed. Accordingly, generators must be cognizant of the increased risks associated with the use of multiple vendors.

There are also numerous sites on the NPL that handled wastes considered to be nonhazardous at the time, such as empty drums, waste oil, asbestos, and batteries, where the generators of these "nonhazardous" wastes have been held accountable as PRPs under CERCLA. Waste generators must also consider the risks associated with the treatment or disposal of these nonhazardous wastes, which can include precious metal bearing wastes, Ni-Cd batteries, and other electronic scrap. The vendors handling these non-RCRA wastes may not be as carefully monitored or controlled as TSD facilities that are regulated under RCRA, TSCA, or state equivalents.

Considering the range of potential liabilities associated with waste management, responsible solid and hazardous wastes generators are anxious to avoid using poorly operated, improperly managed, and insufficiently financed TSD facilities in order to limit their future exposure. In addition to the potential for future financial liability under CERCLA, the possibility of both financial impact and negative public relations exposure—due to private party "toxic tort" suits for real or perceived health impacts, or to property devaluation—is forcing corporations to take a closer look at the commercial TSD facilities that handle their wastes.

Waste vendor audit programs are also increasingly driven by simple economics. As options for waste treatment and disposal become more limited, many generators are forced to pay higher prices for waste disposal and/or transport their wastes much greater distances to reach their selected TSD facility. In some cases, generators start waste vendor audit programs simply as a way to identify and evaluate less expensive but equally suitable alternatives for the management of the their wastes.

OBJECTIVE AND SCOPE OF A TSD FACILITY AUDIT PROGRAM

The basic objective of any TSD facility audit program should be a simple one: to identify and minimize the generator's liabilities that are associated with the off-site treatment, storage, and disposal of their wastes. The vast majority of generators do not have captive treatment or disposal facilities and, therefore, must rely on commercial facilities to handle some, if not all, of these wastes. Accordingly, control over a significant portion of the liabilities associated with the treatment and disposal of hazardous wastes thereby rests in the hands of third-party contractors (i.e., transporters, brokers, and the TSD facility), although under RCRA the generator is responsible in perpetuity for assuring their proper fate. The TSD audit program should be designed to identify the potential liabilities associated with the use of these third-party vendors. Once the potential problems have been identified, the program should allow for some type of quantitative analysis by which different TSD facilities can be evaluated, compared, and selected.

Ideally, the selection of TSD facilities to be audited should not be limited to those facilities that are currently handling a generator's RCRA hazardous wastes, because RCRA-regulated facilities tend to be more closely monitored by regulatory agencies than solid waste, oil, or precious metal recovery operations. Many of these non-RCRA facilities present significant environmental, operational, and demographic concerns, which could result in generator liability. Since the financial assurance requirements for non-RCRA facilities are typically less stringent than for RCRA-regulated facilities (or are nonexistent), the management and financial stability of these facilities may be of concern to a large deep-pocket generator in the event of an environmental problem.

The TSD facility audit program should assist waste generators in identifying those transporters, brokers, and/or TSD facilities that are best suited to handle the generator's particular waste streams. By thoroughly assessing the capabilities and operations of these vendors, generators can often reduce the number of contractors that they utilize for waste transportation, treatment, and disposal, resulting in a more focused and cost-effective waste management program. As an additional benefit, the commercial waste vendor audit program allows the generator to identify and eliminate the use of contractors who present unreasonable environmental risks that otherwise would not have been evident without a comprehensive, risk-based review.

INTERNAL PROGRAMS VS. EXTERNAL PROGRAMS

Waste generators typically conduct commercial waste vendor and audit programs in one of two different ways: (1) through the use of internal staff or (2) by using independent professional environmental consultants.

The use of company employees to conduct a commercial waste vendor audit program usually requires a lengthy start-up period for:

- the training of audit staff,

- selection of the program elements (i.e., what will be covered in the audit),

- development of audit checklists and report formats, and

- establishment of the audit infrastructure.

Depending upon the scope of the program, the development of an internal, comprehensive commercial waste vendor audit program may require dedicated staff and a significant amount of resources. Once the program is implemented, large expenditures are infrequent, but the program management can be overwhelming, especially for corporate environmental staff with other responsibilities. For this reason, most internal commercial waste vendor audit programs are very limited in scope.

Although using consultants to develop and implement a commercial waste vendor audit program will minimize the managerial burden on corporate staff, program start-up costs can be large, and the program implementation costs become directly proportional to the number of audits that are assigned. The design and product of company-specific audit protocols, checklists, scoring models, and financial analysis models can be expensive if a truly comprehensive audit program is desired. Of course, the amount of information that the generator needs to assess the suitability of a waste vendor will ultimately determine the cost of program start-up. Once the program is in place, the costs to have the consultant conduct the audits can range from several thousand dollars to $20,000 per site, based upon the characteristics of the TSD facility, its location, the complexity of the audit, and the scope of the audit report. The advantage to having an independent, outside consultant conduct the audits is that experienced and trained engineers and scientists can conduct as many audits as the generator is willing to assign without draining the generator's available manpower and resources.

In some cases, generators with common interests in conducting commercial waste vendor audits can arrange to have one contractor develop the program and conduct the audits on behalf of the group. The information can then be distributed on a cost-sharing basis. There are several major industry-oriented programs in place today, which employ external consultants to conduct commercial waste vendor audits using pre-established, proprietary, and confidential audit protocols, report formats, and risk-ranking models.

For example, the Commercial Hazardous Waste Management Evaluation Group (CHWMEG) is a trade association of over fifty waste generating companies formed in 1987 and incorporated in 1995 to obtain independent evaluations of TSD facilities. An independent administrator and escrow agent are employed to operate CHWMEG and handle all transactions on a confidential basis. Member companies' decisions to audit or utilize a particular TSD facility are strictly confidential. Each member company selects TSD facilities to be audited, and the audits are then conducted according to a CHWMEG-developed protocol by independent, nationally recognized environmental consulting firms. The member companies who have chosen to sponsor the audit of that particular facility share the cost of each audit. Each sponsor then receives a complete copy of the audit report. The CHWMEG group has sponsored the development of a specially designed database management system (DBMS), which allows computer access to key audit information, data sorts, and extractions. CHWMEG's audit procedure is very comprehensive, and includes a proprietary financial analysis model as well. CHWMEG has also sponsored the development of a quantitative Risk Assessment System (RAS), which considers the environmental, operational, and financial risks posed by a TSD facility. CHWMEG routinely evaluates from 30 to over 100 different TSD facilities annually. The annual membership fee is less than $3,000 and individual audit reports cost less than $800 each. Further information on CHWMEG can be obtained at their website (www.chwmeg.org).

CONDUCTING THE TSD FACILITY AUDIT

Waste generators should design their commercial waste vendor audit programs to incorporate *all* of their waste vendors, including transporters and brokers. However, since the core aspects of most commercial waste vendor programs center around auditing and evaluating TSD facilities, for the purposes of this chapter we will use the example of a TSD facility audit to describe the basic steps in the waste vendor audit process. The same audit tasks and principles will apply to waste transporters and brokers as well, but the specific risk management issues associated with these vendors will focus on waste handling and transportation rather than treatment and disposal.

Waste vendor facility audits are similar to internal plant audits in that they have several different, distinct phases: pre-audit, on-site, and post-audit activities. However, the approach to conducting waste vendor facility audits differs in some key respects:

■ Although regulatory compliance is an important factor in evaluating the relative liability posed by a waste vendor, the audit must focus on risk-related aspects of the waste management operation as well.

■ The relative financial strength of the waste vendor (and its parent company, if applicable) is an important area of evaluation.

■ Staff cooperation, available auditing time, and access to data may be limited by the fact that the auditor is not an employee of the waste management company or a regulatory agency inspector. Therefore, proper pre-audit preparation assumes an even more critical role in conducting waste vendor facility audits. Trying to complete a comprehensive audit of a very large commercial TSD facility without proper pre-audit preparation is akin to attempting to complete your federal income tax return on April 14th without reading the instructions first.

The following sections discuss the elements of conducting a successful waste vendor audit at a commercial TSD facility. The discussion is meant to serve as an addition to the basic audit instructions presented elsewhere in the text, by highlighting the areas that are appropriate to auditing commercial waste management facilities.

PRE-AUDIT PREPARATION

Once a TSD facility has been selected as a candidate to be audited, the audit team leader or project manager should implement the following steps:

■ Obtain basic location, operation, and regulatory agency information about the TSD facility (i.e., the facility pre-audit screening).

Obtain basic financial information about the TSD facility (e.g., ownership, financial health, insurance information, litigation status).

Speak directly with TSD facility representatives to confirm facility operations and to schedule the audit date and activities.

Review the appropriate federal, state, and local regulations pertinent to the TSD facility operations.

Select the audit team staff most suited for the TSD facility, based upon the items above.

The importance of the pre-audit preparation steps described above cannot be overemphasized. The first three steps may, in some cases, serve to eliminate immediately some sites from further consideration due to major regulatory problems, scheduled phase-out or closure of certain operations, financial distress, or shutdown of the entire site. More often, however, the completion of the pre-audit activities prior to arriving on site for the audit will ensure that the audit objectives are met.

Several methodologies are usually employed in order to obtain location, operational, and regulatory information about a TSD facility. The use of telephone interviews, electronic databases, and other readily available sources of information such as maps, aerial photographs, and publications are presented in Figure 24.1. The information obtained during the pre-audit activities should be sufficient to:

Determine if the facility has been the subject of legal action such as Administrative Consent Orders or private party litigation

Determine the legal status and financial condition of the company owner(s) and operator(s)

Identify the basic waste management operations and corresponding environmental compliance issues at the facility

Determine the specific outside contractor or client audit policies that the TSD facility may require you follow before, during, and after the on-site audit

Give the TSD facility staff an understanding of the scope, complexity, time constraints, and objectives of your audit activities

Give the audit team a good understanding of the facility location and demographics with respect to nearby potential environmental and human receptors

Determine if a serious (e.g., major groundwater contamination, permit application denial) or recurring (e.g., repeated spills and releases, poor inspection history) environmental condition or regulatory compliance problem exists at the facility.

Figure 24.1 Sources for Obtaining the Pre-Audit Information

Location

- U.S. Geological Survey maps
- Local historical and current aerial photographs
- U.S. Census data
- Local historical societies, real estate groups, and chamber of commerce
- County and city municipal government interviews.

Regulatory Status and Compliance

- Personal or telephone interviews with federal, state, regional, and local regulatory agencies
- Freedom of Information Act (FOIA) requests
- U.S. EPA, OSHA, and private subscription databases regarding permit status and compliance (e.g., www.epa.gov/envirofacts, www.osha.gov/oshstats)
- Independent commercial database services that monitor TSD facilities, such as EDR and VISTA
- Regulation and compliance-oriented publications.

TSD Facility Operations

- Direct telephone contact with TSD facility technical representatives
- Review of corporate promotional literature and pre-audit information packages
- Review of federal, state, regional, and local regulatory agency files
- Use of a pre-audit questionnaire.

TSD Facility Financial Information

- Annual reports and audited balance sheets
- SEC 10-Q and 10-K forms and other corporate filings
- Financial information services such as Dun and Bradstreet, SEC Online, Dow Jones News Retrieval, and Robert Morris and Associates
- Credit, banking, and vendor references.

Key regulatory compliance parameters that should be ascertained during the pre-audit phase include permit status, facility-specific permit-mandated compliance requirements, recurring or serious compliance problems, existing or suspected environmental contamination issues, RCRA corrective actions status and/or CERCLA involvement, recent regulatory agency inspection results, and closure/post-closure financial assurance information.

Be sure to leave enough time to obtain the pre-audit information prior to commencing the on-site portion of the audit. In some states, regulatory agency personnel are literally inundated with requests for compliance information on TSD facilities and will not answer phone inquiries regarding TSD facility compliance. These agencies may require you to submit a formal Freedom of Information Act (FOIA) request in order to obtain the information you need. This process can take up to several weeks. Certain agencies may allow the review of compliance records for a particular facility in person if you make an appointment ahead of time. If at all possible, this is a valuable way to both review the actual inspection records and correspondence as well as possibly question the agency contact in person. Remember, you'll need to get information regarding air, water, and other regulatory compliance issues, as well as the RCRA compliance files, so allow time to coordinate between the different federal, state, and local contacts.

The use of a brief, pre-audit questionnaire to obtain information about the TSD facility is a good idea for several reasons. First, it gives the TSD facility a good indication of the type of information needed to complete the audit. To that end, the questionnaire should contain a list of the information and documents that will be requested for review or copying during the audit. Second, it will provide a facility contact (or contacts) who will be able to assist during the information gathering stage. Third, it will provide a good indication of both how well the facility is prepared for an audit and what level of cooperation can be expected from the TSD facility staff. Because of the increasing number of generators conducting waste vendor audits, many waste management contractors have prepared "audit information packages" that are designed to provide a prospective auditor with the pertinent facts regarding the facility, such as waste acceptance criteria, operations, permit status, and so on.

Figure 24.2 lists the topics that are most often addressed in a TSD facility audit program.

SPECIAL PRE-AUDIT CONSIDERATIONS

At this stage of the pre-audit activities, several other important aspects of the auditor-TSD facility relationship must be defined, such as the need for confidentiality agreements, the audit schedule, and the exchange of information following the audit.

It is not uncommon for TSD facilities to request that a detailed confidentiality statement be drafted and signed prior to granting a request for an audit. Many small,

Figure 24.2 Areas Most Often Addressed in Commercial TSD Facility Audit Programs

- Compliance with applicable federal, state, and local environmental regulations and permit conditions

- Assessment of the historical operations at the site, especially pre-RCRA or non-RCRA regulated activities

- An evaluation of the facility's environmental setting, such as hydrogeology, topography, distance to surface waters, wind patterns, climate, critical habitats, etc.

- An evaluation of the facility's demographic setting, including distance to nearest human receptors, population density, critical receptors, and other information

- A review of the adequacy and implementation of the facility's key waste management operations and controls, such as the waste analysis plan, emergency and contingency plans, operational plan, training plans, and environmental monitoring systems

- A detailed review of the waste management operations, including processing, treatment and disposal of all incoming waste and residuals

- An evaluation of the company's management practices and attitudes

- A financial analysis of the facility/parent corporation, including a determination of the company's financial status, applicable insurance coverages, and disclosure of contingent environmental liabilities and litigation

- A detailed review of all operational/regulatory compliance documentation, such as Part B and TSCA operating permits, NPDES permits, closure/post-closure plan, inspection records, waste analysis plan and records, manifests, etc.

- A review of any ongoing or anticipated RCRA corrective actions investigations

- A review of any consent agreements, consent orders, or other legal documents affecting the site operations.

privately owned non-RCRA waste management companies (such as precious metal recyclers, drum reconditioners, and brokers) may be reluctant to provide details concerning special waste handling, treatment, or disposal processes; financial data and management-related information; or groundwater monitoring results, unless they are satisfied that the information will remain confidential.

The auditor should be prepared for such a request by either preparing a confidentiality statement in advance, or by asking the TSD facility if they will require the auditor to sign their own agreement before they release any information. This determination should be made well in advance of the scheduled date of the on-site visit, since negotiating a confidentiality agreement or other additional legal agreements between a waste contractor and a generator can be a lengthy and time-consuming process. An additional confidentiality request may be required if the generator is using a third party, such as an environmental consultant, to conduct the audit. One common waste contractor auditing horror story tends to repeat itself time and time again: The audit team shows up at the TSD facility, is denied access to the site, and is asked to sign a confidentiality agreement before they are allowed to conduct the on-site audit or review sensitive documents. Is there a lawyer in the house?

In order to ensure that the on-site activities flow smoothly, it is necessary to establish a schedule for the audit activities well in advance. This means clearly identifying a mutually agreeable date for the audit as well as defining the particular operations you will want to see, the audit scope and level of detail, and the TSD facility staff with whom you intend to speak. Most commercial TSD facilities are audited by federal, state, and local agencies on a fairly routine basis, as well as by other generators, corporate environmental staff members, civic groups, and concerned parties. It is often difficult to schedule a generator audit because of these other concerns, so be prepared to be flexible in your schedule. You don't want to show up on site the same day as the U.S. EPA's National Enforcement Investigation Center (NEIC) auditors, or on the day that the site technical manager is leaving for vacation. Also, remember that you may be one of a hundred waste generators that want to schedule their audit at a TSD facility in southern California in February. Similarly, it is important to let the TSD facility know in advance whether you intend to conduct a comprehensive facility audit, or if you merely want to tour the site in a van, watch the promotional video, have lunch, and leave.

Prior to conducting the on-site audit, you will need to establish what the TSD facility will require in terms of reviewing copies of the audit report, photographs, or other audit-generated information. Some facilities will require that, at a minimum, they are provided with copies of all photographs taken, whereas others may allow you to take pictures only if the film is developed and screened by the site management to eliminate unfavorable pictures. Many waste management facilities will permit a generator-sponsored audit only if they receive a copy of the audit checklist and/or report. Ask if there are any special limitations on making copies of permits and other compliance documentation, or accessing generator-related information such as manifests. Knowing these limitations in advance will prevent misunderstandings and potential confrontations during the on-site audit.

SELECTING THE AUDIT TEAM

The selection of the audit team, irrespective of whether the audit is conducted by the generator or an environmental consultant, is an important element in ensuring the success of the audit. Some key factors that should be considered include:

- Never send an audit team composed entirely of auditors who have never been to a TSD facility before. This is the cardinal rule of selecting audit teams. The facility staff is not going to make it easy for you in the first place. A TSD facility is quite unlike any operating facility that your company might own. Simply put, there is too much to observe and too much liability at stake to risk having an entire audit team overwhelmed and/or under-trained.

- Choose team members who have educational and career backgrounds commensurate with the type of operations to be audited. It doesn't make sense to send two or three hydrogeologists to audit a TSD facility that has a complex incinerator or chemical treatment process. Ideally, the audit team should be composed of no more than three professionals that have compatible skills, which are commensurate to the operations at the TSD facility. As an example, a team composed of one hydrogeologist, one chemical engineer, and one regulatory specialist would be able to successfully understand and audit most of the typical TSD facilities in the country.

- Concerning team size, the same guidelines apply as for in-house audits. Usually a team of two or three auditors will be sufficient. Four or more auditors are not only difficult for the facility to accommodate, but they are also likely to overpower an already overworked and limited TSD facility staff. Conversely, in most cases, there is simply too much to see and read for only one auditor to handle. Unless the facility is very small or the scope of the audit is quite minimal, consider two auditors to be the starting point when selecting the size of the team.

- Although it sounds trite to say it, choose TSD facility auditors that work well together and are most likely not to be rattled or annoyed by scheduling problems, abrasive or uncooperative facility staff, cramped conditions, and other typical audit problems. It is imperative to select audit team members who are not prone to confrontational standoffs. It's no fun to audit a landfill during a heavy rainstorm, but a well-picked audit team with "foul weather fortitude" will at least make the exercise less miserable and ensure that the audit objectives are met. (By the way, auditing a TSD facility in the rain is a *good* idea, since it can give you an indication of surface runoff and stormwater management practices, which are important in evaluating the risks posed by releases that may occur during the waste handling and transfer operations.)

As recently as the mid-1980s, generator audits of waste management facilities were the exception rather than the rule. As such, TSD facility staff were receptive to generator audits in order to attract and maintain new customer relationships. More recently, however, TSD facility auditing has increased at a rapid rate, with more and more companies requesting to conduct time-consuming audits. At the same time, many of the smaller waste treatment and disposal contractors have fallen on hard times as a result of increased regulatory vigilance, inability to meet stringent technical and financial requirements, and stiffened regional and national competition by larger, better financed firms. The waste treatment and disposal market today is dominated by these larger firms, and the entrance of new hazardous waste management firms into the market is extremely difficult, if not impossible. This is largely due to the reasons cited above as well as increased public awareness and a reluctance on the part of communities to accept these types of facilities (i.e., the "not in my backyard," or NIMBY, syndrome).

The end product of this changed market is increased reluctance on behalf of waste management companies to provide *carte blanche* privileges to generators requesting TSD facility audits. Although most TSD facilities respond favorably to inquiries and understand the generator's desire for requesting the audit, the open door policy has somewhat cooled. This change in perspective manifests itself via overly restrictive confidentiality agreements, limited scheduling windows, a reluctance to share details of proprietary treatment technologies, and a reserved approach to meeting auditor's requests for key audit information. Accordingly, the audit team must be cognizant of these factors and highly adaptable to somewhat less than ideal auditing conditions as they arise. Notwithstanding these legitimate TSD concerns, if a facility refuses an audit outright, find another company to handle your wastes.

THE ON-SITE AUDIT

Although the auditing process is similar, conducting a TSD facility audit is fundamentally different in nature from an internal environmental compliance audit at one of your own facilities. Because the primary interest of the TSD facility is to either attract new business or keep an existing customer satisfied, it is natural for the facility management to downplay any problems that exist at the facility. As a result, the auditors must rely more heavily on their ability to uncover potential problems through document review, interviewing key employees, and direct observation of facility practices and operations. Figure 24.3 lists a recommended protocol for conducting the on-site audit.

Figure 24.3 Proposed TSD Facility Audit Agenda

Day One

- Auditors arrive at TSD facility

- TSD facility representatives summarize facility capabilities and operations to familiarize auditors with the site (half-hour to one hour)

- TSD facility tour guide and audit liaison are assigned to the audit team

- TSD facility tour is conducted, preferably in the following sequence:

  - Waste arrival and acceptance procedures at site

  - Waste sampling procedure

  - Manifest verification

  - Waste analysis procedures, including a tour of the laboratory, description of QA/QC, equipment and capabilities, and treatment/disposal option decisions

  - Treatment, storage, and disposal procedures, including a tour of operations to cover all regulated units and a discussion of design and operation controls

  - Training records and inspection logs.

- Auditors conduct interviews with TSD facility representative(s). The purpose of the interviews is to summarize all regulatory correspondence and permits, as well as to identify any discrepancies between current operations and permit conditions. General interview areas will include:

  - Discussion of company structure

  - Current use of the facility by generator(s)

  - The environmental setting of the facility

  - Site history

  - Site operations

  - Waste volumes and types

  - Regulatory compliance history

  - Environmental incidents or releases of waste

  - Involvement in third-party litigation

  - Financial assurance

Figure 24.3 *(cont'd)*

- Management qualifications

- Recordkeeping

- Transportation capabilities

- Process specifications

- Air, surface water, and groundwater monitoring results

- Proposed facility modifications.

■ Auditors review RCRA Part B permit application, other permits, and regulatory correspondence to evaluate TSD facility procedures and determine whether risk factors are adequately mitigated.

Day Two

■ Auditors continue document review

■ Particular areas of interest are revisited to observe waste management practices, safety procedures, environmental monitoring, waste sampling, etc.

■ Follow-up interviews are conducted with key TSD facility personnel

■ Closing meeting is done with facility personnel.

The document review portion of the audit should focus on several key topics. First, the auditors must determine if the proper documentation (e.g., permits, reports, records) is in place so as to ensure facility compliance. Second, the auditors should observe if the documents are complete and adequate, not only to ensure compliance, but also to protect the generator's interests. For example, auditors should carefully review procedures and records that directly involve the generator, such as manifests, the waste analysis plan, and the ultimate disposal records for wastes and residuals, as well as treatment, solvent recovery, or landfill disposal logs.

In order to assess the facility's waste tracking system, it is helpful to track random waste shipments from initial receipt at the facility through ultimate treatment, disposal, and, most importantly, trans-shipment or treatment at another site. The TSD facility should be able to easily document the path of any incoming waste shipment through the facility. Many generators test the adequacy of the TSD facility's waste tracking and recordkeeping system by bringing several manifests (from both old and recent shipments) to determine whether the facility can rapidly and accurately determine the ultimate fate or current location of each particular manifest item.

Records should be carefully reviewed to assess whether employees have been properly trained, whether the contingency and emergency response plans are appropriate for the risks presented by the facility operations, and whether the environmental monitoring systems in place are adequate to determine if contamination is leaving the site via groundwater, surface water, or air pathways. A careful review of the completeness and organization of a facility's recordkeeping system will tell a savvy auditor much about the site's compliance status, safety, and general management attitudes.

Interviewing facility management and operations staff is a critical part of any audit, but it is particularly informative when assessing the relative risks at a TSD facility. Facility management should be intimately familiar with the site operations and should be willing to discuss how waste handling, treatment, and disposal decisions are made. Concerns over confidentiality are often presented when auditors request information concerning waste treatment decisions, so it is important to identify if there will be any such problems during the pre-audit phase. Ask to interview the employees who actually conduct the waste handling activities, such as sampling technicians, waste processing staff, and laboratory personnel, not just the site manager or audit liaison. The purpose of interviewing these employees is to make sure they know exactly what it is they are responsible for, instead of assuming that they have been trained in accordance with the written training plan in the RCRA Part B permit the auditors have reviewed. Be sure to question employees on key risk areas such as waste receipt and analysis, waste handling, treatment decision making (how it is determined what wastes are sent where), training, preventative maintenance, and emergency response procedures. Remember that your overall goal is to ensure that your waste is being handled properly and that your liabilities are being minimized through the use of sound, well-conceived operational practices.

The visual observation of the general appearance and housekeeping practices at the TSD facility will provide a good initial overall picture as to the safety and operation of the site. Look for evidence of poor oversight or inattentive management such as sloppy housekeeping, indication of repeated spills and releases, nonexistent or poorly maintained emergency response equipment, or accumulation of precipitation in secondary containment areas. If possible, observe actual waste handling operations such as tanker truck transfers, container decanting, waste stabilization, active landfilling, or waste sampling practices. Obvious signs of poor facility management may include evidence of repeated spillage, damaged or ineffective secondary containment areas, damaged or unsecured groundwater monitoring wells, poor segregation of incompatible materials, and absence of stormwater runoff control practices. Some typical findings that should lead the auditor to ask additional questions include:

- multiple, confusing labels on containers;
- containers which are staged outside of containment areas;

- lack of respect for health and safety warning signs;

- airborne dispersion of vapors or particulates during transfer operations; and

- cracked or poorly maintained containment areas.

Figure 24.4 provides some examples of typical problems encountered during TSD facility audits.

Upon completion of the on-site audit, some companies prefer to brief the TSD facility staff on the general findings of the audit, in order to provide the TSD facility with the opportunity to either correct misinterpreted information or provide additional verification or evidence of compliance. It is in the generator's best interests to ensure that the information collected during the audit is accurate and complete. Therefore, it's a good idea to discuss, at a minimum, any confusing or unresolved issues prior to leaving the site. The auditors should leave the TSD facility knowing that their information is correct and understanding whether the TSD facility expects to receive a copy of the written report or other conclusions about the generator's findings.

THE TSD FACILITY AUDIT REPORT

The information obtained during the TSD facility audit should be presented in a fashion that allows a comparison of the positive features of the facility and the existing or potential environmental, operational, and financial risks of the site. The audit report should be concise in nature and should be arranged in the following fashion:

- An overall description of the site history, location, and operational parameters, including an identification of any associated risk factors

- A summary and assessment of the site's demographic and environmental setting, aimed at the development of a source-pathway-receptor analysis

- A description of the site's waste management operations, focusing on the positive and negative issues associated with waste receipt, processing, and ultimate treatment/disposal procedures

- A review of the site's regulatory compliance history and current compliance status

- An evaluation of the site's environmental risk management procedures, operational oversight, and attitudes towards employee safety and community awareness

- An analysis of the adequacy and feasibility of the site closure/post-closure plan and cost estimates

- A financial analysis of the site and its parent company, if applicable

Figure 24.4 Typical Problems Encountered during TSD Facility Audits

Regulatory Compliance Issues

- Failure to conduct or document proper inspections as required

- Improper, inaccurate, or illegible labeling practices

- Segregation problems

- Inadequate or improperly designed secondary containment areas

- Minimal employee training programs and/or incomplete training records

- Poor implementation of personal protective equipment requirements, such as failure to wear face shields, gloves, respirators, long-sleeved shirts, etc.

- Poorly organized or incomplete recordkeeping system, or an inability to easily track waste shipments to final disposition

- Drums/bungs left open at all times, uncovered roll-off boxes, or lack of vapor controls for volatile liquids

- Containers in contact with accumulated rainwater

- Inadequate or incomplete waste characterization, or failure to identify and reject contaminated loads

- Inability to carefully track ultimate disposal for trans-shipped wastes or residuals, such as tank bottoms, empty drums, or wastewater treatment sludges

- Closure/post-closure plans that do not reflect accurate waste volumes or technical requirements, or plans containing insufficient closure cost estimates or financial assurance.

Safety and Environmental Risk Issues

- Improper electrical grounding during tanker or drum transfers of flammable liquids

- Questionable groundwater monitoring programs, in terms of well construction, sampling, and QA/QC procedures

- Lack of management oversight for emergency response procedures, such as failure to remove rainfall or accumulated spillage from secondary containment areas

- Inadequate supply and/or poor location of emergency response equipment

- Inadequate employee health monitoring programs

- Lack of compliance with facility safety requirements in restricted areas (i.e., use of hard hats, steel toe shoes, respirators, etc.)

■ An overall assessment of the risks posed by the site, using both qualitative and quantitative methods so as to allow direct comparison of different sites.

Remember that the ultimate objective of the audit program is to identify and manage the inherent liabilities associated with waste treatment and disposal, not to prepare a classical treatise of the subject site. The reports should limit the discussion of factors that do not directly affect the decision-making process.

CONCLUSION

All off-site commercial waste TSD facilities will present some level of risk to a waste generator. The handling and treatment of hazardous and toxic wastes is by nature fraught with environmental, human health, and regulatory-related risks. It is the proper management of those risks that the commercial TSD audit program is designed to facilitate. Generators should seek to limit their liabilities through both the reduction of the amount of wastes that they generate and through the use of commercial TSD facilities that are located, designed, operated, and managed in a fashion that reduces the generator's risk to an acceptable level.

Chapter 25

WASTE MINIMIZATION OR POLLUTION PREVENTION AUDITS

No matter how well you perform there's always somebody of intelligent opinion who thinks it's lousy.

– Laurence Olivier, Baron Olivier of Brighton, 1907-1989

WHY A POLLUTION PREVENTION FOCUS?

As EH&S audit programs have evolved over the past few years, companies have very often modified and honed their initial multimedia focus to reflect the findings of baseline audits. More often than not, this has meant incorporating a significant waste minimization component into the program. There have been several reasons for this development:

- **Historical Noncompliance.** Many of the noncompliance findings identified in the early audits have been a result of poor waste management practices.

- **Regulatory Requirements.** Hazardous waste manifests require large quantity generators to certify that they have a program in place to reduce the volume and toxicity of waste generated. The Pollution Prevention Act of 1990 and the Emergency Planning and Community Right-to-Know Act also call for active pollution prevention programs.

- **Regulatory Trends.** Several U.S. EPA initiatives, such as the Persistent, Bioaccumulative, and Toxic (PBT) Pollutants and High Production Volume (HPV) Chemicals strategies, will apply considerable pressure on industry to minimize the manufacture and/or waste generation of the covered chemicals.

- **Non-Regulatory Initiatives.** As discussed elsewhere, the ISO 14001 Environmental Management Systems Standard was issued in late 1996. In some industries, there is considerable pressure from customers to become ISO-registered. The Standard requires that an environmental policy be developed that "includes a commitment to continual improvement and prevention of pollution."[1]

■ **Economics.** Waste disposal is becoming considerably more expensive. It is now a visible element of the balance sheet.

Successful waste minimization can mean having to meet less stringent regulatory standards, not having to rely on other companies to ultimately dispose of wastes, and paying substantially less for waste disposal. Accomplishment of these goals can do much to improve compliance at individual plants and minimize the liabilities of the corporation.

THE GENERAL APPROACHES

Conducting waste minimization audits can typically be accomplished in two ways. They can be included as part of the standard audit process, or the company can create waste minimization "hit squads," using staff with specialties in manufacturing and process control who travel from plant to plant attacking the specific problem of waste minimization. The first approach is less resource-intensive but is also less likely to achieve significant reductions.

Either approach can be successful, but one needs to be aware of the distinctions between the more traditional audit approach and what is required to complete a waste minimization audit. Historically, environmental audits have been designed to verify that adequate compliance assurance systems (organizational and physical) are in place at the operating facilities. Therefore, audits are not meant to substitute for good, effective site environmental management, which is required day-in and day-out and not simply when the audit team is on site.

Waste minimization audits differ in that more is involved than simply verification. The audit team is usually asked to work with the site staff to review waste generation operations, analyze the potential for waste reductions, and jointly identify solutions to the high-priority problem streams. In this way, the audit team is asked to become more intimately involved in the operations of the facility.

Of course, these differences in waste minimization audits bring with them some advantages and disadvantages. On the plus side, the audit can be seen as more helpful than otherwise might be the case. However, it is also more intrusive. Thus, the auditors must be very diplomatic in their investigations; good technical skills will accomplish only so much.

---

[1] "Environmental Management Systems," ISO 14001:1996(E), International Organization for Standardization, Section 4.2.

LIMITATIONS AND CONSTRAINTS

The objective of a waste minimization audit generally is to reduce the volume and/ or toxicity of wastes. However, meeting this commendable objective is fraught with frustrations. Auditors should be especially aware of the following roadblocks:

- **Waste minimization audits are very site-specific.** Therefore, it is often very difficult to apply the lessons of the past to the case at hand.

- **Like many things in life, waste minimization suffers from the 90/10 rule.** Ninety percent of the reductions are often achieved with the first 10 percent of the effort. Thus, it becomes exponentially more difficult to attain significant reductions as time goes on.

- **Waste minimization can be as much an organizational issue as a technical one.** Seemingly simple steps recommended by the audit team will result in scores of responses by the purchasing, manufacturing, and sales force as to why the steps are impossible to implement. For example, based on a corporate directive, purchasing staff will typically buy materials at the lowest available unit cost. This can often mean obtaining chemicals in 55-gallon drum quantities, even though 10-gallon pails would be easier to handle and each might last as long as two to three months based on production requirements. Thus, a built-in conflict can exist with purchasing.

- Also, research and development (R&D) staff are notorious for experimenting with chemicals and then accumulating the unused portions in a nearby storeroom that was designed to be a coat room. These materials can accumulate for years and, in many cases, in containers that are inadequately labeled. Research and development staff could be directed to use only suppliers who have a chemical "take-back" policy, but if their favored supplier has no policy, they may fight the change.

- Finally, manufacturing and sales staffs have been making and selling successful product lines for years. When it is suggested that substitutions should be made for certain chemicals, they often have a million reasons why their customers would not tolerate the switch.

METHODOLOGY

Notwithstanding these limitations, waste minimization audits can be a worthwhile exercise. In general, the analytical approach is similar to conducting a more routine environmental audit. In fact, the U.S. EPA provides guidance in its published protocols on how to conduct a RCRA waste minimization audit: "Review the generator's waste minimization program to determine if the program includes practical methods for reducing the volume of hazardous wastes generated. Determine whether any or all of the following methods suggested by EPA are incorporated into the program:

- The generator retains information that documents waste minimization activities.

- The program includes:

    - Provisions for top management assurance that waste minimization is a company-wide effort

    - Characterization of waste generation and waste management costs

    - Periodic waste minimization assessments

    - A cost allocation system

    - Encourages technology transfer

    - Program implementation and evaluation

    - Waste minimization employee awareness plans

    - Adequate funding

    - Clearly delineated roles both within the company and among each facility generating waste.

- Conclude if facility actions are resulting in the reduction of hazardous wastes."[2]

Within this framework, the audit team reviews the available written records, interviews key site environmental and operational staff, and inspects the plant's facilities. In conducting this exercise, the auditors are generally attempting to identify the following:

- **The "Devil's" Chemicals.** In most manufacturing, there will be a few chemicals that are extremely toxic and/or troublesome (e.g., phosgene). A waste audit's goal should be to identify where these chemicals are used and what by-products or waste products their use generates.

- **High-Production Volume (HPV) Waste Streams.** The 90/10 rule often applies here as well. In many cases, 10 percent of the waste streams generate

---

[2] U.S. EPA, *Protocol for Conducting Environmental Compliance Audits of Hazardous Waste Generators under the Resource Conservation and Recovery Act* (October 1998). See also *Interim Final Guidance to Hazardous Waste Generators on the Elements of a Waste Minimization Program*, 58 *FR* 31114 (May 28, 1993).

90 percent of the volume. Investigating these waste streams first is likely to result in the most cost-effective reductions.

■ **Highly Regulated Wastes.** Wastes such as PBTs, dioxins, PCBs, chlorinated solvents, and RCRA acutely hazardous wastes should receive considerable attention during the audit. They should receive this attention, if for no other reason, because, in many cases, they have become "political" wastes.

■ **Land-Disposed Wastes or Residuals.** Wastes or treatment residuals that are land disposed present special problems for generators. Strict, joint, and several liability tenets suggest that the generator maintains liability, even when indemnified by a disposal company.

Identifying waste streams that fall into the classes presented above will help set priorities for the audit, which, by its nature, is a time- and resource-limited exercise. There are ways to use readily available data to identify these streams. Some of the more common are listed below:

■ Material safety data sheets (MSDSs)

■ RCRA annual or biennial reports

■ RCRA hazardous waste manifests

■ RCRA list of acutely hazardous wastes

■ PBT and HPV lists

■ SARA Title III lists, reports, and submissions

■ State air toxics lists

■ U.S. EPA Clean Air Act NESHAPS chemicals and candidate chemicals

■ Air emissions and asbestos inventories

■ PCB electrical equipment inventories

■ U.S. EPA Clean Water Act priority pollutants

■ Waste disposal companies' records and invoices

■ Sludge disposal records

■ Records of pollution control equipment and operations, and maintenance expenditures.

Once these sources are reviewed, each of the priority waste streams can be investigated for its reduction potential. It should be clear from the nature of the sources that the waste minimization audit must be more encompassing than simply a review of RCRA-generated hazardous wastes. Wastewaters, air emissions, and other sources of toxic releases must be considered as well.

Evaluating the reduction potential involves analyzing each waste stream against a number of options. Although it is difficult to make generic suggestions on possible waste minimization strategies, some of the more common reduction solutions generally fall into the control strategies listed below:

- **Material Conservation.** Until the last few years, there has been little incentive to conserve many raw materials. Yet, better management and/or more careful use of paints, solvents, and maintenance chemicals could significantly reduce chemicals being emitted through vents, washed down the drains, or sent out for disposal. Vehicle and machinery maintenance should be scheduled at proper, but not overly conservative, intervals. Where process vessels are used to manufacture different products, line management should schedule runs such that chemical cleaning of the vessels is minimized.

- **Material Substitution.** Many companies using this strategy have made significant inroads. Typical substitutions include fiberglass for asbestos and urea formaldehyde insulation, non-chlorinated for chlorinated solvents, and water-based for solvent-based coatings and paints.

- **Inventory Management.** Even at the risk of displeasing the discount-minded purchasing agent, many companies are buying chemicals in much smaller quantities. Where at all possible, five- and ten-gallon pails are often preferred to the tanker truck or ubiquitous 55-gallon drum. In fact, one company has a policy that 55-gallon drums can be purchased on an exception basis only. Companies are also becoming more fastidious about requiring a first-in, first-out inventory policy for chemicals. This minimizes the potential for old drums to accumulate and deteriorate in the rear of a warehouse.

- **Recycling/Segregation.** These two approaches fit hand-in-glove; often, materials cannot be recycled because they have not been segregated properly. Used oils are occasionally so contaminated with solvents that they are not reclaimable. Where wastes must be generated, it is often prudent to search for a waste exchange—one man's waste might be another man's raw material. In this regard, some companies use their corporate environmental department as a clearinghouse. The departments search for both intra-company and commercial users or buyers of excess inventory, past-shelf-life materials, or recoverable wastes.

- **Process Modifications.** Significant gains can be achieved using this strategy. Some potential approaches were mentioned above (e.g., the use of water-based coatings). Other waste reductions can be attained by looking closely at the manufacturing process with trained eyes. One company was able to develop a sophisticated plastic extrusion process that allowed them to fabricate composite conduit directly, as opposed to fabricating two separate pieces and binding them together with adhesive. The new process was especially cost-effective when the cost of waste-adhesive disposal was factored into the analysis.

Waste Treatment and Destruction. This is the waste minimization strategy of last resort. If all else fails, do your best to detoxify or destroy the wastes. Land disposal, or long-term storage if you will, is an extremely questionable approach in this day of Superfund-mandated cleanups; presently, however, some wastes and treatment residuals have no other alternative. Yet, many companies have developed a policy that land disposal of any wastes will be allowed on an exception basis only. Biological, chemical, and physical treatment technologies are evolving rapidly; it is likely that fewer and fewer waste streams will become exceptions under this type of policy.

EXAMPLES OF THE PRESENCE OF A WASTE MINIMIZATION EFFORT

Adopting the above strategies can result in defining some very specific opportunities for waste minimization. Some of the more common techniques are presented below. The auditor should be watchful of these, as their presence is evidence of a waste minimization effort.

- Using non-chlorinated solvents for cleaning (e.g., Simple Green)
- Using water-based coatings and paints
- Adopting purchase-by-exception for 55-gallon drums
- Adopting purchase-by-exception for toxic ("the devil's") chemicals
- Placing emphasis on maintenance chemicals as well as process chemicals
- Setting schedules of vessel runs to minimize the need for frequent cleanouts
- Adopting a first-in, first-out inventory control
- Minimizing the cross-contamination of used oil with solvents
- Developing an internal clearinghouse function for excess inventory, old chemicals, and recoverable wastes
- Revising processes (e.g., using composite plastic extrusion manufacturing vs. simple extrusion and adhesion to eliminate the generation of adhesive wastes)
- Improving housekeeping (e.g., keeping lids on degreasers, minimizing spills during materials transfer and dispensing)
- Using oil-water separators in sewer systems

- Requiring R&D staff to purchase chemicals in small quantities, to not accept salesmen samples indiscriminately, and to work with vendors with return policies

- Training R&D staff to be aware of environmental consequences of design

- Requiring all capital improvements to be signed off by corporate environmental departments

- Requiring secondary containment at all fill and dispensing areas (e.g., tank farm manifolds, underground storage tank fill ports)

- Segregating chemical storage from waste storage; isolating solid wastes from hazardous wastes

- Evaluating the integrity of all floor drains and septic tank systems

- Using the full-service capabilities of reputable waste disposal contractors

- Above all, making waste minimization a *real* corporate policy by instituting an incentive program for plant managers. They will make it happen!

In summary, waste minimization audits are not unlike any analytical exercise. First, high priority waste streams are identified through a review of documents, discussions with site staff, and an inspection of the site. These streams are typically ranked and analyzed for potential reduction strategies, such as material substitution and process modifications. Where potential strategies are identified, a detailed study is made of the costs and benefits. This study includes the concerns of purchasing, manufacturing, and sales. In other words, recommended changes must incorporate use of equivalent and readily available materials and processes that do not materially affect the quality of the product or the cost of its manufacture, including the cost of waste disposal.

Chapter 26

EVALUATING MANAGEMENT SYSTEMS ON EH&S AUDITS[1]

Rules and models destroy genius and art.

– William Hazlett, 1778-1830

WHY EVALUATE MANAGEMENT SYSTEMS?

For the past few years, there has been much discussion in the EH&S auditing profession about evaluating management systems as part of a facility audit. Some people have gone so far as to say that the management systems evaluation should be the *principal* objective of an EH&S audit. It is probably fair to say that many people, while espousing this approach, are not quite sure what it means.

The ISO 14001 Environmental Management Systems Standard published in 1996 has gone a long way in defining the content of an acceptable environmental (and by default health and safety) management system and an environmental management systems audit. There have been other initiatives as well. The European Community has implemented an Eco-Management and Audit Scheme (EMAS) that encourages companies to conduct environmental audits and to focus heavily on systems during the exercise.[2]

So, even with all this recent activity, one can still ask the question: Does this "management systems" approach add value to an EH&S audit? Well, it most assuredly does. Focusing on management systems allows one to identify the underlying or root causes, as opposed to the symptoms, which are typically at the heart of noncompliance at a site.

---

[1] Originally published in *Total Quality Environmental Management*, (New York: Executive Enterprises, Inc., 1992). Updated for this edition.

[2] "Proposal for a Council Regulation (EEC) allowing voluntary participation by companies in the industrial sector in a Community Eco-Audit scheme," 92/C 76/02 (March 6, 1992), *Official Journal of the European Communities*, No. C 76/2 (March 27, 1992).

For example, if an auditor were to observe something as simple as a label missing from a waste solvent drum, the resultant finding could be described as just that: "a drum had a missing label." The site staff would immediately place a label on the drum, and the matter would be considered closed. However, if that same site were to be audited a year later, it is likely that *at least* one drum would be missing labels. Why?

Well, the auditor has failed to address the underlying cause of the problem and, nine times out of ten, this is likely to be the breakdown of a management system. In the case of the problem drum, the label could be missing for a variety of reasons, including:

- The person responsible for drum storage and management has not been trained properly.

- It is unclear as to who maintains responsibility for the drum while it moves to various locations on the site, from accumulation near the point of generation, to a "90-day" accumulation pad, to a permitted storage facility.

- The drum has been sitting around for quite a while and no one is sure of its contents. A sample has been sent out for analysis and the decision has been made to not label the drum until the results are known.

- The purchasing department bought "cheap" labels and they cannot withstand the rigors of outdoor storage—they keep falling off the drums.

- The site inadvertently ran out of labels and the normal purchasing process for re-supply takes two weeks.

Now when we look at the problem, it takes on a different light. Maybe the solution is more complicated than simply placing a label on the drum. Maybe, for example, the site's training programs are not including the right people or job position responsibilities are unclear, and so on. Thus, the corrective actions can now focus on underlying causes and might, for instance, state that the site needs to train its operators better, or assign drum management responsibilities more clearly, or do something as simple as incorporating minimum quality specifications into the label purchasing process. By identifying and remedying the true problem, it is more likely that in a year's time when the next audit takes place, there will be no repeat occurrence. In this way, focusing on management systems can result in long-term environmental compliance improvements, not quick fixes.

WHAT IS A MANAGEMENT SYSTEM?

The ISO 14001 Standard defines an environmental management system as "that part of the overall management system that includes organizational structure, planning activities, responsibilities, practices, procedures, processes and resources for developing, implementing, achieving, reviewing, and maintaining the environmental policy."[3] Within this context, the Standard suggests that an environmental management system should contain five elements:

Environmental policy

Planning

Implementation and operation

Checking and corrective action

Management review.

These elements are, of course, quite consistent with the plan-do-check-act cycle of Total Quality Management.

In addition, "the environmental management system should be designed so that emphasis is placed on the prevention of adverse environmental effects, rather than on detection and amelioration after occurrence. It should:

Identify and assess the environmental effects arising from the organization's existing or proposed activities, products, or services

Identify and assess the environmental effects arising from incidents, accidents, and potential emergency situations

Identify the relevant regulatory requirements

Enable priorities to be identified and pertinent environmental objectives and targets to be set

Facilitate planning, control, monitoring, auditing, and review activities to ensure both that the policy is complied with and that it remains relevant

Be capable of evolution to suit changing circumstances."[4]

Although the above elements should be at the core of a site's environmental management system, they are often difficult to audit against because a site's programs frequently are not structured that way. Typically, the site's environmental management system is the sum of separate programs, which would include most, if not all, of the following:

Specific programs designed to address corporate environmental policies and procedures

---

[3] "Environmental Management Systems," ISO 14001:1996(E), Section 3.5.

[4] "Specification for Environmental Management Systems," British Standard BS 7750:1992, Annex (March 1992): 9.

- Employee training and statements of job accountabilities
- Regulatory tracking system
- Environmental review of new activities
- Waste minimization planning
- Release prevention/emergency response planning
- Environmental auditing including noncompliance follow-up and reporting
- Community outreach program/complaint management
- Product stewardship
- On-site contractor reviews and evaluations
- Off-site contractor reviews and evaluations.

These are the *auditable* program elements of a site's environmental management system.

HOW DO YOU DO IT?

First and foremost, the auditor should recognize that management systems audits are quite different from compliance audits, as Figure 26.1 demonstrates.

These differences must be taken into account throughout the process.

To conduct an audit of a management system, an auditor needs to select those programs that are to be evaluated and to audit the following components of each of the selected programs:

- Organization
- Administrative procedures

Figure 26.1 Differences between Management Systems and Compliance Auditing

Criterion	Compliance Audit	EMS Audit
Focus	End Result	Process
Verification Challenge	Easier	Harder
Best Auditor Skill	Regulatory Knowledge	Ability to Probe
Question Format	What?	Why?
Test	Compliance	Conformance

- Staff assignments

- Documentation, reports, and records

- Implementation.

An auditor needs to be careful that the evaluation is of the program and not simply the written procedures or plans. There are two questions to be answered: Does the system meet the requirements, regulatory, corporate or otherwise? And is it working? It is generally much easier to answer the first question.

For example, if a site is required to have an emergency response program, it could be because of Contingency Plan requirements under the Resource Conservation and Recovery Act (RCRA), Spill Prevention Control and Countermeasure (SPCC) requirements under the Clean Water Act (CWA), Hazardous Materials Response requirements under OSHA's Hazardous Waste Operations (HAZWOPER) rule, requirements under a mandated corporate procedure, or all of the above. The auditor would first have to determine which of these requirements apply and then evaluate the program organization, procedures, documentation, and implementation against those requirements.

When a facility falls under more than one set of requirements in one program area, the auditor would have to determine both if the site has been responsive to each requirement *and* if the overall program is workable. In the emergency response area, for example, some sites will attempt to develop one site emergency response plan, or Integrated Contingency Plan, that addresses all applicable regulatory requirements. The advantage of this approach is that the site management does not have to determine what kind of incident has occurred before utilizing the actions recommended by the plan. On the other hand, having an individual plan developed for each set of requirements simplifies the regulatory response and allows for a more direct assurance to agency inspectors and others that the regulatory requirements have been met. Yet this approach, while valid, can create response-time problems when an incident does occur. In either case, the workability criterion becomes paramount.

Much of the organizational and procedural review of management systems can be conducted through interviews and evaluations of the programs' documentation. If the systems can be identified ahead of time, protocols or checklists can be developed to guide the auditors in their investigations.

One of the most important aspects of the audit, however, is to ensure that written procedures are, in fact, carried out effectively. This can best be explained by way of example. Take again, for instance, emergency response planning. One can review the organization and planning documents designed to respond to an emergency and find that they respond well to regulatory requirements. However, the real test of effectiveness is in the implementation. In practice, this effectiveness can be tested either through evaluations of the response to actual emergencies, or through drills or simulations. Thus, the auditor can only determine that the system is effective if there are assurances that it is tested or evaluated on a routine basis. In other words, any audit of management systems should include an evaluation of actual practices as well as documented procedures.

Given this philosophy of evaluating a program and/or management system, the auditor might want to pose and answer the following ten questions, which in essence are based on the five elements of the ISO 14001 EMS Standard. Any EH&S program could be evaluated using this framework.

1. Is there a regulatory or internal standard driving the need for a program? Is a written program, standard operating procedure, or permit required?

2. Does an inventory or the equivalent need to be developed (e.g., high noise areas, air emissions sources, confined spaces)?

3. What are the essential performance measures for the program (e.g., successful confined space entries, no wastewater exceedances, hearing protection, no spills)?

4. Who is accountable for meeting program objectives?

5. How is management of change handled?

6. What training and communications are required? At what frequency?

7. Is equipment involved? Is it maintained? Is it calibrated?

8. Are routine inspections or self-assessments required? Is there a corrective-action program for identified deficiencies?

9. What records must be maintained?

10. Is there a periodic (e.g., annual) review of the program?

PRACTICAL TIPS

Evaluating management systems is not an easy exercise. It often involves probing interviews with senior staff and managers at a site. Thus, the process can be very intimidating. Keep the following in mind:

- ■ It will be "messy." Verification will be challenge. Attempt to use defined standards and expectations. Steer clear of personal opinions.

- ■ Do not expect site systems and programs to track the corporate expectations exactly. They must meet the test of equivalency and should reflect the size and complexity of the site.

- ■ Be wary of recently developed plans and procedures. Management systems are not developed overnight.

■ Look for the presence of the core elements: a communicated policy, organizational accountability, measured goals and objectives, and a viable self-assessment program.

■ Focus on management of change. This is where most programs fail. Change is not only capital improvements; it includes people, products, raw materials, processes, regulatory requirements, and many other elements of the system. Ask yourself, what if this person were "hit by a truck?" Would the system survive?

WHY IS IT SO HARD?

Many companies have considerable experience in assessing management systems on environmental audits. Yet, observation of numerous audits suggests that even those with experience have difficulties in applying consistent review techniques. This is for a number of reasons, including:

■ **Viewing the Audit as a Performance Appraisal.** An audit of management systems is truly an indicator of personnel performance, and therefore, it will always have a performance appraisal flavor to it. This means that interviews will have an additional tension that must be dealt with by the auditor.

■ **Difficulty in Assessing Root Causes.** Identifying the root causes of a problem requires extra digging and investigation by the auditor. This will often take even a very experienced auditor additional time. These are two luxuries that may not be available to the team.

■ **Lack of Clear Standards.** There will be many requirements placed on an organization (e.g., increased environmental awareness), which will have no standards against which they can be evaluated.

■ **Shared Roles and Responsibilities.** Assessing management systems is difficult because responsibilities typically cut across media, and therefore, necessary review techniques would be counter to the more traditional approaches.

In addition, developing management systems findings on an audit is just plain difficult. Building the case for a management breakdown requires a certain mindset that has to be learned. For example, an auditor might conclude that the "hazardous waste management system at the site is inadequate." Immediately, staff personnel will justifiably ask the question, "Why do you feel that way?" The response is all too often, "Well, I'm not sure, but I just wasn't comfortable after looking at the records and talking with a few of the staff." This is an insufficient evaluation.

The above conclusion related to the hazardous waste management system may, in fact, be correct, but the conclusion must be verified and substantiated with evidence. Accordingly, a deficiency statement or conclusion should have the structure of the following example:

"The hazardous waste management program at the site is not completely responsive to Corporate Directive HW-100. Deficiencies include:

(1) Five drums at the accumulation point had no labels.

(2) Accumulation point inspection logs had not been completed for the past month.

(3) Two of the maintenance staff had not received their annual training."

Developing findings in this fashion begins to build a strong case that the system is breaking down and needs rebuilding.

CONCLUSION

Evaluating management systems is a crucial component of any EH&S audit. Evolving regulations and directives acknowledge this importance. Further, remedying management deficiencies can result in long-term, lasting improvements of EH&S compliance with external requirements and internal policies. This is indeed what EH&S audits are designed to accomplish. Finally, management systems auditing by its nature brings line management formally into the process, often resulting in shared responsibilities and accountabilities. The site EH&S coordinator will no longer carry all the responsibility with none of the authority.

Chapter 27

INTERNATIONAL EH&S AUDITS[1]

The International Chamber of Commerce believes that effective protection of the environment is best achieved by an appropriate combination of legislation/regulation and of policies and programs established voluntarily by industry.... Environmental auditing is an important component of such voluntary policies.[2]

International EH&S audits are receiving increased attention from multinational companies. The ISO 14000 Environmental Management Systems Standards and the European Eco-Management and Audit Scheme (EMAS) have been among the principal drivers. In the U.S., the great majority of major companies with an international presence have conducted routine audits of their overseas facilities for many years.

Most multinational industrial companies that have worldwide EH&S audit programs developed them with objectives that closely parallel objectives and goals of domestic audit programs. Typical objectives of a cross-section of several Fortune 500 companies' worldwide audit programs include:

- To provide independent verification that the corporation's operations are in compliance with the laws of the host nation

- To insure that the corporation's EH&S policies, procedures, and practices are being followed in overseas locations

- To identify and evaluate all hazardous conditions, operations, or activities that pose a risk to the plant and the public

---

[1] For a more extensive treatment of this topic see David D. Nelson, *International Environmental Auditing* (Rockville, MD: Government Institutes, Inc., 1998).

[2] ICC Position Paper on Environmental Auditing, adopted by the ICC Executive Board at its 56th Session (November 29, 1988).

■ To insure that procedures have been established for handling EH&S incidents and emergencies.

This last objective, concerning incidents and emergencies, might lead one to think that the Bhopal tragedy of December 1984 was the primary factor leading to the development of international audit programs. In fact, many U.S.-based firms with worldwide facilities had already established audit programs prior to Bhopal. What Bhopal did was to make these companies take a harder look at their program objectives and strengthen them where necessary.

As a result, most worldwide audit programs today seem to focus more on "risk assessment" of hazardous operations and activities than on the detailed regulatory compliance audits prevalent in many domestic audit programs. This is especially true in developing nations and Third World countries, where EH&S regulations are less stringent than those found in the U.S. and Western Europe. As many multinational corporations seek to set up or expand their presence in the developing nations in Asia and Latin America, international EH&S audit programs are taking on more of a total risk assessment and management-systems approach.

Worldwide EH&S audit programs are sometimes structured totally separate from domestic audit programs within a company's organization. In many cases, an individual or group dedicated specifically to operating the worldwide audit program is established within the company's corporate management. This is because the demands of long-distance travel, overseas communications, keeping up with international laws and regulations, and other similar factors require a full-time effort. In addition, a dedicated international audit team develops an understanding over time of the key EH&S risk management issues that similar facilities face throughout the world. As a result, the audit team can assist management in developing corporate procedures and programs that are designed to incorporate a broad-spectrum approach to risk management suitable for implementation across social, economic, regulatory, and cultural lines.

In most cases, U.S.-based corporate management issues a written policy statement that clearly puts the burden of EH&S compliance and protection on the backs of the managing directors or officers of the worldwide facilities. This policy statement typically requires that all facilities regardless of location meet a set of corporate standards, which provide a minimum set of performance expectations. A few excerpts from different Fortune 500 companies' worldwide policies on EH&S protection illustrate the clear message:

"...Wherever a Bristol-Myers Squibb facility is located, it must meet stringent companywide EHS requirements. At a minimum, each facility must comply with local regulations. In addition, the facility must implement 16 principles of our EHS Codes of Practice. ..."[3]

---

[3] Bristol-Myers Squibb 1999 Report on Environmental Health and Safety Progress.

"...Kodak's HSE management system is supported by its vision of HSE responsibility, HSE Policy, Guiding Principles, and Performance Standards, and is operated consistently with international standards for environmental management systems. Facilities worldwide, including subsidiaries, are routinely evaluated against these standards. ...."[4]

"... With the direction of the Corporate Environment and Safety Council, the company develops Good Environmental Practices (GEPs) and Good Safety Practices (GSPs), and the company's audit group independently assesses compliance at all facilities worldwide. ..."[5]

"... All Unilever companies must adopt the same standards for occupational health and safety, environmental care and consumer safety. These are defined in our framework standards that follow the ISO structure. Our environmental management standards follow the Plan/Do/Check/Review approach and consist of the same 17 elements in the ISO 14001 standard. ..."[6]

One issue that is unique to international audit programs is the degree to which these corporate policies and procedures are enforceable by the firm. Clearly, for worldwide subsidiaries and operating companies in which the U.S.-based parent has a majority ownership, compliance is simply dictated. However, many U.S. companies only hold a 50/50 or minority interest in their overseas plants, making mandatory adherence to corporate EH&S policy difficult to achieve. In these cases, the management of the minority owner is usually careful to suggest and recommend that the major owner of the facilities adopt the minority owner's policy or issue one of its own that addresses top management support of sound EH&S practices. In the most conscientious multinational companies, compliance with applicable local laws and regulations is merely the baseline for EH&S risk management policy. It is the acceptance and implementation of sound, standardized risk management practices (that go above and beyond local standards, where appropriate) at all of a corporation's locations worldwide that define an effective global EH&S policy.

ROLE OF CORPORATE MANAGEMENT

The role of the U.S.-based corporate management in worldwide audit programs does not end with the promulgation of the EH&S policies discussed above, but includes involvement in other activities as well, such as:

---

[4] Eastman Kodak's 1997 Health, Safety and Environment Report.

[5] *Schering-Plough 1998 Report on Environment, Health and Safety.*

[6] *Unilever Internet Site.*

■ Providing EH&S technical advice and support to foreign subsidiaries or operating units from domestic divisions or units

■ Conducting training programs for facility EH&S managers and others with related responsibilities

■ Providing information and clearinghouse functions to ensure that access to technological information and databases is readily obtainable

■ Participating in international conferences, seminars, and symposiums to demonstrate U.S.-based corporate support to foreign nations' EH&S programs

■ Assisting in the development of written EH&S guidelines and procedures to help overseas facilities operate in accordance with good management practices

■ Conducting EH&S audits and/or risk assessments, either independently or in conjunction with foreign operating units.

The size of the corporate staff dedicated to international EH&S programs in most major companies is typically small and ranges from one to three people. Surprisingly, many of the largest U.S. firms have only one corporate person assigned to international programs. With the formal acknowledgment that we now are truly a global economy, some companies have expanded their corporate international staffs or hired outside consulting firms to assist them. In addition, there is a growing trend in multinational corporations to "regionalize" corporate EH&S management staff. This practice effectively reduces the number of staff located at corporate headquarters that are dedicated to EH&S matters, while placing senior-level managers in regional management positions and assigning them the responsibility of overseeing EH&S issues in a specific region such as Europe or Asia.

The number of international audits and risk assessments conducted varies substantially, based on factors such as locations of the plants, degree of risk and concern, stringency of EH&S laws in the host country, and financial or resource limitations. Interestingly, several major U.S. multinational companies are focusing only on conducting audits in countries having weak EH&S laws, based on the assumption that their risks are greater there than in countries with sound EH&S laws.

DESIGN OF INTERNATIONAL AUDIT PROGRAMS

It is important to understand both the basic approach of international audit programs and the standards against which compliance is evaluated. The common two-phased approach that is used, along with highlights of some important issues that one faces in the international arena, is discussed below.

Two-Phased Approach

Most international audit programs appear to be designed in two phases. Phase 1 audits are broad-based, general surveys that focus on understanding the EH&S requirements and actual operating practices at the facilities. Typically a general checklist is used, which is designed more as a tool to record relevant information about plant operations, chemicals and practices, and information on the surrounding environment (e.g., groundwater, surface water, soils). In addition, detailed regulatory compliance information such as copies of pertinent national and local EH&S laws and regulations are gathered and evaluated to determine the scope and extent of future, compliance-oriented audits.

From this information, a judgment is made by the auditor about the risk to the employees, the public, and the environment that the facility presents, and about the regulatory compliance requirements that apply to the facility. This ranking is a subjective, relative risk rating that allows decisions to be made about which facilities need additional attention and the frequency and scope of subsequent audits.

In Phase 2, facilities that were determined to have a high risk are subjected to a more detailed audit/risk assessment that is tailored to a verification of the potential hazard, developing solutions to mitigating or eliminating existing or potential risk, and assessing regulatory compliance issues. In practice, Phase 1 general surveys for some facilities may be scheduled at the same time that the more detailed Phase 2 risk assessment is occurring for other facilities.

This approach allows corporations to constantly focus on those facilities that present the greatest risk to the employees, the environment, the public, and the company. As noted earlier, international audit program designs seem to have a common denominator in that initial auditing efforts are focused more heavily on an evaluation of "EH&S risk" rather than on compliance with administrative and procedural requirements in the regulations. It is only after these risk issues are identified and addressed that most programs zero in on more traditional regulatory compliance. In countries where EH&S laws and regulations are weak and/or poorly enforced, the identification, assessment, and ongoing management of EH&S risks at the facility remains the primary function of the auditing program, even after multiple facility visits.

Audit Standards and Criteria

Notwithstanding the risk assessment approach discussed above, international audit programs should include all appropriate EH&S regulations promulgated by cognizant agencies and regulatory bodies. Most countries have their own EH&S regulations, which should also be consulted when implementing an international audit program. These regulations cover many of the same areas as do U.S. federal and state EH&S regulations (e.g., hazardous waste, air emissions, waste water discharges, PCBs, confined space, personal protective equipment), but they differ in scope, procedural requirements, limitations, and enforcement policy. For example, the German federal government has no power to collect emissions data directly from chemical companies; it has to request the state governments to provide it. Even developing nations such as China, the Philippines, and Malaysia have both national and local laws and regulations addressing wastewater discharges, air emissions, and other EH&S concerns. In many of these locations, the specific permits and approvals that are required prior to construction and operation of new facilities or expansions have specific stipulations governing EH&S issues.

There are many significant differences between the United States' and other countries' approaches to EH&S regulation. Companies with operating units or subsidiaries in foreign countries need to understand these regulatory philosophies and attitudes and how they may affect their facilities. For example, the reality of regulatory compliance and enforcement practices in many countries differs significantly from the programs described in the published law. Many U.S.- and foreign-owned joint venture companies in China have quickly learned that they now face much stricter performance standards, higher discharge fees, and more prevalent enforcement practices than their formerly state-owned entities did before their acquisition or formation of the foreign joint venture. International auditors must attempt to understand these local differences and ensure that EH&S policies and programs are designed to reflect and incorporate such conditions.

Perhaps the most significant difference is the non-adversarial nature of the relationship between industry and national governments in Europe and other foreign countries. Foreign industry has easily adapted to EH&S regulation because they have been subject to it longer than U.S.-based companies. Europeans believe that "good law is good order," as Aristotle once taught. Philosophically, European industry faced up to the realities of the need for regulation long before the U.S. did because it had little choice. The population density of many European countries alone necessitated central control of new industrial development. Germany, for example, which is about the size of Oregon and has a population of 60 million people, has a population density over seven times that of the continental U.S. Is it any wonder why there is little opposition to stringent air emissions limitations in Germany?

Because European countries have a long tradition of regulation that stretches back as far as the Industrial Revolution, environmental control is characterized more as "compromise and negotiation," as compared to the litigious nature of EH&S enforcement in the U.S. However, legislation and implementation of EH&S laws within Third World nations has traditionally been well behind more developed nations. Because pollution control and technology requires capital and continued investment, countries where the average wage base and standard of living is well below European or U.S. standards have failed to set aside money and resources for EH&S control, as other more pressing priorities (such as raising the country's domestic output and improving poor socioeconomic conditions) are addressed. In these countries, EH&S controls, although sorely needed, have been viewed as luxuries that only more wealthy nations could afford. As a result, companies seeking to impose more advanced EH&S control and policies may be stymied by both cultural barriers and apathy driven by a low prioritization of EH&S issues. Unfortunately, many of the countries with the greatest need of improved EH&S regulations are those with the least ability to achieve these goals in the short term. Multinationals with facilities in these locations must seek to achieve commensurate results from their audit programs, starting with increased employee awareness of EH&S matters and basic risk management practices such as improved training.

Another difference between the United States' and other countries' EH&S regulation is the power and prestige of the EH&S bureaucracy. For example, the "best and the brightest" university graduates in European countries seek long-term careers in public administration. This creates an atmosphere of trust, confidence, and consistency in the development and implementation of EH&S laws and regulations. Because the people carrying out EH&S policy in Europe are well respected and not in the job for only a few years until a higher paying job in the private sector comes along, there is greater stability and predictability to EH&S regulation in the European Community. It is simply expected that industry will comply with EH&S laws because a competent, fair, and powerful bureaucracy has brought them about.

A third aspect of EH&S compliance in the international arena is that there is a smaller tradition of litigation in settling EH&S conflicts. Unlike in the U.S., where attorneys pervade the environmental business, lawyers are not popular, are fewer in number, and do not control the implementation of laws in Europe as much as they do in the U.S. Regulators normally deal with plant technical staff in the private sector and have developed the skill of working out differences without hanging the threat of legal action over industry's head.

A final element of difference between U.S. and international implementation of EH&S law is that there is no tradition of the public's right to access to private sector information, as exists in the U.S. There is no formal Freedom of Information Act (FOIA), and the EH&S regulators have wide discretion in choosing to consult and inform interested parties on EH&S laws and regulations. This is not to say that there is no public disclosure of EH&S issues, but it is not implemented with the formality and inflexibility of the "notice and comment" approach taken for new EH&S regulations in the U.S. With its call for disclosure, the Eco-Management and Audit Scheme (EMAS) may alter this historical pattern in Europe.

Largely because of the above factors, international private sector facilities are not subject to as much inspection and monitoring as exists in the U.S. International EH&S regulators expect that because control requirements have been brought about in the spirit of negotiation and compromise, industry is therefore complying or is making best faith efforts to comply. This is an underlying reason why U.S.-based international audit programs tend to focus more on risk assessment than on regulatory compliance.

In summary, U.S. companies with overseas operating units should ensure that the appropriate national EH&S regulations have been researched and evaluated for any impact on their facilities and operations. In countries where there is an absence of EH&S regulations, it is a practice of many U.S. companies operating overseas to extend U.S. EH&S standards to facilities and operations in all worldwide locations. Many companies feel that the absence of any foreign national EH&S regulations puts them at even greater risk; therefore, they have adopted policies that require conformance to U.S.-based standards and requirements as part of their overall corporate risk management philosophy. Interestingly, as witnessed by the Bhopal incident, a U.S. company found itself in litigation in the U.S. courts even though the event occurred in India, a country not known for its tough EH&S regulations.

CONDUCTING INTERNATIONAL AUDITS

Many of the same steps discussed elsewhere in this book, relative to conducting audits, apply to both domestic and international audits. Therefore, this section will focus only on the differences or unique problems encountered when conducting worldwide audits. Using the same three phases of an audit—(1) pre-audit, (2) on-site, and (3) post-audit activities—the key issues that multinational companies have run into in their audit programs are discussed below.

Pre-Audit Activities

As noted previously, additional effort is needed to research and evaluate the EH&S laws and regulations in the country where the plants and facilities are located. This is not as difficult as it seems. Through the use of the Internet and industry consortia, companies have been able to readily obtain EH&S regulations, in English, for many countries. For example, Thailand has published its EH&S regulations in English, and they are available in book or electronic form. There are several additional sources that can be consulted in the U.S. that can provide this information. The foreign embassies in Washington, DC are helpful in this area, as are some private-sector databases such as Enflex and the International Environment Reporter of the Bureau of National Affairs.[7]

Notice and confirmation of the audit dates and scope need to occur much earlier in the process than is required for a domestic audit. This is particularly true when pre-audit questionnaires are used (since translation and interpretation issues are likely to arise) and when multiple facility audits are scheduled for one trip (which, as noted below, is a common practice employed by companies to reduce the overall per-site audit cost). Most companies send a letter outlining the requirements of the audit to the overseas facility at least a month in advance, and lead times of up to

---

[7] Texts are also available in many cases, but they become outdated quickly. An example of one text is Thomas Handler, ed., *Regulating the European Environment,* 2nd ed. (New York: John Wiley and Sons, Inc., 1997).

three months prior to the on-site visit are not unusual. One week prior to the audit, a second confirmation is typically made via the telephone or telex.

As described above, distribution of the audit questionnaire or protocols is usually made well in advance of the on-site visit to acquaint the plant management with the scope of the audit. In many cases, the plant is asked to complete the informational parts of the questionnaire (i.e., permits, discharge points, number and type of air emissions points, number of confined spaces, etc.) prior to the auditor arriving on site. This practice establishes a good starting point for the audit, as the facility representatives can be asked to describe the information presented in the pre-visit questionnaire as a kick-off exercise during the on-site portion of the audit (following the opening conference).

Effort should be made to understand, ahead of time, any language barrier problems that may be encountered during the audit. Interestingly, very few multinational companies seem to have a problem with non-English-speaking plant management. However, often second- and third- level supervisors do not understand English well enough for an auditor to conduct a thorough interview. It is apparently not a common practice that the U.S.-based corporate staff conducting international audits are multilingual, so it is important to inquire, prior to arriving on site, about the degree to which English is understood by key plant staff. Every effort to ease the translation and interpretation problems should be considered, such as using local employees or consultants to assist the audit team and the facility staff as necessary. The audits will be difficult enough without the uncertainty of knowing whether someone really understands a question or a response.

Being aware of any unique cultural customs or traditions in the country prior to traveling abroad is important so that inadvertent indiscretions that can cause a strain between the auditors and plant staff do not occur. Attitudes and traditions on such things as religious observances, holidays, courtesies, and other common protocols should be known ahead of time. Auditors of a certain religious or ethnic backgrounds may feel uncomfortable in certain countries if they are not aware of these sensitivities; the gender of the auditor can also be an issue in some locations. As unfortunate as it is in today's society, in many places throughout the world both age and gender can play an important role in establishing an effective relationship with site management, which is essential to an effective audit. Also, certain practices and comments, although seemingly innocuous and not meant to be defensive or accusatory, can cause employees to "lose face" with local management, so auditors should be cognizant of these cultural concerns.[8]

---

[8] There are two excellent business sources that describe the differing cultures throughout the world. They are Terri Morrison, et.al., *Dun & Bradstreet's Guide to Doing Business around the World* (Englewood, NJ: Prentice Hall, Inc., 1997) and Terri Morrison, et.al., *Kiss, Bow, or Shake Hand* (Bob Adams, Inc., 1994). For information on these resources, please see www.getcustoms.com.

On-Site Activities

Once on-site, there are very few differences in conducting the audit in a domestic facility or in an international plant. They generally follow the same approach.

An initial orientation meeting is held with plant management and key staff to discuss the objectives of the audit and go over a detailed agenda. Typically, international audits seem to be limited to one or two auditors who spend anywhere from one to three days on site, meaning that the effort expended to conduct the audit ranges from one- to six-person days. There appears to be a trend among multinational companies to spend less effort per facility than is typically expended on a domestic audit. This is because there is sensitivity to overpowering the foreign plant with a large group of corporate staff, and secondly, the time and cost to implement an international program can become excessive if audits are not conducted efficiently. Most U.S.-based auditors will plan their trip to visit several plants in several countries when conducting overseas audits. That is another reason why spending more time than is necessary at any one plant is normally not done. The schedule is sometimes very demanding, and travel among several countries and multiple time zones can be much more complicated than is typically experienced between states in the U.S.

The on-site activities of an international audit follow the same general plan as in a domestic audit. Interviews are conducted with key plant staff, physical inspections of operations and facilities are made, and EH&S records and files are reviewed. Often this written documentation is in the native language, giving rise to the need for an English translation. The audit questionnaire referred to previously is completed during the course of the on-site review, and copies of any local or municipal laws, ordinances, or regulations are usually obtained so that the auditor can maintain a file of these requirements back in the U.S.

A closing conference is typically held after the auditors are finished, so that plant management is aware of the findings and recommendations. The post-audit conference can take on a huge importance in the international audit process. It is not uncommon for numerous key managers and other personnel deemed to be important by local management to attend the closing conference. Many of these people may perceive that the findings of the auditors may be used as a measuring stick by their managers and will reflect on their standing and level of respect within the local company organization. For this reason, auditors must once again be respectful of local customs and practices and be certain to present the findings in a factual and low-key manner that will both inform and educate the facility representatives present at the closing conference.

Post-Audit Activities

As in domestic audit programs, an audit report is normally prepared, which presents the findings and recommendations of the auditors. The report is submitted to the audited facility for comment at the same time the corporate law department receives a copy. After comments and necessary revisions are made, a final audit report is submitted to the operating unit's senior management and the corporate director of EH&S affairs. The final audit report is often transmitted with a letter that requires the facility management to develop an action plan to address the findings and recommendations in the audit report.

Typically, the corporate EH&S auditor who conducted the audit receives the action plan, only to confirm that the final report has been understood and that the response is consistent with the findings of the report. Action plans are normally prepared within one to two months of the issuance of the final report. At this point the auditor's role has been completed, and follow-up on the action plan is the responsibility of plant management and the corporate audit program manager. The subsequent audit of the facility would normally include an evaluation of the progress made in the correction of the problems in the action plan since the previous audit.

There is a trend to transmit the audit reports, the corrective action plan, and any periodic status reports entirely by email. In some cases, the email itself is the report, but more often the report is included as an attachment. Using email makes for a much more efficient process.

Few multinational companies appear to manage their international audit programs through their legal departments or classify their audit reports as "Privileged and Confidential" to protect them from discovery. This may be due to the fact that these U.S.-based legal doctrines are not recognized in international settings as binding, and the U.S. judicial system has no jurisdiction in foreign countries.

SUMMARY OF KEY CHALLENGES IN INTERNATIONAL AUDITS

Based on several auditors' experiences overseas, there are a number of special factors to consider when conducting international audits. These are:

- Preparation time for overseas audits needs to be much greater than for domestic audits. Obtaining copies of foreign regulations can take weeks or months and sometimes requires translation. Additionally, audit protocols will have to be revised to reflect these often very different regulations. It is important to understand these regulations since they may be completely different than U.S. regulations in terms of concept and implementation.

- As in the U.S., many foreign countries enable regional and local jurisdictions to develop additional regulations and/or requirements and implement stricter limitations than those found in the national laws and regulations. In addition, permits to operate may impose specific standards. It is important for auditors to determine whether these conditions exist and to incorporate these relevant local compliance concerns into the audit scope.

■ There are great differences in how European countries implement rational regulations in order to meet the European Union's (EU) environmental directives. Members of the EU are free to design and implement regulations as long as they meet the intent of the directives. Consequently, there can be problems with important areas such as transfrontier shipments of hazardous waste since the definitions of "hazardous" or "toxic" wastes may vary from country to country, leaving potential loopholes in the "cradle to grave" concept.

■ Although regulations may exist in some countries, there may simply be no easy way for facilities to comply with the stated requirements. As an example, the Philippines has an environmental law patterned after RCRA, which requires the manifesting of specific hazardous wastes to a "licensed" disposal facility. At present, no licensed hazardous waste disposal facilities are in place for certain types of wastes in the Philippines, making compliance with an existing law a difficult endeavor.

■ When conducting EH&S audits in lesser-developed countries, auditors must be cognizant of the fact that EH&S controls will be secondary to socioeconomic concerns. Control and regulation of EH&S issues is perceived as being much less critical than raising the country's standard of living. It is difficult to audit facilities in lesser-developed countries using U.S. standards. The overall goal of doing these types of audits should be to minimize the EH&S impacts and to educate the employees to make them aware of environmental and health issues.

■ Do not underestimate logistics. Have a clear understanding of how you will travel between the airport, hotel, and plant site. In many countries, renting a car is not recommended. Find out how long it will take each day to travel from the hotel to the plant site. In some locations, suitable hotels are a good two hours away. This will affect the schedule for the day.

■ The auditor should take the time to become familiar with the local customs and practices prior to arriving on site. In many countries, and particularly in the Middle East and Asian countries, traditional customs and practices are revered above all other regulations or protocols.

■ Local timetables and working hours vary greatly throughout the world, so the auditor should be thoughtful of the employees' schedules. In Spain, for instance, expect to break for several hours in the afternoon and not eat the evening meal until very late in the day. Asian countries typically have very strict work habits, so be prepared for a very structured, efficient schedule.

■ The use of a pre-audit questionnaire is critical, particularly in those countries where English is not widely spoken. Solid preparation is paramount.

- Everything takes longer than you would expect. Plan ahead to spend at least twice as long to conduct the audit as you would expect for a similar U.S. operation. Because there is little enforcement action in many countries, EH&S recordkeeping may be scattered and/or disorganized. Interviews may be difficult due to language problems, so plan ahead.

- Although the auditor should be willing to adhere to the local customs and schedules, do not let the scope or time frame of the audit get away from you. It is easy to become distracted and disoriented in unfamiliar facilities where no English language signs are present. Keep a facility plot plan handy at all times as a reference. Stick to the pre-arranged audit schedule and topics as best as possible.

- Although it may sound trite, learning a few simple phrases in the native language will endear you to your hosts and serve as a good icebreaker. This is particularly helpful when interviewing or debriefing employees and management.

- Do not assume that management and employees comprehend everything you say, regardless of the nods of approval they may give you. Be prepared to repeat yourself several times, or change the statement to a question to ensure the correct answer is known. Do not hesitate to ask plant management to translate for you. This is often a very effective way to get the attention of your audience.

- The auditor should be sensitive to conflicts between compliance with national regulations versus corporate policies and/or U.S. standards. It is best to have a corporate policy statement in place regarding these issues prior to conducting the audit program. Be careful not to make too many "good management practice" suggestions when the existing conditions are in compliance with local regulations.

- Get a copy of everything you think you may need, and even the material you don't need. When it comes time for writing the report, it's too late to confirm any questions you may have, as the facility may be over 10,000 miles away. Also, it is a good idea to get photographs, if possible.

- Above all, keep things in their proper perspective. Remember that it is difficult to be concerned over secondary containment or storage practices when the majority of the country's population is starving.

Even when the auditor follows these guidelines, an international audit is a difficult assignment at best. Those that have completed them know that the challenge of doing a thorough and accurate job often takes the edge off the "glamour of international travel."

APPENDICES

Appendix A

REFERENCES

ASTM. *Standard Practice for Environmental Regulatory Compliance Audits*. E 2107 (Draft).

ASTM. *Standard Practice for Environmental Site Assessments: Phase I Environmental Site Assessment Process*. E 1527-00 (July 2000).

ASTM. *Standard Practice for Environmental Site Assessments: Transaction Screen Process*. E 1528-00 (July 2000).

Barton, Hugh and Noel Bruder, *Guide to Local Environmental Auditing*. Washington, DC: Island Press, 1995.

Blakeslee, H.W. and T.M. Grabowski. *A Practical Guide to Plant Environmental Audits*. New York: Van Nostrand Reinhold, 1985.

Blumenfeld, Mark. "Conducting an Environmental Audit." In *Environmental Audit Handbook Series: Volume 1*. New York: Executive Enterprises Publications, 1991.

Board of Environmental, Health and Safety Auditor Certifications. *Standards for the Professional Practice of Environmental, Health and Safety Auditing*. 1999.

Brealey, Mark. *Environmental Liabilities and Regulation in Europe*. The Hague: International Business Publishing Ltd., 1993.

Cheremisinoff, Paul N. and Nicholas P. Cheremisinoff. *Professional Environmental Auditors' Guidebook*. Park Ridge, NJ: Noyes, 1993.

Corporate Counsel's Guide to Environmental Compliance and Audits. no. 105. N.p, 1992.

Crist, Joseph G. "Reporting, Recordkeeping and Disclosure Requirements for an Environmental Audit." In *Environmental Audit Handbook Series: Volume Two* New York: Executive Enterprises Publications, 1989.

Environmental, Health and Safety Auditing Roundtable. *Standards for the Performance of Environmental, Health and Safety Audits.* 1993.

Environmental, Health and Safety Auditing Roundtable. *Standard for the Design and Implementation of an Environmental, Health, and Safety Audit Program.* 1996.

European Union Regulation 1836/93. *Allowing Voluntary Participation in an Eco-Management and Audit Scheme (EMAS).* O.J.L. 168/1 (July 10, 1993).

Grayson, Lesley. *Environmental Auditing: A Guide to Best Practice in the U.K. and Europe.* London: Stanley Thornes Publishers Ltd., 1994.

Greeno, J.L., et. al. *Environmental Auditing: Fundamentals and Techniques.* New York: John Wiley and Sons, 1985.

Handler, Thomas, ed. *Regulating the European Environment.* 2nd ed. New York: John Wiley and Sons, 1997.

Harrison, L., ed. *Environmental Health and Safety Auditing Handbook.* 2nd ed. New York: McGraw-Hill, 1995.

Hillary, Ruth. "The Eco-Management and Audit Scheme: A Practical Guide." In *Business and the Environment Practitioner Series (C).* London: Stanley Thornes Publishers Ltd., 1994.

Hoffman, Stephen A. *Planning, Staffing and Contracting for an Environmental Audit.* New York: John Wiley and Sons, 1994.

International Organization for Standardization (ISO). *Guidelines for Environmental Auditing, ISO 14010 (General Principles), 14011 (Audit Procedures) and 14012 (Qualification Criteria for Environmental Auditors).* (Fall 1996).

Jones, David, ed. *EC Auditing and Environmental Management.* New York: John Wiley and Sons, 1993.

Kato, Hiroki and Joan Kato. *Understanding and Working with the Japanese Business World.* Englewood Cliffs, NJ: Prentice Hall, 1992.

Ledgerwood, Grant. *Implementing an Environmental Audit: How to Gain a Competitive Advantage Using Quality and Environmental Responsibility.* Burr Ridge, IL: Irwin Professional Publishing, 1994.

Lotter, Donald W. *Earthscore: Your Personal Environmental Audit and Guide*. N.p: Morning Sun Press, 1993.

McGaw, David. *Environmental Auditing and Compliance Manual*. New York: Van Nostrand Reinhold, 1993.

Morrison, Terri, et.al. *Dun and Bradstreet's Guide to Doing Business around the World*. Englewood Cliffs, NJ: Prentice Hall, Inc., 1997.

Morrison, Terri, et.al. *Kiss, Bow, or Shake Hands*. Holbrook, MA: Bob Adams, Inc., 1994.

Moskowitz, Joel S. *Environmental Liability and Real Estate Property Transactions: Law and Practice*. 2nd ed. New York: John Wiley and Sons, 1995.

Nelson, David D. *International Environmental Auditing*. Rockville, MD: Government Institutes, 1998.

Ruiz, M.A. and Paul N. Cheremisinoff. *Pocket Guidebook on Environmental Auditing*. 2nd ed. Mendham, NJ: SciTech Publications, 1989.

SEC v. Allied Chemical Corp., No. 77-0373 (D.D.C., March 4, 1977); *SEC v. United States Steel Corp.*, (1979-1980 Transfer Binder) Fed. Sec. L. Rep. (CCH) 82,319 (1979); *SEC v. Occidental Petroleum Corp.*, (1980 Transfer Binder) Fed. Sec. L. Rep. (CCH) 82,622 (1980).

Shanahan, John M. *The Most Brilliant Thoughts of All Time (In Two Lines or Less)*. New York: Harper Collins Inc., 1999.

Shields, J., ed. *Air Emissions, Baselines, and Environmental Auditing*. New York: Van Nostrand Reinhold, 1993.

Smith, Ann C. and William A. Yodis. "Environmental Auditing Quality Management." In *Environmental Auditing Handbook Series: Volume 3* PLACE: Executive Enterprises Publications, 1989.

Sullivan, Thomas F.P., et. al. *Environmental Law Handbook*. 15th ed. Rockville, MD: Government Institutes, 1999.

Truitt, T.H., et. al. *Environmental Auditing Handbook: Basic Principles of Environmental Compliance Auditing*. 2nd ed. Washington, DC: Wald, Harkrader and Ross, 1983.

U.S. Environmental Protection Agency. *Environmental Auditing Policy Statement.* Final Policy Statement (July 9, 1986).

U.S. Environmental Protection Agency. *Incentives for Self-Policing: Discovery, Disclosure, Correction and Prevention of Violations.* Final Policy Statement (January 22, 1996).

U.S. Environmental Protection Agency. *Incentives for Self-Policing: Discovery, Disclosure, Correction and Prevention of Violations.* Final Policy Statement (May 11, 2000).

U.S. Environmental Protection Agency. *Multi-Media Investigation Manual.* EPA-330/9-89-003-R (1992).

U.S. Environmental Protection Agency. *Enforcement and Compliance Assurance Accomplishments Report—FY 1998.* (June 1999).

U.S. Sentencing Commission. *Draft Corporate Sentencing Guidelines for Environmental Violations* (November 16, 1993).

Willig, John T., ed. *Auditing for Environmental Quality Leadership: Beyond Compliance to Environmental Excellence.* New York: John Wiley and Sons, 1995.

Young, Steven S. *Environmental Auditing.* Houston, TX: Gulf Publishing Company, 1994.

Appendix B

FEDERAL REGISTER NOTICES

U.S. EPA's Environmental Auditing Policy Statement (July 9, 1986)

U.S. EPA's Incentives for Self-Policing: Discovery, Disclosure, Correction and Prevention of Violations (December 22, 1995)

U.S. EPA's Incentives for Self-Policing: Discovery, Disclosure, Correction and Prevention of Violations (April 11, 2000)

OSHA's Final Policy Concerning the Occupational Safety and Health Administration's Treatment of Voluntary Employer Safety and Health Self-Audits (July 28, 2000)

U.S. EPA's 1986 Environmental Auditing Policy Statement

25004   Federal Register / Vol. 51, No. 131 / Wednesday, July 9, 1986 / Notices

ENVIRONMENTAL PROTECTION AGENCY

[OPPE-FRL-3046-6]

Environmental Auditing Policy Statement

AGENCY: Environmental Protection Agency (EPA).

ACTION: Final policy statement.

SUMMARY: It is EPA policy to encourage the use of environmental auditing by regulated entities to help achieve and maintain compliance with environmental laws and regulations, as well as to help identify and correct unregulated environmental hazards. EPA first published this policy as interim guidance on November 8, 1985 (50 FR 46504). Based on comments received regarding the interim guidance, the Agency is issuing today's final policy statement with only minor changes.

This final policy statement specifically:

• Encourages regulated entities to develop, implement and upgrade environmental auditing programs;

• Discusses when the Agency may or may not request audit reports;

• Explains how EPA's inspection and enforcement activities may respond to regulated entities' efforts to assure compliance through auditing;

• Endorses environmental auditing at federal facilities;

• Encourages state and local environmental auditing initiatives; and

• Outlines elements of effective audit programs.

Environmental auditing includes a variety of compliance assessment techniques which go beyond those legally required and are used to identify actual and potential environmental problems. Effective environmental auditing can lead to higher levels of overall compliance and reduced risk to human health and the environment. EPA endorses the practice of environmental auditing and supports its accelerated use by regulated entities to help meet the goals of federal, state and local environmental requirements. However, the existence of an auditing program does not create any defense to, or otherwise limit, the responsibility of any regulated entity to comply with applicable regulatory requirements.

States are encouraged to adopt these or similar and equally effective policies in order to advance the use of environmental auditing on a consistent, nationwide basis.

DATES: This final policy statement is effective July 9, 1986.

FOR FURTHER INFORMATION CONTACT: Leonard Fleckenstein, Office of Policy, Planning and Evaluation, (202) 382-2726;

or

Cheryl Wasserman, Office of Enforcement and Compliance Monitoring, (202) 382-7550.

SUPPLEMENTARY INFORMATION:

ENVIRONMENTAL AUDITING POLICY STATEMENT

I. Preamble

On November 8, 1985 EPA published an Environmental Auditing Policy Statement, effective as interim guidance, and solicited written comments until January 7, 1986.

Thirteen commenters submitted written comments. Eight were from private industry. Two commenters represented industry trade associations. One federal agency, one consulting firm and one law firm also submitted comments.

Twelve commenters addressed EPA requests for audit reports. Three comments per subject were received regarding inspections, enforcement response and elements of effective environmental auditing. One commenter addressed audit provisions as remedies in enforcement actions, one addressed environmental auditing at federal facilities, and one addressed the relationship of the policy statement to state or local regulatory agencies. Comments generally supported both the concept of a policy statement and the interim guidance, but raised specific concerns with respect to particular language and policy issues in sections of the guidance.

General Comments

Three commenters found the interim guidance to be constructive, balanced and effective at encouraging more and better environmental auditing.

Another commenter, while considering the policy on the whole to be constructive, felt that new and identifiable auditing "incentives" should be offered by EPA. Based on earlier comments received from industry, EPA believes most companies would not support or participate in an "incentives-based" environmental auditing program with EPA. Moreover, general promises to forgo inspections or reduce enforcement responses in exchange for companies' adoption of environmental auditing programs—the "incentives" most frequently mentioned in this context—are fraught with legal and policy obstacles.

Several commenters expressed concern that states or localities might use the interim guidance to *require* auditing. The Agency disagrees that the policy statement opens the way for states and localities to require auditing. No EPA policy can grant states or localities any more (or less) authority than they already possess. EPA believes that the interim guidance effectively encourages *voluntary* auditing. In fact, Section II.B. of the policy states: "because audit quality depends to a large degree on genuine management commitment to the program and its objectives, auditing should remain a voluntary program."

Another commenter suggested that EPA should not expect an audit to identify all potential problem areas or conclude that a problem identified in an audit reflects normal operations and procedures. EPA agrees that an audit report should clearly reflect these realities and should be written to point out the audit's limitations. However, since EPA will not routinely request audit reports, the Agency does not believe these concerns raise issues which need to be addressed in the policy statement.

A second concern expressed by the same commenter was that EPA should acknowledge that environmental audits are only part of a successful environmental management program and thus should not be expected to cover every environmental issue or solve all problems. EPA agrees and accordingly has amended the statement of purpose which appears at the end of this preamble.

Yet another commenter thought EPA should focus on environmental performance results (compliance or non-compliance), not on the processes or vehicles used to achieve those results. In general, EPA agrees with this statement and will continue to focus on environmental results. However, EPA also believes that such results can be improved through Agency efforts to identify and encourage effective environmental management practices, and will continue to encourage such practices in non-regulatory ways.

A final general comment recommended that EPA should sponsor seminars for small businesses on how to start auditing programs. EPA agrees that such seminars would be useful. However, since audit seminars already are available from several private sector organizations, EPA does not believe it should intervene in that market with the possible exception of seminars for government agencies, especially federal agencies, for which EPA has a broad mandate under Executive Order 12088 to

U.S. EPA's 1986 Environmental Auditing Policy Statement *(cont'd)*

Federal Register / Vol. 51, No. 131 / Wednesday, July 9, 1986 / Notices **25005**

provide technical assistance for environmental compliance.

Requests for Reports

EPA received 12 comments regarding Agency requests for environmental audit reports, far more than on any other topic in the policy statement. One commenter felt that EPA struck an appropriate balance between respecting the need for self-evaluation with some measure of privacy, and allowing the Agency enough flexibility of inquiry to accomplish future statutory missions. However, most commenters expressed concern that the interim guidance did not go far enough to assuage corporate fears that EPA will use audit reports for environmental compliance "witch hunts." Several commenters suggested additional specific assurances regarding the circumstances under which EPA will request such reports.

One commenter recommended that EPA request audit reports only "when the Agency can show the information it needs to perform its statutory mission cannot be obtained from the monitoring, compliance or other data that is otherwise reportable and/or accessible to EPA, or where the Government deems an audit report material to a criminal investigation." EPA accepts this . recommendation in part. The Agency believes it would not be in the best interest of human health and the environment to commit to making a "showing" of a compelling information need before ever requesting an audit report. While EPA may normally be willing to do so, the Agency cannot rule out in advance all circumstances in which such a showing may not be possible. However, it would be helpful to further clarify that a request for an audit report or a portion of a report normally will be made when needed information is not available by alternative means. Therefore, EPA has revised Section III.A., paragraph two and added the phrase: "and usually made where the information needed cannot be obtained from monitoring, reporting or other data otherwise available to the Agency."

Another commenter suggested that (except in the case of criminal investigations) EPA should limit requests for audit documents to specific questions. By including the phrase "or relevant portions of a report" in Section III.A., EPA meant to emphasize it would not request an entire audit document when only a relevant portion would suffice. Likewise, EPA fully intends not to request even a portion of a report if needed information or data can be otherwise obtained. To further clarify this point EPA has added the phrase,

"most likely focused on particular information needs rather than the entire report," to the second sentence of paragraph two, Section III.A. Incorporating the two comments above, the first two sentences in paragraph two of final Section III.A. now read: "EPA's authority to request an audit report, or relevant portions thereof, will be exercised on a case-by-case basis where the Agency determines it is needed to accomplish a statutory mission or the Government deems it to be material to a criminal investigation. EPA expects such requests to be limited, most likely focused on particular information needs rather than the entire report, and usually made where the information needed cannot be obtained from monitoring, reporting or other data otherwise available to the Agency."

Other commenters recommended that EPA not request audit reports under any circumstances, that requests be "restricted to only those legally required," that requests be limited to criminal investigations, or that requests be made only when EPA has reason to believe "that the audit programs or reports are being used to conceal evidence of environmental non-compliance or otherwise being used in bad faith." EPA appreciates concerns underlying all of these comments and has considered each carefully. However, the Agency believes that these recommendations do not strike the appropriate balance between retaining the flexibility to accomplish EPA's statutory missions in future, unforeseen circumstances, and acknowledging regulated entities' need to self-evaluate environmental performance with some measure of privacy. Indeed, based on prime informal comments, the small number of formal comments received, and the even smaller number of adverse comments, EPA believes the final policy statement should remain largely unchanged from the interim version.

Elements of Effective Environmental Auditing

Three commenters expressed concerns regarding the seven general elements EPA outlined in the Appendix to the interim guidance.

One commenter noted that were EPA to further expand or more fully detail such elements, programs not specifically fulfilling each element would then be judged inadequate. EPA agrees that presenting highly specific and prescriptive auditing elements could be counter-productive by not taking into account numerous factors which vary extensively from one organization to another, but which may still result in effective auditing programs.

Accordingly, EPA does not plan to expand or more fully detail these auditing elements.

Another commenter asserted that states and localities should be cautioned not to consider EPA's auditing elements as mandatory steps. The Agency is fully aware of this concern and in the interim guidance noted its strong opinion that "regulatory agencies should not attempt to prescribe the precise form and structure of regulated entities' environmental management or auditing programs." While EPA cannot require state or local regulators to adopt this or similar policies, the Agency does strongly encourage them to do so, both in the interim and final policies.

A final commenter thought the Appendix too specifically prescribed what should and what should not be included in an auditing program. Other commenters, on the other hand, viewed the elements described as very general in nature. EPA agrees with these other commenters. The elements are in no way binding. Moreover, EPA believes that most mature, effective environmental auditing programs do incorporate each of these general elements in some form, and considers them useful yardsticks for those considering adopting or upgrading audit programs. For these reasons EPA has not revised the Appendix in today's final policy statement.

Other Comments

Other significant comments addressed EPA inspection priorities for, and enforcement responses to, organizations with environmental auditing programs.

One commenter, stressing that audit programs are *internal* management tools, took exception to the phrase in the second paragraph of section III.B.1. of the interim guidance which states that environmental audits can 'complement' regulatory oversight. By using the word 'complement' in this context, EPA does not intend to imply that audit reports must be obtained by the Agency in order to supplement regulatory inspections. 'Complement' is used in a broad sense of being in addition to inspections and providing something (i.e., self-assessment) which otherwise would be lacking. To clarify this point EPA has added the phrase "by providing self-assessment to assure compliance" after "environmental audits may complement inspections" in this paragraph.

The same commenter also expressed concern that, as EPA sets inspection priorities, a company having an audit program could appear to be a 'poor performer' due to complete and accurate reporting when measured against a

U.S. EPA's 1986 Environmental Auditing Policy Statement *(cont'd)*

25006   **Federal Register** / Vol. 51, No. 131 / Wednesday, July 9, 1986 / Notices

company which reports something less than required by law. EPA agrees that it is important to communicate this fact to Agency and state personnel, and will do so. However, the Agency does not believe a change in the policy statement is necessary.

A further comment suggested EPA should commit to take auditing programs into account when assessing all enforcement actions. However, in order to maintain enforcement flexibility under varied circumstances, the Agency cannot promise reduced enforcement responses to violations at all audited facilities when other factors may be overriding. Therefore the policy statement continues to state that EPA may exercise its discretion to consider auditing programs as evidence of honest and genuine efforts to assure compliance, which would then be taken into account in fashioning enforcement responses to violations.

A final commenter suggested the phrase "expeditiously correct environmental problems" not be used in the enforcement context since it implied EPA would use an entity's record of correcting nonregulated matters when evaluating regulatory violations. EPA did not intend for such an inference to be made. EPA intended the term "environmental problems" to refer to the underlying circumstances which eventually lead up to the violations. To clarify this point, EPA is revising the first two sentences of the paragraph to which this comment refers by changing "environmental problems" to "violations and underlying environmental problems" in the first sentence and to "underlying environmental problems" in the second sentence.

In a separate development EPA is preparing an update of its January 1984 *Federal Facilities Compliance Strategy*, which is referenced in section III. C. of the auditing policy. The Strategy should be completed and available on request from EPA's Office of Federal Activities later this year.

EPA thanks all commenters for responding to the November 8, 1985 publication. Today's notice is being issued to inform regulated entities and the public of EPA's final policy toward environmental auditing. This policy was developed to help (a) encourage regulated entities to institutionalize effective audit practices as one means of improving compliance and sound environmental management, and (b) guide internal EPA actions directly related to regulated entities' environmental auditing programs.

EPA will evaluate implementation of this final policy to ensure it meets the above goals and continues to encourage

better environmental management, while strengthening the Agency's own efforts to monitor and enforce compliance with environmental requirements.

II. General EPA Policy on Environmental Auditing

A. Introduction

Environmental auditing is a systematic, documented, periodic and objective review by regulated entities [1] of facility operations and practices related to meeting environmental requirements. Audits can be designed to accomplish any or all of the following: verify compliance with environmental requirements; evaluate the effectiveness of environmental management systems already in place; or assess risks from regulated and unregulated materials and practices.

Auditing serves as a quality assurance check to help improve the effectiveness of basic environmental management by verifying that management practices are in place, functioning and adequate. Environmental audits evaluate, and are not a substitute for, direct compliance activities such as obtaining permits, installing controls, monitoring compliance, reporting violations, and keeping records. Environmental auditing may verify but does not include activities required by law, regulation or permit (e.g., continuous emissions monitoring, composite correction plans at wastewater treatment plants, etc.). Audits do not in any way replace regulatory agency inspections. However, environmental audits can improve compliance by complementing conventional federal, state and local oversight.

The appendix to this policy statement outlines some basic elements of environmental auditing (e.g., auditor independence and top management support) for use by those considering implementation of effective auditing programs to help achieve and maintain compliance. Additional information on environmental auditing practices can be found in various published materials. [2]

[1] "Regulated entities" include private firms and public agencies with facilities subject to environmental regulation. Public agencies can include federal, state or local agencies as well as special-purpose organizations such as regional sewage commissions.

[2] See, e.g., "Current Practices in Environmental Auditing," EPA Report No. EPA-230-09-83-006, February 1984; "Annotated Bibliography on Environmental Auditing," Fifth Edition, September 1985, both available from: Regulatory Reform Staff, PM-223, EPA, 401 M Street SW, Washington, DC 20460.

Environmental auditing has developed for sound business reasons, particularly as a means of helping regulated entities manage pollution control affirmatively over time instead of reacting to crises. Auditing can result in improved facility environmental performance, help communicate effective solutions to common environmental problems, focus facility managers' attention on current and upcoming regulatory requirements, and generate protocols and checklists which help facilities better manage themselves. Auditing also can result in better-integrated management of environmental hazards, since auditors frequently identify environmental liabilities which go beyond regulatory compliance. Companies, public entities and federal facilities have employed a variety of environmental auditing practices in recent years. Several hundred major firms in diverse industries now have environmental auditing programs, although they often are known by other names such as assessment, survey, surveillance, review or appraisal.

While auditing has demonstrated its usefulness to those with audit programs, many others still do not audit. Clarification of EPA's position regarding auditing may help encourage regulated entities to establish audit programs or upgrade systems already in place.

B. EPA Encourages the Use of Environmental Auditing

EPA encourages regulated entities to adopt sound environmental management practices to improve environmental performance. In particular, EPA encourages regulated entities subject to environmental regulations to institute environmental auditing programs to help ensure the adequacy of internal systems to achieve, maintain and monitor compliance. Implementation of environmental auditing programs can result in better identification, resolution and avoidance of environmental problems, as well as improvements to management practices. Audits can be conducted effectively by independent internal or third party auditors. Larger organizations generally have greater resources to devote to an internal audit team, while smaller entities might be more likely to use outside auditors.

Regulated entities are responsible for taking all necessary steps to ensure compliance with environmental requirements, whether or not they adopt audit programs. Although environmental laws do not require a regulated facility to have an auditing program, ultimate responsibility for the environmental

U.S. EPA's 1986 Environmental Auditing Policy Statement *(cont'd)*

Federal Register / Vol. 51, No. 131 / Wednesday, July 9, 1986 / Notices   **25007**

performance of the facility lies with top management, which therefore has a strong incentive to use reasonable means, such as environmental auditing, to secure reliable information of facility compliance status.

EPA does not intend to dictate or interfere with the environmental management practices of private or public organizations. Nor does EPA intend to mandate auditing (though in certain instances EPA may seek to include provisions for environmental auditing as part of settlement agreements, as noted below). Because environmental auditing systems have been widely adopted on a voluntary basis in the past, and because audit quality depends to a large degree upon genuine management commitment to the program and its objectives, auditing should remain a voluntary activity.

III. EPA Policy on Specific Environmental Auditing Issues

A. Agency Requests for Audit Reports

EPA has broad statutory authority to request relevant information on the environmental compliance status of regulated entities. However, EPA believes routine Agency requests for audit reports [3] could inhibit auditing in the long run, decreasing both the quantity and quality of audits conducted. Therefore, as a matter of policy, EPA will *not* routinely request environmental audit reports.

EPA's authority to request an audit report, or relevant portions thereof, will be exercised on a case-by-case basis where the Agency determines it is needed to accomplish a statutory mission, or where the Government deems it to be material to a criminal investigation. EPA expects such requests to be limited, most likely focused on particular information needs rather than the entire report, and usually made where the information needed cannot be obtained from monitoring, reporting or other data otherwise available to the Agency. Examples would likely include situations where: audits are conducted under consent decrees or other settlement agreements; a company has placed its management practices at issue by raising them as a defense; or state of mind or intent are a relevant element of inquiry, such as during a criminal investigation. This list

is illustrative rather than exhaustive, since there doubtless will be other situations, not subject to prediction, in which audit reports rather than information may be required.

EPA acknowledges regulated entities' need to self-evaluate environmental performance with some measure of privacy and encourages such activity. However, audit reports may not shield monitoring, compliance, or other information that would otherwise be reportable and/or accessible to EPA, even if there is no explicit 'requirement' to generate that data.[4] Thus, this policy does not alter regulated entities' existing or future obligations to monitor, record or report information required under environmental statutes, regulations or permits, or to allow EPA access to that information. Nor does this policy alter EPA's authority to request and receive any relevant information—including that contained in audit reports—under various environmental statutes (e.g., Clean Water Act section 308, Clean Air Act sections 114 and 208) or in other administrative or judicial proceedings.

Regulated entities also should be aware that certain audit findings may by law have to be reported to government agencies. However, in addition to any such requirements, EPA encourages regulated entities to notify appropriate State or Federal officials of findings which suggest significant environmental or public health risks, even when not specifically required to do so.

B. EPA Response to Environmental Auditing

1. General Policy

EPA will not promise to forgo inspections, reduce enforcement responses, or offer other such incentives in exchange for implementation of environmental auditing or other sound environmental management practices. Indeed, a credible enforcement program provides a strong incentive for regulated entities to audit.

Regulatory agencies have an obligation to assess source compliance status independently and cannot eliminate inspections for particular firms or classes of firms. Although environmental audits may complement inspections by providing self-assessment to assure compliance, they are in no way a substitute for regulatory oversight. Moreover, certain statutes (e.g. RCRA) and Agency policies

establish minimum facility inspection frequencies to which EPA will adhere.

However, EPA will continue to address environmental problems on a priority basis and will consequently inspect facilities with poor environmental records and practices more frequently. Since effective environmental auditing helps management identify and promptly correct actual or potential problems, audited facilities' environmental performance should improve. Thus, while EPA inspections of self-audited facilities will continue, to the extent that compliance performance is considered in setting inspection priorities, facilities with a good compliance history may be subject to fewer inspections.

In fashioning enforcement responses to violations, EPA policy is to take into account, on a case-by-case basis, the honest and genuine efforts of regulated entities to avoid and promptly correct violations and underlying environmental problems. When regulated entities take reasonable precautions to avoid noncompliance, expeditiously correct underlying environmental problems discovered through audits or other means, and implement measures to prevent their recurrence, EPA may exercise its discretion to consider such actions as honest and genuine efforts to assure compliance. Such consideration applies particularly when a regulated entity promptly reports violations or compliance data which otherwise were not required to be recorded or reported to EPA.

2. Audit Provisions as Remedies in Enforcement Actions

EPA may propose environmental auditing provisions in consent decrees and in other settlement negotiations where auditing could provide a remedy for identified problems and reduce the likelihood of similar problems recurring in the future.[5] Environmental auditing provisions are most likely to be proposed in settlement negotiations where:

• A pattern of violations can be attributed, at least in part, to the absence or poor functioning of an environmental management system; or

• The type or nature of violations indicates a likelihood that similar noncompliance problems may exist or occur elsewhere in the facility or at other facilities operated by the regulated entity.

---

[3] An "environmental audit report" is a written report which candidly and thoroughly presents findings from a review, conducted as part of an environmental audit as described in section II.A., of facility environmental performance and practices. An audit report is not a substitute for compliance monitoring reports or other reports or records which may be required by EPA or other regulatory agencies.

[4] See, for example, "Duties to Report or Disclose Information on the Environmental Aspects of Business Activities," Environmental Law Institute report to EPA, final report, September 1985.

[5] EPA is developing guidance for use by Agency negotiators in structuring appropriate environmental audit provisions for consent decrees and other settlement negotiations.

U.S. EPA's 1986 Environmental Auditing Policy Statement *(cont'd)*

25008 Federal Register / Vol. 51, No. 131 / Wednesday, July 9, 1986 / Notices

Through this consent decree approach and other means, EPA may consider how to encourage effective auditing by publicly owned sewage treatment works (POTWs). POTWs often have compliance problems related to operation and maintenance procedures which can be addressed effectively through the use of environmental auditing. Under its National Municipal Policy EPA already is requiring many POTWs to develop composite correction plans to identify and correct compliance problems.

C. Environmental Auditing at Federal Facilities

EPA encourages all federal agencies subject to environmental laws and regulations to institute environmental auditing systems to help ensure the adequacy of internal systems to achieve, maintain and monitor compliance. Environmental auditing at federal facilities can be an effective supplement to EPA and state inspections. Such federal facility environmental audit programs should be structured to promptly identify environmental problems and expeditiously develop schedules for remedial action.

To the extent feasible, EPA will provide technical assistance to help federal agencies design and initiate audit programs. Where appropriate, EPA will enter into agreements with other agencies to clarify the respective roles, responsibilities and commitments of each agency in conducting and responding to federal facility environmental audits.

With respect to inspections of self-audited facilities (see section III.B.1 above) and requests for audit reports (see section III.A above), EPA generally will respond to environmental audits by federal facilities in the same manner as it does for other regulated entities, in keeping with the spirit and intent of Executive Order 12088 and the EPA *Federal Facilities Compliance Strategy* (January 1984, update forthcoming in late 1986). Federal agencies should, however, be aware that the Freedom of Information Act will govern any disclosure of audit reports or audit-generated information requested from federal agencies by the public.

When federal agencies discover significant violations through an environmental audit, EPA encourages them to submit the related audit findings and remedial action plans expeditiously to the applicable EPA regional office (and responsible state agencies, where appropriate) even when not specifically required to do so. EPA will review the audit findings and action plans and either provide written approval or

negotiate a Federal Facilities Compliance Agreement. EPA will utilize the escalation procedures provided in Executive Order 12088 and the EPA *Federal Facilities Compliance Strategy* only when agreement between agencies cannot be reached. In any event, federal agencies are expected to report pollution abatement projects involving costs (necessary to correct problems discovered through the audit) to EPA in accordance with OMB Circular A-106. Upon request, and in appropriate circumstances, EPA will assist affected federal agencies through coordination of any public release of audit findings with approved action plans once agreement has been reached.

IV. Relationship to State or Local Regulatory Agencies

State and local regulatory agencies have independent jurisdiction over regulated entities. EPA encourages them to adopt these or similar policies, in order to advance the use of effective environmental auditing in a consistent manner.

EPA recognizes that some states have already undertaken environmental auditing initiatives which differ somewhat from this policy. Other states also may want to develop auditing policies which accommodate their particular needs or circumstances. Nothing in this policy statement is intended to preempt or preclude states from developing other approaches to environmental auditing. EPA encourages state and local authorities to consider the basic principles which guided the Agency in developing this policy:

• Regulated entities must continue to report or record compliance information required under existing statutes or regulations, regardless of whether such information is generated by an environmental audit or contained in an audit report. Required information cannot be withheld merely because it is generated by an audit rather than by some other means.

• Regulatory agencies cannot make promises to forgo or limit enforcement action against a particular facility or class of facilities in exchange for the use of environmental auditing systems. However, such agencies may use their discretion to adjust enforcement actions on a case-by-case basis in response to honest and genuine efforts by regulated entities to assure environmental compliance.

• When setting inspection priorities regulatory agencies should focus to the extent possible on compliance performance and environmental results.

• Regulatory agencies must continue to meet minimum program requirements

(e.g., minimum inspection requirements, etc.).

• Regulatory agencies should not attempt to prescribe the precise form and structure of regulated entities' environmental management or auditing programs.

An effective state/federal partnership is needed to accomplish the mutual goal of achieving and maintaining high levels of compliance with environmental laws and regulations. The greater the consistency between state or local policies and this federal response to environmental auditing, the greater the degree to which sound auditing practices might be adopted and compliance levels improve.

Dated: June 28, 1986.

Lee M. Thomas,

Administrator.

Appendix—Elements of Effective Environmental Auditing Programs

Introduction: Environmental auditing is a systematic, documented, periodic and objective review by a regulated entity of facility operations and practices related to meeting environmental requirements.

Private sector environmental audits of facilities have been conducted for several years and have taken a variety of forms, in part to accommodate unique organizational structures and circumstances. Nevertheless, effective environmental audits appear to have certain discernible elements in common with other kinds of audits. Standards for internal audits have been documented extensively. The elements outlined below draw heavily on two of these documents: "Compendium of Audit Standards" (°1983, Walter Willborn, American Society for Quality Control) and "Standards for the Professional Practice of Internal Auditing" (°1981, The Institute of Internal Auditors, Inc.). They also reflect Agency analyses conducted over the last several years.

Performance-oriented auditing elements are outlined here to help accomplish several objectives. A general description of features of effective, mature audit programs can help those starting audit programs, especially federal agencies and smaller businesses. These elements also indicate the attributes of auditing EPA generally considers important to ensure program effectiveness. Regulatory agencies may use these elements in negotiating environmental auditing provisions for consent decrees. Finally, these elements can help guide states and localities considering auditing initiatives.

U.S. EPA's 1986 Environmental Auditing Policy Statement *(cont'd)*

Federal Register / Vol. 51, No. 131 / Wednesday, July 9, 1986 / Notices **25009**

An effective environmental auditing system will likely include the following general elements:

I. *Explicit top management support for environmental auditing and commitment to follow-up on audit findings.* Management support may be demonstrated by a written policy articulating upper management support for the auditing program, and for compliance with all pertinent requirements, including corporate policies and permit requirements as well as federal, state and local statutes and regulations.

Management support for the auditing program also should be demonstrated by an explicit written commitment to follow-up on audit findings to correct identified problems and prevent their recurrence.

II. *An environmental auditing function independent of audited activities.* The status or organizational locus of environmental auditors should be sufficient to ensure objective and unobstructed inquiry, observation and testing. Auditor objectivity should not be impaired by personal relationships, financial or other conflicts of interest, interference with free inquiry or judgment, or fear of potential retribution.

III. *Adequate team staffing and auditor training.* Environmental auditors should possess or have ready access to the knowledge, skills, and disciplines needed to accomplish audit objectives. Each individual auditor should comply with the company's professional, standards of conduct. Auditors, whether full-time or part-time, should maintain their technical and analytical competence through continuing education and training.

IV. *Explicit audit program objectives, scope, resources and frequency.* At a minimum, audit objectives should include assessing compliance with applicable environmental laws and evaluating the adequacy of internal compliance policies, procedures, and personnel training programs to ensure continued compliance.

Audits should be based on a process which provides auditors: all corporate policies, permits, and federal, state, and local regulations pertinent to the facility; and checklists or protocols addressing specific features that should be evaluated by auditors.

Explicit written audit procedures generally should be used for planning audits, establishing audit scope, examining and evaluating audit findings, communicating audit results, and following-up.

V. *A process which collects, analyzes, interprets and documents information sufficient to achieve audit objectives.* Information should be collected before and during an onsite visit regarding environmental compliance(1), environmental management effectiveness(2), and other matters (3) related to audit objectives and scope. This information should be sufficient, reliable, relevant and useful to provide a sound basis for audit findings and recommendations.

a. *Sufficient* information is factual, adequate and convincing so that a prudent, informed person would be likely to reach the same conclusions as the auditor.

b. *Reliable* information is the best attainable through use of appropriate audit techniques.

c. *Relevant* information supports audit findings and recommendations and is consistent with the objectives for the audit.

d. *Useful* information helps the organization meet its goals.

The audit process should include a periodic review of the reliability and integrity of this information and the means used to identify, measure, classify and report it. Audit procedures, including the testing and sampling techniques employed, should be selected in advance, to the extent practical, and expanded or altered if circumstances warrant. The process of collecting, analyzing, interpreting, and documenting information should provide reasonable assurance that audit objectivity is maintained and audit goals are met.

VI. *A process which includes specific procedures to promptly prepare candid, clear and appropriate written reports on audit findings, corrective actions, and schedules for implementation.* Procedures should be in place to ensure that such information is communicated to managers, including facility and corporate management, who can evaluate the information and ensure correction of identified problems. Procedures also should be in place for determining what internal findings are reportable to state or federal agencies.

VII. *A process which includes quality assurance procedures to assure the accuracy and thoroughness of environmental audits.* Quality assurance may be accomplished through supervision, independent internal reviews, external reviews, or a combination of these approaches.

Footnotes to Appendix

(1) A comprehensive assessment of compliance with federal environmental regulations requires an analysis of facility performance against numerous environmental statutes and implementing regulations. These statutes include:
Resource Conservation and Recovery Act
Federal Water Pollution Control Act
Clean Air Act
Hazardous Materials Transportation Act
Toxic Substances Control Act
Comprehensive Environmental Response, Compensation and Liability Act
Safe Drinking Water Act
Federal Insecticide, Fungicide and Rodenticide Act
Marine Protection, Research and Sanctuaries Act
Uranium Mill Tailings Radiation Control Act

In addition, state and local government are likely to have their own environmental laws. Many states have been delegated authority to administer federal programs. Many local governments' building, fire, safety and health codes also have environmental requirements relevant to an audit evaluation.

(2) An environmental audit could go well beyond the type of compliance assessment normally conducted during regulatory inspections, for example, by evaluating policies and practices, regardless of whether they are part of the environmental system or the operating and maintenance procedures. Specifically, audits can evaluate the extent to which systems or procedures:

1. Develop organizational environmental policies which: a. implement regulatory requirements; b. provide management guidance for environmental hazards not specifically addressed in regulations;

2. Train and motivate facility personnel to work in an environmentally-acceptable manner and to understand and comply with government regulations and the entity's environmental policy;

3. Communicate relevant environmental developments expeditiously to facility and other personnel;

4. Communicate effectively with government and the public regarding serious environmental incidents;

5. Require third parties working for, with or on behalf of the organization to follow its environmental procedures;

U.S. EPA's 1986 Environmental Auditing Policy Statement *(cont'd)*

25010   Federal Register / Vol. 51, No. 131 / Wednesday, July 9, 1986 / Notices

6. Make proficient personnel available at all times to carry out environmental (especially emergency) procedures;

7. Incorporate environmental protection into written operating procedures;

8. Apply best management practices and operating procedures, including "good housekeeping" techniques;

9. Institute preventive and corrective maintenance systems to minimize actual and potential environmental harm;

10. Utilize best available process and control technologies;

11. Use most-effective sampling and monitoring techniques, test methods, recordkeeping systems or reporting protocols (beyond minimum legal requirements);

12. Evaluate causes behind any serious environmental incidents and establish procedures to avoid recurrence;

13. Exploit source reduction, recycle and reuse potential wherever practical; and

14. Substitute materials or processes to allow use of the least-hazardous substances feasible.

(1) Auditors could also assess environmental risks and uncertainties.

[FR Doc. 86-15423 Filed 7-8-86 8:45 am]

BILLING CODE 6560-50-M

U.S. EPA's 1995 Incentives for Self-Policing

66706   Federal Register / Vol. 60, No. 246 / Friday, December 22, 1995 / Notices

ENVIRONMENTAL PROTECTION AGENCY

[FRL–5400–1]

Incentives for Self-Policing: Discovery, Disclosure, Correction and Prevention of Violations

AGENCY: Environmental Protection Agency (EPA).

ACTION: Final Policy Statement.

SUMMARY: The Environmental Protection Agency (EPA) today issues its final policy to enhance protection of human health and the environment by encouraging regulated entities to voluntarily discover, and disclose and correct violations of environmental requirements. Incentives include eliminating or substantially reducing the gravity component of civil penalties and not recommending cases for criminal prosecution where specified conditions are met, to those who voluntarily self-disclose and promptly correct violations. The policy also restates EPA's long-standing practice of not requesting voluntary audit reports to trigger enforcement investigations. This policy was developed in close consultation with the U.S. Department of Justice, states, public interest groups and the regulated community, and will be applied uniformly by the Agency's enforcement programs.

DATES: This policy is effective January 22, 1996.

FOR FURTHER INFORMATION CONTACT: Additional documentation relating to the development of this policy is contained in the environmental auditing public docket. Documents from the docket may be obtained by calling (202) 260–7548, requesting an index to docket #C–94–01, and faxing document requests to (202) 260–4400. Hours of operation are 8 a.m. to 5:30 p.m., Monday through Friday, except legal holidays. Additional contacts are Robert Fentress or Brian Riedel, at (202) 564–4187.

SUPPLEMENTARY INFORMATION:

I. Explanation of Policy

A. Introduction

The Environmental Protection Agency today issues its final policy to enhance protection of human health and the environment by encouraging regulated entities to discover voluntarily, disclose, correct and prevent violations of federal environmental law. Effective 30 days from today, where violations are found through voluntary environmental audits or efforts that reflect a regulated entity's due diligence, and are promptly disclosed and expeditiously corrected, EPA will not seek gravity-based (i.e., non-economic benefit) penalties and will generally not recommend criminal prosecution against the regulated entity. EPA will reduce gravity-based penalties by 75% for violations that are voluntarily discovered, and are promptly disclosed and corrected, even if not found through a formal audit or due diligence. Finally, the policy restates EPA's long-held policy and practice to refrain from routine requests for environmental audit reports.

The policy includes important safeguards to deter irresponsible behavior and protect the public and environment. For example, in addition to prompt disclosure and expeditious correction, the policy requires companies to act to prevent recurrence of the violation and to remedy any environmental harm which may have occurred. Repeated violations or those which result in actual harm or may present imminent and substantial endangerment are not eligible for relief under this policy, and companies will not be allowed to gain an economic advantage over their competitors by delaying their investment in compliance. Corporations remain criminally liable for violations that result from conscious disregard of their obligations under the law, and individuals are liable for criminal misconduct.

The issuance of this policy concludes EPA's eighteen-month public evaluation of the optimum way to encourage voluntary self-policing while preserving fair and effective enforcement. The incentives, conditions and exceptions announced today reflect thoughtful suggestions from the Department of Justice, state attorneys general and local prosecutors, state environmental agencies, the regulated community, and public interest organizations. EPA believes that it has found a balanced and responsible approach, and will conduct a study within three years to determine the effectiveness of this policy.

B. Public Process

One of the Environmental Protection Agency's most important responsibilities is ensuring compliance with federal laws that protect public health and safeguard the environment. Effective deterrence requires inspecting, bringing penalty actions and securing compliance and remediation of harm. But EPA realizes that achieving compliance also requires the cooperation of thousands of businesses and other regulated entities subject to these requirements. Accordingly, in

May of 1994, the Administrator asked the Office of Enforcement and Compliance Assurance (OECA) to determine whether additional incentives were needed to encourage voluntary disclosure and correction of violations uncovered during environmental audits.

EPA began its evaluation with a two-day public meeting in July of 1994, in Washington, D.C., followed by a two-day meeting in San Francisco on January 19, 1995 with stakeholders from industry, trade groups, state environmental commissioners and attorneys general, district attorneys, public interest organizations and professional environmental auditors. The Agency also established and maintained a public docket of testimony presented at these meetings and all comment and correspondence submitted to EPA by outside parties on this issue.

In addition to considering opinion and information from stakeholders, the Agency examined other federal and state policies related to self-policing, self-disclosure and correction. The Agency also considered relevant surveys on auditing practices in the private sector. EPA completed the first stage of this effort with the announcement of an interim policy on April 3 of this year, which defined conditions under which EPA would reduce civil penalties and not recommend criminal prosecution for companies that audited, disclosed, and corrected violations.

Interested parties were asked to submit comment on the interim policy by June 30 of this year (60 FR 16875), and EPA received over 300 responses from a wide variety of private and public organizations. (Comments on the interim audit policy are contained in the Auditing Policy Docket, hereinafter, "Docket".) Further, the American Bar Association SONREEL Subcommittee hosted five days of dialogue with representatives from the regulated industry, states and public interest organizations in June and September of this year, which identified options for strengthening the interim policy. The changes to the interim policy announced today reflect insight gained through comments submitted to EPA, the ABA dialogue, and the Agency's practical experience implementing the interim policy.

C. Purpose

This policy is designed to encourage greater compliance with laws and regulations that protect human health and the environment. It promotes a higher standard of self-policing by waiving gravity-based penalties for

U.S. EPA's 1995 Incentives for Self-Policing *(cont'd)*

Federal Register / Vol. 60. No. 246 / Friday. December 22, 1995 / Notices   **66707**

violations that are promptly disclosed and corrected, and which were discovered through voluntary audits or compliance management systems that demonstrate due diligence. To further promote compliance, the policy reduces gravity-based penalties by 75% for any violation voluntarily discovered and promptly disclosed and corrected, even if not found through an audit or compliance management system.

EPA's enforcement program provides a strong incentive for responsible behavior by imposing stiff sanctions for noncompliance. Enforcement has contributed to the dramatic expansion of environmental auditing measured in numerous recent surveys. For example. more than 90% of the corporate respondents to a 1995 Price-Waterhouse survey who conduct audits said that one of the reasons they did so was to find and correct violations before they were found by government inspectors. (A copy of the Price-Waterhouse survey is contained in the Docket as document VIII–A–76.)

At the same time, because government resources are limited, maximum compliance cannot be achieved without active efforts by the regulated community to police themselves. More than half of the respondents to the same 1995 Price-Waterhouse survey said that they would expand environmental auditing in exchange for reduced penalties for violations discovered and corrected. While many companies already audit or have compliance management programs, EPA believes that the incentives offered in this policy will improve the frequency and quality of these self-monitoring efforts.

D. Incentives for Self-Policing

Section C of EPA's policy identifies the major incentives that EPA will provide to encourage self-policing, self-disclosure, and prompt self-correction. These include not seeking gravity-based civil penalties or reducing them by 75%, declining to recommend criminal prosecution for regulated entities that self-police, and refraining from routine requests for audits. (As noted in Section C of the policy, EPA has refrained from making routine requests for audit reports since issuance of its 1986 policy on environmental auditing.)

1. Eliminating Gravity-Based Penalties

Under Section C(1) of the policy, EPA will not seek gravity-based penalties for violations found through auditing that are promptly disclosed and corrected. Gravity-based penalties will also be waived for violations found through any documented procedure for self-policing. where the company can show that it has a compliance management program that meets the criteria for due diligence in Section B of the policy.

Gravity-based penalties (defined in Section B of the policy) generally reflect the seriousness of the violator's behavior. EPA has elected to waive such penalties for violations discovered through due diligence or environmental audits, recognizing that these voluntary efforts play a critical role in protecting human health and the environment by identifying, correcting and ultimately preventing violations. All of the conditions set forth in Section D, which include prompt disclosure and expeditious correction. must be satisfied for gravity-based penalties to be waived.

As in the interim policy, EPA reserves the right to collect any economic benefit that may have been realized as a result of noncompliance, even where companies meet all other conditions of the policy. Economic benefit may be waived, however, where the Agency determines that it is insignificant.

After considering public comment, EPA has decided to retain the discretion to recover economic benefit for two reasons. First, it provides an incentive to comply on time. Taxpayers expect to pay interest or a penalty fee if their tax payments are late; the same principle should apply to corporations that have delayed their investment in compliance. Second, it is fair because it protects responsible companies from being undercut by their noncomplying competitors, thereby preserving a level playing field. The concept of recovering economic benefit was supported in public comments by many stakeholders. including industry representatives (see. e.g.. Docket. II–F–39. II–F–28. and II–F–18).

2. 75% Reduction of Gravity

The policy appropriately limits the complete waiver of gravity-based civil penalties to companies that meet the higher standard of environmental auditing or systematic compliance management. However. to provide additional encouragement for the kind of self-policing that benefits the public, gravity-based penalties will be reduced by 75% for a violation that is voluntarily discovered. promptly disclosed and expeditiously corrected, even if it was not found through an environmental audit and the company cannot document due diligence. EPA expects that this will encourage companies to come forward and work with the Agency to resolve environmental problems and begin to develop an effective compliance management program.

Gravity-based penalties will be reduced 75% only where the company meets all conditions in Sections D(2) through D(9). EPA has eliminated language from the interim policy indicating that penalties may be reduced "up to" 75% where "most" conditions are met, because the Agency believes that all of the conditions in D(2) through D(9) are reasonable and essential to achieving compliance. This change also responds to requests for greater clarity and predictability.

3. No Recommendations for Criminal Prosecution

EPA has never recommended criminal prosecution of a regulated entity based on voluntary disclosure of violations discovered through audits and disclosed to the government before an investigation was already under way. Thus, EPA will not recommend criminal prosecution for a regulated entity that uncovers violations through environmental audits or due diligence, promptly discloses and expeditiously corrects those violations, and meets all other conditions of Section D of the policy.

This policy is limited to good actors. and therefore has important limitations. It will not apply, for example. where corporate officials are consciously involved in or willfully blind to violations, or conceal or condone noncompliance. Since the regulated entity must satisfy all of the conditions of Section D of the policy, violations that caused serious harm or which may pose imminent and substantial endangerment to human health or the environment are not covered by this policy. Finally, EPA reserves the right to recommend prosecution for the criminal conduct of any culpable individual.

Even where all of the conditions of this policy are not met, however, it is important to remember that EPA may decline to recommend prosecution of a company or individual for many other reasons under other Agency enforcement policies. For example. the Agency may decline to recommend prosecution where there is no significant harm or culpability and the individual or corporate defendant has cooperated fully.

Where a company has met the conditions for avoiding a recommendation for criminal prosecution under this policy, it will not face any civil liability for gravity-based penalties. That is because the same conditions for discovery, disclosure, and correction apply in both cases. This represents a clarification of the interim policy, not a substantive change.

U.S. EPA's 1995 Incentives for Self-Policing *(cont'd)*

66708   **Federal Register** / Vol. 60, No. 246 / Friday, December 22, 1995 / Notices

4. No Routine Requests for Audits

EPA is reaffirming its policy, in effect since 1986, to refrain from routine requests for audits. Eighteen months of public testimony and debate have produced no evidence that the Agency has deviated, or should deviate, from this policy.

If the Agency has independent evidence of a violation, it may seek information needed to establish the extent and nature of the problem and the degree of culpability. In general, however, an audit which results in prompt correction clearly will reduce liability, not expand it. Furthermore, a review of the criminal docket did not reveal a single criminal prosecution for violations discovered as a result of an audit self-disclosed to the government.

E. Conditions

Section D describes the nine conditions that a regulated entity must meet in order for the Agency not to seek (or to reduce) gravity-based penalties under the policy. As explained in the Summary above, regulated entities that meet all nine conditions will not face gravity-based civil penalties, and will generally not have to fear criminal prosecution. Where the regulated entity meets all of the conditions except the first (D(1)), EPA will reduce gravity-based penalties by 75%.

1. Discovery of the Violation Through an Environmental Audit or Due Diligence

Under Section D(1), the violation must have been discovered through either (a) an environmental audit that is systematic, objective, and periodic as defined in the 1986 audit policy, or (b) a documented, systematic procedure or practice which reflects the regulated entity's due diligence in preventing, detecting, and correcting violations. The interim policy provided full credit for any violation found through "voluntary self-evaluation," even if the evaluation did not constitute an audit. In order to receive full credit under the final policy, any self-evaluation that is not an audit must be part of a "due diligence" program. Both "environmental audit" and "due diligence" are defined in Section B of the policy.

Where the violation is discovered through a "systematic procedure or practice" which is not an audit, the regulated entity will be asked to document how its program reflects the criteria for due diligence as defined in Section B of the policy. These criteria, which are adapted from existing codes of practice such as the 1991 Criminal Sentencing Guidelines, were fully discussed during the ABA dialogue. The criteria are flexible enough to accommodate different types and sizes of businesses. The Agency recognizes that a variety of compliance management programs may develop under the due diligence criteria, and will use its review under this policy to determine whether basic criteria have been met.

Compliance management programs which train and motivate production staff to prevent, detect and correct violations on a daily basis are a valuable complement to periodic auditing. The policy is responsive to recommendations received during public comment and from the ABA dialogue to give compliance management efforts which meet the criteria for due diligence the same penalty reduction offered for environmental audits. (See, *e.g.*, II–F–39, II–E–18, and II–G–18 in the Docket.)

EPA may require as a condition of penalty mitigation that a description of the regulated entity's due diligence efforts be made publicly available. The Agency added this provision in response to suggestions from environmental groups, and believes that the availability of such information will allow the public to judge the adequacy of compliance management systems, lead to enhanced compliance, and foster greater public trust in the integrity of compliance management systems.

2. Voluntary Discovery and Prompt Disclosure

Under Section D(2) of the final policy, the violation must have been identified voluntarily, and not through a monitoring, sampling, or auditing procedure that is required by statute, regulation, permit, judicial or administrative order, or consent agreement. Section D(4) requires that disclosure of the violation be prompt and in writing. To avoid confusion and respond to state requests for greater clarity, disclosures under this policy should be made to EPA. The Agency will work closely with states in implementing the policy.

The requirement that discovery of the violation be voluntary is consistent with proposed federal and state bills which would reward those discoveries that the regulated entity can legitimately attribute to its own voluntary efforts.

The policy gives three specific examples of discovery that would not be voluntary, and therefore would not be eligible for penalty mitigation: emissions violations detected through a required continuous emissions monitor, violations of NPDES discharge limits found through prescribed monitoring, and violations discovered through a compliance audit required to be performed by the terms of a consent order or settlement agreement.

The final policy generally applies to any violation that is voluntarily discovered, regardless of whether the violation is required to be reported. This definition responds to comments pointing out that reporting requirements are extensive, and that excluding them from the policy's scope would severely limit the incentive for self-policing (see, *e.g.*, II–C–48 in the Docket).

The Agency wishes to emphasize that the integrity of federal environmental law depends upon timely and accurate reporting. The public relies on timely and accurate reports from the regulated community, not only to measure compliance but to evaluate health or environmental risk and gauge progress in reducing pollutant loadings. EPA expects the policy to encourage the kind of vigorous self-policing that will serve these objectives, and not to provide an excuse for delayed reporting. Where violations of reporting requirements are voluntarily discovered, they must be promptly reported (as discussed below). Where a failure to report results in imminent and substantial endangerment or serious harm, that violation is not covered under this policy (see Condition D(8)). The policy also requires the regulated entity to prevent recurrence of the violation, to ensure that noncompliance with reporting requirements is not repeated. EPA will closely scrutinize the effect of the policy in furthering the public interest in timely and accurate reports from the regulated community.

Under Section D(4), disclosure of the violation should be made within 10 days of its discovery, and in writing to EPA. Where a statute or regulation requires reporting be made in less than 10 days, disclosure should be made within the time limit established by law. Where reporting within ten days is not practical because the violation is complex and compliance cannot be determined within that period, the Agency may accept later disclosures if the circumstances do not present a serious threat and the regulated entity meets its burden of showing that the additional time was needed to determine compliance status.

This condition recognizes that it is critical for EPA to get timely reporting of violations in order that it might have clear notice of the violations and the opportunity to respond if necessary, as well as an accurate picture of a given facility's compliance record. Prompt disclosure is also evidence of the regulated entity's good faith in wanting

U.S. EPA's 1995 Incentives for Self-Policing *(cont'd)*

Federal Register / Vol. 60, No. 246 / Friday, December 22, 1995 / Notices   **66709**

to achieve or return to compliance as soon as possible.

In the final policy, the Agency has added the words, "or may have occurred," to the sentence, "The regulated entity fully discloses that a specific violation has occurred, or may have occurred * * *." This change, which was made in response to comments received, clarifies that where an entity has some doubt about the existence of a violation, the recommended course is for it to disclose and allow the regulatory authorities to make a definitive determination.

In general, the Freedom of Information Act will govern the Agency's release of disclosures made pursuant to this policy. EPA will, independently of FOIA, make publicly available any compliance agreements reached under the policy (see Section H of the policy), as well as descriptions of due diligence programs submitted under Section D.1 of the Policy. Any material claimed to be Confidential Business Information will be treated in accordance with EPA regulations at 40 C.F.R. Part 2.

3. Discovery and Disclosure Independent of Government or Third Party Plaintiff

Under Section D(3), in order to be "voluntary", the violation must be identified and disclosed by the regulated entity prior to: the commencement of a federal state or local agency inspection, investigation, or information request; notice of a citizen suit; legal complaint by a third party; the reporting of the violation to EPA by a "whistleblower" employee; and imminent discovery of the violation by a regulatory agency.

This condition means that regulated entities must have taken the initiative to find violations and promptly report them, rather than reacting to knowledge of a pending enforcement action or third-party complaint. This concept was reflected in the interim policy and in federal and state penalty immunity laws and did not prove controversial in the public comment process.

4. Correction and Remediation

Section D(5) ensures that, in order to receive the penalty mitigation benefits available under the policy, the regulated entity not only voluntarily discovers and promptly discloses a violation, but expeditiously corrects it, remedies any harm caused by that violation (including responding to any spill and carrying out any removal or remedial action required by law), and expeditiously certifies in writing to appropriate state, local and EPA

authorities that violations have been corrected. It also enables EPA to ensure that the regulated entity will be publicly accountable for its commitments through binding written agreements, orders or consent decrees where necessary.

The final policy requires the violation to be corrected within 60 days, or that the regulated entity provide written notice where violations may take longer to correct. EPA recognizes that some violations can and should be corrected immediately, while others (*e.g.*, where capital expenditures are involved), may take longer than 60 days to correct. In all cases, the regulated entity will be expected to do its utmost to achieve or return to compliance as expeditiously as possible.

Where correction of the violation depends upon issuance of a permit which has been applied for but not issued by federal or state authorities, the Agency will, where appropriate, make reasonable efforts to secure timely review of the permit.

5. Prevent Recurrence

Under Section D(6), the regulated entity must agree to take steps to prevent a recurrence of the violation, including but not limited to improvements to its environmental auditing or due diligence efforts. The final policy makes clear that the preventive steps may include improvements to a regulated entity's environmental auditing or due diligence efforts to prevent recurrence of the violation.

In the interim policy, the Agency required that the entity implement appropriate measures to prevent a recurrence of the violation, a requirement that operates prospectively. However, a separate condition in the interim policy also required that the violation not indicate "a failure to take appropriate steps to avoid repeat or recurring violations"Ða requirement that operates retrospectively. In the interest of both clarity and fairness, the Agency has decided for purposes of this condition to keep the focus prospective and thus to require only that steps be taken to prevent recurrence of the violation after it has been disclosed.

6. No Repeat Violations

In response to requests from commenters (*see, e.g.*, II–F–39 and II–G–18 in the Docket), EPA has established "bright lines" to determine when previous violations will bar a regulated entity from obtaining relief under this policy. These will help protect the public and responsible companies by ensuring that penalties are not waived

for repeat offenders. Under condition D(7), the same or closely-related violation must not have occurred previously within the past three years at the same facility, or be part of a pattern of violations on the regulated entity's part over the past five years. This provides companies with a continuing incentive to prevent violations, without being unfair to regulated entities responsible for managing hundreds of facilities. It would be unreasonable to provide unlimited amnesty for repeated violations of the same requirement.

The term "violation" includes any violation subject to a federal or state civil judicial or administrative order, consent agreement, conviction or plea agreement. Recognizing that minor violations are sometimes settled without a formal action in court, the term also covers any act or omission for which the regulated entity has received a penalty reduction in the past. Together, these conditions identify situations in which the regulated community has had clear notice of its noncompliance and an opportunity to correct.

7. Other Violations Excluded

Section D(8) makes clear that penalty reductions are not available under this policy for violations that resulted in serious actual harm or which may have presented an imminent and substantial endangerment to public health or the environment. Such events indicate a serious failure (or absence) of a self-policing program, which should be designed to prevent such risks, and it would seriously undermine deterrence to waive penalties for such violations. These exceptions are responsive to suggestions from public interest organizations, as well as other commenters. (See, *e.g.*, II–F–39 and II–G–18 in the Docket.)

The final policy also excludes penalty reductions for violations of the specific terms of any order, consent agreement, or plea agreement. (See, II–E–60 in the Docket.) Once a consent agreement has been negotiated, there is little incentive to comply if there are no sanctions for violating its specific requirements. The exclusion in this section applies to violations of the terms of any response, removal or remedial action covered by a written agreement.

8. Cooperation

Under Section D(9), the regulated entity must cooperate as required by EPA and provide information necessary to determine the applicability of the policy. This condition is largely unchanged from the interim policy. In the final policy, however, the Agency has added that "cooperation" includes

U.S. EPA's 1995 Incentives for Self-Policing *(cont'd)*

66710   **Federal Register** / Vol. 60, No. 246 / Friday, December 22, 1995 / Notices

assistance in determining the facts of any related violations suggested by the disclosure, as well as of the disclosed violation itself. This was added to allow the agency to obtain information about any violations indicated by the disclosure, even where the violation is not initially identified by the regulated entity.

F. Opposition to Privilege

The Agency remains firmly opposed to the establishment of a statutory evidentiary privilege for environmental audits for the following reasons:

1. Privilege, by definition, invites secrecy, instead of the openness needed to build public trust in industry's ability to self-police. American law reflects the high value that the public places on fair access to the facts. The Supreme Court, for example, has said of privileges that, "[w]hatever their origins, these exceptions to the demand for every man's evidence are not lightly created nor expansively construed, for they are in derogation of the search for truth." *United States* v. *Nixon*, 418 U.S. 683 (1974). Federal courts have unanimously refused to recognize a privilege for environmental audits in the context of government investigations. See, *e.g., United States* v. *Dexter*, 132 F.R.D. 8, 9–10 (D.Conn. 1990) (application of a privilege "would effectively impede [EPA's] ability to enforce the Clean Water Act, and would be contrary to stated public policy.")

2. Eighteen months have failed to produce any evidence that a privilege is needed. Public testimony on the interim policy confirmed that EPA rarely uses audit reports as evidence. Furthermore, surveys demonstrate that environmental auditing has expanded rapidly over the past decade without the stimulus of a privilege. Most recently, the 1995 Price Waterhouse survey found that those few large or mid-sized companies that do not audit generally do not perceive any need to; concern about confidentiality ranked as one of the least important factors in their decisions.

3. A privilege would invite defendants to claim as "audit" material almost any evidence the government needed to establish a violation or determine who was responsible. For example, most audit privilege bills under consideration in federal and state legislatures would arguably protect factual informationDsuch as health studies or contaminated sediment dataDand not just the conclusions of the auditors. While the government might have access to required monitoring data under the law, as some industry commenters have suggested, a privilege of that nature would cloak

underlying facts needed to determine whether such data were accurate.

4. An audit privilege would breed litigation, as both parties struggled to determine what material fell within its scope. The problem is compounded by the lack of any clear national standard for audits. The "*in camera*" (i.e., non-public) proceedings used to resolve these disputes under some statutory schemes would result in a series of time-consuming, expensive mini-trials.

5. The Agency's policy eliminates the need for any privilege as against the government, by reducing civil penalties and criminal liability for those companies that audit, disclose and correct violations. The 1995 Price Waterhouse survey indicated that companies would expand their auditing programs in exchange for the kind of incentives that EPA provides in its policy.

6. Finally, audit privileges are strongly opposed by the law enforcement community, including the National District Attorneys Association, as well as by public interest groups. (See, *e.g.,* Docket, II–C–21, II–C–28, II–C–52, IV–G–10, II–C–25, II–C–33, II–C–52, II–C–48, and II–G–13 through II–G–24.)

G. Effect on States

The final policy reflects EPA's desire to develop fair and effective incentives for self-policing that will have practical value to states that share responsibility for enforcing federal environmental laws. To that end, the Agency has consulted closely with state officials in developing this policy, through a series of special meetings and conference calls in addition to the extensive opportunity for public comment. As a result, EPA believes its final policy is grounded in common-sense principles that should prove useful in the development of state programs and policies.

As always, states are encouraged to experiment with different approaches that do not jeopardize the fundamental national interest in assuring that violations of federal law do not threaten the public health or the environment, or make it profitable not to comply. The Agency remains opposed to state legislation that does not include these basic protections, and reserves its right to bring independent action against regulated entities for violations of federal law that threaten human health or the environment, reflect criminal conduct or repeated noncompliance, or allow one company to make a substantial profit at the expense of its law-abiding competitors. Where a state has obtained appropriate sanctions

needed to deter such misconduct, there is no need for EPA action.

H. Scope of Policy

EPA has developed this document as a policy to guide settlement actions. EPA employees will be expected to follow this policy, and the Agency will take steps to assure national consistency in application. For example, the Agency will make public any compliance agreements reached under this policy, in order to provide the regulated community with fair notice of decisions and greater accountability to affected communities. Many in the regulated community recommended that the Agency convert the policy into a regulation because they felt it might ensure greater consistency and predictability. While EPA is taking steps to ensure consistency and predictability and believes that it will be successful, the Agency will consider this issue and will provide notice if it determines that a rulemaking is appropriate.

II. Statement of Policy: Incentives for Self-Policing

Discovery, Disclosure, Correction and Prevention

A. Purpose

This policy is designed to enhance protection of human health and the environment by encouraging regulated entities to voluntarily discover, disclose, correct and prevent violations of federal environmental requirements.

B. Definitions

For purposes of this policy, the following definitions apply:

"Environmental Audit" has the definition given to it in EPA's 1986 audit policy on environmental auditing, i.e., "a systematic, documented, periodic and objective review by regulated entities of facility operations and practices related to meeting environmental requirements."

"Due Diligence" encompasses the regulated entity's systematic efforts, appropriate to the size and nature of its business, to prevent, detect and correct violations through all of the following:

(a) Compliance policies, standards and procedures that identify how employees and agents are to meet the requirements of laws, regulations, permits and other sources of authority for environmental requirements;

(b) Assignment of overall responsibility for overseeing compliance with policies, standards, and procedures, and assignment of specific responsibility for assuring compliance at each facility or operation;

U.S. EPA's 1995 Incentives for Self-Policing *(cont'd)*

Federal Register / Vol. 60, No. 246 / Friday, December 22, 1995 / Notices   **66711**

(c) Mechanisms for systematically assuring that compliance policies, standards and procedures are being carried out, including monitoring and auditing systems reasonably designed to detect and correct violations, periodic evaluation of the overall performance of the compliance management system, and a means for employees or agents to report violations of environmental requirements without fear of retaliation;

(d) Efforts to communicate effectively the regulated entity's standards and procedures to all employees and other agents;

(e) Appropriate incentives to managers and employees to perform in accordance with the compliance policies, standards and procedures, including consistent enforcement through appropriate disciplinary mechanisms; and

(f) Procedures for the prompt and appropriate correction of any violations, and any necessary modifications to the regulated entity's program to prevent future violations.

"Environmental audit report" means the analysis, conclusions, and recommendations resulting from an environmental audit, but does not include data obtained in, or testimonial evidence concerning, the environmental audit.

"Gravity-based penalties" are that portion of a penalty over and above the economic benefit, i.e., the punitive portion of the penalty, rather than that portion representing a defendant's economic gain from non-compliance. (For further discussion of this concept, see "A Framework for Statute-Specific Approaches to Penalty Assessments", #GM–22, 1980, U.S. EPA General Enforcement Policy Compendium).

"Regulated entity" means any entity, including a federal, state or municipal agency or facility, regulated under federal environmental laws.

C. Incentives for Self-Policing

1. No Gravity-Based Penalties

Where the regulated entity establishes that it satisfies all of the conditions of Section D of the policy, EPA will not seek gravity-based penalties for violations of federal environmental requirements.

2. Reduction of Gravity-Based Penalties by 75%

EPA will reduce gravity-based penalties for violations of federal environmental requirements by 75% so long as the regulated entity satisfies all of the conditions of Section D(2) through D(9) below.

3. No Criminal Recommendations

(a) EPA will not recommend to the Department of Justice or other prosecuting authority that criminal charges be brought against a regulated entity where EPA determines that all of the conditions in Section D are satisfied, so long as the violation does not demonstrate or involve:

(i) a prevalent management philosophy or practice that concealed or condoned environmental violations; or

(ii) high-level corporate officials' or managers' conscious involvement in, or willful blindness to, the violations.

(b) Whether or not EPA refers the regulated entity for criminal prosecution under this section, the Agency reserves the right to recommend prosecution for the criminal acts of individual managers or employees under existing policies guiding the exercise of enforcement discretion.

4. No Routine Request for Audits

EPA will not request or use an environmental audit report to initiate a civil or criminal investigation of the entity. For example, EPA will not request an environmental audit report in routine inspections. If the Agency has independent reason to believe that a violation has occurred, however, EPA may seek any information relevant to identifying violations or determining liability or extent of harm.

D. Conditions

1. Systematic Discovery

The violation was discovered through:

(a) an environmental audit; or

(b) an objective, documented, systematic procedure or practice reflecting the regulated entity's due diligence in preventing, detecting, and correcting violations. The regulated entity must provide accurate and complete documentation to the Agency as to how it exercises due diligence to prevent, detect and correct violations according to the criteria for due diligence outlined in Section B. EPA may require as a condition of penalty mitigation that a description of the regulated entity's due diligence efforts be made publicly available.

2. Voluntary Discovery

The violation was identified voluntarily, and not through a legally mandated monitoring or sampling requirement prescribed by statute, regulation, permit, judicial or administrative order, or consent agreement. For example, the policy does not apply to:

(a) emissions violations detected through a continuous emissions monitor (or alternative monitor established in a permit) where any such monitoring is required;

(b) violations of National Pollutant Discharge Elimination System (NPDES) discharge limits detected through required sampling or monitoring;

(c) violations discovered through a compliance audit required to be performed by the terms of a consent order or settlement agreement.

3. Prompt Disclosure

The regulated entity fully discloses a specific violation within 10 days (or such shorter period provided by law) after it has discovered that the violation has occurred, or may have occurred, in writing to EPA;

4. Discovery and Disclosure Independent of Government or Third Party Plaintiff

The violation must also be identified and disclosed by the regulated entity prior to:

(a) the commencement of a federal, state or local agency inspection or investigation, or the issuance by such agency of an information request to the regulated entity;

(b) notice of a citizen suit;

(c) the filing of a complaint by a third party;

(d) the reporting of the violation to EPA (or other government agency) by a "whistleblower" employee, rather than by one authorized to speak on behalf of the regulated entity; or

(e) imminent discovery of the violation by a regulatory agency;

5. Correction and Remediation

The regulated entity corrects the violation within 60 days, certifies in writing that violations have been corrected, and takes appropriate measures as determined by EPA to remedy any environmental or human harm due to the violation. If more than 60 days will be needed to correct the violation(s), the regulated entity must so notify EPA in writing before the 60-day period has passed. Where appropriate, EPA may require that to satisfy conditions 5 and 6, a regulated entity enter into a publicly available written agreement, administrative consent order or judicial consent decree, particularly where compliance or remedial measures are complex or a lengthy schedule for attaining and maintaining compliance or remediating harm is required;

6. Prevent Recurrence

The regulated entity agrees in writing to take steps to prevent a recurrence of the violation, which may include improvements to its environmental auditing or due diligence efforts;

U.S. EPA's 1995 Incentives for Self-Policing *(cont'd)*

66712   **Federal Register** / Vol. 60, No. 246 / Friday, December 22, 1995 / Notices

7. No Repeat Violations

The specific violation (or closely related violation) has not occurred previously within the past three years at the same facility, or is not part of a pattern of federal, state or local violations by the facility's parent organization (if any), which have occurred within the past five years. For the purposes of this section, a violation is:

(a) any violation of federal, state or local environmental law identified in a judicial or administrative order, consent agreement or order, complaint, or notice of violation, conviction or plea agreement; or

(b) any act or omission for which the regulated entity has previously received penalty mitigation from EPA or a state or local agency.

8. Other Violations Excluded

The violation is not one which (i) resulted in serious actual harm, or may have presented an imminent and substantial endangerment to, human health or the environment, or (ii) violates the specific terms of any judicial or administrative order, or consent agreement.

9. Cooperation

The regulated entity cooperates as requested by EPA and provides such information as is necessary and requested by EPA to determine applicability of this policy. Cooperation includes, at a minimum, providing all requested documents and access to employees and assistance in investigating the violation, any noncompliance problems related to the disclosure, and any environmental consequences related to the violations.

E. Economic Benefit

EPA will retain its full discretion to recover any economic benefit gained as a result of noncompliance to preserve a "level playing field" in which violators do not gain a competitive advantage over regulated entities that do comply. EPA may forgive the entire penalty for violations which meet conditions 1 through 9 in section D and, in the Agency's opinion, do not merit any penalty due to the insignificant amount of any economic benefit.

F. Effect on State Law, Regulation or Policy

EPA will work closely with states to encourage their adoption of policies that reflect the incentives and conditions outlined in this policy. EPA remains firmly opposed to statutory environmental audit privileges that shield evidence of environmental violations and undermine the public's right to know, as well as to blanket immunities for violations that reflect criminal conduct, present serious threats or actual harm to health and the environment, allow noncomplying companies to gain an economic advantage over their competitors, or reflect a repeated failure to comply with federal law. EPA will work with states to address any provisions of state audit privilege or immunity laws that are inconsistent with this policy, and which may prevent a timely and appropriate response to significant environmental violations. The Agency reserves its right to take necessary actions to protect public health or the environment by enforcing against any violations of federal law.

G. Applicability

(1) This policy applies to the assessment of penalties for any violations under all of the federal environmental statutes that EPA administers, and supersedes any inconsistent provisions in media-specific penalty or enforcement policies and EPA's 1986 Environmental Auditing Policy Statement.

(2) To the extent that existing EPA enforcement policies are not inconsistent, they will continue to apply in conjunction with this policy. However, a regulated entity that has received penalty mitigation for satisfying specific conditions under this policy may not receive additional penalty mitigation for satisfying the same or similar conditions under other policies for the same violation(s), nor will this policy apply to violations which have received penalty mitigation under other policies.

(3) This policy sets forth factors for consideration that will guide the Agency in the exercise of its prosecutorial discretion. It states the Agency's views as to the proper allocation of its enforcement resources. The policy is not final agency action, and is intended as guidance. It does not create any rights, duties, obligations, or defenses, implied or otherwise, in any third parties.

(4) This policy should be used whenever applicable in settlement negotiations for both administrative and civil judicial enforcement actions. It is not intended for use in pleading, at hearing or at trial. The policy may be applied at EPA's discretion to the settlement of administrative and judicial enforcement actions instituted prior to, but not yet resolved, as of the effective date of this policy.

H. Public Accountability

(1) Within 3 years of the effective date of this policy, EPA will complete a study of the effectiveness of the policy in encouraging:

(a) changes in compliance behavior within the regulated community, including improved compliance rates;

(b) prompt disclosure and correction of violations, including timely and accurate compliance with reporting requirements;

(c) corporate compliance programs that are successful in preventing violations, improving environmental performance, and promoting public disclosure;

(d) consistency among state programs that provide incentives for voluntary compliance.

EPA will make the study available to the public.

(2) EPA will make publicly available the terms and conditions of any compliance agreement reached under this policy, including the nature of the violation, the remedy, and the schedule for returning to compliance.

I. Effective Date

This policy is effective January 22, 1996.

Dated: December 18, 1995.

Steven A. Herman,

Assistant Administrator for Enforcement and Compliance Assurance.

[FR Doc. 95±31146 Filed 12±21±95; 8:45 am]

BILLING CODE 6560–50–P

U.S. EPA's 2000 Incentives for Self-Policing

19618   **Federal Register** / Vol. 65. No. 70 / Tuesday. April 11. 2000 / Notices

ENVIRONMENTAL PROTECTION AGENCY

[FRL–6576–3]

Incentives for Self-Policing: Discovery, Disclosure, Correction and Prevention of Violations

AGENCY: Environmental Protection Agency (EPA. or Agency).

ACTION: Final Policy Statement.

SUMMARY: EPA today issues its revised final policy on "Incentives for Self-Policing: Discovery, Disclosure, Correction and Prevention of Violations," commonly referred to as the "Audit Policy." The purpose of this Policy is to enhance protection of human health and the environment by encouraging regulated entities to voluntarily discover, promptly disclose and expeditiously correct violations of Federal environmental requirements. Incentives that EPA makes available for those who meet the terms of the Audit Policy include the elimination or substantial reduction of the gravity component of civil penalties and a determination not to recommend criminal prosecution of the disclosing entity. The Policy also restates EPA's long-standing practice of not requesting copies of regulated entities' voluntary audit reports to trigger Federal enforcement investigations. Today's revised Audit Policy replaces the 1995 Audit Policy (60 FR 66706) which was issued on December 22, 1995, and took effect on January 22, 1996. Today's revisions maintain the basic structure and terms of the 1995 Audit Policy while clarifying some of its language, broadening its availability, and conforming the provisions of the Policy to actual Agency practice. The revisions being released today lengthen the prompt disclosure period to 21 days, clarify that the independent discovery condition does not automatically preclude penalty mitigation for multi-facility entities, and clarify how the prompt disclosure and repeat violation conditions apply to newly acquired companies. The revised Policy was developed in close consultation with the U.S. Department of Justice (DOJ), States, public interest groups and the regulated community. The revisions also reflect EPA's experience implementing the Policy over the past five years.

DATES: This revised Policy is effective May 11, 2000.

FOR FURTHER INFORMATION CONTACT: Catherine Malinin Dunn (202) 564–2629 or Leslie Jones (202) 564–5123. Documentation relating to the development of this Policy is contained in the environmental auditing public docket (#C–94–01). An index to the docket may be obtained by contacting the Enforcement and Compliance Docket and Information Center (ECDIC) by telephone at (202) 564–2614 or (202) 564–2119. by fax at (202) 501–1011. or by email at docket.oeca@epa.gov. ECDIC office hours are 8:00 am to 4:00 pm Monday through Friday except for Federal holidays. An index to the docket is available on the Internet at www.epa.gov/oeca/polguid/enfdock.html. Additional guidance regarding interpretation and application of the Policy is also available on the Internet at www.epa.gov/oeca/ore/apolguid.html.

SUPPLEMENTARY INFORMATION: This Notice is organized as follows:

I. Explanation of Policy

A. Introduction
B. Background and History
C. Purpose
D. Incentives for Self-Policing
  1. Eliminating Gravity-Based Penalties
  2. 75% Reduction of Gravity-Based Penalties
  3. No Recommendations for Criminal Prosecution
  4. No Routine Requests for Audit Reports
E. Conditions
  1. Systematic Discovery of the Violation Through an Environmental Audit or a Compliance Management System
  2. Voluntary Discovery
  3. Prompt Disclosure
  4. Discovery and Disclosure Independent of Government or Third-Party Plaintiff
  5. Correction and Remediation
  6. Prevent Recurrence
  7. No Repeat Violations
  8. Other Violations Excluded
  9. Cooperation
F. Opposition to Audit Privilege and Immunity
G. Effect on States
H. Scope of Policy
I. Implementation of Policy
  1. Civil Violations
  2. Criminal Violations
  3. Release of Information to the Public
II. Statement of Policy—Incentives for Self-Policing: Discovery. Disclosure. Correction and Prevention
A. Purpose
B. Definitions
C. Incentives for Self-Policing
  1. No Gravity-Based Penalties
  2. Reduction of Gravity-Based Penalties by 75%
  3. No Recommendation for Criminal Prosecution
  4. No Routine Request for Environmental Audit Reports
D. Conditions
  1. Systematic Discovery
  2. Voluntary Discovery
  3. Prompt Disclosure
  4. Discovery and Disclosure Independent of Government or Third-Party Plaintiff
  5. Correction and Remediation
  6. Prevent Recurrence
  7. No Repeat Violations
  8. Other Violations Excluded
  9. Cooperation
E. Economic Benefit
F. Effect on State Law, Regulation or Policy
G. Applicability
H. Public Accountability
I. Effective Date

I. Explanation of Policy

A. Introduction

On December 22, 1995, EPA issued its final policy on "Incentives for Self-Policing: Discovery, Disclosure, Correction and Prevention of Violations" (60 FR 66706) (Audit Policy, or Policy). The purpose of the Policy is to enhance protection of human health and the environment by encouraging regulated entities to voluntarily discover, disclose, correct and prevent violations of Federal environmental law. Benefits available to entities that make disclosures under the terms of the Policy include reductions in the amount of civil penalties and a determination not to recommend criminal prosecution of disclosing entities.

Today, EPA issues revisions to the 1995 Audit Policy. The revised Policy reflects EPA's continuing commitment to encouraging voluntary self-policing while preserving fair and effective enforcement. It lengthens the prompt disclosure period to 21 days, clarifies that the independent discovery condition does not automatically preclude Audit Policy credit in the multi-facility context, and clarifies how the prompt disclosure and repeat violations conditions apply in the acquisitions context. The revised final Policy takes effect May 11, 2000.

B. Background and History

The Audit Policy provides incentives for regulated entities to detect, promptly disclose, and expeditiously correct violations of Federal environmental requirements. The Policy contains nine conditions, and entities that meet all of them are eligible for 100% mitigation of any gravity-based penalties that otherwise could be assessed. ("Gravity-based" refers to that portion of the penalty over and above the portion that represents the entity's economic gain from noncompliance, known as the "economic benefit.") Regulated entities that do not meet the first condition—systematic discovery of violations—but meet the other eight conditions are eligible for 75% mitigation of any gravity-based civil penalties. On the criminal side, EPA will generally elect not to recommend criminal prosecution

U.S. EPA's 2000 Incentives for Self-Policing *(cont'd)*

Federal Register / Vol. 65, No. 70 / Tuesday, April 11, 2000 / Notices **19619**

by DOJ or any other prosecuting authority for a disclosing entity that meets at least conditions two through nine—regardless of whether it meets the systematic discovery requirement—as long as its self-policing, discovery and disclosure were conducted in good faith and the entity adopts a systematic approach to preventing recurrence of the violation.

The Policy includes important safeguards to deter violations and protect public health and the environment. For example, the Policy requires entities to act to prevent recurrence of violations and to remedy any environmental harm that may have occurred. Repeat violations, those that result in actual harm to the environment, and those that may present an imminent and substantial endangerment are not eligible for relief under this Policy. Companies will not be allowed to gain an economic advantage over their competitors by delaying their investment in compliance. And entities remain criminally liable for violations that result from conscious disregard of or willful blindness to their obligations under the law, and individuals remain liable for their criminal misconduct.

When EPA issued the 1995 Audit Policy, the Agency committed to evaluate the Policy after three years. The Agency initiated this evaluation in the Spring of 1998 and published its preliminary results in the **Federal Register** on May 17, 1999 (64 FR 26745). The evaluation consisted of the following components:

• An internal survey of EPA staff who process disclosures and handle enforcement cases under the 1995 Audit Policy;

• A survey of regulated entities that used the 1995 Policy to disclose violations;

• A series of meetings and conference calls with representatives from industry, environmental organizations, and States;

• Focused stakeholder discussions on the Audit Policy at two public conferences co-sponsored by EPA's Office of Enforcement and Compliance Assurance (OECA) and the Vice President's National Partnership for Reinventing Government, entitled "Protecting Public Health and the Environment through Innovative Approaches to Compliance";

• A **Federal Register** notice on March 2, 1999, soliciting comments on how EPA can further protect and improve public health and the environment through new compliance and enforcement approaches (64 FR 10144); and

• An analysis of data on Audit Policy usage to date and discussions amongst EPA officials who handle Audit Policy disclosures.

The same May 17, 1999, **Federal Register** notice that published the evaluation's preliminary results also proposed revisions to the 1995 Policy and requested public comment. During the 60-day public comment period, the Agency received 29 comment letters, copies of which are available through the Enforcement and Compliance Docket and Information Center. (See contact information at the beginning of this notice.) Analysis of these comment letters together with additional data on Audit Policy usage has constituted the final stage of the Audit Policy evaluation. EPA has prepared a detailed response to the comments received; a copy of that document will also be available through the Docket and Information Center as well on the Internet at www.epa.gov/oeca/ore/apolguid.html.

Overall, the Audit Policy evaluation revealed very positive results. The Policy has encouraged voluntary self-policing while preserving fair and effective enforcement. Thus, the revisions issued today do not signal any intention to shift course regarding the Agency's position on self-policing and voluntary disclosures but instead represent an attempt to fine-tune a Policy that is already working well.

Use of the Audit Policy has been widespread. As of October 1, 1999, approximately 670 organizations had disclosed actual or potential violations at more than 2700 facilities. The number of disclosures has increased each of the four years the Policy has been in effect.

Results of the Audit Policy User's Survey revealed very high satisfaction rates among users, with 88% of respondents stating that they would use the Policy again and 84% stating that they would recommend the Policy to clients and/or their counterparts. No respondents stated an unwillingness to use the Policy again or to recommend its use to others.

The Audit Policy and related documents, including Agency interpretive guidance and general interest newsletters, are available on the Internet at www.epa.gov/oeca/ore/apolguid. Additional guidance for implementing the Policy in the context of criminal violations can be found at www.epa.gov/oeca/oceft/audpol2.html.

In addition to the Audit Policy, the Agency's revised Small Business Compliance Policy ("Small Business Policy") is also available for small entities that employ 100 or fewer individuals. The Small Business Policy provides penalty mitigation, subject to certain conditions, for small businesses that make a good faith effort to comply with environmental requirements by discovering, disclosing and correcting violations. EPA has revised the Small Business Policy at the same time it revised the Audit Policy. The revised Small Business Policy will be available on the Internet at www.epa.gov/oeca/smbusi.html.

C. Purpose

The revised Policy being announced today is designed to encourage greater compliance with Federal laws and regulations that protect human health and the environment. It promotes a higher standard of self-policing by waiving gravity-based penalties for violations that are promptly disclosed and corrected, and which were discovered systematically—that is, through voluntary audits or compliance management systems. To provide an incentive for entities to disclose and correct violations regardless of how they were detected, the Policy reduces gravity-based penalties by 75% for violations that are voluntarily discovered and promptly disclosed and corrected, even if not discovered systematically.

EPA's enforcement program provides a strong incentive for compliance by imposing stiff sanctions for noncompliance. Enforcement has contributed to the dramatic expansion of environmental auditing as measured in numerous recent surveys. For example, in a 1995 survey by Price Waterhouse LLP, more than 90% of corporate respondents who conduct audits identified one of the reasons for doing so as the desire to find and correct violations before government inspectors discover them. (A copy of the survey is contained in the Docket as document VIII–A–76.)

At the same time, because government resources are limited, universal compliance cannot be achieved without active efforts by the regulated community to police themselves. More than half of the respondents to the same 1995 Price Waterhouse survey said that they would expand environmental auditing in exchange for reduced penalties for violations discovered and corrected. While many companies already audit or have compliance management programs in place, EPA believes that the incentives offered in this Policy will improve the frequency and quality of these self-policing efforts.

D. Incentives for Self-Policing

Section C of the Audit Policy identifies the major incentives that EPA

U.S. EPA's 2000 Incentives for Self-Policing *(cont'd)*

19620   **Federal Register** / Vol. 65, No. 70 / Tuesday, April 11, 2000 / Notices

provides to encourage self-policing, self-disclosure, and prompt self-correction. For entities that meet the conditions of the Policy, the available incentives include waiving or reducing gravity-based civil penalties, declining to recommend criminal prosecution for regulated entities that self-police, and refraining from routine requests for audits. (As noted in Section C of the Policy, EPA has refrained from making routine requests for audit reports since issuance of its 1986 policy on environmental auditing.)

1. Eliminating Gravity-Based Penalties

In general, civil penalties that EPA assesses are comprised of two elements: the economic benefit component and the gravity-based component. The economic benefit component reflects the economic gain derived from a violator's illegal competitive advantage. Gravity-based penalties are that portion of the penalty over and above the economic benefit. They reflect the egregiousness of the violator's behavior and constitute the punitive portion of the penalty. For further discussion of these issues, see "Calculation of the Economic Benefit of Noncompliance in EPA's Civil Penalty Enforcement Cases," 64 FR 32948 (June 18, 1999) and "A Framework for Statute-Specific Approaches to Penalty Assessments," #GM–22 (1984), U.S. EPA General Enforcement Policy Compendium.

Under the Audit Policy, EPA will not seek gravity-based penalties for disclosing entities that meet all nine Policy conditions, including systematic discovery. ("Systematic discovery" means the detection of a potential violation through an environmental audit or a compliance management system that reflects the entity's due diligence in preventing, detecting and correcting violations.) EPA has elected to waive gravity-based penalties for violations discovered systematically, recognizing that environmental auditing and compliance management systems play a critical role in protecting human health and the environment by identifying, correcting and ultimately preventing violations.

However, EPA reserves the right to collect any economic benefit that may have been realized as a result of noncompliance, even where the entity meets all other Policy conditions. Where the Agency determines that the economic benefit is insignificant, the Agency also may waive this component of the penalty.

EPA's decision to retain its discretion to recover economic benefit is based on two reasons. First, facing the risk that the Agency will recoup economic

benefit provides an incentive for regulated entities to comply on time. Taxpayers whose payments are late expect to pay interest or a penalty: the same principle should apply to corporations and other regulated entities that have delayed their investment in compliance. Second, collecting economic benefit is fair because it protects law-abiding companies from being undercut by their noncomplying competitors, thereby preserving a level playing field.

2. 75% Reduction of Gravity-based Penalties

Gravity-based penalties will be reduced by 75% where the disclosing entity does not detect the violation through systematic discovery but otherwise meets all other Policy conditions. The Policy appropriately limits the complete waiver of gravity-based civil penalties to companies that conduct environmental auditing or have in place a compliance management system. However, to encourage disclosure and correction of violations even in the absence of systematic discovery, EPA will reduce gravity-based penalties by 75% for entities that meet conditions D(2) through D(9) of the Policy. EPA expects that a disclosure under this provision will encourage the entity to work with the Agency to resolve environmental problems and begin to develop an effective auditing program or compliance management system.

3. No Recommendations for Criminal Prosecution

In accordance with EPA's Investigative Discretion Memo dated January 12, 1994, EPA generally does not focus its criminal enforcement resources on entities that voluntarily discover, promptly disclose and expeditiously correct violations, unless there is potentially culpable behavior that merits criminal investigation. When a disclosure that meets the terms and conditions of this Policy results in a criminal investigation, EPA will generally not recommend criminal prosecution for the disclosing entity, although the Agency may recommend prosecution for culpable individuals and other entities. The 1994 Investigative Discretion Memo is available on the Internet at http://www.epa.gov/oeca/ore/aed/comp/acomp/a11.html.

The "no recommendation for criminal prosecution" incentive is available for entities that meet conditions D(2) through D(9) of the Policy. Condition D(1) "systematic discovery" is not required to be eligible for this incentive.

although the entity must be acting in good faith and must adopt a systematic approach to preventing recurring violations. Important limitations to the incentive apply. It will not be available, for example, where corporate officials are consciously involved in or willfully blind to violations, or conceal or condone noncompliance. Since the regulated entity must satisfy conditions D(2) through D(9) of the Policy, violations that cause serious harm or which may pose imminent and substantial endangerment to human health or the environment are not eligible. Finally, EPA reserves the right to recommend prosecution for the criminal conduct of any culpable individual or subsidiary organization.

While EPA may decide not to recommend criminal prosecution for disclosing entities, ultimate prosecutorial discretion resides with the U.S. Department of Justice, which will be guided by its own policy on voluntary disclosures ("Factors in Decisions on Criminal Prosecutions for Environmental Violations in the Context of Significant Voluntary Compliance or Disclosure Efforts by the Violator," July 1, 1991) and by its 1999 Guidance on Federal Prosecutions of Corporations. In addition, where a disclosing entity has met the conditions for avoiding a recommendation for criminal prosecution under this Policy, it will also be eligible for either 75% or 100% mitigation of gravity-based civil penalties, depending on whether the systematic discovery condition was met.

4. No Routine Requests for Audit Reports

EPA reaffirms its Policy, in effect since 1986, to refrain from routine requests for audit reports. That is, EPA has not and will not routinely request copies of audit reports to trigger enforcement investigations. Implementation of the 1995 Policy has produced no evidence that the Agency has deviated, or should deviate, from this Policy. In general, an audit that results in expeditious correction will reduce liability, not expand it. However, if the Agency has independent evidence of a violation, it may seek the information it needs to establish the extent and nature of the violation and the degree of culpability.

For discussion of the circumstances in which EPA might request an audit report to determine Policy eligibility, see the explanatory text on cooperation, section I.E.9.

E. Conditions

Section D describes the nine conditions that a regulated entity must

U.S. EPA's 2000 Incentives for Self-Policing *(cont'd)*

Federal Register / Vol. 65, No. 70 / Tuesday, April 11, 2000 / Notices   **19621**

meet in order for the Agency to decline to seek (or to reduce) gravity-based penalties under the Policy. As explained in section I.D.1 above, regulated entities that meet all nine conditions will not face gravity-based civil penalties. If the regulated entity meets all of the conditions except for D(1)—systematic discovery—EPA will reduce gravity-based penalties by 75%. In general, EPA will not recommend criminal prosecution for disclosing entities that meet at least conditions D(2) through D(9).

1. Systematic Discovery of the Violation Through an Environmental Audit or a Compliance Management System

Under Section D(1), the violation must have been discovered through either (a) an environmental audit, or (b) a compliance management system that reflects due diligence in preventing, detecting and correcting violations. Both "environmental audit" and "compliance management system" are defined in Section B of the Policy.

The revised Policy uses the term "compliance management system" instead of "due diligence," which was used in the 1995 Policy. This change in nomenclature is intended solely to conform the Policy language to terminology more commonly in use by industry and by regulators to refer to a systematic management plan or systematic efforts to achieve and maintain compliance. No substantive difference is intended by substituting the term "compliance management system" for "due diligence," as the Policy clearly indicates that the compliance management system must reflect the regulated entity's due diligence in preventing, detecting and correcting violations.

Compliance management programs that train and motivate employees to prevent, detect and correct violations on a daily basis are a valuable complement to periodic auditing. Where the violation is discovered through a compliance management system and not through an audit, the disclosing entity should be prepared to document how its program reflects the due diligence criteria defined in Section B of the Policy statement. These criteria, which are adapted from existing codes of practice—such as Chapter Eight of the U.S. Sentencing Guidelines for organizational defendants, effective since 1991—are flexible enough to accommodate different types and sizes of businesses and other regulated entities. The Agency recognizes that a variety of compliance management programs are feasible, and it will determine whether basic due diligence

criteria have been met in deciding whether to grant Audit Policy credit.

As a condition of penalty mitigation, EPA may require that a description of the regulated entity's compliance management system be made publicly available. The Agency believes that the availability of such information will allow the public to judge the adequacy of compliance management systems, lead to enhanced compliance, and foster greater public trust in the integrity of compliance management systems.

2. Voluntary Discovery

Under Section D(2), the violation must have been identified voluntarily, and not through a monitoring, sampling, or auditing procedure that is required by statute, regulation, permit, judicial or administrative order, or consent agreement. The Policy provides three specific examples of discovery that would not be voluntary, and therefore would not be eligible for penalty mitigation: emissions violations detected through a required continuous emissions monitor, violations of NPDES discharge limits found through prescribed monitoring, and violations discovered through a compliance audit required to be performed by the terms of a consent order or settlement agreement. The exclusion does not apply to violations that are discovered pursuant to audits that are conducted as part of a comprehensive environmental management system (EMS) required under a settlement agreement. In general, EPA supports the implementation of EMSs that promote compliance, prevent pollution and improve overall environmental performance. Precluding the availability of the Audit Policy for discoveries made through a comprehensive EMS that has been implemented pursuant to a settlement agreement might discourage entities from agreeing to implement such a system.

In some instances, certain Clean Air Act violations discovered, disclosed and corrected by a company prior to issuance of a Title V permit are eligible for penalty mitigation under the Policy. For further guidance in this area, see "Reduced Penalties for Disclosures of Certain Clean Air Act Violations," Memorandum from Eric Schaeffer, Director of the EPA Office of Regulatory Enforcement, dated September 30, 1999. This document is available on the Internet at www.epa.gov/oeca/ore/apolguid.html.

The voluntary requirement applies to discovery only, not reporting. That is, any violation that is voluntarily discovered is generally eligible for Audit Policy credit, regardless of

whether reporting of the violation was required after it was found.

3. Prompt Disclosure

Section D(3) requires that the entity disclose the violation in writing to EPA within 21 calendar days after discovery. If the 21st day after discovery falls on a weekend or Federal holiday, the disclosure period will be extended to the first business day following the 21st day after discovery. If a statute or regulation requires the entity to report the violation in fewer than 21 days, disclosure must be made within the time limit established by law. (For example, unpermitted releases of hazardous substances must be reported immediately under 42 U.S.C. 9603.) Disclosures under this Policy should be made to the appropriate EPA Regional office or, where multiple Regions are involved, to EPA Headquarters. The Agency will work closely with States as needed to ensure fair and efficient implementation of the Policy. For additional guidance on making disclosures, contact the Audit Policy National Coordinator at EPA Headquarters at 202–564–5123.

The 21-day disclosure period begins when the entity discovers that a violation has, or may have, occurred. The trigger for discovery is when any officer, director, employee or agent of the facility has an objectively reasonable basis for believing that a violation has, or may have, occurred. The "objectively reasonable basis" standard is measured against what a prudent person, having the same information as was available to the individual in question, would have believed. It is not measured against what the individual in question thought was reasonable at the time the situation was encountered. If an entity has some doubt as to the existence of a violation, the recommended course is for the entity to proceed with the disclosure and allow the regulatory authorities to make a definitive determination. Contract personnel who provide on-site services at the facility may be treated as employees or agents for purposes of the Policy.

If the 21-day period has not yet expired and an entity suspects that it will be unable to meet the deadline, the entity should contact the appropriate EPA office in advance to develop disclosure terms acceptable to EPA. For situations in which the 21-day period already has expired, the Agency may accept a late disclosure in the exceptional case, such as where there are complex circumstances, including where EPA determines the violation could not be identified and disclosed within 21 calendar days after discovery.

U.S. EPA's 2000 Incentives for Self-Policing *(cont'd)*

19622   **Federal Register** / Vol. 65, No. 70 / Tuesday, April 11, 2000 / Notices

EPA also may extend the disclosure period when multiple facilities or acquisitions are involved.

In the multi-facility context, EPA will ordinarily extend the 21-day period to allow reasonable time for completion and review of multi-facility audits where: (a) EPA and the entity agree on the timing and scope of the audits prior to their commencement; and (b) the facilities to be audited are identified in advance. In the acquisitions context, EPA will consider extending the prompt disclosure period on a case-by-case basis. The 21-day disclosure period will begin on the date of discovery by the acquiring entity, but in no case will the period begin earlier than the date of acquisition.

In summary, Section D(3) recognizes that it is critical for EPA to receive timely reporting of violations in order to have clear notice of the violations and the opportunity to respond if necessary. Prompt disclosure is also evidence of the regulated entity's good faith in wanting to achieve or return to compliance as soon as possible. The integrity of Federal environmental law depends upon timely and accurate reporting. The public relies on timely and accurate reports from the regulated community, not only to measure compliance but to evaluate health or environmental risk and gauge progress in reducing pollutant loadings. EPA expects the Policy to encourage the kind of vigorous self-policing that will serve these objectives and does not intend that it justify delayed reporting. When violations of reporting requirements are voluntarily discovered, they must be promptly reported. When a failure to report results in imminent and substantial endangerment or serious harm to the environment, Audit Policy credit is precluded under condition D(8).

4. Discovery and Disclosure Independent of Government or Third Party Plaintiff

Under Section D(4), the entity must discover the violation independently. That is, the violation must be discovered and identified before EPA or another government agency likely would have identified the problem either through its own investigative work or from information received through a third party. This condition requires regulated entities to take the initiative to find violations on their own and disclose them promptly instead of waiting for an indication of a pending enforcement action or third-party complaint.

Section D(4)(a) lists the circumstances under which discovery and disclosure

will not be considered independent. For example, a disclosure will not be independent where EPA is already investigating the facility in question. However, under subsection (a), where the entity does not know that EPA has commenced a civil investigation and proceeds in good faith to make a disclosure under the Audit Policy, EPA may, in its discretion, provide penalty mitigation under the Audit Policy. The subsection (a) exception applies only to civil investigations; it does not apply in the criminal context. Other examples of situations in which a discovery is not considered independent are where a citizens' group has provided notice of its intent to sue, where a third party has already filed a complaint, where a whistleblower has reported the potential violation to government authorities, or where discovery of the violation by the government was imminent. Condition D(4)(c)—the filing of a complaint by a third party—covers formal judicial and administrative complaints as well as informal complaints, such as a letter from a citizens' group alerting EPA to a potential environmental violation.

Regulated entities that own or operate multiple facilities are subject to section D(4)(b) in addition to D(4)(a). EPA encourages multi-facility auditing and does not intend for the "independent discovery" condition to preclude availability of the Audit Policy when multiple facilities are involved. Thus, if a regulated entity owns or operates multiple facilities, the fact that one of its facilities is the subject of an investigation, inspection, information request or third-party complaint does not automatically preclude the Agency from granting Audit Policy credit for disclosures of violations self-discovered at the other facilities, assuming all other Audit Policy conditions are met. However, just as in the single-facility context, where a facility is already the subject of a government inspection, investigation or information request (including a broad information request that covers multiple facilities), it will generally not be eligible for Audit Policy credit. The Audit Policy is designed to encourage regulated entities to disclose violations before any of their facilities are under investigation, not after EPA discovers violations at one facility. Nevertheless, the Agency retains its full discretion under the Audit Policy to grant penalty waivers or reductions for good-faith disclosures made in the multi-facility context. EPA has worked closely with a number of entities that have received Audit Policy credit for multi-facility disclosures, and entities contemplating multi-facility auditing

are encouraged to contact the Agency with any questions concerning Audit Policy availability.

5. Correction and Remediation

Under Section D(5), the entity must remedy any harm caused by the violation and expeditiously certify in writing to appropriate Federal, State, and local authorities that it has corrected the violation. Correction and remediation in this context include responding to spills and carrying out any removal or remedial actions required by law. The certification requirement enables EPA to ensure that the regulated entity will be publicly accountable for its commitments through binding written agreements, orders or consent decrees where necessary.

Under the Policy, the entity must correct the violation within 60 calendar days from the date of discovery, or as expeditiously as possible. EPA recognizes that some violations can and should be corrected immediately, while others may take longer than 60 days to correct. For example, more time may be required if capital expenditures are involved or if technological issues are a factor. If more than 60 days will be required, the disclosing entity must so notify the Agency in writing prior to the conclusion of the 60-day period. In all cases, the regulated entity will be expected to do its utmost to achieve or return to compliance as expeditiously as possible.

If correction of the violation depends upon issuance of a permit that has been applied for but not issued by Federal or State authorities, the Agency will, where appropriate, make reasonable efforts to secure timely review of the permit.

6. Prevent Recurrence

Under Section D(6), the regulated entity must agree to take steps to prevent a recurrence of the violation after it has been disclosed. Preventive steps may include, but are not limited to, improvements to the entity's environmental auditing efforts or compliance management system.

7. No Repeat Violations

Condition D(7) bars repeat offenders from receiving Audit Policy credit. Under the repeat violations exclusion, the same or a closely-related violation must not have occurred at the same facility within the past 3 years. The 3-year period begins to run when the government or a third party has given the violator notice of a specific violation, without regard to when the original violation cited in the notice

U.S. EPA's 2000 Incentives for Self-Policing *(cont'd)*

Federal Register / Vol. 65, No. 70 / Tuesday, April 11, 2000 / Notices   **19623**

actually occurred. Examples of notice include a complaint, consent order, notice of violation, receipt of an inspection report, citizen suit, or receipt of penalty mitigation through a compliance assistance or incentive project.

When the facility is part of a multi-facility organization, Audit Policy relief is not available if the same or a closely-related violation occurred as part of a pattern of violations at one or more of these facilities within the past 5 years. If a facility has been newly acquired, the existence of a violation prior to acquisition does not trigger the repeat violations exclusion.

The term "violation" includes any violation subject to a Federal, State or local civil judicial or administrative order, consent agreement, conviction or plea agreement. Recognizing that minor violations sometimes are settled without a formal action in court, the term also covers any act or omission for which the regulated entity has received a penalty reduction in the past. This condition covers situations in which the regulated entity has had clear notice of its noncompliance and an opportunity to correct the problem.

The repeat violation exclusion benefits both the public and law-abiding entities by ensuring that penalties are not waived for those entities that have previously been notified of violations and fail to prevent repeat violations. The 3-year and 5-year "bright lines" in the exclusion are designed to provide regulated entities with clear notice about when the Policy will be available.

8. Other Violations Excluded

Section D(8) provides that Policy benefits are not available for certain types of violations. Subsection D(8)(a) excludes violations that result in serious actual harm to the environment or which may have presented an imminent and substantial endangerment to public health or the environment. When events of such a consequential nature occur, violators are ineligible for penalty relief and other incentives under the Audit Policy. However, this condition does not bar an entity from qualifying for Audit Policy relief solely because the violation involves release of a pollutant to the environment, as such releases do not necessarily result in serious actual harm or an imminent and substantial endangerment. To date, EPA has not invoked the serious actual harm or the imminent and substantial endangerment clauses to deny Audit Policy credit for any disclosure.

Subsection D(8)(b) excludes violations of the specific terms of any order, consent agreement, or plea agreement.

Once a consent agreement has been negotiated, there is little incentive to comply if there are no sanctions for violating its specific requirements. The exclusion in this section also applies to violations of the terms of any response, removal or remedial action covered by a written agreement.

9. Cooperation

Under Section D(9), the regulated entity must cooperate as required by EPA and provide the Agency with the information it needs to determine Policy applicability. The entity must not hide, destroy or tamper with possible evidence following discovery of potential environmental violations. In order for the Agency to apply the Policy fairly, it must have sufficient information to determine whether its conditions are satisfied in each individual case. In general, EPA requests audit reports to determine the applicability of this Policy only where the information contained in the audit report is not readily available elsewhere and where EPA decides that the information is necessary to determine whether the terms and conditions of the Policy have been met. In the rare instance where an EPA Regional office seeks to obtain an audit report because it is otherwise unable to determine whether Policy conditions have been met, the Regional office will notify the Office of Regulatory Enforcement at EPA headquarters.

Entities that disclose potential criminal violations may expect a more thorough review by the Agency. In criminal cases, entities will be expected to provide, at a minimum, the following: access to all requested documents; access to all employees of the disclosing entity; assistance in investigating the violation, any noncompliance problems related to the disclosure, and any environmental consequences related to the violations; access to all information relevant to the violations disclosed, including that portion of the environmental audit report or documentation from the compliance management system that revealed the violation; and access to the individuals who conducted the audit or review.

F. Opposition to Audit Privilege and Immunity

The Agency believes that the Audit Policy provides effective incentives for self-policing without impairing law enforcement, putting the environment at risk or hiding environmental compliance information from the public. Although EPA encourages environmental auditing, it must do so without compromising the integrity and

enforceability of environmental laws. It is important to distinguish between EPA's Audit Policy and the audit privilege and immunity laws that exist in some States. The Agency remains firmly opposed to statutory and regulatory audit privileges and immunity. Privilege laws shield evidence of wrongdoing and prevent States from investigating even the most serious environmental violations. Immunity laws prevent States from obtaining penalties that are appropriate to the seriousness of the violation, as they are required to do under Federal law. Audit privilege and immunity laws are unnecessary, undermine law enforcement, impair protection of human health and the environment, and interfere with the public's right to know of potential and existing environmental hazards.

Statutory audit privilege and immunity run counter to encouraging the kind of openness that builds trust between regulators, the regulated community and the public. For example, privileged information on compliance contained in an audit report may include information on the cause of violations, the extent of environmental harm, and what is necessary to correct the violations and prevent their recurrence. Privileged information is unavailable to law enforcers and to members of the public who have suffered harm as a result of environmental violations. The Agency opposes statutory immunity because it diminishes law enforcement's ability to discourage wrongful behavior and interferes with a regulator's ability to punish individuals who disregard the law and place others in danger. The Agency believes that its Audit Policy provides adequate incentives for self-policing but without secrecy and without abdicating its discretion to act in cases of serious environmental violations.

Privilege, by definition, invites secrecy, instead of the openness needed to build public trust in industry's ability to self-police. American law reflects the high value that the public places on fair access to the facts. The Supreme Court, for example, has said of privileges that, " [w]hatever their origins, these exceptions to the demand for every man's evidence are not lightly created nor expansively construed, for they are in derogation of the search for truth." *United States* v. *Nixon*, 418 U.S. 683, 710 (1974). Federal courts have unanimously refused to recognize a privilege for environmental audits in the context of government investigations. See, *e.g.*, *United States* v. *Dexter Corp.*, 132 F.R.D. 8, 10 (D.Conn. 1990)

U.S. EPA's 2000 Incentives for Self-Policing *(cont'd)*

19624   **Federal Register** / Vol. 65. No. 70 / Tuesday. April 11. 2000 / Notices

(application of a privilege "would effectively impede [EPA's] ability to enforce the Clean Water Act. and would be contrary to stated public policy.") Cf. In re Grand Jury Proceedings, 861 F. Supp. 386 (D. Md. 1994) (company must comply with a subpoena under Food. Drug and Cosmetics Act for self-evaluative documents).

G. Effect on States

The revised final Policy reflects EPA's desire to provide fair and effective incentives for self-policing that have practical value to States. To that end, the Agency has consulted closely with State officials in developing this Policy. As a result, EPA believes its revised final Policy is grounded in commonsense principles that should prove useful in the development and implementation of State programs and policies.

EPA recognizes that States are partners in implementing the enforcement and compliance assurance program. When consistent with EPA's policies on protecting confidential and sensitive information, the Agency will share with State agencies information on disclosures of violations of Federally-authorized, approved or delegated programs. In addition, for States that have adopted their own audit policies in Federally-authorized, approved or delegated programs, EPA will generally defer to State penalty mitigation for self-disclosures as long as the State policy meets minimum requirements for Federal delegation. Whenever a State provides a penalty waiver or mitigation for a violation of a requirement contained in a Federally-authorized, approved or delegated program to an entity that discloses those violations in conformity with a State audit policy, the State should notify the EPA Region in which it is located. This notification will ensure that Federal and State enforcement responses are coordinated properly.

For further information about minimum delegation requirements and the effect of State audit privilege and immunity laws on enforcement authority, see "Statement of Principles: Effect of State Audit/Immunity Privilege Laws on Enforcement Authority for Federal Programs," Memorandum from Steven A. Herman et al, dated February 14, 1997, to be posted on the Internet under www.epa.gov/oeca/oppa.

As always, States are encouraged to experiment with different approaches to assuring compliance as long as such approaches do not jeopardize public health or the environment, or make it profitable not to comply with Federal environmental requirements. The Agency remains opposed to State legislation that does not include these basic protections, and reserves its right to bring independent action against regulated entities for violations of Federal law that threaten human health or the environment. reflect criminal conduct or repeated noncompliance. or allow one company to profit at the expense of its law-abiding competitors.

H. Scope of Policy

EPA has developed this Policy to guide settlement actions. It is the Agency's practice to make public all compliance agreements reached under this Policy in order to provide the regulated community with fair notice of decisions and to provide affected communities and the public with information regarding Agency action. Some in the regulated community have suggested that the Agency should convert the Policy into a regulation because they feel doing so would ensure greater consistency and predictability. Following its three-year evaluation of the Policy, however. the Agency believes that there is ample evidence that the Policy has worked well and that there is no need for a formal rulemaking. Furthermore. as the Agency seeks to respond to lessons learned from its increasing experience handling self-disclosures, a policy is much easier to amend than a regulation. Nothing in today's release of the revised final Policy is intended to change the status of the Policy as guidance.

I. Implementation of Policy

1. Civil Violations

Pursuant to the Audit Policy. disclosures of civil environmental violations should be made to the EPA Region in which the entity or facility is located or. where the violations to be disclosed involve more than one EPA Region. to EPA Headquarters. The Regional or Headquarters offices decide whether application of the Audit Policy in a specific case is appropriate. Obviously, once a matter has been referred for civil judicial prosecution, DOJ becomes involved as well. Where there is evidence of a potential criminal violation, the civil enforcement offices coordinate with criminal enforcement offices at EPA and DOJ.

To resolve issues of national significance and ensure that the Policy is applied fairly and consistently across EPA Regions and at Headquarters, the Agency in 1995 created the Audit Policy Quick Response Team (QRT). The QRT is comprised of representatives from the Regions. Headquarters. and DOJ. It meets on a regular basis to address issues of interpretation and to coordinate self-disclosure initiatives. In addition, in 1999 EPA established a National Coordinator position to handle Audit Policy issues and implementation. The National Coordinator chairs the QRT and, along with the Regional Audit Policy coordinators, serves as a point of contact on Audit Policy issues in the civil context.

2. Criminal Violations

Criminal disclosures are handled by the Voluntary Disclosure Board (VDB), which was established by EPA in 1997. The VDB ensures consistent application of the Audit Policy in the criminal context by centralizing Policy interpretation and application within the Agency.

Disclosures of potential criminal violations may be made directly to the VDB, to an EPA regional criminal investigation division or to DOJ. In all cases, the VDB coordinates with the investigative team and the appropriate prosecuting authority. During the course of the investigation. the VDB routinely monitors the progress of the investigation as necessary to ensure that sufficient facts have been established to determine whether to recommend that relief under the Policy be granted.

At the conclusion of the criminal investigation, the Board makes a recommendation to the Director of EPA's Office of Criminal Enforcement, Forensics, and Training. who serves as the Deciding Official. Upon receiving the Board's recommendation, the Deciding Official makes his or her final recommendation to the appropriate United States Attorney's Office and/or DOJ. The recommendation of the Deciding Official, however, is only that—a recommendation. The United States Attorney's Office and/or DOJ retain full authority to exercise prosecutorial discretion.

3. Release of Information to the Public

Upon formal settlement, EPA places copies of settlements in the Audit Policy Docket. EPA also makes other documents related to self-disclosures publicly available, unless the disclosing entity claims them as Confidential Business Information (and that claim is validated by U.S. EPA), unless another exemption under the Freedom of Information Act is asserted and/or applies, or the Privacy Act or any other law would preclude such release. Presumptively releasable documents include compliance agreements reached under the Policy (see Section H) and descriptions of compliance management systems submitted under Section D(1).

U.S. EPA's 2000 Incentives for Self-Policing *(cont'd)*

Federal Register / Vol. 65, No. 70 / Tuesday, April 11, 2000 / Notices   **19625**

Any material claimed to be Confidential Business Information will be treated in accordance with EPA regulations at 40 CFR Part 2. In determining what documents to release, EPA is guided by the Memorandum from Assistant Administrator Steven A. Herman entitled "Confidentiality of Information Received Under Agency's Self-Disclosure Policy," available on the Internet at www.epa.gov/oeca/sahmemo.html.

II. Statement of Policy—Incentives for Self-Policing: Discovery, Disclosure, Correction and Prevention of Violations

A. Purpose

This Policy is designed to enhance protection of human health and the environment by encouraging regulated entities to voluntarily discover, disclose, correct and prevent violations of Federal environmental requirements.

B. Definitions

For purposes of this Policy, the following definitions apply:

"Environmental Audit" is a systematic, documented, periodic and objective review by regulated entities of facility operations and practices related to meeting environmental requirements.

"Compliance Management System" encompasses the regulated entity's documented systematic efforts, appropriate to the size and nature of its business, to prevent, detect and correct violations through all of the following:

(a) Compliance policies, standards and procedures that identify how employees and agents are to meet the requirements of laws, regulations, permits, enforceable agreements and other sources of authority for environmental requirements;

(b) Assignment of overall responsibility for overseeing compliance with policies, standards, and procedures, and assignment of specific responsibility for assuring compliance at each facility or operation;

(c) Mechanisms for systematically assuring that compliance policies, standards and procedures are being carried out, including monitoring and auditing systems reasonably designed to detect and correct violations, periodic evaluation of the overall performance of the compliance management system, and a means for employees or agents to report violations of environmental requirements without fear of retaliation;

(d) Efforts to communicate effectively the regulated entity's standards and procedures to all employees and other agents;

(e) Appropriate incentives to managers and employees to perform in accordance with the compliance policies, standards and procedures, including consistent enforcement through appropriate disciplinary mechanisms; and

(f) Procedures for the prompt and appropriate correction of any violations, and any necessary modifications to the regulated entity's compliance management system to prevent future violations.

"Environmental audit report" means the documented analysis, conclusions, and recommendations resulting from an environmental audit, but does not include data obtained in, or testimonial evidence concerning, the environmental audit.

"Gravity-based penalties" are that portion of a penalty over and above the economic benefit, *i.e.*, the punitive portion of the penalty, rather than that portion representing a defendant's economic gain from noncompliance.

"Regulated entity" means any entity, including a Federal, State or municipal agency or facility, regulated under Federal environmental laws.

C. Incentives for Self-Policing

1. No Gravity-Based Penalties

If a regulated entity establishes that it satisfies all of the conditions of Section D of this Policy, EPA will not seek gravity-based penalties for violations of Federal environmental requirements discovered and disclosed by the entity.

2. Reduction of Gravity-Based Penalties by 75%

If a regulated entity establishes that it satisfies all of the conditions of Section D of this Policy except for D(1)—systematic discovery—EPA will reduce by 75% gravity-based penalties for violations of Federal environmental requirements discovered and disclosed by the entity.

3. No Recommendation for Criminal Prosecution

(a) If a regulated entity establishes that it satisfies at least conditions D(2) through D(9) of this Policy, EPA will not recommend to the U.S. Department of Justice or other prosecuting authority that criminal charges be brought against the disclosing entity, as long as EPA determines that the violation is not part of a pattern or practice that demonstrates or involves:

(i) A prevalent management philosophy or practice that conceals or condones environmental violations; or

(ii) High-level corporate officials' or managers' conscious involvement in, or willful blindness to, violations of Federal environmental law;

(b) Whether or not EPA recommends the regulated entity for criminal prosecution under this section, the Agency may recommend for prosecution the criminal acts of individual managers or employees under existing policies guiding the exercise of enforcement discretion.

4. No Routine Request for Environmental Audit Reports

EPA will neither request nor use an environmental audit report to initiate a civil or criminal investigation of an entity. For example, EPA will not request an environmental audit report in routine inspections. If the Agency has independent reason to believe that a violation has occurred, however, EPA may seek any information relevant to identifying violations or determining liability or extent of harm.

D. Conditions

1. Systematic Discovery

The violation was discovered through:

(a) An environmental audit; or

(b) A compliance management system reflecting the regulated entity's due diligence in preventing, detecting, and correcting violations. The regulated entity must provide accurate and complete documentation to the Agency as to how its compliance management system meets the criteria for due diligence outlined in Section B and how the regulated entity discovered the violation through its compliance management system. EPA may require the regulated entity to make publicly available a description of its compliance management system.

2. Voluntary Discovery

The violation was discovered voluntarily and not through a legally mandated monitoring or sampling requirement prescribed by statute, regulation, permit, judicial or administrative order, or consent agreement. For example, the Policy does not apply to:

(a) Emissions violations detected through a continuous emissions monitor (or alternative monitor established in a permit) where any such monitoring is required;

(b) Violations of National Pollutant Discharge Elimination System (NPDES) discharge limits detected through required sampling or monitoring; or

(c) Violations discovered through a compliance audit required to be performed by the terms of a consent order or settlement agreement, unless the audit is a component of agreement terms to implement a comprehensive environmental management system.

U.S. EPA's 2000 Incentives for Self-Policing *(cont'd)*

19626   **Federal Register** / Vol. 65. No. 70 / Tuesday. April 11, 2000 / Notices

3. Prompt Disclosure

The regulated entity fully discloses the specific violation in writing to EPA within 21 days (or within such shorter time as may be required by law) after the entity discovered that the violation has, or may have, occurred. The time at which the entity discovers that a violation has, or may have, occurred begins when any officer, director, employee or agent of the facility has an objectively reasonable basis for believing that a violation has, or may have, occurred.

4. Discovery and Disclosure Independent of Government or Third-Party Plaintiff

(a) The regulated entity discovers and discloses the potential violation to EPA prior to:

(i) The commencement of a Federal. State or local agency inspection or investigation, or the issuance by such agency of an information request to the regulated entity (where EPA determines that the facility did not know that it was under civil investigation, and EPA determines that the entity is otherwise acting in good faith, the Agency may exercise its discretion to reduce or waive civil penalties in accordance with this Policy);

(ii) Notice of a citizen suit;

(iii) The filing of a complaint by a third party;

(iv) The reporting of the violation to EPA (or other government agency) by a "whistleblower" employee, rather than by one authorized to speak on behalf of the regulated entity; or

(v) imminent discovery of the violation by a regulatory agency.

(b) For entities that own or operate multiple facilities, the fact that one facility is already the subject of an investigation, inspection, information request or third-party complaint does not preclude the Agency from exercising its discretion to make the Audit Policy available for violations self-discovered at other facilities owned or operated by the same regulated entity.

5. Correction and Remediation

The regulated entity corrects the violation within 60 calendar days from the date of discovery, certifies in writing that the violation has been corrected. and takes appropriate measures as determined by EPA to remedy any environmental or human harm due to the violation. EPA retains the authority to order an entity to correct a violation within a specific time period shorter than 60 days whenever correction in such shorter period of time is feasible and necessary to protect public health

and the environment adequately. If more than 60 days will be needed to correct the violation. the regulated entity must so notify EPA in writing before the 60-day period has passed. Where appropriate. to satisfy conditions D(5) and D(6). EPA may require a regulated entity to enter into a publicly available written agreement. administrative consent order or judicial consent decree as a condition of obtaining relief under the Audit Policy. particularly where compliance or remedial measures are complex or a lengthy schedule for attaining and maintaining compliance or remediating harm is required.

6. Prevent Recurrence

The regulated entity agrees in writing to take steps to prevent a recurrence of the violation. Such steps may include improvements to its environmental auditing or compliance management system.

7. No Repeat Violations

The specific violation (or a closely related violation) has not occurred previously within the past three years at the same facility, and has not occurred within the past five years as part of a pattern at multiple facilities owned or operated by the same entity. For the purposes of this section, a violation is:

(a) Any violation of Federal, State or local environmental law identified in a judicial or administrative order. consent agreement or order. complaint. or notice of violation. conviction or plea agreement; or

(b) Any act or omission for which the regulated entity has previously received penalty mitigation from EPA or a State or local agency.

8. Other Violations Excluded

The violation is not one which (a) resulted in serious actual harm. or may have presented an imminent and substantial endangerment. to human health or the environment, or (b) violates the specific terms of any judicial or administrative order. or consent agreement.

9. Cooperation

The regulated entity cooperates as requested by EPA and provides such information as is necessary and requested by EPA to determine applicability of this Policy.

E. Economic Benefit

EPA retains its full discretion to recover any economic benefit gained as a result of noncompliance to preserve a "level playing field" in which violators do not gain a competitive advantage

over regulated entities that do comply. EPA may forgive the entire penalty for violations that meet conditions D(1) through D(9) and, in the Agency's opinion, do not merit any penalty due to the insignificant amount of any economic benefit.

F. Effect on State Law, Regulation or Policy

EPA will work closely with States to encourage their adoption and implementation of policies that reflect the incentives and conditions outlined in this Policy. EPA remains firmly opposed to statutory environmental audit privileges that shield evidence of environmental violations and undermine the public's right to know, as well as to blanket immunities, particularly immunities for violations that reflect criminal conduct, present serious threats or actual harm to health and the environment, allow noncomplying companies to gain an economic advantage over their competitors, or reflect a repeated failure to comply with Federal law. EPA will work with States to address any provisions of State audit privilege or immunity laws that are inconsistent with this Policy and that may prevent a timely and appropriate response to significant environmental violations. The Agency reserves its right to take necessary actions to protect public health or the environment by enforcing against any violations of Federal law.

G. Applicability

(1) This Policy applies to settlement of claims for civil penalties for any violations under all of the Federal environmental statutes that EPA administers. and supersedes any inconsistent provisions in media-specific penalty or enforcement policies and EPA's 1995 Policy on "Incentives for Self-Policing: Discovery, Disclosure, Correction and Prevention of Violations."

(2) To the extent that existing EPA enforcement policies are not inconsistent, they will continue to apply in conjunction with this Policy. However, a regulated entity that has received penalty mitigation for satisfying specific conditions under this Policy may not receive additional penalty mitigation for satisfying the same or similar conditions under other policies for the same violation, nor will this Policy apply to any violation that has received penalty mitigation under other policies. Where an entity has failed to meet any of conditions D(2) through D(9) and is therefore not eligible for penalty relief under this Policy, it may still be eligible for penalty

U.S. EPA's 2000 Incentives for Self-Policing *(cont'd)*

Federal Register / Vol. 65, No. 70 / Tuesday, April 11, 2000 / Notices **19627**

relief under other EPA media-specific enforcement policies in recognition of good faith efforts, even where, for example, the violation may have presented an imminent and substantial endangerment or resulted in serious actual harm.

(3) This Policy sets forth factors for consideration that will guide the Agency in the exercise of its enforcement discretion. It states the Agency's views as to the proper allocation of its enforcement resources. The Policy is not final agency action and is intended as guidance. This Policy is not intended, nor can it be relied upon, to create any rights enforceable by any party in litigation with the United States. As with the 1995 Audit Policy, EPA may decide to follow guidance provided in this document or to act at variance with it based on its analysis of the specific facts presented. This Policy may be revised without public notice to reflect changes in EPA's approach to providing incentives for self-policing by regulated entities, or to clarify and update text.

(4) This Policy should be used whenever applicable in settlement negotiations for both administrative and civil judicial enforcement actions. It is not intended for use in pleading, at hearing or at trial. The Policy may be applied at EPA's discretion to the settlement of administrative and judicial enforcement actions instituted prior to, but not yet resolved, as of the effective date of this Policy.

(5) For purposes of this Policy, violations discovered pursuant to an environmental audit or compliance management system may be considered voluntary even if required under an Agency "partnership" program in which the entity participates, such as regulatory flexibility pilot projects like Project XL. EPA will consider application of the Audit Policy to such partnership program projects on a project-by-project basis.

(6) EPA has issued interpretive guidance addressing several applicability issues pertaining to the Audit Policy. Entities considering whether to take advantage of the Audit Policy should review that guidance to see if it addresses any relevant questions. The guidance can be found on the Internet at www.epa.gov/oeca/ore/apolguid.html.

H. Public Accountability

EPA will make publicly available the terms and conditions of any compliance agreement reached under this Policy, including the nature of the violation, the remedy, and the schedule for returning to compliance.

I. Effective Date

This revised Policy is effective May 11, 2000.

Dated: March 30, 2000.

Steven A. Herman,

Assistant Administrator for Enforcement and Compliance Assurance.

[FR Doc. 00–8954 Filed 4–10–00; 8:45 am]

BILLING CODE 6560–50–P

OSHA's 2000 Self-Audit Policy

46498   Federal Register / Vol. 65, No. 146 / Friday, July 28, 2000 / Notices

WA000011 (Feb. 11, 2000)
WA000023 (Feb. 11, 2000)

Volume VII

California
CA000001 (Feb. 11, 2000)
CA000002 (Feb. 11, 2000)
CA000004 (Feb. 11, 2000)
CA000009 (Feb. 11, 2000)
CA000027 (Feb. 11, 2000)
CA000028 (Feb. 11, 2000)
CA000029 (Feb. 11, 2000)
CA000030 (Feb. 11, 2000)
CA000031 (Feb. 11, 2000)
CA000032 (Feb. 11, 2000)
CA000033 (Feb. 11, 2000)
CA000034 (Feb. 11, 2000)
CA000035 (Feb. 11, 2000)
CA000036 (Feb. 11, 2000)
CA000037 (Feb. 11, 2000)
CA000038 (Feb. 11, 2000)
CA000039 (Feb. 11, 2000)
CA000040 (Feb. 11, 2000)
CA000041 (Feb. 11, 2000)

General Wage Determination Publication

General wage determinations issued under the Davis-Bacon and related Acts, including those noted above, may be found in the Government Printing Office (GPO) document entitled "General Wage Determinations Issued Under The Davis-Bacon and Related Acts." This publication is available at each of the 50 Regional Government Depository Libraries and many of the 1,400 Government Depository Libraries across the country.

The general wage determinations issued under the Davis-Bacon and related Acts are available electronically by subscription to the FedWorld Bulletin Board System of the National Technical Information Service (NTIS) of the U.S. Department of Commerce at 1–800–363–2068.

Hard-copy subscriptions may be purchased from: Superintendent of Documents, U.S. Government Printing Office, Washington, DC 20402, (202) 512–1800.

When ordering hard-copy subscription(s), be sure to specify the State(s) of interest, since subscriptions may be ordered for any or all of the seven separate volumes, arranged by State. Subscriptions include an annual edition (issued in January or February) which includes all current general wage determinations for the States covered by each volume. Throughout the remainder of the year, regular weekly updates are distributed to subscribers.

Signed at Washington, DC this 20th day of July 2000.

Carl J. Poleskey,
Chief, Branch of Construction Wage Determinations.

[FR Doc. 00–18869 Filed 7–27–00: 8:45 am]
BILLING CODE 4510–27–M

DEPARTMENT OF LABOR

Occupational Safety and Health Administration

[Docket No. W–100]

Final Policy Concerning the Occupational Safety and Health Administration's Treatment of Voluntary Employer Safety and Health Self-Audits

AGENCY: Occupational Safety and Health Administration, USDOL.

ACTION: Notice of final policy

Authority: Sec. 8(a) and 8(b), Pub. L. 91–596, 84 Stat. 1599 (29 U.S.C. 657)

SUMMARY: The Occupational Safety and Health Administration (OSHA) has developed a final policy describing the Agency's treatment of voluntary employer self-audits that assess workplace safety and health conditions, including compliance with the Occupational Safety and Health Act (Act). The policy provides that the Agency will not routinely request self-audit reports at the initiation of an inspection, and the Agency will not use self-audit reports as a means of identifying hazards upon which to focus during an inspection. In addition, where a voluntary self-audit identifies a hazardous condition, and the employer has corrected the violative condition prior to the initiation of an inspection (or a related accident, illness, or injury that triggers the OSHA inspection) and has taken appropriate steps to prevent the recurrence of the condition, the Agency will refrain from issuing a citation, even if the violative condition existed within the six month limitations period during which OSHA is authorized to issue citations. Where a voluntary self-audit identifies a hazardous condition, and the employer promptly undertakes appropriate measures to correct the violative condition and to provide interim employee protection, but has not completely corrected the violative condition when an OSHA inspection occurs, the Agency will treat the audit report as evidence of good faith, and not as evidence of a willful violation of the Act.

FOR FURTHER INFORMATION CONTACT:
Richard E. Fairfax, Occupational Safety and Health Administration, Directorate of Compliance Programs, Room N–3603, U.S. Department of Labor, 200 Constitution Avenue, NW, Washington, DC 20210, Telephone: 202–693–2100.

SUPPLEMENTARY INFORMATION:

I. Background Information

On October 6, 1999, OSHA published a "Proposed Policy Statement Concerning the Occupational Safety and Health Administration's Use of Voluntary Employer Safety and Health Self-Audits" in the **Federal Register**. 64 FR 54358 (1999). The policy statement described the Agency's proposal regarding the manner in which it would treat voluntary employer self-audits that assess workplace safety and health conditions, including compliance with the Act. The proposed policy statement provided that the Agency would not routinely request voluntary employer self-audit reports at the initiation of an inspection. Further, the proposed policy provided that, where an employer identified a hazardous condition through a voluntary self-audit, and the employer promptly undertook appropriate corrective measures, OSHA would treat the audit report as evidence of good faith, and not as evidence of a willful violation. It was, and remains, the Agency's intention to develop and implement a policy that recognizes the value of voluntary self-audit programs that are designed to allow employers, or their agents, to identify and promptly correct hazardous conditions. In limited situations, however, documentation related to voluntary self-audits plays an important role in the Agency's ability to effectively and faithfully carry out its inspection and enforcement obligations under the Act.

Although the Agency is not required by the Administrative Procedures Act, 5 U.S.C. 551, *et seq.*, to engage in notice and comment rulemaking procedures prior to the adoption and implementation of this policy, OSHA requested public comment regarding its proposed policy statement in order to gain input and insight from employers, employees, employee representatives, and other interested parties. OSHA received and thoroughly reviewed comments from a variety of sources. The Agency has modified the proposed policy to incorporate those comments that further OSHA's dual purposes in proposing the voluntary self-audit policy—*i.e.*, to provide appropriate, positive treatment that is in accord with the value that voluntary self-audits have for employers' safety and health compliance efforts, while maintaining the Agency's authority to gain access to voluntary self-audit documentation in limited circumstances in which access is important to effectively and faithfully enforce the Act. The Agency has not incorporated those comments that it considered to be contrary to its purposes in proposing this policy or that it

OSHA's 2000 Self-Audit Policy *(cont'd)*

Federal Register / Vol. 65, No. 146 / Friday, July 28, 2000 / Notices   **46499**

considered to be beyond the scope of its intent in proposing the policy.

II. Substantive Modifications to the Proposed Policy

Based upon input that the Agency received from interested parties, OSHA has made several substantive changes to its proposed policy on the treatment of voluntary employer self-audits.

1. Modifications to Certain Definitions in the Policy

In the final policy, the Agency has defined the term "self-audit" to include health and safety audits conducted for an employer by a third party. In addition, in defining the terms "systematic" and "documented," the Agency has added the words "or for" before the phrase "the employer" to clarify that an audit conducted by a third party for an employer is covered by the final policy. OSHA values the role that independent safety and health professionals play in furthering occupational safety and health and encourages employers to utilize their services when appropriate.

The Agency has changed the definition of the word "objective" by deleting reference to "safety and health professional[s]" and by broadening the class of persons who may conduct an "objective" self-audit to include competent employees and management officials. Thus, in the final policy, a self-audit is "objective" if it is conducted "by or under the direction of an individual or group of individuals who are competent to identify workplace safety or health hazards, given the scope and complexity of the processes under review." This modification is responsive to suggestions from small business employers, organizations such as the National Advisory Committee on Occupational Safety and Health, and other members of the public. Employers, particularly small business employers, who might not have the financial resources to hire an independent consultant, may use their own personnel who do not have professional certification, but who do have the necessary experience or training to conduct an effective and thorough self-audit. In addition, the Agency recognizes the expertise that many joint labor-management safety committees have developed with respect to workplace safety and health issues and acknowledges that audits conducted by such committees should qualify for recognition under this policy.

2. Training for Compliance Safety and Health Officers

In the final policy, the Agency has added the following statement: "All OSHA personnel applying this policy will receive instruction in order to ensure the consistent and appropriate application of the policy." The Agency received comments from employers expressing their concerns regarding the potential for inconsistent implementation and application of the policy. OSHA agrees that an effective policy can be achieved only through consistent implementation and application. Thus, in the final policy, OSHA has explicitly stated that training will be provided, over a period of time, to all personnel who will apply this policy in order to ensure its consistent and proper implementation.

3. Citation Policy for Violative Conditions Identified and Corrected Through Voluntary Self-Audits

In response to numerous suggestions from commenters, the Agency has added a provision explicitly stating that OSHA will not issue citations for violative conditions discovered during a voluntary self-audit and corrected prior to the initiation of an inspection (or a related accident, illness, or injury that triggers the inspection), even if the violative condition existed within the six month limitations period during which OSHA is authorized to issue citations. OSHA encourages employers to conduct voluntary self-audits and to promptly correct all violations of the Act that are discovered in order to ensure safety and health in the workplace. Thus, in the final policy, the Agency has incorporated its current enforcement practice and will refrain from issuing a citation for a violative condition that an employer discovered as a result of a voluntary self-audit, if the employer corrects the condition prior to the initiation of an OSHA inspection (or a related accident, illness, or injury that triggers the OSHA inspection), and if the employer has taken appropriate steps to prevent a recurrence of the violative condition.

4. Employers' Prerogative to Voluntarily Provide Self-Audit Documentation

Several parties requested that the Agency provide that, in those situations in which the Agency has not requested or used voluntary self-audit documentation in conducting its inspection, employers be permitted to take advantage of the policy by providing the Agency with evidence of their voluntary self-audit program. Since OSHA inspectors rarely request

voluntary self-audit documentation when conducting inspections, and this policy states the Agency's intent that inspectors should request such documentation only in limited situations, OSHA recognizes that there will be a significant number of instances in which the Agency is unaware of an employer's voluntary self-audit activities, and thus the employer would not be considered for recognition under the policy. Therefore, the final policy provides that an employer voluntarily may provide the Agency with self-audit documentation, and the employer may be eligible to receive the benefits that are detailed in this policy.

III. Comments Not Incorporated Into Final Policy

A number of parties offered comments that have not been included in the final policy. While the Agency considered thoroughly each of the comments that it received, OSHA considered the following comments either to be inconsistent with the Agency's dual purposes in proposing the policy or to be beyond the scope of the proposed policy.

1. Employee Participation in the Voluntary Self-Audit Process

Two union representatives maintained that OSHA should require employers to disclose self-audit results to their employees and their representatives and that OSHA should not grant good faith credit to any employer who has not disclosed all of the audit results both to OSHA and to its employees. OSHA agrees that the interests of workplace safety and health are advanced when employers share self-audit results with employees and employee representatives. However, because this is not a rulemaking procedure, the Agency considers it to be inappropriate to use this policy to adopt a practice that may be deemed to modify the legal duties of employers. Moreover, insofar as the purpose of this statement is to clarify current OSHA practices and to provide appropriate, positive treatment that is in accord with the value of voluntary self-audits, the Agency believes that it may be counterproductive to impose additional requirements on employers in order to qualify for inclusion under the policy.

2. More Significant Proposed Penalty Reductions

Several parties suggested that OSHA should provide a more significant proposed penalty reduction for an employer's "good faith" by offering proposed penalty reductions in excess of 25 percent to employers who identify

OSHA's 2000 Self-Audit Policy *(cont'd)*

46500 **Federal Register** / Vol. 65, No. 146 / Friday, July 28, 2000 / Notices

violative conditions during voluntary self-audits and who have begun to correct the conditions, but who have not completed abatement prior to the initiation of an OSHA inspection. OSHA's current guidelines account for an employer's "good faith" when the Agency calculates a proposed penalty for a violation of the Act. These guidelines allow a penalty reduction of up to 25 percent in recognition of an employer's "good faith," if the employer has developed and implemented a written health and safety program, which provides for appropriate management commitment and employee involvement; worksite analysis for the purpose of hazard identification; hazard prevention and control measures; and safety and health training. The Agency has stated that it will treat a voluntary self-audit, which results in prompt corrective action and appropriate steps to prevent similar violations, as strong evidence of the employer's good faith with respect to the matters covered by the voluntary self-audit. However, a voluntary self-audit is only one of the many steps that employers can and do undertake to protect the health and safety of their employees, and OSHA does not believe that the goals of the Act would be furthered by an additional "good faith" penalty reduction that is keyed directly and exclusively to voluntary self-audits. Rather, the Agency believes that its current "good faith" penalty reduction provisions, in conjunction with the inherent advantages that employers gain by conducting voluntary self-audits and the treatment that this policy provides for voluntary self-audits, provide appropriate, positive recognition for voluntary self-audits.

3. *Total Prohibition Against the Use of Voluntary Self-Audit Documentation*

Many employers and employer associations stated that OSHA should refrain totally from using voluntary self-audit information as a part of the Agency's enforcement efforts under the Act. The Agency has not incorporated this comment into its policy because it believes that a complete prohibition is unnecessary in order to provide appropriate, positive treatment for voluntary self-audits. In addition, the Agency believes that, in some circumstances, a complete prohibition would prevent it from effectively enforcing the Act.

The implementation of this policy will publicly state the Agency's policy to request voluntary self-audit documentation only in limited situations. A substantial number of employers already conduct voluntary

self-audits for their own benefit and for the benefit of their employees. The Agency believes that this policy, with its explicit provisions concerning the Agency's use of voluntary self-audit documentation, will provide the assurances that additional employers may need in order to conduct voluntary self-audits. Indeed, under the policy, employers who respond promptly and appropriately to hazardous conditions that are identified in a voluntary self-audit can only be rewarded for having conducted the self-audit.

On the other hand, there are legitimate circumstances in which voluntary self-audit data are important to enable the Agency to effectively enforce the Act. For example, such information may allow an inspector, who has already identified a hazard, to determine the scope of the hazard or to assess the manner in which the condition can be abated. In addition, pursuant to Occupational Safety and Health Review Commission precedent, the Secretary of Labor has the obligation to demonstrate that an employer had knowledge of a cited violative condition, and, in certain situations, the obligation to demonstrate that an employer was so indifferent to recognized occupational health or safety hazards that more significant penalties are justified in order to effectuate the provisions of the Act. Thus, the Agency believes that a complete prohibition against the use of voluntary self-audit documentation would be an imprudent policy because it would hamper OSHA's ability to enforce the Act effectively.

4. *More Precisely Defined Limitations on the Agency's Use of Voluntary Self-Audit Documentation*

In the proposed policy statement, the Agency had proposed to "refrain from routinely requesting reports of voluntary self-audits at the initiation of an enforcement inspection." OSHA explained that it intended to seek access to such reports only in limited situations in which the Agency had an independent basis to believe that a specific safety or health hazard warrants investigation, and had determined that such records may be relevant to identify or determine the circumstances or nature of the hazardous condition. However, several employers asked that the Agency more precisely detail the specific situations in which its inspectors may request voluntary self-audit documentation.

The Agency has decided not to attempt to modify its proposed policy in this manner for several reasons. First, OSHA believes that, given the diversity of circumstances that inspectors

encounter in conducting thousands of workplace inspections each year, it is not feasible to comprehensively list or to describe with any specificity each of those situations in which it would be appropriate for an inspector to request voluntary self-audit documentation. Rather, the Agency believes that the implementation of this policy will provide sufficient specificity to assure employers that inspectors will seek voluntary self-audit documentation only in limited and generally defined situations. Second, OSHA recognizes the skill and experience of its inspectors and believes that it is essential for the Agency and its inspectors to have some discretion in implementing this policy in order to effectively and efficiently fulfill the Act's mandate to detect and identify occupational safety and health hazards. Third, in refraining from an attempt to more specifically define those discrete circumstances in which inspectors may request voluntary self-audit documentation, the Agency has adopted the comment offered by several employers and their representatives who expressed concern that such specificity may in practice increase the frequency with which inspectors request voluntary self-audit documentation, given the natural human inclination to interpret specific examples as situations in which a request for self-audit documentation is mandated, as opposed to merely permitted, pursuant to the policy.

5. *Adoption of a Formal Rule Regarding the Agency's Treatment of Voluntary Self-Audits*

Several commenters suggested that the Agency should adopt the "Final Policy Concerning the Occupational Safety and Health Administration's Treatment of Voluntary Employer Safety and Health Self-Audits" as a formal rule that would be legally binding on the Agency. However, OSHA has declined to incorporate this comment and believes that the policy, as adopted, provides sufficient assurance that employers who conduct voluntary self-audits, and who take prompt and appropriate steps to address occupational hazards that are identified in such audits, will not be penalized by OSHA for conducting voluntary self-audits. In addition, since this policy is an internal policy that is intended only to provide OSHA inspectors with guidance regarding the circumstances under which the Agency considers it appropriate to review and consider documentation generated by employers as a result of voluntary self-audits, the Agency believes it is imprudent and unnecessary to expend the time, money,

OSHA's 2000 Self-Audit Policy *(cont'd)*

Federal Register / Vol. 65, No. 146 / Friday, July 28, 2000 / Notices   **46501**

and other resources required to promulgate a formal rule. Finally, the Agency believes that a rule that creates legal rights for third parties would be more likely to produce unproductive litigation than will a policy that only provides guidance to OSHA inspectors. This type of litigation would not further the health and safety purposes of the Act.

6. No Citation for Partial or Planned Correction of Violative Conditions Identified through a Voluntary Self-Audit

A number of employers stated that the Agency should refrain from issuing a citation in any situation in which an employer has identified a hazardous condition and is in the process of correcting that condition, or has developed a plan or program for correcting that condition, at the time that OSHA conducts an inspection of the employer's facility. OSHA has decided not to incorporate this comment into the final policy for several reasons. First, the agency recognizes that the prompt correction of hazardous workplace conditions is essential for the prevention of occupational illnesses, injuries, and fatalities. The Agency is concerned that a policy that excuses an employer for an abatement plan alone, or for abatement actions that do not constitute the complete elimination of the hazard, may serve to diminish an employer's incentive to promptly and completely eliminate workplace hazards. Second, the Agency believes that such a policy would be inconsistent with the Act's mandate, which is to assure, so far as possible, safe and healthful working conditions for every working man and woman in the Nation. In enforcing the Act, OSHA only issues citations in cases in which employees actually are exposed to hazards associated with violative conditions. While the final policy recognizes that employers who identify hazardous conditions through the use of voluntary self-audits, and are in the process of correcting those hazards, may deserve a "good faith" reduction in the penalty that OSHA proposes for the violation, the Agency does not believe that the Act contemplates that OSHA will refrain totally from issuing citations in situations in which employees are working in an environment in which they are exposed to serious occupational hazards.

IV. Description of the Final Policy

The policy applies to audits (1) that are systematic, documented, and objective reviews conducted by, or for,

employers to review their operations and practices to ascertain compliance with the Act, and (2) that are not mandated by the Act, rules or orders issued pursuant to the Act, or settlement agreements. A systematic audit is planned, and it is designed to be appropriate to the scope of the hazards that it addresses and to provide a basis for corrective action. Ad hoc observations and other ad hoc communications concerning a hazardous condition made during the ordinary course of business are not included within the definition of a "self-audit" or "voluntary self-audit report." The findings resulting from the systematic self-audit must be documented contemporaneously (at the time the condition is discovered or immediately after completion of the audit) so as to assure that they receive prompt attention.

The self-audit also must be conducted by or supervised by a competent person who is capable of identifying the relevant workplace hazards. Employees or management officials who have the training or experience that is necessary to identify workplace safety or health hazards, given the scope and complexity of the processes under review, are considered to be competent persons under the policy, even though they may not maintain engineering, scientific, industrial hygiene, or other relevant professional accreditation.

In order to qualify for inclusion under the policy, a self-audit need not review or analyze an entire plant, facility, or operation. For example, a voluntary self-audit designed to identify hazards associated with a particular process or hazard (as opposed to an entire plant, facility, or operation) will qualify for consideration under the policy.

The policy provides that OSHA will not routinely request voluntary self-audit reports when initiating an inspection, and that the Agency will not use voluntary self-audit reports as a means of identifying hazards upon which to focus during an inspection. Rather, OSHA intends to seek access to such reports only in limited situations in which the Agency has an independent basis to believe that a specific safety or health hazard warrants investigation, and has determined that such records may be relevant to identify or determine the circumstances of the hazardous condition. For example, an inspector might seek access to self-audit documentation following a fatal or catastrophic accident when OSHA is investigating the circumstances of the accident to assess compliance and to assure that hazardous conditions are abated. Likewise, it would be consistent

with this policy to request self-audit documentation when the Agency has an independent basis for believing that a hazard exists. The Agency believes that this provision is responsive to the concerns of employers who sought assurances that OSHA would not use voluntary self-audit documentation during an inspection as a "road map" to identify violations of the Act.

OSHA emphasizes that it is not seeking through this policy to expand the situations in which it requests production of voluntary self-audit reports beyond its present practice. In addition, OSHA intends to seek access only to those audit reports, or portions of those reports, that are relevant to the particular matters that it is investigating.

OSHA has defined "voluntary self-audit report" to include information obtained in the audit, as well as analyses and recommendations. The effect is to include audit information in the documents that OSHA will not routinely request at the initiation of the inspection. OSHA has defined the term this way because the Agency believes that the definition responds to the concerns raised by employers about the effect of routine OSHA requests for voluntary self-audit findings.

The policy also contains provisions designed to assure that employers who respond with prompt corrective actions will receive corresponding benefits following an OSHA inspection. These provisions would come into play when OSHA obtains a voluntary self-audit report, either because the employer has voluntarily provided it to OSHA, as commonly occurs, or because OSHA has required production of the report. In response to public comment, OSHA has expressly stated in the final policy that employers may voluntarily provide OSHA with self-audit documentation and that those employers may be eligible to receive the benefits detailed in the policy.

The policy explains that OSHA will refrain from issuing a citation for a violative condition that an employer has discovered through a voluntary self-audit and has corrected prior to the initiation of an inspection (or a related accident, illness, or injury that triggers the inspection), if the employer also has taken appropriate steps to prevent the recurrence of the condition. In situations in which the corrective steps have not been completed at the time of the inspection, OSHA will treat the voluntary self-audit report as evidence of good faith, not as evidence of a willful violation, provided that the employer has responded promptly with appropriate corrective action to the violative conditions identified in the

OSHA's 2000 Self-Audit Policy *(cont'd)*

46502   **Federal Register** / Vol. 65, No. 146 / Friday, July 28, 2000 / Notices

audit. Accordingly, if the employer is responding in good faith and in a timely manner to correct a violative condition discovered in a voluntary self-audit, and OSHA detects the condition during an inspection, OSHA will not use the report as evidence of willfulness. A timely, good faith response includes promptly taking diligent steps to correct the violative condition, while providing effective interim employee protection, as necessary.

OSHA will treat a voluntary self-audit that results in prompt corrective action of the nature described above and appropriate steps to prevent similar violations, as strong evidence of the employer's good faith with respect to the matters addressed. Good faith is one of the statutory factors that OSHA is directed to take into account in assessing penalties. 29 U.S.C. 666(j). Where OSHA finds good faith, OSHA's Field Inspection Reference Manual (the "FIRM") authorizes up to a 25 percent reduction in the penalty that otherwise would be assessed. The FIRM treats the presence of a comprehensive safety and health program as a primary indicator of good faith. A comprehensive safety and health program includes voluntary self-audits, but is broader in concept, covering additional elements. In this policy, OSHA has concluded that a voluntary self-audit/correction program is evidence of good faith. OSHA believes that the policy will provide appropriate positive recognition of the value of voluntary self-audits, while simultaneously enabling the Agency to enforce the provisions of the Occupational Safety and Health Act effectively.

V. Final Policy Concerning the Occupational Safety and Health Administration's Treatment of Voluntary Employer Safety and Health Self-Audits

A. Purpose

1. This policy statement describes how the Occupational Safety and Health Administration (OSHA) will treat voluntary self-audits in carrying out Agency civil enforcement activities. Voluntary self-audits, properly conducted, may discover conditions that violate the Occupational Safety and Health Act (Act) so that those conditions can be corrected promptly and similar violations prevented from occurring in the future. This policy statement is intended to provide appropriate, positive treatment that is in accord with the value voluntary self-audits have for employers' safety and health compliance efforts, while also recognizing that access to relevant

information is important to the Secretary of Labor's inspection and enforcement duties under the Act.

2. This policy statement sets forth factors that guide OSHA in exercising its informed discretion to request and use the information contained in employers' voluntary self-audit reports. All OSHA personnel applying this policy will receive instruction in order to ensure the consistent and appropriate application of the policy. The policy statement is not a final Agency action. It is intended only as general, internal OSHA guidance, and is to be applied flexibly, in light of all appropriate circumstances. It does not create any legal rights, duties, obligations, or defenses, implied or otherwise, for any party, or bind the Agency.

3. This policy statement has four main components:

(a.) It explains that OSHA will refrain from routinely requesting reports of voluntary self-audits at the initiation of an enforcement inspection;

(b.) It explains that OSHA will refrain from issuing a citation for a violative condition that an employer has discovered through a voluntary self-audit and has corrected prior to the initiation of an OSHA inspection (or a related accident, illness, or injury that triggers the inspection), if the employer also has taken appropriate steps to prevent the recurrence of the condition;

(c.) It contains a safe-harbor provision under which, if an employer is responding in good faith to a violative condition identified in a voluntary self-audit report, and OSHA discovers the violation during an enforcement inspection, OSHA will not treat that portion of the report as evidence of willfulness;

(d.) It describes how an employer's response to a voluntary self-audit may be considered evidence of good faith, qualifying the employer for a substantial civil penalty reduction, when OSHA determines a proposed penalty. *See* 29 U.S.C. 666(j). Under this section of the Act, a proposed penalty for an alleged violation is calculated giving due consideration to the "good faith" of the employer.

B. Definitions

1. "Self-Audit" means a systematic, documented, and objective review by or for an employer of its operations and practices related to meeting the requirements of the Act.

(a.) "Systematic" means that the self-audit is part of a planned effort to prevent, identify, and correct workplace safety and health hazards. A systematic self-audit is designed by or for the employer to be appropriate to the scope

of hazards it is aimed at discovering, and to provide an adequate basis for corrective action;

(b.) "Documented" means that the findings of the self-audit are recorded contemporaneously and maintained by or for the employer;

(c.) "Objective" means that the self-audit is conducted by or under the direction of an individual or group of individuals who are competent to identify workplace safety or health hazards, given the scope and complexity of the processes under review.

2. "Voluntary" means that the self-audit is not required by statute, rule, order, or settlement agreement. Voluntary self-audits may assess compliance with substantive legal requirements (e.g., an audit to assess overall compliance with the general machine guarding requirement in 29 CFR 1910.212).

3. "Voluntary self-audit report" means the written information, analyses, conclusions, and recommendations resulting from a voluntary self-audit, but does not include matters required to be disclosed to OSHA by the records access rule, 29 CFR 1910.1020, or other rules.

4. "Good faith" response means an objectively reasonable, timely, and diligent effort to comply with the requirements of the Act and OSHA standards.

C. OSHA's Treatment of Voluntary Self-Audit Reports

1. No Routine Initial Request for Voluntary Self-Audit Reports

(a.) OSHA will not routinely request voluntary self-audit reports at the initiation of an inspection. OSHA will not use such reports as a means of identifying hazards upon which to focus inspection activity.

(b.) However, if the Agency has an independent basis to believe that a specific safety or health hazard warranting investigation exists. OSHA may exercise its authority to obtain the relevant portions of voluntary self-audit reports relating to the hazard.

(c.) An employer voluntarily may provide OSHA with self-audit documentation and may be eligible to receive the benefits that are detailed in this policy.

2. No Citations for Violative Conditions Discovered During a Voluntary Self-Audit and Corrected Prior to an Inspection (or a Related Accident, Illness, or Injury That Triggers the Inspection)

It is OSHA's current enforcement practice to refrain from issuing a citation for a violative condition that an

OSHA's 2000 Self-Audit Policy *(cont'd)*

Federal Register / Vol. 65, No. 146 / Friday, July 28, 2000 / Notices   **46503**

employer has corrected prior to the initiation of an OSHA inspection (and prior to a related accident, illness, or injury that triggers the inspection), if the employer has taken appropriate steps to prevent a recurrence of the violative condition, even if the violative condition existed within the six month limitations period during which OSHA is authorized to issue citations. Consistent with this enforcement practice, OSHA will not issue a citation for a violative condition that an employer has discovered as a result of a voluntary self-audit, if the employer has corrected the violative condition prior to the initiation of an inspection (and prior to a related accident, illness, or injury that triggers the inspection) and has taken appropriate steps to prevent a recurrence of the violative condition that was discovered during the voluntary self-audit.

3. Safe Harbor—No Use of Voluntary Self-Audit Reports as Evidence of Willfulness

A violation is considered willful if the employer has intentionally violated a requirement of the Act, shown reckless disregard for whether it was in violation of the Act, or demonstrated plain indifference to employee safety and health. Consistent with the prevailing law on willfulness, if an employer is responding in good faith to a violative condition discovered through a voluntary self-audit and OSHA detects the condition during an inspection, OSHA will not use the voluntary self-audit report as evidence that the violation is willful.

This policy is intended to apply when, through a voluntary self-audit, the employer learns that a violative condition exists and promptly takes diligent steps to correct the violative condition and bring itself into compliance, while providing effective interim employee protection, as necessary.

4. "Good Faith" Penalty Reduction

Under the Act, an employer's good faith normally reduces the amount of the penalty that otherwise would be assessed for a violation. 29 U.S.C. 666(j). OSHA's FIRM provides up to a 25 percent penalty reduction for employers who have implemented an effective safety and health program, including voluntary self-audits. OSHA will treat a voluntary self-audit that results in prompt action to correct violations found, in accordance with paragraph C.3. above, and appropriate steps to prevent similar violations, as strong evidence of an employer's good faith with respect to the matters covered by

the voluntary self-audit. This policy does not apply to repeat violations.

D. Federal Program Change

This policy statement describes a Federal OSHA Program change for which State adoption is not required; however, in the interest of national consistency, States are encouraged to adopt a similar policy regarding voluntary self-audits.

E. Effective Date

This policy is effective July 28, 2000.

This document was prepared under the direction of Charles N. Jeffress, Assistant Secretary for Occupational Safety and Health, US Department of Labor, 200 Constitution Avenue, NW., Washington, DC 20210.

Signed at Washington, D.C. this 24th day of July, 2000.

Charles N. Jeffress,

Assistant Secretary of Labor.

[FR Doc. 00–19067 Filed 7–27–00; 8:45 am]

BILLING CODE 4510–26–P

LEGAL SERVICES CORPORATION

Sunshine Act Meeting of the Board of Directors

TIME AND DATE: The Legal Services Corporation's Board of Directors will meet by teleconference on Tuesday, August 1, 2000, at 4 p.m. EDT.

STATUS OF MEETING: Open.

LOCATION: Members of the Board will participate by way of telephonic conferencing equipment allowing them all to hear one another. Members of the Corporation's staff and the public will be able to hear and participate in the meeting by means of telephonic conferencing equipment set up for this purpose in the Corporation's Conference Room, on the 11th floor of 750 First Street, NE., Washington, DC 20002.

MATTERS TO BE CONSIDERED:

1. Approval of agenda.

2. Consider and act on a proposed resolution recognizing and thanking the law firm of Nelson, Mullins, Riley & Scarborough for their *pro bono* representation of LSC in the case of *Regional Management Corp. et al.* v. *Legal Services Corporation.*

3. Consider and act on a proposed resolution recognizing and thanking the law firm of Porter, Wright, Morris & Arthur for their *pro bono* representation of LSC in the case of *Ashtabula County Legal Aid Corporation* v. *Legal Services Corporation.*

4. Consider and act on proposed extension of John McKay's tenure as President of LSC to September 30, 2001.

5. Consider and act on other business.

CONTACT PERSON FOR INFORMATION: Victor M. Fortuno, Vice President for Legal Affairs, General Counsel & Secretary, (202) 336–8800.

SPECIAL NEEDS: Upon request, meeting notices will be made available in alternate formats to accommodate visual and hearing impairments. Individuals who have a disability and need an accommodation to attend the meeting may notify Shannon N. Adaway, at (202) 336–8800.

Dated: July 25, 2000.

Victor M. Fortuno,

Vice President of Legal Affairs, General Counsel & Corporate Secretary.

[FR Doc. 00–19200 Filed 7–25–00; 4:59 pm]

BILLING CODE 7050–01–P

NATIONAL FOUNDATION ON THE ARTS AND THE HUMANITIES

Privacy Act of 1974: Republication of Notice of Systems of Records

AGENCY: National Endowment for the Arts.

ACTION: Notice of republication of systems of records, proposed systems of records, and new routine uses.

SUMMARY: The National Endowment for the Arts (Endowment) is publishing a notice of its systems of records with descriptions of the systems and the ways in which they are maintained, as required by the Privacy Act of 1974, 5 U.S.C. 552a(e)(4). This notice reflects administrative changes that have been made at the Endowment since the last publication of a notice of its systems of records. This notice also will enable individuals who wish to access information maintained in Endowment systems to make accurate and specific requests for such information.

DATES: In accordance with 5 U.S.C. 552a(r), on July 17, 2000, the Endowment filed a report as to the changes proposed in this notice with the Committee on Government Reform of the House of Representatives; the Committee on Governmental Affairs of the Senate; and the Administrator, Office of Information and Regulatory Affairs, Office of Management and Budget (OMB). The proposed changes to the Endowment's systems of records will become effective 40 days from the date the report was submitted to Congress and the OMB, or 30 days from the date of this publication in the **Federal Register**, whichever is later.

ADDRESSES: Karen Elias; Deputy General Counsel; National Endowment for the Arts; 1100 Pennsylvania Avenue, NW;

SAMPLE EPCRA AUDIT PROTOCOL

Note: Appendix A to this protocol is not provided in this text. The entirety of this protocol is available from Government Institutes or at the U.S. EPA website (www.epa.gov).

United States Environmental Protection Agency	Enforcement and Compliance Assurance (2224A)	EPA-305-B-98-007 December 1998

♻EPA

Protocol for Conducting Environmental Compliance Audits under the Emergency Planning and Community Right-to-Know Act

EPA Office of Compliance

Protocol for Conducting Environmental Compliance Audits under EPCRA

Notice

This document has been developed to assist in conducting environmental audits. The use of this document should be restricted to environmental audits only. For example, areas such as safety, transportation, occupational health, and fire protection are mentioned solely for clarification purposes. It is a summary of environmental regulations under EPCRA, but it is not a substitute for a comprehensive knowledge of the regulations themselves. Any variation between applicable regulations and the summaries contained in this guidance document are unintentional, and, in the case of such variations, the requirements of the regulations govern.

This document is intended solely as guidance to explain performance objectives for environmental auditors. Following the steps set forth in this guidance generally should result in compliance with those aspects of the regulations that it covers. The U.S. Environmental Protection Agency (EPA) does not make any guarantee or assume any liability with respect to the use of any information or recommendations contained in this document. Regulated entities requiring additional information or advice should consult a qualified professional.

This guidance does not constitute rulemaking by the EPA and may not be relied on to create a substantive or procedural right or benefit enforceable, at law or in equity, by any person. EPA may take action at variance with this guidance and its internal procedures.

Acknowledgments

EPA would like to gratefully acknowledge the support of the U.S. Army Corps of Engineers Construction Engineering Research Laboratories (CERL) for providing suggestions for the overall format of this document. In addition, acknowledgment is given to the representatives of the Chemical Manufacturers Association (CMA) who contributed their comments.

Protocol for Conducting Environmental Compliance Audits under EPCRA

Table of Contents

Protocol for Conducting Environmental Compliance Audits under EPCRA

Section I
Introduction

Background

The Environmental Protection Agency (EPA) is responsible for ensuring that businesses and organizations comply with federal laws that protect the public health and the environment. Recently, EPA has begun combining traditional enforcement activities with more innovative compliance approaches. In its Strategic Plan, the Agency recognizes the need to assist the regulated community by providing compliance assistance and guidance that will promote improved compliance and overall environmental performance (see Exhibit 1). EPA encourages regulated entities to recognize compliance as the floor, rather than the ceiling, of environmental performance by internalizing and implementing sound environmental practices. As part of that effort, EPA is encouraging the development of self-assessment programs at individual facilities. Voluntary audit programs play an important role in helping companies meet their obligation to comply with environmental requirements. Such assessments can be a critical link, not only to improved compliance, but also to improvements in other aspects of an organization's performance. For example, environmental audits may identify pollution prevention opportunities that can substantially reduce an organization's operating costs.

Over the years, EPA has encouraged regulated entities to initiate environmental audit programs that support and document compliance with environmental regulations. EPA has developed this audit protocol to provide regulated entities with specific guidance in periodically evaluating their compliance with federal environmental requirements.

Exhibit 1 - EPA's Credible Deterrent Goal

Within its Strategic Plan, EPA has established a goal to ensure full compliance with the laws intended to protect human health and the environment. Within the framework of this goal, EPA's objectives are as follows:
- Identify and reduce significant non-compliance in high priority program areas, while maintaining a strong enforcement presence in all regulatory program areas,
- Promote the regulated communities' voluntary compliance with environmental requirements through compliance incentives and assistance programs.

EPA's Policy on Environmental Audits

In 1986, in an effort to encourage the use of environmental auditing, EPA published its "Environmental Auditing Policy Statement" (see 51 FR 25004). The 1986 audit policy states that "it is EPA policy to encourage the use of environmental auditing by regulated industries to help achieve and maintain compliance with environmental laws and regulation, as well as to help identify and correct unregulated environmental hazards." In addition, EPA defined environmental auditing as a systematic, documented, periodic, and objective review of facility operations and practices related to meeting environmental requirements. The policy also identified several objectives for environmental audits:
- verifying compliance with environmental requirements,
- evaluating the effectiveness of in-place environmental management systems, and
- assessing risks from regulated and unregulated materials and practices.

This document is intended solely for guidance. No statutory or regulatory requirements are in any way altered by any statement(s) contained herein.

ii

Protocol for Conducting Environmental Compliance Audits under EPCRA

Exhibit 2 – EPA's 1995 Audit Policy

Under the final Audit/Self Policing Policy, EPA will not seek gravity-based penalties and will not recommend criminal prosecutions for companies that meet the requirements of the policy. Gravity-based penalties represent the "seriousness" or punitive portion of penalties over and above the portion representing the economic gain from non-compliance. The policy requires companies:

- to promptly disclose and correct violations,
- to prevent recurrence of the violation, and
- to remedy environmental harm.

The policy excludes:

- repeated violations,
- violations that result in serious actual harm, and
- violations that may present an imminent and substantial endangerment.

Corporations remain criminally liable for violations resulting from conscious disregard of their legal duties, and individuals remain liable for criminal wrongdoing. EPA retains discretion to recover the economic benefit gained as a result of noncompliance, so that companies will not be able to obtain an economic advantage over their competitors by delaying investment in compliance. Where violations are discovered by means other than environmental audits or due diligence efforts, but are promptly disclosed and expeditiously corrected, EPA will reduce gravity-based penalties by 75% provided that all of the other conditions of the policy are met.

As a result of EPA's new audit policy, through March 1998, 247 companies have disclosed environmental violations at more than 760 facilities and EPA has reduced or waived penalties for 89 companies and 433 facilities.

The final Audit/Self-Policing Policy was published in the Federal Register on December 22, 1995 (60 FR 66706). It took effect on January 22, 1996. For further information, contact the Audit Policy Docket at (202) 260-7548 or call (202) 564-4187.

In 1995, EPA published "Incentives for Self-Policing: Discovery. Disclosure, Correction and Prevention of Violations" which both reaffirmed and expanded its 1986 audit policy. The 1995 audit policy offers major incentives for entities to discover, disclose and correct environmental violations. Under the 1995 policy, EPA will not seek gravity-based penalties or recommend criminal charges be brought for violations that are discovered through an "environmental audit" (as defined in the 1986 audit policy) or a management system reflecting "due diligence" and that are promptly disclosed and corrected, provided that other important safeguards are met (see Exhibit 2). These safeguards protect health and the environment by precluding policy relief for violations that cause serious environmental harm or may have presented imminent and substantial endangerment, for example.

Purpose of the Protocols for Conducting Environmental Compliance Audits

This protocol, which is part of a set containing other area or statutory specific audit protocols, is a tool to assist you in conducting environmental audits, which should inform you whether your facility is in compliance with federal regulations. EPA has developed these audit protocols to assist and encourage businesses and organizations to perform environmental audits and disclose violations in accordance with EPA's audit policy. The audit protocols are intended to promote consistency among regulated entities when conducting environmental audits and to ensure that audits are conducted in a thorough and comprehensive manner.

Protocol for Conducting Environmental Compliance Audits under EPCRA

Each protocol provides guidance on key requirements, defines regulatory terms, and gives an overview of the federal laws affecting a particular environmental management area. It also includes a checklist containing detailed procedures for conducting a review of facility conditions. In order to use these documents effectively, you should be familiar with basic environmental auditing practices and the relevant environmental regulations under Title 40 of the Code of Federal Regulations (CFR). The audit protocols are not intended to be exclusive or limiting with respect to procedures that may be followed. EPA recognizes that other audit approaches and techniques may be effective in identifying and evaluating a facility's environmental status and in formulating recommendations to correct observed deficiencies.

These protocols can be used as a basis to implement, upgrade, or benchmark environmental management activities. The protocols are a management tool for measuring and improving environmental performance by correcting deficiencies uncovered by the audit (see Exhibit 3). This process is perhaps the key element to a high quality environmental management program and will function best when an organization identifies the "root causes" of each audit finding. Root causes are those breakdowns in management oversight, information exchange, and evaluation that allow environmental problems to recur. Thus, while an organization may have developed an excellent record of dealing with a symptom, such as spill response, the underlying problem or "root cause" has not been addressed. Furthermore, identifying the root cause of an audit finding can mean identifying not only the failures that require correction but also the successes. In each case a root cause analysis should uncover the failures while promoting the successes so that an organization can make continual progress toward environmental excellence.

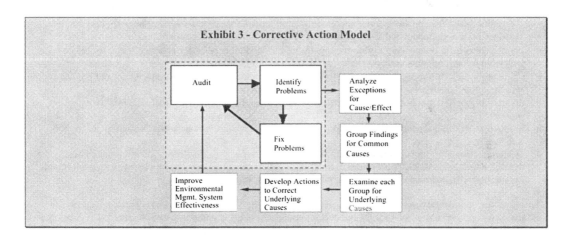

Exhibit 3 - Corrective Action Model

How to Use This Protocol

To conduct effective compliance audits, the auditor or audit team needs to possess sound working knowledge of the operations and processes to be reviewed, the relevant regulations that apply to a given facility, and of acceptable auditing practices. The audit protocol should be used as a planning tool to assist the auditor in understanding the requirements for conducting a comprehensive audit. This document will provide the user with a generic audit approach to regulatory issues that may require closer examination. Once the general issues are identified through the use of this protocol, the auditor should perform a more detailed investigation to determine the specific area of noncompliance to be corrected. The auditor should review federal, state and local

This document is intended solely for guidance. No statutory or regulatory requirements are in any way altered by any statement(s) contained herein.

iv

Protocol for Conducting Environmental Compliance Audits under EPCRA

environmental requirements and annotate the protocol, as required, to include other applicable requirements not included in the protocol.

The auditor also should determine which regulatory agency has authority for implementing an environmental program so that the proper set of regulations is consulted. State programs that implement federally mandated programs may contain more stringent requirements. This protocol should not be used as a substitute for the applicable regulations.

The collective set of the audit protocols developed by EPA is designed to support a wide range of environmental auditing needs; therefore several of the protocols in this set or sections of an individual protocol may not be applicable to a particular facility. Each protocol is not intended to be an exhaustive set of procedures; rather it is meant to inform the auditor, about the degree and quality of evaluation essential to a thorough environmental audit. EPA is aware that other audit approaches may provide an effective means of identifying and assessing facility environmental status and in developing corrective actions.

Each protocol contains the following information:
- List of acronyms and abbreviations used in the document,
- Applicability - provides guidance on the major activities and operations included in the protocol and a brief description of how the protocol is applied,
- Review of federal legislation - identifies key issues associated with the subject protocol area,
- State and local regulations - identifies typical issues normally addressed in state and local regulations but does not present individual state/local requirements,
- Key compliance requirements - summarizes the overall thrust of the regulations for that particular protocol,
- Key compliance definitions - defines important terms,
- Typical records to review - highlights documents, permits and other pertinent paperwork that should be reviewed by an auditor and reconciled against regulatory requirements,
- Typical physical features to inspect - highlights pollution control equipment, manufacturing and process equipment and other areas that should be visited and evaluated during an audit,
- Index for checklist users - outlines different areas of the checklist that may pertain to the facility being audited,
- Checklist - matches the regulatory requirements with the tasks that should be accomplished by the auditor, and
- Appendices - supporting information for the checklist (e.g., regulatory deadlines, lists of contaminants, wastes, and required testing procedures). Note: information contained in the appendices is dated and should be verified with a current version of the applicable federal regulations.

The checklist delineates what should be evaluated during an audit. The left column states either a requirement mandated by regulation or a good management practice that exceeds the requirements of the federal regulations. Good management practices are distinguished from regulatory requirements in the checklist by the acronym (MP) and are printed in italics. The regulatory citation is given in parentheses after the requirement. The right column gives instructions to help conduct the evaluation. These instructions are performance objectives that should be accomplished by the auditor. Some of the performance objectives may be simple documentation checks that take only a few minutes; others may require a time-intensive physical inspection of a facility.

EPA is presently is the process of developing a series of audit protocol application guides to serve as companion documents to the set of protocols. The application guides will provide the auditor with a matrix that identifies and cross-references certain site-specific activities or unit operations with particular environmental aspects of that activity. For example, managing hazardous waste containers is a site-specific activity with environmental concerns, such as possible releases to air, and water, that may require additional review through auditing. By using the application guide the user can identify facility specific practices that require more in-depth review. In

Protocol for Conducting Environmental Compliance Audits under EPCRA

addition, the application guides will also direct the user to specific protocols and sections (e.g., checklist items) of the protocol to determine areas that are regulated and require auditing.

List of Acronyms and Abbreviations

CAA	Clean Air Act
CAS	Chemical Abstract Service
CERCLA	Comprehensive Environmental Response, Compensation, and Liability Act (or Superfund)
CFR	Code of Federal Regulations
CWA	Clean Water Act
EHS	Extremely hazardous substance
EPA	Environmental Protection Agency
EPCRA	Emergency Planning and Community Right-to-Know Act of 1986
FR	Federal Register
gal.	Gallon
kg	Kilogram
lb.	Pound
LEPC	Local Emergency Planning Committee
MP	Management practice
MSDS	Material Data Safety Sheet
NOV	Notice of violation
NRC	National Response Center
OSHA	Occupational Health and Safety Act
PAC	Polycyclic aromatic compound
POTW	Publicly owned treatment works
PPA	Pollution Prevention Act of 1990
RCRA	Resource Conservation and Recovery Act
RQ	Reportable quantity
SARA	Superfund Amendments and Reauthorization Act of 1986
SERC	State Emergency Response Commission
SIC	Standard Industrial Classification
SPCC	Spill Prevention, Control and Countermeasures
TPQ	Threshold planning quantity
TRI	Toxic release inventory
yr	Year

Section II
Audit Protocol

Applicability

This protocol addresses facilities that manufacture, process, store, or otherwise use extremely hazardous substances (EHSs) defined in 40 CFR 355, hazardous chemicals defined in 29 CFR 1910.1200, and toxic chemicals defined in 40 CFR 372.

There are numerous environmental regulatory requirements administered by federal, state, and local governments. Each level of government may have a major impact on areas at the facility that are subject to the audit. Therefore, auditors are advised to review federal, state, and local regulations in order to perform a comprehensive assessment.

Federal Legislation

Emergency Planning and Community Right-to-Know Act of 1986 (EPCRA)
This act, also known as SARA Title III, was designed to promote emergency planning and preparedness at both the state and local level. It provides citizens, local governments, and local response authorities with information regarding the potential hazards in their community. EPCRA requires the use of emergency planning and designates state and local governments as recipients of information regarding certain chemicals used in the community. EPCRA has four major components:
- Emergency planning (Sections 301-303)
- Emergency release notification (Section 304)
- Community right-to-know reporting (Sections 311-312)
- Toxic chemical release reporting (Section 313)

Pollution Prevention Act of 1990 (PPA)
The goals of PPA were the following: preventing or reducing pollution at the source whenever feasible; pollution that cannot be prevented should be recycled in an environmentally safe manner whenever feasible; pollution that cannot be prevented or recycled should be treated in an environmentally safe manner whenever feasible; and disposal or other release into the environment should be employed only as a last resort and conducted in an environmentally safe manner. Section 6607 of the PPA requires owners or operators of facilities who have to file an annual toxic chemical release form (Form R) under EPCRA Section 313 to include a toxic chemical source reduction and recycling report for the preceding calendar year which has been incorporated into the Form R.

State/Local Regulations

State and local emergency response agencies may establish additional and/or more stringent reporting requirements under Section 312 of EPCRA and may require the use of state-specific reporting forms.

Key Compliance Requirements

Emergency Planning (40 CFR 355.30) (EPCRA Section 302)
A facility with quantities of extremely hazardous substances equal to or greater than the limits found in the third column of Appendix A is required to notify the state emergency response commission within 60 days that the facility is subject to emergency planning requirements. The facility must designate a representative to participate in local emergency planning as a facility emergency response coordinator. The facility must also submit additional information

This document is intended solely for guidance. No statutory or regulatory requirements are in any way altered by any statement(s) contained herein.

1

Protocol for Conducting Environmental Compliance Audits under EPCRA

to the local emergency planning committee upon request and notify them of any changes at the facility which might be relevant to emergency planning (i.e., designation of the emergency response coordinator, material changes in inventory) (40 CFR 355.10-355.30 and 355 Appendices A & B).

Emergency Release Notification (40 CFR 355.40) (EPCRA Section 304)
Under Section 304 of EPCRA, a facility which produces, uses, or stores a hazardous chemical must immediately notify the designated state and local emergency response authorities if there is a release of a listed EHS or a hazardous substance that equals or exceeds the reportable quantity for that substance. Refer to Appendix A column 4 or 40 CFR 355 Appendices A & B for the EHSs. The hazardous substances are designated under CERCLA (see Appendix A column 5 or 40 CFR 302 Table 302.4). If the release is a CERCLA-listed hazardous substance, the National Response Center (NRC) in Washington, DC, must also be notified (1-800-424-8802). If the release is transportation-related, a 911 call will meet the requirement of notification to the state and local authorities. The NRC must always be contacted for reportable transportation-related releases.

The initial notice should give as much information as possible about the release as long as notification is not delayed. The initial notification of a release can be made by telephone, radio, or in person, but must be followed by a written notice to the state and local emergency response authorities as soon as practicable (40 CFR 355.40(b)(3)).

Community Right-to-Know Requirements
• **MSDS Reporting** (40 CFR 370.21)
Under Section 311 of EPCRA, those facilities which are required under OSHA's Hazard Communication Standard regulations to prepare or have Material Safety Data Sheets (MSDSs) available are also required to submit copies of the MSDSs (or corresponding lists as described below) to the state emergency response commission (SERC), local emergency planning committee (LEPC), and the fire department with jurisdiction over the facility. MSDSs (or corresponding lists) must be submitted for each hazardous chemical present at the facility according to the following thresholds:

• All hazardous chemicals present at the facility at any one time in amounts equal to or greater than 10,000 lb. (4540 kg) (Note: not all hazardous chemicals requiring an MSDS are listed in Appendix A; these are chemicals designated by OSHA under 29 CFR 1910.1200), and
• All extremely hazardous substances present at the facility in amounts equal to or greater than 500 lb. (227 kg - approximately 55 gallons) or the threshold planning quantity, whichever is lower (see Appendix A column 3).

If a hazardous chemical is present in a mixture, the facility can either provide information on the mixture or on each hazardous chemical component of the mixture.

Instead of submitting the MSDSs, the facility can submit a list of hazardous chemicals for which MSDSs are required, grouped by hazard category (e.g., immediate health hazard, delayed health hazard, fire hazard, sudden release of pressure hazard, and reactive hazard). The list must include the chemical or common name of each substance. If the facility provides a list, it must provide a copy of the MSDS for any chemical on the list within 30 days of a request from the local emergency planning committee.

If a new hazardous chemical exceeds the threshold limit or significant new information is discovered, the facility has 3 months to submit the revised list of chemicals or new MSDS.

• **Inventory Reporting** (40 CFR 370.25, 370.40, 370.41)
Under Section 312 of EPCRA, those facilities which are required under OSHA's Hazard Communication Standard regulations to prepare or have MSDSs available are also required to submit annual emergency and hazardous chemical inventory forms to the state emergency response commission, the local emergency planning committee, and the fire department which has jurisdiction over the facility. The Tier I form includes chemical categories, quantities, and locations of hazardous chemicals on-site. More detailed information may be requested by emergency response organizations, in which case facilities must submit a Tier II form within 30 days. Facilities also can choose to submit the Tier II form instead of a Tier I report. Either report must be submitted on or before March 1 of each year.

This document is intended solely for guidance. No statutory or regulatory requirements are in any way altered by any statement(s) contained herein.

2

Protocol for Conducting Environmental Compliance Audits under EPCRA

The information in these reports does not include accidental releases or permitted discharges and is specifically targeted toward hazardous chemicals requiring MSDSs that are present on-site above the following threshold levels:

- All hazardous chemicals present at the facility at any one time in amounts equal to or greater than 10,000 lb. (4540 kg) (Note: not all hazardous chemicals requiring an MSDS are listed in Appendix A), and
- All extremely hazardous substances present at the facility in amounts equal to or greater than 500 lb. (227 kg - approximately 55 gallons) or the threshold planning quantity, whichever is lower (see Appendix A column 3).

Facilities who submit inventory forms must allow the fire department to inspect the site upon request and must provide specific location information about hazardous chemicals at the facility.

Toxic Chemical Release Reporting (40 CFR 372)
Section 313 of EPCRA and Section 6607 of the PPA require certain facilities to report to the federal and state governments the annual quantity of toxic chemicals (listed in 40 CFR 372.65) entering each environmental medium, either through normal operations or as the result of an accident, quantities transferred offsite in waste, as well as other information. Facilities subject to this requirement must submit to EPA and state officials a toxic chemical release form (Form R) for each toxic chemical manufactured, processed, or otherwise used in quantities exceeding minimum threshold values during the preceding calendar year. Facilities that have a "reportable waste quantity" of 500 pounds of a listed toxic chemical may take advantage of an alternate threshold of one million pounds. If the facility does not manufacture, process or otherwise use more than one million pounds, it may certify by filing a Form A certification statement rather than a Form R. Releases that must be reported include those to air, water, and land (including land disposal and underground injection). In addition, discharges to a POTW and transfers to off-site locations for treatment, disposal, energy recovery, and recycling must also be reported. Facilities must also report on the quantities of the chemicals treated, recycled, or combusted for energy recovery on-site.

Form R/Form A reports must be submitted to both the EPA and the state on or before July 1. Copies of Form R/Form A reports and related documentation must be kept at the facility for three years after the report is submitted.

The Pollution Prevention Act requires facilities subject to Form R/Form A reporting to also submit information on source reduction.

For further information regarding the EPCRA regulations, contact U.S. EPA's EPCRA, RCRA/UST, and Superfund Hotline at 800-424-9346 (or 703-412-9810 in the D.C. area) from 9 a.m. to 6 p.m., Monday through Friday.

This EPA hotline provides up-to-date information on regulations developed under EPCRA, as well as RCRA, CERCLA (Superfund), and the Oil Pollution Act. The hotline can assist with Section 112(r) of the Clean Air Act (CAA) and Spill Prevention, Control and Countermeasures (SPCC) regulations. The hotline also responds to requests for relevant documents and can direct the caller to additional tools that provide a more detailed discussion of specific regulatory requirements.

Key Terms and Definitions (40 CFR 355.20, 370.2, 372.3)

Commission or State Emergency Response Commission (SERC)
As of April 17, 1987, the governor of each state was required to have appointed a State Emergency Response Commissioner. For Indian tribes, commission means the emergency response commission for the tribe under whose jurisdiction the facility is located. In absence of an emergency response commission, the governor and the chief executive officer, respectively, shall be the commission. Where there is a cooperative agreement between a state and a tribe, the commission shall be the entity identified in the agreement.

Protocol for Conducting Environmental Compliance Audits under EPCRA

Committee or Local Emergency Planning Committee (LEPC)
The local emergency planning committee appointed by the state emergency response commission.

Extremely Hazardous Substance
A substance listed in Appendices A and B of 40 CFR 355.

Facility
All buildings, equipment, structures, and other stationary items that are located on a single site or on contiguous or adjacent sites and which are owned or operated by the same person (or by any person which controls, is controlled by, or under common control with, such person). A facility may contain more than one establishment. Facility shall include manmade structures as well as all natural structures in which chemicals are purposefully placed or removed through human means such that it functions as a containment structure for human use. For purposes of emergency release notification, the term includes motor vehicles, rolling stock, and aircraft.

Full-time Employee
2000 hours per year of full-time equivalent employment. To calculate the number of full-time employees, total the hours worked during the calendar year by all employees, including contract employees, and divide the total by 2000 hours.

Hazardous Chemical
Any hazardous chemical as defined under 29 CFR 1910.1200(c), except for the following substances:
- Any food, food additive, color additive, drug, or cosmetic regulated by the Food and Drug Administration.
- Any substance present as a solid in any manufactured item to the extent that exposure to the substance does not occur under normal conditions of use.
- Any substance to the extent it is used for personal, family, or household purposes, or is present in the same form and concentration as a product packaged for distribution and use by the general public.
- Any substance to the extent it is used in a research laboratory or a hospital or other medical facility under the direct supervision of a technically qualified individual.
- Any substance to the extent it is used in routine agricultural operations or is fertilizer held for sale by a retailer to the ultimate customer.

Import
To intend a chemical to be imported into the customs territory of the United States and to control the identity of the imported chemical and the amount to be imported.

Inventory Form
The Tier I and Tier II emergency and hazardous chemical inventory forms set forth in Subpart D of 40 CFR 370.

Material Safety Data Sheet or MSDS
The sheet required to be developed under 29 CFR 1910.1200(g).

Manufacture
To produce, prepare, import, or compound a toxic chemical. Manufacture also includes coincidental production of a toxic chemical during the manufacture, processing, use, or treatment of another chemical or mixture of chemicals, including a toxic chemical that is separated from that other chemical or mixture of chemicals as a byproduct, and a toxic chemical that remains in that other chemical or mixture as an impurity (>0.1% for carcinogens; otherwise >1%).

Management Practice
Practice that, although not mandated by law, is encouraged to promote safe operating procedures.

Protocol for Conducting Environmental Compliance Audits under EPCRA

Mixture (EPCRA 311, 312, and 313)
Any combination of two or more chemicals, if the combination is not, in whole or in part, the result of a chemical reaction. However, if the combination was produced by a chemical reaction but could have been produced without a chemical reaction, it is also treated as a mixture. A mixture also includes any combination that consists of a chemical and associated impurities (40 CFR 372.3).

Mixture (EPCRA 304)
A heterogeneous association of substances where the various individual substances retain their identities and can usually be separated by mechanical means. Includes solutions or compounds but does not include alloys or amalgams (40 CFR 355.20).

Otherwise Use
Any use of a toxic chemical that is not covered by the terms "manufacture" or "process" and includes use of a toxic chemical contained in a mixture, trade name product or waste. Otherwise use includes use as a cleaner, degreaser, fuel, lubricant, chemical processing aid, manufacturing aid, or a chemical used for treating waste. Disposal, stabilization or treatment for destruction is not included unless the toxic chemical was received from off-site for further waste management or was manufactured as a result of waste management activities on materials received from off-site for further waste management. Relabeling or redistributing a container of a toxic chemical where no repackaging of the toxic chemical occurs is not included.

Process
The preparation of a listed toxic chemical, after its manufacture, for distribution in commerce:
- In the same or different form or physical state from which it was received by the person preparing such substance, or
- As part of an article containing the toxic chemical. Process also applies to the processing of a toxic chemical contained in a mixture or trade name product.

Release
Any spilling, leaking, pumping, pouring, emitting, emptying, discharging, injecting, escaping, leaching, dumping, or disposing into the environment (including the abandonment or discarding of barrels, containers, and other closed receptacles) of any hazardous chemical, extremely hazardous substance, or CERCLA hazardous substance.

Reportable Quantity
For a CERCLA hazardous substance, the reportable quantity is the amount established in 40 CFR 302 Table 302.4. For an extremely hazardous substance, the reportable quantity is the amount established in 40 CFR 355, Appendices A and B.

Threshold Planning Quantity
The threshold planning quantity for an extremely hazardous substance as listed in 40 CFR 355 Appendices A and B.

Toxic Chemical
A chemical or chemical category listed in 40 CFR 372.65.

Protocol for Conducting Environmental Compliance Audits under EPCRA

Typical Records to Review

- Emergency response plan(s)
- Emergency Release Notification Reports
- Chemical inventory forms
- MSDSs
- Pollution prevention plan (optional)
- Tier I/Tier II reports
- Toxic chemical source reduction and recycling reports (for facilities subject to Form R reporting)
- Toxic release inventory (TRI) reports (Form R/Form A) and related documentation
- Hazardous communication plan
- Contingency plan.

Typical Physical Features to Inspect

- Chemical storage areas
- Chemical manufacturing or processing areas (generation sites)
- Recordkeeping system
- Shop activities
- Hazardous material/waste transfer areas
- Treatment units
- Recycling sites
- Disposal sites
- Surface impoundments

Index for Checklist Users

Category	Refer To	
	Checklist Items	Page Numbers
General	E.1 through E.3	7
Planning	E.4	7
Release Notification/Reporting	E.5 through E.8	8-11
Recordkeeping	E.9	12

Protocol for Conducting Environmental Compliance Audits under EPCRA

Checklist

Compliance Category: Emergency Planning and Community Right-to-Know Act (EPCRA)	
Regulatory Requirement or Management Practice:	**Reviewer Checks:**
General	
E.1 The current status of any ongoing or unresolved Consent Orders, Compliance Agreements, Notices of Violation (NOVs), or equivalent state enforcement actions should be examined.	Determine if noncompliance issues have been resolved by reviewing a copy of the previous report, Consent Orders, Compliance Agreements, NOVs, or equivalent state enforcement actions. For those open items, indicate what corrective action is planned and milestones established to correct problems.
E.2 Facilities are required to comply with all applicable federal regulatory requirements not contained in this checklist.	Determine if any new regulations have been issued since the finalization of the guide. If so, annotate checklist to include new standards. Determine if the facility has activities or facilities which are federally regulated, but not addressed in this checklist. Verify that the facility is in compliance with all applicable and newly issued regulations.
E.3 Facilities are required to abide by state and local regulations concerning hazardous materials.	Verify that the facility is abiding by state and local requirements. Verify that the facility is operating according to permits issued by the state or local agencies. (NOTE: Issues typically regulated by state and local agencies include: - Notification requirements - Response plan requirements - Spill response requirements.)
Planning	
E.4. Facilities with quantities of extremely hazardous substances equal to or greater than the threshold limits are required to follow specific emergency planning procedures (40 CFR 355.30 and 355 Appendices A & B).	Determine if the facility has any extremely hazardous substances in amounts equal to or greater than the limits listed in Appendix A column 3. Verify that the facility notified the state emergency response commission, or governor if there is no emergency response commission, that the facility is subject to emergency planning requirements within 60 days after the facility first became subject to these requirements. Determine whether the facility has representatives for contact by internal and external parties. Verify that the facility has notified the local emergency planning committee, or governor if there is no committee, of the facility environmental response coordinator. Verify that the facility is actively participating in off-site planning by interviewing the facility point of contact and reviewing the files. Verify that a procedure is in place to notify the local emergency planning committee of changes at the facility that are relevant to emergency planning.

This document is intended solely for guidance. No statutory or regulatory requirements are in any way altered by any statement(s) contained herein.

7

Protocol for Conducting Environmental Compliance Audits under EPCRA

Compliance Category: Emergency Planning and Community Right-to-Know Act (EPCRA)	
Regulatory Requirement or Management Practice:	**Reviewer Checks:**

Release Notification/Reporting

E.5. Facilities where any hazardous chemical is produced, used or stored at which there is a release of a reportable quantity of any listed hazardous substance in amounts equal to or greater than the reportable quantity are required to provide emergency release notification (40 CFR 302, 355.40 and 355 Appendices A & B).	Determine if there has been a spill or release of an extremely hazardous substance (see Appendix A column 4) or a CERCLA hazardous substance (see Appendix A column 5) in an amount exceeding the reportable quantity. Verify that if a spill or release has occurred in excess of the reportable quantity, the facility immediately notified the following: - Community emergency coordinator for the local emergency planning committee of any area likely to be affected by the release - State emergency response commission of any state likely to be affected by the release - Local emergency response personnel if there is no local emergency planning committee - The National Response Center if a CERCLA-listed hazardous substance was released - A 911 operator can be notified instead of state and local emergency organizations if the release is transportation-related. Verify that the notice contained the following, to the extent known at the time of notice, so long as no delay in notice or emergency response resulted: - The chemical name or identity of any substance involved in the release - An indication of whether the substance is an extremely hazardous substance - An estimate of the quantity that was released into the environment - The time and duration of the release - The medium or media into which the release occurred - Any known or anticipated acute or chronic health risks associated with the emergency and, where appropriate, advice regarding medical attention necessary for exposed individuals - Proper precautions to take as a result of the release, including evacuation (unless such information is readily available to the community emergency coordination because of the local emergency plan) - The names and telephone numbers of the persons to be contacted for further information. Verify that after the immediate verbal notification, a follow-up written emergency notification was submitted to the SERC and LEPC which contained the same information detailed in the verbal notice plus: - Actions taken to respond to and contain the release - Any known or anticipated acute or chronic health risks associated with the release - Advice regarding medical attention for exposed individuals, as necessary. (NOTE: These release notification requirements do not apply to the following: - Any release which results in exposure to persons solely within the boundaries of the facility and there is no potential for any part of the release to go off-site - Any release which is a federally permitted release as defined in CERCLA Section 101 - Any release that is continuous and stable in quantity and rate (initial notices, statistically significant increases, new releases and changes in the normal range of the release are not exempted) - Any release of a pesticide product exempt from CERCLA Section 103 reporting - Any release not meeting the CERCLA definition of a release - Any radionuclide release which occurs naturally in soil, from land disturbances except that which occurs at uranium, phosphate, tin, zircon, hafnium, vanadium, monazite, and rare earth mines (40 CFR 355.40(a)(2)(ii)) or from dumping or piles of coal and coal ash at utility and industrial facilities with coal-fired boilers.)

This document is intended solely for guidance. No statutory or regulatory requirements are in any way altered by any statement(s) contained herein.

8

Protocol for Conducting Environmental Compliance Audits under EPCRA

Compliance Category: Emergency Planning and Community Right-to-Know Act (EPCRA)	
Regulatory Requirement or Management Practice:	**Reviewer Checks:**

E.6. Facilities which are required to prepare or have available a MSDS for a hazardous chemical under OSHA are required to meet specific MSDS reporting requirements for planning purposes (40 CFR 370.20, 370.21, and 370.28).	Verify that MSDS sheets or a list as described below are submitted to the state emergency response commission (SERC), local emergency planning committee (LEPC) and the fire department with jurisdiction over the facility for each hazardous chemical present at the facility according to the following thresholds:
	- All hazardous chemicals requiring MSDSs present at the facility at any one time in amounts equal to or greater than 10,000 lb. (4540 kg) (NOTE: Not all hazardous chemicals requiring an MSDS are listed in Appendix A. Commonly overlooked substances requiring MSDSs are propane, petroleum-based fuels, and many other mixtures and trade name products.)
	- All extremely hazardous substances present at the facility in amounts greater than or equal to 500 lb. (227 kg) or the threshold planning quantity, whichever is lower (see Appendix A column 3).
	
	Verify that if the facility has not submitted MSDSs, the following have been submitted:
	- A list of hazardous chemicals for which the MSDS is required, grouped by hazard category (e.g., immediate health hazard, delayed health hazard, fire hazard, sudden release of pressure hazard, and reactive hazard)
	- The chemical or common name of each hazardous chemical
	- Any hazardous component of each hazardous chemical unless reported as a mixture.
	
	(NOTE: The facility may fulfill these reporting requirements for a hazardous chemical that is a mixture of hazardous chemicals by doing one of the following:
	  - Providing the required information on each hazardous component in the mixture, or
	  - Providing the required information on the mixture itself.)
	
	(NOTE: Although the facility may provide information either on the mixture or the hazardous components, in calculating whether the amount of EHSs meets the threshold, it must do so by component. In calculating the amounts present of non-EHS chemicals, the facility can consider either the mixture or the hazardous components, so long as it does so consistently throughout the facility.)
	
	Verify that revised MSDS sheets are provided within 3 months after the discovery of significant new information concerning the hazardous chemical or after a chemical crosses the threshold limit.

Protocol for Conducting Environmental Compliance Audits under EPCRA

Compliance Category: Emergency Planning and Community Right-to-Know Act (EPCRA)	
Regulatory Requirement or Management Practice:	**Reviewer Checks:**
E.7. Facilities which are required to prepare or have available a MSDS sheet for a hazardous chemical under OSHA are required to meet specific inventory reporting requirements for planning purposes (40 CFR 370.25, 370.40, and 370.41).	Verify that the Tier I (or Tier II) forms are submitted annually to the state emergency response commission (SERC), local emergency planning committee (LEPC) and the fire department with jurisdiction over the facility. Hazardous chemicals that must be included are: - All hazardous chemicals requiring MSDSs present at the facility at any one time in amounts equal to or greater than 10,000 lb. (4540 kg) (NOTE: Not all hazardous chemicals requiring an MSDS are listed in Appendix A. Commonly overlooked substances requiring MSDSs are propane, petroleum-based fuels, and many other mixtures and trade name products.) - All extremely hazardous substances present at the facility in amounts greater than or equal to 500 lb. (227 kg) or the threshold planning quantity, whichever is lower (see Appendix A column 3). (NOTE: The facility may fulfill these reporting requirements for a hazardous chemical that is a mixture of hazardous chemicals by doing one of the following: - Providing the required information on each component in the mixture which is a hazardous chemical - Providing the required information on the mixture itself.) (NOTE: Although the facility may provide information either on the mixture or the hazardous components, in calculating whether the amount of EHSs meets the threshold, it must do so by component. In calculating the amounts present of non-EHS chemicals, the facility can consider either the mixture or the hazardous components, so long as it does so consistently throughout the facility.) Verify that reports are submitted on or before March 1.

Protocol for Conducting Environmental Compliance Audits under EPCRA

Compliance Category: Emergency Planning and Community Right-to-Know Act (EPCRA)	
Regulatory Requirement or Management Practice:	**Reviewer Checks:**
E.8. Covered facilities that manufacture, process, or otherwise use a toxic chemical (see Appendix A column 6) are subject to certain reporting requirements (40 CFR 372.22-372.65).	Determine if the facility meets the criteria for a covered facility: - Has 10 or more full-time employees; - Is in SIC codes 10 (except 1011, 1081 & 1094), 12 (except 1241), 20 through 39, 4911, 4931 (limited to facilities that combust coal and/or oil for the purpose of generating power for distribution in commerce), 4939 (limited to facilities that combust coal and/or oil for the purpose of generating power for distribution in commerce), 4953 (limited to facilities regulated under RCRA, Subtitle C), 5169, 5171, and 7389 (limited to facilities primarily engaged in solvent recovery services on a contract or fee basis); and - Manufactured, processed, or otherwise used a toxic chemical in excess of its threshold amounts noted below. Determine if the facility exceeded the following threshold levels: - Manufactured or processed 25,000 lb/yr [11,340 kg/yr] or more of a toxic chemical (Appendix A column 6). - Otherwise used 10,000 lb. [4540 kg] or more of a toxic chemical during the year. - When more than one threshold applies, if any threshold is exceeded then releases and other waste management activities associated with all activities (except those specifically exempt) must be reported. - When a facility manufactures, processes or otherwise uses more than one member of a chemical category listed in 40 CFR 372.65, if the total weight of all the members in that category exceeds the threshold, then it must be reported. (NOTE: Some thresholds only apply to the manufacturer or for certain forms of a chemical (see 40 CFR 372.65).) (NOTE: Articles containing toxic chemicals are not included in calculations of total toxic chemical manufactured, processed, or used at the facility. See 40 CFR 372.30(b)(3) for procedure to determine whether a threshold has been exceeded.) Determine if supplier notification is required under 40 CFR 372.45 (required if a facility in SIC codes 20-39 sells or otherwise distributes a mixture or trade name product containing a toxic chemical to a covered facility). Verify that the facility annually submits a completed Form R/Form A to the EPA and state on or before July 1 for each toxic chemical exceeding a reporting threshold.

Protocol for Conducting Environmental Compliance Audits under EPCRA

Compliance Category: Emergency Planning and Community Right-to-Know Act (EPCRA)	
Regulatory Requirement or Management Practice:	**Reviewer Checks:**
Recordkeeping	

E.9. Covered facilities that manufacture, process, or otherwise use a toxic chemical in excess of a reporting threshold (see Appendix A column 6) are subject to certain recordkeeping requirements (40 CFR 372.10).	Verify that the facility retains the following records at the facility for 3 years:
	- A copy of each toxic chemical release inventory report (EPA Form R or Form A) submitted.
	- All supporting materials and documentation used to determine if the facility is a covered facility under 372.22 or 372.45.
	- Documentation supporting the Form R report, including:
	  -- Documentation supporting exemptions
	  -- Data showing if a reporting threshold applies for each toxic chemical
	  -- Calculations of the quantity of each reported chemical released or otherwise managed as waste including toxic chemicals in waste transferred off-site
	  -- Use indications and quantity on-site reported, including dates of manufacturing, processing or otherwise use
	  -- Documentation supporting estimates for releases and off-site transfers
	  -- Receipts or manifests for off-site transfers of reported chemicals in waste
	  -- Documentation supporting reported waste treatment methods, estimates of treatment efficiencies, ranges of influent concentration to such treatment, sequential nature of treatment steps (if applicable) and the actual operating data (if applicable) to support the waste treatment efficiency estimate for each reported chemical.
	- Supporting materials and documentation determining if supplier notification is required under 40 CFR 372.45 (required if a facility in SIC codes 20-39 sells or otherwise distributes a mixture or a product containing a toxic chemical to a covered facility).
	- Documentation used in developing, and copies of, such notices.
	- Documentation related to applying alternate thresholds (if applicable).

**Protocol for Conducting Environmental Compliance
Audits under the Emergency Planning and Community
Right-to-Know Act**

**Appendix A:
Consolidated List of Chemicals Covered in EPCRA**

Appendix D

PROBLEM SOLVING EXERCISES

Audit Verification
Interviewing Skills
Management Systems Assessments
Report Writing
Audit Conferences

Audit Verification

CONFINED SPACES

Background

You have been assigned to review the confined spaces program during the audit of a facility. The site provided you with the following information about on-site confined spaces:

- Thirty-five (35) confined spaces

- Twenty (25) spaces are permit-required

- Thirty (30) employees are trained in/ qualified for confined spaces

- Twenty (20) permits issued all of last year

- Ten (15) permits issued in the first quarter of this year.

The OSHA confined space standard (29 CFR 1910.146) defines a confined space as a space that is large enough for an employee to enter, has restricted means of entry or exit, and is not designed for continuous employee occupancy. Examples include ship compartments, missile fuel tanks, vats, silos, sewers, tunnels and vaults. Confined space hazards include physical hazards, oxygen deficiency, combustibility and toxic air contaminants.

Assignment

1. List the following activities in the order in which you would do them:

    _____ Review written permit entry program

    _____ Inspect training records

    _____ Review emergency procedures

    _____ Inspect the confined spaces

    _____ Review canceled permits

    _____ Review results of annual review

    _____ Review lockout/tagout program

    _____ Interview employees

2. Using the attached sampling methodology, how many permit-required confined spaces and non-permit confined spaces would you review. What kind of sampling strategy (e.g., random, block, stratified, interval) would you use?

3a. Upon inspecting a confined space entry that is underway you discover that no entry permit has been issued. A certificate is posted at the entry portal that explains that all hazards have been eliminated. What conclusion can you make with regard to the status of this confined space?

3b. What if welders enter the space to make a repair?

4. At a minimum, which type of employees would you need to interview to understand the program and verify compliance? How do you distinguish a good program from a bad one?

5. Based on a review of the confined space activities at the site over the past couple of years, what management issue might you want to investigate? What types of questions would you ask?

SELECTING A SAMPLE SIZE ON ENVIRONMENTAL AUDITS

Population Size	Suggested Minimum Sample Size			
	A	B	C	D
10	98%	88%	72%	50%
25	94%	74%	49%	28%
50	89%	58%	32%	18%
100	80%	41%	19%	9%
250	61%	21%	8%	4%
500	43%	12%	4%	2%
1000	28%	6%	2%	1%
2000	16%	3%	1%	0.5%

A Suggested minimum sample size for a population(s) being reviewed which is considered to be extremely important in terms of verifying compliance with applicable requirements, and/or is of critical concern to the corporation in terms of potential or actual impacts associated with non-compliance. A confidence interval of 95% is assumed.

B Suggested minimum sample size for a population(s) being reviewed that will provide additional information to substantiate compliance or non-compliance and/or is of considerable importance to the corporation in terms of potential or actual impacts associated with non-compliance. A confidence interval of 90% is assumed.

C Suggested minimum sample size for a population(s) being reviewed that will provide ancillary information in terms of verifying overall compliance with a requirement. A confidence interval of 85% is assumed.

D Suggested minimum sample size for a population(s) being reviewed that will provide ancillary information in terms of verifying overall compliance with a requirement. A confidence interval of 80% is assumed.

AUDIT SAMPLING

Sampling theory can provide a means to identifying the number of items to be reviewed to be fairly confident the results are representative. That is, when a confidence interval given width is desired for an unknown proportion, p (in this case the proportion of sources that are in compliance), the sample size, n, required can be obtained using a formula given by Inman and Conover[1]. However, the formula applies to an infinite population. A correction for finite population is given by Cochran[2]. The finite population correction close to unity when the sampling fraction n/N remains low (approximately 5% or less). Combining the two formulae gives:

$$n = (4z[a/2]^2 pqN)/(w^2N - w^2 + 4z[a/2]^2 pq)$$

Where,

n is the required number of sources in the sample

z[a/2] is the (1–a/2) quantile from the standard normal probability function that is:

Confidence Level	a	1–a/2	z[a/2]
95%	0.05	0.975	1.96
90%	0.10	0.950	1.65
85%	0.15	0.925	1.44

p is the proportion of interest (proportion of sources in compliance); when p is unknown it is set equal to 0.5 to give the most conservative possible value of n

q is (1–p)

N is the total population being sampled
w is 2a

---

[1] Inman, R.L. and Conover. W.J., *A Modern Approach to Statistics,* John Wiley and Sons. New York, NY.

[2] Cochran. *W.G., Sampling Techniques.* Second Edition. John Wiley and Sons. New York, NY.

HAZARD COMMUNICATION

Background

You have been assigned the review of the hazard communication program during the audit of a facility. The written program has procedures for requesting a MSDS if one is not received automatically from a supplier of a hazardous chemical. It also includes the OSHA Guide for Reviewing MSDS Completeness, which is attached.

Assignment

1. Using questions 4 and 5 of the OSHA Guide, perform a review of the MSDS for BIO BETTY™ to determine whether the facility is implementing this hazard communication procedure. What, if any, obvious inadequacies were found with the MSDS for BIO BETTY™?

2. Review the label on the container of BIO BETTY™ for the identity of the material, appropriate hazard warnings, and the name and address of the producer. What, if any, obvious inadequacies were found with the label for BIO BETTY™?

3. Is the label prepared below adequate for a container into which you might subsequently transfer the BIO BETTY™? What, if any, are its obvious inadequacies?

BIO BETTY™

Contains Water Base Willie
and dry chlorine

CSHA Instruction CPL 2-2.38C
Office of Health Compliance Assistance

Appendix D

Guide for Reviewing MSDS Completeness

NOTE: This guide has been developed for use as an optional aid during inspections.

During CSHO review for Material Safety Data Sheet completeness, the following questions may be helpful:

1. Do chemical manufacturers and importers have an MSDS for each hazardous chemical produced or imported into the United States?

2. Do employers have an MSDS for each hazardous chemical used?

3. Is each MSDS in at least English?

4. Does each MSDS contain at least the:

    (a) Identity used on the label?

    (b) Chemical and common name(s) for single substance hazardous chemicals?

    (c) For mixtures tested as a whole:

        (1)   Chemical and common name(s) of the ingredients which contribute to the known hazards?

        (2)   Common name(s) of the mixture itself?

    (d) For mixtures not tested as a whole:

        (1)   Chemical and common name(s) of all ingredients which are health hazards (1 percent concentration or greater), including carcinogens (0.1 percent concentration or greater)?

        (2)   Chemical and common name(s) of all ingredients which are health hazards and present a risk to employees, even though they are present in the mixture in concentrations of less than 1 percent of 0.1 percent for carcinogens?

    (e) Chemical and common name(s) of all ingredients which have been determined to present a physical harm when present in the mixture?

(f) Physical and chemical characteristics of the hazardous chemical (vapor pressure, flash point, etc.)?

(g) Physical hazards of the hazardous chemical including the potential for fire, explosion, and reactivity?

(h) Health hazards of the hazardous chemical (including signs and symptoms and medical conditions aggravated)?

(i) Primary routes of entry?

(j) OSHA permissible exposure limit (PEL)? The American Conference of Governmental Industrial Hygienists (ACGIH) Threshold Limit Value (TLV)? Other exposure limit(S) (including ceiling and other short term limits)?

(k) Information on carcinogen listings (reference OSHA regulated carcinogens, those indicated in the National Toxicology Program (NTP) Annual Report on Carcinogens and/or those listed by the International Agency for Research on Carcinogens (IARC))?

　　NOTE:　Negative conclusions regarding carcinogenicity, or the fact that there is no information, do not have to be reported unless there is a specific space or blank for carcinogenicity on the form.

(l) Generally applicable procedures and precautions for safe handling and use of the chemical (hygienic practices, maintenance and spill procedures)?

(m) Generally applicable control measures (engineering controls, work practices and personal protective equipment)?

(n) Pertinent emergency and first aid procedures?

(o) Date that the MSDS was prepared or the date of the last change?

(p) Name, address and telephone number of the responsible party?

5. Are all sections of the MSDS completed?

BIO BETTY™

American Health & Safety, INC.
6250 Nesbitt Ad.
Madison, WI 53719
800-522-7554

SECTION 1- CHEMICAL PRODUCT AND COMPANY INFORMATION

Date Prepared: November 8,1989
Product Name: B IO BETTY™
Chemical Name(s):   Sodium Polyacrylate and Calcium Hypochlorite
Emergency Telephone: 608-273-4000

SECTION 2 -COMPOSITIONAL INFORMATION

Name:	CAS#	Approximate Weight (% wt,):
Sodium Polyacrylate	9003-04-07	99.9
Calcium Hypochlorite	7778-54-3	.1

SECTION 3 -POTENTIAL HEAL1H EFFECTS

Effects of Overexposure:
   Excessive exposure to dust may irritate eyes, nose and respiratory system.

Acute effects: not available

Chronic effects:

Medical Conditions Generally Aggravated by Exposure: None known

Chemical Listed as Carcinogen or Potential Carcinogen: Not Available

        NIP: No
        IARC: No
        OSHA: No

SECTION 4- FIRST AID MEASURES

Eye Contact:
   Flush with gently running water for 20 minutes. Consult a physician.
Skin Contact:
   Wash with soap and water. If irritation persists consult a physician.
Inhalation:
   Remove to fresh air. Consult a physician if necessary.
Ingestion:
   Drink large quantities of water. Do not induce vomiting, consult a physician.

Emergency and First Aid Procedures:

Obtain medical advice except for minor exposure.

SECTION 5 -FIRE FIGHTING MEASURES

Flash Point:	Not Applicable
Lower Explosive Limit:	Not Applicable
Upper Explosive Limit:	Not Applicable
Autoignition Temperature:	Not Applicable

Extinguishing Media:

Carbon Dioxide, Dry Chemical or Foam.

Unusual Fire Hazard–Explosion Hazards:

Not applicable

Fire Fighting Procedures:

Wear self-contained breathing apparatus when fighting fire.

SECTION 6- ACCIDENTAL RELEASE MEASURES

Releases:

In case of a release or spill, vacuum, sweep or shovel up material and dispose of in a waste container in accordance with local, state, federal and provincial authorities.

Water may make the area slippery.

SECTION 7- HANDLING AND STORAGE

Store in a dry place under 100°F. Avoid exposure to direct sunlight and high humidity.

Other Precautions:

Keep dust levels low, wear personal protective equipment if excessive dust is present.

SECTION 8- EXPOSURE CONTROLS/PERSONAL PROTECTION

ACGIH Threshold Limit Value

N/A

OSHA Permissible Exposure Limit

N/A

Other Exposure Limits

N/A

Engineering Controls:

Ventilation Requirements:

Local exhaust suggested.

Personal Protective Equipment:

Respiratory Protection:

Dust or filter type respirator when working with excessive amounts of product.

Eye Protection:

Chemical goggles recommended.

Skin Protection:

Plastic or rubber chemical resistant.

Hygienic Practices:

Wash hands with soap and water after using product.

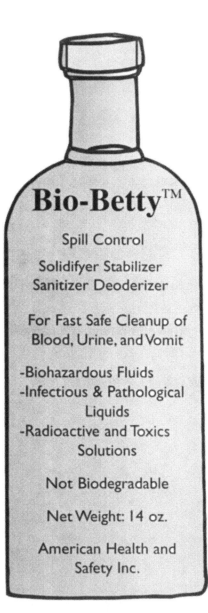

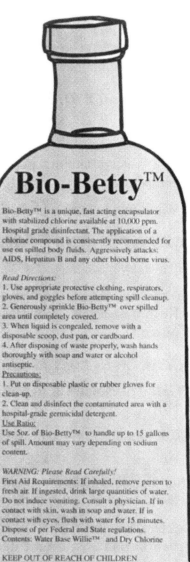

SECTION 9 -PHYSICAL AND CHEMICAL PROPERTIES

Appearance:	White Powder
Color:	White
Odor:	Chlorine Fragrance
Vapor Pressure (mm Hg):	Not Applicable
Vapor Density (Air=l):	Not Applicable
Boiling Point:	Not Available
Melting Point:	Decomposition at 350°F
Specific Gravity (Water=l):	Not Available
Solubility in Water:	Insoluble (Swells in Water)
Reactivity in	Water Swells in Water

SECTION 10- STABILIIY AND REACTIVITY

Stability:

This material is stable.

Conditions to Avoid:

None Known

Hazardous Decomposition Products:

Thermo decomposition may produce Carbon Monoxide/Carbon Dioxide.

Incompatibility (Materials to Avoid):

Strong Oxidizing Agents

AIR EMISSIONS

Background

In the course of preparing to audit air emissions compliance you discover that the facility has several sources which are regulated for opacity (fuel burners, incinerators). The facility also has about 20 stacks and vents on the roofs of three buildings, some of which may be exempted from permitting. The actual audit is scheduled for the next day and you are working by yourself.

Assignment

1. How would you schedule activities for the next day to perform the audit efficiently and accurately.

2. Would you physically go up on the roofs and record ALL the stacks and attempt to match them with equipment/operations inside the buildings?

3. How would you best determine what stacks or vents were exempted from any licenses or permits?

4. How would you determine if all sources of volatile organic compounds (VOC) emissions are identified at the facility? What would you do to verify compliance with VQC emission standards?

5. Later in the day, you observe asbestos is being removed from a boiler and piping system by an outside contractor. You had not anticipated this because your escort forgot to tell you it was happening. What would you do? What would some of your key questions be? Who would you address them to?

Wastewater Discharges

Background

The facility you are about to audit has industrial wastewater that discharges *directly* the local river. The facility's wastewater discharge permit, which has been issued by regulatory authority, requires monthly sampling. The permit expires six months from n Permitted effluent parameters include flow, BOD, TSS, TOC, Ph, and several priority pollutants. The treatment plant includes primary clarifiers, activated sludge tanks, settling tanks.

The facility also has recently received an *indirect* discharge permit from Onondaga County. Two pages from this permit are included with this exercise. You notice during your tour that the facility is testing the fire water systems and the discharge is going into County Sewer System. Your facility contact tells you they test the fire water systems twice per month.

The facility also has an unpermitted stormwater outfall. Your job is to audit wastewater storm water compliance at the site.

Assignment

1. What is the logical sequence of tasks you would undertake to evaluate wastewater discharge permit compliance at the facility?

    _____ Observe technician taking a sample for proper technique

    _____ Determine if lab is certified

    _____ Inspect effluent discharge

    _____ Inspect treatment plant/interview operator

    _____ Inspect wastewater discharge monitoring reports

    _____ Review permit from the regulatory authority

2. You notice from the monitoring reports that the flow and pH exceeded the limits specified in the permit twelve times during the last 12 months. How would you react to this? What would you ask the facility contact?

3. What key scheduling question might you want to ask about the wastewater discharge permit?

4. Is the fire water system discharge to the municipal sewer system permitted or prohibited?

5. How would you verify stormwater discharge compliance?

6. What general wastewater *management issue* might you want to discuss with the facility contact based on your overall review of the wastewater discharges?

ONONDAGA MUNICIPAL SEWER ORDINANCE

I. AUTHORITY

A. This permit is hereby promulgated by the Commissioner of the Onondaga Municipal Department of Drainage and Sanitation (OMDDs) to regulate the discharge of wastewater, polluted or unpolluted, to the sanitary sewer system, under the authority of The Onondaga Municipal Rules and Regulations Relating to the Use of Public Sewer System (the Rules and Regulations) and the Onondaga Municipal Administrative Code.

B. Article VII of the Rules and Regulations provides that any violation of this permit may subject the permittee to a fine of one thousand dollars per day per violation. In addition Articles VI and VII of the Rules c Regulations specify other penalties and procedures the Department may employ for any violation of this permit or the Rules and Regulations.

II. PERMI1TED WASTEWATER DISCHARGE

A. The permittee is authorized to discharge the following to the municipal sewer system:

1. Sanitary wastewater;

2. Boiler blowdown, wastewater including that from vehicle washing, EP 10 Outdoor Sump and EP 9 Basement Sump discharged via the Building 10 oil/water separator.

3. Filtered wastewater with the addition of peroxide originating from production and operation of ceramic sonar transducer element cylinders and lids (Transducer Products Operations (TPO) -Building #5);

4. Wastewater generated froll\ the fabrication of semiconductors, cleaning of facilities and equipment and the cleaning of parts ir the Electronics Laboratory (Building 3), and the cleaning of par in the Electronics Lab Model Shop in Building 7.

5. Contact cooling water blowdown from the cooling towers located outside of Buildings 7 and 10; and non-contact cooling water associated with the operation of air conditioners and process equipment and basement sump in EP-6 until such time as permission from the state is obtained to reroute through the EP storm drains.

6. Photographic laboratory wastewater.

7. Wastewater from Projection Display Products Operations (PDPO) group production, parts cleaning and silk screening in Building 7.

8. Wastewater discharges from the Environmental Test Chambers, the Conformal Coat Process, and the cleaning of air filters in the calibration laboratory in EP-5.

9. Sump water contaminated with low levels of trichloroethene (less than 25 parts per billion) from building EP-6. This discharge shall be prohibited after May 1, 1993.

B. All wastewater discharged to the sanitary sewer system must comply with the effluent limitations set forth in Section IV of this permit and Article ill of the Onondaga Municipal Rules and Regulations Relating to the Use of the Public Sewer System, unless otherwise indicated in this permit expressly or by implication.

III. PROHIBITED DISCHARGES

A. In accordance with Article ill of the Rules and Regulations, the following wastes shall not be introduced into the Onondaga Municipal Sanitary Sewer System.

1. Wastewater constituents which by their introduction to the sewer system, cause pass-through (in accordance with Sections 3.01 (d), 3.01(f), and 3.01(8)).

2. Wastewater constituents which by their introduction to the sewer system, cause interference (in accordance with Sections 3.01(b), 3.01(d), 3.01(i), and 3.01(j)).

3. Wastewater which has the potential to create a fire or explosion hazard in the publicly-owned treatment works (POTW), including wastewater having a closed-cup flashpoint less than 140°F, (pursuant to Section 3.01(a)).

4. Wastewater having a pH lower than 5.5 or higher than 9.5 Standard Units (in accordance with Section 3.01)).

5. Wastewater constituents which result in the presence of toxic gases, vapors or fumes within the POTW in a quantity that may cause acute worker health and safety problems (pursuant to Sections 3.01 (a), 3.01(e)).

6. The introduction of wastewater having a temperature greater than 150°F into the sanitary sewer system <u>or</u> at a quantity such that the temperature at the headworks of the POTW exceeds 104°F (Section 3.01(i)).

7. Batch discharges without prior written approval from the Commissioner. Any request to discharge such wastewater must be submitted in writing to this office and is subject to the approval of the Commissioner on a case-by-case basis.

8. Any wastewater which will subject the receiving POTW to reporting and permitting requirements of the federal hazardous waste rules.

9. Non-contact cooling water and other unpolluted wastewater (in accordance with Section 3.02).

10. All other wastes which are prohibited by Article ill of the Rules and Regulations.

B. In addition to the above prohibitions, dilution shall not be used as a substitute for pretreatment.

HAZARDOUS WASTE MANAGEMENT

Background

You are on a three-person team about to conduct an audit of a major manufacturing facility. Your responsibility is hazardous waste. From the pre-audit questionnaire you have determined that the facility is a large quantity generator (LQG) with a wide variety of characteristic and listed hazardous wastes coming from laboratory, maintenance and manufacturing operations. There are five satellite accumulation points, two 90-day accumulation points and one permitted storage area on the site.

Assignment

1. How would *you* begin your hazardous waste audit of the site? That is, what specifically would you do in the first couple of hours to assure an efficient review?

2. What are the key items you need to evaluate at the 90-day accumulation point? What are some of the key differences among the requirements for satellite, 90-day and storage areas?

3. Review the attached manifest and identify any deficiencies. Are any of these significant? What other things should you be looking for in the manifest file?

4. You have given yourself only two hours to review the manifest file, which contains 1000 manifests. Using the attached Sample Size table, how many manifests would you look at to obtain a representative sample? If, as you conduct your review you discover some major discrepancies in the first few manifests, would you (1) increase your sample size, (2) stop where you are, or (3) retain the original sampling scheme? Pick only one and explain your rationale.

5. Review the attached two-page inspection log for the storage area and identify any deficiencies. Speculate on the likely underlying causes for the deficiencies.

Bureau of Waste Management
P. O. Box 8550
Harrisburg, PA 17105-8550

ER-WM-51 REV. 11/89

UNIFORM HAZARDOUS WASTE MANIFEST	1. Generator's US EPA ID No. 1PAD 000000789		2. Page 1 of 1	Information in the shaded areas is not required by Federal law but is required by State law.

A. State Manifest Document Number
PAC 3025131

B. State Gen. ID
DAD 000000789

3. Generator's Name and Mailing Address	
XYZ Company 123 Anystreet Ourtown, PA 11131	

4. Generator's Phone ( )

5. Transporter 1 Company Name WE DRIVE TRUCKS	6. US EPA ID Number 1PAD 555 123 47

C. State Trans. ID
PA-1AH1 123451

7. Transporter 2 Company Name Specialty Transporters	8. US EPA ID Number 1NJD 555 123 489

D. Transporter's Phone ( )

E. State Trans. ID
PA-1AH1 345121

9. Designated Facility Name and Site Address	
ABC Disposal Industrial Park Somewhere, PA 11132	10. US EPA ID Number 1PAT 111 454 769

F. Transporter's Phone (609) 222-7777

G. State Facility's ID

H. Facility's Phone (412) 000-3131

11. US DOT Description (Including Proper Shipping Name, Hazard Class, and ID Number)	12. Containers No.	Type	13. Total Quantity	14. Unit Wt/Vol	I. Waste No.
a. Paint, Flammable Liquid UN 1263	10	DM	550	G	D001
b. Waste Flammable Liquid, N.O.S. (Xylene) Flammable Liquid UN 1993	10	DM		G	D001
c. Waste Corrosive Liquid, N.O.S. (sulfuric Acid, chromic Acid) Corrosive Material	15	DF	1000	P	D002
d.					

J. Additional Descriptions for Materials Listed Above				K. Handling Codes for Wastes Listed Above
Lab Pack / Physical State	Lab Pack / Physical State			a. S01 b. S01
a. ☐ b. ☐	c. ☐ d. ☐			c. S01 d.
e. ☐ f. ☐	g. ☐ h. ☐			

15. Special Handling Instructions and Additional Information

15- empty Drums (previously contained Flammable solvents)

1- Drum of unknown Material

16. GENERATOR'S CERTIFICATION: I hereby declare that the contents of this consignment are fully and accurately described above by proper shipping name and are classified, packed, marked, and labeled and are in all respects in proper condition for transport by highway according to applicable international and national government regulations.

If I am a large quantity generator, I certify that I have a program in place to reduce the volume and toxicity of waste generated to the degree I have determined to be economically practicable and that I have selected the practicable method of treatment, storage, or disposal currently available to me which minimizes the present and future threat to human health and the environment; OR, if I am a small quantity generator, I have made a good faith effort to minimize my waste generation and select the best waste management method that is available to me and that I can afford.

Printed/Typed Name John C. Generator	Signature JC Gen	Month 5	Day 15	Year 93

17. Transporter 1 Acknowledgement of Receipt of Materials

Printed/Typed Name Bill M. Driver	Signature Bill M Driver	Month 5	Day 15	Year 93

18. Transporter 2 Acknowledgement of Receipt of Materials

Printed/Typed Name Mark Miwords	Signature Mark Miwords	Month 5	Day 25	Year 93

19. Discrepancy Indication Space

20. Facility Owner or Operator: Certification of receipt of hazardous materials covered by this manifest except as noted in Item 19.

Printed/Typed Name Mike T. Owner	Signature Mike T Owner	Month 5	Day 11	Year 93

EPA Form 8700-22 (Rev. 9/88) Previous editions are obsolete.

21

SELECTING A SAMPLE SIZE ON ENVIRONMENTAL AUDITS

Population Size	Suggested Minimum Sample Size			
	A	B	C	D
10	98%	88%	72%	50%
25	94%	74%	49%	28%
50	89%	58%	32%	18%
100	80%	41%	19%	9%
250	61%	21%	8%	4%
500	43%	12%	4%	2%
1000	28%	6%	2%	1%
2000	16%	3%	1%	0.5%

A   Suggested minimum sample size for a population(s) being reviewed which is considered to be extremely important in terms of verifying compliance with applicable requirements, and/or is of critical concern to the corporation in terms of potential or actual impacts associated with non-compliance. A confidence interval of 95% is assumed.

B   Suggested minimum sample size for a population(s) being reviewed that will provide additional information to substantiate compliance or non-compliance and/or is of considerable importance to the corporation in terms of potential or actual impacts associated with non-compliance. A confidence interval of 90% is assumed.

C   Suggested minimum sample size for a population(s) being reviewed that will provide ancillary information in terms of verifying overall compliance with a requirement. A confidence interval of 85% is assumed.

D   Suggested minimum sample size for a population(s) being reviewed that will provide ancillary information in terms of verifying overall compliance with a requirement. A confidence interval of 80% is assumed.

AUDIT SAMPLING

Sampling theory can provide a means to identifying the number of items to be reviewed be fairly confident the results are representative. That is, when a confidence interval of a given width is desired for an unknown proportion, p (in this case the proportion of sources that are in compliance), the sample size, n, required can be obtained using a formula given by Inman and Conover[1]. However, the formula applies to an infinite population. A correction for finite population is given by Cochran[2]. The finite population correction close to unity when the sampling fraction n/N remains low (approximately 5% or less). Combining the two formulae gives:

$$n = (4z[a/2]^2pqN)/(w^2N - w^2 + 4z[a/2]^2pq)$$

Where,

n is the required number of sources in the sample

z[a/2] is the (1–a/2) quantile from the standard normal probability function that is:

Confidence Level	a	1–a/2	z[a/2]
95%	0.05	0.975	1.96
90%	0.10	0.950	1.65
85%	0.15	0.925	1.44

p is the proportion of interest (proportion of sources in compliance); when p is unknown it is set equal to 0.5 to give the most conservative possible value of n

q is (1–p)

N is the total population being sampled
w is 2a

---

[1] Inman, R.L. and Conover. W.J., *A Modern Approach to Statistics,* John Wiley and Sons. New York, NY.

[2] Cochran. *W.G., Sampling Techniques.* Second Edition. John Wiley and Sons. New York, NY.

ABC Chemical Company

Hazardous Waste Storage Facility
Weekly Inspection Log

Date	Time	Inspector	No. of Drums	Status OK	Status Needs Att'n	Comments
4/12/93	8 AM	C. More	20	ℓ		
4/19/93	8 AM	C. More	20	ℓ		
4/26/93	8 AM	C. More	20	ℓ		
5/3/93	8:00	L. Jones	21		X	Acid waste drum leaking. Pumped into new drum on 5/7
5/17/93	8:00 AM	J. Smith	21	✓		
5/24/93	8:00 AM	J. Smith	29		✓	missing bung on drum of spent paint gun cleaner. Being replaced on 5/28
6/4	8:00	L. Jones	29	X		
6/11	8:00	D. Jones	29	✓		
6/18	8:00	D.J.	29	✓		
6/25	8:00	Jones	29	✓		
7/2	8:00 AM	J.S.	11	✓		
7/9	8:15	Smith	11	✓		
7/16	8 AM	C.M.	6	ℓ		

ABC Chemical Company

Hazardous Waste Storage Facility
Weekly Inspection Log

Date	Time	Inspector	No. of Drums	Status OK	Status Needs Act'n	Comments
1/4/93	8:00AM	J. Smith	10	✓		
1/11/93	8:00AM	J. Smith	12	✓		
1/19/93	9:00	J. Jones	12	X		
1/25/93	8:00	J. Jones	12	X		
2/1/93	8AM	C. Myse	11	?		
2/5/93	8:15	J. Jones	12	X		
2/12/93	8:15	J. Jones	12	X		
2/19/93	8:20	J. Jones	12	X		
2/29/93	8:00AM	J. Smith	13	✓		
3/5/93	9:00AM	J. Smith	21	✓		Acid waste drum leaking / pumped into new drum on 3/8
3/15/93	9:00AM	J. Smith	21	✓		
3/24/93	8AM	E. Ryen	20	?		
3/30/93	8:00	J. Jones	21	✓		
4/5/93	9:00AM	J. Smith	21		✓	wall between acid waste and cyanide waste area damaged by forklift truck

SPILL CONTROL

Background

As part of a multimedia comprehensive environmental audit scheduled to last five days, you will be examining the facility's Spill Prevention Control and Counter-measures (SPCC) Plan. After reviewing the entire facility layout and SPCC Plan, you note that, according to the Plan, there are 20 oil storage tanks of various capacities that have a system of diking installed. You have decided that you will physically inspect only five (5) tanks, which you consider to be a representative sample.

You look at the first tank and discover that, contrary to the Plan, there is no diking. You confirm that you are at the right tank and that you are reading the Plan accurately.

You continue on to the second oil storage tank. Here you find a somewhat different situation. While there is diking installed, your rough calculation indicates that it is about half the capacity indicated in the SPCC Plan which calls for secondary containment of 150% of tank volume. Additionally, you note that the dike walls are made of concrete and the base (inside the diked area) is natural ground. Your escort tells you that he has repeatedly put in work requests to management to get the base of the dike paved but nothing seems to happen.

Assignment

1. Would you at this point modify your original audit plan? How? Have you seen enough? Would you decide to look at more than the 5 original tanks?

2. What would be your reactions relative to the first tank?

3. How would you react to the problems at the second tank? What specifically would you look for, do or ask at this tank?

4. How and when would you discuss this with the Plant Manager?

CALLING REGULATORY AUTHORITIES

Background

You have just completed an environmental review of a major process unit. On this unit you have discovered a small incinerator burning hydrogen sulfide off-gas. You later determine that hydrogen sulfide is regulated as a hazardous waste. This incinerator is presently covered under the facility's air permit but does not have a hazardous waste permit.

To determine the need for a hazardous waste permit you make a "blind" phone call to the regulatory authority. They tell you in no uncertain terms that the incinerator must have a permit and it is your legal and ethical duty to report the non-compliance instance immediately to them for possible enforcement. You are now beginning to understand the true meaning of the phrase "What did he know and when did he know it?"

Assignment

1. How would you end your phone call with the regulatory authority representative?

2. What should your next steps be?

3. How would you determine your personal liability? How will this affect your actions?

WORKING PAPERS

Background

You are the team leader of an audit team of four (4) people. Part of your responsibility is to review the working papers of the team members. It's lO:00pm on the second day of a four day audit. You're in your hotel room and begin to review John's notes. John is responsible for assessing site compliance with hazardous waste regulations. The first page is as follows:

Hazardous Waste Audit
May 6, 1991

Noted some empty drums stacked on their side. Oily substance on the ground; probably a major source of groundwater contamination. Locked tractor trailer; should come back later and open it; could have chemicals inside. Unlabeled transformers: not a hazardous waste issue. Probably some violations here; review regulations. Site should clean this place up immediately; don't want a Regulatory Authority to see this.

Your job is to give counsel to John the next morning at breakfast about improving working papers. John has been with the Company for twenty (20) years and is currently an Environmental Coordinator at another Plant. He is a headstrong and quite opinionated individual.

Assignment

1. How would you begin your conversation with John?

2. When would you have the discussion? Before, during or right after breakfast?

3. The audit has not been going that smoothly so far. Would you consider not having the discussion with John until after the audit is over to avoid a potentially messy scene and possible non-performing auditor?

4. When you do get around to having your conversation, what are some of the specific statements in his notes that you might comment on?

TANK FARM MANAGEMENT

Background

You are an EH&S auditor at a major manufacturing facility. There is a tank farm on the site in the utilities area with secondary containment. All the tanks are at atmospheric pressure and contain either sodium hypochlorite, sulfuric acid, or No. 4 fuel oil. They support boiler and wastewater treatment plant operations located nearby. Your job is to identify any EH&S deficiencies for the defined area. You are provided with area plan drawings of the tank farm and the loading and unloading area, a materials compatibility chart, and the MSDSs for the materials in the tank farm (see Figures D.1 through D.7).

Assignment

1. Local regulations require that the containment capacity for any hazardous materials storage tank farm be large enough to hold the contents of the largest tank plus a contingency for rainfall. This contingency can be either 10 percent of the largest tank's contents or the maximum amount of rainfall that cocurs over a 24-

Figure D.1 Tank Farm Plan View

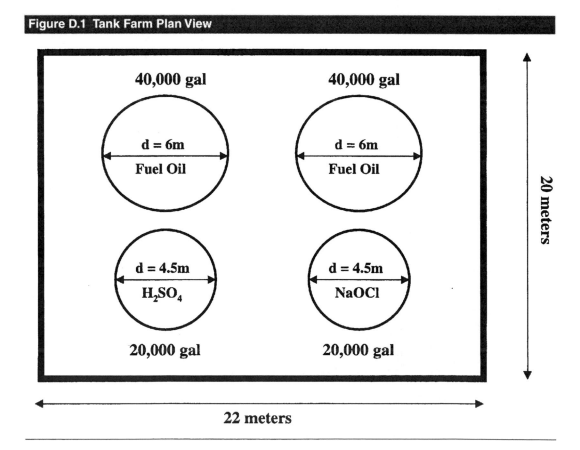

Figure D.2 Tanker Truck Unloading Area Containment Design

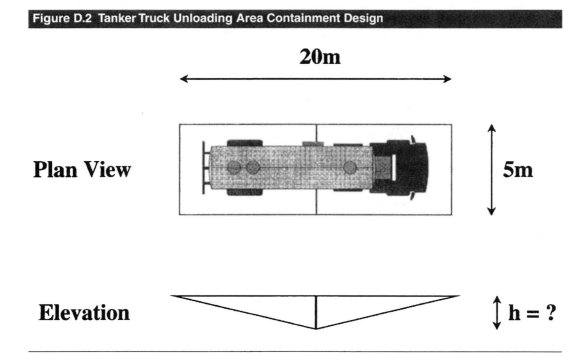

20m

Plan View

5m

Elevation

h = ?

hour period once in 25 years (10 cm in this case), whichever is more stringent. You note that the containment wall is about 2-feet high. Is this sufficient? How high or low should the wall be to meet the standard? (Note: 1 U.S. gallon = 0.0038 cubic meters.) (Hint: Do the calculations using metric units.)

2. Due to space constraints, the site has put all three materials (sodium hypochlorite, sulfuric acid, or No. 4 fuel oil) in the same containment area. Is there any problem with this? Are any of the materials incompatible with one another? How do you know? If there are incompatibilities, could the site simply construct internal walls between the problem tanks?

3. During a sulfuric acid unloading operation last week, there was a release of 75 gallons of the material outside the tank containment area. The hose connection to the truck broke free and there was no containment for the truck station. The release drained onto both paved and unpaved ground nearby. The spill was attended to immediately and no obvious harm to the environment resulted. The site did not report the spill to any regulatory agency. Do you think that this was correct? Why or why not? How would you address this issue with repect to the audit?

4. After the spill, the EH&S Coordinator was given the responsibility to design containment for the unloading area. He decided that the simplest containment approach for the unloading area would be to regrade and repave the area where the trucks unload. The containment conceputal design is shown in Figure D.2. He wants to know how deep the containment should be in the middle of the area (h = ? cm) in order for it to be able to hold the entire contents of the largest truck that uses the area to unload? This is a single-compartment, 20,000-liter tanker truck. He also wants to know the slope (as a percentage) of the containment area? Is it gradual enough so that the trucks can enter and exit without any problems? He is not very good at geometry and is asking you to help. Should you? Can you? What is the height requirement?

5. The EH&S Coordinator also needs to develop a new standard operating procedure (SOP) for the unloading of any materials at the tank farm. He has a generic SOP provided by the EH&S Excellence Center that includes such things as verification of paperwork, mandatory driver attendance during unloading, checking the condition of hoses and connections, wheel chocking, the use of drip pans, and so forth. The Coordinator does not plan to modify this SOP at all. Using the MSDS forms provided in Figures D.3, D.4, and D.5, is there any advice you might want to provide with regard to special provisions to be included in the SOP or safety equipment to have available at the unloading area?

Figure D.3 Sodium Hypochlorite MSDS

Material Safety Data Sheet

Revision Issued: 7/06/99   Supercedes: 5/17/96   First Issued: 6/17/87

Section I - Chemical Product And Company Identification

Product Name: Sodium Hypochlorite

CAS Number: 7681-52-9   HBCC MSDS No. CC17000

 HILL BROTHERS *Chemical Co.*

1675 NORTHMAIN STREET   •   ORANGE, CALIFORNIA 92867-3499
(714) 998-8800   •   FAX: (714) 998-6310
http://hillbrothers.com

1675 No. Main Street, Orange, California 92867
Telephone No: 714-998-8800 | Outside Calif: 800-821-7234 | Chemtrec: 800-424-9300

Section II - Composition/Information On Ingredients

Chemical Name	CAS Number	%	Exposure Limits (TWAs) in Air		
			ACGIH TLV	OSHA PEL	STEL
Sodium Hypochlorite	7681-52-9	10-15	N/A	N/A	N/A

Section III - Hazard Identification

Routes of Exposure: Sodium hypochlorite may affect the body either through ingestion, inhalation, or contact with the eyes and/or skin.

Summary of Acute Health Hazards

Ingestion: May cause irritation of the membranes of the mouth and throat, stomach pain and possible ulceration.

Inhalation: May cause irritation to the mucous membranes of the respiratory tract.

Skin: May cause moderate skin irritation and reddening of the skin.

Eyes: May cause severe irritation.

Carcinogenicity Lists: No **NTP:** No **IARC Monograph:** No **OSHA Regulated:** No

Summary of Chronic Health Hazards: Irritating effects increase with strength of solution and time of exposure.

Medical Conditions Generally Aggravated by Exposure: N/A

Section IV - First Aid Measures

Ingestion: Do not give any liquid to an unconscious person. Drink large quantities of gelatin solution or milk. If these are not available, drink large quantities of water. Do NOT give vinegar, baking soda or acidic antidotes. GET MEDICAL ATTENTION IMMEDIATELY.

Inhalation: Remove the victim to fresh air at once.

Skin: Wash with soap and water, flush with plenty of water.

Eyes: Flush with plenty of water for 15 minutes, lifting the lower and upper lids occasionally. GET MEDICAL ATTENTION IMMEDIATELY. Contact lenses should not be worn when working with this chemical.

Section V - Fire Fighting Measures

Figure D.3 *(cont'd)*

Flash Point: Nonflammable **Autoignition Temperature:** Nonflammable

Lower Explosive Limit: Nonflammable **Upper Explosive Limit:** Nonflammable

Unusual Fire and Explosion Hazards: Heat and acid contamination will produce irritating and toxic fumes. May decompose, generating irritating chlorine gas.

Extinguishing Media: N/A

Special Firefighting Procedures: N/A

Section VI - Accidental Release Measures

[Spills may need to be reported to the National Response Center (800/424-8802) DOT Reportable Quantity (RQ) is 100 pounds** Ventilate the area of the spill or leak. For large spills, evacuate the hazard area of unprotected personnel. Wear appropriate protective clothing. Dike and contain. Neutralize with sodium sulfite, bisulfite or thiosulfite. Remove with vacuum trucks or pump to storage vessels. Soak up residue with an absorbent such as clay, sand or other suitable material; place in non-leaking containers for proper disposal. Flush area with water to remove trace residue; dispose of flush solutions as above. For small spills, take up with an absorbent material and place in non-leaking containers; seal tightly for proper disposal.

Section VII - Handling and Storage

Store in vented, closed, clean non-corrosive containers in a cool, dry location away from direct sunlight and not adjacent to chemicals which may react with the bleach if spillage occurs. If closed containers become heated, the containers should be vented to release decomposition products (mainly oxygen under normal decomposition). Do not mix or contaminate with ammonia, hydrocarbons, acids, alcohols or ethers.

Section VIII - Exposure Controls/Personal Protection

Respiratory Protection: Always use only NIOSH/MSHA-approved respirators with acid type canisters or in the case of a fire use self-contained breathing apparatus.

Ventilation: No special ventilation is required unless bleach is exposed to decomposition conditions, i.e. heat or acidic conditions.

Protective Clothing: Avoid contact with the eyes. Wear chemical goggles and/or face shield if there is the likelihood of contact with the eyes. Avoid prolonged or repeated contact with the skin. Wear chemical-resistant gloves and other clothing as required to minimize contact.

Other Protective Clothing or Equipment: Safety showers and eyewash fountains should be available in storage and handling areas.

Work/Hygienic Practices: All employees who handle sodium hypochlorite should wash their hands before eating, smoking, or using the toilet facilities.

Section IX - Physical and Chemical Properties

Physical State: Liquid **pH:** 12

Melting Point/Range: N/A **Boiling Point/Range:** 48-76°C (120-170°F) for 15% (Decomposes)

Appearance/Color/Odor: Green to Yellow watery liquid with a pungent chlorine odor

Solubility in Water: 100% **Vapor Pressure(mmHg):** < 17.5

Specific Gravity(Water=1): 1.20-1.26 **Molecular Weight:** N/A

Vapor Density(Air=1): 1 **% Volatiles (by volume):** Variable-Water plus products of Decomposition

How to detect this compound : N/A

Section X - Stability and Reactivity

Figure D.3 *(cont'd)*

Stability: Unstable   **Hazardous Polymerization:** Will Not Occur

Conditions to Avoid: Stability decreases with concentration, heat, light exposure, decrease in pH and contamination with heavy metals, such as nickel, cobalt, copper and iron.

Materials to Avoid: Strong acids, strong oxidizers, heavy metals(which act as catalysts), reducing agents, ammonia, ether, and many organic and inorganic chemicals such as paint, kerosene, paint thinners, shellac, etc.

Hazardous Decomposition Products: Chlorine, hydrochloric acid, hypochlorous acid (HOCL). Composition depends upon temperature and decrease in pH. Additional decomposition products which depend upon pH, temperature and time are sodium chloride, sodium chlorate and oxygen.

Section XI - Toxicological Information

Toxicity Data: By ingestion, Grade 1: oral rat LD_{50}=8.91 g/kg IDLH Value: Data not availabe

Section XII - Ecological Information

N/A

Section XIII - Disposal Considerations

Can be neutralized with weak reducing agents such as sodium sulfite, bisulfite, or thiosulfite (DO NOT USE SULFATES OR BISULFATES). Dispose of in accordance with all applicable local, county, state and federal regulations.

Section XIV - Transport Information

DOT Proper Shipping Name: Hypochlorite Solution
DOT Hazard Class/ I.D. No.: 8, UN1791, III

Section XV - Regulatory Information

Reportable Quantity: 1000 Pounds (45.4 Kilograms)
NFPA Rating: Health - 2; Fire - 0; Reactivity - 1
0=Insignificant 1=Slight 2=Moderate 3=High 4=Extreme
Carcinogenicity Lists: No **NTP:** No **IARC Monograph:** No **OSHA Regulated:** No
NSF Standard 60   Maximum Use   210 mg/L

Section XVI - Other Information

Hazardous Ingredients: Sodium hypochlorite is manufactured only in solution form. Industrial grade sodium hypochlorite contains from 10 - 15% by weight NaOCL (10 - 17.8% available chlorine) with about 0.50-1.00% excess NaOH for stability control.
Synonyms/Common Names: Liquid Bleach
Chemical Family/Type: Halogen Compound

IMPORTANT! Read this MSDS before use or disposal of this product. Pass along the information to employees and any other persons who could be exposed to the product to be sure that they are aware of the information before use or other exposure. This MSDS has been prepared according to the OSHA Hazard Communication Standard [29 CFR 1910.1200]. The MSDS information is based on sources believed to be reliable. However, since data, safety standards, and government regulations are subject to change and the conditions of handling and use, or misuse are beyond our control, **Hill Brothers Chemical Company** makes no warranty, either expressed or implied, with respect to the completeness or continuing accuracy of the information contained herein and disclaims all liability for reliance thereon. Also, additional information may be necessary or helpful for specific conditions and circumstances of use. It is the user's responsibility to determine the suitability of this product and to evaluate risks prior to use, and then to exercise appropriate precautions for protection of employees and others.

Figure D.4 Sulfuric Acid MSDS

Material Safety Data Sheet

Revision Issued: 6/17/99   Supercedes: 1/27/97   First Issued: 1/02/86

Section I - Chemical Product And Company Identification

Product Name: Sulfuric Acid

CAS Number: 7664-93-9   HBCC MSDS No. CS18100

HILL BROTHERS *Chemical Co.*

1675 NORTH MAIN STREET • ORANGE, CALIFORNIA 92867-3409
(714) 998-8800 • FAX: (714) 998-0310
http://hillbrothers.com

1675 No. Main Street, Orange, California 92867
Telephone No: 714-998-8800 I Outside Calif: 800-821-7234 I Chemtrec: 800-424-9300

Section II - Composition/Information On Ingredients

| Chemical Name | CAS Number | % | Exposure Limits (TWAs) in Air | | |
			ACGIH TLV	OSHA PEL	STEL
Sulfuric Acid (H$_2$SO$_4$)	7664-93-9	93-99	1 mg/m³	1 mg/m³	3 mg/m³
Sulfur Dioxide	7446-09-5	< 2	2 ppm	5 ppm	5 ppm

Section III - Hazard Identification

Routes of Exposure: Sulfuric acid can affect the body if it is inhaled or if it comes in contact with the eyes or skin. It can also affect the body if it is swallowed.

Points of Attack: Sulfuric acid attacks the respiratory system, eyes, skin, teeth, and lungs.

Summary of Acute Health Hazards: Concentrated sulfuric acid will effectively remove the elements of water from many organic materials with which it comes in contact. It is even more rapidly injurious to mucous membranes and exceedingly dangerous to the eyes.

Ingestion: Causes serious burns of the mouth or perforation of the esophagus or stomach. May be fatal if swallowed.

Inhalation: Corrosive and highly toxic. May be harmful or fatal if inhaled. May cause severe irritation and burns of the nose, throat and respiratory tract.

Skin: Splashes on the skin will cause severe skin burns. Burning and charring of the skin are a result of the great affinity for, and strong exothermic reaction with, water. Direct contact can be severely irritating to the skin and may result in redness, swelling, burns and severe skin damage.

Eyes: Direct contact with the liquid or exposure to vapors or mists may cause stinging, tearing, redness, swelling, corneal damage and irreversible eye damage. Splashes in the eyes will cause severe burns. Contact lenses should not be worn when working with this chemical.

Effects of Overexposure: May cause severe irritation and burns of the mouth,, nose, throat, respiratory and digestive tract, coughing, nausea, vomiting, abdominal pain, chest pain, pneumonitis (inflammation of the fluid in the lungs), pulmonary edema (accumulation of the fluid in the lungs), and perforation of the stomach. Overexposure to acid mists has been reported to cause erosion to tooth enamel.

Medical Conditions Generally Aggravated by Exposure: Persons with pre-existing skin disorders and/or respiratory disorders (e.g. Asthma-like conditions) may be more susceptible to the effects of this material, and may be aggravated by exposure to this material.

Note to Physicians: Sulfuric acid is reported to cause pulmonary function impairment. Periodic surveillance is indicated. Sulfuric acid may cause acute lung damage. Surveillance of the lungs is

Figure D.4 *(cont'd)*

indicated. Ingestion may cause gastroesophageal perforation. Perforation may occur within 72 hours, but along with abscess formation, can occur weeks later. Long term complications may include esophageal, gastric or pyloric strictures or stenosis.

Section IV - First Aid Measures

Ingestion: If liquid sulfuric acid or solutions containing sulfuric acid have been swallowed and the person is conscious, give him one glass of water (1/2 glass of water to children under 5), immediately to dilute the sulfuric acid. Do NOT induce vomiting. Do not attempt to make the exposed person vomit. Do not leave victim unattended. GET MEDICAL ATTENTION IMMEDIATELY.

Inhalation: If a person breathes in large amounts of sulfuric acid, move the exposed person to fresh air at once. If breathing has stopped, perform artificial respiration. If breathing is difficult, give oxygen. Keep the affected person warm and at rest. GET MEDICAL ATTENTION AS SOON AS POSSIBLE.

Skin: If liquid sulfuric acid or solutions containing sulfuric acid get on the skin, immediately flush the contaminated skin with water for at least 15 minutes. If skin surface is damaged, apply a clean dressing. If liquid sulfuric acid or solutions containing sulfuric acid penetrate through the clothing, immediately remove the clothing, shoes and constrictive jewelry under a safety shower and continue to wash the skin for at least 15 minutes. GET MEDICAL ATTENTION IMMEDIATELY.

Eyes: If liquid sulfuric acid or solutions containing sulfuric acid get into the eyes, flush eyes immediately with a directed stream of water for at least 30 minutes while forcibly holding eyelids apart to ensure complete irrigation of all eye and lid tissue. GET MEDICAL ATTENTION IMMEDIATELY. Contact lenses should not be worn when working with this chemical.

Section V - Fire Fighting Measures

Flash Point: Non-flammable   **Autoignition Temperature:** N/A

Lower Explosive Limit: N/A   **Upper Explosive Limit:** N/A

Unusual Fire and Explosion Hazards: Not flammable but highly reactive and capable of igniting finely divided combustible materials on contact. Reacts violently with water and organic materials with evolution of heat. If involved in fire, may release hazardous oxides of sulfur. Vapors are heavier than air and may accumulate in low areas. Containers exposed to extreme heat may rupture due to pressure buildup. Contact with common metals may generate hydrogen, which can form flammable mixture with air.

Extinguishing Media: Fires involving small amount of combustibles may be smothered with suitable dry chemical, soda ash, lime, sand or CO2. Use water on combustibles burning in vicinity of this material but use care as water applied directly to this acid results in evolution of heat and causes splattering.

Special Firefighting Procedures: Causes severe, deep burns to tissue; very corrosive effect. Sulfuric Acid is extremely slippery. Emergency responders in the danger area should wear bunker gear and self contained breathing apparatus for fires beyond the incipient stage (29CFR 1910.156). In addition, wear other appropriate protective equipment as conditions warrant (see Section 8). Water reactive. Contact with water may generate heat. Isolate damage area, keep unauthorized personnel out. If tank, railcar, or tank truck is involved in a fire, isolate for 1/2 mile in all directions. Consider initial evacuation for 1/2 mile in all directions. Stop spill/release if it can be done with minimal risk. Move undamaged containers from danger area if it can be done with minimal risk. Fires involving small amounts of combustibles may be smothered with suitable dry chemicals. Use water on combustibles burning but avoid using water directly on acid as it results in evolution of heat and causes splattering.

Section VI - Accidental Release Measures

If sulfuric acid is spilled or leaked, ventilate area. Wear appropriate protective equipment including respiratory protection as conditions warrant (see Section 8). Collect spilled or leaked material in the most convenient and safe manner for reclamation or for disposal in a secured sanitary landfill. Sulfuric acid

Figure D.4 *(cont'd)*

should be absorbed in vermiculite, dry sand, earth, or a similar material. It may also be diluted and neutralized. Add slowly to solution of soda ash and slaked lime with stirring. Use Caution around spill area, Sulfuric Acid is extremely slippery. Stay upwind and away from spill release.

Section VII - Handling and Storage

Protect against physical damage and water. Keep containers closed. Sulfuric Acid is extremely slippery. Do not enter confined spaces such as tanks or pits without following proper entry procedures such as ASTM D–4276. To prevent ignition of hydrogen gas generated in metal containers (from metal contact) smoking, open flames and sparks must not be permitted in storage areas. This product has a great affinity for water, abstracting it from the air and also from many organic substances; hence it will char wood, etc.. When diluting, the acid should be added to the diluent. Separate from carbides, chlorates, fulminates, nitrates, picrates, powdered metals, and combustible materials. Keep away from strong oxidizing agents including oxygen and chlorine.

Other Precautions: Persons not wearing protective equipment and clothing should be restricted from areas of spills or leaks until cleanup has been completed.

Section VIII - Exposure Controls/Personal Protection

Respiratory Protection: Good industrial hygiene practices recommend that engineering controls be used to reduce environmental concentrations to the permissible exposure level. However, there are some exceptions where respirators may be used to control exposure. Respirators may be used when engineering and work practice controls are not technically feasible, when such controls are in the process of being installed, or when they fail and need to be supplemented. If the use of respirators is necessary, a NIOSH/MSHA approved air purifying respirator with N95 filter may be used under conditions where airborne concentrations are expected to exceed exposure limits (see Section II). Protection provided by air purifying respirators is limited (see manufactureres respirator selection guide). Use a positive pressure air supplied respirator if there is potential for an uncontrolled release, exposure levels are not known, or any other circumstances where air purifying respirators may not provide adequate protection. A respiratory protection program that meets OSHA'a 29 CFR 1910.134 and ANSI Z88.2 requirements must be followed whenever workplace conditions warrant a respirator's use.

Ventilation: General mechanical ventilation may be sufficient to keep sulfuric acid vapor concentrations within specified time-weighted TLV range. If general ventilation proves inadequate to maintain safe vapor concentrations, supplemental local exhaust may be required.

Protective Clothing: Employees should be provided with and required to use impervious clothing, gloves, face shields (eight-inch minimum), and other appropriate protective clothing necessary to prevent any possibility of skin contact with liquid sulfuric acid or solutions containing more than 1% sulfuric acid by weight.

Eye Protection: Employees should be provided with and required to use splash-proof safety goggles where there is any possibility of liquid sulfuric acid or solutions containing sulfuric acid contacting the eyes. Contact lenses should not be worn when working with this chemical.

Other Protective Clothing or Equipment: Rubber apron, rubber boots, eyewash stations and safety showers must be available in the immediate work area for emergency use.

Work/Hygienic Practices: Avoid contact with the skin and avoid breathing vapors. Do not eat, drink, or smoke in work area. Wash hands before eating, drinking, or using restroom.

Section IX - Physical and Chemical Properties

Figure D.4 *(cont'd)*

Physical State: Liquid   **pH:** 1.0

Melting Point/Range: 3° C; 37°F   **Boiling Point/Range:** 260° F; 315° C

Appearance/Color/Odor: Colorless to dark brown; odorless unless hot, then choking

Solubility in Water: 100%   **Vapor Pressure(mmHg):** 1 @ 145.8°F

Specific Gravity(Water=1): 1.82-1.84   **Molecular Weight:** 98

Vapor Density(Air=1): 3.4%   **% Volatiles:** Negligible

Evaporation Rate (N-Butyl Acetate=1): < 1   **Weight/Gallon:** 15.2 Lbs.

How to detect this compound : Sampling and analyses may be performed by collection of sulfuric acid on a cellulose membrane filter, followed by extraction with distilled water and isopropyl alcohol, treatment with perchloric acid, and titration with barium perchlorate. Also, detector tubes certified by NIOSH under 42 CFR Part 84 or other direct-reading devices calibrated to measure sulfuric acid may be used.

Section X - Stability and Reactivity

Stability: Stable   **Hazardous Polymerization:** Will not occur

Conditions to Avoid: Temperatures above 150°F

Materials to Avoid: Contact of acid with organic materials (such as chlorates, carbides, fulminates, and picrates), alkaline materials and water may cause fires and explosions. Contact of acid with metals may form toxic sulfur dioxide fumes and flammable hydrogen gas. Contact with hypochlorites (e.g., chlorine bleach), sulfides, or cyanides will produce toxic gases.

Hazardous Decomposition Products: Toxic gases and vapors (such as sulfuric acid fume, sulfur dioxide, and carbon monoxide) may be released when sulfuric acid decomposes. Decomposes to water and sulfur trioxide above 644°F.

Section XI - Toxicological Information

(Sulfuric acid) mist severely irritates the eyes, respiratory tract, and skin. Concentrated sulfuric acid destroys tissue due to its severe dehydrating action, whereas the dilute form acts as a mild irritant due to acid properties. The LC50 of mist of 1-micron particle size for an 8 hour exposure was 50 mg/m³ for adult guinea pigs and 18 mg/m³ for young animals. Continuous exposure of guinea pigs to 2 mg/m³ for 5 days caused pulmonary edema and thickening of the alveolar walls; exposure of guinea pigs to 2 mg/m³ for 1 hour caused an increase in pulmonary airway resistance from reflex bronchoconstriction. A worker sprayed in the face with liquid fuming sulfuric acid suffered skin burns of the face and body, as well as pulmonary edema from inhalation. Sequelae were pulmonary fibrosis, residual bronchitis, and pulmonary emphysema; in addition, necrosis of the skin resulted in marked scarring. In human subjects, concentrations of about 5 mg/m³ were objectionable, usually causing cough, an increase in respiratory rate, and impairment of ventilatory capacity. Workers exposed to concentrations of 12.6 to 35 mg/m³ had a markedly higher incidence of erosion and discoloration of teeth than was noted in unexposed individuals. Splashed in the eye, the concentrated acid causes extremely severe damage, often leading to blindness, whereas dilute acid produces more transient effects from which recovery may be complete. Repeated exposure of workers to the mist causes chronic conjunctivitis, tracheobronchitis, stomatitis, and dermatitis, as well as dental erosion. While ingestion of the liquid is unlikely in ordinary industrial use, the highly corrosive nature of the substance may be expected to produce serious mucous membrane burns of the mouth and esophagus.

Section XII - Ecological Information

N/A

Section XIII - Disposal Considerations

Sulfuric acid may be placed in sealed containers or absorbed in vermiculite, dry sand, earth, or a similar

Figure D.4 *(cont'd)*

material and disposed of in a secured sanitary landfill. It may also be diluted and neutralized. Check with your Federal, State, and Local authorities as neutralized sulfuric acid may be allowed to be flushed down the drain. Empty conatiners must be handled with care due to material residue.

Section XIV - Transport Information

DOT Proper Shipping Name: RQ Sulfuric Acid
DOT Hazard Class/ I.D. No.: 8, UN1830, II

Section XV - Regulatory Information

Reportable Quantity: 1,000 Pounds (454 Kilograms) (66.71 Gal.)
NFPA Rating: Health - 3; Fire - 0; Reactivity - 2
0=Insignificant 1=Slight 2=Moderate 3=High 4=Extreme
Carcinogenicity Lists: Yes **NTP:** No **IARC Monograph:** No **OSHA Regulated:** Yes

Section 313 Supplier Notification: This product contains the following toxic chemcial(s) subject to the reporting requirements of SARA TITLE III Section 313 of the Emergency Planning and Community Right-To Know Act of 1986 and of 40 CFR 372:

<u>CAS #</u>	<u>Chemical Name</u>	<u>% By Weight</u>
7664-93-9	Sulfuric Acid	93-99

Section XVI - Other Information

Synonyms/Common Names: H2SO4; Oil of Vitriol; Spirit of Sulfur; Hydrogen Sulfate; Oleum
Chemical Family/Type: Inorganic Acid

<u>**IMPORTANT!** Read this MSDS before use or disposal of this product. Pass along the information to employees and any other persons who could be exposed to the product to be sure that they are aware of the information before use or other exposure.</u> This MSDS has been prepared according to the OSHA Hazard Communication Standard [29 CFR 1910.1200]. The MSDS information is based on sources believed to be reliable. However, since data, safety standards, and government regulations are subject to change and the conditions of handling and use, or misuse are beyond our control, **Hill Brothers Chemical Company** makes no warranty, either expressed or implied, with respect to the completeness or continuing accuracy of the information contained herein and disclaims all liability for reliance thereon. Also, additional information may be necessary or helpful for specific conditions and circumstances of use. It is the user's responsibility to determine the suitability of this product and to evaluate risks prior to use, and then to exercise appropriate precautions for protection of employees and others.

Figure D.5 #4 Fuel Oil MSDS

COASTAL — FUEL OIL #4 - FUEL OIL,BURNER
MATERIAL SAFETY DATA SHEET
NSN: 9140002474361
Manufacturer's CAGE: 46684
Part No. Indicator: A
Part Number/Trade Name: FUEL OIL #4

General Information

Item Name: FUEL OIL,BURNER
Company's Name: COASTAL CORP
Company's Street: 9 GREENWAY PLAZA
Company's City: HOUSTON
Company's State: TX
Company's Country: US
Company's Zip Code: 77046
Company's Emerg Ph #: 713-877-6732,713-877-1400
Company's Info Ph #: 713-877-1400
Record No. For Safety Entry: 004
Tot Safety Entries This Stk#: 005
Status: SE
Date MSDS Prepared: 07FEB90
Safety Data Review Date: 19SEP91
Supply Item Manager: KY
MSDS Serial Number: BKQTM
Spec Type, Grade, Class: GRADE 4
Hazard Characteristic Code: F4
Unit Of Issue: DR
Unit Of Issue Container Qty: 55.0 GALLONS
Type Of Container: DRUM, 16 GAGE
Net Unit Weight: 412.2 LBS

Ingredients/Identity Information

Proprietary: NO
Ingredient: FUEL OIL NO. 4
Ingredient Sequence Number: 01
Percent: 100
NIOSH (RTECS) Number: 1006946FO
CAS Number: 68476-31-3
OSHA PEL: 5 MG/M3
ACGIH TLV: 5 MG/M3
Other Recommended Limit: STEL 10 MG/M3 OIL MI

Figure D.5 *(cont'd)*

Physical/Chemical Characteristics

Appearance And Odor: BLACK LIQUID WITH MILD PETROLEUM ODOR.
Boiling Point: 400F,204C
Specific Gravity: 0.90-1.0
Decomposition Temperature: UNKNOWN
Evaporation Rate And Ref: <0.01 (BU ACETATE=1)
Solubility In Water: INSOLUBLE
Viscosity: 90-120 SUS
Autoignition Temperature: 765F

Fire and Explosion Hazard Data

Flash Point: >140F,60C
Flash Point Method: PMCC
Lower Explosive Limit: 1.0
Upper Explosive Limit: 5.0
Extinguishing Media: USE HALON, CARBON DIOXIDE, FOAM, OR DRY CHEMICAL.
Special Fire Fighting Proc: WEAR FIRE FIGHTING PROTECTIVE EQUIPMENT AND A
FULL FACED SELF CONTAINED BREATHING APPARATUS. COOL FIRE EXPOSED
CONTAINERS
WITH WATER SPRAY. CONTAIN RUNOFF.
Unusual Fire And Expl Hazrds: COMBUSTION OR HEAT OF FIRE MAY PRODUCE
HAZARDOUS DECOMPOSITION PRODUCTS AND VAPORS.

Reactivity Data

Stability: YES
Cond To Avoid (Stability): EXTREMELY HIGH TEMPERATURES, OPEN FLAMES
Materials To Avoid: STRONG OXIDIZING AGENTS
Hazardous Decomp Products: FUMES,SMOKE,CARBON MONOXIDE, AND OTHER
DECOMPOSITION PRODUCTS IN THE CASE OF INCOMPLETE COMBUSTION.
Hazardous Poly Occur: NO
Conditions To Avoid (Poly): NOT APPLICABLE

Health Hazard Data

LD50-LC50 Mixture: ORAL LD50 (RAT) UNKNOWN
Route Of Entry - Inhalation: YES
Route Of Entry - Skin: YES
Route Of Entry - Ingestion: YES
Health Haz Acute And Chronic: ACUTE-INGESTION:HARMFUL OR FATAL.
ASPIRATION

Figure D.5 *(cont'd)*

INTO LUNGS CAN CAUSE CHEMICAL PNEUMONIA AND CAN BE FATAL. INHALATION OF
IRRITATION. CHRONIC-PROLONGED/REPEATED SKIN CONTACT MAY CAUSE IRRITATION,
DERMATITIS.
Carcinogenicity - NTP: NO
Carcinogenicity - IARC: NO
Carcinogenicity - OSHA: NO
Signs/Symptoms Of Overexp: INHALATION MAY CAUSE IRRITATION OF NOSE, THROAT
AND DIZZINESS. PROLONGED OR REPEATED SKIN CONTACT MAY CAUSE SKIN
IRRITATION. EYE CONTACT MAY CAUSE EYE IRRITATION.INGESTION:VOMITING,
WEEKNESS, COMA, CONVUSIONS.
Med Cond Aggravated By Exp: PERSONS WITH SKIN & PULMONARY DISORDERS SHOULD
AVOID PROLONGED CONTACT WHEN HANDLING OR USING THIS PRODUCT.
Emergency/First Aid Proc: SKIN: REMOVE CONTAMINATED CLOTHING. WASH WITH
REMOVE TO FRESH AIR & RESTORE BREATHING IF NECESSARY. GET MEDICAL
ATTENTION. EYE: IMMEDIATELY FLUSH WITH WATER FOR 15 MINUTES WHILE HOLDING
EYELIDS OPEN. GET MEDICAL ATTENTION. INGESTION: GET IMMEDIATE MEDICAL
ATTENTION. DO NOT INDUCE VOMITING. NOTHING BY MOUTH IF UNCONSCIOUS.

Precautions for Safe Handling and Use

Steps If Matl Released/Spill: RECOVER FREE PRODUCT, OR ABSORB WITH
DIATOMACEOUS EARTH OR OTHER INERT MATERIAL. STORE IN APPROPRIATE CONTAINER
FOR DISPOSAL. KEEP PRODUCT OUT OF SEWERS AND WATERCOURSES BY DIKING OR
IMPOUNDING. MINIMIZE SKIN CONTACT AND BREATHING VAPORS.
Neutralizing Agent: NOT APPLICABLE
Waste Disposal Method: DISPOSE OF WASTE IN ACCORDANCE WITH LOCAL, STATE
AND FEDERAL REGULATIONS. THIS PRODUCT IS SUBJECT TO 40 CFR PT. 268.30 LAND
BAN, 40 CFR PT 370 & 372.
Precautions-Handling/Storing: AVOID STORAGE NEAR OPEN FLAME OR OTHER
SOURCES OF IGNITION,AND STRONG OXIDANTS. KEEP CONTAINERS CLOSED.
Other Precautions: EMPTY CONTAINERS RETAIN RESIDUE. DO NOT PRESSURIZE,
CUT, WELD OR EXPOSE TO HEAT, FLAME, STATIC ELECTRICITY, OR OTHER SOURCES OF
IGNITION; THEY MAY EXPLODE AND CAUSE INJURY.

Figure D.5 *(cont'd)*

Control Measures

Respiratory Protection: USE SUPPLIED-AIR RESPIRATORY PROTECTION IN CONFINED OR ENCLOSED SPACES, IF NEEDED.
Ventilation: SUFFICIENT TO MAINTAIN ATMOSPHERE BELOW TLV LIMIT.
Protective Gloves: NEOPRENE, NITRILE, OR POLYVINYL ALCOHOL
Eye Protection: USE CHEMICAL SAFETY GOGGLES
Other Protective Equipment: EYE WASH STATION & SAFETY SHOWER. CHEMICALLY RESISTANT BOOTS AND APRONS RECOMMENDED.
Work Hygienic Practices: DO NOT TAKE INTERNALLY. AVOID SKIN/EYE CONTACT. WASH SKIN AFTER USING PRODUCT. DO NOT EAT, DRINK OR SMOKE IN WORK AREA.
Suppl. Safety & Health Data: WASH OR TAKE SHOWER IF GENERAL CONTACT OCCURS. REMOVE OIL-SOAKED CLOTHING AND LAUNDER BEFORE REUSE. DISCARD
CONTAMINATED LEATHER GLOVES AND SHOES.

Transportation Data

Trans Data Review Date: 91262
DOT PSN Code: GTF
DOT Proper Shipping Name: GAS OIL OR DIESEL FUEL OR HEATING OIL, LIGHT
DOT Class: 3
DOT ID Number: UN1202
DOT Pack Group: III
DOT Label: FLAMMABLE LIQUID
IMO PSN Code: HRR
IMO Proper Shipping Name: GAS OIL
IMO Regulations Page Number: 3375
IMO UN Number: 1202
IMO UN Class: 3.3
IMO Subsidiary Risk Label: -
IATA PSN Code: MTX
IATA UN ID Number: 1202
IATA Proper Shipping Name: GAS OIL
IATA UN Class: 3
IATA Label: FLAMMABLE LIQUID
AFI PSN Code: MTX
AFI Prop. Shipping Name: GAS OIL OR DIESEL FUEL OR HEATING OIL, LIGHT
AFI Class: 3
AFI ID Number: UN1202
AFI Pack Group: III
AFI Basic Pac Ref: 7-7

Figure D.5 *(cont'd)*

Disposal Data

Label Data

Label Required: YES
Technical Review Date: 19SEP91
MFR Label Number: UNKNOWN
Label Status: F
Common Name: FUEL OIL #4
Signal Word: WARNING!
Acute Health Hazard-Moderate: X
Contact Hazard-Slight: X
Fire Hazard-Moderate: X
Reactivity Hazard-None: X
Special Hazard Precautions: ACUTE-INGESTION:HARMFUL OR FATAL. INHALATION
OF MIST MAY CAUAE IRRITATION OF NOSE & THROAT. FURTHER EXPOSURE MAY
CAUSE
IRRITATION. CHRONIC-PROLONGED/REPEATED SKIN CONTACT MAY CAUSE
IRRITATION,
DERMATITIS. RECOVER FREE PRODUCT, OR ABSORB WITH DIATOMACEOUS
EARTH OR
OTHER INERT MATERIAL. STORE IN APPROPRIATE CONTAINER FOR DISPOSAL.
KEEP
PRODUCT OUT OF SEWERS AND WATERCOURSES BY DIKING OR IMPOUNDING.
MINIMIZE
SKIN CONTACT AND BREATHING VAPORS. AVOID STORAGE NEAR OPEN FLAME
OR OTHER
SOURCES OF IGNITION,AND STRONG OXIDANTS. KEEP CONTAINERS CLOSED.
Protect Eye: Y
Protect Skin: Y
Protect Respiratory: Y
Label Name: COASTAL CORP
Label Street: 9 GREENWAY PLAZA
Label City: HOUSTON
Label State: TX
Label Zip Code: 77046
Label Country: US
Label Emergency Number: 713-877-1400

Figure D.6 Materials Compatibility Chart

Reactivity group

No.	Name
1	Acids, minerals, non-oxidizing
2	Acids, minerals, oxidizing
3	Acids, organic
4	Alcohols & glycols
5	Aldehydes
6	Amides
7	Amines, aliphatic & aromatic
8	Azo compounds, diazo comp. & hydrazines
9	Carbamates
10	Caustics
11	Cyanides
12	Dithiocarbamates
13	Esters
14	Ethers
15	Fluorides, inorganic
16	Hydrocarbons, aromatic
17	Halogenated organics
18	Isocyanates
19	Ketones
20	Mercaptans & other organic sulfides
21	Metals, alkali & alkaline earth, elemental
22	Metals, other elemental & alloys as powders, vapors or sponges
23	Metals, other elemental & alloys as sheets, rods, drops, moldings, etc.
24	Metals & metal compounds, toxic
25	Nitrides
26	Nitrites
27	Nitro compounds, organic
28	Hydrocarbons, aliphatic, unsaturated
29	Hydrocarbons, aliphatic, saturated
30	Peroxides & hydroperoxides, organic
31	Phenols & cresols
32	Organophosphates, phosphothioates, phosphodithioates
33	Sulfides, inorganic
34	Epoxides
101	Combustible & flammable materials, misc.
102	Explosives
103	Polymerizable compounds
104	Oxidizing agents, strong
105	Reducing agents, strong
106	Water & mixtures containing water
107	Water reactive substances

KEY

Reactivity code	Consequences
H	Heat generation
F	Fire
G	Innocuous and non-flammable gas generation
GT	Toxic gas generation
GF	Flammable gas generation
E	Explosion
P	Violent polymerization
S	Solubilization of toxic substances
U	May be hazardous but unknown

Example:

H
F
GT

Heat generation, fire, and toxic gas generation

Row 107 (Water reactive substances): Extremely Reactive! Do Not Mix with Any Chemical or Waste Material

Column footer numbers: 1, 2, 3, 4, 5, 6, 7, 8, 9, 10, 11, 12, 13, 14, 15, 16, 17, 18, 19, 20, 21, 22, 23, 24, 25, 26, 27, 28, 29, 30, 31, 32, 33, 34, 101, 102, 103, 104, 105, 106, 107

Figure D.7 Excerpt of Hazardous Chemical List

Table 1 Hazardous Chemical List (continued)

Chemical Name	Reactivity Group No.	Chemical Name	Reactivity Group No.
Raney nickel	22	Soda niter	104
RDX	27, 102	Sodium	21, 105, 107
Refuse	101	Sodium acid fluoride	15
Resins	101	Sodium aluminate	10, 105
Resorcinol	31	Sodium aluminate hydride	105, 107
Rubidium	21	Sodium amide	10, 107
Salicylated mercury	24	Sodium arsenate	24
Saligenin	31	Sodium arsenite	24
Saltpeter	102, 104	Sodium azide	102
Schradan	6, 32	Sodium bichromate	24, 104
Selenious acid	1, 24	Sodium bifluoride	15
Selenium	22, 23, 24	Sodium bromate	104
Selenium diethyldithiocarbamate	12, 24	Sodium cacodylate	24
Selenium fluoride	15, 24	Sodium carbonate	10
Selenous acid	1, 24	Sodium carbonate peroxide	104
Silicochloroform	107	Sodium chlorate	104
Silicon tetrachloride	107	Sodium chlorite	104
Silicon tetrafluoride	15, 107	Sodium chromate	24
Silver acetylide	24, 102, 105, 107	Sodium cyanide	11
Silver azide	24, 102	Sodium dichloroisocyanurate	104
Silver cyanide	11, 24	Sodium dichromate	24, 104
Silver nitrate	24, 104	Sodium dimethylarsenate	24
Silver nitride	24, 25, 102	Sodium fluoride	15
Silver styphnate	24, 27, 102	Sodium hydride	105, 107
Silver sulfide	24, 33, 105	Sodium hydroxide	10
Silver tetrazene	24, 102	Sodium hypochlorite	10, 104
Silver trinitroresorcinate	24, 27, 102	Sodium hyposulfite	105
Slaked lime	10, 107	Sodium methylate	10, 107
Smokeless powder	102	Sodium methoxide	10, 107
Sodamide	10, 107	Sodium molybdate	24

Figure D.7 *(cont'd)*

Table 1 Hazardous Chemical List (continued)

Chemical Name	Reactivity Group No.	Chemical Name	Reactivity Group No.
Sodium monoxide	10, 107	Succinic acid	3
Sodium nitrate	104	Succinic acid peroxide	30
Sodium nitride	25	Sulfonyl chloride	107
Sodium nitrite	104	Sulfonyl fluoride	107
Sodium oxide	10, 107	Sulfotepp	32
Sodium pentachlorophenate	31	Sulfur chloride	107
Sodium perchlorate	104	Sulfur (elemental)	101
Sodium permanganate	24, 104	Sulfuric acid	2, 107
Sodium peroxide	104, 107	Sulfuricanhydride	104, 107
Sodium phenolsulfonate	31	Sulfur monochloride	107
Sodium picramate	27, 102	Sulfur mustard	20
Sodium polysulfide	101	Sulfur oxychloride	107
Sodium potassium alloy	21, 107	Sulfur pentafluoride	15, 107
Sodium salenate	24	Sulfur trioxide	104, 107
Sodium sulfide	24, 33, 105	Sulfuryl chloride	107
Sodium thiosulfate	105	Sulfuryl fluoride	107
Stannic chloride	24, 107	Supracide*	32
Stannic sulfide	33, 105	Surecide*	32
Starch nitrate	27, 102	Synthetic rubber	101
Stilbene	16	TCDD	14, 17
Stoddard solvent	101	TEDP	32
Strontium	24	TEL	24
Strontium arsenate	24	TEPA	6, 32
Strontium dioxide	24, 104	TEPP	32
Strontium monosulfide	24, 33, 105	THF	14
Strontium nitrate	24, 104	TMA	7
Strontium peroxide	104	TML	24
Strontium tetrasulfide	24, 33, 105	TNB	27, 102
Styphnic acid	27, 31, 102	TNT	27, 102
styrene	16, 28, 103	Tall oil	101

Interviewing Skills

INTERVIEWING ROLE PLAYING EXERCISE

Background

Interviewing is a central part of any EH&S audit. During the course of an audit, the auditors may be talking with plant managers, EH&S managers, purchasing agents, laboratory staff with doctoral degrees, and unit operators with 35 years of experience with the company. Information gained from these discussions is vital to making valid and persuasive findings and recommendations. However, obtaining valuable information through the interview is the most difficult way to gather evidence. In some ways, audits will always seem like performance evaluations to those being audited; no matter how much they are assured that "we're from corporate and we're here to help you." Let's explore some key interviewing issues by completing the five following exercises.

Assignment

1. What percent of an interviewer's time is *typically* spent:

    Listening?   ____%
    Taking Notes?   ____%
    Talking?   ____%
    Observing?   ____%
    Thinking?   ____%

    TOTAL   ____%

    Is the interviewer doing anything else during the interview? What should the interviewer do once the interview is over?

2. Under what circumstances do you write up a finding solely based on the results of an interview?

3. What do you do if an interviewee is non-responsive?

4. What is right or wrong about the following questions?

    (1) Do you inspect weekly as required by the hazardous waste regulations?

    (2) Can you tell me about your Preparedness and Prevention Program?

    (3) Do you have any concerns about maintaining compliance at this site?

    (4) What concerns do you have about maintaining compliance at this site?

    (5) Have you ever been cited by a regulatory agency?

    (6) Do you have any confined spaces at this site?

    (7) Why is housekeeping so poor in this area?

    (8) Could you find that exemption letter that you mentioned you received from the regulatory authority eight years ago?

    (9) Does the plant look any different during other times of the year? Is there more activity at other times? Does the plant ever have planned maintenance shutdowns?

    (10) Who is responsible for the labels missing from these containers?

    (11) What haven't you told me that might help me be complete in my review?

    (12) What do you think is the best way to begin our review of this part of the facility?

    (13) Can we go over this again? I need help in understanding how the regulations apply to this operation.

    (14) Would you mind if I recorded our conversation? It would be a great help.

    (15) I've heard you have a nice operation here. Can we talk a bit about what happens on a day-to-day basis?

5. Listen to the role-playing exercise that will be performed in class. This exercise involves two auditors with very different approaches interviewing a site EH&S staff person. There are many good things and bad things that will happen during the simulated interviews. Keep track of these and be ready to discuss them at the conclusion of the exercise.

Background

The following is a scripted role-playing exercise. The exercise involves two auditors with very different approaches to interviewing a site engineer responsible for hazardous waste management, among other things. As we begin, the first auditor enters the engineer's office and begins the interview. After a while, the first auditor leaves and some time later the second auditor shows up to continue the investigation. There are many good things and as many bad things that will happen during the interviews. Keep track of these and be ready to discuss them at the conclusion of the exercise.

ACT I:	FIRST AUDITOR INTERVIEWING THE SITE ENGINEER IN HIS OR HER OFFICE

AUDITOR: *Good morning Mr./Ms. _____, my name is _____ and I'm here to conduct an EH&S audit of the hazardous waste storage facility here at your plant. The purpose of this audit is to uncover poor practices and negligent operations and report them to responsible officials, so that corrective actions can be taken. Those actions might be to fund needed maintenance and repair or to arrange for personnel action to remove or replace incompetent staff. Do you understand this or have any questions?*

ENGINEER: Well, no ...Except that the waste regulations are pretty overwhelming and I'm doing the best I can. Mr./Ms. _____, my supervisor, said you were coming over, but I figured this as more of a regulatory type of inspection. We had one of those last month and we did very well, except for three items that I'm working on right now. They said we should have more specific training and I've arranged for a company to come in and help with ......

AUDITOR: *[INTERRUPTING] That's all very interesting Mr./Ms. _____, but I have an inspection protocol that I have to follow and I'm sure some of it will cover all the same areas that the agency inspector touched on.*

ENGINEER: Okay. It was kind of interesting, what we did, but whatever you want to do is fine with me.

AUDITOR: *Good. Can you tell me how your storage facility complies with the hazardous waste regulations? Specifically, how do you comply with the security requirements?*

ENGINEER: Well, the place is secure, you know. It's inside the plant and it has a fence and we keep people out. So it's secure.

AUDITOR: *How about signs?*

ENGINEER: We have signs and we keep people out of the storage area.

AUDITOR: *Well, what do the signs say?*

ENGINEER: They say to keep out ... I don't remember the exact wording. It's whatever the regulations require. I remember having to get the exact wording from the regulations to give to the sign shop. They made up the signs with the wording from the regulations.

AUDITOR: *How big are the signs? And the lettering, how big is that?*

ENGINEER: Oh, they're about like this [USES HANDS] . I don't know.

AUDITOR: *How far away can the signs be read?*

ENGINEER: I guess that depends on how good your eyes are ... [ACTING AN-NOYED]

AUDITOR: *Mr./Ms _____, I'm trying to conduct a serious effort here and your present attitude isn't helping at all.*

ENGINEER: Well, Mr./Ms. _____, your questions are not exactly to the point. You seem to be playing some sort of game here. If you could be more specific in your questions, I could probably give you better answers.

AUDITOR: *All right Mr./Ms. _____, how about this? Are the signs legible from a distance of 10 meters?*

ENGINEER: Yeah, I guess, I think. I don't know. Why don't we go outside and look at the signs and you can see for yourself?

AUDITOR: *We can't. I have to finish this checklist first and then I want to review all your permits, plans, and manifests. Another auditor will look at the physical layout.*

ENGINEER: Well, I would guess that the average person could read the signs from 10 meters, but I really can't say for sure.

AUDITOR: *Look, let's move on. With regard to inspections, do you inspect the facility at least weekly?*

ENGINEER: Yes.

AUDITOR: *Do you have a written inspection plan?*

ENGINEER: Sure.

AUDITOR: *Can I see it?*

ENGINEER: [REACHES FOR MOCK PLAN] Well, let me see. Here it is.

AUDITOR: *This shows that you inspect the facility daily. Why do you do that? You just said that you inspected weekly.*

ENGINEER: Well, *you* said weekly and I figured that was what I was supposed to do.

AUDITOR: *Okay, Mr./Ms. _____, let's go over this again. You actually inspect the storage area daily?*

ENGINEER: Yeah, that's right. Is there something wrong with that?

AUDITOR: *Well, you only have to do it weekly. And where do you record the results of the inspections?*

ENGINEER: [REACHES FOR MOCK FORM] We write up the problems on this form and send it over to plant maintenance for them to repair. [REACHES FOR MOCK FOLDER] We keep copies here in this folder.

AUDITOR: *So, you only note exceptions on the inspection report?*

ENGINEER: Yeah, I guess you could say that.

AUDITOR: *Mr./Ms. _____, you should be aware that the hazardous waste regulations require you to keep a log of inspections which includes, at a minimum, a separate entry for each inspection including the date and time of each inspection; the name of the inspector, not simply the initials as you have done here; notations of observations made, both positive and negative; and the date and nature of any repairs. Mr./Ms. _____, the inspection recording procedures you have here are totally inadequate and are in violation of the regulations!*

ENGINEER: Hey! Wait a minute! I'm doing my best. We know what the problems are and we fix anything we find. If you would go out and see the facility, you would see that we put any leaking containers in over-pack drums; we have our spill cleanup equipment in place; the facility is dry; and everything is okay. So, I don't have the proper forms. What are you concerned about anyway, the paperwork or how we manage the waste?

AUDITOR: *Mr./Ms. _____, the hazardous waste program is a paper intensive effort and if you can't deal with these requirements, I don't see how this facility can ever be brought into compliance.*

ENGINEER: What else do you want to see? [ACTING ANNOYED]

AUDITOR: *Well, we're way behind schedule here but I would like to discuss personnel training. Has everyone who works here completed a program of training to teach them to perform their duties?*

ENGINEER: Yes.

AUDITOR: *The person who directs the training must also be trained in hazardous waste management. Who directs the training?*

ENGINEER: I do.

AUDITOR: *Are you yourself trained, Mr./Ms. _____?*

ENGINEER: I am.

AUDITOR: *Where did you get trained?*

ENGINEER: I took a course with _____ .

AUDITOR: *Do you feel that such a course qualifies you to train people?*

ENGINEER: I do. Why, do you have some kind of problem with that?

AUDITOR: *No, no, Mr./Ms. _____. One last question and then I really must leave. Do any newly hired people, people who have not completed training, do any of these people work alone or unsupervised?*

ENGINEER: No. We closely supervise all our new employees.

AUDITOR: *Good. What about the young fellow over there. [POINTS TO A MAN IN THE CLASS] Is he a new employee?*

ENGINEER: Yes.

AUDITOR: *Is anyone supervising him?*

ENGINEER: Well, he's only eating his lunch. I think he can do that by himself! [PAUSE] Look, is there anything else? It's getting kind of late.

AUDITOR: *No, I don't think so. Oh, yeah! I'm also supposed to audit electrical safety while I'm here. I don't normally audit this topic, but let's give it a try.*

ENGINEER: Okay, but this is not my strongest area, either. How about if we ask the master electrician to come over?

AUDITOR: *That probably won't be necessary. We'll just blast through these questions. Between you and me, these questions on the audit protocol are really overkill ... they just go on and on. I'll tell you what, why don't we begin this area after lunch?*

[CONTINUING] Well, Mr./Ms. _____, thanks for your time. By the way, my associate, Mr./Ms. _____, will be coming along later this afternoon to discuss container storage standards. This has been most interesting!

ENGINEER: Okay. [SARCASTICALLY] Watch your step on the way out. I wouldn't want anything unpleasant to happen to you.

ACT II: **SECOND AUDITOR INTERVIEWING THE SITE ENGINEER IN HIS OR HER OFFICE AND THEN PROCEEDING OUT INTO THE YARD**

AUDITOR: *Well, hello Mr./Ms. _____, Mr./Ms. _____ said he/she had finished his/her portion of the audit and that you were ready to talk about container storage standards.*

ENGINEER: Okay, I guess I can spare some time. How long will this take?

AUDITOR: *I know you're a busy person and I really won't take any more of your time than is necessary. Probably no more than an hour.*

ENGINEER: Okay.

AUDITOR: *Let's see ... You know there is so much involved in these regulations, I can hardly keep up myself and I deal with this every day. How do you keep track of all these regulations?*

ENGINEER: Well, the Corporate EH&S staff send us notices on changes and Mr./Ms. _____, the site EH&S coordinator, and I talk about changes every few weeks. I have a copy of the latest hazardous waste regulations and I refer to that.

AUDITOR: *Do you keep copies of that around here?*

ENGINEER: Yes, I have to in order to conduct my inspections and everything. It's a big job to keep up to date.

AUDITOR: *Yes, it really is. Well, I want to see how you store containers, so I guess the best thing to do is to go out and see the drum storage area.*

ENGINEER: Okay. You're the boss, Mr./Ms. _____.

AUDITOR: *Well, is there anything else you think we should do first? This is your facility and you know it best, so I guess I'm asking you if that would be a good place to start.*

ENGINEER: You're right. We should probably see the facility first.

[THE TWO ACTORS SIMULATE GOING OUT TO THE DRUM STORAGE AREA]

AUDITOR: *What do you store here?*

ENGINEER: Mostly waste solvents, paint stripper, and paint sludge.

AUDITOR: *Are those flammable?*

ENGINEER: Yes. We had some of the wastes tested and they are flammable.

AUDITOR: *Is there anything special about any of the waste?*

ENGINEER: No, I don't think so.

AUDITOR: *What do you think is in this drum labeled "solvent and sludge?"*

ENGINEER: Oh, those guys over at the metal shop have a small plating line and they often drop the sludge into a solvent drum and mix the whole mess together. Now it looks like they've done it again.

AUDITOR: *Will you have to do anything special with this waste?*

ENGINEER: Yes. I will probably have to pay the waste hauler more money, since he can't reclaim the solvent with all the metal hydroxides in it now. Those guys have no ideas what problems they cause.

AUDITOR: *It sure makes your job difficult. By the way, why is that respirator hanging on the hook?*

ENGINEER: Oh, we leave it there so that when the technicians empty solvent into the drums they have protection from the fumes.

AUDITOR: *Really. All the technicians use the same respirator?*

ENGINEER: Sure. It only takes a short while to empty the solvent, so it's not that critical.

AUDITOR: *And those drums over there that are all dented, are they full of hazardous waste?*

ENGINEER: Yes, that's one of our designated waste accumulation points.

AUDITOR: *Can we look at them?*

ENGINEER: Sure, I inspected it just the other day.

AUDITOR: *I notice you have funnels on the top of the drums. That's good to prevent spillage. Do you keep the funnels in the drums all the time?*

ENGINEER: Yes, you never know when these guys are going to put something in the drums and half the time they're always rushing around and would probably spill the waste if it wasn't for the funnel.

AUDITOR: *Yes, I know what you mean. That's a good idea. I think it would be wise to use the funnel that has the spring-loaded top instead of the open top one you're using here. That would keep the drum sealed and prevent emissions of any volatiles.*

ENGINEER: Yes, you're right. I never realized that. We've been doing it like this for years. But I'll change the funnel.

AUDITOR: *I see you've put the accumulation start date on all the drums.*

ENGINEER: Yes, we're always careful to do that.

AUDITOR: *You know, 90 days is the limit for this type of storage. Why do you think the two drums over there have been stored for longer than 90 days?*

ENGINEER: Where? Oh, those drums. Those are just old labels from the last time we used them. The new labels are on the other side of the drums. See they show [INSERT MONTH AND DAY THAT IS LESS THAN 90 DAYS) and that's less than 90 days.

AUDITOR: *Okay. I think you understand the requirement, but that could be confusing. I think you should make sure only the correct start dates are on the drums.*

ENGINEER: Yes, I'll do that.

AUDITOR: *Also, these other drums are damaged. A few are dented and some corrosion is starting to work its way through. It's probably a good idea to change these as soon as you can.*

ENGINEER: Will do. Gee, it looks like I'm failing this test.

AUDITOR: *Don't look at this audit as a test. We're trying to focus your attention on some things that could cause problems if not managed properly. These little problems I'm finding are typical at other plants, too. They may seem trivial but they are important. These are potential risks to the company. This region is highly dependent on groundwater for drinking water and with all these sandy soils, contamination from leaking drums could put us all in a bad position. A lot of companies are paying out a lot of money for major problems that all started out as small items like these.*

ENGINEER: Yes, I think we all need a little refresher training on some of these procedures.

AUDITOR: *Yes, I think so too. Okay, that completes this part of the audit. Thanks for your time. Is there anything else you want to mention before I go?*

ENGINEER: No, I don't think so.

AUDITOR: *Okay, we'll be summarizing our findings at the closing meeting on Friday for the plant manager. If you want to talk to me about anything else before then, let me know. Also, I think you might find it useful to attend the closing meeting.*

ENGINEER: Okay, there is one thing though.

AUDITOR: *What's that?*

ENGINEER: The auditor who visited me earlier today, does he/she work for you?

AUDITOR: *Yes, he/she does.*

ENGINEER: Well, no offense intended but, I think he/she could use a little refresher training, too.

AUDITOR: *Really, in what area?*

ENGINEER: In the proper way to conduct these audits.

Management Systems Assessments

CONDUCTING PROCESS FLOW ANALYSES

Background

One of the most valuable techniques used in identifying root causes and systemic failures on environmental, health and safety audits, is to develop a flow diagram for the process being reviewed. An example process flow diagram for the generation of a solvent waste by the maintenance department is provided with this exercise. This charting effort can help in identifying and defining inefficient systems, critical path constraints and process gaps. Evaluating processes in this way is what re-engineering is all about. EHS auditors must develop this charting skill if they are to be responsive to the new requirements to evaluate management systems.

Assignment

1. Examine the attached flow diagram and identify any parts of the process that have not been included, which would be critical in determining if the *management system* is deficient in any way. That is, what else would you need to know to complete a management systems audit?

2. Review the photograph provided with this exercise. Pose a series of questions to your instructor about the management of the drums in the picture so that you can accurately draw a process flow diagram for the delivery, storage and disposal of the drums. Be prepared to share the diagram with the class and discuss your view of the system deficiencies.

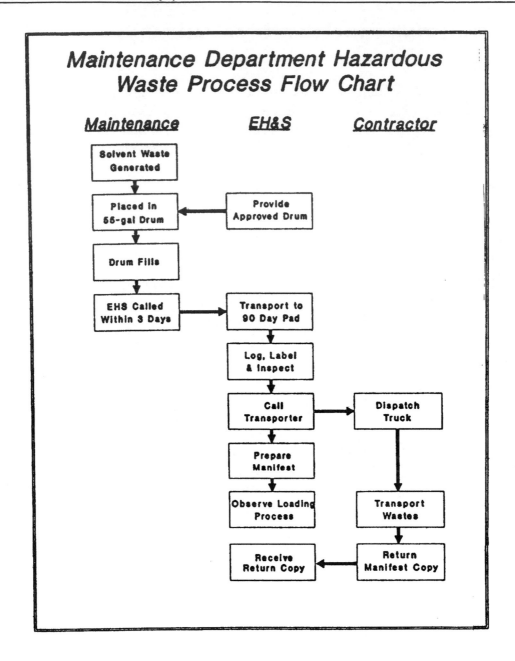

Inspection of Facilities

ROOT CAUSE ANALYSIS

Background

Root cause analysis is an important part of what auditors do on environmental management systems audits. Unfortunately for auditors, root cause analysis is both difficult to do and relatively time consuming. Yet, significant value is added to the process when auditors can identify the underlying cause of a problem (e.g., lack of training) as opposed to the symptom (e.g., improperly labeled drums). Corrective actions can then be designed to resolve not just the observed deficiency but what caused it to begin with (e.g., strengthening the training program as well as fixing the labels on the drums).

Undertaking root cause analysis, while both difficult and time consuming, is nonetheless conceptually quite simple. It involves little more than continuously asking the question "why?" as opposed to "what?". The attached hypothetical investigation models the process that an auditor would go through in doing a root cause analysis. The symptom or deficiency is traced back through its derivative causes until a root cause is identified. The hypothetical investigation ends in a startling conclusion that is deliberately far-fetched (or is it?).

Assignment

Your assignment is to do a similar analysis for the symptoms listed on the attached page. The idea is to analyze the symptoms and speculate on what the causes might be and work your way back through the chain. Use a "fishbone" diagram if that is helpful. Attempt to identify enough underlying causes to get you through at least three or four levels of analysis. Once you have identified the "root" cause, propose a corrective action that you believe will resolve the problem.

As opposed to the hypothetical case, don't worry about being too "cute" in identifying the ultimate causes; treat the symptoms as though they were real audit findings. Be prepared to formally discuss your analysis with the class.

ROOT CAUSE ANALYSIS SAMPLE SYMPTOMS

Symptom No. 1: A newly built process unit, that has been up and running for two months, does not have the required air emissions permits for construction and operation.

Symptom No.2: The wastewater treatment plant is routinely exceeding its permit limits for pH in four months out of the year. There are no exception reports in the files.

Symptom No.3: The site has a confined space entry permit program. However, the audit team observed an employee entering a tank for cleanout with no other employee around and no evidence a permit was obtained.

Symptom No.4: The site's 5,000 gallon above ground diesel oil tank does not have the secondary containment that is described in the Spill Prevention Control and Countermeasure (SPCC) Plan. It has no apparent containment at all.

Symptom No.5: The site's Environmental Coordinator was not aware that he will be required to have permits for several sources under the Title V Permit Program of the 1990 Clean Air Act Amendments. He has done nothing to prepare for this eventuality and it is likely that the site will not meet the regulatory deadline for permit applications.

Symptom No.6: It was recommended in the previous audit report, which is now two years old, that the site should have a written respiratory protection program. This is required by company policy and OSHA regulations. The quarterly corrective-action status reports indicated that this was done, and the audit was formally closed-out. You observed on the current audit that it was, indeed, never done.

ROOT CAUSE ANALYSIS HYPOTHETICAL INVESTIGATION

LEVEL	DEFICIENCY/SYMPTOM
I (Baseline)	WHAT??? A label is missing from a hazardous waste drum at the site's accumulation point WHY???
II	The label weathered, fell to the ground and blew away. WHY???
III	The label's adhesive was of poor quality. WHY???
IV	The site's Purchasing Department recently bought less expensive labels without notifying the site environmental coordinator. WHY???
V	The Department was told by the Plant Manager to quickly reduce the annual costs of goods purchased by 20%. WHY???
VI	The Plant Manager is under pressure to improve profitability and has responded by cutting costs where he can. WHY???
VII	The CEO has asked all Plant Managers in this Division to improve profitability by 15%. WHY???
VIII	The Company's overall profits are declining and large institutional investors (i.e., pension funds) are putting pressure on the Board of Directors and CEO to improve performance. WHY???
IX	The individual investors in the pension funds are concerned about its performance and are putting pressure on fund managers to get a better return. WHY???
X	The investors are concerned that Social Security (SS) will not be there when they retire, so they must rely solely on their pensions. WHY???
XI	They know the SS System is in trouble and the U.S. Government "can't manage its way out of a paper bag!"
Root Cause:	**It's the Government's fault!!!**
Corrective Action:	**Vote out all the Incumbents!!!**

FISHBONE DIAGRAM ANALYSIS
HAZARDOUS WASTE LABEL

A Label Was Missing From a Hazardous Waste Drum

WHAT?

No One Was Accountable

The Label "Fell Off"

There Was No Hazardous Waste Training

WHY?

The Drum Was in a Caustic Environment

The Label's Adhesive Was of Poor Quality

The Drum Had Been Around for Years and the Label Deteriorated

WHY?

The Adhesive Specification Was Incorrect

The Purchasing Agent Bought Cheaper Labels

The Supplier Provided a Bad Batch of Labels

WHY?

The Change in Label Type Was not Cleared by Env'l Coordinator

ROOT CAUSE!

Example Fishbone Diagram for a "Missing Hazardous Waste Label"

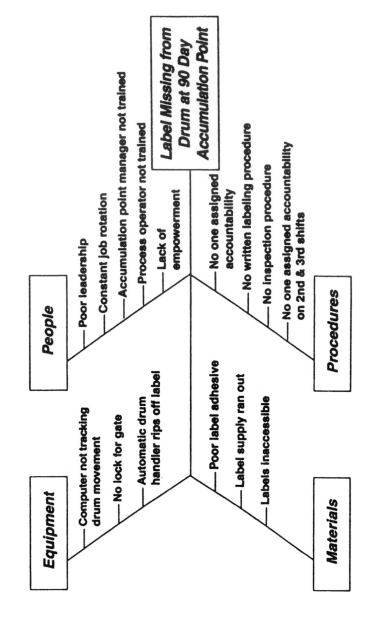

Label Missing from Drum at 90 Day Accumulation Point

People
- Poor leadership
- Constant job rotation
- Accumulation point manager not trained
- Process operator not trained
- Lack of empowerment

Equipment
- Computer not tracking drum movement
- No lock for gate
- Automatic drum handler rips off label

Procedures
- No one assigned accountability
- No written labeling procedure
- No inspection procedure
- No one assigned accountability on 2nd & 3rd shifts

Materials
- Poor label adhesive
- Label supply ran out
- Labels inaccessible

14993 5.10 95 DL

Report Writing

AUDIT REPORTS "TIPS for Success"

1. Separate the Process from the Product

2. Use pyramid/logical thinking/topic sentences

3. Present activities/findings/conclusions:

    • What you saw

    • What you found

    • What it means

4. Look for underlying causes

5. Keep findings in perspective

6. Organize daily

7. Write findings as you go

8. Aim for direct, factual, informative style

9. Hunt for bad words

10. Avoid conjecture ("conclusions deduced by guesswork")

11. Use evidence (inquiry, observation, test)

12. Use proper grammar

13. Bottom line your interviews

14. Copy important documents

15. Complete at least an annotated outline before you leave

16. Start early

17. Challenge each other

18. Agree on report format

19. Don't indict the staff

20. KISS

THE EVOLUTION OF AN EH&S AUDIT FINDING

1. Hazardous waste management at the site needs improvement.

2. Hazardous waste management at the site was deficient.

3. Hazardous waste drum management at the site's accumulation point was not adequate.

4. The drum storage area contained a drum that had a funnel in it.

5. The site's accumulation point contained a drum that had a funnel in it.

6. One of the four hazardous waste drums at the site's 90-day accumulation point was not closed and no operators were nearby. RCRA requires drums to be closed except when adding or removing waste. (40 CFR 265.14)

Combining the management system finding with the compliance finding is probably the best approach, but . . .

AUDIT REPORTS "WHAT'S WRONG WITH THIS PICTURE"

1. The respiratory protection program was deficient and could be improved. This is a serious concern.

2. The audit team inspected 20 transformers and 10 capacitors, of which 3 showed past signs of leaks.

3. Several of the drums at the hazardous waste storage area had no labels, as required by RCRA.

4. Three fire extinguishers at the site did not have the required inspection tags.

5. The hazardous waste 90 day accumulation area had no secondary containment.

6. It is possible that some previous spillage occurred at the bulk loading transfer station.

7. A unit operator reported that the wastewater treatment plant is bypassed during severe storms events. This violates the site's wastewater discharge permit.

8. Because of the possibility of solvent releases into the sewers, the wastewater treatment ponds might have to be permitted as a hazardous waste surface impoundment.

9. The blood-borne pathogen program should be improved to reflect the most recent OSHA regulations.

10. The permitted hazardous waste storage facility at Building 51 was recently inspected by the New Jersey DEP and found to be in compliance with environmental standards. Used oil at the site is accumulated at Building 52 and disposed of monthly by Used Oil Reclamation Company. Used oil is exempt from hazardous waste regulations.

11. The fire training area has reportedly been contaminated with waste solvents, used as recently as 5 years ago as supplementary fuel for the fires. The audit team recommends that the facility file for a hazardous waste permit as a treatment/disposal facility and immediately excavate the contaminated soils.

12. As part of the hazardous waste audit we went to the point where the hazardous wastes are accumulated at the site and we reviewed whether the drums had labels and whether there was enough aisle space for a fork truck and whether the hazardous waste accumulation point was inspected weekly and whether all the other hazardous waste regulations were complied with. There was a plethora of violations.

AUDIT FINDINGS FORM

Description of Finding:

Statement of Observation:

Statement of Requirement:

Citation/Source:

Compliance Area (e.g., Wastewater, HazCom):

Type: [ ] Regulatory   [ ] Policy   [ ] Management Practice

Level: [ ] Level I   [ ] Level II   [ ] Level III

Recommendation (Immediate/Long-term):

Code: **Auditor:**   **Date:**

Audit Conferences

ENVIRONMENTAL AUDITS OPENING CONFERENCE QUESTIONS

1. I've been called out of town for the rest of the week. I won't be available for the closing conference. Is that okay?

2. I've been having problems with my accumulation point manager. Could you give me a third-party evaluation of his performance?

3. I'm sure we've removed all of our PCB equipment and Underground Storage Tanks. You could eliminate your review of these areas and save time. Okay? What do you think?

4. We just received notice this morning that we're to have an EPA inspection this week, starting today. Can you cancel or postpone the audit?

5. I've got some bad news. Due to the torrential rains we've bad this week, we've bad to shut down the plant because the lagoons are overflowing. Does that mean you can't do the audit?

ENVIRONMENTAL AUDITS CLOSING CONFERENCE QUESTIONS

Plant Manager

1. You've been on many audits this year. Tell me, how does my plant stack up?

2. On a scale of 1 to 10 how would you rate our performance on the audit?

3. Which of the findings are high priority requiring my immediate attention?

4. Can you make sure that you indicate all the positive things we are doing at the plant *in* the report?

5. It seems some of the findings are repeated from the last audit. We just haven't had the resources. How will you handle those in the report?

Environmental Manager

1. I don't think I can get the corrective action plan completed in the required time frame. Can I have another three to four weeks to get it done?

2. Will I be given a chance to review the audit report and make comments? Will there be anything new in the report that has not been addressed at the closing conference?

3. If I f1X some of the problems today, can you go back out and look at them? If they're okay, do the findings have to go in the report?

4. Do you have any feelings about our people? Performance is crucial as we re-structure. Any staff who are doing an outstanding job?

5. We're having an agency inspection next week. Will this audit guarantee a good result if we fix everything?

Appendix E

Summary of Audit Programs

SUMMARY OF AN ENVIRONMENTAL AUDIT PROGRAM

COMPANY:	FORTUNE 500 CHEMICAL COMPANY
Program Name:	Environmental, Health and Safety Audit Program
Start Date:	1993 in its current form
Purpose:	Achieve compliance with regulations and company policies and assess the efficacy of environmental management systems
Organization:	One corporate manager who leads management systems audits with consultants on the teams; Compliance audits done by 2 business units, also with consultants as team members; Evolving strategy with no formal plan for integration; Conducted under attomey-client privilege protections
Audit Scope:	Global; Environmental, Health and Safety; Multi-media
Staffing:	2-3 technical staff either consultants or borrowed from line organization; 10-25 years experience; No formal internal training program
Duration:	2-5 days; 3 days on the average
Number:	About 15 corporate management systems audits per year; same level of activity for business compliance audits
Frequency:	Every 2, 3 or 4 years; No risk evaluation
Methodology:	Standard approach; Management systems oriented checklists at corporate level; Scoring system used
Reporting:	Brief exception reports which include recommendations; Legal not typically involved; Goal of leaving the draft report with the site at the closing conference
Follow-up:	Corrective action plans and quarterly reporting required; Formal tracking implemented

SUMMARY OF AN ENVIRONMENTAL AUDIT PROGRAM

COMPANY:	**FORTUNE 200 CONSUMER PRODUCTS COMPANY**
Program Name:	Environmental Audit Program
Start Date:	Re-engineered in 1995
Purpose:	Achieve compliance with regulations and company policies and assess the efficacy of environmental management systems; Developed a formal set of environmental standards and guidelines (e.g., secondary containment required for all hazardous materials tanks) as part of re-engineering roll-out
Organization:	One corporate manager with four audit program managers responsible for geographical regions; Managers lead every audit; Corporate manager established standards of performance for audits; Annual third-party program evaluation; Conducted under attorney-client privilege protections in the U.S. but not overseas
Audit Scope:	Global; Environmental; Multi-media
Staffing:	3-5 technical staff borrowed from other facilities within geographical region; 5-20 years experience; Formal internal training program
Duration:	2-5 days; 3 days on the average
Number:	About 30 audits per year; Third party does 10% with corporate program manager in attendance as a quality assurance check
Frequency:	Every 3, 4 or 5 years depending on risk evaluation
Methodology:	Standard approach; Detailed compliance checklists covering regulations and corporate standards; Detailed management systems checklist as well
Reporting:	Brief exception reports which include recommendations; Findings categorized into one of three risk groups; Legal involved in U.S.; Goal of leaving the draft report with the site at the closing conference
Follow-up:	Corrective action plans and quarterly reporting required

SUMMARY OF AN ENVIRONMENTAL AUDIT PROGRAM

COMPANY:	FORTUNE 50 CHEMICAL COMPANY
Program Name:	Environmental Review Program
Start Date:	1988 in its current form
Purpose:	Achieve compliance with regulations and company policies and assess the efficacy of environmental management systems
Organization:	One corporate manager with program delegated to about 20 business units and 3 geographical regions for implementation; Corporate manager established standards of performance for business programs and undertakes formal quality assurance review of 1/3 of business programs each year; Also, annual third-party evaluation; Not conducted under attorney-client privilege protections
Audit Scope:	Global; Environmental; Multi-media
Staffing:	3-5 technical staff borrowed from corporate, other facilities and business units; 10-25 years experience; Formal internal training program
Duration:	2-5 days; 3 days on the average
Number:	About 50 audits per year
Frequency:	Annual or every 2, 3 or 4 years depending on risk evaluation
Methodology:	Standard approach; Management systems oriented checklists; covers TSCA and CDTA; On occasion allows for community participation
Reporting:	Brief exception reports which include recommendations; Findings categorized into one of three risk groups; Legal involved as needed; Goal of leaving the draft report with the site at the closing conference
Follow-up:	Corrective action plans and quarterly reporting required; Implementation in the businesses very uneven

SUMMARY OF AN ENVIRONMENTAL AUDIT PROGRAM

COMPANY:	**LARGE U.S. CHEMICAL COMPANY SUBSIDIARY OF EUROPEAN PARENT**
Program Name:	Environmental, Health and Safety Audit Program
Start Date:	1988 in its current form
Purpose:	Achieve compliance with regulations and company policies and assess the efficacy of environmental management systems
Organization:	One corporate Vice President with four full-time audit program managers who lead every audit; Conducted under attomey-client privilege protections; Annual third-party program evaluation
Audit Scope:	North America only; Environmental, Health and Safety; Multi-media plus focused audits (e.g., product stewardship)
Staffing:	3-5 technical staff borrowed from corporate, other facilities and business units; 10-25 years experience; Formal internal training program
Duration:	2-5 days; 3 days on the average
Number:	About 30 audits per year
Frequency:	Every 3 years
Methodology:	Standard approach; Management systems oriented checklists, with move towards detailed compliance checklists
Reporting:	Brief exception reports which include recommendations; Findings categorized into one of two risk groups; Legal reviews and issues all reports and attends closing conferences; Goal of leaving the draft report with the site at the closing conference
Follow-up:	Corrective action plans and quarterly reporting required; Formal computerized tracking system; Formal verification follow-up audits on 10% of audits each year

SUMMARY OF AN ENVIRONMENTAL AUDIT PROGRAM

COMPANY:	**BILLION DOLLAR MINING AND MINERALS COMPANY**

Program Name:	Environmental Audit Program
Start Date:	Program re-engineered in 1994
Purpose:	Achieve compliance with regulations and company policies and assess the efficacy of environmental management systems
Organization:	One corporate manager with small Audit Core Team made up of rotating Business representatives; Corporate manager established standards of performance; Annual third-party program evaluation; Conducted under attomey-client privilege protections
Audit Scope:	Global; Environmental; Multi-media; Will be integrating health and safety in the future
Staffing:	2-4 technical staff borrowed from other facilities and business units; 10-25 years experience; Formal internal training program
Duration:	2-5 days; 3 days on the average
Number:	About 10 audits per year
Frequency:	Every 2, 3 or 4 years depending on risk evaluation
Methodology:	Standard approach; Detailed compliance checklists
Reporting:	Brief exception reports which include recommendations; Findings categorized into one of three risk groups; Legal involved; Goal of leaving the draft report with the site at the closing conference
Follow-up:	Corrective action plans and quarterly reporting required

SUMMARY OF AN ENVIRONMENTAL AUDIT PROGRAM

COMPANY:	**FORTUNE 100 CHEMICAL COMPANY**
Program Name:	Environmental Audit Program
Start Date:	1984
Purpose:	To anticipate problems; assure of compliance
Organization:	One corporate staff member from Safety, Health and Environmental Department; rotating senior environmental staff from sister divisions
Audit Scope:	U.S., environmental, multi-media
Staffing:	3-4 senior technical staff (10-25 years experience)
Duration:	1-3 days; 2 days on the average
Number:	10 facilities/year
Frequency:	18 month cycle
Methodology:	standard approach; open-ended detailed checklists; plants do annual vendor audits with corporate direction
Reporting:	Good & bad findings; oral reports to legal; draft report to plant management; no recommendations; 3-5 page reports
Follow-up:	Informal; no auditing of follow-up no action plan required

SUMMARY OF AN ENVIRONMENTAL AUDIT PROGRAM

COMPANY:	**FORTUNE 500 MINERAL PRODUCTS COMPANY**
Program Name:	Environmental Auditing Program
Start Date:	1976
Purpose:	Increase awareness; assure compliance; data collection for litigation
Organization:	Six part-time corporate auditors in corporate environmental department; audits done under direction of General Counsel
Audit Scope:	U.S., environmental plus right-to-know and natural resources {e.g., mining}; multi-media
Staffing:	2 technical staff (plus an attorney where sites are under litigation)
Duration:	One week
Number:	10 audits/year
Frequency:	Two year cycle on the average (1-4 year cycle based on risk)
Methodology:	Standard approach; detailed worksheets; some sampling done; some contact with regulatory authorities
Reporting:	One to four page reports; very limited distribution; report sent to Division President with plant manager's comments; reports for plants under litigation are sometimes verbal; good & bad findings; no recommendations
Follow-up:	Informal; auditors provide technical assistance

SUMMARY OF AN ENVIRONMENTAL AUDIT PROGRAM

COMPANY:	**FORTUNE 200 CHEMICAL COMPANY**
Program Name:	Regulatory Audits
Start Date:	1978
Purpose:	Compliance
Organization:	Five Full-time Corporate Auditors with at least 10 years experience in Financial Audit Department
Audit Scope:	International, comprehensive, multi-media
Staffing:	3 technical staff
Duration:	Up to 2 weeks
Number:	60/year
Frequency:	Once a year
Methodology:	Surprise audits, comprehensive check-lists, standard approach
Reporting:	Good & bad findings, brief off-site report with recommendations, no pro-forma legal reviev
Follow-up:	60 day formal response required

SUMMARY OF AN ENVIRONMENTAL AUDIT PROGRAM

COMPANY:	**FORTUNE 100 MANUFACTURING COMPANY**

Program Name:	Plant Audits
Start Date:	1972
Purpose:	Environmental Engineering Evaluation, Awareness, Compliance (GMP's)
Organization:	10 Corporate Full-time auditors in Environmental Department
Audit Scope:	U.S. and Canada, Environmental, Multi-media

Staffing:	Technical staff, up to 4 auditors
Duration:	Up to one week
Number:	Up to 75 facilities/year
Frequency:	Four year cycle (or less based on risk)

Methodology:	Detailed checklists and procedures, standard approach
Reporting:	Bad findings only, brief off-site written report, no recommendations, no pro-forma legal review
Follow-up:	Formal response required by plant manager

SUMMARY OF AN ENVIRONMENTAL AUDIT PROGRAM

COMPANY:	FORTUNE 100 DIVERSIFIED CONGLOMERATE
Program Name:	Environmental Surveillance
Start Date:	1978
Purpose:	Compliance (GMP's)
Organization:	3 Full-time auditors in Corporate Environmental Affairs Department
Audit Scope:	International, Comprehensive, Single-medium
Staffing:	2-3 Technical staff
Duration:	3-4 days
Number:	35 plants/year
Frequency:	2-3 year cycle
Methodology:	Detailed checklists and procedures, standard approach
Reporting:	Bad findings only, brief on-site preliminary written report, no pro-forma legal review
Follow-up:	60 day formal response required

SUMMARY OF AN ENVIRONMENTAL AUDIT PROGRAM

COMPANY:	**MAJOR ELECTRIC UTILITY**
Program Name:	Assessment Program
Start Date:	1976
Purpose:	Compliance (GMP's) and Awareness
Organization:	5 Full-time Corporate staff reporting to VP-System Power & Engineering
Audit Scope:	U.S., Environmental, Multi-media
Staffing:	2-3 auditors
Duration:	3 days
Number:	30/year
Frequency:	2 year cycle
Methodology:	Detailed checklists and procedures, some sampling is conducted, some surprise audits
Reporting:	Good & bad findings, 30 page off-site report with recommendations, no pro-forma legal review
Follow-up:	30 day formal response required

SUMMARY OF AN ENVIRONMENTAL AUDIT PROGRAM

COMPANY:	**CHEMICAL SUBSIDIARY OF FORTUNE 100 COMPANY**

Program Name:	Environmental Surveillance
Start Date:	1979
Purpose:	Compliance (GMP's)
Organization:	Run by Division in concert with separate Corporate program; One full-time auditor with several part-time auditors out of Environmental Affairs Department
Audit Scope:	International, Comprehensive, Multi-Media

Staffing:	2-3 Technical Staff
Duration:	3-4 days
Number:	25/year
Frequency:	2-3 year cycle

Methodology:	Multi-lingual checklists, standard approach
Reporting:	Bad findings only, brief off-site written report with recommendations, no pro-forma legal review
Follow-up:	60 day formal response required

SUMMARY OF AN ENVIRONMENTAL AUDIT PROGRAM

COMPANY:	**FORTUNE 1000 HIGH-TECHNOLOGY COMPANY**
Program Name:	Regulatory Affairs Audit Program
Start Date:	1981
Purpose:	Compliance (GMP's), Technology Transfer, Prevention
Organization:	Half-time Corporate Manager in Regulatory Affairs Department under the Office of General Counsel
Audit Scope:	International, Comprehensive, Multi-media
Staffing:	2 Corporate/Division Technical staff with 2-5 plant staff
Duration:	3-5 days
Number:	6 per year
Frequency:	Annual audits
Methodology:	Detailed checklists and procedures, standard approach
Reporting:	Bad findings only; off-site 15 page written report, no recommendations, no pro-forma legal review; space is left for action plan to be filled in
Follow-up:	Action plans submitted to corporate within 2-4 weeks; audit manager follows-up on significant items within 30 days

SUMMARY OF AN ENVIRONMENTAL AUDIT PROGRAM

COMPANY:	**FORTUNE 100 PETROCHEMICAL COMPANY**

Program Name:	Environmental Assessment Program
Start Date:	1978
Purpose:	Compliance (GMP's), Awareness
Organization:	Run out of Corporate Environmental Department with two staff: auditors come from 2 Divisions and plant being audited
Audit Scope:	International, Environmental, Multi-media

Staffing:	3 Technical Staff
Duration:	2-3 days
Number:	15/year
Frequency:	Varied: one year cycle for major facilities

Methodology:	Detailed checklists and procedures: standard approach
Reporting:	Good & bad findings with recommendations; pro-forma legal review
Follow-up:	Computerited action plan tracking system, with monthly reports and scoring of plants responsiveness

SUMMARY OF AN ENVIRONMENTAL AUDIT PROGRAM

COMPANY:	**FORTUNE 500 CHEMICAL COMPANY**

Program Name:	Compliance Audits
Start Date:	1981
Purpose:	Compliance (GMP's)
Organization:	Run by Regional Regulatory Manager; with no permanent auditors (participation at all levels)
Audit Scope:	International, Comprehensive, Multi-media (including product stewardship)

Staffing:	3-6 technical/regulatory staff
Duration:	3-4 days
Number:	15/year
Frequency:	2 year cycle

Methodology:	Detailed checklists and procedures, standard approach
Reporting:	Good & bad findings, several oral reports before final brief written report with recommendations; legal review
Follow-up:	Reporting and follow-up to President of Company

SUMMARY OF AN ENVIRONMENTAL AUDIT PROGRAM

COMPANY:	**FORTUNE 500 SPECIALTY PRODUCTS COMPANY**
Program Name:	Environmental Audit Program
Start Date:	1980
Purpose:	Compliance (GMP's)
Organization:	Run from Corporate Environmental Department; no permanent auditors, rotating Divisional/plant staff
Audit Scope:	U.S., Environmental, Multi-media
Staffing:	4 Technical staff
Duration:	3 days
Number:	10/year
Frequency:	2 year cycle
Methodology:	Detailed checklists and procedures
Reporting:	Good & bad findings; elaborate drafting and submission of audit report with recommendations; scoring system is used
Follow-up:	Informal follow-up procedures

SUMMARY OF AN ENVIRONMENTAL AUDIT PROGRAM

COMPANY:	**FORTUNE 500 OIL COMPANY**
Program Name:	Systems Review Program
Start Date:	1980
Purpose:	System compliance (GMP's)
Organization:	Run with large core (50) of part-time auditors from separate Corporate Environmental Council
Audit Scope:	U.S., Environmental, Multi-media
Staffing:	3-4 Technical staff
Duration:	Up to 10 days
Number:	10 per year
Frequency:	Four year cycle
Methodology:	Checklists based on 10 management systems criteria that cut across media; very detailed instructions to auditors
Reporting:	Bad findings only; on-site preliminary written report; report has recommendations
Follow-up:	45 day formal follow-up required

SUMMARY OF AN ENVIRONMENTAL AUDIT PROGRAM

COMPANY:	**FORTUNE 100 DIVERSIFIED CHEMICAL COMPANY**
Program Name:	Environmental Protection Audit Program
Start Date:	1985
Purpose:	Provide management with verification of compliance and good management practices
Organization:	Corporate group with 30 full-time auditors with consultant support
Audit Scope:	International, OSHA, Environmental & Product Safety, Multi-Media
Staffing:	Varied
Duration:	A week or less
Number:	Unknown
Frequency:	Phased based on risk assessments of facilities
Methodology:	Standard approach; detailed checklists, focus on management systems; both compliance and process audits
Reporting:	Report good and bad findings; sent to group vice president; no pro-forma legal review
Follow-up:	Formal action plans required by plants; loaded onto MIS for computerized tracking

SUMMARY OF AN ENVIRONMENTAL AUDIT PROGRAM

COMPANY:	**FORTUNE 100 FOOD PRODUCTS COMPANY**
Program:	Environmental Compliance Survey
Start Date:	1986
Purpose:	Compliance
Organization:	Two part-time corporate auditors supplemented by consultants
Audit Scope:	U.S. only, environmental, multi-media
Staffing:	1 technical staff
Duration:	2 days
Number:	80/year
Frequency:	Annual
Methodology:	Standard approach, comprehensive previsit questionnaire requiring emissions/effluent inventories, summary checklists
Reporting:	Good & bad findings, brief off-site report with recommendations, no pro-forma legal review
Follow-up:	Informal follow-up; actions required by both corporate and plant personnel

SUMMARY OF AN ENVIRONMENTAL AUDIT PROGRAM

COMPANY:	**DEFENSE AND SPACE EQUIPMENT MANUFACTURER**
Program:	Environmental Audit Program
Start Date:	1983
Purpose:	Compliance, assist operations, assure management
Organization:	One full time on-site auditor from corporate staff function
Audit Scope:	One major facility in U.S., environmental, three compliance areas
Staffing:	1 technical staff
Duration:	One-half day
Number:	60 auditable units at one site
Frequency:	Major units quarterly; others semi-annual
Methodology:	No previsit questionnaire: no checklists; reliance on environmental standards and auditor's skill
Reporting:	Bad findings only; brief two page report; no pro-forma legal review
Follow-up:	Very formal: unit response plan required in 14 days: if non-responsive "red tag" can be placed on equipment shutting it down.

SUMMARY OF AN ENVIRONMENTAL AUDIT PROGRAM

COMPANY:	**FORTUNE 500 CHEMICAL COMPANY**
Program Name:	Environmental Audits
Start Date:	1979
Purpose:	Compliance
Organization:	Four part-time auditors in Corporate Legal and Enviornmental Departments
Audit Scope:	U.S., Environmental, Multi-media
Staffing:	Technical and legal staff, 2 auditors
Duration:	2-3 days
Number:	20/year
Frequency:	Two year cycle
Methodology:	Open-ended checklists and procedures, principally review of last audit findings, standard approach
Reporting:	Bad findings only, off-site written report, some recommendations, legal review
Follow-up:	Formal response required in 30 days, automated corporate "tickler file"

SUMMARY OF AN ENVIRONMENTAL AUDIT PROGRAM

COMPANY:	LARGE GOVERNMENTAL AGENCY
Program Name:	Environmental Survey
Start Date:	1985-1986
Purpose:	Identification of environmental problems
Organization:	Headquarters management with field support by consultants
Audit Scope:	U.S, environmental, multi-media (including radioactive)
Staffing:	7-10 technical staff
Duration:	2 weeks
Number:	10/year
Frequency:	One time
Methodology:	Standard approach, very detailed checklists; pre-survey visit by team leader; sampling included
Reporting:	Good and bad findings; comprehensive off-site report; no pro-forma legal review
Follow-up:	Major follow-up program anticipated

SUMMARY OF AN ENVIRONMENTAL AUDIT PROGRAM

COMPANY:	**MID-SIZED CHEMICAL COMPANY**
Program Name:	Environmental Audits
Start Date:	1983
Purpose:	Compliance
Organization:	One part-time auditor in the major division
Audit Scope:	International, environmental, multi-media
Staffing:	1 technical staff
Duration:	1-2 days
Number:	5/year
Frequency:	Once every 3 years
Methodology:	No detailed checklists; reliance on expertise of auditor
Reporting:	Good and bad findings, comprehensive off-site report, no pro-forma legal legal review
Follow-up:	Very informal outside consultant used to conduct follow-up audits, 1-2 years later

SUMMARY OF AN ENVIRONMENTAL AUDIT PROGRAM

COMPANY:	**FORTUNE 100 BASIC MANUFACTURING COMPANY**
Program Name:	Environmental Evaluation
Start Date:	1981
Purpose:	"Improve Environmental Performance"
Organization:	Two Corporate staff in Environmental Department; Corporate teams with one plant environmental staff
Audit Scope:	Primarily U.S., Environmental, Multi-media
Staffing:	2-3 Technical staff
Duration:	1-5 days
Number:	20/year
Frequency:	Varied; large plants on one year cycle; small plants on 4 year cycle
Methodology:	Detailed checklists and procedures; standard approach
Reporting:	(Some) good & bad findings with recommendations; reports vary from 2-50 pages; pro-forma legal review
Follow-up:	No formal follow-up approach

SUMMARY OF AN ENVIRONMENTAL AUDIT PROGRAM

COMPANY:	**FORTUNE 500 MANUFACTURER**

Program Name:	Environmental Compliance Audit Program
Start Date:	1987
Purposes:	Assure environmental stewardship: reduce liability; increase awareness; transfer information; assess management practices; create good record
Organization:	Run from corporate environmental/legal departments; no permanent auditors; rotating plant participants
Audit Scope:	All environmental laws and regulations, both Federal and state, for all media

Staffing:	1 legal, 1 corporate technical, 1 plant technical (rotating)
Duration:	2-3 days for environmentally complex plants; 1 day for smaller plants
Number:	6/year
Frequency:	2 year cycle for complex plants; 4 year cycle for smaller plants

Methodology:	Detailed checklist and procedures; scheduled in advance; no sampling; no contact with agencies; detailed instructions to auditors
Reporting:	Positive and negative findings; no recommendations; oral on-site report to plant management; 3-5 page written report within one month; limited distribution.
Follow-up:	Informal, with plant action plan; quarterly review between plant management and corporate environmental manager; assurance letters.

Appendix F

Model EH&S Audit Program Manual

Note: This appendix is also available on CD-ROM as an electronic template to be tailored to your company's individual needs.

MODEL AUDIT MANUAL

Model EH&S Audit Program Manual

August 5, 2000

Caution

This is a sample EH&S Audit Program Manual, which can be used as a model in structuring an audit program. The model should be modified to meet any particular organization's specific objectives (e.g., ISO 14000).

TABLE OF CONTENTS

ABC CORPORATION
Model EH&S Audit Program Guidance Manual

1.0 EXECUTIVE SUMMARY

This Manual describes how ABC Corporation will conduct environmental, health, and safety (EH&S) audits of its facilities and operations. Providing this written guidance helps to: (1) broadly communicate the objectives and scope of the Program, (2) improve the consistency of the Corporation's audits, and (3) allow the Program to be evaluated regularly against established performance criteria. The Guidance Manual will be revised each year to reflect: (1) the internal experiences of the company in conducting audits on a continuing basis, and (2) any external initiatives that are deemed applicable to the Program (e.g., the ISO 14000 Environmental Auditing Guidelines).

The ABC EH&S Audit Program initially is directed by the Director, EH&S Compliance Audits, in conjunction with the Law Department. Reporting to the Director are three Audit Program Managers, who manage various aspects of the Program and lead the audits. As the organization chart on the following page shows, the Director reports to the Vice President for EH&S Affairs. Auditors are drawn from throughout the Corporation but will only include those individuals who can qualify by relevant experience or by attending an ABC audit training course.

Virtually all ABC facilities and/or operations will be covered by the EH&S Audit Program. Operating sites will be audited every 3-5 years, depending on size and complexity. Sites will be evaluated against federal, state, and local EH&S laws and regulations, Company policies and procedures and good management practices. Individual audits will last from 2-5 days and will involve 2-4 auditors. Group management will be accountable for responding appropriately to the audit findings and reporting quarterly to the Program Director on the status of all outstanding items.

The EH&S Audit Program will be evaluated formally each year and improvements made accordingly. The Audit Program Director will report to the Audit Committee of the Board of Directors each year on the progress the Program has made in achieving its objectives. Timely and effective closure of all audit findings will be considered one of the most important criteria for determining the success of the Program. All participants, including corporate, Group, and site staff, will share accountability in achieving this goal.

ABC CORPORATION
Model EH&S Audit Program Guidance Manual

TABLE 1

ABC Company Audit Program

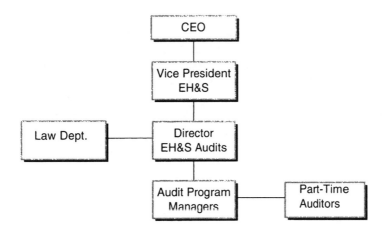

ABC CORPORATION
Model EH&S Audit Program Guidance Manual

2.0   INTRODUCTION

All ABC EH&S audits will be conducted consistent with this Guidance Manual. The Manual is designed to provide audit program and process information to auditors, those being audited and management staff who will be responsible for assuring that audit findings are responded to appropriately.

Assuring EH&S compliance has become a tremendous challenge for U.S. corporations operating both domestically and overseas. Statutes passed by legislatures and requirements established by federal, state, regional, and local agencies continue to increase in both volume and complexity. This increasing complexity is occurring at a time when the general public, shareholders, and other interested parties are asking to know more, much more, about EH&S issues. Regulatory agency enforcement is also on the rise. The consequences of poor EH&S performance have never been more troubling.

Conducting routine EH&S audits of facilities can provide assurances that an organization is responding adequately to constantly changing statutory and regulatory requirements. They can also help to identify situations where a company may wish to do more than simply meet rules and regulations in order to better manage EH&S liabilities and risks. Audit programs are a cost-effective management tool, not simply an additional burden. Audit programs are consistent with Total Quality Management principles and are an integral element of the existing ISO 14000 Standards. They have become an expected component of a sound EH&S management system.

The EH&S audit is not a new concept. Hundreds of U.S. companies have developed some form of program. In fact, ABC has conducted EH&S audits of its operations for some years now. We are improving the program with the goal of achieving a more articulated, structured, and documented program. We anticipate that this will result in audits that are consistent and increase understanding of the audits' objectives.

ABC CORPORATION
Model EH&S Audit Program Guidance Manual

3.0   OBJECTIVES OF THE EH&S AUDIT PROGRAM

The ABC EH&S Audit Program is a supportive one. The Program is designed to provide assistance to the sites, while at the same time independently and objectively evaluating the site's EH&S performance. Sites will not be "scored" (good or bad) or "ranked" (best or worst) based on the results of the audit. The audit team will be asked to work with the sites in developing appropriate responses to audit findings. However, line management will be responsible for implementing timely and effective corrective action plan actions.

Environmental, health, and safety audits are a management tool that will assist the Corporation in meeting its goals for EH&S excellence. At the very least, audits will seek to assure full compliance and the minimization of potential EH&S risks.

An audit program is first and foremost a verification program. It is not meant to supplant existing EH&S management systems in the line organization. It is meant to *verify* that these systems exist, are in use, and are effective; moreover, audits should foster the creation of new systems to manage any identified deficiencies.

The specific objectives of the ABC EH&S Audit Program are:

- *Program Objective 1:* Assure regulatory compliance, minimize potential EH&S risks, and evaluate the adequacy of EH&S management systems to meet the Corporation's goals

- *Program Objective 2:* Increase EH&S awareness and continuous learning by audited personnel and auditors

- *Program Objective 3:* Transfer EH&S technologies and innovations across the Corporation

- *Program Objective 4:* Assure adequate EH&S performance and continuous improvement to the Board of Directors.

The Program will achieve these objectives in a way that:

- Maximizes the use and leveraging of internal resources

- Eliminates duplication of effort

ABC CORPORATION
Model EH&S Audit Program Guidance Manual

- Promotes continuous improvement of the auditors and the sites being audited

- Provides for a consistent approach.

The Audit Program will be evaluated annually against these objectives to assure that the Program continues to add value to the corporation. The specific performance criteria that will be used in the evaluation are discussed later in this Manual.

4.0   ROLES AND RESPONSIBILITIES

The EH&S Audit Program will involve many parts of the ABC organization. The relative roles and responsibilities of the different organizational entities are discussed in this section.

4.1   *Senior Management*

Senior management, namely the Board of Directors, has directed that the Audit Program be developed and implemented. The Board of Directors will receive periodic reports discussing the status of the Audit Program and an overview of the results of the audits. Senior Management will be apprised by the Audit Program Director promptly, with counsel from the Law Department, of any issues identified by the Audit Program that could adversely affect the Corporation in a significant way.

4.2   *Corporate EH&S Compliance and Audits*

The Corporate Director of EH&S Compliance and Audits will direct the Program in conjunction with the Law Department. The specific responsibilities of the Audit Program Director include those listed below. The Program Director may delegate some responsibilities to the Audit Program Managers.

- Maintain and update Program materials including this Manual, the pre-audit questionnaire, and the audit protocols

- Maintain the auditor training program, including updating the qualified auditor database

ABC CORPORATION
Model EH&S Audit Program Guidance Manual

- Review draft and final audit reports

- Track the status of corrective action plans and formally "close out" audits when all findings are corrected

- Provide to the audit teams, on an as needed basis, state regulatory information

- Conduct an annual evaluation of the Program

- Periodically report on Program status to the Board of Directors

- With the advice of Counsel, manage the Program files, consistent with the Corporation's established records retention policy.

Reporting to the Director for EH&S Compliance and Audits are three Audit Program Managers. The responsibilities of the Managers include:

- Serve as Team Leaders on audits (See Section 4.6)

- Track the status of the CAPs for the audits they have led

- Conduct auditor training seminars

- Maintain audit files consistent with corporate retention policies

4.3   Corporate Law

The Corporate Law Department will have a vital role in the management of the Program. The Department's responsibilities include:

- Assure that Program procedures are consistent with maintaining document confidentiality

- Receive and review copies of all draft and final audit reports

- Provide legal advice on issues identified by the audit teams.

4.5   Group and Plant Management

ABC CORPORATION
Model EH&S Audit Program Guidance Manual

Group and plant management (i.e., line management) are essential partners in the Audit Program. They are responsible to:

- Provide an appropriate number of qualified staff to serve as auditors during the course of the year to assure that the facility audit schedule is met

- Provide appropriate resources, information, and data in preparation for and during the site audits

- Assure that full disclosure is made to the audit team during the audit

- Assure that a senior plant/line manager is made available for the audit opening and closing conferences

- Complete feedback questionnaires evaluating the individual audits

- Implement audit action items and communicate the status of open action items on a periodic basis, as determined by the Audit Program Director.

4.6 Audit Team Leaders

Audit Team Leaders will be selected from the among the Audit Program Managers. Their responsibilities will include:

- Become qualified by experience or attendance at an ABC audit training seminar or its equivalent

- Working with the Director, choose the appropriate number of auditors from the qualified pool for each audit

- For each audit:
  - Assign audit protocols to each auditor
  - Review audit protocols
  - Review applicable state regulatory data
  - Notify site management and send pre-audit questionnaire
  - Review the completed pre-audit questionnaire
  - Set the agenda and arrange for logistics for the audit
  - Lead the opening and closing conferences

ABC CORPORATION
Model EH&S Audit Program Guidance Manual

- Manage the audit process while at the site
- Do the audits for the assigned protocols
- Develop and distribute the draft and final reports
- Assure document management meets records retention policies.

- To remain qualified, lead or participate in at least five audits per year.

4.7 Auditors

Auditors will be selected from among qualified individuals within the Corporate, Group, and site organizations. Their responsibilities will include:

- Become qualified by experience or attendance at an ABC audit training seminar or its equivalent

- For each audit:
  - Review assigned audit protocols and the completed pre-audit questionnaire
    - Review applicable state regulatory data
    - Arrange for personal logistics for the audit
    - Participate in the opening and closing conferences
    - Do audits for the assigned protocols
    - Develop draft and final findings and recommendations for the assigned protocols
    - Assure document management meets records retention policies.

- To remain qualified, participate in at least one audit per year.

5.0   SCOPE AND COVERAGE OF THE PROGRAM

Any audit program must have some bounds under which it operates. Accordingly, this section defines the facilities and regulations that are covered by the Program. In addition, it discusses the audit protocols (i.e., checklists) that will be used to assess site compliance against applicable laws, regulations, and corporate policies.

5.1   Facilities Covered

ABC CORPORATION
Model EH&S Audit Program Guidance Manual

Essentially all North America ABC and subsidiary operations will be subject to the EH&S Audit Program. This includes facilities that are owned and operated by ABC, facilities that are leased to and operated by ABC, and joint venture sites where ABC has majority ownership or operational responsibility. For joint ventures where ABC does not have majority ownership or operational responsibility, ABC will attempt to influence the partner(s) to participate in ABC's Program or ensure that the partner(s) has an equivalent program. ABC owned property leased or rented to others initially will not be covered by the Program where the lease stipulates that the lessee will comply with all applicable EH&S laws and regulations.

Distribution centers, warehouses, administrative buildings, real estate, as well as manufacturing facilities are covered under the Program. Any on-site contractors will be covered as well. This Program will not *directly* address off-site commercial waste disposal contractors or property/business acquisitions or divestitures.

5.2   Topical Coverage

The ABC EH&S Audit Program focuses principally on the site's compliance with EH&S requirements. The EH&S Audit Program will encompass corporate policies and procedures, good management practices, and federal, state, and local regulations, including the following federal statutes, when applicable:

- Clean Air Act (including CFC's) (CAA)
- Clean Water Act (CWA)
- Safe Drinking Water Act (SDWA)
- Resource Conservation and Recovery Act (not including corrective action plan actions) (RCRA)
- Comprehensive EH&S Response, Compensation and Liability Act (not including site remediation) (CERCLA)
- Emergency Planning and Community Right-to-Know Act (EPCRA)
- Pollution Prevention Act (PPA)
- Oil Pollution Act (OPA)
- Toxic Substances Control Act (TSCA)
- Hazardous Materials Transportation Act (HMTA) (pre-transport only)
- Federal Insecticide, Fungicide and Rodenticide Act (FIFRA)
- Occupational Safety and Health Act (OSHA)

State and local laws and regulations that are separate but related to the above federal statutes (e.g., wetlands regulations in New Jersey, residual wastes regulations in Pennsylvania, Proposition 65 in California) will be covered as well,

ABC CORPORATION
Model EH&S Audit Program Guidance Manual

where applicable. The Audit Program Director can provide applicable state requirements to the auditors, on an as needed basis.

As indicated by the exceptions listed above under RCRA and CERCLA, the Audit Program will focus on current and recent past facility operations. Historical practices and site remediation activities will be addressed under a separate program. Facility operations will be reviewed for the past three years or since the time of the last audit, whichever is shorter.

International sites will be audited against the local country standards and company policies and procedures. Where company policies and procedures are more stringent, they will apply. The Audit Program Director will be responsible for providing applicable country requirements to the Audit Team Leaders.

5.3   Audit Types

The audits will address both compliance with laws and regulations and the adequacy of the site's management systems. The vast majority of audits will be comprehensive, multimedia EH&S audits. However, targeted audits of one or more compliance areas may be conducted where appropriate.

On occasion, verification audits will be used to assess the effectiveness of site corrective action plan programs. On these audits one or two auditors will revisit a site that has been audited in the past year with the sole objective to determine the site's progress in meeting its corrective action plan commitments.

For certain "low-risk" facilities, the Audit Program Director may institute a self-audit program. If a site qualifies under this program, there will be no independent audit of the site. Rather, an audit checklist will be distributed to the site EH&S coordinator or appropriate responsible parties. The coordinator will complete the checklist annually and report the results of the self-audit to the Audit Program Director in the first quarter of the year following the audit.

5.4   Audit Protocols

Audit protocols or checklists will be developed for use by the audit teams. The protocols will cover all of the federal requirements listed above and corporate policies and procedures but will not address directly any state or local requirements. At the option of the Audit Program Director, state exception checklists may be developed. The audit protocols will be developed in-house or purchased and will be updated annually.

ABC CORPORATION
Model EH&S Audit Program Guidance Manual

6.0   AUDITOR TRAINING AND SELECTION

Audit teams will be made up of qualified, trained auditors from Group and site staff, corporate EH&S affairs and law departments, and other individuals as deemed appropriate by the Audit Program Director. Each organization will be responsible for nominating appropriate candidates each year.

When possible, the site EH&S coordinator from the site that is next in line to be audited will be a member of the team on the current audit. This will help prepare this individual for the upcoming audit at his or her site.

The Audit Program Director will be responsible for developing and holding a formal auditor training course. The course will be held on an as needed basis to replace auditors lost through attrition. It will emphasize auditing skills, especially the writing of effective audit reports. Those auditor candidates in need of training on regulatory requirements should not rely exclusively on this course for that knowledge. A refresher training course will also be developed and will be held on an as needed basis but no less frequent than once every two years. The emphasis of the refresher training will be based on the feedback received from audit team leaders and site survey questionnaires. The need for both courses will be decided based on the requirements discussed directly below.

All auditors must be trained prior to conducting their first audit. They must complete ABC's audit training course, complete an equivalent course (as determined by the Audit Program Director), or be able to demonstrate equivalent experience (as determined by the Audit Program Director). An individual meeting any one of these criteria will be classified as a *qualified auditor*. The Audit Program Director will maintain a current record of all qualified auditors and will assure that enough auditors are qualified and available each year to meet the facility audit schedule for that year. Audit Program Managers must lead or participate in five audits per year and audit team members must participate in one audit per year to maintain their qualified status.

7.0   AUDIT PROCEDURES

The core of any audit program lies in the actual completion of facility audits. There are three major phases to an audit. They are: pre-audit, on-site, and post-audit activities. This section discusses ABC's *general* approach to each of these phases. The overall audit process and the timeline for each audit, from initial notification to the site to completion of the site corrective action plan, are shown

ABC CORPORATION
Model EH&S Audit Program Guidance Manual

in Table 2. The more detailed tasks associated with conducting an EH&S audit are covered in the ABC audit training courses.

7.1   Pre-Audit Activities

In preparation for the actual site audit, the Audit Team Leader and auditors need to accomplish the following tasks.

Team Selection and Formation

The audit team will consist of a Team Leader and one or more auditors. In general, ABC sites will require anywhere from 2-4 auditors on site for 2-5 days depending upon the complexity of the site. It will be the responsibility of the Audit Program Director to decide for each audit how many team members will be required and how long the audit will be. (See the section discussing resource allocations.) Within this guideline, the Team Leader will select the team from the list of qualified auditors. No auditor can be selected who is directly involved in the site's management or operations. It is expected that the Group EH&S Coordinators will participate in their Group's audits, but not as a formal member of the audit team.

Setting of Scope and Assignment of Responsibilities

The Team Leader will define the scope of the audit and assign protocol responsibilities to the team members. In general, the scope should assume a broad-based review of the site addressing all applicable EH&S requirements. Therefore, each auditor likely will be assigned more than one compliance area. These assignments will be made based on the relative skills of the team. The Team Leader will be expected to take responsibility for one or more compliance areas.

ABC CORPORATION
Model EH&S Audit Program Guidance Manual

TABLE 2

EH&S Audit Process Timeline

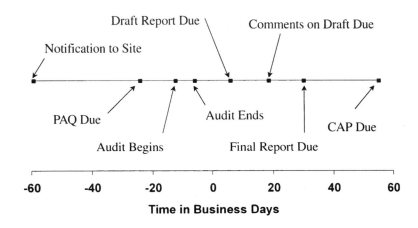

ABC CORPORATION
Model EH&S Audit Program Guidance Manual

Protocol Review and Regulatory Research

The audit team members are responsible for reviewing the protocols they have been assigned and conducting any necessary independent research of applicable federal and state regulations. The auditors will rely on information provided by the pre-audit questionnaire to assist them in determining applicability. Even though the audit protocols will provide background on applicable federal regulations, the team members are expected to conduct a review of current federal rules, as the protocols may not reflect the most recent changes. Any calls to regulatory agencies should be made only if needed and generally should be cleared through the Audit Program Director or Law Department.

Distribution and Review of Pre-Audit Questionnaire

The pre-audit questionnaire is used to highlight regulatory compliance areas that are applicable at the site and to help the site prepare for the audit. A standard questionnaire will be sent to the site EH&S coordinator by the Team Leader at least eight weeks (40 business days) prior to the audit. The coordinator will deliver the completed questionnaire to the Team Leader two weeks prior to the audit. The Team Leader will distribute the questionnaire to the team members immediately upon receipt.

Development of Site Agenda and Notification of Site Management

The Audit Team Leader is responsible for notifying site management eight weeks (40 business days) prior to the audit. This can and should be done concurrent with the distribution of the pre-audit questionnaire. The notification can be done by phone or in writing. At a minimum, a proposed agenda should be sent to the site at this time. An example of an agenda for a three-day audit is presented in Table 3. At the time of the notification, the Audit Team Leader should be certain that the following items are handled:

ABC CORPORATION
Model EH&S Audit Program Guidance Manual

TABLE 3
Sample Audit Agenda for a Three-Day Audit

Day	Activity
Sunday Evening	Pre-Audit Team Meeting
Monday Morning	Opening Conference and Orientation Tour
Monday Afternoon	Meetings with EH&S Staff and Initial Records Review
Monday Evening	Audit Team Planning Meeting and Development of Initial Findings
Tuesday Morning	Review Meeting with Site EH&S Staff; Further Records Review and Initial Field Verification Inspections
Tuesday Afternoon	Continuous Field and Interview Verification Activities
Tuesday Evening	Audit Team Planning Meeting and Development of Draft Findings
Wednesday Morning	Review Meeting with Site EH&S Staff; Continuous Field and Interview Verification Activities
Wednesday Early Afternoon	Corrective Action Plan on Unresolved Issues and Finalization of Draft Findings or Report; Final Review Meeting with Site EH&S Staff
Wednesday Late Afternoon	Closing Conference with Site Management

ABC CORPORATION
Model EH&S Audit Program Guidance Manual

- Discuss the scope of and agenda for the audit with site management
- Obtain directions to the site and a hotel recommendation
- Identify the audit team members and review safety and security requirements
- Set exact time of arrival and time of opening conference; assure participation by the site manager
- Request office space and telephone access while on site
- Request a list of key site staff or organization chart
- Determine if a hazardous waste pick-up, emergency response drill, confined space entry, or the like could be scheduled during the audit week.

The Audit Team Leader should also make one last confirming phone call a few days before the audit to assure the site is prepared.

Pre-Audit Team Meeting

The Audit Team Leader will assure that a meeting of the team takes place prior to the audit. This meeting might constitute a face-to-face meeting a week prior to the audit if team members are located near one another, a teleconference among the team, or a meeting the evening prior to the audit at the local hotel. During the meeting, the audit team will discuss the completed pre-audit questionnaire and will discuss any issues that arose as a result of their pre-audit research.

7.2 *On-Site Activities*

Once the team arrives on site, the audit proper begins. The team should request and receive a site safety orientation. A number of tasks are undertaken during the site visit. These are highlighted below.

Opening and Daily Conferences

The opening conference is normally held when the audit team first arrives on site. It is attended by the audit team and site line and EH&S management. Key operational personnel also attend. The Audit Team Leader will utilize a set of standard slides for the conference, which will explain the objectives and approach for the audit. These slides are available on the company's Intranet.

The opening conference with site management should last no more than one hour. Typically, after half an hour, line management departs and the meeting

ABC CORPORATION
Model EH&S Audit Program Guidance Manual

continues with the audit team and site EH&S staff. The pre-audit questionnaire is reviewed in detail and site management's concerns are solicited. A topical agenda for the opening conference is provided below:

- Audit objectives and scope
- Audit flow including corrective action plan and closure
- Identification of key interview candidates and availability (including relevant organization charts)
- A summary review of facility operations
- Identification of important site activities occurring during the week
- A review of the pre-audit information including the pre-visit questionnaire and the previous audit report
- Scheduling the daily and closing conferences
- Identification of the audit team work room and phone protocol
- Identification of the site work hours and visitor safety and security protocols
- Identification of computer/printer support
- Discussion of the site escort protocol for visitors.

Note that the sample agenda assumes that the audit team will meet amongst themselves each evening to review their findings. The first thing each morning they will meet with site EH&S staff to go over these findings and to set the agenda for the day. These daily meetings with site staff help to enhance the communications on the audit.

In the opening conference, the audit team should emphasize the fact that not every record or operation will necessarily be reviewed in detail. The team may only look at a representative sample of items to determine whether there is a deficiency or problem. Thus, there is no *guarantee* that the audit will identify *all* EH&S compliance problems.

The audit team will also be recording notes in the field. These notes will be reviewed by the Audit Team Leader to assure that they contain simple statements of fact and not supposition or inappropriate comments.

Orientation Tour

Immediately following the opening conference the audit team will go on a site orientation tour. This should take no more than 1-1/-2 hours and should be designed to give the team an overview of the site. If the team members are

ABC CORPORATION
Model EH&S Audit Program Guidance Manual

familiar with the site they may elect to forego the tour. Plot plans of the site should be provided to the audit team.

Records Reviews

It is important that the audit team spend some time reviewing the site's EH&S compliance records (e.g., permits, plans, and procedures) before interviewing the staff or inspecting the operating facilities. This is because many of the compliance requirements are found in these records. The audit team will review the records for the applicable requirements and verify compliance through interviews, inspections, or a review of compliance data.

The auditors should be thorough in the investigation of records. However, this does not mean that every record is to be evaluated. The auditor is free to use statistical or otherwise representative sampling in the review. Where the auditor does not review every record and there is a finding of noncompliance, the auditor should reflect the sampling method in the statement of finding.

Interviews

Interviews will be conducted with plant management, EH&S staff, and operating personnel. To the extent possible, the interviews will be conducted one-on-one and in the employee's workspace. The use of tape recorders is strongly discouraged.

Facility Inspections

Inspections of the site with special attention given to critical compliance areas (e.g., hazardous waste accumulation and storage areas, wastewater treatment plants, permitted confined spaces) will be conducted following a review of records. The site should be fully covered during these inspections. This would include rooftops, electrical utilities, fencelines, and remote areas.

In the event that an auditor believes that he or she has observed an imminent safety or environmental hazard during the course of the audit, the situation will be reported to site management immediately.

Closing Conference

The closing conference is a crucial element of the audit. The Audit Team Leader should assure that site management is in attendance. Where this is not feasible, in

ABC CORPORATION
Model EH&S Audit Program Guidance Manual

the event of an emergency, the Team Leader should debrief the site manager independently, by phone, or in person. A typical agenda for the closing conference would be as follows:

- General reintroductions
- Restatement of objectives, scope, and approach
- Overall summary of the audit, highlighting particularly commendable items and significant deficiencies
- Review of findings by compliance area
- Discussion of the audit report format and schedule
- Discussion of the corrective action plan action report format and schedule.

To the extent possible, the audit team should be prepared to leave a written list of findings or a draft report with the site at the closing conference. This will allow the site to begin immediately to develop and implement the corrective action plan. Each auditor will be responsible for developing the findings for his or her compliance areas. Both the list of findings and the draft report will be distributed to the Law Department.

It is important to note that when the audit team presents the list of findings or the draft report during the closing conference, the site is expected to provide input into the accuracy and precision of the findings. The closing conference is a negotiating session in which both the audit team and the site staff should resolve all differences. Where differences cannot be resolved, the final arbiter will be the Audit Program Director, with counsel from the Law Department.

7.3   Post-Audit Activities

Once the on-site audit is completed, there are several important tasks remaining for the audit team and site staff. These are discussed below.

Report Preparation

The Audit Team Leader, with input from the audit team, is required to develop draft and final audit reports consistent with the schedule and format depicted in later sections of this manual. The report should include any findings from the previous audit report that have not been corrected. The draft report is due within ten business days of the last day of the audit. Comments from the site are due within ten business days of receipt of the draft report. The final report is due ten business days later.

ABC CORPORATION
Model EH&S Audit Program Guidance Manual

The Corrective Action Plan

Within 20 business days of receipt of the final audit report, the site is responsible for developing a corrective action plan (CAP) that responds to the findings in the report. An electronic version of the CAP form is available on the company's Intranet. While on site, the audit team should feel free to work with site staff in the formulation of the CAP.

Site Evaluation

A site audit evaluation questionnaire will be used as a quality assurance check for the Program. The form, which requires site feedback on the perceived value of the audit, is completed by site staff and returned directly to the Audit Program Director within ten business days of the last day of the audit. The Program Director will use the results of the questionnaires to improve the Program.

Quarterly Status Reports

Corrective action planning is a critical part of the audit process. Failing to respond to identified noncompliance issues can result in "willful and knowing" sanctions from regulatory agencies. Thus, site management is required to submit a CAP quarterly status report to the Audit Program Director. The Program Director will input this information into a database of all "open" audits, and revise the status of the Group's progress, as appropriate. The Program Managers will conduct sporadic verification audits as deemed necessary by the Program Director.

8.0   FACILITY AUDIT SCHEDULES AND RESOURCE ALLOCATIONS

The Audit Program Director will develop the audit schedule for each year and assign audit team leaders from his staff of Managers. The audit team members will be selected from the list of qualified auditors (See the section on training for a discussion of "qualified" auditor.) The audit team leaders will be responsible for selecting the audit team members, from a pool of qualified auditors, and will make any adjustments necessary if scheduling conflicts arise at any time prior to the audit.

The frequency at which a site is audited, how long the audit will take and how many auditors will participate will be based on the perceived risks of the site. An evaluation of these parameters will be made by the end of each year by the Audit

ABC CORPORATION
Model EH&S Audit Program Guidance Manual

Program Director in consultation with Group EH&S Coordinators based on the criteria presented in Table 4. The criteria will be used as a guide not as a quantitative scoring system. So, a site will not necessarily have to have all of the characteristics associated with a Category I site to be classified as Category I. It may only have one or more of those characteristics to be classified as such. Based on the Coordinators' evaluations, an annual schedule will be published and distributed by the Audit Program Director in December of each year to Corporate and Group management. Site and Group management may request to have any site audited more, but not less, frequently than as determined by the annual Program schedule.

9.0   REPORT STRUCTURE, DISTRIBUTION, AND RECORDS RETENTION

This section discusses the structure, schedule, and distribution of reports, and records retention.

9.1   Report Structure

All ABC reports will have the same basic structure. A sample audit report is provided on the Intranet. The outline for the report is as follows:

> 1.0   Executive summary
> Highlights of deficiencies
> Deficiencies requiring capital expenditures
> Noteworthy or commendable items
>
> 2.0   Introduction
> Audit background and scope
>
> 3.0   Overview of the facility
>
> 4.0   Audit findings and recommendations by compliance area

The report will be an exception report in that only findings of deficiency will be listed in the fourth section. This permits better tracking of the findings as each numbered finding will require a corrective action. If the audit team observes something especially noteworthy, this can be highlighted in the Executive Summary.

ABC CORPORATION
Model EH&S Audit Program Guidance Manual

TABLE 4
Risk Factors Used in Assigning Site Audit Frequency

Site Characteristics	Category I (Every Three Years)	Category II (Every Four Years)	Category III (Every Five Years)
Size and Type	Major Manufacturing, Mining, or Processing	Minor Manufacturing, Mining, or Processing	Warehouses, Real Estate, or Administration Buildings
Employee Safety	Lost Workday Case Incident Rate Worse than Industry Average	Lost Workday Case Incident Rate at Industry Average	Lost Workday Case Incident Rate Better than Industry Average
Process Safety	Covered by the Process Safety Management Rule	Covered by the Process Safety Management Rule	Not Covered by the Process Safety Management Rule
Chemical Exposure	Covered Under >10 1910.1001-50 Chemicals	Covered Under 3-10 1910.1001-50 Chemicals	Covered Under <3 1910.1001-50 Chemicals
Air Emissions	Major Source of Air Toxics or Significant Emissions; Multiple Permits	Moderate Emissions; Some Air Permits	No Sources Require Air Permits
Community Relations	Major Documented Problems with the Community	Periodic Formal Complaints	No or Isolated Complaints
Hazardous Materials Releases	Has Three or More §313 Chemicals	Has One or Two §313 Chemicals	Has No §313 Chemicals
Hazardous Waste	Large Quantity Generator	Small Quantity Generator	Conditionally Exempt Small Quantity Generator
Wastewater	Operates On-Site Treatment or Pre-Treatment Plant	Discharges Process Wastewater to POTW	Discharges Only Sanitary Wastewater or No Discharges

ABC CORPORATION
Model EH&S Audit Program Guidance Manual

Spill Potential	On-Site Bulk Petroleum or Hazardous Substances Storage of >50,000 Gallons	On-Site Bulk Petroleum or Hazardous Substances Storage of 1000 to 50,000 Gallons	On-Site Bulk Petroleum or Hazardous Substances Storage of <1000 Gallons

ABC CORPORATION
Model EH&S Audit Program Guidance Manual

In the reports, each audit finding will be classified by type and degree of importance, as shown in Table 5. This classification system will help in setting priorities. For example, a Level I Regulatory Finding should receive immediate and significant attention from site management. Conversely, a Level III Management Practice Finding may be something that the site could defer while it focuses on other, higher-priority issues. It is important to remember, however, that a Level III (and every) finding will have to be responded to in the corrective action plan. It is also important to note that it is not always the case that a Regulatory Finding will be more significant than a Company Policy or Management Practice Finding of the same level.

Thus, in the findings and recommendations section, the format for *each* finding will be as follows:

- Finding (a statement of fact)
- Requirement (a statement of the relevant requirement)
- Type of finding (with citation if appropriate)
- Level of Finding (I, II, or III)
- Recommendation (immediate and long-term).

Where a finding is corrected prior to the departure of the audit team, the report will contain the finding but indicate that it was corrected. If a finding is repeated from a previous audit report, then the report will indicate it is a repeat finding. The audit team will consider whether repeat findings should be given a higher classification level than otherwise might be the case. Sample findings and recommendations can be observed in the example report.

9.2   *Confidentiality*

All materials prepared in connection with the EH&S Audit Program, including but not limited to draft and final audit reports, are confidential and proprietary information of ABC Corporation. Distribution guidelines for audit materials are provided in Tables 6 and 7. Audit materials should only be distributed in accordance with these guidelines, and access to these materials should be strictly limited.

ABC CORPORATION
Model EH&S Audit Program Guidance Manual

TABLE 5
Classification of Audit Findings

Type of Finding
Regulatory: A finding involving laws, ordinances, or regulations, which are external to the Company. These include government regulations and international treaties. Any deficiencies associated with plans required by regulations (e.g., SPCC Plans, RCRA Contingency Plans) are considered regulatory.
Policy: A finding involving Corporate policies, guidelines, or operating standards.
Management Practice: A finding involving physical situations posing a risk, or EH&S management programs/systems at the site that are not covered by external regulations or company policy.

Level of Finding
Level I: HIGHEST PRIORITY ACTION REQUIRED. Situations which could result in substantial risk to the environment, the public, employees, stockholders, customers, the Company, or in criminal or civil liability for knowing violations. Some administrative issues could be categorized as Level I (e.g., failure to report a significant release when required).
Level II : PRIORITY ACTION REQUIRED. Does not meet the criteria for Level I but is more than an isolated or occasional situation. Should not continue beyond the short term. This category can usually result in a notice of violation from regulatory agencies. It could also be a serious void and/or breakdown in a management system.
Level III: ACTION REQUIRED. Findings may be administrative in nature or involve an isolated or occasional situation. They may involve temporary or occasional instances of noncompliance. They may also involve opportunities for substantive system improvement.

ABC CORPORATION
Model EH&S Audit Program Guidance Manual

TABLE 6
Schedule and Assignments for Audit Documentation and Reports

Document	Responsible Party	Timetable and Distribution
Pre-Audit Questionnaire	Site or Group EH&S Coordinator	Returned completed to Team Leader ten business days prior to the audit
Working Papers (i.e., Field Notes)	Individual Auditors	Returned to Audit Team Leader once draft report is issued
Draft Findings	Audit Team Leader	Left at the site if draft report is not left at the site
Draft Reports	Audit Team Leader	Left at the site (preferred) or within ten business days of the end of the audit; Distributed to Corporate EH&S Affairs and Law and the site/Group EH&S coordinators
Audit Evaluation Questionnaire	Site Management	Due within ten business days after the audit; Distributed to Audit Program Director
Comments on Draft	Site and Group EH&S Coordinator, Law, and Corporate EH&S Affairs	Due within ten business days of receipt of the draft report by the Audit Team Leader
Final Report	Audit Team Leader	Due within ten business days of due date for receipt of comments; Distributed to Corporate EH&S Affairs and Law, Plant Manager, Operations Director, Group President, and Environmental Coordinator
Corrective Action Plans and Quarterly Updates	Plant Manager	Due within 20 business days of final report and quarterly thereafter; Distributed to Corporate Environmental Affairs and Law, and Group Coordinator
Status Reports	Group EH&S Coordinator	Quarterly for all open audits; Due on the 15th of the month following the calendar quarter; Summary distributed to Corporate EH&S Affairs and Law

ABC CORPORATION
Model EH&S Audit Program Guidance Manual

TABLE 7
Audit Document Retention Procedures

Document	Retention Procedure
Pre-Audit Questionnaire	Is coupled with Final Report (See Below)
Working Papers (i.e., field notes)	Collected and Destroyed by Team Leader Once Final Report Is Issued
Draft Findings	Collected and Destroyed by Team Leader Once Draft Report Is Issued
Draft Report	Collected and Destroyed by Audit Team Leader Once Final Report Is Issued
Audit Evaluation Questionnaires	Retained by Audit Program Director until Annual Program Evaluation Is Completed
Comments on Draft Report	Destroyed by Audit Team Leader Once Final Report Is Issued
Final Report	Destroyed by Recipients Once a More Recent Audit Report Exists
Corrective Action Plans	Destroyed Once Final Report Is Destroyed
Status Reports	Destroyed Once Final Report Is Destroyed

ABC CORPORATION
Model EH&S Audit Program Guidance Manual

9.3   Report Schedule and Distribution

A variety of documents are created during the audit process. The schedule and responsibilities for each of these are listed in Table 6. The schedule is somewhat accelerated but this is done purposely to assure that the momentum of the audit is not lost.

9.4   Records Retention

Records retention is another important element of an audit program. For ABC's EH&S Audit Program the applicable Program document retention procedures are presented in Table 7.

10.0   AUDIT PROGRAM MANAGEMENT AND EVALUATION

Managing an EH&S audit program typically involves a number of tasks. These are discussed below.

10.1   Annual Audit Planning

As discussed previously, the Audit Program Director, with the Program Managers, will meet in the last quarter of each calendar year. The principal objectives of this meeting are to set the facility audit schedule, assign audit team leaders, assure that the current pool of qualified auditors is sufficient to meet the schedule, and determine how the annual program evaluation will be done.

10.2   Response Tracking

The Audit Program Director, in consultation with the Group EH&S Coordinators, is responsible for tracking the status of all corrective action plans and assuring that quarterly status reports are received for each open audit. Based on a quarterly summary report of corrective action plan status provided by the Group EH&S Coordinator, the Program Director will maintain statistics on site response by Group and report these to Senior Management and the Core Team quarterly. Since the Groups have agreed to the CAP's for each site, it will be expected that there will be virtually 100 percent compliance with the CAP's unless something extraordinary occurs. These extraordinary circumstances must be documented in the CAP.

ABC CORPORATION
Model EH&S Audit Program Guidance Manual

The Audit Program Director will officially "close-out" each audit once all CAP actions have been completed. If actions remain outstanding at the time of the next scheduled audit for any given site, these findings and actions will be incorporated into the new audit report and the old report and plans will be destroyed consistent with this Manual's records retention policy.

10.3 Management Reports

Every year, the Audit Program Director will report to the Audit Committee of the Board of Directors on the results of the EH&S Audit Program. The submittals will be concise reports on the status of the Program and will, at a minimum, contain the following:

- Number of audits completed during the time period and number planned for the next time period

- Highlights of liabilities most affecting the Corporation

- Trends in the types of noncompliance items to identify potential corporate-wide issues

- Statistics on Group success rates in meeting corrective action plan action schedules

- Trends in the number of repeat and Level I findings

- Results of the annual (self- or third-party) evaluation of the Program.

The reporting to senior management may be done in person by the Audit Program Director. However, a written report will be required regardless of whether this presentation takes place or not. This report can be integrated with the annual program evaluation report, which is discussed below.

10.4 Program Evaluation and Quality Assurance

One of the key challenges with any management program is assuring that it meets its stated objectives. In this light, the ABC EH&S Audit Program will be evaluated annually using the following objectives-based criteria:

ABC CORPORATION
Model EH&S Audit Program Guidance Manual

- *Program Objective 1: Assure regulatory compliance, minimize potential EH&S risks, and evaluate the adequacy of EH&S management systems to meet the Corporation's goals*

  - Completion of planned audits
  - Site responsiveness in meeting CAP action plans
  - Auditor responsiveness in meeting report deadlines
  - Long-term reduction in facility noncompliance findings
  - Reduction in number of Level I findings in the company
  - Reduction in number of repeat findings at a given site
  - Formal feedback from those who are audited
  - Development and annual update of audit protocols.

- *Program Objective 2: Increased EH&S awareness and continuous learning by audited personnel and auditors*

  - Development and implementation of an auditor training program
  - All auditors trained prior to their first audit
  - Maintaining a current list of qualified auditors
  - Auditors meeting utilization target (frequency of audits)
  - Audit reports are consistent and meet Program expectations.

- *Program Objective 3: Transfer of EH&S technologies and innovations across the Corporation*

  - Issuance of periodic information exchange reports focusing on key learnings and root-cause analysis
  - Audit teams consistently have cross-Group participation

- *Program Objective 4: Assure adequate EH&S performance and continuous improvement to the Board of Directors*

  - Third-party annual assessment of the Program
  - Periodic oversight audits (or peer review)
  - Periodic report to the Audit Committee of the Board of Directors
  - Annual update of the Program Guidance Manual.

The program evaluation can be done internally or by a third party. The evaluation report will be due on March 1st of each year, for the preceding year.

ABC CORPORATION
Model EH&S Audit Program Guidance Manual

The report will be distributed to the Board, Corporate EH&S Affairs, and the Law Department.

Appendix G

Model Pre-Audit Questionnaire
for an EH&S Audit

Note: This appendix is also available on CD-ROM as an electronic template to be tailored to your company's individual needs.

Model Pre-Audit Questionnaires for EH&S Audits

August 5, 2000

Caution

The following Pre-Audit Questionnaires can be used as models in preparing for an EH&S audit. The models should be modified to meet any particular organization's specific objectives (e.g., ISO 14000).

Environmental Audit Program
Model Pre-Audit Questionnaire

Privileged and Confidential

This pre-audit questionnaire is intended to elicit background information from the operating facility pertaining to its environmental management activities. This background information will assist the audit team in planning and conducting facility audits. Accurate and timely completion is requested. Please return the completed questionnaire to the person designated below at least <u>five business days</u> prior to the scheduled audit.

> John Smith, Audit Program Manager
> ABC Company
> 100 Main Street
> Downingtown, PA 19335
> Phone: (610) 555-1212
> Fax: (610) 555-1213

Please call if you have questions or wish to discuss your response. If a yes or no response is not appropriate, please provide a narrative response or attach the information.

GENERAL

Facility Name: _____ SIC: _____

Business _____

Street: _____

City: _____

County/Parish: _____

Facility Manager: _____ Email: _____

Environmental Coordinator: _____ Email: _____

Phone No.: _____ Fax No.: _____

Date Completed: _____ Completed By: _____

FACILITY DESCRIPTION

On a separate sheet, provide a one-page narrative description of the facility and its operations. Topics that should be addressed include:

- Location, size, and age of the facility
- Number of employees
- Description of operations
- Manufacturing or processing square footage
- Number of shifts and days per week of operation
- Any important environmental factors (e.g., wetlands, groundwater recharge, non-attainment area, or near a major water course)

Environmental Audit Program
Model Pre-Audit Questionnaire

Privileged and Confidential

1. Total Area   _____ acres

2. Total Personnel   _____ people

3. Can the area surrounding the facility be described as:

   a. Commercial?   _____%

   b. Industrial?   _____%

   c. Residential?   _____%

   d. Agricultural, undeveloped, or rural?   _____%

	Check One		
4. Surrounding population characteristics	Y (Yes)	N (No)	DK (Don't Know)
a. Are there any schools, day care centers, nursing homes, prisons, churches, or hospitals within 1.0 mile of your facility?	☐	☐	☐
b. Is the distance to the nearest residential structure from the facility fence line:			
- Less than 0.5 mile?	☐	☐	☐
- 0.5 to 1.0 mile?	☐	☐	☐
- Greater than 1.0 mile?	☐	☐	☐
c. Is the distance to the nearest industrial structure from the facility fence line:			
- Less than 0.5 mile?	☐	☐	☐
- 0.5 to 1.0 mile?	☐	☐	☐
- Greater than 1.0 mile?	☐	☐	☐
d. What is the approximate population within 1.0 mile of your facility? _____ people			

Environmental Audit Program
Model Pre-Audit Questionnaire

Privileged and Confidential

5. Local Topography

    Can the area surrounding your facility be described as:

    a. Coastal?   _____ %

    b. Hilly/mountainous?   _____ %

    c. Flood plain?   _____ %

    d. Desert?   _____ %

    e. Valley?   _____ %

    f. Other (describe)?   _____ %   _____

    _____

	Y	N	DK

6. Surrounding population characteristics

    a. Are there any off-site locations (e.g., warehouses, processing plants) that fall under the direct control of plant management? ☐ ☐ ☐

    b. Does the site audit any on-site contractor operations? ☐ ☐ ☐

FACILITY ENVIRONMENTAL MANAGEMENT SYSTEMS

1. Please give the names, titles, and areas of responsibility of the designated Environmental Coordinator(s) at the facility.

2. To whom do they report?

    Name: _____   Title: _____

3. What percentage of the coordinators' time is actually spent on environmentally related activities?   _____ %

**Environmental Audit Program
Model Pre-Audit Questionnaire**

Privileged and Confidential

	Y	N	DK

4. Have the coordinators' responsibilities been clearly defined and communicated by plant management to site personnel? ☐ ☐ ☐

5. Are the coordinators' performance evaluations influenced by the execution of environmental responsibilities? ☐ ☐ ☐

6. How do the coordinators keep up with regulatory developments and company environmental policies and guidelines?

7. Briefly describe the facility's overall system for reviewing the performance of its environmental programs (e.g., self-audits or inspections, environmental self-evaluation, review of records and reports, etc.), and for identifying departures from established standards and policies (governmental or company).

8. What system is in place for review of environmental impacts when new products, process/operational changes, new raw materials, etc. are anticipated? When is this review undertaken (e.g., several months prior to initiation, the week before)?

	Y	N	DK

9. Are facility and company management kept informed of ongoing environmental activities? If yes, what mechanisms are used? ☐ ☐ ☐

Environmental Audit Program
Model Pre-Audit Questionnaire

Privileged and Confidential

	Y	N	DK
10. Are facility and company management made aware of environmental problems or incidents (e.g., reportable releases)?	☐	☐	☐

   a. What mechanisms are used?

   b. Who is notified?

	Y	N	DK
11. Did the site pay any penalties for either an investigation deficiency or as a result of a spill or release in the previous year?	☐	☐	☐

   a. How much? $_____

   b. How many?   _____

c. Any pending fines?	☐	☐	☐

AIR EMISSIONS

	Y	N	DK
1. Has a site air emissions inventory been conducted within the last two years?	☐	☐	☐
2. Have emissions inventories included fugitive emissions?	☐	☐	☐
3. Does the site have any of the following types of air emissions sources?			
a. Flares	☐	☐	☐
b. Stacks and Vents	☐	☐	☐
c. Storage Tanks	☐	☐	☐
d. Incinerators	☐	☐	☐
e. Boilers	☐	☐	☐
f. Other Point Sources (describe)	☐	☐	☐
g. Other Fugitive Sources (describe)	☐	☐	☐

ENVIRONMENTAL AUDIT PROGRAM - GUIDANCE MANUAL - PAGE 5
DISTRIBUTION DATE: 7/15/00
DATE OF NEXT REVISION: 7/15/01

Environmental Audit Program
Model Pre-Audit Questionnaire

Privileged and Confidential

	Y	N	DK

4. Is the facility required to register or permit air emissions sources? ☐ ☐ ☐

    a. If yes, provide a brief description of major air permits, including "grandfathered" sources by facility area.

    b. Which, if any, grandfathered sources are likely to become subject to permitting within the next two years?

	Y	N	DK

    c. Are site or surrounding area emissions subject to PSD Standards? ☐ ☐ ☐

    d. Are site or area emissions subject to NSPS? ☐ ☐ ☐

5. Does the site have any air permits pending? Is so, in what operations? ☐ ☐ ☐

Environmental Audit Program
Model Pre-Audit Questionnaire

Privileged and Confidential

	Y	N	DK
6. Do any of the pending permits involve PSD review, offsets, banked emissions, or bubbles? If yes, please describe.	☐	☐	☐

If yes, associated with which permits? For which chemicals?

	Y	N	DK
7. Does the facility conduct fence line monitoring of any air emissions?	☐	☐	☐
8. Have the area's NAAQS attainment/non-attainment designations changed since the last audit?	☐	☐	☐
9. Is the facility subject to federal and/or state air emissions standards?	☐	☐	☐
10. Are any of the following Hazardous Air Pollutants (HAPs) present in the facility's emissions?			
a. Beryllium	☐	☐	☐
b. Asbestos	☐	☐	☐
c. Mercury	☐	☐	☐
d. Vinyl Chloride	☐	☐	☐
e. Benzene	☐	☐	☐
f. VOCs	☐	☐	☐
g. Arsenic	☐	☐	☐
h. Radionuclides	☐	☐	☐
11. Has the facility evaluated the impact of pending HAP regulations (1990 Clean Air Act Amendments)?	☐	☐	☐
12. Is the facility subject to HAP regulations?	☐	☐	☐
13. Has the facility experienced any air pollution incidents in the past two years? If yes, please describe the incidents.	☐	☐	☐

ENVIRONMENTAL AUDIT PROGRAM - GUIDANCE MANUAL - PAGE 7
DISTRIBUTION DATE: 7/15/00
DATE OF NEXT REVISION: 7/15/01

Environmental Audit Program
Model Pre-Audit Questionnaire

Privileged and Confidential

	Y	N	DK

14. Have facility emissions resulted in complaints from the general public due to:

    a. Odors? ☐ ☐ ☐

    b. Irritants? ☐ ☐ ☐

    c. Fugitive Dusts? ☐ ☐ ☐

    d. Visible Discharges? ☐ ☐ ☐

    e. Other (describe): _____

    _____

15. Has the facility received air violations within the past two years, including notices of violation, administrative orders, or enforcement actions? If yes, please describe the incident and status of enforcement. ☐ ☐ ☐

16. Are environmental coordinators notified when a permit limit or condition is exceeded? If yes, describe the notification process and site procedures. ☐ ☐ ☐

17. Does the site have an Air Pollution Alert Plan? ☐ ☐ ☐

18. Does the site conduct indoor air pollution monitoring? ☐ ☐ ☐

19. Are aspects of the air program expected to change in the next two years due to new regulations or permit conditions in the following areas:

    a. Air Toxics? ☐ ☐ ☐

    b. SO_2 Emissions? ☐ ☐ ☐

    c. Particulates? ☐ ☐ ☐

    d. CO_2 Controls? ☐ ☐ ☐

    e. Fugitives ID and Monitoring? ☐ ☐ ☐

    f. Regional Air Monitoring? ☐ ☐ ☐

    g. New Permit Conditions? ☐ ☐ ☐

Environmental Audit Program
Model Pre-Audit Questionnaire

Privileged and Confidential

	Y	N	DK
20. Does the site have any project activities that will impact overall air emissions? If yes, what is the impact? How does this relate to the site's waste minimization goals?	☐	☐	☐

WASTEWATER AND STORMWATER DISCHARGES

	Y	N	DK
1. Does the facility have an NPDES permit?	☐	☐	☐
2. Does the facility discharge any of the following into a waterway (e.g., river, stream brook, lake)? If yes, please name the waterway.	☐	☐	☐
a. Non-contact cooling water	☐	☐	☐
b. Manufacturing/storage area, parking area, roadway, non-precipitation-related runoff, washwaters, or rinsewaters containing detergents or other cleansers	☐	☐	☐
c. Undeveloped area non-precipitation-related and non-irrigation-related runoff	☐	☐	☐
d. Dredge and fill solids drainage water	☐	☐	☐
e. Wastewater treatment plant effluent	☐	☐	☐
f. Process wastewater	☐	☐	☐
g. Other (describe): _____			
3. Is the facility subject to point source effluent limitations?	☐	☐	☐
4. Does the facility discharge any of the following into a publicly owned treatment works (POTW)?			
a. Process Water	☐	☐	☐
b. Domestic (Sanitary) Wastewater	☐	☐	☐
c. Wastewater Treatment Plant Effluent	☐	☐	☐
5. Does the facility treat wastewater on site before discharge (including septic systems)?	☐	☐	☐
6. Is the facility subject to stormwater permitting?	☐	☐	☐

Environmental Audit Program
Model Pre-Audit Questionnaire

Privileged and Confidential

	Y	N	DK
7. Is the facility subject to any NPDES limitations?	☐	☐	☐
8. What type of stormwater permit do you have? _____			
9. Does the permit require certified laboratory analysis?	☐	☐	☐
10. Is the facility NPDES permit up for renewal within the next two years?	☐	☐	☐
11. Are NPDES samples analyzed on site?	☐	☐	☐
12. Are all monitoring records required by the permit, including instrumentation calibration records, retained for three years or as the permit requires?	☐	☐	☐
13. Have any incidents occurred in the last year in which the treatment system was bypassed and wastewater discharge occurred without treatment? If yes, describe the incident(s).	☐	☐	☐
14. Have there been any fines or citations from wastewater/stormwater discharges? If yes, please describe briefly.	☐	☐	☐
15. Are other wastewater regulatory impacts (e.g., stormwater) anticipated during the next two years?	☐	☐	☐
16. Are there any project activities planned for the next two years which will significantly affect wastewater flow or composition?	☐	☐	☐

DRINKING WATER

	Y	N	DK
1. Does any portion of the facility's drinking water supply come from on-site wells or surface water sources?	☐	☐	☐
2. Does the facility monitor on-site drinking water sources?	☐	☐	☐

Environmental Audit Program
Model Pre-Audit Questionnaire

Privileged and Confidential

	Y	N	DK
3. Has a qualified technical supervisor or sanitarian surveyed the facility's drinking water system within the past 24 months?	☐	☐	☐
4. Are reports and records retained in accordance with regulations?			
a. Bacteriological analysis (five years)	☐	☐	☐
b. Chemical analysis (ten years)	☐	☐	☐
c. Actions taken to correct violations (three years)	☐	☐	☐
d. Documents relating to sanitary surveys	☐	☐	☐
5. Has the drinking water system been constructed or significantly modified in the last two years?	☐	☐	☐
6. Has a program been undertaken to ensure that lead and copper limits in drinking water meet applicable regulatory standards?	☐	☐	☐

GROUNDWATER

	Y	N	DK
1. Has the facility evaluated groundwater quality?	☐	☐	☐
2. Does the facility monitor groundwater?	☐	☐	☐
3. Is there groundwater contamination?	☐	☐	☐
4. Are there any abatement, remediation and/or groundwater treatment operations underway?	☐	☐	☐

OIL AND HAZARDOUS SUBSTANCE STORAGE
SPILL AND PREVENTION CONTROL

	Y	N	DK
1. Does the facility store oil in volumes greater than 42,000 gallons below ground, 1,320 gallons above ground, or 660 gallons in a single container above ground?	☐	☐	☐
2. Does the facility have a procedure for reporting releases of hazardous substances?	☐	☐	☐
3. Is secondary containment provided for all bulk oil or hazardous substance storage tanks?	☐	☐	☐

Environmental Audit Program
Model Pre-Audit Questionnaire

Privileged and Confidential

	Y	N	DK
4. Does the facility have any underground tanks in or out of service? (Please have a list available.)	☐	☐	☐
5. Does the facility have a written Spill Prevention Control and Countermeasures (SPCC) Plan or its state equivalent?	☐	☐	☐
6. Has the plant discharged more than 1,000 gallons of oil into or upon the navigable waters of the United States or adjoining shoreline in a single spill event, or reported two spills within the last 12 months?	☐	☐	☐
7. Does the facility maintain records of reportable spills?	☐	☐	☐
8. Does the facility conduct training in spill response?	☐	☐	☐
9. Can an exercise or spill drill be scheduled during the audit?	☐	☐	☐
10. Does the facility respond to emergency situations involving hazardous substances and wastes off site?	☐	☐	☐
11. Has the facility been cited for any SPCC or other spill deficiencies by a regulatory agency within the past year? If yes, please describe.	☐	☐	☐

CERCLA

	Y	N	DK
1. Did any release or spill report in the past year initiate a visit from a regulatory agency? If yes, describe each incident and its status.	☐	☐	☐

2. Who at the site is responsible for phoning in release reports to the regulatory agencies?

Name: _____

Environmental Audit Program
Model Pre-Audit Questionnaire

Privileged and Confidential

3. What outside agencies are notified in the event of a CERCLA release (including local groups and LEPCs)?

4. Please list any significant incidents which occurred in the last two years.

WASTE AND WASTE MINIMIZATION

	Y	N	DK
1. Does the facility have a program for recycling solid wastes (e.g., paper, glass, aluminum, plastic)?	☐	☐	☐
2. Does the facility have a documented waste minimization program?	☐	☐	☐
3. Have all waste streams (including wastes that are recycled) been evaluated for hazardous waste status?	☐	☐	☐
4. Under RCRA or appropriate state regulations, is the site a:			
a. Conditionally-exempt small quantity generator (less than 100 kg hazardous waste per month)?	☐	☐	☐
b. Small quantity generator (less than 100 kg and less than 1,000 kg hazardous waste per month)?	☐	☐	☐
c. Large quantity generator (greater than 1,000 kg hazardous waste per month)?	☐	☐	☐
5. How are wastes classified?			
a. Analytical Testing	☐	☐	☐
b. Process Knowledge (Engineering Logic)	☐	☐	☐
6. Does the facility have permits for hazardous waste:			
a. Treatment?	☐	☐	☐
b. Storage?	☐	☐	☐
c. Disposal?	☐	☐	☐

Environmental Audit Program
Model Pre-Audit Questionnaire

Privileged and Confidential

	Y	N	DK

7. Does the facility generate any materials classified as:

    a. Listed RCRA or state hazardous wastes? ☐ ☐ ☐

    b. Ignitable wastes? ☐ ☐ ☐

    c. Corrosive wastes? ☐ ☐ ☐

    d. Reactive wastes? ☐ ☐ ☐

    e. Toxic (as determined by the Toxicity Characteristic/Leaching Procedure or more stringent state test)? ☐ ☐ ☐

    f. Other (please describe): _____

_____

8. Does the facility:

    a. Store hazardous wastes for longer than 90 days, or treat or dispose of hazardous waste? ☐ ☐ ☐

    b. Generate, treat, or store medical or infectious wastes? ☐ ☐ ☐

    c. Treat, store, or dispose nonhazardous industrial wastes on site? ☐ ☐ ☐

    d. Treat, store, or dispose trash ("municipal" solid waste) on site? ☐ ☐ ☐

9. Are there corrective action programs (RCRA, state, or voluntary) underway at the site? If yes, briefly describe the status. ☐ ☐ ☐

10. Which of the following types of nonhazardous waste facilities are currently in operation at the facility?

    a. Surface impoundment ☐ ☐ ☐

    b. Waste piles ☐ ☐ ☐

    c. Land treatment facility ☐ ☐ ☐

    d. Landfill ☐ ☐ ☐

    e. Incinerator ☐ ☐ ☐

    f. Boiler ☐ ☐ ☐

    g. Thermal treater (specify type) ☐ ☐ ☐

    h. Biological treatment facility ☐ ☐ ☐

    i. Other (please describe): _____

_____

Environmental Audit Program
Model Pre-Audit Questionnaire

Privileged and Confidential

	Y	N	DK
11. Is the site involved in any of the following activities?			
a. Recyclable materials used in a manner which constitutes disposal	☐	☐	☐
b. Hazardous waste burned for energy recovery	☐	☐	☐
c. Used oil burned for energy recovery	☐	☐	☐
d. Recyclable materials used for precious metals recovery	☐	☐	☐
e. Spent lead-acid battery reclamation	☐	☐	☐
12. Has the facility received any regulatory notices or citations for hazardous or solid waste management deficiencies during the past two years?	☐	☐	☐
13. Can a hazardous waste contractor pickup be scheduled during the audit?	☐	☐	☐

TSCA/PCBs

	Y	N	DK
1. Does the facility have a TSCA Section 8 reporting and recordkeeping program?	☐	☐	☐
2. Have there been any reported instances of reactions to chemicals at the site? If yes, has a report to U.S. EPA been made?	☐	☐	☐
3. Are PCB or PCB-contaminated soils and/or equipment in use or stored at the facility? If yes, are PCBs in:	☐	☐	☐
a. Transformers?	☐	☐	☐
b. Capacitors?	☐	☐	☐
c. Hydraulic fluid?	☐	☐	☐
d. Heat transfer fluid?	☐	☐	☐
e. Lubricating oils?	☐	☐	☐
4. Is there a utility-owned transformer on the site?	☐	☐	☐
5. If yes, does it contain PCBs?	☐	☐	☐

Environmental Audit Program
Model Pre-Audit Questionnaire

Privileged and Confidential

PESTICIDES/HERBICIDES/OTHER CHEMICALS COVERED BY FIFRA

		Y	N	DK
1.	Does the facility use any pesticides, herbicides, or biocides on site?	☐	☐	☐
2.	Do contractors apply the pesticides? (If applied by contractors, have available a list of those contractors.)	☐	☐	☐

EMERGENCY PLANNING AND COMMUNITY RIGHT-TO-KNOW (EPCRA)

		Y	N	DK
1.	Did the facility have to notify the LEPC that it is subject to CRTK requirements?	☐	☐	☐
2.	Has the facility submitted §311/312 Tier I or II reports to the LEPC in the past three years?	☐	☐	☐
3.	Has the facility submitted a §313 Form R report to the U.S. EPA in the past three years?	☐	☐	☐
4.	Has the facility established a community advisory council or similar group?	☐	☐	☐
5.	Did the facility notify the state by May 17, 1987 or later that it was subject to the requirements created by SARA Title III (Community Right-to-Know)?	☐	☐	☐
6.	Has the facility designated an emergency response coordinator? Please provide the person's name and job title.	☐	☐	☐

Name: _____ Title: _____

		Y	N	DK
7.	Has the facility evaluated chemical inventory information to determine whether threshold quantities for inventory reporting (Tier I and Tier II reports) have been exceeded, and if so, submitted these reports to the state and local authorities?	☐	☐	☐
8.	Does the site manufacture, process, or use a "toxic" chemical above the reporting thresholds as defined in Section 313 of Title III?	☐	☐	☐

Environmental Audit Program
Model Pre-Audit Questionnaire

Privileged and Confidential

OTHER/MISCELLANEOUS

		Y	N	DK
1.	Is the facility subject to the Surface Mining Control and Reclamation Act or its state equivalent?	☐	☐	☐
2.	Is the facility subject to the Oil Pollution Act?	☐	☐	☐
3.	Does the facility transport hazardous chemicals or wastes off site?	☐	☐	☐
4.	Does the facility have any regulated radiation sources (e.g., instruments)?	☐	☐	☐
5.	Has the facility had any involvement with NEPA requirements (e.g., EIAs, EISs) in the past two years?	☐	☐	☐

PRE-AUDIT INFORMATION COLLECTION CHECKLIST

Information to be made available during the audit:

		Available	Not Available	Not Applicable
A.	Air Emissions			
	1. Copies of all current air permits	☐	☐	☐
	2. Air monitoring data for the past 12 months	☐	☐	☐
	3. Air emission inventor	☐	☐	☐
	4. Air emission reports submitted to regulatory agencies for past 12 months	☐	☐	☐
	5. Copies of any violation notices received in the past three years	☐	☐	☐
B.	Wastewater/Stormwater			
	1. Copies of all U.S. EPA, state, or municipal sewer permits	☐	☐	☐
	2. Copies of discharge monitoring data for last two years for flow and permit parameters	☐	☐	☐
	3. Any complete (organic and inorganic) analysis of process, cooling, or stormwater streams	☐	☐	☐
	4. Water-use records for the past 12 months	☐	☐	☐
	5. Copies of any violation notices received in the past three years	☐	☐	☐

Environmental Audit Program
Model Pre-Audit Questionnaire

Privileged and Confidential

	Available	Not Available	Not Applicable
C. Hazardous Wastes			
1. RCRA Permits	☐	☐	☐
2. Hazardous Waste Manifests for the past 13 months	☐	☐	☐
3. Copies of Preparedness and Prevention/Contingency Plans	☐	☐	☐
4. Waste Analysis data for all hazardous waste streams	☐	☐	☐
5. Latest Generator Report to U.S. EPA and state	☐	☐	☐
6. Copies of any violation notices received in the past three years	☐	☐	☐
7. Copies of any notices of involvement at "Superfund" sites	☐	☐	☐
8. Copy of the Waste Minimization Plan	☐	☐	☐
9. List of all wastes generated in the past year	☐	☐	☐
D. Tanks			
1. A listing of all aboveground storage tanks that includes capacity, contents, use, and volume capacity of secondary containment system	☐	☐	☐
2. A copy of the underground tank registration form(s) submitted to any authority or removal/closure records	☐	☐	☐
3. A copy of the site's Spill Prevention Control and Countermeasure (SPCC) Plan	☐	☐	☐
4. Map indicating location of USTs	☐	☐	☐
	☐	☐	☐
E. TSCA/Polychlorinated Biphenyls (PCBs)			
1. Any TSCA adverse reaction reports	☐	☐	☐
2. A copy of an annual PCB report	☐	☐	☐
3. PCB test results from analysis on electrical equipment	☐	☐	☐
4. Copies of any violation notices received in the past three years	☐	☐	☐
5. Asbestos inventory, testing and classification, and disposal records.	☐	☐	☐

**Environmental Audit Program
Model Pre-Audit Questionnaire**

Privileged and Confidential

		Available	Not Available	Not Applicable
F.	**Groundwater**			
1.	Well construction diagrams for on-site water supply or groundwater monitoring wells	☐	☐	☐
2.	Water quality analyses from water supply or groundwater monitoring wells for the past 12 months	☐	☐	☐
G.	**Community Right-to-Know**			
1.	Copies of lists of chemicals or MSDSs sent to LEPC	☐	☐	☐
2.	Copies of §311/312 Tier I and II reports	☐	☐	☐
3.	Copies of §313 Form R Submissions	☐	☐	☐
4.	List of all chemical substances on site	☐	☐	☐
H.	**Management Systems**			
1.	List of responsible party for each environmental activity	☐	☐	☐
2.	All environmentally-related training records	☐	☐	☐
3.	All environmental policies and procedures	☐	☐	☐
4.	Organization chart	☐	☐	☐
5.	Site diagram identifying storage areas, tanks, etc.	☐	☐	☐

Health and Safety Audit Program
Model Pre-Audit Questionnaire

Privileged and Confidential

This pre-audit provides background information from facilities about their health and safety management activities. This background information will assist auditors in planning and conducting facility audits; thus, please complete this questionnaire accurately and on a timely basis. Please return the completed questionnaire to the person designated below at least <u>five business days</u> prior to the scheduled audit.

> John Smith, Audit Program Manager
> ABC Company
> 100 Main Street
> Downingtown, PA 19335
> Phone: (610) 555-1212
> Fax: (610) 555-1213

Company Name	
Street Address	
City/Country	
State/Province	
Zip Code/Postal Code	
Phone/Fax Number	
Date Questionnaire Completed	
SIC Code	

General

1. What types of operations are or have been conducted at this location (e.g., extruding, refining, chemical manufacturing, assembly of parts, etc.)?

   _____

   _____

   _____

2. What are the primary products and services supplied by this location?

   _____

   _____

   _____

Health and Safety Audit Program
Model Pre-Audit Questionnaire

Privileged and Confidential

3. How many employees work at the site (full/part time, salaried/hourly)?

    _____

    _____

    _____

4. How many shifts does the plant operate? What are the hours of operation?

    _____

    _____

    _____

5. How large is the facility or site (e.g., number of buildings, square footage, acres, etc.)?

    _____

    _____

    _____

Facility Health and Safety Management

Position	Name	Telephone Number
Facility Manager		
Health & Safety Coordinator		

Who is responsible for the development, implementation, and administration of programs for compliance with applicable government and company/business requirements for each of the following functional areas?

Functional Area	Program Development	Program Implementation
Hazardous energy control programs (i.e., lockout/tagout)		
Confined space entry		
Hot work		
Laboratory safety		
Contractor safety		
First aid or medical services		
Respirator program		
Hearing protection		
Hazard communication		

Health and Safety Audit Program
Model Pre-Audit Questionnaire

Privileged and Confidential

Functional Area	Program Development	Program Implementation
Bloodborne pathogens		
Fire protection equipment		
Fire brigade		
Emergency response		
Incident investigation		
Accident recordkeeping		

Employee Safety

	Yes	No	N/A

1. Are there written programs for:

    a. Hazardous energy control (i.e., lockout/tagout)? ☐ ☐ ☐

    b. Confined space entry? ☐ ☐ ☐

    c. Hot work? ☐ ☐ ☐

    d. Contractor safety? ☐ ☐ ☐

    e. Electrical safety-related work practices? ☐ ☐ ☐

2. Does the facility have programs (e.g., audits, inspections, etc.) to monitor:

    a. Safe work practices? ☐ ☐ ☐

    b. Contractor safety? ☐ ☐ ☐

3. Does the facility use or have any of the following:

    a. Powered industrial trucks (e.g., forklifts)? ☐ ☐ ☐

    b. Cranes? ☐ ☐ ☐

    c. Hoisting equipment and slings? ☐ ☐ ☐

    d. Aboveground walking/working surfaces ☐ ☐ ☐

    e. Portable ladders? ☐ ☐ ☐

    f. Fixed ladders? ☐ ☐ ☐

    g. Scaffolding? ☐ ☐ ☐

    h. Emergency eyewashes? ☐ ☐ ☐

Health and Safety Audit Program
Model Pre-Audit Questionnaire

Privileged and Confidential

Employee Safety	**Yes**	**No**	**N/A**

i.   Safety showers? ☐ ☐ ☐

4.   Does the facility have equipment on site requiring guarding? ☐ ☐ ☐
      If yes, describe the types of equipment (e.g., grinders, saws,
      drill presses, robotic equipment, lathes, etc.) and where a
      majority of the equipment is located.

      _____

      _____

      _____

5.   Does the facility have routine inspection/preventive ☐ ☐ ☐
      maintenance programs for any of the above equipment?
      If yes, specify the frequency for each equipment type.

      _____

      _____

6.   Does the facility maintain live electrical equipment ☐ ☐ ☐
      (e.g., transformers)? If yes, specify the highest voltage
      with which the facility employees have to work.

      _____

      _____

7.   Has the facility conducted job safety analyses? ☐ ☐ ☐

8.   Does the facility have the following laboratories on site:

      a.   Clinical/biological? ☐ ☐ ☐

      b.   Quality control? ☐ ☐ ☐

      c.   Research and development? ☐ ☐ ☐

9.   Does the facility have medical services on site? If yes, specify the ☐ ☐ ☐
      type of coverage (e.g., full-time, all shifts, part-time, first shift only,
      etc.). If not, how far away are the nearest medical services?

      _____

      _____

10.   Does the facility employ contract workers? If yes, are they ☐ ☐ ☐
      covered under the facility's health and safety programs?

      _____

      _____

Health and Safety Audit Program
Model Pre-Audit Questionnaire

Privileged and Confidential

Industrial Hygiene	Yes	No	N/A
1. Are there formal written programs for:			
a. Respiratory protection?	☐	☐	☐
b. Hearing protection?	☐	☐	☐
c. Hazard communication?	☐	☐	☐
d. Laboratory safety?	☐	☐	☐
e. Personal protective equipment?	☐	☐	☐
2. Has the facility conducted a noise exposure survey? Are employees exposed to noise exposure levels of 85 dBA for an 8-hour time-weighted average or greater?	☐	☐	☐
3. Has the facility conducted a workplace hazard assessment for the need for personal protective equipment?	☐	☐	☐
4. Does the facility provide any of the following personal protective equipment for employees' use:			
a. Hearing protection? If yes, where?	☐	☐	☐
b. Respirators? If yes, what types of respirators are used (e.g., two-strap dust mask, half-mask (negative pressure), full-face (negative pressure), PAPRs, supplied air, SCBAs, etc.) and where?	☐	☐	☐
c. Protective eyewear (e.g., safety glasses, goggles, face shields, etc.)? If yes, where?	☐	☐	☐
d. Safety shoes? If yes, where?	☐	☐	☐

Health and Safety Audit Program
Model Pre-Audit Questionnaire

Privileged and Confidential

Industrial Hygiene (continued)	Yes	No	N/A

    e.   Head protection? If yes, where?   ☐ ☐ ☐

_____

_____

    f.   Hand protection? If yes, where?   ☐ ☐ ☐

_____

_____

5.   Does the facility provide employees with initial and periodic medical evaluations for the following:

    a.   Employees working in high noise areas?   ☐ ☐ ☐

    b.   Respirator wearers?   ☐ ☐ ☐

    c.   Industrial powered truck operators (e.g., forklift drivers, DOT MV operators)?   ☐ ☐ ☐

    d.   Emergency/spill response team members?   ☐ ☐ ☐

    e.   Fire brigade members?   ☐ ☐ ☐

    f.   Employees working with regulated substances (e.g., benzene, lead, formaldehyde, etc.)? If yes, please specify.   ☐ ☐ ☐

_____

_____

    g.   Other?   ☐ ☐ ☐

_____

_____

6.   Has the facility conducted a hazard assessment to determine priorities for exposure monitoring?   ☐ ☐ ☐

7.   Does or has the facility conducted any exposure monitoring? If yes, for what contaminants and how often is it done?   ☐ ☐ ☐

_____

_____

8.   Does the facility have an exposure monitoring schedule/plan?   ☐ ☐ ☐

Health and Safety Audit Program
Model Pre-Audit Questionnaire

Privileged and Confidential

Industrial Hygiene (continued)	**Yes**	**No**	**N/A**

9. Does the facility have any of the following sources?

   a. Non-ionizing radiation? If yes, specify where. ☐ ☐ ☐

_____

_____

   b. Ionizing radiation? If yes, specify where. ☐ ☐ ☐

_____

_____

   c. Lasers? If yes, specify where. ☐ ☐ ☐

_____

_____

10. Are ventilation systems used to control chemical exposures? ☐ ☐ ☐

11. Are other engineering controls used for control of hazards (e.g., noise enclosures, controlled atmosphere control rooms)? If yes, please specify. ☐ ☐ ☐

_____

_____

12. Are any administrative controls used for hazard control (e.g., limiting exposure time)? If yes, please specify. ☐ ☐ ☐

_____

_____

Loss Prevention and Emergency Response	**Yes**	**No**	**N/A**

1. Does the facility have the following?

   a. Fire prevention plan? ☐ ☐ ☐

   b. Emergency action plan? ☐ ☐ ☐

   c. Emergency response plan? If yes, list the type of response(s). ☐ ☐ ☐

_____

_____

2. Does the facility train and expect all or designated employees to use portable fire extinguisher and/or hoses? (Specify whether all ☐ ☐ ☐

Health and Safety Audit Program
Model Pre-Audit Questionnaire

Privileged and Confidential

Industrial Hygiene (continued)	Yes	No	N/A
employees or designated employees.)			

_____

_____

3.   Does the facility have the following fire protection equipment:

    a.   Automatic sprinkler systems? If yes, specify whether they are inspected by vendors or in-house personnel. ☐ ☐ ☐

_____

    b.   Fixed extinguishing systems? If yes, specify what type (e.g., CO_2, halon, etc.) and indicate whether they are inspected by vendors or in-house personnel. ☐ ☐ ☐

_____

    c.   Fire detection systems? If yes, specify whether they are inspected by vendors or in-house personnel. ☐ ☐ ☐

_____

    d.   Fire alarm systems? If yes, specify what type (e.g., PA system, sounding alarm, etc.) and indicate whether they are inspected by vendors or in-house personnel. ☐ ☐ ☐

_____

4.   Does the facility have the following:

    a.   Fire brigade? ☐ ☐ ☐

    b.   Emergency response team? ☐ ☐ ☐

5.   Does the facility store flammable liquids in:

    a.   Bulk storage tanks? If yes, specify the type of equipment (e.g., flame arresters, internal floating roofs, foam dispensers, etc.) the tanks are supplied with. ☐ ☐ ☐

_____

    b.   Inside storage areas/rooms? ☐ ☐ ☐

Health and Safety Audit Program
Model Pre-Audit Questionnaire

Privileged and Confidential

Industrial Hygiene (continued)	**Yes**	**No**	**N/A**
c. Outside storage buildings?	☐	☐	☐
d. Warehouse?	☐	☐	☐
6. Does the facility dispense flammable liquids?	☐	☐	☐
7. Does the facility conduct spray painting operations?	☐	☐	☐

General Health and Safety Management	**Yes**	**No**	**N/A**
1. Does the facility have a safety manual or safety guidelines?	☐	☐	☐
2. Are new and modified processes reviewed for occupational safety and health issues?	☐	☐	☐
3. Does the facility track health and safety national regulations? If yes, how?	☐	☐	☐

_____

_____

_____

Appendix H

Model EH&S Audit Opening Conference Presentation

Note: This appendix is also available on CD-ROM as an electronic template to be tailored to your company's individual needs.

MODEL OPENING CONFERENCE

Model EH&S Audit Opening Conference Presentation

August 5, 2000

Caution

This is a model EH&S Audit Opening Conference Presentation, which can be used as a model to assure consistent communication of program goals and approach. The model should be modified to meet any particular organization's specific objectives (e.g., ISO 14000).

EH&S Audit
Opening Conference

Audit Objectives

To Verify Compliance with

- ◆ Regulations
- ◆ Company Policies & Procedures
- ◆ Good Management Practices

To Assess the Effectiveness of EH&S Management Systems

Audit Scope & Approach

- Four-Day Review
- Three Team Members
- All EH&S Compliance Areas Addressed
- Remediation Not Covered
- Conducted under Attorney-Client Privilege

On-Site Process

- Opening Conference
- Orientation Tour
- Records Review, Interviews and Observations
- Daily Conferences
- Preparation of Draft Findings
- Closing Conference

Key Audit Issues

- There Will Be Findings
- Audits Require Verification
- Activities Will Be Observed
- Fixed Findings Are Typically Included
- Known Noncompliances Are Included
- Compliance Guarantees Cannot Be Made

Expected Outputs

- Written Draft Findings On-Site
- Exception-Based Draft Report within Two Weeks of Closing Conference
- Final Report within One Week of Receipt of Comments

Audit Report Structure

■ Executive Summary

■ Background and Approach

■ Audit Findings and Recommendations

◆ Overall Management Issues

◆ By Compliance Area

Structure of Findings and Recommendations

■ Statement of Observation

■ Statement of Requirement

■ Citation

■ Finding Type (Reg, Corp Std, GMP)

■ Finding Level (I, II, III)

■ Immediate Recommendation

■ Long-Term Recommendation

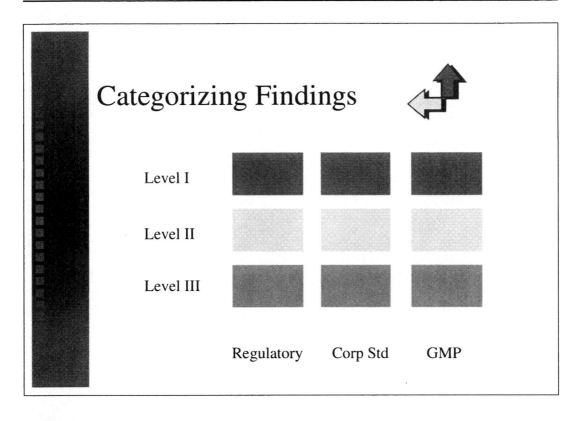

Categorizing Findings

Level I

Level II

Level III

Regulatory   Corp Std   GMP

What to Expect...

- A Rigorous Review
- A Supportive Process
- A Practical Approach
- A "Road Map" to Improvement
- The Audit Is Just the Beginning...

Model Environmental Audit Report

Note: This appendix is also available on CD-ROM as an electronic template to be tailored to your company's individual needs.

MODEL REPORT

Model Environmental Audit Report

August 5, 2000

Caution

This is a sample environmental audit report, which can be used as a model in developing audit reports for individual sites and facilities. The sample findings are illustrative only and do not necessarily reflect current federal, state, or local regulatory requirements. The model should be modified to meet any particular organization's specific objectives (e.g., ISO 14000).

TABLE OF CONTENTS

ABC COMPANY ENVIRONMENTAL AUDIT PROGRAM
Audit of *[Indicate Name and Location of Facility]*

1.0   EXECUTIVE SUMMARY

An environmental audit was conducted at the *[Plant Name]* from *[Dates]*. This section summarizes the results of the audit. Overall, the facility .... *[Provide a summary statement or, if an overall ranking is desired, select one of the following options:*

> ...... *meets governmental and internal requirements.*
> ...... *substantially meets governmental and internal requirements.*
> ...... *generally meets governmental and internal requirements, except as noted.*
> ...... *requires improvement to meet governmental and internal requirements.*
> ...... *requires substantial improvement to meet governmental and internal requirements.]*

During the course of the audit, the team observed the following especially commendable practices:

> *[Bullet list 2-4 commendable practices that are truly worthy of special mention.]*

The team was impressed with your efforts in these areas.

The audit team did identify a number of deficiencies that need to be addressed by the site. Table 1 summarizes these audit findings and Table 2 describes the definitions used to classify each finding. As shown, there were a total of *[Provide Number]* findings identified. The most significant findings include:

> *[Bullet list the most significant findings.]*

All findings are discussed in detail in Section 4.0 of this report. All findings are to be addressed in a Follow-up Action Plan (FAP) to be developed by site management. The FAP is due to the Corporate Audit Program Manager within 20 business days of issuance of the final audit report.

ABC COMPANY ENVIRONMENTAL AUDIT PROGRAM
Audit of *[Indicate Name and Location of Facility]*

TABLE 1
Summary of Environmental Audit Findings
[This table is to be completed based on the final tally of findings.]

CATEGORY	LEVEL I			LEVEL II			LEVEL III		
	REG	POL	GMP	REG	POL	GMP	REG	POL	GMP
Management Systems									
Air Emissions, Noise, and Odor									
Wastewater and Stormwater									
Drinking Water									
Spill Control									
Solid and Hazardous Waste									
Underground Storage Tanks									
Toxic Substances									
PCBs									
Asbestos									
Pesticides									
Community Right-to-Know									
TOTALS	•	•	•	•	•	•	•	•	•

Table Key: REG - Government Regulation; POL - Corporate Environmental Policy or Procedure; GMP - Good Management Practice

ABC COMPANY ENVIRONMENTAL AUDIT PROGRAM
Audit of *[Indicate Name and Location of Facility]*

TABLE 2
Classification of Audit Findings

TYPE OF FINDING

Regulatory: A finding involving laws, ordinances, or regulations, which are external to the Company. These include government regulations and international treaties.

Policy: A finding involving Corporate policies, guidelines, or operating standards.

Good Management Practice: A finding involving environmental management programs or systems at the site.

LEVEL OF FINDING

Level I: IMMEDIATE ACTION REQUIRED. Situations that could result in substantial risk to the environment, the public, employees, stockholders, customers, the Company, or in criminal or civil liability for knowing violations. Some administrative issues could be categorized as Level I (e.g., failure to report a significant release when required).

Level II : PRIORITY ACTION REQUIRED. Does not meet the criteria for Level I but is more than an isolated or occasional situation. Should not continue beyond the short term. This category can usually result in a notice of violation from regulatory agencies. It could also be a serious void and/or breakdown in a management system.

Level III: ACTION REQUIRED. Findings may be administrative in nature or involve an isolated or occasional situation. They may involve temporary or occasional instances of noncompliance. They may also offer opportunities for substantive systems improvements.

ABC COMPANY ENVIRONMENTAL AUDIT PROGRAM
Audit of *[Indicate Name and Location of Facility]*

2.0   INTRODUCTION

An environmental audit was conducted at *[Plant Name]* on *[Dates]*. The objectives of the audit were to: (1) assess the site's compliance with government laws and regulations, corporate policies and procedures, and good management practices and (2) determine if management systems were in place for ensuring continued compliance. The audit focused on the following areas:

[List areas (e.g., air emissions, hazardous waste, wastewater, management systems).]

The audit team generally reviewed records and performance *[Choose and insert an alternative: "since the last audit, which occurred during the week of [Date];" or "over the past 12 [or 24] months"]*.

The audit team leader was *[Provide Name]*. Audit team members are listed below with their areas of responsibility on the audit:

Team Member	Organizational Affiliation	Areas of Responsibility
[Provide Name]	*[Provide Organization]*	*[List Areas]*
"	"	"
"	"	"
"	"	"
"	"	"

The audit required substantial participation by the site staff. Principal participants included:

Site Staff	Title	Areas of Involvement
[Provide Name]	*[Provide Title]*	*[List Areas]*
"	"	"
"	"	"
"	"	"
"	"	"

ABC COMPANY ENVIRONMENTAL AUDIT PROGRAM
Audit of *[Indicate Name and Location of Facility]*

The audit was conducted consistent with the requirements of the *[Insert Corporate Environmental Audit Guidance Manual or equivalent]*. The process included a review of records, interviews with site staff, and physical observation of facilities. All findings were verified. Consistent with generally accepted audit practices, in some cases the audit team may have reviewed only a representative sample of records or equipment. Therefore, no compliance guarantees can be made with respect to areas that were not found deficient. No obstacles were encountered that prevented the audit team from completing the audit as designed.

This report presents the results of the audit. An Executive Summary is provided and a detailed discussion of findings with appropriate recommendations is presented. These findings are categorized as either regulatory, company policy, or good management practice. Findings are further classified by priority Level I, II, or III. Definitions for these levels are provided in Table 2. It should be noted that this is an exception report in that only deficiencies are recorded as findings. Where especially innovative or commendable practices are identified, these are highlighted in the Executive Summary.

3.0   *FACILITY OVERVIEW*

[This section should provide a brief overview of the facility. Topics that should be addressed include:

- *Location and age of facilities*
- *Site size (acres)*
- *Manufacturing or processing square footage*
- *Number of employees*
- *Number of shifts and days per week of operation*
- *Brief description of operations*
- *Overview of any environmentally important factors (e.g., wetlands, groundwater recharge area, non-attainment area, nearly major watercourse).]*

ABC COMPANY ENVIRONMENTAL AUDIT PROGRAM
Audit of *[Indicate Name and Location of Facility]*

4.0   FINDINGS AND RECOMMENDATIONS

This section presents the findings and recommendations for each area reviewed by the audit team. Each subsection contains a brief overview of the site's activities relevant to the area. Findings are classified according to the scheme presented in Table 2. Citations are provided where appropriate.

[Note: Example findings are provided below for each of the compliance areas. These findings are provided for instructional purposes only. If the audit team identifies any overall or linked management systems deficiencies, they are discussed in the first section. Note that where individual compliance findings are "rolled-up" into a management systems finding, these are not repeated in the individual compliance areas. Note also that management systems findings are type-categorized based on a hierarchy. That is, if any of the symptoms are regulatory deficiencies, then the entire finding is considered regulatory.]

4.1   MANAGEMENT SYSTEMS

There is an environmental coordinator at the site. The coordinator reports to the Human Resources Manager, who, in turn, reports to the Plant Manager. The site is organized using a high-commitment work system approach. The team identified some management systems at the site, which were not operating at full effectiveness.

4.1.1   Hazardous Waste Training

Finding: Management training for the hazardous waste coordinator was deficient as evidenced by the following findings. (Regulatory/I)

- The weekly inspection log for the accumulation point showed no record of inspections for the weeks of June 6 and 13. (40 CFR 265.174)

- Labels were missing from three of the five drums at the accumulation point. (40 CFR 262.32)

- There were no return copies for manifest numbers CA34077 and CA34099. (40 CFR 262.23)

ABC COMPANY ENVIRONMENTAL AUDIT PROGRAM
Audit of *[Indicate Name and Location of Facility]*

- There is no Hazardous Waste Contingency Plan for the site. Although this is not required by the Federal rule for Small Quantity Generators, the state does require it. (CA Code 25-7)

Recommendation: The site environmental coordinator should remedy the existing deficiencies and contract with an outside firm or request that Corporate Environmental Affairs conduct focused generator training at the site.

4.1.2 Management of Change

Finding: The management of change process does not effectively incorporate EH&S review into new activities. (Regulatory/II)

- A new air source in the painting area was built without a pre-construction permit. (CA Code 25-4)

- New chemicals are brought on site by R&D staff without submitting MSDSs to the Environmental Coordinator. (Corporate EH&S Policy 12-3)

- A new process using new hazardous chemicals was started eight months ago and no hazard communication refresher training has been conducted. (29 CFR 1910.1200)

Recommendation: The site manager and environmental coordinator should alter the management processes to assure change is addressed.

4.1.3 Regulatory Updating

Finding: The site has discontinued its subscription to a regulatory database service in anticipation of installation of a corporate wide-area network regulatory database service. Due to some unanticipated technical problems, that service has not yet been fully installed. This has resulted in a gap in regulatory information support. Corporate policy requires that the facility have an established procedure to identify and maintain legal and other requirements. (Policy/III) (Corporate Policy 1-4)

Recommendation: Expedite the installation of the corporate regulatory database or provide an interim procedure to fulfill the requirement of regulatory monitoring.

ABC COMPANY ENVIRONMENTAL AUDIT PROGRAM
Audit of *[Indicate Name and Location of Facility]*

4.2 *AIR EMISSIONS, NOISE, AND ODOR*

The site has the following air sources: one on-site boiler, three dust collectors associated with processing equipment, a 10,000-gallon diesel oil aboveground tank, a paint-spray booth, and numerous fugitive sources. The major sources are covered under a single state air permit (CA-OP7532).

4.2.1 Emissions Inventory

Finding: The site has not completed an air emissions inventory. Corporate Policy requires emissions inventories. (Policy/II) (Corporate EHS Policy 3-2)

Recommendation: The site environmental coordinator should complete the inventory in accordance with Corporate reporting requirements.

4.2.2 Boiler Fuel Sulfur Content

Finding: The boiler permit requires documentation that less than 1% sulfur fuel oil is used as fuel. The site had no records available indicating the sulfur content of the fuel. (Regulatory/II) (Permit No. CA-OP7532)

Recommendation: The site environmental coordinator should contact the fuel oil supplier and obtain the appropriate historical records.

4.2.3 Boundary Noise

Finding: The facility has conducted a property boundary noise survey, which identified areas where daytime and nighttime noise standards are exceeded. Not all areas with exceedances have been addressed. City regulations require the facility to comply with Zone III area daytime (70 dBA) and nighttime (60 dBA) noise standards at the property boundaries. (Regulatory/II) (City of Medford Ordinance 72-310)

Recommendation: Provide sound attenuation equipment and/or barriers capable of reducing noise levels below regulatory standards in areas where exceedances have been detected. Following the implementation of the above corrective actions,

ABC COMPANY ENVIRONMENTAL AUDIT PROGRAM
Audit of *[Indicate Name and Location of Facility]*

perform the necessary confirmatory sound level measurements to ensure that regulatory standards are being met.

4.3   *WASTEWATER AND STORMWATER*

The site discharges sanitary and process wastewaters into the Medford Sanitary District system. There is a local permit (MED 84-312), which requires monthly monitoring. The site also has an NPDES permit for stormwater discharges (CA-7657), which also requires periodic monitoring.

4.3.1   Discharge Monitoring Report Administration

Finding: The Medford Sanitary District requires that a duly authorized representative sign the monthly discharge monitoring reports that are submitted to the district. The site must submit the names of the duly authorized representatives in writing to the District. Only the Plant Manager had been duly authorized. A consultant has been signing/certifying the monthly reports. Additionally, there is no confirmation (e.g., cover letter, certified mail receipt) that the reports have been submitted, as required, by the tenth of the month following the monitoring period. (Regulatory/II) (Permit No. MED 84-312)

Recommendation: Submit a letter to the District listing the people who are duly authorized representatives. Develop a method to verify that monthly reports are submitted on time.

4.3.2   Annual Stormwater Reports

Finding: An annual stormwater report with results of any sampling data and/or visual inspections is to be submitted to the state by January 28 of the following year. The site submitted these reports for 1993 and 1994. The requirement to submit the report is listed in the site's compliance calendar but was inadvertently overlooked in 1996, so the report covering calendar year 1995 was not submitted on time. (Regulatory/III) (Permit No. CA-7657)

Recommendation: Upon discovery of the omission, the site submitted the report during the audit, on March 13, 1996. No further action is necessary.

ABC COMPANY ENVIRONMENTAL AUDIT PROGRAM
Audit of *[Indicate Name and Location of Facility]*

4.4   DRINKING WATER

There are two sources of potable water for the site: municipal and two on-site wells. The well water is treated with sodium hypochlorite (or chlorine gas as a backup). Residual chlorine is managed at 0.5-1.5 ppm for the system to prevent bacteriological contamination. Residual chlorine is monitored once per day at several locations, including a point that is remote from the chemical addition station. Bacteriological sampling is completed once per week. A review of a sample of recent records indicated acceptable residual chlorine concentrations and no unacceptable bacteriological (i.e., coliform) contamination.

4.3.2   Backflow Preventor Inspections

Finding: The site is provided water by the City of Medford. Twice a year the Board of Health inspects the three main backflow preventors on the site. The site could not provide records of the results of these inspections. (Management Practice/III)

Recommendation: The site environmental coordinator should obtain copies of the results of the most recent inspections.

4.5   SPILL PREVENTION AND CONTROL

According to current plant drawings, twenty tanks are in active use to store a variety of raw materials, intermediates, and finished product. Horizontal and vertical tanks are used for the storage of liquid raw materials, and silos are used for the storage of granular or powdered solids. Major raw materials include solvents, acids, caustics, and oils. A tank inventory is maintained with pertinent tank and containment specifications.

4.5.1   Secondary Containment Integrity

Finding: Section 6 of the site's 1993 SPCC Plan states that there will be a containment system constructed around the tanker unloading area at the liquid tank area. This was done. However, the three valves for draining the secondary containment system were either missing or open. Secondary containment systems must utilize outlet valves (allow outward flow of the containment system) that lock closed. (Regulatory/I) (SPCC Plan, November 1, 1993, 40 CFR 112)

ABC COMPANY ENVIRONMENTAL AUDIT PROGRAM
Audit of *[Indicate Name and Location of Facility]*

Recommendation: Replace the valves so the valves lock closed and contain any liquids prior to discharge.

4.5.2 Tank Integrity Inspections

Finding: The SPCC Plan requires that the facility conduct visual integrity inspections of each tank on a quarterly basis. The facility conducts these inspections annually. The facility must follow the requirements as outlined in the SPCC Plan. (Regulatory/III) (SPCC Plan, November 1, 1993, 40 CFR 112)

Recommendation: Either conduct the quarterly inspections or revise the Plan to reflect current practices if the risks warrant the reduced frequency.

4.5.3 Loading and Unloading Procedures

Finding: Site procedures for the loading and unloading of bulk chemicals do not require that blocking or covering of nearby drains. Corporate policy requires that mats or valves be used to close stormwater drains during material transfer operations. (Policy/II) (Corporate Policy 5-6)

Recommendation: The bulk chemical loading procedures should be revised to require the blocking or covering of drains during material transfers. The facility should utilize drain covers or other barriers for use during material transfer operations.

4.6 SOLID AND HAZARDOUS WASTE MANAGEMENT

The site is a Small Quantity Generator (less than 1,000 kg/mo.). There is one 180-day accumulation point and two satellite accumulation areas. Wastes generated include non-chlorinated solvents and contaminated hydraulic oil. All wastes are recycled at Waste Recyclers, Inc.

4.6.1 Satellite Accumulation

Finding: The satellite accumulation area at the machine shop is located outside on gravel. (Management Practice/II)

Recommendation: The site should move the area indoors or construct a small pad with containment.

ABC COMPANY ENVIRONMENTAL AUDIT PROGRAM
Audit of *[Indicate Name and Location of Facility]*

4.6.2 Open Containers

Finding: The 5-gallon plastic drum storing hazardous waste solvent in the main laboratory was observed to be open. Federal regulations require that containers storing hazardous waste must always be closed during storage except when it is necessary to add or remove waste. (Regulatory/II) (40 CFR 265.173 (a))

Recommendation: Ensure that all containers storing hazardous waste are closed. The facility should incorporate this requirement into its general environmental awareness training.

4.7 *UNDERGROUND STORAGE TANKS*

Currently, two out-of-service underground storage tanks (USTs) are present at the facility. The tanks are 2,800 gallons each. These formerly held No. 6 fuel oil for the boilers, which have been switched to natural gas. The tanks were reported to be constructed of steel. Each tank has two vertical pipes with open flanges at the top. Plant personnel reported that the tanks were empty but not filled with inert materials.

4.7.1 UST Closure

Finding: For the two underground storage tanks formerly used to hold No. 6 fuel oil for the boilers, the following observations were made:

- The fill piping has not been disconnected;
- An oily liquid was observed in a pit over one of the tanks;
- What appeared to be fresh oil was staining the concrete near the fill port of one of the tanks; and
- Liquid could be seen in the tanks through the fill ports.

Corporate policy requires that out-of-service underground tanks be closed in place or removed from the ground. (Policy/I) (Corporate Policy 6-7)

Recommendation: The facility has indicated that excavation is not a viable option. Therefore it is recommended that the tanks be properly closed in place. The tanks should be emptied and cleaned,

ABC COMPANY ENVIRONMENTAL AUDIT PROGRAM
Audit of *[Indicate Name and Location of Facility]*

then filled with an inert material such as sand. The oily material and any contaminated soil should be removed for proper disposal.

4.8   TOXIC SUBSTANCES

The site does not manufacture chemicals. Appropriate measures are in place to assure that imported chemicals are on the TSCA inventory. There is a procedure in place for employees to report any adverse reactions to chemicals.

No Findings.

4.9   PCB MANAGEMENT

There is one in-service PCB Transformer (1,000 ppm) and two PCB-contaminated transformers (250 ppm and 405 ppm) in storage at the site. The site owns the transformers.

4.9.1   PCB Transformer Marking

Finding: The PCB transformer did not have a PCB label. TSCA requires all PCB transformers to have the M_L marking. (Regulatory/III) (40 CFR 761.40)

Recommendation: The site environmental coordinator should label the transformer accordingly.

4.9.2   Out-of-Service PCB-Contaminated Transformer Storage

Finding: The PCB-contaminated transformers have been in storage for two years awaiting disposal by PCB Disposal Inc. TSCA permits storage for only one year prior to disposal. (Regulatory/II) (40 CFR 761.65)

Recommendation: The site environmental coordinator should investigate the possibility of using an alternate vendor and have the transformer removed and disposed as soon as possible.

ABC COMPANY ENVIRONMENTAL AUDIT PROGRAM
Audit of *[Indicate Name and Location of Facility]*

4.10   ASBESTOS

There are asbestos-containing materials on the site. These include floor and ceiling tiles, transite wall board, and pipe insulation. An inventory has been completed. Also, an asbestos management plan has been developed for the facility.

4.10.1 Inventory

> **Finding:** The facility has identified the quantity of asbestos-containing material on site but has not specifically identified the locations of the material. Corporate policy requires that an up-to-date inventory of asbestos-containing materials be maintained, which identifies the locations. The inventory should be updated annually or when asbestos-containing materials are removed. (Policy/III) (Corporate Policy 3-2)
>
> **Recommendation:** Develop an accurate asbestos inventory to identify the specific locations and quantity of asbestos-containing materials.

4.11   PESTICIDES MANAGEMENT

The facility uses an outside, licensed contractor to apply all restricted-use pesticides. The facility does apply two non-restricted-use pesticides. Pesticide containers are stored in a locked room within a containment pan.

No Findings.

4.12   COMMUNITY RIGHT-TO-KNOW (SARA TITLE III)

The site does not exceed any thresholds that would result in the operations being covered by the Community Right-to-Know inventory (Section 312) or toxic release inventory (Section 313) reporting requirements.

No findings.

Model Environmental Audit Appraisal Questionnaire

Note: This appendix is also available on CD-ROM as an electronic template to be tailored to your company's individual needs.

MODEL AUDIT QUESTIONNAIRE

Model Environmental Audit Appraisal Questionnaire

August 5, 2000

Caution

This is a sample Environmental Audit Appraisal Questionnaire, which can be used as a model should an organization wish to have site management and staff independently evaluate the performance of an audit team. The model should be modified to meet any particular organization's specific objectives (e.g., ISO 14000).

ABC COMPANY
Corporate Environmental Affairs
Environmental Audit Appraisal Questionnaire

Corporate Environmental Affairs is very interested in constructive feedback regarding the effectiveness of its environmental audits. As a customer of the audit program, we would appreciate your completing the questionnaire provided below. Return the questionnaire to: Audit Program Manager, Corporate Environmental Affairs, Boston, MA. Thank you for your assistance.

Name_____   Position_____

Facility _____   Date _____

Indicate the extent to which you agree or disagree with the following statements by circling the appropriate code, as follows:

5 = Strongly Agree	2 = Disagree
4 = Agree	1 = Strongly Disagree
3 = Undecided	0 = Cannot Rate

If you cannot rate a particular question due to limited involvement, <u>please select the "0" column</u>.

Audit Planning

1. I was given a clear indication of the scope and purpose of the audit   0 1 2 3 4 5
before commencement.

2. I was given a clear indication of who would receive copies of the report   0 1 2 3 4 5
after completion, the required site response, follow-up and timing.

Audit Process

3. The audit did not inappropriately focus on detail checking or trivial issues.   0 1 2 3 4 5

4. The audit did not result in excessive disruption to the operation of this facility.   0 1 2 3 4 5

5. The audit was effective and was conducted in a professional manner.   0 1 2 3 4 5

6. The audit struck a good balance between evaluating the compliance status   0 1 2 3 4 5
and the management systems at the facility.

7. The length of the audit was appropriate for the facility.   0 1 2 3 4 5

Audit Team

8. The audit team had sufficient knowledge and understanding of the operations
and systems of this facility.   0 1 2 3 4 5

9. The audit team had sufficient regulatory knowledge, technical skill, and experience.   0 1 2 3 4 5

10. The audit team showed a good awareness of current events relevant to this facility.   0 1 2 3 4 5

ABC COMPANY
February 9, 2001

ABC COMPANY
Corporate Environmental Affairs
Environmental Audit Appraisal Questionnaire

11. The audit team was willing to lend advice and assistance to facility staff.   0 1 2 3 4 5

12. The audit team showed interest and enthusiasm for their job.   0 1 2 3 4 5

13. The audit team was organized adequately and functioned as a team.   0 1 2 3 4 5

Audit Closing Conference

14. The close-out meeting was factual and accurate.   0 1 2 3 4 5

15. The close-out meeting contained adequate explanation of findings and recommendations. 0 1 2 3 4 5

16. There was adequate discussion of audit results between the audit team and   0 1 2 3 4 5
facility management.

17. The meeting provided a good overview of both compliance and management   0 1 2 3 4 5
systems issues of significance to the facility.

18. The closing conference was useful to the management of this facility.   0 1 2 3 4 5

19. Comments:

_____

_____

_____

_____

_____

_____

_____

_____

_____

_____

_____

Model Management Presentation

Note: This appendix is also available on CD-ROM as an electronic template to be tailored to your company's individual needs.

MODEL PRESENTATION

Model Management Presentation

August 8, 2000

Caution

This is a sample audit program management presentation. The model should be modified to meet any particular organization's specific objectives (e.g., ISO 14000).

Reporting to Management

Why So Important?

* "Management Ignorance Is No Defense!" *(U.S. EPA General Counsel)*
* "Explicit Top Management Support, Including Written Commitment to Follow-Up" *(U.S. EPA Audit Policy)*
* Directors and Officers Can Be Held Both Accountable and Liable

What Should Management See?

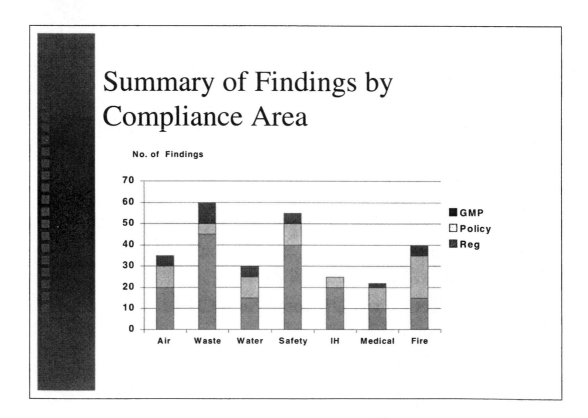

- Progress in Completing Audits
- Timeliness of Reports
- Corrective Action Closure Rate
- Highlights of Significant and Common Issues
- Trends in Regulatory Noncompliance
- Trends in Repeat Findings

Summary of Findings by Compliance Area

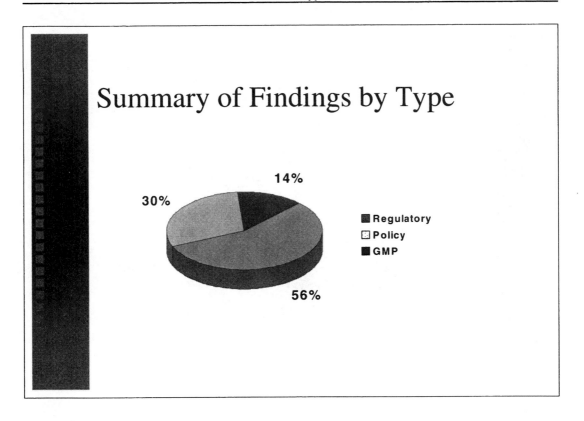

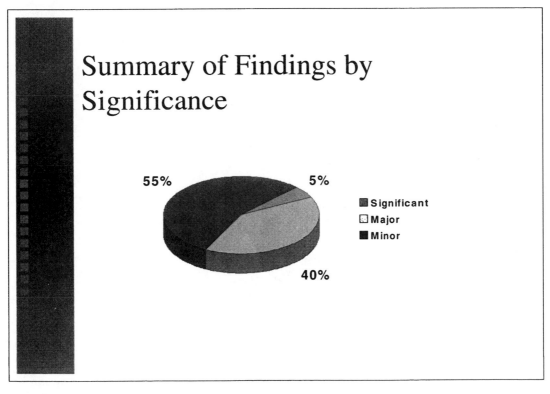

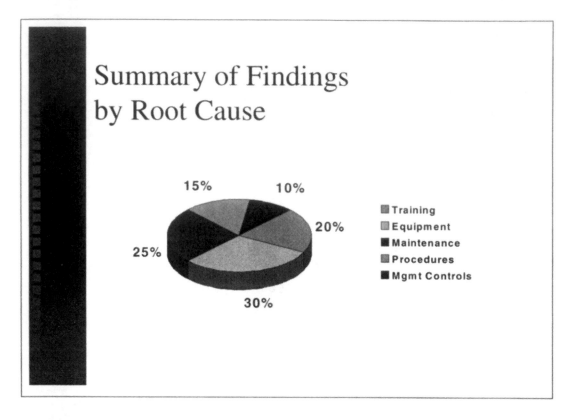

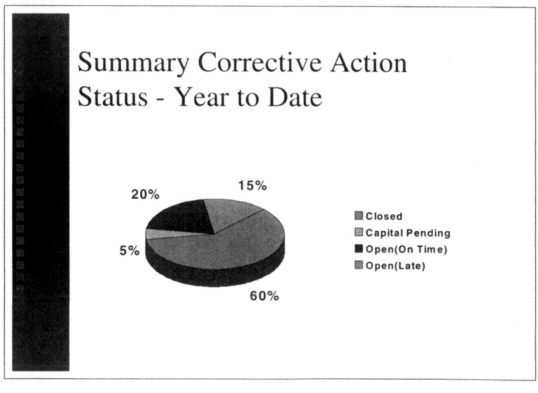

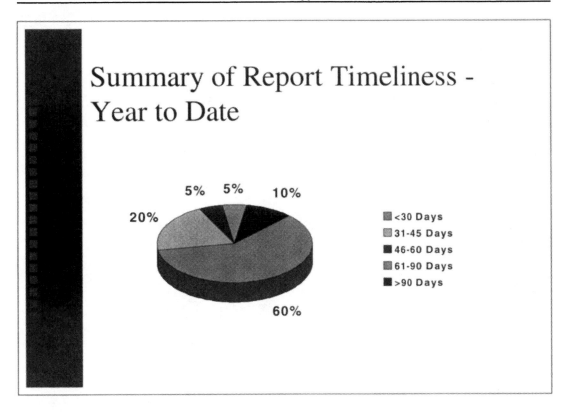

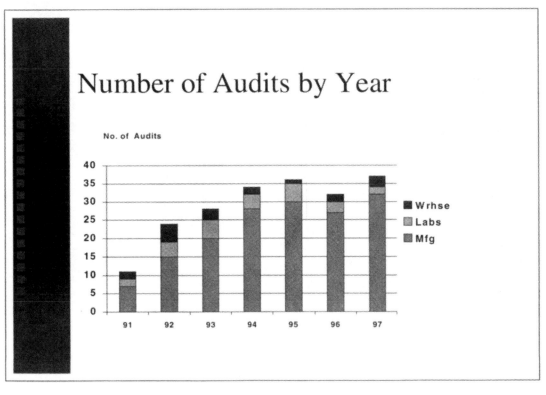

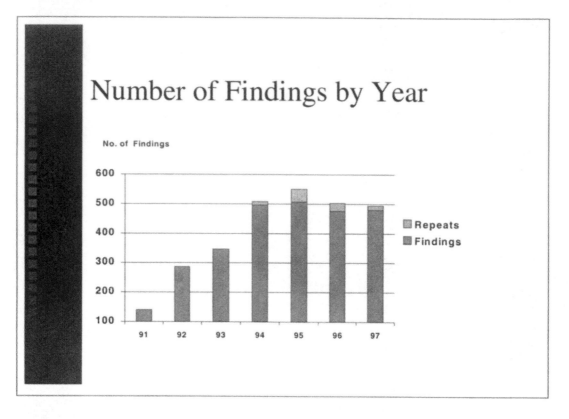

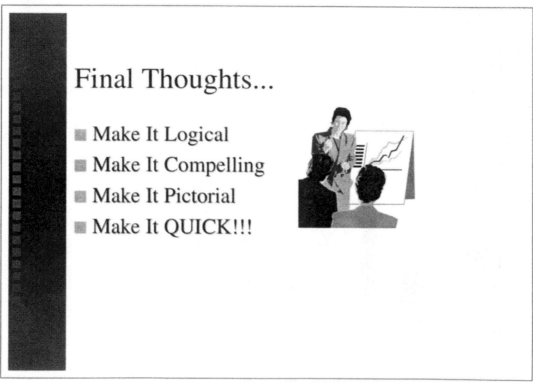

Appendix L

Sample Site Assessment Report

Note: The information contained in this appendix is publicly and freely available from federal and state databases.

SITE ASSESSMENT REPORT

PROPERTY INFORMATION	CLIENT INFORMATION
Project Name/Ref #: Not Provided 6856 ROSEFIELD DR LA MESA, CA 91941 Latitude/Longitude: (32.765934, 117.048243)	SAMPLE REPORT

Site Distribution Summary			*within 1/8 mile*	*1/8 to 1/4 mile*	*1/4 to 1/2 mile*	*1/2 to 1 mile*
Agency / Database - Type of Records						
A) Databases searched to 1 mile:						
US EPA	NPL	National Priority List	0	0	0	0
US EPA	CORRACTS (TSD)	RCRA Corrective Actions and associated TSD	0	0	0	0
STATE	SPL	State equivalent priority list	0	0	0	0
B) Databases searched to 1/2 mile:						
STATE	SCL	State equivalent CERCLIS list	0	0	0	-
US EPA	CERCLIS / NFRAP	Sites currently or formerly under review by US EPA	0	0	0	-
US EPA	TSD	RCRA permitted treatment, storage, disposal facilities	0	0	0	-
STATE	LUST	Leaking Underground Storage Tanks	0	5	3	-
STATE	SWLF	Permitted as solid waste landfills, incinerators, or transfer stations	0	0	0	-
C) Databases searched to 1/4 mile:						
STATE	UST	Registered underground storage tanks	0	6	-	-
STATE	AST	Registered aboveground storage tanks	0	0	-	-
D) Databases searched to 1/8 mile:						
US EPA	ERNS	Emergency Response Notification System of spills	0	-	-	-
US EPA	LG GEN	RCRA registered large generators of hazardous waste	0	-	-	-
US EPA	SM GEN	RCRA registered small generators of hazardous waste	0	-	-	-
STATE	SPILLS	State spills list	0	-	-	-

For more information call VISTA Information Solutions, Inc. at **1 - 800 - 767 - 0403.**
Report ID: **980914-002**
Version 2.6

Date of Report: **September 14, 1998**
Page #1

This report meets the ASTM standard E-1527 for standard federal and state government database research in a Phase I environmental site assessment. A (-) indicates a distance not searched because it exceeds these ASTM search parameters.

NOTES

For more information call VISTA Information Solutions, Inc. at **1 - 800 - 767 - 0403.**
Report ID: **980914-002**
Version 2.6

Date of Report: **September 14, 1998**
Page #2

SITE ASSESSMENT REPORT

SITE INVENTORY

MAP ID	PROPERTY AND THE ADJACENT AREA (within 1/8 mile) VISTA ID / DISTANCE / DIRECTION	NPL	CORRACTS(TSD)	SPL	SCL	CERCLIS/NFRAP	TSD	LUST	SWLF	UST	AST	ERNS	LG GEN	SM GEN	SPILLS
	No Records Found														

MAP ID	SITES IN THE SURROUNDING AREA (within 1/8 - 1/4 mile) VISTA ID / DISTANCE / DIRECTION	NPL	CORRACTS(TSD)	SPL	SCL	CERCLIS/NFRAP	TSD	LUST	SWLF	UST	AST	ERNS	LG GEN	SM GEN	SPILLS
1A	MOBIL STATION #18 PWJ 7003 EL CAJON BLVD SAN DIEGO, CA 92115 935035 / 0.14 MI / N							X		X					
1A	BARRY W O'BRIEN INC 7003 EL CAJON SAN DIEGO, CA 92115 1235613 / 0.14 MI / N									X					
1A	BAGSHAW SHELL SERVICE 7006 EL CAJON SAN DIEGO, CA 92115 3195114 / 0.15 MI / N							X		X					
1B	70TH ST CHEVRON SERVICE 6992 EL CAJON SAN DIEGO, CA 92115 1152092 / 0.15 MI / N							X		X				•	
2	FRANK HABETLER FOREIGN CAR SER 7075 EL CAJON SAN DIEGO, CA 92115 1584223 / 0.16 MI / N							X		X					
3	RUSSNAK, GEORGE 6880 EL CAJON BLVD SAN DIEGO, CA 92115 1194881 / 0.20 MI / NW							X							
4	WESTERN TOWING 7182 EL CAJON SAN DIEGO, CA 92115 3195115 / 0.24 MI / NE									X					

X = search criteria; • = tag-along (beyond search criteria).
For more information call VISTA Information Solutions, Inc. at **1 - 800 - 767 - 0403.**
Report ID: **980914-002**
Version 2.6
Date of Report: **September 14, 1998**
Page #6

MAP ID	SITES IN THE SURROUNDING AREA (within 1/4 - 1/2 mile) VISTA ID DISTANCE DIRECTION	A NPL	CORRACTS(TSD)	SPL	SCL	B CERCLIS/NFRAP	TSD	LUST	SWLF	C UST	AST	D ERNS	LG GEN	SM GEN	SPILLS
5	THE PEP BOYS #647 6714 EL CAJON SAN DIEGO, CA 92115 325397 0.33 MI W							X		•					
6	EXXON LOCATION 7-7047 5151 70TH ST N LA MESA, CA 92041 126272 0.49 MI N							X							
7	ITNS RECYCLING 6554 EL CAJON BLVD SAN DIEGO, CA 92115 3078200 0.49 MI W							X							

MAP ID	SITES IN THE SURROUNDING AREA (within 1/2 - 1 mile) VISTA ID DISTANCE DIRECTION	A NPL	CORRACTS(TSD)	SPL	SCL	B CERCLIS/NFRAP	TSD	LUST	SWLF	C UST	AST	D ERNS	LG GEN	SM GEN	SPILLS
	No Records Found														

X = search criteria; • = tag-along (beyond search criteria).
For more information call VISTA Information Solutions, Inc. at **1 - 800 - 767 - 0403.**
Report ID: **980914-002**   Date of Report: **September 14, 1998**
Version 2.6   *Page #7*

UNMAPPED SITES		A		B				C		D			
	VISTA ID	NPL	CORRACTS(TSD)	SPL	SCL	CERCLIS/NFRAP	TSD	LUST	SWLF	UST	AST	ERNS	LG GEN	SM GEN	SPILLS
No Records Found														

X = search criteria; • = tag-along (beyond search criteria).
For more information call VISTA Information Solutions, Inc. at **1 - 800 - 767 - 0403.**
Report ID: **980914-002**   Date of Report: **September 14, 1998**
Version 2.6   *Page #8*

SITE ASSESSMENT REPORT

DETAILS

PROPERTY AND THE ADJACENT AREA (within 1/8 mile)

No Records Found

SITES IN THE SURROUNDING AREA (within 1/8 - 1/4 mile)

VISTA Address*:	MOBIL STATION #18 PWJ 7003 EL CAJON BLVD SAN DIEGO, CA 92115	VISTA ID#:	935035	Map ID
		Distance/Direction:	0.14 MI / N	
		Plotted as:	Point	**1A**

STATE LUST - State Leaking Underground Storage Tank / SRC# 4828		EPA/Agency ID:	N/A
Agency Address:	MOBIL STATION #18 PWJ 7003 EL CAJON BLVD SAN DIEGO, CA 921151825		
Facility ID:	9UT3153		
Leak Report Date:	01/26/1996		
Site Assessment Plan Submitted:	03/12/1996		
Site Assessment Began:	03/15/1996		
Substance:	WASTE OIL		
Quantity / Units: 0	**Units:**	NOT REPORTED	
Remediation Status:	PRELIMINARY SITE ASSESSMENT UNDERWAY		
Media Affected:	SOIL ONLY		
Description / Comment:	SAN DIEGO REGION		
Description / Comment:	REVIEW DATE: 12/18/1996		

STATE LUST - State Leaking Underground Storage Tank / SRC# 4828		EPA/Agency ID:	N/A
Agency Address:	MOBIL SERVICE STATION 7003 EL CAJON BLVD SAN DIEGO, CA 92115		
Facility ID:	9UT885		
Leak Report Date:	01/05/1988		
Tank Inspection Date:	01/11/1988		
Site Assessment Began:	01/15/1988		
Remediation Plan Date:	10/13/1989		
Case Closed Date:	08/15/1991		
Substance:	WASTE OIL		
Remediation Event:	EXCAVATE AND DISPOSE		
Remediation Status:	CASE CLOSED		
Media Affected:	SOIL ONLY		
Description / Comment:	CROSS STREET: 70TH		
Description / Comment:	SAN DIEGO REGION		
Description / Comment:	REVIEW DATE: 09/10/1991		

* **VISTA address includes enhanced city and ZIP.**
For more information call VISTA Information Solutions, Inc. at **1 - 800 - 767 - 0403.**
Report ID: **980914-002**   Date of Report: **September 14, 1998**
Version 2.6   Page #9

SITES IN THE SURROUNDING AREA (within 1/8 - 1/4 mile) CONT.

STATE LUST - State Leaking Underground Storage Tank / SRC# 4917	EPA/Agency ID:	N/A
Agency Address:	MOBIL SERVICE STATION 7003 EL CAJON BLVD SAN DIEGO, CA 92115	
Facility ID:	9UT885	
Leak Date:	12/30/1987	
Leak Report Date:	01/05/1988	
Site Assessment Began:	01/15/1988	
Contamination Confirmed Date:	01/11/1988	
Remediation Plan Date:	10/13/1989	
Case Closed Date:	08/15/1991	
Leak Detection Method:	TANK CLOSURE	
Leak Cause:	CORROSION	
Leak Source:	TANK	
Substance:	WASTE OIL	
Remediation Event:	EXCAVATE AND DISPOSE	
Remediation Event:	LEAK STOPPED BY: NEW TANK	
Remediation Event:	LEAK STOP DATE: 19871230	
Remediation Status:	CASE CLOSED	
Media Affected:	SOIL ONLY	
Description / Comment:	PILOT PROGRAM: YES INTERIM REMEDIAL ACTION: YES LOCAL CASE NUM:H05480-002	
Description / Comment:	BASIN NUM: 90 GW DEPTH: CAONUM: WDRNUM: NPDES NUM: FILEDISP: DISCARDED	
Description / Comment:	PRIORITY: LOW	

STATE LUST - State Leaking Underground Storage Tank / SRC# 4917	EPA/Agency ID:	N/A
Agency Address:	MOBIL STATION #18 PWJ 7003 EL CAJON BLVD SAN DIEGO, CA 921151825	
Facility ID:	9UT3153	
Leak Date:	01/04/1996	
Leak Report Date:	01/26/1996	
Site Assessment Plan Submitted:	03/12/1996	
Site Assessment Began:	03/15/1996	
Leak Detection Method:	OTHER MEANS	
Substance:	WASTE OIL	
Quantity / Units: 0	**Units:**	NOT REPORTED
Remediation Event:	LEAK STOPPPED BY : UNKNOWN	
Remediation Status:	PRELIMINARY SITE ASSESSMENT UNDERWAY	
Media Affected:	SOIL ONLY	
Description / Comment:	PILOT PROGRAM: YES INTERIM REMEDIAL ACTION: LOCAL CASE NUM: H05480-003 BENEFICIAL: NO BENEFICIAL GROUNDWATER USE	
Description / Comment:	BASIN NUM: 908.22 GW DEPTH: CAONUM: WDRNUM: NPDES NUM: FILEDISP: DATABASE	
Description / Comment:	PRIORITY: MINOR OR NO POTENTIAL WATER RESOURCE IMPACTS EXIST	

STATE UST - State Underground Storage Tank / SRC# 5041	Agency ID:	H05480
Agency Address:	70TH MOBIL 7003 EL CAJON BL SAN DIEGO, CA 92115	
Underground Tanks:	5	
Aboveground Tanks:	NOT REPORTED	
Tanks Removed:	NOT REPORTED	

* VISTA address includes enhanced city and ZIP.
For more information call VISTA Information Solutions, Inc. at **1 - 800 - 767 - 0403.**
Report ID: **980914-002**   Date of Report: **September 14, 1998**
Version 2.6   Page #10

SITES IN THE SURROUNDING AREA (within 1/8 - 1/4 mile) CONT.

Tank ID:	T001U	**Tank Status:**	ACTIVE/IN SERVICE
Tank Contents:	UNLEADED GAS	**Leak Monitoring:**	NOT AVAILABLE
Tank Age:	14	**Tank Piping:**	PRESSURIZED
Tank Size (Units):	10000 (GALLONS)	**Tank Material:**	DOUBLE WALLED OR SINGLE WALLED
Tank ID:	T002U	**Tank Status:**	ACTIVE/IN SERVICE
Tank Contents:	UNLEADED GAS	**Leak Monitoring:**	NOT AVAILABLE
Tank Age:	14	**Tank Piping:**	PRESSURIZED
Tank Size (Units):	12000 (GALLONS)	**Tank Material:**	DOUBLE WALLED OR SINGLE WALLED
Tank ID:	T003U	**Tank Status:**	ACTIVE/IN SERVICE
Tank Contents:	UNLEADED GAS	**Leak Monitoring:**	NOT AVAILABLE
Tank Age:	14	**Tank Piping:**	PRESSURIZED
Tank Size (Units):	6000 (GALLONS)	**Tank Material:**	DOUBLE WALLED OR SINGLE WALLED
Tank ID:	T004U	**Tank Status:**	CLOSED REMOVED
Tank Contents:	WASTE OIL	**Leak Monitoring:**	NOT AVAILABLE
Tank Age:	27	**Tank Piping:**	NONE
Tank Size (Units):	280 (GALLONS)	**Tank Material:**	DOUBLE WALLED OR SINGLE WALLED
Tank ID:	T005U	**Tank Status:**	ACTIVE/IN SERVICE
Tank Contents:	WASTE OIL	**Leak Monitoring:**	NOT AVAILABLE
Tank Age:	11	**Tank Piping:**	GRAVITY
Tank Size (Units):	550 (GALLONS)	**Tank Material:**	DOUBLE WALLED OR SINGLE WALLED

VISTA Address*:	**BARRY W O'BRIEN INC** **7003 EL CAJON** **SAN DIEGO, CA 92115**	VISTA ID#:	1235613	Map ID
		Distance/Direction:	0.14 MI / N	**1A**
		Plotted as:	Point	

STATE UST - State Underground Storage Tank / SRC# 1612		EPA/Agency ID:	N/A
Agency Address:	SAME AS ABOVE		
Underground Tanks:	5		
Aboveground Tanks:	NOT REPORTED		
Tanks Removed:	NOT REPORTED		
Tank ID:	1U	**Tank Status:**	ACTIVE/IN SERVICE
Tank Contents:	LEADED GAS	**Leak Monitoring:**	UNKNOWN
Tank Age:	NOT REPORTED	**Tank Piping:**	UNKNOWN
Tank Size (Units):	10000 (GALLONS)	**Tank Material:**	FIBERGLASS
Tank ID:	2U	**Tank Status:**	ACTIVE/IN SERVICE
Tank Contents:	UNLEADED GAS	**Leak Monitoring:**	UNKNOWN
Tank Age:	NOT REPORTED	**Tank Piping:**	UNKNOWN
Tank Size (Units):	12000 (GALLONS)	**Tank Material:**	FIBERGLASS
Tank ID:	3U	**Tank Status:**	ACTIVE/IN SERVICE
Tank Contents:	LEADED GAS	**Leak Monitoring:**	UNKNOWN
Tank Age:	NOT REPORTED	**Tank Piping:**	UNKNOWN
Tank Size (Units):	6000 (GALLONS)	**Tank Material:**	FIBERGLASS
Tank ID:	4U	**Tank Status:**	CLOSED REMOVED
Tank Contents:	PETROLEUM	**Leak Monitoring:**	UNKNOWN
Tank Age:	NOT REPORTED	**Tank Piping:**	UNKNOWN
Tank Size (Units):	280 (GALLONS)	**Tank Material:**	OTHER DESCRIPTIONS
Tank ID:	5U	**Tank Status:**	ACTIVE/IN SERVICE
Tank Contents:	PETROLEUM	**Leak Monitoring:**	UNKNOWN
Tank Age:	NOT REPORTED	**Tank Piping:**	UNKNOWN
Tank Size (Units):	550 (GALLONS)	**Tank Material:**	FIBERGLASS

* VISTA address includes enhanced city and ZIP.
For more information call VISTA Information Solutions, Inc. at **1 - 800 - 767 - 0403.**
Report ID: **980914-002**
Version 2.6

Date of Report: **September 14, 1998**
Page #11

SITES IN THE SURROUNDING AREA (within 1/8 - 1/4 mile) CONT.

VISTA Address*:	**BAGSHAW SHELL SERVICE** **7006 EL CAJON** **SAN DIEGO, CA 92115**		VISTA ID#:	3195114
			Distance/Direction:	0.15 MI / N
			Plotted as:	Point

Map ID

1A

STATE UST - State Underground Storage Tank / SRC# 1612		EPA/Agency ID:	N/A
Agency Address:	*SAME AS ABOVE*		
Underground Tanks:	*4*		
Aboveground Tanks:	*NOT REPORTED*		
Tanks Removed:	*NOT REPORTED*		

Tank ID:	*1U*	**Tank Status:**	*ACTIVE/IN SERVICE*
Tank Contents:	*UNLEADED GAS*	**Leak Monitoring:**	*UNKNOWN*
Tank Age:	*NOT REPORTED*	**Tank Piping:**	*UNKNOWN*
Tank Size (Units):	*10000 (GALLONS)*	**Tank Material:**	*FIBERGLASS*
Tank ID:	*2U*	**Tank Status:**	*ACTIVE/IN SERVICE*
Tank Contents:	*LEADED GAS*	**Leak Monitoring:**	*UNKNOWN*
Tank Age:	*NOT REPORTED*	**Tank Piping:**	*UNKNOWN*
Tank Size (Units):	*10000 (GALLONS)*	**Tank Material:**	*FIBERGLASS*
Tank ID:	*3U*	**Tank Status:**	*ACTIVE/IN SERVICE*
Tank Contents:	*LEADED GAS*	**Leak Monitoring:**	*UNKNOWN*
Tank Age:	*NOT REPORTED*	**Tank Piping:**	*UNKNOWN*
Tank Size (Units):	*10000 (GALLONS)*	**Tank Material:**	*FIBERGLASS*
Tank ID:	*4U*	**Tank Status:**	*ACTIVE/IN SERVICE*
Tank Contents:	*PETROLEUM*	**Leak Monitoring:**	*UNKNOWN*
Tank Age:	*NOT REPORTED*	**Tank Piping:**	*UNKNOWN*
Tank Size (Units):	*550 (GALLONS)*	**Tank Material:**	*FIBERGLASS*

STATE LUST - State Leaking Underground Storage Tank / SRC# 4828		EPA/Agency ID:	N/A
Agency Address:	*SHELL SERVICE STATION #* *7006 EL CAJON BLVD* *SAN DIEGO. CA 92115*		
Facility ID:	*9UT1971*		
Leak Report Date:	*04/09/1991*		
Tank Inspection Date:	*04/22/1991*		
Site Assessment Plan Submitted:	*04/23/1991*		
Site Assessment Began:	*12/21/1992*		
Substance:	*GASOLINE*		
Remediation Status:	*PRELIMINARY SITE ASSESSMENT UNDERWAY*		
Media Affected:	*OTHER GROUND WATER*		
Description / Comment:	*CROSS STREET: 70TH ST*		
Description / Comment:	*SAN DIEGO REGION*		
Description / Comment:	*REVIEW DATE: 07/08/1993*		

STATE LUST - State Leaking Underground Storage Tank / SRC# 4917		EPA/Agency ID:	N/A
Agency Address:	*SHELL SERVICE STATION #* *7006 EL CAJON BLVD* *SAN DIEGO. CA 92115*		
Facility ID:	*9UT1971*		
Leak Date:	*04/09/1991*		
Leak Report Date:	*04/09/1991*		
Site Assessment Plan Submitted:	*04/23/1991*		
Site Assessment Began:	*12/21/1992*		
Contamination Confirmed Date:	*04/22/1991*		
Leak Detection Method:	*OTHER MEANS*		

* VISTA address includes enhanced city and ZIP.
For more information call VISTA Information Solutions, Inc. at **1 - 800 - 767 - 0403.**
Report ID: **980914-002**
Version 2.6

Date of Report: **September 14, 1998**
Page #12

SITES IN THE SURROUNDING AREA (within 1/8 - 1/4 mile) CONT.

Leak Cause:	*UNKNOWN*
Leak Source:	*UNKNOWN*
Substance:	*GASOLINE*
Remediation Event:	*LEAK STOPPED BY: OTHER MEANS*
Remediation Event:	*LEAK STOP DATE: 19910409*
Remediation Event:	*ENFORCEMENT: NONE TAKEN*
Remediation Status:	*PRELIMINARY SITE ASSESSMENT UNDERWAY*
Media Affected:	*OTHER GROUND WATER*
Description / Comment:	*PILOT PROGRAM: YES INTERIM REMEDIAL ACTION: NO LOCAL CASE NUM: H12307-001 BENEFICIAL: MUNICIPAL GROUNDWATER USE*
Description / Comment:	*BASIN NUM: 908.22 GW DEPTH: 63' CAONUM: WDRNUM: NPDES NUM: FILEDISP: DISCARDED*
Description / Comment:	*PRIORITY: WATER RESOURCE OTHER THAN DRINKING WATER IS/MAY BE IMPACTED*

STATE UST - State Underground Storage Tank / SRC# 5041		Agency ID:	H12307
Agency Address:	*AZTEC SHELL* *7006 EL CAJON BL* *SAN DIEGO, CA 92115*		
Underground Tanks:	*4*		
Aboveground Tanks:	*NOT REPORTED*		
Tanks Removed:	*NOT REPORTED*		

Tank ID:	*T001U*	**Tank Status:**	*ACTIVE/IN SERVICE*
Tank Contents:	*UNLEADED GAS*	**Leak Monitoring:**	*NOT AVAILABLE*
Tank Age:	*16*	**Tank Piping:**	*PRESSURIZED*
Tank Size (Units):	*10000 (GALLONS)*	**Tank Material:**	*SINGLE WALLED*
Tank ID:	*T002U*	**Tank Status:**	*ACTIVE/IN SERVICE*
Tank Contents:	*LEADED GAS*	**Leak Monitoring:**	*NOT AVAILABLE*
Tank Age:	*16*	**Tank Piping:**	*PRESSURIZED*
Tank Size (Units):	*10000 (GALLONS)*	**Tank Material:**	*SINGLE WALLED*
Tank ID:	*T003U*	**Tank Status:**	*ACTIVE/IN SERVICE*
Tank Contents:	*UNLEADED GAS*	**Leak Monitoring:**	*NOT AVAILABLE*
Tank Age:	*16*	**Tank Piping:**	*PRESSURIZED*
Tank Size (Units):	*10000 (GALLONS)*	**Tank Material:**	*SINGLE WALLED*
Tank ID:	*T004U*	**Tank Status:**	*ACTIVE/IN SERVICE*
Tank Contents:	*WASTE OIL*	**Leak Monitoring:**	*NOT AVAILABLE*
Tank Age:	*13*	**Tank Piping:**	*GRAVITY*
Tank Size (Units):	*550 (GALLONS)*	**Tank Material:**	*DOUBLE WALLED OR SINGLE WALLED*

VISTA Address*:	**70TH ST CHEVRON SERVICE** **6992 EL CAJON** **SAN DIEGO, CA 92115**	VISTA ID#:	1152092	Map ID
		Distance/Direction:	0.15 MI / N	**1B**
		Plotted as:	Point	

STATE UST - State Underground Storage Tank / SRC# 1612		EPA/Agency ID:	N/A
Agency Address:	*SAME AS ABOVE*		
Underground Tanks:	*4*		
Aboveground Tanks:	*NOT REPORTED*		
Tanks Removed:	*NOT REPORTED*		

Tank ID:	*1U*	**Tank Status:**	*ACTIVE/IN SERVICE*
Tank Contents:	*UNLEADED GAS*	**Leak Monitoring:**	*UNKNOWN*
Tank Age:	*NOT REPORTED*	**Tank Piping:**	*UNKNOWN*
Tank Size (Units):	*7500 (GALLONS)*	**Tank Material:**	*OTHER DESCRIPTIONS*

* VISTA address includes enhanced city and ZIP.
For more information call VISTA Information Solutions, Inc. at **1 - 800 - 767 - 0403.**

Report ID: **980914-002**

Date of Report: **September 14, 1998**

Version 2.6

SITES IN THE SURROUNDING AREA (within 1/8 - 1/4 mile) CONT.

Tank ID:	2U	Tank Status:	ACTIVE/IN SERVICE
Tank Contents:	LEADED GAS	Leak Monitoring:	UNKNOWN
Tank Age:	NOT REPORTED	Tank Piping:	UNKNOWN
Tank Size (Units):	6000 (GALLONS)	Tank Material:	OTHER DESCRIPTIONS
Tank ID:	3U	Tank Status:	ACTIVE/IN SERVICE
Tank Contents:	LEADED GAS	Leak Monitoring:	UNKNOWN
Tank Age:	NOT REPORTED	Tank Piping:	UNKNOWN
Tank Size (Units):	2000 (GALLONS)	Tank Material:	OTHER DESCRIPTIONS
Tank ID:	4U	Tank Status:	ACTIVE/IN SERVICE
Tank Contents:	PETROLEUM	Leak Monitoring:	UNKNOWN
Tank Age:	NOT REPORTED	Tank Piping:	UNKNOWN
Tank Size (Units):	550 (GALLONS)	Tank Material:	OTHER DESCRIPTIONS

STATE LUST - State Leaking Underground Storage Tank / SRC# 4828   EPA/Agency ID: N/A

Agency Address:	CHEVRON SERV. STA. 6992 EL CAJON BLVD SAN DIEGO, CA 92115
Facility ID:	9UT1197
Leak Report Date:	11/28/1988
Tank Inspection Date:	01/25/1989
Site Assessment Began:	01/25/1989
Pollution Characterization Date:	09/30/1989
Remediation Complete Date:	04/29/1992
Substance:	UNLEADED GASOLINE
Quantity / Units: 5000 Units:	NOT REPORTED
Remediation Status:	POST REMEDIAL ACTION UNDERWAY
Media Affected:	OTHER GROUND WATER
Description / Comment:	SAN DIEGO REGION
Description / Comment:	REVIEW DATE: 06/08/1993

STATE LUST - State Leaking Underground Storage Tank / SRC# 4917   EPA/Agency ID: N/A

Agency Address:	CHEVRON SERV. STA. 6992 EL CAJON BLVD SAN DIEGO, CA 92115
Facility ID:	9UT1197
Leak Date:	01/25/1989
Leak Report Date:	11/28/1988
Site Assessment Began:	01/25/1989
Contamination Confirmed Date:	01/25/1989
Pollution Characterization Date:	09/30/1989
Post Remediation Monitoring Began:	04/29/1992
Leak Detection Method:	TANK CLOSURE
Substance:	UNLEAD GASOL
Quantity / Units: 5000 Units:	NOT REPORTED
Remediation Event:	EXCAVATE AND DISPOSE
Remediation Event:	LEAK STOPPED BY: REPAIR TANK
Remediation Event:	LEAK STOP DATE: 19890125
Remediation Event:	ENFORCEMENT: NONE TAKEN
Remediation Status:	POST REMEDIAL ACTION UNDERWAY
Media Affected:	OTHER GROUND WATER
Description / Comment:	PILOT PROGRAM: YES INTERIM REMEDIAL ACTION: YES LOCAL CASE NUM:H05658-001 BENEFICIAL: MUNICIPAL GROUNDWATER USE
Description / Comment:	BASIN NUM: 908.22 GW DEPTH: 28 CAONUM: WDRNUM: NPDES NUM: FILEDISP: DISCARDED
Description / Comment:	PRIORITY: WATER RESOURCE OTHER THAN DRINKING WATER IS/MAY BE IMPACTED

* VISTA address includes enhanced city and ZIP.
For more information call VISTA Information Solutions, Inc. at **1 - 800 - 767 - 0403.**
Report ID: **980914-002**
Version 2.6

Date of Report: **September 14, 1998**
Page #14

SITES IN THE SURROUNDING AREA (within 1/8 - 1/4 mile) CONT.					

STATE UST - State Underground Storage Tank / SRC# 5041			Agency ID:		H05658
Agency Address:		70TH ST CHEVRON SERVICE 6992 EL CAJON BL SAN DIEGO, CA 92115			
Underground Tanks:		4			
Aboveground Tanks:		NOT REPORTED			
Tanks Removed:		NOT REPORTED			
Tank ID:	T001U		**Tank Status:**	OTHER	
Tank Contents:	UNLEADED GAS		**Leak Monitoring:**	NOT AVAILABLE	
Tank Age:	38		**Tank Piping:**	PRESSURIZED	
Tank Size (Units):	7500 (GALLONS)		**Tank Material:**	DOUBLE WALLED OR SINGLE WALLED	
Tank ID:	T002U		**Tank Status:**	OTHER	
Tank Contents:	LEADED GAS		**Leak Monitoring:**	NOT AVAILABLE	
Tank Age:	38		**Tank Piping:**	PRESSURIZED	
Tank Size (Units):	6000 (GALLONS)		**Tank Material:**	DOUBLE WALLED OR SINGLE WALLED	
Tank ID:	T003U		**Tank Status:**	OTHER	
Tank Contents:	SUPER UNLEADED		**Leak Monitoring:**	NOT AVAILABLE	
Tank Age:	38		**Tank Piping:**	PRESSURIZED	
Tank Size (Units):	2000 (GALLONS)		**Tank Material:**	DOUBLE WALLED OR SINGLE WALLED	
Tank ID:	T004U		**Tank Status:**	OTHER	
Tank Contents:	WASTE OIL		**Leak Monitoring:**	NOT AVAILABLE	
Tank Age:	38		**Tank Piping:**	NONE	
Tank Size (Units):	550 (GALLONS)		**Tank Material:**	DOUBLE WALLED OR SINGLE WALLED	

VISTA Address*:	**FRANK HABETLER FOREIGN CAR SER** **7075 EL CAJON** **SAN DIEGO, CA 92115**		VISTA ID#:	1584223	Map ID
			Distance/Direction:	0.16 MI / N	**2**
			Plotted as:	Point	

STATE UST - State Underground Storage Tank / SRC# 1612			EPA/Agency ID:		N/A
Agency Address:		SAME AS ABOVE			
Underground Tanks:		2			
Aboveground Tanks:		NOT REPORTED			
Tanks Removed:		NOT REPORTED			
Tank ID:	1U		**Tank Status:**	CLOSED REMOVED	
Tank Contents:	PETROLEUM		**Leak Monitoring:**	UNKNOWN	
Tank Age:	NOT REPORTED		**Tank Piping:**	UNKNOWN	
Tank Size (Units):	300 (GALLONS)		**Tank Material:**	OTHER DESCRIPTIONS	
Tank ID:	2U		**Tank Status:**	CLOSED REMOVED	
Tank Contents:	PETROLEUM		**Leak Monitoring:**	UNKNOWN	
Tank Age:	NOT REPORTED		**Tank Piping:**	UNKNOWN	
Tank Size (Units):	500 (GALLONS)		**Tank Material:**	OTHER DESCRIPTIONS	

STATE LUST - State Leaking Underground Storage Tank / SRC# 4828		EPA/Agency ID:		N/A
Agency Address:	FRANK HABETLER'S AUTO REPAIR 7075 EL CAJON BLVD SAN DIEGO, CA 92115			
Facility ID:	9UT1608			
Leak Report Date:	01/09/1990			
Tank Inspection Date:	01/09/1990			
Site Assessment Began:	08/02/1993			
Substance:	WASTE OIL			
Remediation Status:	PRELIMINARY SITE ASSESSMENT UNDERWAY			
Media Affected:	SOIL ONLY			

* VISTA address includes enhanced city and ZIP.
For more information call VISTA Information Solutions, Inc. at **1 - 800 - 767 - 0403.**
Report ID: **980914-002**
Version 2.6

Date of Report: **September 14, 1998**
Page #15

SITES IN THE SURROUNDING AREA (within 1/8 - 1/4 mile) CONT.

Description / Comment:	SAN DIEGO REGION
Description / Comment:	REVIEW DATE: 08/30/1993

STATE LUST - State Leaking Underground Storage Tank / SRC# 4917		EPA/Agency ID:	N/A
Agency Address:	FRANK HABETLER'S AUTO REPAIR 7075 EL CAJON BLVD SAN DIEGO, CA 92115		
Facility ID:	9UT1608		
Leak Date:	01/09/1990		
Leak Report Date:	01/09/1990		
Site Assessment Began:	08/02/1993		
Contamination Confirmed Date:	01/09/1990		
Leak Detection Method:	TANK CLOSURE		
Leak Cause:	CORROSION		
Leak Source:	TANK		
Substance:	WASTE OIL		
Remediation Event:	LEAK STOPPED BY: CLOSE TANK		
Remediation Event:	LEAK STOP DATE: 19900109		
Remediation Event:	ENFORCEMENT: NONE TAKEN		
Remediation Status:	PRELIMINARY SITE ASSESSMENT UNDERWAY		
Media Affected:	SOIL ONLY		
Description / Comment:	PILOT PROGRAM: YES INTERIM REMEDIAL ACTION: YES LOCAL CASE NUM:H12544-001 BENEFICIAL: NO BENEFICIAL GROUNDWATER USE		
Description / Comment:	BASIN NUM: 908.22 GW DEPTH: CAONUM: WDRNUM: NPDES NUM: FILEDISP: DISCARDED		
Description / Comment:	PRIORITY: ADMINISTRATIVE NEED EXISTS		

STATE UST - State Underground Storage Tank / SRC# 5041		Agency ID:	H12544
Agency Address:	FRANK HABETLER FOREIGN CAR SER 7075 EL CAJON BL SAN DIEGO, CA 92115		
Underground Tanks:	2		
Aboveground Tanks:	NOT REPORTED		
Tanks Removed:	NOT REPORTED		

Tank ID:	T001U	Tank Status:	CLOSED REMOVED
Tank Contents:	WASTE OIL	Leak Monitoring:	NOT AVAILABLE
Tank Age:	NOT REPORTED	Tank Piping:	UNKNOWN
Tank Size (Units):	300 (GALLONS)	Tank Material:	DOUBLE WALLED OR SINGLE WALLED
Tank ID:	T002U	Tank Status:	CLOSED REMOVED
Tank Contents:	WASTE OIL	Leak Monitoring:	NOT AVAILABLE
Tank Age:	NOT REPORTED	Tank Piping:	UNKNOWN
Tank Size (Units):	500 (GALLONS)	Tank Material:	DOUBLE WALLED OR SINGLE WALLED

VISTA Address*:	**RUSSNAK, GEORGE 6880 EL CAJON BLVD SAN DIEGO, CA 92115**	VISTA ID#:	1194881	Map ID
		Distance/Direction:	0.20 MI / NW	**3**
		Plotted as:	Point	

STATE LUST - State Leaking Underground Storage Tank / SRC# 4828		EPA/Agency ID:	N/A
Agency Address:	SAME AS ABOVE		
Facility ID:	9UT1653		
Leak Report Date:	03/14/1990		
Tank Inspection Date:	02/23/1990		
Site Assessment Began:	06/27/1990		
Remediation Plan Date:	02/09/1994		
Substance:	GASOLINE		
Remediation Status:	REMEDIATION PLAN SUBMITTED		

* **VISTA address includes enhanced city and ZIP.**
For more information call VISTA Information Solutions, Inc. at **1 - 800 - 767 - 0403.**
Report ID: **980914-002**
Version 2.6

Date of Report: **September 14, 1998**
Page #16

SITES IN THE SURROUNDING AREA (within 1/8 - 1/4 mile) CONT.

Media Affected:	SOIL ONLY
Description / Comment:	SAN DIEGO REGION
Description / Comment:	REVIEW DATE: 05/15/1990

STATE LUST - State Leaking Underground Storage Tank / SRC# 4917		EPA/Agency ID:	N/A
Agency Address:	SAME AS ABOVE		
Facility ID:	9UT1653		
Leak Date:	02/23/1990		
Leak Report Date:	03/14/1990		
Site Assessment Began:	06/27/1990		
Contamination Confirmed Date:	02/23/1990		
Remediation Plan Date:	02/09/1994		
Leak Detection Method:	TANK CLOSURE		
Leak Cause:	CORROSION		
Leak Source:	TANK		
Substance:	GASOLINE		
Remediation Event:	LEAK STOPPED BY: CLOSE TANK		
Remediation Event:	LEAK STOP DATE: 19900223		
Remediation Event:	ENFORCEMENT: NONE TAKEN		
Remediation Status:	REMEDIATION PLAN SUBMITTED		
Media Affected:	SOIL ONLY		
Description / Comment:	PILOT PROGRAM: YES INTERIM REMEDIAL ACTION: YES LOCAL CASE NUM:H29978-001 BENEFICIAL: MUNICIPAL GROUNDWATER USE		
Description / Comment:	BASIN NUM: 907.11 GW DEPTH: CAONUM: WDRNUM: NPDES NUM: FILEDISP: DISCARDED		
Description / Comment:	PRIORITY: LOW POTENTIAL HEALTH/SAFETY/ENVIRONMENTAL IMPACT EXISTS AFTER INVESTIG		

VISTA Address*:	WESTERN TOWING 7182 EL CAJON SAN DIEGO, CA 92115		VISTA ID#:	3195115	Map ID
			Distance/Direction:	0.24 MI / NE	**4**
			Plotted as:	Point	

STATE UST - State Underground Storage Tank / SRC# 1612			EPA/Agency ID:	N/A
Agency Address:	SAME AS ABOVE			
Underground Tanks:	4			
Aboveground Tanks:	NOT REPORTED			
Tanks Removed:	NOT REPORTED			

Tank ID:	1U	Tank Status:	CLOSED REMOVED
Tank Contents:	PETROLEUM	Leak Monitoring:	UNKNOWN
Tank Age:	NOT REPORTED	Tank Piping:	UNKNOWN
Tank Size (Units):	225 (GALLONS)	Tank Material:	OTHER DESCRIPTIONS
Tank ID:	2U	Tank Status:	CLOSED REMOVED
Tank Contents:	LEADED GAS	Leak Monitoring:	UNKNOWN
Tank Age:	NOT REPORTED	Tank Piping:	UNKNOWN
Tank Size (Units):	6000 (GALLONS)	Tank Material:	OTHER DESCRIPTIONS
Tank ID:	3U	Tank Status:	CLOSED REMOVED
Tank Contents:	UNLEADED GAS	Leak Monitoring:	UNKNOWN
Tank Age:	NOT REPORTED	Tank Piping:	UNKNOWN
Tank Size (Units):	7500 (GALLONS)	Tank Material:	OTHER DESCRIPTIONS
Tank ID:	4U	Tank Status:	CLOSED REMOVED
Tank Contents:	LEADED GAS	Leak Monitoring:	UNKNOWN
Tank Age:	NOT REPORTED	Tank Piping:	UNKNOWN
Tank Size (Units):	7500 (GALLONS)	Tank Material:	OTHER DESCRIPTIONS

* VISTA address includes enhanced city and ZIP.
For more information call VISTA Information Solutions, Inc. at **1 - 800 - 767 - 0403.**
Report ID: **980914-002**
Version 2.6

Date of Report: **September 14, 1998**
Page #17

SITES IN THE SURROUNDING AREA (within 1/8 - 1/4 mile) CONT.

STATE UST - State Underground Storage Tank / SRC# 5041 — Agency ID: H03588

Agency Address:		WESTERN TOWING 7182 EL CAJON BL SAN DIEGO, CA 92115
Underground Tanks:		4
Aboveground Tanks:		NOT REPORTED
Tanks Removed:		NOT REPORTED

Tank ID:	T001U	Tank Status:	CLOSED REMOVED
Tank Contents:	WASTE OIL	Leak Monitoring:	NOT AVAILABLE
Tank Age:	NOT REPORTED	Tank Piping:	UNKNOWN
Tank Size (Units):	225 (GALLONS)	Tank Material:	UNKNOWN

Tank ID:	T002U	Tank Status:	CLOSED REMOVED
Tank Contents:	SUPER UNLEADED	Leak Monitoring:	NOT AVAILABLE
Tank Age:	22	Tank Piping:	UNKNOWN
Tank Size (Units):	6000 (GALLONS)	Tank Material:	UNKNOWN

Tank ID:	T003U	Tank Status:	CLOSED REMOVED
Tank Contents:	UNLEADED GAS	Leak Monitoring:	NOT AVAILABLE
Tank Age:	NOT REPORTED	Tank Piping:	UNKNOWN
Tank Size (Units):	7500 (GALLONS)	Tank Material:	UNKNOWN

Tank ID:	T004U	Tank Status:	CLOSED REMOVED
Tank Contents:	LEADED GAS	Leak Monitoring:	NOT AVAILABLE
Tank Age:	NOT REPORTED	Tank Piping:	UNKNOWN
Tank Size (Units):	7500 (GALLONS)	Tank Material:	UNKNOWN

SITES IN THE SURROUNDING AREA (within 1/4 - 1/2 mile)

VISTA Address*:	THE PEP BOYS #647 6714 EL CAJON SAN DIEGO, CA 92115	VISTA ID#:	325397	Map ID
		Distance/Direction:	0.33 MI / W	**5**
		Plotted as:	Point	

STATE LUST - State Leaking Underground Storage Tank / SRC# 4828 — EPA/Agency ID: N/A

Agency Address:		PEP BOYS 6714 EL CAJON BLVD SAN DIEGO, CA 92115
Facility ID:		9UT868
Leak Report Date:		10/30/1987
Remediation Plan Date:		10/05/1987
Case Closed Date:		04/05/1988
Quantity / Units:	0	Units: NOT REPORTED
Remediation Status:		CASE CLOSED
Media Affected:		SOIL ONLY
Description / Comment:		CROSS STREET: MONTEZUMA
Description / Comment:		SAN DIEGO REGION
Description / Comment:		REVIEW DATE: 12/05/1987

STATE LUST - State Leaking Underground Storage Tank / SRC# 4917 — EPA/Agency ID: N/A

Agency Address:		PEP BOYS 6714 EL CAJON BLVD SAN DIEGO, CA 92115
Facility ID:		9UT868
Leak Date:		09/22/1987
Leak Report Date:		10/30/1987
Remediation Plan Date:		10/05/1987

* VISTA address includes enhanced city and ZIP.
For more information call VISTA Information Solutions, Inc. at **1 - 800 - 767 - 0403.**
Report ID: **980914-002**
Version 2.6

Date of Report: **September 14, 1998**
Page #18

SITES IN THE SURROUNDING AREA (within 1/4 - 1/2 mile) CONT.	
Case Closed Date:	04/05/1988
Leak Detection Method:	TANK CLOSURE
Leak Cause:	CORROSION
Leak Source:	TANK
Quantity / Units: 0	Units: NOT REPORTED
Remediation Event:	LEAK STOPPED BY: CLOSE TANK
Remediation Event:	LEAK STOP DATE: 19870922
Remediation Status:	CASE CLOSED
Media Affected:	SOIL ONLY
Description / Comment:	PILOT PROGRAM: YES INTERIM REMEDIAL ACTION: YES LOCAL CASE NUM:H13139-001
Description / Comment:	BASIN NUM: 90 GW DEPTH: CAONUM: WDRNUM: NPDES NUM: FILEDISP: DISCARDED
Description / Comment:	PRIORITY: LOW

VISTA Address*:	EXXON LOCATION 7-7047 5151 70TH ST N LA MESA, CA 92041	VISTA ID#:	126272	Map ID
		Distance/Direction:	0.49 MI / N	**6**
		Plotted as:	Point	

STATE LUST - State Leaking Underground Storage Tank / SRC# 4828		EPA/Agency ID:	N/A
Agency Address:	SAME AS ABOVE		
Facility ID:	9UT168		
Leak Report Date:	12/02/1985		
Site Assessment Began:	12/11/1986		
Remediation Start Date:	11/24/1987		
Case Closed Date:	11/20/1987		
Substance:	GASOLINE		
Remediation Status:	CASE CLOSED		
Media Affected:	SOIL ONLY		
Description / Comment:	CROSS STREET: ALVARADO		
Description / Comment:	SAN DIEGO REGION		
Description / Comment:	REVIEW DATE: 11/24/1987		

STATE LUST - State Leaking Underground Storage Tank / SRC# 4917		EPA/Agency ID:	N/A
Agency Address:	SAME AS ABOVE		
Facility ID:	9UT168		
Leak Date:	12/02/1985		
Leak Report Date:	12/02/1985		
Site Assessment Began:	12/11/1986		
Remediation Start Date:	11/24/1987		
Case Closed Date:	11/20/1987		
Leak Detection Method:	TANK CLOSURE		
Leak Cause:	OVERFILL		
Leak Source:	PIPING		
Substance:	GASOLINE		
Remediation Event:	LEAK STOPPED BY: CLOSE TANK		
Remediation Status:	CASE CLOSED		
Media Affected:	SOIL ONLY		
Description / Comment:	PILOT PROGRAM: YES INTERIM REMEDIAL ACTION: YES LOCAL CASE NUM:H13427-001		
Description / Comment:	BASIN NUM: 907.11 GW DEPTH: CAONUM: WDRNUM: NPDES NUM: FILEDISP: DISCARDED		
Description / Comment:	PRIORITY: LOW		

* VISTA address includes enhanced city and ZIP.
For more information call VISTA Information Solutions, Inc. at **1 - 800 - 767 - 0403.**
Report ID: **980914-002**
Version 2.6

Date of Report: **September 14, 1998**
Page #19

SITES IN THE SURROUNDING AREA (within 1/4 - 1/2 mile) CONT.

VISTA Address*:	ITNS RECYCLING 6554 EL CAJON BLVD SAN DIEGO, CA 92115		VISTA ID#:	3078200	Map ID
			Distance/Direction:	0.49 MI / W	7
			Plotted as:	Point	

STATE LUST - State Leaking Underground Storage Tank / SRC# 4828   EPA/Agency ID: N/A

Agency Address:	SAME AS ABOVE
Facility ID:	9UT2165
Leak Report Date:	01/10/1992
Tank Inspection Date:	01/10/1992
Site Assessment Plan Submitted:	01/30/1992
Site Assessment Began:	04/12/1993
Remediation Plan Date:	08/28/1996
Substance:	GASOLINE
Quantity / Units: 0 **Units:**	NOT REPORTED
Remediation Status:	REMEDIATION PLAN SUBMITTED
Media Affected:	OTHER GROUND WATER
Description / Comment:	CROSS STREET: ROLANDO
Description / Comment:	SAN DIEGO REGION
Description / Comment:	REVIEW DATE: 02/28/1994

STATE LUST - State Leaking Underground Storage Tank / SRC# 4917   EPA/Agency ID: N/A

Agency Address:	SAME AS ABOVE
Facility ID:	9UT2165
Leak Date:	01/10/1992
Leak Report Date:	01/10/1992
Site Assessment Plan Submitted:	01/30/1992
Site Assessment Began:	04/12/1993
Contamination Confirmed Date:	01/10/1992
Remediation Plan Date:	08/28/1996
Leak Detection Method:	OTHER MEANS
Leak Cause:	UNKNOWN
Leak Source:	UNKNOWN
Substance:	GASOLINE
Quantity / Units: 0 **Units:**	NOT REPORTED
Remediation Event:	LEAK STOPPED BY: OTHER MEANS
Remediation Event:	LEAK STOP DATE: 19920110
Remediation Event:	ENFORCEMENT: NONE TAKEN
Remediation Status:	REMEDIATION PLAN SUBMITTED
Media Affected:	OTHER GROUND WATER
Description / Comment:	PILOT PROGRAM: YES INTERIM REMEDIAL ACTION: NO LOCAL CASE NUM: H21227-001 BENEFICIAL: MUNICIPAL GROUNDWATER USE
Description / Comment:	BASIN NUM: 907.11 GW DEPTH: 6' CAONUM: WDRNUM: NPDES NUM: FILEDISP: DISCARDED
Description / Comment:	PRIORITY: ADMINISTRATIVE NEED EXISTS

SITES IN THE SURROUNDING AREA (within 1/2 - 1 mile)

No Records Found

* VISTA address includes enhanced city and ZIP.
For more information call VISTA Information Solutions, Inc. at **1 - 800 - 767 - 0403.**
Report ID: **980914-002**
Version 2.6
Date of Report: **September 14, 1998**
Page #20

UNMAPPED SITES
No Records Found

* VISTA address includes enhanced city and ZIP.
For more information call VISTA Information Solutions, Inc. at **1 - 800 - 767 - 0403.**
Report ID: **980914-002**   Date of Report: **September 14, 1998**
Version 2.6   *Page #21*

SITE ASSESSMENT REPORT

DESCRIPTION OF DATABASES SEARCHED

A) DATABASES SEARCHED TO 1 MILE

NPL
SRC#: 4938

VISTA conducts a database search to identify all sites within 1 mile of your property.
The agency release date for NPL was July, 1998.

The National Priorities List (NPL) is the EPA's database of uncontrolled or abandoned hazardous waste sites identified for priority remedial actions under the Superfund program. A site must meet or surpass a predetermined hazard ranking system score, be chosen as a state's top priority site, or meet three specific criteria set jointly by the US Dept of Health and Human Services and the US EPA in order to become an NPL site.

SPL
SRC#: 4808

VISTA conducts a database search to identify all sites within 1 mile of your property.
The agency release date for Calsites Database: Annual Workplan Sites was May, 1998.

This database is provided by the Cal. Environmental Protection Agency, Dept. of Toxic Substances Control. The agency may be contacted at: 916-323-3400.

CORRACTS
SRC#: 4467

VISTA conducts a database search to identify all sites within 1 mile of your property.
The agency release date for HWDMS/RCRIS was February, 1998.

The EPA maintains this database of RCRA facilities which are undergoing "corrective action". A "corrective action order" is issued pursuant to RCRA Section 3008 (h) when there has been a release of hazardous waste or constituents into the environment from a RCRA facility. Corrective actions may be required beyond the facility's boundary and can be required regardless of when the release occurred, even if it predates RCRA.

B) DATABASES SEARCHED TO 1/2 MILE

CERCLIS
SRC#: 4941

VISTA conducts a database search to identify all sites within 1/2 mile of your property.
The agency release date for CERCLIS was June, 1998.

The CERCLIS List contains sites which are either proposed to or on the National Priorities List(NPL) and sites which are in the screening and assessment phase for possible inclusion on the NPL. The information on each site includes a history of all pre-remedial, remedial, removal and community relations activiies or events at the site, financial funding information for the events, and unrestricted enforcement activities.

NFRAP
SRC#: 4942

VISTA conducts a database search to identify all sites within 1/2 mile of your property.
The agency release date for CERCLIS-NFRAP was June, 1998.

NFRAP sites may be sites where, following an initial investigation, no contamination was found, contamination was removed quickly, or the contamination was not serious enough to require Federal Superfund action or NPL consideration.

SCL
SRC#: 4807

VISTA conducts a database search to identify all sites within 1/2 mile of your property.
The agency release date for Calsites Database: All Sites except Annual Workplan Sites (incl. ASPIS) was May, 1998.

This database is provided by the Department of Toxic Substances Control. The agency may be contacted at: .

The CalSites database includes both known and potential sites. Two- thirds of these sites have been classified, based on available information, as needing "No Further Action" (NFA) by the Department of Toxic Substances Control. The remaining sites are in various stages of review and remediation to determine if a problem exists at the site. Several hundred sites have been remediated and are considered certified. Some of these sites may be in long term operation and maintenance.

RCRA-TSD
SRC#: 4467

VISTA conducts a database search to identify all sites within 1/2 mile of your property.
The agency release date for HWDMS/RCRIS was February, 1998.

The EPA's Resource Conservation and Recovery Act (RCRA) Program identifies and tracks hazardous waste from the point of generation to the point of disposal. The RCRA Facilities database is a compilation by the EPA of facilities which report generation, storage, transportation, treatment or disposal of hazardous waste. RCRA TSDs are facilities which treat, store and/or dispose of hazardous waste.

SWLF
SRC#: 5043

VISTA conducts a database search to identify all sites within 1/2 mile of your property.
The agency release date for Ca Solid Waste Information System (SWIS) was July, 1998.

This database is provided by the Integrated Waste Management Board. The agency may be contacted at: 916-255-4021.

The California Solid Waste Information System (SWIS) database consists of both open as well as closed and inactive solid waste disposal facilities and transfer stations pursuant to the Solid Waste Management and Resource Recovery Act of 1972, Government Code Section 2.66790(b). Generally, the California Integrated Waste Management Board learns of locations of disposal facilities through permit applications and from local enforcement agencies.

LUST
SRC#: 4828

VISTA conducts a database search to identify all sites within 1/2 mile of your property.
The agency release date for Lust Information System (LUSTIS) was April, 1998.

This database is provided by the California Environmental Protection Agency. The agency may be contacted at: 916-445-6532.

C) DATABASES SEARCHED TO 1/4 MILE

UST's
SRC#: 1612

VISTA conducts a database search to identify all sites within 1/4 mile of your property.
The agency release date for Underground Storage Tank Registrations Database was January, 1994.

This database is provided by the State Water Resources Control Board, Office of Underground Storage Tanks. The agency may be contacted at: 916-227-4337; Caution-Many states do not require registration of heating oil tanks, especially those used for residential purposes.

UST's
SRC#: 4814

VISTA conducts a database search to identify all sites within 1/4 mile of your property.
The agency release date for City of San Leandro UST Listing was May, 1998.

This database is provided by the San Leandro Fire Department. The agency may be contacted at: 510-577-3331; Caution-Many states do not require registration of heating oil tanks, especially those used for residential purposes.

UST's
SRC#: 4815

VISTA conducts a database search to identify all sites within 1/4 mile of your property.
The agency release date for City of Anaheim UST Listing was May, 1998.

This database is provided by the City of Anaheim. The agency may be contacted at: 714-765-4050; Caution-Many states do not require registration of heating oil tanks, especially those used for residential purposes.

UST's
SRC#: 4818

VISTA conducts a database search to identify all sites within 1/4 mile of your property.
The agency release date for City of Hayward UST Report was May, 1998.

This database is provided by the City of Hayward Fire Department. The agency may be contacted at: 510-583-4900; Caution-Many states do not require registration of heating oil tanks, especially those used for residential purposes.

UST's
SRC#: 4819

VISTA conducts a database search to identify all sites within 1/4 mile of your property.
The agency release date for Bakersfield City Tanks - In Compliance and Out of Compliance was May, 1998.

This database is provided by the Bakersfield Fire Department Office of Environmental Services. The agency may be contacted at: 805-326-3979; Caution-Many states do not require registration of heating oil tanks, especially those used for residential purposes.

UST's
SRC#: 4821

VISTA conducts a database search to identify all sites within 1/4 mile of your property.
The agency release date for Sebastopol City Owner List of USTs was May, 1998.

This database is provided by the City of Sebastopol Fire Department. The agency may be contacted at: 707-823-8061; Caution-Many states do not require registration of heating oil tanks, especially those used for residential purposes.

UST's
SRC#: 5041

VISTA conducts a database search to identify all sites within 1/4 mile of your property.
The agency release date for San Diego County Environmental Health Services Database-UST Sites was July, 1998.

This database is provided by the San Diego County Department of Health Services. The agency may be contacted at: 619-338-2268; Caution-Many states do not require registration of heating oil tanks, especially those used for residential purposes.

UST's
SRC#: 5047

VISTA conducts a database search to identify all sites within 1/4 mile of your property.
The agency release date for City of Santa Clara Underground Storage Tanks was May, 1998.

This database is provided by the City of Santa Clara, Fire Department. The agency may be contacted at: 408-984-4109; Caution-Many states do not require registration of heating oil tanks, especially those used for residential purposes.

UST's
SRC#: 5054

VISTA conducts a database search to identify all sites within 1/4 mile of your property.
The agency release date for City of Oakland Underground Storage Tank List was June, 1998.

This database is provided by the City of Oaklan Fire Department, Office of Emergency Services. The agency may be contacted at: 510-238-3938; Caution-Many states do not require registration of heating oil tanks, especially those used for residential purposes.

UST's
SRC#: 5056

VISTA conducts a database search to identify all sites within 1/4 mile of your property.
The agency release date for City of Union Underground Storage Tanks List was May, 1998.

This database is provided by the Union City Fire Department. The agency may be contacted at: 510-471-1424; Caution-Many states do not require registration of heating oil tanks, especially those used for residential purposes.

For more information call VISTA Information Solutions, Inc. at **1 - 800 - 767 - 0403.**
Report ID: **980914-002**
Version 2.6

Date of Report: **September 14, 1998**
Page #24

UST's
SRC#: 5057
VISTA conducts a database search to identify all sites within 1/4 mile of your property.
The agency release date for City of Petaluma Underground Storage Tank List was July, 1998.

This database is provided by the City of Petaluma Fire Department. The agency may be contacted at: 707-778-4389; Caution-Many states do not require registration of heating oil tanks, especially those used for residential purposes.

UST's
SRC#: 5061
VISTA conducts a database search to identify all sites within 1/4 mile of your property.
The agency release date for City of El Segundo Open Tanks List was May, 1998.

This database is provided by the City of El Segundo Fire Department. The agency may be contacted at: 310-607-2239; Caution-Many states do not require registration of heating oil tanks, especially those used for residential purposes.

UST's
SRC#: 5062
VISTA conducts a database search to identify all sites within 1/4 mile of your property.
The agency release date for City of Mountain View Underground Storage Tank List was May, 1998.

This database is provided by the Mountain View Fire Department. The agency may be contacted at: 415-903-6378; Caution-Many states do not require registration of heating oil tanks, especially those used for residential purposes.

UST's
SRC#: 5063
VISTA conducts a database search to identify all sites within 1/4 mile of your property.
The agency release date for City of Oxnard Underground Storage Tank List was May, 1998.

This database is provided by the City of Oxnard Wastewater Division. The agency may be contacted at: 805-271-2206; Caution-Many states do not require registration of heating oil tanks, especially those used for residential purposes.

UST's
SRC#: 5066
VISTA conducts a database search to identify all sites within 1/4 mile of your property.
The agency release date for City of Livermore UST List was July, 1998.

This database is provided by the City of Livermore Fire Department. The agency may be contacted at: 510-454-2361; Caution-Many states do not require registration of heating oil tanks, especially those used for residential purposes.

UST's
SRC#: 5067
VISTA conducts a database search to identify all sites within 1/4 mile of your property.
The agency release date for City of Hollister Underground Storage Tank List was July, 1998.

This database is provided by the City of Hollister Environmental Services Department. The agency may be contacted at: 408-636-4325; Caution-Many states do not require registration of heating oil tanks, especially those used for residential purposes.

UST's
SRC#: 5068
VISTA conducts a database search to identify all sites within 1/4 mile of your property.
The agency release date for City of Torrance Underground Storage Tank List was July, 1998.

This database is provided by the City of Torrance Fire Prevention Division. The agency may be contacted at: 310-618-2973; Caution-Many states do not require registration of heating oil tanks, especially those used for residential purposes.

UST's
SRC#: 5070
VISTA conducts a database search to identify all sites within 1/4 mile of your property.
The agency release date for City of Santa Rosa Underground Storage Tank List was July, 1998.

This database is provided by the City of Santa Rosa Fire Department. The agency may be contacted at: 707-543-3500; Caution-Many states do not require registration of heating oil tanks, especially those used for residential purposes.

UST's
SRC#: 5071

VISTA conducts a database search to identify all sites within 1/4 mile of your property.
The agency release date for City of Orange Underground Storage Tank List was July, 1998.

This database is provided by the City of Orange Fire Department. The agency may be contacted at: 714-288-2541; Caution-Many states do not require registration of heating oil tanks, especially those used for residential purposes.

AST's
SRC#: 4320

VISTA conducts a database search to identify all sites within 1/4 mile of your property.
The agency release date for Aboveground Storage Tank Database was December, 1997.

This database is provided by the State Water Resources Control Board. The agency may be contacted at: 916-227-4364.

D) DATABASES SEARCHED TO 1/8 MILE

ERNS
SRC#: 4939

VISTA conducts a database search to identify all sites within 1/8 mile of your property.
The agency release date for was July, 1998.

The Emergency Response Notification System (ERNS) is a national database used to collect information on reported releases of oil and hazardous substances. The database contains information from spill reports made to federal authorities including the EPA, the US Coast Guard, the National Response Center and the Department of transportation. A search of the database records for the period October 1986 through January 1998 revealed information regarding reported spills of oil or hazardous substances in the stated area.

RCRA-LgGen
SRC#: 4467

VISTA conducts a database search to identify all sites within 1/8 mile of your property.
The agency release date for HWDMS/RCRIS was February, 1998.

The EPA's Resource Conservation and Recovery Act (RCRA) Program identifies and tracks hazardous waste from the point of generation to the point of disposal. The RCRA Facilities database is a compilation by the EPA of facilities which report generation, storage, transportation, treatment or disposal of hazardous waste. RCRA Large Generators are facilities which generate at   least 1000 kg./month of non-acutely hazardous waste (or 1 kg./month of acutely hazardous waste).

RCRA-SmGen
SRC#: 4467

VISTA conducts a database search to identify all sites within 1/8 mile of your property.
The agency release date for HWDMS/RCRIS was February, 1998.

The EPA's Resource Conservation and Recovery Act (RCRA) Program identifies and tracks hazardous waste from the point of generation to the point of disposal. The RCRA Facilities database is a compilation by the EPA of facilities which report generation, storage, transportation, treatment or disposal of hazardous waste. RCRA Small and Very Small generators are facilities which generate less than 1000 kg./month of non-acutely hazardous waste.

SPILL
SRC#: 161

VISTA conducts a database search to identify all sites within 1/8 mile of your property.
The agency release date for California Hazardous Materials Incident Report was December, 1990.

This database is provided by the Office of Emergency Services. The agency may be contacted at: .

SPILL
SRC#: 5036

VISTA conducts a database search to identify all sites within 1/8 mile of your property.
The agency release date for Region #1-Active Toxic Site Investigations-Spills was July, 1998.

This database is provided by the Regional Water Quality Control Board, Region #1 (North Coast Region). The agency may be contacted at: 707-576-2220.

SPILL
SRC#: 5041

VISTA conducts a database search to identify all sites within 1/8 mile of your property.
The agency release date for San Diego County Environmental Health Services Database-Spill Sites was July, 1998.

This database is provided by the San Diego County Department of Health Services. The agency may be contacted at: 619-338-2268.

End of Report

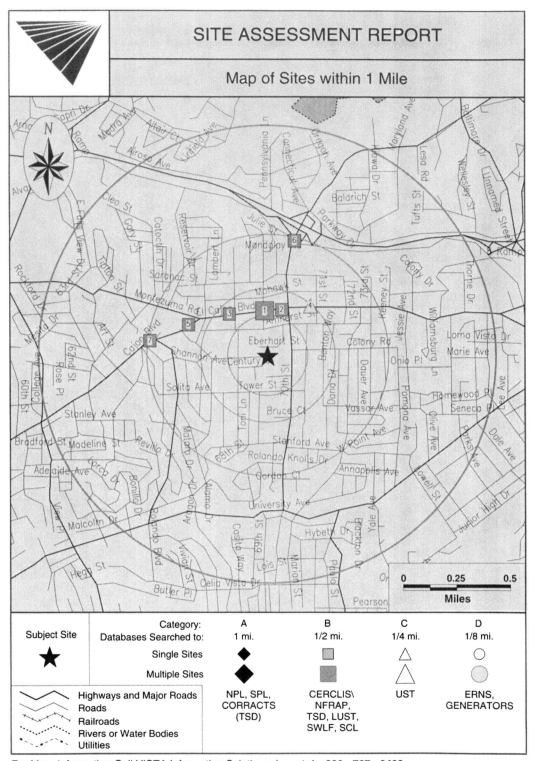

SITE ASSESSMENT REPORT

Map of Sites within 1 Mile

	Category: Databases Searched to:	A 1 mi.	B 1/2 mi.	C 1/4 mi.	D 1/8 mi.
Subject Site ★	Single Sites	◆	▣	△	○
	Multiple Sites	◆	▣	△	○
		NPL, SPL, CORRACTS (TSD)	CERCLIS\ NFRAP, TSD, LUST, SWLF, SCL	UST	ERNS, GENERATORS

Highways and Major Roads
Roads
Railroads
Rivers or Water Bodies
Utilities

For More Information Call VISTA Information Solutions, Inc. at **1 - 800 - 767 - 0403**
Report ID: **980914002**   Date of Report: **September 14, 1998**
Page #3

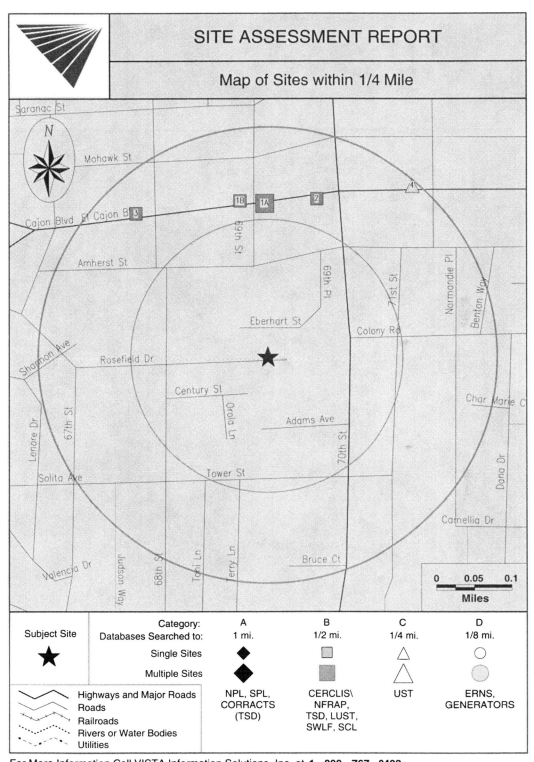

SITE ASSESSMENT REPORT

Map of Sites within 1/4 Mile

	Category: Databases Searched to:	A 1 mi.	B 1/2 mi.	C 1/4 mi.	D 1/8 mi.
Subject Site	Single Sites	◆	▢	△	○
★	Multiple Sites	◆	▣	△	◯

Highways and Major Roads
Roads
Railroads
Rivers or Water Bodies
Utilities

A	B	C	D
NPL, SPL, CORRACTS (TSD)	CERCLIS\ NFRAP, TSD, LUST, SWLF, SCL	UST	ERNS, GENERATORS

For More Information Call VISTA Information Solutions, Inc. at **1 - 800 - 767 - 0403**
Report ID: **980914002**

Date of Report: **September 14, 1998**

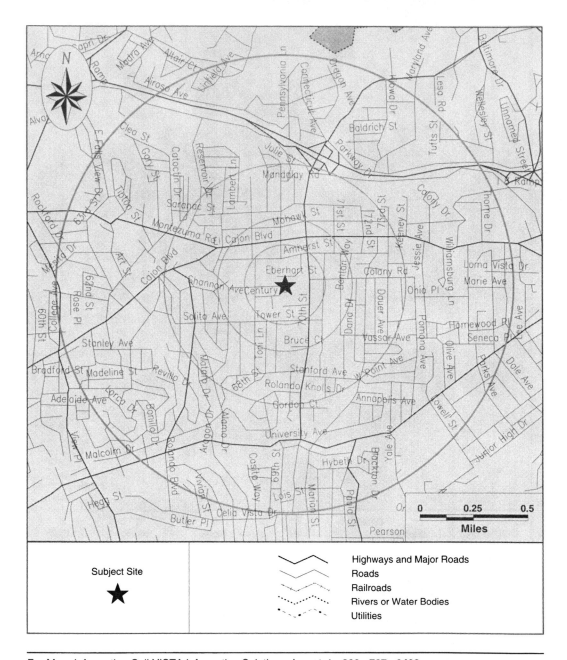

SITE ASSESSMENT REPORT

Street Map

Subject Site

★

Highways and Major Roads
Roads
Railroads
Rivers or Water Bodies
Utilities

For More Information Call VISTA Information Solutions, Inc. at **1 - 800 - 767 - 0403**
Report ID: **980914002**   Date of Report: **September 14, 1998**
Page #5

Index

Breinigsville, PA USA
01 August 2010
242573BV00006B/2/P